BESTSELLING Annual Bible Commentary

Standard LESSON COMMENTARY®

KJV SEPTEMBER–AUGUST 2023–2024

KING JAMES VERSION

Jane Ann Kenney
Ronald L. Nickelson
Taylor Z. Stamps

Volume 71

part of the David C Cook family

In This Volume

Fall Quarter 2023 (page 1)
God's Law Is Love

Lesson Development . . . . Mark W. Hamilton (1–2, 10), Lauren Parliament (3–4), Mark S. Krause (5–6), Walt Harper (7–9), Doug Redford (11, 13), Chad Summa (12)
Verbal Illustrations . . . . Andrew Wood (1–3), Marsella Evans (4, 10–11), Ronald L. Nickelson (5), Mark S. Krause (5), Noah Goodwin (6–7, 13), Jane Ann Kenney (8), Jon Miller (9, 12)
Involvement Learning . . . . Mark Taylor (1–3), Andrew Wood (4–7), Connie Chandler (8–10), Ann Diaz (11–13)
What Do You Think? . . . . Andrew Wood (1–13)

Winter Quarter 2023–2024 (page 113)
Faith That Pleases God

Lesson Development . . . . Lauren Parliament (1–2), Mark S. Krause (3, 5), Chad Summa (4, 6, 9), Andrew Wood (7, 13), Doug Redford (8, 10), Mark W. Hamilton (11–12)
Verbal Illustrations . . . . Andrew Wood (1, 3, 5, 8), David Daniels (2, 4, 6, 11), Noah Goodwin (7, 9), Jon Miller (10, 12–13)
Involvement Learning . . . . Andrew Wood (1–4), Connie Chandler (5–9), Mark Taylor (10–13)
What Do You Think? . . . . Andrew Wood (1–13)

Spring Quarter 2024 (page 225)
Examining Our Faith

Lesson Development . . . . John Mark Hicks (1–2), Taylor Z. Stamps (3), Mark S. Krause (4, 7–8), Jason Hitchcock (5), Jon Miller (6), Chad Summa (9–10), Mark Hamilton (11–13)
Verbal Illustrations . . . . Andrew Wood (1–3), David Daniels (4, 8), Omar Palafox (5, 9, 13), Noah Goodwin (6, 11), Petra L. Miller (7), Jon Miller (10, 12)
Involvement Learning . . . . Connie Chandler (1–4), Mark Taylor (5, 7–9), Andrew Wood (10–13)
What Do You Think? . . . . Andrew Wood (1–5, 7–13), Jon Miller (6)

Summer Quarter 2024 (page 337)
Hope In The Lord

Lesson Development . . . . Omar Palafox (1–3, 11), Jon Miller (4), Jason Hitchcock (5), Kevin Youngblood (6), Mark Hamilton (7–9), Doug Hoffer (10), John Mark Hicks (12–13)
Verbal Illustrations . . . . Petra L. Miller (1), Chad Summa (2–3, 6), Andrew Wood (4–5, 7–8), Jon Miller (9, 12), Laura McKillip Wood (10–11, 13)
Involvement Learning . . . . Mark Taylor (1–2, 3, 5), Jon Miller (4), Andrew Wood (6–7, 8–9), Connie Chandler (10–13)
What Do You Think? . . . . Andrew Wood (1–3, 5–13), Jon Miller (4)

Index of Printed Texts

The printed texts for 2023–2024 are arranged here in the order in which they appear in the Bible.

We are committed to serving you by providing excellent resources that inspire, educate, and motivate you in a growing relationship with Jesus Christ. Please tell us about your experience with Standard Lesson Commentary by completing the survey at: StandardLesson.com/survey.

On mobile devices, scan the QR Code with the camera app:

Don't forget the visuals!

The thumbnail visuals in the lessons are small reproductions of 18″ x 24″ full-color posters that are included in the *Adult Resources* packet for each quarter. Order numbers 978-0-784739-13-6 (Fall 2023), 978-0-784739-63-1 (Winter 2023–2024), 978-0-784740-13-2 (Spring 2024), and 978-0-784740-63-7 (Summer 2024) from either your supplier, by calling 1.800.323.7543, or at www.standardlesson.com.

Cumulative Index

A cumulative index for Scripture passages used in the Standard Lesson Commentary *for September 2022–August 2026 is provided below.*

Notes

Notes

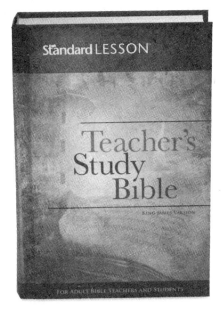

God's Law Is Love

Special Features

Lessons

Unit 1: Love Completes, Law Falls Short

Unit 2: Faith Triumphs, Law Fails

Unit 3: Christ Frees, Law Enslaves

Quarterly Quiz

Use these questions as a pretest or as a review. The answers are on page iv of This Quarter in the Word.

Lesson 1

1. The Pharisee was surprised that Jesus did not do what? (pray, wash, sing) *Luke 11:38*

2. Jesus chastised the Pharisees for loving the "uppermost" seats in the __________. *Luke 11:43*

Lesson 2

1. Jesus asked if healing on the Sabbath was __________. *Luke 14:3*

2. The Pharisees and the law experts responded to Jesus' question with silence. T/F. *Luke 14:4*

Lesson 3

1. Jesus' __________ was not His own, but from the one who sent Him. *John 7:16*

2. Jesus warned against judgment based on appearance. T/F. *John 7:24*

Lesson 4

1. The religious leaders told Jesus that the woman had committed what offense? (adultery, blasphemy, murder) *John 8:3*

2. Jesus proclaimed that "before __________ was, I am." *John 8:58*

Lesson 5

1. Where is the "work of the law" written? (stones, minds, hearts) *Romans 2:15*

2. Circumcision of the __________ is what defines who is a "Jew." *Romans 2:29*

Lesson 6

1. People have been released from the law in order to serve in the "newness of spirit." T/F. *Romans 7:6*

2. Paul was "deceived" by what? (sin, people, angels) *Romans 7:11*

Lesson 7

1. People are justified by faith and by their works of the law. T/F. *Galatians 2:16*

2. Paul was "__________ with Christ." *Galatians 2:20*

Lesson 8

1. Paul accused the Galatians of having been "bewitched." T/F. *Galatians 3:1*

2. Christ redeemed us from the law by becoming "a ________ for us." *Galatians 3:13*

Lesson 9

1. Because faith has come, "we are no longer under a __________." *Galatians 3:25*

2. God sent His Son so that we might receive adoption. T/F. *Galatians 4:5*

Lesson 10

1. Certain people taught that salvation required what? (tithes, circumcision, offerings) *Acts 15:1*

2. Who was appointed to go to Jerusalem along with Paul and other believers? (Barabbas, Bartholomew, Barnabas) *Acts 15:2*

Lesson 11

1. Love does what to the law? (fulfills it, transcends it, cancels it) *Romans 13:10*

2. Paul taught that ________ never fails. *1 Corinthians 13:8*

Lesson 12

1. Some practices and observances are described as what in relation to the things to come? (whisper, vapor, shadow) *Colossians 2:16-17*

2. We are alive in Christ to follow the "rudiments of the world." T/F. *Colossians 2:20*

Lesson 13

1. Eating and drinking should be for "the __________ of God." *1 Corinthians 10:31*

2. Paul advised others to follow his example because he first followed the example of whom? (Abraham, Moses, Christ) *1 Corinthians 11:1*

Quarter at a Glance

by Mark S. Krause

One point of conflict in the first-century church concerned the authority and relevancy of the Law of Moses. This quarter will explore the relationship between faith and law through Jesus' teachings and writings to the first-century church.

Jesus, the Pharisees, and the Law

During His earthly ministry, Jesus experienced conflict with certain Pharisees. This sect of Judaism was strict and passionate regarding obedience to the Law of Moses and its related commentary. To ensure obedience, they had established traditions to guide their actions.

However, Jesus identified disparities between the requirements of the Law of Moses and the Pharisees' obedience. One inconsistency involved their devotion to the law at the expense of acting with love (see Luke 11:42, lesson 1). Other inconsistencies regarded their observance of the Sabbath (see Luke 14:1-6; John 7:14-24; lessons 2 and 3).

On one occasion, some Pharisees and scribes brought a woman to Jesus, charging her with the crime of adultery. The leaders planned to use the opportunity to trap Jesus. However, Jesus flipped their expectations. He suggested that following the requirements of the Law of Moses for this woman—in this case, capital punishment—should be initiated by the person "without sin" (John 8:7, lesson 4). Jesus' action was not in violation of the Law of Moses. On the contrary, He taught that keeping the law should follow God's requirements for justice and mercy.

Paul, the Church, and the Law

After Jesus' ascension, the composition of churches became diverse. These communities consisted of Jews raised under the Law of Moses and Gentiles not accustomed to that law. This mix created the opportunity for turmoil in the church. Certain Jewish believers insisted that all followers of Jesus—Jew or Gentile—must follow the Law of Moses. As a result, these believers emphasized that converted Gentile men should undergo circumcision.

Conflict regarding circumcision and the role of the Law of Moses came to a head during the events described in Acts 15 (lesson 10). Church leaders gathered in Jerusalem to discuss the relevance of the law for Gentile believers. Did Gentiles have to adhere to the law to become part of the people of God? The apostle Peter answered, *no*! All people can receive salvation by faith "through the grace of the Lord Jesus Christ" (Acts 15:11).

> *Through faith in Jesus, a person . . . receives God's Spirit.*

Paul taught that observing the Law of Moses was not enough for salvation. God's people seek to have a circumcision of the heart, not the flesh (Romans 2:29, lesson 5). While the law is "holy, and just, and good" (7:12, lesson 6), it cannot bring salvation. If people could gain right standing before God through the law, Christ would have died in vain (see Galatians 2:21, lesson 7).

The Law of Moses cannot bring the presence of the Spirit (see Galatians 3:2-6, 11-12, lesson 8). Through faith in Jesus, a person becomes a child of God and receives God's Spirit (see 4:6, lesson 9). Because of the Spirit's indwelling, believers' lives would bear the fruit of their transformation (see 5:22-23).

Paul never condoned ungodly behavior. Christian liberty is not a license for sin. Instead, a believer's display of love to others fulfills the requirements of the law (Romans 13:10, lesson 11). Exhibiting personal freedom may cause weaker Christians to stumble (see 1 Corinthians 10:23-30, lesson 13). The people of God should use their freedom to love God and others.

Get the Setting

by Andrew Wood

The Jews of Jesus' day were not one homogeneous group. Instead, we can divide first-century Jews into different political and philosophical groups. The four most well-known were the Pharisees, Sadducees, Zealots, and Essenes. Participation in these groups was diverse and voluntary. These groups remained small in number when compared to the population of first-century Palestine. A better understanding of these groups can help us comprehend the challenges that Jesus and the first-century church faced.

The Pharisees

The sect of the Pharisees was influential with the Jewish people and appeared prominently in the New Testament. Members of the sect were not members of the priesthood. However, the people still regarded them as experts in the Law of Moses. Therefore, they carried influence in the synagogue.

Pharisees set up traditions based on their strict interpretation of the Law of Moses (see Mark 7:5). These traditions went beyond the actual requirements of the law. These traditions separated the Pharisees' religious identity from others and ensured that adherents appropriately followed the Pharisees' interpretations of the law.

Their tradition and interpretation placed the Pharisees into frequent conflict with Jesus. For instance, they criticized Jesus for eating with tax collectors (Matthew 9:9-13) and doing work on the Sabbath (Luke 6:1-5).

Additionally, the Pharisees believed in a bodily resurrection of the dead and the existence of angels and demons (Matthew 9:34; Acts 23:8). After the Romans destroyed Jerusalem in AD 70, the Pharisees were the only surviving major faction of Judaism.

The Sadducees

The Sadducees appear less frequently in the Gospels than the Pharisees. However, they were influential members of the Sanhedrin, the Jewish governing body. Many Sadducees were from priestly families (see Acts 5:17). Therefore, they were concerned with matters related to the temple (example: 4:1-3). The Sadducees' influence was most substantial in Jerusalem, so they are presented in the Gospel narratives more frequently as Jesus nears the city.

Their belief system centered on the Law of Moses while rejecting doctrines like the existence of angels and bodily resurrection (see Acts 23:8). Despite doctrinal differences with the Pharisees, they united in testing Jesus (see Matthew 16:1).

The Zealots

The Zealots were a political party of revolt against foreign occupation. Their influence inspired events that led to the destruction of Jerusalem by the Romans in AD 70. Zealots opposed the Roman occupation and desired to have God as the only king of Israel. One of Jesus' disciples was called "Zelotes" (Luke 6:15; Acts 1:13), another name for Zealot. However, such a name could refer to his zealous character rather than his membership in the faction. Zealots committed sabotage, carried out assassinations, and seeded uprisings against Rome.

The Essenes

The Bible does not mention the Jewish sect of the Essenes. Our knowledge of them comes from nonbiblical writings that date from approximately 200 BC–AD 100. The Essenes were exclusive in their membership. By one estimate, there were approximately 4,000 members during the time of Jesus. They held that the temple in Jerusalem had been defiled. Therefore, they believed that their physical bodies were temples of God. As a result, they adhered firmly to rules of personal conduct and ritual cleanliness. Such observations consisted of certain practices of self-denial, such as strict vows of celibacy.

Mon, Nov. 13	**The Lord's Spirit Brings Freedom**	2 Corinthians 3:12-18
Tue, Nov. 14	**Judged by the Law of Liberty**	James 2:8-13
Wed, Nov. 15	**Proclaim Liberty Throughout the Land**	Leviticus 25:8-17
Thu, Nov. 16	**Jesus Announces Freedom and Release**	Luke 4:14-22
Fri, Nov. 17	**God Provides and Comforts**	Psalm 23
Sat, Nov. 18	**Rooted and Built Up in Christ**	Colossians 2:6-15
Sun, Nov. 19	**Hold Fast to Christ**	Colossians 2:16-23
Mon, Nov. 20	**Remember God's Goodness**	Joshua 24:1-14
Tue, Nov. 21	**Choose Whom You Will Serve**	Joshua 24:15-24
Wed, Nov. 22	**Obey God Only**	Acts 5:27-32
Thu, Nov. 23	**The Perfect Law of Liberty**	James 1:19-27
Fri, Nov. 24	**Love and Delight in God's Commands**	Psalm 119:41-56
Sat, Nov. 25	**Do Not Cause Your Neighbor to Fall**	1 Corinthians 8
Sun, Nov. 26	**Strength in the Lord**	1 Corinthians 10:23–11:1

Answers to the Quarterly Quiz on page 2

Lesson 1—1. wash. 2. synagogues. **Lesson 2**—1. lawful. 2. True. **Lesson 3**—1. doctrine. 2. True. **Lesson 4**—1. adultery. 2. Abraham. **Lesson 5**—1. hearts. 2. heart. **Lesson 6**—1. True. 2. sin. **Lesson 7**—1. False. 2. crucified. **Lesson 8**—1. True. 2. curse. **Lesson 9**—1. schoolmaster. 2. True. **Lesson 10**—1. circumcision. 2. Barnabas. **Lesson 11**—1. fulfills it. 2. charity. **Lesson 12**—1. shadow. 2. False. **Lesson 13**—1. glory. 2. Christ.

This Quarter in the Word

Mon, Aug. 28	**Follow God, Not Human Traditions**	Mark 7:1-8
Tue, Aug. 29	**Obedience, Not Sacrifice**	1 Samuel 1:19-23
Wed, Aug. 30	**Be Gracious to Me, O Lord**	Psalm 6
Thu, Aug. 31	**Jesus, a Friend of Sinners**	Luke 7:24-34
Fri, Sep. 1	**Humility Before God and Others**	Luke 14:7-14
Sat, Sep. 2	**Cleanliness and Holiness**	Exodus 30:17-21
Sun, Sep. 3	**Be Cleansed Inside and Out**	Luke 11:37-44
Mon, Sep. 4	**Bless the Lord Who Heals**	Psalm 103:1-12
Tue, Sep. 5	**Praise the Lord of Compassion**	Psalm 103:13-22
Wed, Sep. 6	**Remember the Sabbath Day**	Exodus 20:8-11
Thu, Sep. 7	**Rest for God's People**	Hebrews 4:1-10
Fri, Sep. 8	**Enter God's Rest**	Hebrews 4:11-16
Sat, Sep. 9	**God's People Must Care for Others**	Deuteronomy 22:1-4
Sun, Sep. 10	**The Sabbath Is for Doing Good**	Luke 14:1-6
Mon, Sep. 11	**God Demands Justice**	Isaiah 58:6-14
Tue, Sep. 12	**Do You Want to Be Well?**	John 5:1-9
Wed, Sep. 13	**God's Work Faces Resistance**	John 5:10-16
Thu, Sep. 14	**The Father Works on the Sabbath**	John 5:17-21
Fri, Sep. 15	**Obedience Shows Wisdom**	Deuteronomy 4:1-14
Sat, Sep. 16	**God, Teach Us Your Statutes**	Psalm 119:113-128
Sun, Sep. 17	**Jesus Glorifies the Father**	John 7:14-24

Mon, Sep. 18	**Forgive as You Have Been Forgiven**	Ephesians 4:17-32
Tue, Sep. 19	**God Forgives**	Psalm 130
Wed, Sep. 20	**Adultery in the Heart**	Matthew 5:27-32
Thu, Sep. 21	**You Get the Judgment You Give**	Matthew 7:1-5
Fri, Sep. 22	**Rejoice in God's Forgiveness**	Psalm 32
Sat, Sep. 23	**Let the Wicked Forsake Their Way**	Isaiah 55:6-13
Sun, Sep. 24	**Neither Do I Condemn You**	John 8:1-11
Mon, Sep. 25	**Keep God's Laws in Your Heart**	Deuteronomy 6:4-9
Tue, Sep. 26	**Practice Your Piety in Secret**	Matthew 6:1-8, 16-18
Wed, Sep. 27	**Abide in Christ**	John 15:1-8
Thu, Sep. 28	**God Will Give the Spirit**	Ezekiel 36:25-30
Fri, Sep. 29	**God Will Repay Each One's Deeds**	Romans 2:1-8
Sat, Sep. 30	**God Shows No Partiality**	Romans 2:9-16
Sun, Oct. 1	**God Looks at Your Heart**	Romans 2:17-29
Mon, Oct. 2	**Living Before God**	Deuteronomy 5:1-15
Tue, Oct. 3	**Living with Others**	Deuteronomy 5:16-22
Wed, Oct. 4	**Who Will Rescue Me?**	Romans 7:14-25
Thu, Oct. 5	**God Sees Human Intentions**	Jeremiah 7:1-15
Fri, Oct. 6	**Dead to Sin; Alive in Christ**	Romans 6:1-12
Sat, Oct. 7	**Present Your Bodies to God**	Romans 6:13-23
Sun, Oct. 8	**Dead to the Law Through Christ**	Romans 7:1-13
Mon, Oct. 9	**The Lord Preserves the Faithful**	Psalm 31:1-5, 19-24
Tue, Oct. 10	**Your Faith Has Made You Well**	Mark 10:46-52
Wed, Oct. 11	**My Heart Trusts in God**	Psalm 28
Thu, Oct. 12	**The Gospel Sets Us Free**	Acts 15:22-35
Fri, Oct. 13	**Justice, Kindness, and Humility**	Micah 6:1-8
Sat, Oct. 14	**The Gospel for All People**	Galatians 2:1-10
Sun, Oct. 15	**We Are Justified in Christ**	Galatians 2:11-21

Mon, Oct. 16	**So Great a Salvation**	Hebrews 2:1-9
Tue, Oct. 17	**Christ Destroys the Power of Death**	Hebrews 2:10-18
Wed, Oct. 18	**Delight in the Law of the Lord**	Psalm 1:1-6
Thu, Oct. 19	**Blessed with Every Spiritual Blessing**	Ephesians 1:3-14
Fri, Oct. 20	**The Hope to Which We're Called**	Ephesians 1:15-23
Sat, Oct. 21	**Receiving the Spirit**	Galatians 3:1-5
Sun, Oct. 22	**Redeemed from the Law's Curse**	Galatians 3:6-18
Mon, Oct. 23	**A Promise to Abram's Offspring**	Genesis 12:1-9
Tue, Oct. 24	**An Imperishable Inheritance**	1 Peter 1:3-12
Wed, Oct. 25	**Poor in the World, but Rich in Faith**	James 2:1-7
Thu, Oct. 26	**The Lord Is My Portion**	Psalm 16
Fri, Oct. 27	**God Is the Rock**	Deuteronomy 32:1-14
Sat, Oct. 28	**Heirs of God's Promise**	Hebrews 11:8-19
Sun, Oct. 29	**Children of God**	Galatians 3:23–4:7
Mon, Oct. 30	**Welcoming God's New People**	Acts 15:12-21
Tue, Oct. 31	**The Lord Delivers**	Psalm 37:27-40
Wed, Nov. 1	**My Help Comes from the Lord**	Psalm 121
Thu, Nov. 2	**Many Parts, One Body**	1 Corinthians 12:12-20
Fri, Nov. 3	**God Is Near to Anyone**	Acts 17:22-34
Sat, Nov. 4	**Salvation for All People**	Isaiah 56
Sun, Nov. 5	**Saved Through the Grace of Jesus**	Acts 15:1-11
Mon, Nov. 6	**Let Us Love One Another**	1 John 4:7-13
Tue, Nov. 7	**Perfect Love Casts Out Fear**	1 John 4:14-21
Wed, Nov. 8	**Love and Serve the Lord**	Deuteronomy 10:12-22
Thu, Nov. 9	**Faith Working Through Love**	Galatians 5:1-6
Fri, Nov. 10	**The Greatest Commandment Is Love**	Matthew 22:34-40
Sat, Nov. 11	**Loving Deeds**	Leviticus 19:11-18
Sun, Nov. 12	**Fulfill the Law Through Love**	Romans 13:8-10; 1 Corinthians 13:8-13

Lesson Cycle Chart

International Sunday School Lesson Cycle, September 2022–August 2026

Year	Fall Quarter (Sep, Oct, Nov)	Winter Quarter (Dec, Jan, Feb)	Spring Quarter (Mar, Apr, May)	Summer Quarter (Jun, Jul, Aug)
2022–2023	**God's Exceptional Choice** Genesis, Exodus, Deuteronomy, Judges, 1 Samuel, Ephesians	**From Darkness to Light** 2 Chronicles, Isaiah, Joel, Luke, 1 Corinthians, 2 Timothy, James, 1 Peter	**Jesus Calls Us** Matthew, Mark, Luke, John, Acts	**The Righteous Reign of God** Prophets, Matthew, Romans, 1 Corinthians, Galatians
2023–2024	**God's Law Is Love** Luke, John, Acts, Romans, 1 Corinthians, Galatians, Colossians	**Faith That Pleases God** Ruth, 1 Samuel, 2 Chronicles, Proverbs, Prophets, Matthew, Luke, Romans, Hebrews	**Examining Our Faith** Matthew, Mark, Luke, Acts, Romans, 2 Corinthians, 1 Peter, Jude	**Hope in the Lord** Psalms, Lamentations, Acts, Epistles
2024–2025	**Worship in the Covenant Community** Genesis, Exodus, 2 Samuel, 1 & 2 Kings, 2 Chronicles, Psalms, Isaiah, John	**A King Forever and Ever** Ruth, 2 Samuel, Psalms, Matthew, Luke	**Costly Sacrifices** Exodus, Leviticus, Numbers, Deuteronomy, 1 & 2 Chronicles, Ezra, Matthew, Hebrews, 1 John, Revelation	**Sacred Altars and Holy Offerings** Genesis, Gospels, Romans, 1 Corinthians, Ephesians, Hebrews, 1 Peter
2025–2026	**Judah, From Isaiah to Exile** 2 Kings, 2 Chronicles, Isaiah, Jeremiah, Ezekiel	**Enduring Beliefs of the Church** Exodus, Psalms, Gospels, Acts, Epistles, Revelation	**Social Teachings of the Church** Genesis, Exodus, Deuteronomy, Nehemiah, Psalms, Prophets, Gospels, Acts, Epistles	**Faithful Witnesses** Judges, 1 Samuel, Amos, Gospels, Acts, 2 Timothy, Philemon

Question Quest

Teacher Tips by Ronald L. Nickelson

Expert teachers strive to master the art of posing questions that enhance the learning process. But doing so in an excellent way is not as easy as one might think. We shall approach the issue from a military angle. We are, after all, engaged in spiritual warfare (2 Corinthians 10:4); we need to use our weapons in the most effective way (compare Ephesians 6:11-13). As we consider how to do so, we will focus on two concepts: *strategy* and *tactics,* beginning with the latter.

Tactics of Posing Effective Questions

Tactics can be defined as "optimal maneuvering." For our subject here, this speaks to the nuts and bolts of the positioning and presentation of your questions as appropriate to the nature of your teaching event.

From the familiar investigative list *Who*, *What*, *Where*, *When*, *Why*, and *How*, productive tactics deal with **who** will be responding (level of spiritual maturity? stage of life?), **what** you will be asking for (Scripture reference? personal experience? exceptions to a rule?), **where** you will be asking it (private home? church classroom? campground?), **when** the teaching event will occur (on a cultural holiday? one-on-one over lunch? Sunday morning?), and **how** you will pose the question (verbally? on handouts? on the board?).

Here's a practice exercise in this regard. Take the following question and think about how you would modify it for each of the situations below it:

Considering 1 Thessalonians 5:4-11, what sort of things need to be in your life for you to be considered a child of the "day"? Why?

Situations:

- At a large Sunday morning adult Bible study class of young married couples
- Around a nighttime campfire at an adult retreat
- In a counseling session with a couple considering divorce
- At a support group for people with an addiction

Perhaps right now you're thinking, *That question looks pretty good as-is for all those situations. I wouldn't change it at all.* If that's what you're thinking, let's dig a little deeper and consider just two possible modifications among many:

1. For a large Bible study class, it may be a more efficient use of time to print the question on note cards to distribute to small groups for discussion rather than posing it verbally to the class as a whole.
2. For the retreat, you may have to adjust for the setting being too dark to read the passage from the Bible (if attendees even brought Bibles with them).

As you can see, tactical decisions make the difference between effective and ineffective questions!

Strategies Behind Effective Questions

From the investigative list to the left, we have yet to deal with **why**. That's where strategy comes in. *Strategy* can be defined as "planning what you want to accomplish." The plan should be specific—a plan for "more spiritual growth" or to "value" something is too vague.

Every lesson in the *Standard Lesson Commentary* comes with a strategy in the form of three Lesson Aims, achievement of which is observable by the teacher during class. These follow a time-tested model of stating desired outcomes in terms of what learners are to (1) *know* regarding facts of the lesson, (2) *comprehend* regarding how various facts interrelate, and (3) *apply* as a result of the lesson. You can view these as starting points to be adjusted as appropriate for the nature of your learning environment.

The Nature of Spiritual Warfare

The Chinese general Sun Tzu (who lived about 544–496 BC) said, "Strategy without tactics is the slowest route to victory. Tactics without strategy is the noise before defeat." Indeed!

Jesus Confronts Hypocrisy

Devotional Reading: 1 Samuel 15:19-23
Background Scripture: Luke 11:37-44

Luke 11:37-44

37 And as he spake, a certain Pharisee besought him to dine with him: and he went in, and sat down to meat.

38 And when the Pharisee saw it, he marvelled that he had not first washed before dinner.

39 And the Lord said unto him, Now do ye Pharisees make clean the outside of the cup and the platter; but your inward part is full of ravening and wickedness.

40 Ye fools, did not he that made that which is without make that which is within also?

41 But rather give alms of such things as ye have; and, behold, all things are clean unto you.

42 But woe unto you, Pharisees! for ye tithe mint and rue and all manner of herbs, and pass over judgment and the love of God: these ought ye to have done, and not to leave the other undone.

43 Woe unto you, Pharisees! for ye love the uppermost seats in the synagogues, and greetings in the markets.

44 Woe unto you, scribes and Pharisees, hypocrites! for ye are as graves which appear not, and the men that walk over them are not aware of them.

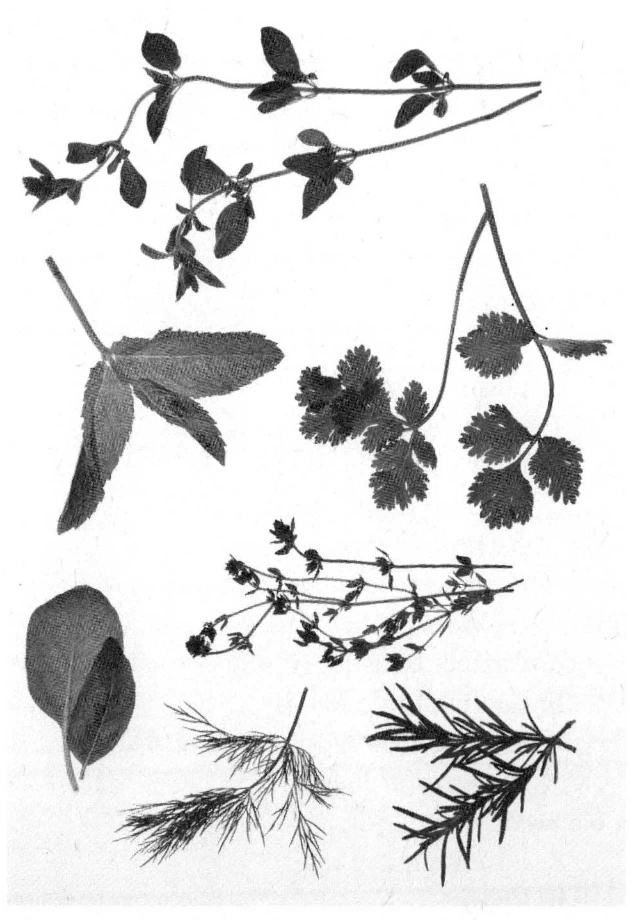

Key Text

The Lord said unto him, Now do ye Pharisees make clean the outside of the cup and the platter; but your inward part is full of ravening and wickedness. **—Luke 11:39**

God's Law

Is Love

Unit 1: Love Completes, Law Falls Short

Lessons 1–4

Lesson Aims

After participating in this lesson, each learner will be able to:

1. Summarize the woes Jesus proclaimed.
2. Explain why the Pharisees were hypocrites.
3. Identify a common area of hypocrisy among Christians and suggest ways to avoid it.

Lesson Outline

Introduction

A. Counterfeit Money, Counterfeit Behavior
B. Lesson Context

I. Two People (Luke 11:37-41)

A. Jesus and a Pharisee (vv. 37-38)
B. Inside and Outside (vv. 39-40)
Beautiful Teeth
C. Generosity and Cleanliness (v. 41)

II. Three Woes (Luke 11:42-44)

A. Against Injustice (v. 42)
B. Against Pride (v. 43)
C. Against Deadly Influence (v. 44)
Hypocritical Behavior

Conclusion

A. Pure Religion
B. Prayer
C. Thought to Remember

Introduction

A. Counterfeit Money, Counterfeit Behavior

After the creation of modern money, an inevitable invention followed: counterfeit money. For example, ancient counterfeiters minted coins made from metals that were less valuable than the authentic coins. The counterfeit coins were dipped in silver to mimic the real coins. In the seventeenth and eighteenth centuries, fraudsters clipped the edges of authentic coins in order to extract bits of the precious metals. From those clippings, they would create a counterfeit coin.

Contemporary money has undergone developments to limit counterfeiters. Many modern coins have grooved or milled edges to show that none of the valuable precious metals have been removed. These efforts, while preventing some counterfeiters, have not done away with the practice altogether. Profits await the successful counterfeiter.

People sometimes "counterfeit" themselves by pretending to be someone they are not. Scandals arise when people say they believe or value one thing but act in a way that opposes that value. Jesus had no tolerance for hypocritical behavior, especially from the religious leaders of His day.

B. Lesson Context

The Gospel of Luke is the first of a two-volume work attributed to "Luke, the beloved physician" (Colossians 4:14). The man Luke was likely the same individual mentioned as the traveling companion of the apostle Paul (2 Timothy 4:11). This would explain the use of "we" throughout the book of Acts (examples: Acts 16:10-12; 20:5-6; 21:1), which is the second volume of Luke's writing (1:1-3). Together, the books of Luke and Acts describe the establishment and expansion of the first-century church.

Today's Scripture is part of a larger section that details Jesus' journey to Jerusalem (Luke 9:51–19:44). Immediately prior to the events of this lesson's Scripture, Jesus had been teaching (11:1-4) and healing (11:14-15). His teaching called out the wickedness of the people (11:29-32) and emphasized the importance of their internal spiritual transformation (11:33-36).

The religious leaders undoubtedly heard what Jesus was teaching and doing as He traveled to Jerusalem. The New Testament Gospels describe Jesus' interactions with the Pharisees more than any other party of first-century Judaism. The Pharisees were a small but influential sect. Their focus was on strict adherence to Judaism (see Acts 26:5), which would have involved obedience to the Law of Moses (also called Torah), the first five books of the Old Testament. The Pharisees believed that by faithfully obeying even the smallest parts of the law, they would experience blessing from God. In an effort to follow the law faithfully, the Pharisees had established a tradition to guide their behavior (see Mark 7:3-5). The Pharisees sought to "build a fence" around the Law of Moses by enforcing their own rules. The expectation was that by following the Pharisees' tradition, a person would faithfully keep God's commands—even down to the most obscure command.

The Pharisees' zeal, however, had caused them to lose sight of the intentions of the law and the extent to which they had been influenced by tradition. They had focused so heavily on their prideful adherence to tradition that they neglected to cultivate hearts of worship that the law required (see Matthew 15:1-9). Jesus denounced the Pharisees for their pride and hypocrisy (examples: 23:1-7; Luke 18:9-14). As a result, instances of conflict between Jesus and the Pharisees arose (examples: 6:1-11; 16:13-14; John 7:28-34; 11:57).

Despite the hostile relationship, Jesus accepted invitations to eat with the Pharisees. Today's Scripture describes the second time in Luke's Gospel that Jesus dined with a Pharisee (see also Luke 7:36-50; 14:1-6). Accounts similar to those found in today's lesson are found in Matthew 15:1-20; 23:5-7, 23-28; and Mark 12:38-39.

How to Say It

czar	zahr.
Deuteronomy	Due-ter-*ahn*-uh-me.
Leviticus	Leh-*vit*-ih-kus.
Pharisees	*Fair*-ih-seez.
synagogues	*sin*-uh-gogs.
Torah (*Hebrew*)	*Tor*-uh.

I. Two People

(Luke 11:37-41)

A. Jesus and a Pharisee (vv. 37-38)

37. And as he spake, a certain Pharisee besought him to dine with him: and he went in, and sat down to meat.

Prior to this verse, Jesus had been teaching the crowds regarding wickedness and judgment (Luke 11:29-32) and how they might live in a manner indicative of spiritual health (11:33-36). The text is silent regarding the reason that this *certain Pharisee* invited Jesus *to dine with him*. Inviting a teacher to a meal was common in the first century AD. The meal allowed the teacher to demonstrate his or her expertise and wisdom. By extending the invitation, the host desired to receive some level of honor from the guest and from the wider community of people. Extending invitations to the socially outcast, people like "publicans and sinners," was generally avoided (see 5:27-31). Perhaps this Pharisee wanted to question Jesus in private. Or perhaps he wanted to demonstrate his own piety by way of extending an invitation to the traveling teacher.

What Do You Think?

How can your sharing a meal with another person give you the opportunity to show God's love to that person?

Digging Deeper

Who will you invite to share a meal with you this upcoming week?

38. And when the Pharisee saw it, he marvelled that he had not first washed before dinner.

It was common for first-century Jews to perform ceremonial washings for purification (examples: John 2:6; 3:25; 11:55). Such occurrences were a way for the people to became ritually clean as described by the Law of Moses (Leviticus 11–15). For Pharisees, cleanliness in general and handwashing in particular were ways to follow the religious tradition (see Mark 7:1-4). Although the Law of Moses required periodic washing (examples: Leviticus 11:28; 15:4-27), the Pharisees had broadened the practice.

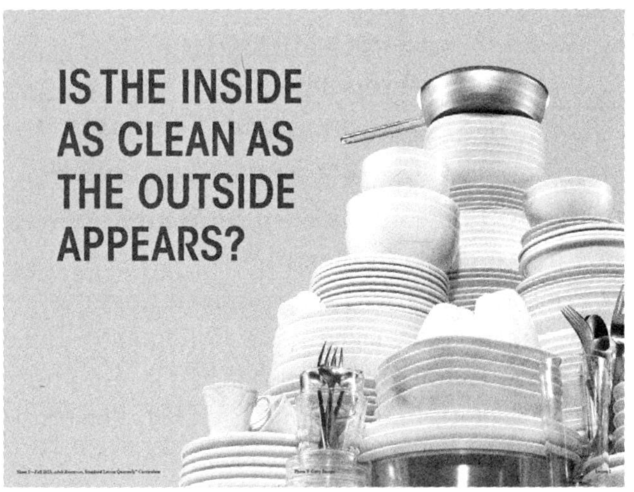

IS THE INSIDE
AS CLEAN AS
THE OUTSIDE
APPEARS?

Visual for Lesson 1. *Start a discussion by pointing to this posted visual and asking, "What's the connection between integrity and spiritual cleanliness?"*

One would expect that a guest would follow the customs and manners of his or her host. Being *marvelled* at someone did not always have positive connotation, as was the case with Jesus (Mark 6:6) and the apostle Paul (Galatians 1:6). This Pharisee did not have positive regard for that fact that Jesus *had not first washed*.

Jesus did not object to washing. He washed the feet of the Twelve (John 13:1-12). He even scolded a host for failing to provide water for washing (Luke 7:44). In this instance, Jesus' refusal to wash served as an act of provocation and gave Him the opportunity to teach those in attendance at the meal.

B. Inside and Outside (vv. 39-40)

39. And the Lord said unto him, Now do ye Pharisees make clean the outside of the cup and the platter; but your inward part is full of ravening and wickedness.

Washing only *the outside of the cup and the platter* presents an obvious problem. While the vessels might appear clean, the inside that touches food or drink will remain unclean. The dish still has potential for contamination. Cleaning dishes for food and drink requires total commitment!

Jesus was not primarily concerned about food safety practices. Instead, He used the example to rebuke the attitudes and behaviors of the *Pharisees*. They were more concerned with outward displays of purity than with the actual purity of their hearts and minds. The Pharisees' inner impurity was evident in their public actions. *Wickedness* is a generic term for evil actions. The apostle Paul used the same term when describing the actions of the unrighteous (Romans 1:28-31). Such actions are indicative of the evil present in a person's heart (see Mark 7:20-23). The word *ravening* means "to devour or plunder greedily" (compare Ezekiel 22:25-27). Greed characterized the desires of many of the Pharisees (Luke 16:14). They engaged in predatory behavior to gain wealth at the expense of vulnerable members of their community (see 11:41, below; 20:46-47).

Beautiful Teeth

Samuel Collins (1619–1670) entered the sumptuous Russian palace, eager to attend his first royal ball. A physician, Collins had been appointed as the personal physician to the Russian czar. As the festivities began, the czar introduced Collins to a group of noblewomen. Samuel greeted the women in broken Russian. The group broke out in laughter and smiles, revealing their teeth that were various shades of black! Soon after, Collins realized that every woman at the ball had inexplicably dyed her teeth this unsettling shade.

Because of poor dental hygiene habits, tooth decay was prevalent during this time. These women had blackened their teeth so that others could not differentiate rotten teeth from heathy teeth. All teeth were the same unnatural color. By doing so, the women preserved a facade of health and beauty.

The Pharisees of Jesus' day had focused on creating a mere facade of righteousness and ritual cleanliness. However, Jesus saw through their display. While the veneer of righteousness might have fooled people, Jesus knew the wickedness of the hearts of the Pharisees. What parts of your life are you "painting over" in order to impress others? Get comfortable being real with the Lord, for He knows the true status of your heart. —A. W.

40. Ye fools, did not he that made that which is without make that which is within also?

Calling the Pharisees *fools* intensified Jesus' indictment of their wicked behavior. In a later parable, Jesus used the designation "fool" when describing a "certain rich man" and the spiritual dangers he faced because of his greed (Luke 12:13-21). Both the Pharisees and that parable's main character were fools because their lives lacked integrity.

Jesus' rhetorical question highlights that God *made* the whole person: the parts seen (*that which is without*) and unseen (*that which is within*). God himself is perfect (Matthew 5:48) and pure (Job 4:17; compare Habakkuk 1:13). Therefore, God desires total purity from His creation. God's wants people to live lives that are pure from the inside out, not concerned only with appearances (see James 4:8). Jesus explained the folly of shallow cleanliness in place of developing actual spiritual purity and lives of integrity.

What Do You Think?

What steps can believers take to develop spiritual purity and personal integrity?

Digging Deeper

How do Romans 12; Ephesians 4:20-32; and Colossians 3:5-17 inform your actions in this regard?

C. Generosity and Cleanliness (v. 41)

41. But rather give alms of such things as ye have; and, behold, all things are clean unto you.

One correction for the Pharisees' greed and wickedness involved giving generously of their wealth. This could be accomplished through charitable gifts (*alms*) given to the poor. Although the Law of Moses contains no reference to these specific gifts, it does include guidance on caring for people in need (Exodus 23:10-11; Leviticus 25:35-43; Deuteronomy 15:7-11; etc.). Therefore, practices of justice in the form of generosity were not a new requirement for the Pharisees. Jesus was calling them to follow the law that they already had claimed to value.

Jesus' command appears to deny the value of one practice (washing) in order to uphold the value of another (giving). However, it is the intent, rather than the act itself, that determines the purity of that act. How a person allocates his or her wealth is one way to indicate the status of his or her heart: a *clean* heart is generous with worldly wealth (see 1 John 3:17-18).

What Do You Think?

How do you practice generosity that comes from having a clean heart?

Digging Deeper

What steps do you take to overcome challenges to demonstrating hospitality?

II. Three Woes
(Luke 11:42-44)

A. Against Injustice (v. 42)

42a. But woe to you, Pharisees!

A *woe* is a proclamation intended to announce pending pain, threat, or grief. Such proclamations are common in the Old Testament prophets (examples: Isaiah 5:8-30; Micah 2:1-2). Jesus also proclaimed such warnings (examples: Matthew 11:21; 26:24; Luke 6:24-26; 17:1). On one occasion, Jesus proclaimed woes upon the scribes and *Pharisees* (Matthew 23:13-32).

42b. For ye tithe mint and rue and all manner of herbs.

The first woe came as a result of the Pharisees' keeping a minor command without showing regard for a weightier command (see Luke 11:42c, below). A *tithe* is a gift of a tenth from the larger whole (example: Genesis 14:18-20). The Law of Moses provided guidelines on how the Israelites should give a tenth of their goods for worship and to support the Levites and the impoverished (Leviticus 27:30-33; Deuteronomy 14:22-29; 26:1-15).

Herbs like *mint and rue* grow wild and can flourish without oversight and care from humans. Determining the appropriate amount of these herbs to tithe would have required great attention to detail from the Pharisees. Several centuries after events of this lesson, extracanonical commentary on the Law of Moses clarified that tithing from these herbs was not required because such plants were difficult to measure and considered insignificant. While the Law of Moses gave no specific command regarding the tithing of wild herbs, the Pharisees practiced such a thing. Their practice hedged all around the law while disregarding the explicit requirements of the law.

Tithing should have been a joyous act of love to

God. The Pharisees had turned the practice into an opportunity to demonstrate their rigorous obedience to the law, even regarding insignificant herbs.

What Do You Think?
In what ways do you tithe to God from your time, energy, or thoughts?
Digging Deeper
How will these types of tithes demonstrate your love for God and for your neighbors?

42c. And pass over judgment and the love of God: these ought ye to have done, and not to leave the other undone.

Judgment in this verse consists of showing justice toward other people, especially the economically vulnerable. The same God who acted with justice and mercy toward His people by rescuing them from Egypt (see Exodus 12:31-42) also required that His people show justice and mercy to others in need (see Zechariah 7:9-10). The Old Testament provides guidance regarding treatment toward people experiencing poverty, many of whom were widows, orphans, and resident aliens (examples: Exodus 22:21-27; Deuteronomy 24:10-22). God judged those who failed to show fair and just treatment toward others (see Amos 2:6-8).

At the heart of the Law of Moses and Jesus' teachings were the dual commands regarding the people's *love of God* (Deuteronomy 6:5; Matthew 22:36-38) and their love for others (Leviticus 19:18; Matthew 22:39; Luke 10:26-27). God's people followed the former command as they demonstrated their willingness to adhere to the latter command.

Jesus declared woe on the Pharisees for their neglect of these two commands. They had *done* the unrequired smaller aspects of law—tithing herbs—while leaving *undone* the command to love others (see Matthew 23:23). They had attempted to honor God while also neglecting the command to show justice to their neighbors. The religious leaders of Jesus' day had shown a lack of regard for people in need (see Luke 20:46-47). Further, they had acted pridefully regarding their observance of the law (see 18:9-14), leading them to show disregard for others (see Matthew 23:1-4). They had failed to live in the manner required of them: a life of humility marked with mercy and justice (see Micah 6:8).

B. Against Pride (v. 43)

43. Woe unto you, Pharisees! for ye love the uppermost seats in the synagogues, and greetings in the markets.

The second *woe* calls out the prideful and arrogant behavior of the Pharisees. Their *love* was misdirected, concerned for their own status rather than the well-being of others.

First-century *synagogues* were the locations for the reading and teaching of Scripture (example: Matthew 4:23). Most synagogues would have lacked sufficient seating, requiring some people to stand or sit on the floor. The religious leaders, however, would not have to take on these positions. They would sit in *the uppermost seats* of honor and prestige, likely visible to all people in the building.

The Pharisees' desire for recognition also included their attitudes in the public square. Jesus warned against similar actions from the scribes as they "[desired] to walk in long robes, and [loved] *greetings in the markets*" (Luke 20:46). The nature of these greetings is unknown, but they likely involved excessive deference by other people to these leaders. God desires that His people act with humility and treat others with respect and dignity, regardless of social status (see Romans 12:3).

What Do You Think?
How can believers ensure worship services do not turn into opportunities for self-promotion?
Digging Deeper
What steps can your congregation take to avoid playing favorites?

C. Against Deadly Influence (v. 44)

44. Woe unto you, scribes and Pharisees, hypocrites! for ye are as graves which appear not, and the men that walk over them are not aware of them.

This final *woe* does not mention a specific sin committed by the *Pharisees*. Instead, the woe introduces a metaphor that demonstrates Jesus' disgust. Additionally, Jesus expanded this woe to include the *scribes*, religious leaders who were experts in the Law of Moses (compare Matthew 23:13-29).

In an ironic twist, Jesus proclaimed that the scribes and the Pharisees—people most concerned with purity—had become not only defiled but also a source of defilement themselves. Jesus considered them *hypocrites* because they claimed to honor the law while ignoring its core: loving God and others (see commentary on Luke 11:42c, above).

If a Jewish person came into contact with a dead body, the person became ritually unclean and would have to take steps to be considered clean (see Numbers 19:11-22). This held true even if a grave was unmarked and the person who came upon it did not realize their proximity to the dead. In a similar manner, people would unknowingly become unclean when they followed the teachings and the practices of the Pharisees. This was like people walking over unmarked *graves* and *not* being *aware* of their own defilement. The behavior and attitudes of the Pharisees were causing others to suffer grave harm.

Hypocritical Behavior

Born into slavery, Harriet Jacobs (approx. 1813–1897) understood firsthand the horror of being controlled by other people. She suffered inhumane conditions as a slave, assault at the hands of slaveholders, and loneliness as a result of her family being torn apart. She eventually escaped to New York City and became a staunch abolitionist. She detailed her experiences in her autobiography, *Incidents in the Life of a Slave Girl.*

In the book, Harriet questioned the religious leaders of her day. Regarding their attitudes toward slavery, she wondered if such leaders were "blind or . . . hypocrites?" She called out the duplicity of Christian leaders who either ignored slavery or used Scripture to justify the practice.

The Pharisees of Jesus' day had acted hypocritically; they had disregarded the parts of the Law of Moses that required demonstrations of care to the most vulnerable members of the community. Although the Pharisees' public displays of observance to the law portrayed one thing, in their hearts was the opposite sentiment. They had failed to show mercy and justice. They had become prideful. They were a deadly influence on others. Hypocrisy is still an issue today. Where do hypocritical impulses arise in your heart? —A. W.

Conclusion

A. Pure Religion

In many ways, faults similar to those Jesus pointed out in the Pharisees can be found in people today. The Pharisees prioritized outward displays of holiness, while failing to do the important work of love, mercy, and justice. Pursuing counterfeit displays of holiness, while potentially easier than going after what God requires, leaves people as hypocrites. God wants His people to experience holiness in all aspects of their lives.

Followers of Jesus must remember to honor the commands to love God, show justice, and demonstrate merciful love, above any other traditions. Only then will believers exercise a "pure religion" before God (James 1:27). A failure to do so indicates that one's heart has not been transformed.

Consider the following questions: Does your behavior lead you to love God more deeply? Does your behavior lead you to act justly or advocate for justice for others? If you can answer positively to both questions, then you are on the right track to loving God and your neighbor.

B. Prayer

Heavenly Father, we desire to be holy people. Take away our need to impress others, and impress on us the image of Your Son, Jesus Christ. Show us how we might be generous with our giftings in order that we might love You and our neighbors. In the name of Your Son, Jesus. Amen

C. Thought to Remember

Pure religion requires that we love God and our neighbors.

Visuals FOR THESE LESSONS

The visual pictured in each lesson (example: page 12) is a small reproduction of a large, full-color poster included in the *Adult Resources* packet for the Fall Quarter. Order ISBN 978-0-784739-13-6 from your supplier.

Involvement Learning

Enhance your lesson with KJV Bible Student *(from your curriculum supplier) and the reproducible activity page (at www.standardlesson.com or in the back of the* KJV Standard Lesson Commentary Deluxe Edition*).*

Into the Lesson

Before class begins, do an online search for a recording of the 1964 song "The 'In' Crowd" by Dobie Gray. Once class begins, divide the class in half and give each half one of the following assignments. Ask one half to listen to the lyrics and answer the following question: "How does the singer know if he is a part of the perceived 'in' crowd?" Ask the other half to listen to the lyrics and answer the following question: "According to the singer, what is great about being in the 'in' crowd?" (*Option.* Print the lyrics or project the lyrics on a screen.) After five minutes, ask groups to present their answers for whole-class discussion.

Have groups discuss the following questions: 1–What are some common situations when people claim to be a part of the perceived "in" crowd? 2–How might it feel to be a part of situations where you were considered to be "in" and others were considered to be "out"? 3–How might it feel to be part of the perceived "out" crowd?

Alternative. Distribute copies of the "Movie Script" exercise from the activity page, which you can download. Have learners work in small groups to complete as indicated. After 10 minutes, reconvene the groups and ask them to share their results.

Transition to Bible study by saying, "Today's Scripture describes how Jesus interacted with some religious leaders who were proud of their status as a part of the perceived 'in' crowd. As we study, notice Jesus' reaction to their attitude."

Into the Word

Before class, recruit two learners to prepare a brief presentation regarding the lesson context. Assign one of the following questions to each learner for them to answer: 1–Why was it considered problematic that Jesus refused to wash His hands? 2–Why was it shocking for Jesus to compare the Pharisees to graves? Invite the learners to share their reports before the whole class.

Ask a volunteer to read Luke 11:37-44 aloud. Write two headers on the board: *What Jesus Condemned* / *What Jesus Encouraged.* Divide the class into two groups. One group will come up with responses to the first header, while the other group will do the same for the second header.

After five minutes, ask a volunteer from each group to give his or her group's responses. Write the responses under the appropriate header on the board. Ask the following questions for whole-class discussion: 1–What attitudes of the Pharisees were at the heart of Jesus' condemnation? 2–How could the actions that Jesus encouraged be an antidote to these negative attitudes?

Into Life

Place learners into groups of three and distribute a sheet of paper and pen to each group. Have groups discuss the following questions and write down their responses: 1–How could the Pharisees correct the hypocrisy for which Jesus criticized them? 2–How have Christians displayed or have continued to display hypocrisy? 3–How can Christians avoid hypocritical behavior?

Option 1. Distribute copies of the "We Still Have a Problem" activity from the activity page. Have learners complete it in pairs before discussing conclusions with the whole class.

Option 2. Ask groups to imagine a visitor to your congregation. List possible reactions that the visitor could have to the visit. Consider questions that the visitor might have regarding expected behavior or the order of service. After two minutes, ask groups to share the lists with the class. Discuss how your congregation may be inconsistent regarding intended attitudes toward visitors and actual behavior toward visitors.

Close class with prayer. Begin with a silent time of repentance for hypocritical attitudes. Finish by asking God to reveal to learners how to live in a consistent way that demonstrates God's love.

September 10
Lesson 2 (KJV)

Jesus Silences Critics

Devotional Reading: Hebrews 4:1-10
Background Scripture: Luke 14:1-6

Luke 14:1-6

1 And it came to pass, as he went into the house of one of the chief Pharisees to eat bread on the sabbath day, that they watched him.
2 And, behold, there was a certain man before him which had the dropsy.
3 And Jesus answering spake unto the lawyers and Pharisees, saying, Is it lawful to heal on the sabbath day?
4 And they held their peace. And he took him, and healed him, and let him go;
5 And answered them, saying, Which of you shall have an ass or an ox fallen into a pit, and will not straightway pull him out on the sabbath day?
6 And they could not answer him again to these things.

Key Text

Jesus answering spake unto the lawyers and Pharisees, saying, Is it lawful to heal on the sabbath day? And they held their peace. And he took him, and healed him, and let him go. **—Luke 13:3-4**

God's Law
Is Love

Unit 1: Love Completes, Law Falls Short

Lessons 1–4

Lesson Aims

After participating in this lesson, each learner will be able to:

1. Identify the Sabbath law at issue.
2. Contrast the viewpoint of the Pharisees with the viewpoint of Jesus.
3. Suggest why the lesson's passage is (or should be) relevant to him or her.

Lesson Outline

Introduction
- A. Loving God by Loving the Least
- B. Lesson Context

I. Tense Hospitality (Luke 14:1-2)
- A. The Meal (v. 1)
- B. The Sick Man (v. 2)

II. Two Questions (Luke 14:3-6)
- A. The First Question (v. 3)
- B. The Healing (v. 4)
  - *A Suspicious Stethoscope*
- C. The Second Question (vv. 5-6)
  - *How Much Is a Pet Worth?*

Conclusion
- A. Holiness in Time
- B. Prayer
- C. Thought to Remember

Introduction

A. Loving God by Loving the Least

As attendees at the memorial service for Dorothy Day (1897–1980) listened to the sermon, they were reminded of the following quote from her writing: "You love God just as much as the one you love least." This quote was her way of paraphrasing Jesus' commands in Luke 10:25-37 to love God and show love and mercy to others. The minister giving the sermon went on to describe how this quote anchored Dorothy's life and work.

Demonstrations of mercy, love, and justice have been the tenets of the Catholic Worker Movement, established by Dorothy and others in the 1930s. The movement consists of over 200 communities ("houses") in 14 countries. Each house works to show hospitality and mercy to the most vulnerable members of their city. This work is done through their feeding of the hungry, tending to the sick, and providing stable housing for the unhoused.

God desires that His people love Him and love their neighbors. People can demonstrate such love toward others through acts of mercy. In doing so, God's people follow Jesus' command to "be ye therefore merciful, as your Father also is merciful" (Luke 6:36). This lesson's Scripture reveals how Jesus responded to a group of people who wanted to add boundaries and limitations to acts of mercy.

B. Lesson Context

This lesson depicts the third occasion in Luke's Gospel that Jesus shared a meal with a Pharisee (see also Luke 7:36-50; 11:37-53). All three interactions share a common pattern of events. First, a Pharisee invited Jesus to join the meal. Second, a tense moment between Jesus and the host led to a conversation regarding issues of religious observance. Third, Jesus used the opportunity to instruct those in attendance on issues regarding how to follow God. In doing so, Jesus taught His fellow diners to act mercifully in their dealings with other people.

The issue of doing work on the Sabbath is the

primary concern of Luke 14:1-6, today's Scripture. The Jewish Sabbath was established based on the day that God rested after six days of creation (see Genesis 2:2-3; Exodus 20:8-11; Deuteronomy 5:12-15). As a result, the people were to cease work on the Sabbath. Such requirements regarding that day were a sign of holiness between God and His people (see Exodus 31:12-17).

As the ancient Israelites left Egypt, they were commanded to take certain steps to prepare for Sabbath observance (example: Exodus 16:21-30). Later, as the people entered the promised land, the Law of Moses provided further descriptions regarding proper observance of the Sabbath (see 34:21; 35:1-3). Defiance of these commands brought harsh consequences to the people (examples: Numbers 15:32-36; Nehemiah 13:15-18; Jeremiah 17:27). The Israelites understood the Sabbath to be "a delight" (Isaiah 58:13) and a day for worship (see Leviticus 23:3). Even certain psalms were to be sung on that day (example: Psalm 92).

By the first century AD, certain expectations regarding proper adherence of the Sabbath had been established by the Jewish religious leaders. In the time between the testaments, an oral tradition later codified as the *Mishna* (rabbinic law) attempted to define the rules regarding proper Sabbath observance. These included nuanced definitions of work, as well as complex regulations regarding what was allowed and disallowed on the Sabbath. Such intricacies made it challenging for most first-century Jews to accurately interpret how they should observe the Sabbath.

Jesus never disputed the importance of the Sabbath. His high regard for it can be seen in His habit of teaching in synagogues on the Sabbath (examples: Mark 1:21; Luke 13:10). Further, He was willing to use the day to show mercy toward suffering people (examples: Mark 1:21-34; Luke 6:6-11; 13:10-17; John 5:1-18). As "Lord . . . of the sabbath" (Mark 2:28), Jesus demonstrated the true intent of the Sabbath: to remind God's people of His mercy (see Deuteronomy 5:15). The day was not to be a religious burden or an excuse to limit works of love and mercy.

How to Say It

Hillel	*Hill*-el.
Judaism	*Joo*-duh-izz-um or Joo-*day*-izz-um.
Mishna	*Mish*-nuh.
Nazareth	*Naz*-uh-reth.
rabbi	*rab*-eye.
Sabbath	*Sab*-buth.
Shammai	*Sham*-eye.

I. Tense Hospitality

(Luke 14:1-2)

A. The Meal (v. 1)

1. And it came to pass, as he went into the house of one of the chief Pharisees to eat bread on the sabbath day, that they watched him.

This Scripture takes place as Jesus traveled to Jerusalem (Luke 9:51–19:44). Immediately before this text, upon being warned regarding Herod's intentions to have Jesus executed, Jesus expressed sorrow for Jerusalem (13:31-35). The phrase *and it came to pass* indicates that some unknown amount of time had passed between that teaching and this meal.

Because Jesus was considered a rabbi by at least one member of the Pharisees (see John 3:2), the group likely deemed Him to be an appropriate guest for a meal. They could spend the meal discussing the law and its associated tradition and commentary.

The Pharisees rose to prominence as a sect of Judaism because of their interpretation of the Law of Moses, its oral commentary, and its related tradition. Several schools of interpretation came from the Pharisees. Teachers from the first century AD, Hillel and Shammai, attracted students to their respective schools of interpretations. Their interpretative work included determining guidelines regarding Sabbath observance for first-century Jews.

As a Pharisee, the host likely enjoyed some degree of wealth (compare Luke 16:14). This assumption is further bolstered by his elevated position as *one of the chief Pharisees.* In addition to financial benefit, this particular Pharisee was likely held in high regard as a teacher of the law (see Matthew 23:1-2, 5-7).

Additionally, the Pharisees had strong concerns regarding ritual purity and physical cleanliness. For this reason, the host likely invited only Pharisees and people who would be considered clean. Other people, such as "publicans and sinners" (Luke 5:30), would not have been invited. Pharisees had certain expectations regarding the cleanliness of the guests and even the dishes of the meal (compare Mark 7:3-5; Luke 11:38).

The timing of this meal (*on the sabbath day*) would have required advance planning by the host in order to observe the Sabbath day as required by the Law of Moses (see Lesson Context). This meal was likely prepared before the Sabbath and served during the 24-hour period beginning at sundown on Friday.

The Pharisees who assembled for this meal treated Jesus with suspicion. *They watched* Jesus in order to find fault with Him, just as they had done previously (see Luke 6:7; 11:53-54; see also 20:20). The atmosphere of the meal had a tense edge, rather than being one of relaxation and conversation. This was not the first time that the Pharisees had presented Jesus with an issue regarding what was acceptable on the Sabbath (see 6:1-10; 13:10-17).

What Do You Think?

How do you behave in situations where it seems like you and your faith are being observed by others?

Digging Deeper

How does Jesus' teaching regarding salt and light (Matthew 5:13-16) inform your response in these situations?

B. The Sick Man (v. 2)

2. And, behold, there was a certain man before him which had the dropsy.

Luke does not describe whether this *certain man* was a guest of the Pharisees, an intruder, or a living "prop" brought to test Jesus. Either the man was a surprise to the entire party, or his presence was the result of the Pharisees' cunning intentions. But Jesus knows the hearts of all people (compare John 2:23-25); He knew the true reason the ailing man was in their midst.

Dropsy is an outdated medical term for a malady characterized by painful swelling of the limbs. The swelling probably resulted from an underlying issue regarding the heart, kidney, or liver. Modern medicine would treat the condition with diuretics. In the first century AD, however, no such treatment was available. The man would have continued to suffer and would have depended on the charity of others to meet his basic needs.

Some students of this Scripture have argued that Luke's description of the man's disease served as a form of literary foreshadowing to Jesus' later criticism of the Pharisees in Luke 16:14-15 regarding their greed. A disease like the one suffered by that man caused insatiable thirst, even as the body retained water. Some first-century philosophers thought of swelling diseases as a metaphor for the disease of greed. Greed caused a swelling of a person's pride, which led that person to seek more wealth. The Pharisees had brought a diseased man before the group in hopes to trap Jesus. Instead, it was the Pharisees who were experiencing a disease in their spirits.

II. Two Questions

(Luke 14:3-6)

A. The First Question (v. 3)

3a. And Jesus answering spake unto the lawyers and Pharisees, saying,

First-century lawyers were not primarily legal advocates in criminal or civil courts as modern-day lawyers are. Instead, these *lawyers* were regarded as experts in the Torah. (The Torah, also known as the Law of Moses, is comprised of the first five books of the Old Testament.) We might compare these individuals to modern-day scholars of the Bible. These lawyers are mentioned more often in Luke's Gospel than in any other Gospel (examples: Luke 10:25; 11:45-52; 14:3). Luke describes them alongside the Pharisees as having "rejected the counsel of God" (7:30).

3b. Is it lawful to heal on the sabbath day?

Jesus' question concerned the heart of the Law

of Moses. The law was never intended to burden the people (compare Deuteronomy 30:11-14). And Jesus never abolished the Law of Moses (see Matthew 5:17-20). Instead, He wanted His audience to consider the principles of goodness and righteousness intrinsic to the Law of Moses (compare Romans 7:12; 1 Timothy 1:8). *To heal on the sabbath* violated the Pharisees' strict reading of the law regarding what was acceptable on that day.

This was not the first time that Jesus taught a lawyer regarding the importance of mercy (see Luke 10:25-37). God does not desire for humans to limit works of mercy, either regarding the timing or the recipient of those works.

What Do You Think?

How can you incorporate the practice of asking questions as an act of accountability or evangelism?

Digging Deeper

What steps will you take to improve your question-asking skills?

B. The Healing (v. 4)

4. And they held their peace. And he took him, and healed him, and let him go.

The Pharisees and the lawyers were speechless and unable to answer Jesus' question. The phrase *held their peace* does not mean that the religious leaders agreed with Jesus or were peaceful regarding Jesus' words or actions. Rather, they avoided confronting Jesus at that particular moment.

Luke does not describe how Jesus *took* the ailing man *and healed him*. Rather than focus on the way that Jesus healed, Luke focused on the results of that healing. Jesus *let* the sick man *go*, thus freeing him from his physical suffering. This healing is similar to another healing that Jesus did on the Sabbath. On that occasion, Jesus healed a woman and declared her free from her bondage (Luke 13:10-17).

Jesus' inaugural sermon in Nazareth describes His work, in part, as one of bringing physical healing (Luke 4:14-21). The arrival of God's kingdom would be demonstrated by such healings (see 9:1-2, 10-11; 10:9). These miraculous works were evidence that the rule of God's Messiah, as promised by the prophet Isaiah (Isaiah 35:1-6; 61:1-2), had come.

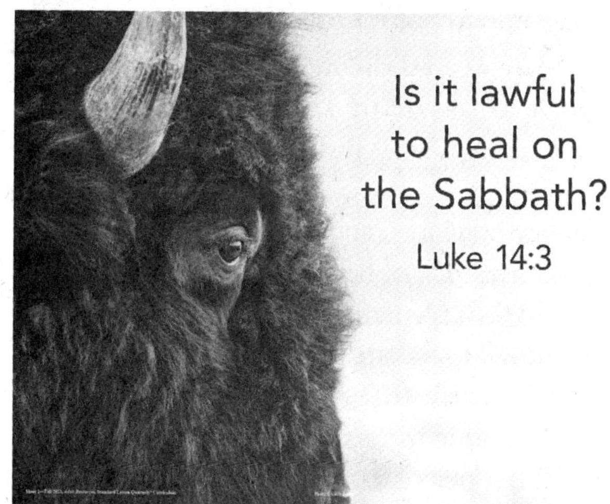
Is it lawful
to heal on
the Sabbath?
Luke 14:3
Visual for Lesson 2. *Point to this visual as you discuss the lesson commentary associated with Luke 14:3b.*

A Suspicious Stethoscope

A comedian once revealed that he always kept a stethoscope in his car's glove compartment. Then, if he was pulled over for breaking the speed limit, he would put the stethoscope around his neck and say, "Officer, I'm a doctor! If I don't get to the hospital *now*, a patient is going to *die*." The comedian claimed he never received a ticket when *correctly* using this strategy.

But once when the comedian was pulled over, the officer looked puzzled by the comedian's lie instead of alarmed about the fake emergency. Still, the officer let the comedian go with only a warning. As the comedian drove away, he realized that instead of a stethoscope around his neck, he was wearing his car's jumper cables! He had bent the rules and been caught.

The Pharisees were hoping to catch Jesus bending the Law of Moses. What they missed, however, was that Jesus had no need to bend the Law of Moses. Rather, He fulfilled the law (see Matthew 5:17-20). Jesus demonstrated this by showing mercy and healing on the Sabbath. To what extent are you willing to show mercy to your neighbors regardless of others' trying to enforce limits on you?

—A. W.

C. The Second Question (vv. 5-6)

5. And answered them, saying, Which of you shall have an ass or an ox fallen into a pit, and will not straightway pull him out on the sabbath day?

The Law of Moses required that people help lost or injured livestock of neighbors and enemies alike (Exodus 23:4-5; Deuteronomy 22:1-4). An attitude of mercy (even to livestock) was at the heart of these commands. By the first century AD, disagreement had arisen among interpreters of the Law of Moses regarding if a person could rescue a stranded animal on the Sabbath. Strict interpretations allowed the animal's owner to feed the animal and ensure its survival until the end of the Sabbath day. Freeing the animal, however, was not allowed. In this interpretation, the work of freeing the animal broke the command to do no work on the Sabbath (see Exodus 20:8-11). Other interpretations were more lenient and allowed for the animal's owner to work to free the animal, even on the Sabbath.

Jesus' question assumed a positive answer: yes, even *on the sabbath* would a person rescue *an ox* that had *fallen into a pit*. Without assistance, the stranded animal was at risk of suffering injury or facing harm from predators. All of the people at the meal likely agreed that saving the life of this hypothetical animal was accepted. If there was disagreement among the guests at the meal, then it was likely regarding the *extent* that work could be done to save the animal. In short, Jesus expected that all of the guests would agree that showing mercy to an animal even on the Sabbath made sense. In that case, how much more legitimate was showing mercy to *people* on the Sabbath?

Older Greek manuscripts of this Scripture include the Greek word for *son* or *child* in place of the word for *ass*. Possible endangerment of a child would also be an appropriate (and necessary) reason for a person to act on the Sabbath. If a person showed effort to save livestock on the Sabbath, then that person would surely show more effort to save a child.

Jesus could have waited until the next day to heal the man. However, the opportunity for Jesus to show mercy presented itself on the Sabbath. The Sabbath served human well-being, not the other way around (see Mark 2:27). If some religious leaders considered that it was acceptable to work on the Sabbath (see Luke 13:15), then Jesus argued that His work was also acceptable, if not all the more so.

Jesus' question in this verse parallels another question that He asked of the Pharisees in Matthew 12:11-14. Both accounts have the same emphasis: doing good and showing mercy on the Sabbath is at the heart of the Sabbath itself.

What Do You Think?

How can an unhealthy focus on human traditions lead a person to fail to show mercy?

Digging Deeper

What steps do you take to overcome any tendencies to be unmerciful?

How Much Is a Pet Worth?

I had known that it was only a matter of time before my young daughter's beloved guinea pig would become sick. These animals are prone to having respiratory issues. The day came when my daughter showed me how her guinea pig struggled to breathe and refused to eat. Her love for the pet was evident. And my love for my daughter meant that I had to help her suffering pet.

The veterinarian confirmed our fears: the guinea pig had pneumonia which was likely to become fatal. Replacing the pet would have been cheaper than treating the pet. But I spent my money on treatment instead, for my daughter's sake. After attentive treatment and several veterinarian visits, the pet's health improved. My daughter was relieved that her beloved—and for me, rather costly!—guinea pig was on the mend.

Love can make us spend a great deal, in time, money, and other resources, to demonstrate our care. Jesus desired that the Pharisees demonstrate their love for God and for others with action. How will you demonstrate your love for God and for others in the upcoming week? —A. W.

6. And they could not answer him again to these things.

For the second time during the meal, the Pharisees were left speechless (compare Luke 14:4, above). Their refusal to answer might have indicated their collective humiliation and shame (compare 13:17; regarding human silence and shame in response to God's work, see Ezekiel 16:63). This tense interaction likely contributed to later hostility that the Pharisees would demonstrate toward Jesus.

These things refers to all that Jesus had done and implied. The Pharisees were well educated in the Law of Moses; they knew what was required of them for good. Their silence and repeated failure to see what Jesus was teaching indicated that their hearts had refused to exercise the capacity to show mercy, even on the Sabbath. The silence of the Pharisees and experts of the law did not end the meal. Instead, Jesus used their silence as an opportunity to question them and teach them (see Luke 14:7-24, not in our printed text).

What Do You Think?

How can a believer know whether or not silence is an appropriate response to observing God's work?

Digging Deeper

How do Psalms 30:11-12; 39:1-2, 9; 40:9; Ecclesiastes 3:7; Lamentations 3:28; Ezekiel 16:63; and Luke 19:37-40 help you answer this question?

Conclusion

A. Holiness in Time

The emphasis of this story is not on the ailing man. Instead, this story at its heart is a caution against focusing on religious practices at the expense of showing mercy. Jesus was not trying to nullify the Pharisees' practice of observing Sabbath. Not only did the Sabbath require a pause on work, but it also provided time for people to consider how they could show mercy to others.

Further, the question of whether or not a person could heal on the Sabbath was an obscure point. Most people are unable to heal another person on any day of the week. Only the one who is the Lord of the Sabbath (see Luke 6:5) has the ability to heal on the Sabbath. Sometimes we unintentionally limit our expectations of what God ought to do. What are some traditions we hold to that perpetuate this? God's work is not limited by human expectations. We are to trust God and His timing of His work. When we exercise faith by trusting Him in this way, we commit to lives of mercy, following the ways of our heavenly Father.

Twentieth-century Jewish scholar Abraham Joshua Heschel (1907–1972) describes the Sabbath as being an expression of holiness based in time. Although Christians today are not required to observe the Jewish Sabbath, we can still apply similar principles. The idea of observing specific time in order to show mercy to others meets a vital spiritual need for Christians. Followers of Jesus should desire to show mercy in sustained and tangible ways. Although we may sometimes get tunnel vision and focus on other parts of our (busy) lives, we must remember to keep mercy at the forefront of our minds, regardless of the situation.

What Do You Think?

How would you answer a person who says that this Scripture is irrelevant to modern-day Christians because they are not required to obey Sabbath laws?

Digging Deeper

How would you communicate the main points of this story by using modern-day examples?

B. Prayer

Heavenly Father, You have shown us great mercy, just as You have shown mercy to Your people throughout history. We want to be people marked by lives of mercy. Heal us from spiritual ailments that cause us to act in unloving ways. Grant us deeper awareness of the needs of our neighbors so that we might show love and mercy. Help us be merciful, just as You are merciful. In the name of Your Son, Jesus. Amen.

C. Thought to Remember

Remember the Lord of the Sabbath
and live accordingly.

Involvement Learning

Enhance your lesson with KJV Bible Student *(from your curriculum supplier) and the reproducible activity page (at www.standardlesson.com or in the back of the* KJV Standard Lesson Commentary Deluxe Edition*).*

Into the Lesson

Before class begins, write the following sentence on the board:

Rules are made to be broken.

Divide learners into two groups: **Rule Breakers Group** and **Rule Followers Group**. Ask the **Rule Breakers Group** to develop arguments that defend and affirm the sentence written on the board. Ask the **Rule Followers Group** to develop arguments that refute the sentence. Challenge groups to include personal experiences in addition to logic- or law-based reasons in their arguments.

After five minutes, ask for two volunteers from each group to take part in a friendly debate. Ask the volunteers from the **Rule Breakers Group** to give one argument in defense of the given sentence. Then ask the volunteers from the **Rule Followers Group** to give one argument in critique of the given sentence. Continue in this manner until each group has given all their arguments. Allow five minutes for the volunteers to respond to the other group's arguments.

Lead in to Bible study by saying, "Today, we will see how Jesus responded to an opinion regarding the interpretations of the Law of Moses. Let's see if we can understand Jesus' reasoning."

Into the Word

Divide learners into groups of three. Distribute a handout (you create) that contains the following statements. Ask groups to read Luke 14:1-6 and decide if each statement is true or false.

1. The Pharisees had little to do with Jesus and only noticed what He was doing with villagers on the street.
2. The Pharisees at the meal closely watched Jesus.
3. While at the meal, Jesus encountered a man who suffered from something like the common cold.
4. Jesus healed this man in secret so as not to stir up the anger of the Pharisees.
5. Jesus healed the man on the Sabbath day.
6. The Pharisees engaged Jesus in a long and complicated debate regarding the issue of healing on the Sabbath.
7. In teaching the Pharisees, Jesus gave the example of an ox and its predator.

(*Answers:* 1. False [v. 1]; 2. True [v. 1]; 3. False [v. 2]; 4. False [v. 4]; 5. True [v. 4]; 6. False [vv. 3-4]; 7. False [v. 5].)

After five minutes, ask for volunteers to share their groups' answers. If needed, provide further information from the lesson commentary.

Alternative. Distribute copies of the "Three Meals, One Pattern" exercise from the activity page, which you can download. Have learners work in pairs to complete as indicated.

Option. Distribute copies of the "Remember the Sabbath" activity from the activity page. Have learners work in pairs to complete as indicated

Into Life

Write the following unfinished statements on the board, with space under each sentence:

Today's Scripture is irrelevant because . . .
Today's Scripture is relevant because . . .
In light of today's Scripture, I will . . .

Ask volunteers to give reasons that some people might perceive today's Scripture to be irrelevant to a modern audience. Write responses on the board under the first phrase.

Ask volunteers to give reasons that today's Scripture is relevant to the lives of believers. Write responses on the board under the second phrase.

Ask learners to join with a partner and complete the third phrase. Close class by having pairs pray for each other to have wisdom and confidence to live in the prescribed manner and complete the given action in the upcoming week.

Jesus Glorifies God

Devotional Reading: Psalm 119:113-128
Background Scripture: John 7:14-24

John 7:14-24

14 Now about the midst of the feast Jesus went up into the temple, and taught.

15 And the Jews marvelled, saying, How knoweth this man letters, having never learned?

16 Jesus answered them, and said, My doctrine is not mine, but his that sent me.

17 If any man will do his will, he shall know of the doctrine, whether it be of God, or whether I speak of myself.

18 He that speaketh of himself seeketh his own glory: but he that seeketh his glory that sent him, the same is true, and no unrighteousness is in him.

19 Did not Moses give you the law, and yet none of you keepeth the law? Why go ye about to kill me?

20 The people answered and said, Thou hast a devil: who goeth about to kill thee?

21 Jesus answered and said unto them, I have done one work, and ye all marvel.

22 Moses therefore gave unto you circumcision; (not because it is of Moses, but of the fathers;) and ye on the sabbath day circumcise a man.

23 If a man on the sabbath day receive circumcision, that the law of Moses should not be broken; are ye angry at me, because I have made a man every whit whole on the sabbath day?

24 Judge not according to the appearance, but judge righteous judgment.

Key Text

He that speaketh of himself seeketh his own glory: but he that seeketh his glory that sent him, the same is true, and no unrighteousness is in him. **—John 7:18**

God's Law

Is Love

Unit 1: Love Completes, Law Falls Short

Lessons 1–4

Lesson Aims

After participating in this lesson, each learner will be able to:

1. Identify the origin of Jesus' teaching.

2. Trace the cause-and-effect dynamic of right and wrong motives of teaching.

3. Suggest a safeguard against having wrong motives in teaching.

Lesson Outline

Introduction

A. "Raccoon" John Smith

B. Lesson Context

I. On Jesus' Teaching (John 7:14-18)

A. Question of Education (vv. 14-15)

B. Answer of Origin (vv. 16-18)

Paul's Teaching Record

"The Lotto Angel"

II. On Moses' Law (John 7:19-24)

A. Questions of Intent (v. 19)

B. Question of Possession (v. 20)

C. How to Answer (vv. 21-24)

Conclusion

A. Whose Glory?

B. Prayer

C. Thought to Remember

Introduction

A. "Raccoon" John Smith

John Smith was born in East Tennessee in 1784 and moved to Kentucky with his family as a teenager. The Smith family lived in a remote area of what was still a state full of wilderness. John did not have much formal education but adhered to the Baptist faith as a child and young man.

Although he was ordained as a preacher, John wrestled with his faith, a struggle that intensified after he lost two of his four children in a fire and his wife to illness. When he heard the preaching of Alexander Campbell, John began to understand the Scripture more clearly and began preaching based on his enhanced knowledge. People affectionately began calling him "Raccoon" John Smith because of his plainspoken style of preaching and approach to life. He never gave up farming but worked to support himself and his family. And John preached to glorify the One who sent him, not himself. His motives shone clear to those who listened.

Our lesson today finds its focus in John 7:18. As you study, consider: Do I teach for my own glory? Or am I seeking the glory of God?

B. Lesson Context

We have four Gospels in the New Testament that tell the story of Jesus. The first three Gospels (Matthew, Mark, and Luke) are very similar in their general structure. The fourth Gospel, John, is quite different from the other three. John wrote 30 or so years after those other three, and he was well acquainted with their material. For this reason he seems to avoid repeating most of their content. Instead, he chose to give new information from his wealth of eyewitness recollections (see John 21:24-25). About 90 percent of John's material is not found in the other three Gospels.

A significant difference among the four Gospels is the way the writers choose to begin their accounts. Mark begins with the ministry of John the Baptist, without any reference to the birth or childhood of Jesus. Luke begins with the birth of John the Baptist and includes the nativity story of

Jesus. Matthew begins with Jesus' genealogy, thus pushing the story of Jesus back to the time of King David (reigned 1010–970 BC).

John the Evangelist (not John the Baptist) pushes the story back to the very beginning of creation and before. Thus John's Gospel is an inclusive account of the entire sweep of human history. Most of this is accomplished in John 1:1-18, often referred to as the prologue of John. Today's lesson explores the implications of the doctrine of the incarnation, especially concerning Jesus' knowledge and teaching of Scripture and God's will.

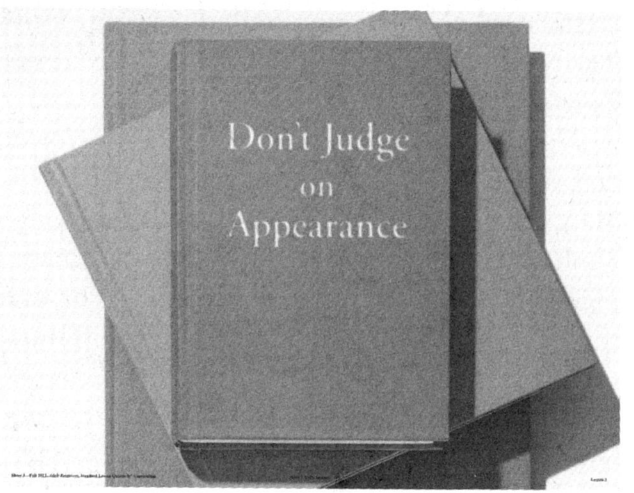

Visual for Lesson 3. *Ask what "book covers" we might judge others by. Then pose the questions associated with verse 24.*

I. On Jesus' Teaching

(John 7:14-18)

A. Question of Education (vv. 14-15)

14. Now about the midst of the feast Jesus went up into the temple, and taught.

Jesus was aware that the religious leaders were seeking to kill Him. This homicidal animosity was part of His stated reason for not being present in Jerusalem at the start of *the feast* of tabernacles (John 7:1-9). God instituted this feast for two reasons. First, it was a time of thanksgiving during the season of the olive and fruit harvests (the September–October time frame). Second, it was as a time to remember deliverance from slavery in Egypt (see Leviticus 23:33-44). As something of an object lesson, many who celebrated this feast would live in tents ("tabernacles") outside the city to reenact the 40 years that the Israelites had lived in tents while wandering in the wilderness. Apparently waiting until *the midst* of the feast was meant to allow Jesus' enemies time to cool their heels. This was the right time for Him to show up (contrast John 7:8).

In the meantime, the crowds watched for Jesus, divided as to whether He was a good man or a deceiver (John 7:12, not in our printed text). They had seen or heard of His signs (examples: 2:1-11; 6:2, 14), His teaching (examples: 5:17-47; 6:25-59), and of the witnesses concerning His identity and the source of His authority (example: 1:6-18). But were these things to be trusted? What did all of this really mean about Jesus? (See commentary on 7:16-17, below.)

The temple was still the center of Jewish life (examples: 2 Chronicles 6; Psalms 27:4; 66:13; Isaiah 2:3; Jeremiah 7:4, 13-14), though the Babylonian exile (beginning with its first wave in 597 BC; 2 Chronicles 36:9-10) saw the beginning of a less centralized religion. The first temple was destroyed in 586 BC during the third and final wave of exiles (36:11-20); the second temple (which stood in Jesus' day) was dedicated in 516 BC (Ezra 6:13-18).

The building's importance was never more evident than during a feast. Religious pilgrims came, sometimes from distant homelands, to celebrate and to learn (examples: Acts 2:8-11). Jesus was never haphazard in His actions; choosing to teach in the temple during this feast was a choice to make His message public, not keeping it a secret (Luke 19:47; John 18:20).

How to Say It

Babylonian	Bab-ih-*low*-nee-un.
Bethesda	Bu-*thez*-duh.
Damascus	Duh-*mass*-kus.
Galilee	*Gal*-uh-lee.
Jerusalem	Juh-*roo*-suh-lem.
Mishna Shabbat (*Hebrew*)	*Mish*-nuh Shab-awt.
Moses	*Mo*-zes or *Mo*-zez.
Pharisees	*Fair*-ih-seez.
rabbinical	ruh-*bin*-ih-kul.
tabernacles	tah-burr-*nah*-kulz.

15. And the Jews marvelled, saying, How knoweth this man letters, having never learned?

The Jews (presumably both the pilgrim crowds and the religious leaders) *marvelled* at what this man was teaching and the profound knowledge He had (compare Luke 2:46-47). Their amazement likely had at least two sources. For one thing, it was known that Jesus was not a trained rabbi; He had no formal education in *letters*—that is, Scripture. He had not attended any rabbinical schools or been taught by a rabbi; by trade, He should have been working as a carpenter, not a teacher (Mark 6:3; compare Acts 4:13). This is no small objection, since sound knowledge is not often achieved without a sound instructor (examples: Nehemiah 8:7-9; Acts 8:30-31). However, they would have done well to remember that God sometimes chose unexpected people for His purposes (examples: Genesis 25:23; 1 Samuel 16:7-13; Amos 1:1).

For another, Jesus' Galilean roots prejudiced people against Him. There was nothing wrong with being from Galilee per se, but as a rural place of no particular historical or cultural significance, no one expected anyone great to come out of the region (examples: John 7:41, 52). Though we do not know exactly what Jesus was teaching that elicited this response from the crowd, we could point to other examples of Jesus' teaching that yielded similar reactions (example: Matthew 5–7).

What Do You Think?

What roadblocks to seeking wisdom might formal education create?

Digging Deeper

How can you encourage students to take their education seriously without losing sight of better sources of wisdom?

B. Answer of Origin (vv. 16-18)

16-17. Jesus answered them, and said, My doctrine is not mine, but his that sent me. If any man will do his will, he shall know of the doctrine, whether it be of God, or whether I speak of myself.

The people seemed to assume that Jesus taught His own thoughts on the Scripture. This would make the *doctrine* His own, without any authority from God, history, tradition, or any other seemingly legitimate source. Though His audience might have expected their question was rhetorical—that no answer would be provided as to the source of Jesus' knowledge—Jesus chose to offer the answer.

His that sent me is both a proclamation of the source of Jesus' knowledge and of Jesus' identity. Jesus' authority and wisdom are from God, just as Jesus' works came from the Father (John 5:36). *If any man will do his will, he shall know of the doctrine* might appropriately remind us of Jesus' refrain, "If any man have ears to hear, let him hear" (Mark 4:23; compare Matthew 11:15; 13:15; Luke 8:8; etc.). The implication is that the heart that is prepared to hear the word of Lord will recognize it as a word from the Lord. This preparation allows a person to recognize the character and source of another's teaching and to discern what is *of God* versus what is mere human ego or understanding.

Paul's Teaching Record

Educated in the Law of Moses, Paul became a Pharisee. He actively participated in the persecution of Christians in the days after Jesus' resurrection. He even participated in the stoning of Stephen, holding the coats of the men who stoned him (Acts 7:58; 8:1; Philippians 3:1-6).

All of that changed when Paul traveled to Damascus to seek out Christians, arrest them, and bring them back to Jerusalem for punishment. On the way, a great light shone around him, and he heard the voice of Jesus (Acts 9:1-19). This introduction to the Lord immediately changed everything in Paul's life. He began traveling the known world, starting churches, and preaching. In 2 Corinthians 11, Paul reported persecutions he endured in the name of Jesus, including beatings, stonings, and shipwrecks.

Paul's teaching did not come from his own understanding but from Jesus (Galatians 1:11-12).

He showed this in his repentance of his prior erroneous beliefs and in his unfailing zeal for the Lord's church. When others ask where your teaching—whether in word or action—comes from, what evidence is there that it is from God? —A. W.

18. He that speaketh of himself seeketh his own glory: but he that seeketh his glory that sent him, the same is true, and no unrighteousness is in him.

Jesus offered a sort of litmus test regarding where His own teaching came from: Whose *glory* was being sought? Those who speak independently do so for personal gain. They promote their ideas for their own ends, and their egos are probably involved. But those who speak what God reveals *seeketh his glory,* not their own. In this, the speaker acts correctly. The proclamation is not made to glorify the one who speaks but the one who gave the message. In short, the reason Jesus taught with such knowledge and authority is because He only taught what He received from the Lord, and He only sought to glorify God.

> **What Do You Think?**
> When do you experience the impulse to glorify yourself?
> **Digging Deeper**
> How does seeking God's glory keep your ego in check?

"The Lotto Angel"

Barbara lived an average life, working in a hospital caring for sick people. That did not change when she won more than ten million dollars. She and her husband, Ray, began looking for ways to use their winnings to help others in their community. They gave some to charities, hospitals, and cancer research. They paid for inner-city children to attend theater productions and veterans to travel to reunions. They funded enough local projects that Barbara was dubbed "The Lotto Angel."

Barbara's humble attitude extended to her understanding of the benefit she received from giving. She loved to see the joy that money well-spent brought to others. Barbara's care showed her heart in the way she used her winnings for others and not for her own glory.

Jesus preached the gospel for God's glory, not His own. How do you know that your words and actions are for God's glory, not yours? —A. W.

II. On Moses' Law
(John 7:19-24)

A. Questions of Intent (v. 19)

19a. Did not Moses give you the law, and yet none of you keepeth the law?

The law was the content of what the scribes and the Pharisees studied and taught (Acts 22:3), along with their own traditions (example: Matthew 15:1-9). The law was referred to more broadly as "letters" above in John 7:15. *Moses* is analogous (though not equal) to God in this question. What Moses gave, the people studied but failed to put into daily practice. Their knowledge without their actions was useless (James 1:22-25). From this lesser example, Jesus' question implies that the people were receiving instruction from God but were not putting this wisdom into action. Some didn't even recognize the source of Jesus' teaching, so how could they possibly keep His teaching?

19b. Why go ye about to kill me?

At first glance, this question has little to do with the previous. However, closer inspection shows the connection. Jesus' teaching was from God; therefore, His teaching was to be absorbed, hearts yielded, and lives changed. However, the spiritual deafness of some in the crowd to Jesus' message prevented them from obeying the Lord. Thus they sought to kill Jesus (see John 7:14, above), on the grounds of blasphemy (Leviticus 24:13-16; see John 10:31-33). But because Jesus came from God and taught only what God gave Him to teach, killing Him was not an apt punishment of sin. There was no sin in Him! Instead, the scribes and Pharisees' desire was a violation of the command "thou shalt not kill" (Exodus 20:13; compare Acts 2:22-23). If the only law they followed was from Moses, they *still* would sin by wanting to execute Jesus because His words were recognized as being from God—by those who were able to recognize it.

B. Question of Possession (v. 20)

20. The people answered and said, Thou hast a devil: who goeth about to kill thee?

The people were ignorant of the schemes of the Pharisees and the scribes (see John 7:1). It made more sense to them that Jesus was possessed by *a devil* that made His thinking paranoid. But, as the following verses reveal, Jesus knew *who goeth about to kill* Him. And His execution would be irrefutable proof of a plot to kill Him (19:6, 17-21).

What Do You Think?

How do you respond to others' inaccurate assessments of you?

Digging Deeper

When might it be best to address the issue? to let it pass without direct refutation?

C. How to Answer (vv. 21-24)

21. Jesus answered and said unto them, I have done one work, and ye all marvel.

The *one work* Jesus had done was the healing of the lame man at the pool of Bethesda. While in Jerusalem for a feast, Jesus visited this pool where many sick people gathered for medical care. There He met a man who had been lame for 38 years. To the great surprise of the crowd—and especially to the surprise of the man himself—Jesus healed him (John 5:1-16).

The authorities objected because Jesus worked on the Sabbath (John 5:16) and told the man to work by carrying his mat (5:10). Sabbath was the weekly day of rest when Jews were not permitted to work (5:9; see Exodus 31:15). Some Jewish authorities who believed that carrying cots and healing were works prohibited on the Sabbath confronted the man and learned what Jesus had done. So in this case, it is clear that *marvel* does not have a positive connotation.

22. Moses therefore gave unto you circumcision; (not because it is of Moses, but of the fathers;) and ye on the sabbath day circumcise a man.

Jesus' answer might not seem to address whether He was paranoid for believing some wanted Him to be killed (John 7:20, above). But in fact, Jesus' response reveals both the motivation for the Jewish leaders' wanting to kill Him and the hypocrisy of their desire (5:18). Their fury came from Jesus' apparent flouting of Sabbath laws according to His own whims (as they thought). But they also broke Sabbath to *circumcise a man*. All male children born in Israel were to be circumcised "in the eighth day" (Leviticus 12:3).

Though this is the law given by Moses, the command predated him, coming from Abraham (here referred to with Isaac and Jacob as *the fathers*; see Genesis 17:9-14). Moses himself faced near-fatal consequence when he failed to have his infant son circumcised (Exodus 4:24-26). Oral law developed over the years regarding circumcision and other intricacies. These were compiled in written form around AD 200 by Rabbi Yehudah ha-Nasi. This non-biblical document, called the Mishna, codified that the circumcision should still go forward regardless of the Sabbath (see the Mishna Shabbat 19.2).

23a. If a man on the sabbath day receive circumcision, that the law of Moses should not be broken.

Jesus pushed the knowledge and authority issue further. The word *if* introduces a fact that should inform the answer to Jesus' question. The facts laid out in verse 22 lead to this justification of healing on *the sabbath day*. Moses gave the law regarding circumcision. Still, the covenant predated the ordinance and went back to the time of Abraham (Genesis 17:10). So, it seems that circumcision took precedence over the law about working on the Sabbath.

Keeping the law by circumcising on the Sabbath could be considered a legal infraction. But it was not. The religious leaders for generations had simply acknowledged that the two laws seemed to collide at times, and in those instances, the law of circumcision would supersede the law of Sabbath.

23b. Are ye angry at me, because I have made a man every whit whole on the sabbath day?

Considering this priority, Jesus challenged His audience regarding the validity of their anger after He *made a man every whit whole on the sabbath*. Jesus' actions were not only justifiable but completely appropriate on the Sabbath. The people had missed something fundamental about what the Sabbath was actually *for*. The concept went together with God's promised peace—more than a break in violence but an end in violence that allowed for human thriving (see Leviticus 26:1-13). Elsewhere, Jesus justified His disciples' picking corn to eat on the Sabbath by reiterating that the Sabbath was created for human benefit (Mark 2:27).

The primary reason for observing Sabbath was God's own rest after creating the world. The secondary reason flowed from the first—namely, that God desired all people to be given rest from their own work (Exodus 20:10-11). The Sabbath rest was given by God as a gift for the wellbeing of His people. Following the letter of the law—doing no work—did not honor the spirit of the law—enabling people to thrive rather than only survive.

What Do You Think?

Do you have any Sabbath-keeping practices? Why or why not?

Digging Deeper

How do Jesus' actions and teachings about Sabbath challenge your own Sabbath activities?

24. Judge not according to the appearance, but judge righteous judgment.

By *appearance*, Jesus' work on the Sabbath was in violation of the law. But by *righteous judgment*, discerning the order of priority based on knowledge of God and His will, Jesus had rightly chosen what was more important. A proper assessment of Jesus' actions would conclude that He was fulfilling the moral obligation of the law. Jesus' argument about circumcision not violating the Sabbath showed that the religious leaders themselves acknowledged that some laws were to be held in higher esteem than literalistic Sabbath-keeping.

Jesus' own actions were in line with His summary of the Law (and the Prophets): "Thou shalt love the Lord thy God with all thy heart, and with all thy soul, and with all thy mind. This is the first and great commandment. And the second is like unto it, Thou shalt love thy neighbour as thyself" (Matthew 22:37-39; see Deuteronomy 6:5; Leviticus 19:18). The law to love the Lord and demonstrate that love in care for others fulfills the Sabbath.

What Do You Think?

How do you guard against judging others by appearance?

Digging Deeper

What acts of repentance are appropriate if you have judged by appearance?

Conclusion

A. Whose Glory?

The beginning of this lesson asked: Do you teach for your own glory? Or are you seeking Someone else's glory?

Answering these questions is not a matter of numbering your years of knowledge, listing your formal Christian education, or quantifying the results of your witness. Instead, it is a heart matter. When you spread the gospel, do you primarily hope to gain something for yourself? Or do you hope to glorify Christ and His heavenly Father?

Our success or failure as disciples is not measured by how people react to us. Time and again, we see that Jesus' own audiences did not like what they heard Him say. They did not always judge His words correctly. The same will happen to us. As with Jesus, so with us: our success is measured in our intention to glorify the Lord. When we speak the truth and live it to the best of our ability—helped by the Holy Spirit—we succeed.

B. Prayer

Lord, teach us to glorify You in all that we do. Diminish our desires to make a name or a fortune for ourselves and increase our desire to bring glory to Your Name. May we rely on the Holy Spirit to guide our thoughts, words, and actions. Thank You for the example we have in Christ. It is in His name we pray. Amen.

C. Thought to Remember

Choose: your glory, or His?

Involvement Learning

Enhance your lesson with KJV Bible Student *(from your curriculum supplier) and the reproducible activity page (at www.standardlesson.com or in the back of the* KJV Standard Lesson Commentary Deluxe Edition*).*

Into the Lesson

Write on the board *What Makes a Good Teacher? / What Makes a Bad Teacher?* as the headers of two columns. Divide class members into pairs and instruct them to share with each other their responses to both prompts. Allow three or four minutes for discussion before having the pairs share their conclusions with the whole class. After filling out both columns with responses, discuss: 1–What do good and bad teachers have in common? 2–How often do you think poor teaching is a result of poor preparation? an inflated sense of self? bad information?

Alternative. Distribute copies of the "Look at the Big Picture" exercise from the activity page, which you can download. Ask pairs or small groups to complete the chart as indicated.

Lead to Bible study by saying, "Jesus, the best teacher in the world, was accused of sharing bad information with wrong motives. Let's see what happened."

Into the Word

Divide the class into four Bible study groups. After asking a volunteer to read the text aloud, distribute a handout (you prepare) with these headings: *Why Jews thought Jesus was wrong / How Jesus argued He was right.* Ask each group to put findings from today's text under both headings. Encourage them to include the verse numbers in their findings. After a few minutes, ask the groups to jot down any obvious or possible motives behind the ways Jesus and His opponents acted and reacted in this case. Come together as a whole class to discuss their findings.

Divide the class in half. One half will spend one minute writing a diary entry from the point of view of a religious leader who heard Jesus. The other half will write from the point of view of a bystander in the crowd. Encourage the class to use their sanctified imaginations as well as any hints in the biblical story. Discuss this exercise as a class, then ask how an entry from one of the disciples might differ from the religious leaders or other bystanders.

Option. Distribute copies of the "Examining the Story" activity from the activity page. Have learners complete it individually in one minute or less before comparing their work with a partner.

Into Life

Say to the class, "Jesus was not the first or the last teacher to be accused of wrong motives. What are some faulty motives that might drive certain teachers today?" Give students two minutes to shout out as many answers as they can, while you list each one on your board. Ask the class: 1–What results tend to follow teaching with faulty motives? 2–What can help teachers guard against these motives?

Write the heading *When I am a teacher* on the board. Preface the brainstorming by reminding learners that not all teaching happens in a formal classroom. Have volunteers provide examples of times when they find themselves in a position to teach. These should include home and work situations. Give the group time to vote on the top three situations in which they find themselves as teachers. Mark each of these situations with a star.

Finish your brainstorming session by giving learners one minute to answer how they guard against having faulty motives when they find themselves in these teaching situations. Before listing responses on the board, encourage learners to think through the focus of the teaching in the various starred situations. Invite them to consider how that focus and what the teacher is called to do affects one's motives in teaching.

Divide learners into pairs. Ask partners to pray for each other regarding specific teaching opportunities they may face in the week ahead, asking God to purify their motives and give them wisdom.

September 24
Lesson 4 (KJV)

Jesus Prevents Two Stonings

Devotional Reading: Matthew 7:1-5
Background Scripture: John 8:1-11, 39-59

John 8:1-11, 56-59

1 Jesus went unto the mount of Olives.
2 And early in the morning he came again
into the temple, and all the people came unto
him; and he sat down, and taught them.
3 And the scribes and Pharisees brought
unto him a woman taken in adultery; and
when they had set her in the midst,
4 They say unto him, Master, this woman
was taken in adultery, in the very act.
5 Now Moses in the law commanded us,
that such should be stoned: but what sayest
thou?
6 This they said, tempting him, that they
might have to accuse him. But Jesus stooped
down, and with his finger wrote on the ground,
as though he heard them not.
7 So when they continued asking him, he
lifted up himself, and said unto them, He that
is without sin among you, let him first cast a
stone at her.
8 And again he stooped down, and wrote on
the ground.
9 And they which heard it, being convicted
by their own conscience, went out one by one,
beginning at the eldest, even unto the last: and
Jesus was left alone, and the woman standing
in the midst.
10 When Jesus had lifted up himself, and
saw none but the woman, he said unto her,
Woman, where are those thine accusers? hath
no man condemned thee?
11 She said, No man, Lord. And Jesus said
unto her, Neither do I condemn thee: go, and
sin no more.

56 Your father Abraham rejoiced to see my
day: and he saw it, and was glad.
57 Then said the Jews unto him, Thou art
not yet fifty years old, and hast thou seen
Abraham?
58 Jesus said unto them, Verily, verily, I say
unto you, Before Abraham was, I am.
59 Then took they up stones to cast at him:
but Jesus hid himself, and went out of the temple, going through the midst of them, and so
passed by.

Key Text

Jesus said unto her, Neither do I condemn thee: go, and sin no more. —John 8:11b

God's Law

Is Love

Unit 1: Love Completes, Law Falls Short

Lessons 1–4

Lesson Aims

After participating in this lesson, each learner will be able to:

1. Identify the "I am."

2. Explain the difference between "forgiving" and "not condemning."

3. Write a prayer of gratitude for escaping condemnation in Christ.

Lesson Outline

Introduction

A. Deciding the Game

B. Lesson Context

I. A Woman's Cause to Rejoice (John 8:1-11)

A. Jesus Prepares to Teach (vv. 1-2)

B. Change of Curriculum (vv. 3-9)

Burning Answers

C. Life-Changing Lesson (vv. 10-11)

Learning from Experience

II. Abraham's Cause to Rejoice (John 8:56-59)

A. Jesus' Day (vv. 56-58)

B. Not Jesus' Time (v. 59)

Conclusion

A. Following I Am

B. Prayer

C. Thought to Remember

Introduction

A. Deciding the Game

Referees can be much-maligned by coaches, players, fans, commentators—almost anyone who is watching the game. They are second-guessed, taunted, and even on occasion blamed for a team's loss. Theirs is a difficult task. Referees must be quick and direct with their decisions. They must work together as a team to effectively officiate a game. And they must trust one another to know and care about the rules and work with integrity and skill to enforce those rules fairly.

The contest Jesus was called on to referee in today's lesson was no game. At stake were Jesus' credibility and a woman's life. Who would come away from this confrontation crying foul?

B. Lesson Context

The events and teachings recorded in John 7 and 8 occurred during one of Jesus' visits to Jerusalem for the feast of tabernacles (see John 7:1-2, 37; 8:20). God instituted this festival for two reasons. First, it was a time of thanksgiving during the season of the olive and fruit harvests (the September–October time frame). Second, it was a time to remember deliverance from slavery in Egypt (see Leviticus 23:33-44).

As something of an object lesson, many who celebrated this festival would live in tents ("tabernacles") outside the city to reenact the 40 years that the Israelites had lived in tents while wandering in the wilderness. "And every man went unto his own house" (John 7:53) closes the day before the events considered in the first half of this lesson (see lesson 3).

The second half of this lesson begins in John 8:56. In John 8:12-55 (not in our printed text), Jesus responded to questions from a crowd of both laypeople (some who believed Him, others who did not) and Pharisees. Of particular interest to the following episode are the conversational threads about being Abraham's descendants. Despite the Jews' confidence that they were Abraham's family, Jesus declared that their own actions revealed them to be children of the devil (John 8:44; compare 1:13)! No crowd would respond well to being called children of the devil, and this crowd was no different. They went so far as to claim Jesus must be demon-possessed to think that if Abraham and all the rest of the prophets died, Jesus' own followers would not (8:52-53).

We do well to note that the contrast Jesus set up can apply broadly to anyone who claims to be a child of Abraham (and therefore chosen by God, including Christians today) but acts in evil ways that contradict this heritage. Neither Jesus' words here nor anywhere else justify violence against Jews, past or present.

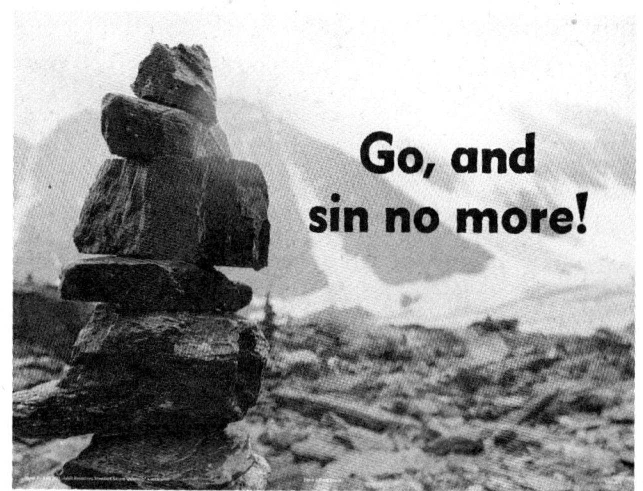

Visual for Lesson 4. *Open the lesson by asking volunteers for examples of times when they experienced mercy and repentance.*

I. A Woman's Cause to Rejoice
(John 8:1-11)

A. Jesus Prepares to Teach (vv. 1-2)

1. Jesus went unto the mount of Olives.

Jesus routinely took time to be in His Father's presence (examples: Luke 5:16; 6:12; 9:18). And *the mount of Olives* was a common stop for Jesus when He was in Jerusalem. Given His prayerful habit, the specific location, and no further information, we surmise that Jesus took this time to pray (consider 21:37; 22:39-45).

The Mount of Olives first appears in the Bible in 2 Samuel 15:30, when David fled Jerusalem during Absalom's rebellion (see 2 Samuel 15:32–16:4). The spot was aptly named due to the proliferation of olives in this area, though the modern reader might suggest it was more of a high hill than a mountain. It did overlook the temple, sitting off to its east side. Other examples of reference to the Mount of Olives in the Old Testament include 1 Kings 11:7; 2 Kings 23:13-14; Ezekiel 11:23; and Zechariah 14:4. The Mount looms large in the Christian faith because it is the location of Jesus' last night of prayer, betrayal by Judas, and arrest (Luke 22:39-54).

2. And early in the morning he came again into the temple, and all the people came unto him; and he sat down, and taught them.

Jesus often began His day *early in the morning* (examples: Matthew 21:18; Mark 1:35; Luke 21:38). *The temple* was the place for religious teachers to meet with and instruct their students (example: Luke 2:46). *All the people* drawing near suggests that they were primed—through recent experience, word of mouth, or other means—to seek out Jesus' teaching. *Again* points to at least one event that would have prepared the people to hear from Jesus on this occasion (see John 7:14). Teachers commonly sat as they taught (Matthew 13:1; 26:55).

B. Change of Curriculum (vv. 3-9)

3a. And the scribes and Pharisees brought unto him a woman taken in adultery.

The relationship between Jesus and *the scribes and Pharisees* was typically contentious (examples: Matthew 23; contrast John 3:1-2). In the generations following the return from Babylonian exile, these two groups of religious leaders came into prominence in the Jewish faith. Their zeal for the law was commendable, intended to prevent the sins that had led to exile in the first place. Unfortunately, several factors, including

How to Say It

Abraham	*Ay*-bruh-ham.
Absalom	*Ab*-suh-lum.
Babylonian	Bab-ih-*low*-nee-un.
Jerusalem	Juh-*roo*-suh-lem.
Messiah	Meh-*sigh*-uh.
Mosaic	Mo-*zay*-ik.
Pharisees	*Fair*-ih-seez.
tabernacles	tah-burr-*nah*-kulz.

mistaken expectations (John 7:52), vested interests (11:48), and hypocrisy (Matthew 23:13-32), prevented these leaders from seeing God's larger picture and made recognizing His Messiah incredibly difficult.

How this *woman* was found *in adultery* but her partner was not is a mystery. There could be perfectly innocent reasons (on the part of her accusers) why this man was not present: he escaped, he fought them off, etc. The most cynical reading (which is refuted by Jesus' instructions in John 8:11, below) would suggest that the woman was unjustly accused or even framed by these religious leaders.

Gender dynamics of the time are the most likely explanation for the male adulterer's absence. Especially in Roman culture, though also present to some degree in Jewish culture, adultery on the part of men was often considered an unfortunate fact of life. The women with whom they committed adultery, however, frequently were held to a higher standard and harshly punished for the role they played (see commentary on John 8:5, below). This double standard dichotomy likely resulted in part from questions of paternity and inheritance should a woman become pregnant by a man who was not her husband (consider Numbers 27:1-11).

> **What Do You Think?**
> How well do you adapt to a sudden change of plans?
> **Digging Deeper**
> Could more flexibility in this regard open doors for ministry? Explain your answer.

3b-4. And when they had set her in the midst, they say unto him, Master, this woman was taken in adultery, in the very act.

Why would Jesus' enemies refer to Him as *Master*? We could assume that the honorific was slathered in sarcasm, since the scribes and Pharisees largely did not consider Jesus to have any authority to teach (compare John 1:38). In addition, using the title might have been a ploy to the crowd that was gathered around Jesus. On the one hand, it could sound like they were being very respectful. On the other, it put the listening audience on alert—would Jesus answer as a learned teacher ought to, or would He reveal himself as a fraud?

> **What Do You Think?**
> Based on verses such as Matthew 18:15-17, what are some situations where it might be necessary to point out another's sin?
> **Digging Deeper**
> What considerations prevent you from pointing out *every* sin you witness?

5a. Now Moses in the law commanded us, that such should be stoned.

The scribes and Pharisees devoted their entire lives to learning and living the Law of Moses faithfully. Given their long years of training and scholarly debate, they no doubt believed they had an edge on Jesus regarding questions of *the law*. Direct reference to *Moses* was unnecessary to establish what law they were talking about; dropping his name, however, raised the stakes of giving any answer that would seem to undercut this revered lawgiver and the God who gave him the law (consider Deuteronomy 34:10-12).

Commands to stone adulterers (found in Deuteronomy 22:20-21, 23-24) were specifically linked to a woman's promiscuity before marriage or during her engagement. In the first instance, the man with whom she had sexual relations apparently was unknown, so she alone would be punished. In the second, the man who was not her fiancé was also to be executed. According to the law, both parties were meant to be held accountable. At least ideally, women in Israel would not face harsher consequences than the men with whom they consorted. The guilty parties were both subject to the death penalty (Leviticus 20:10; Deuteronomy 22:22). The harshness of this punishment reflects how repulsive God finds this unholy faithlessness (22:23-27; Ezekiel 22:11; Malachi 3:5; compare Romans 13:9-10).

5b. But what sayest thou?

For a clearer idea of Jesus' apparent dilemma in answering *what sayest thou*, one should consider two key points. First, Jesus was known to be a friend of the sinners (examples: Matthew 9:10-12;

Luke 7:36-50). What would happen when He was faced with blatant sin, punishable by death? Second, under Roman law the Jews had no authority to carry out the death penalty. Religious leaders were endlessly frustrated that Rome was the final authority (John 18:31). On one significant level, this question had nothing to do with the woman, though her life hung in the balance. Instead, it was a question designed to trap Jesus and thereby discredit Him (compare Mark 12:13-17).

Burning Answers

One of the keys to good debate is mastering the art of asking trick questions. One of my high school debate teammates was particularly good at leading an opponent into a cleverly disguised trap. Such questions would start, "Would you say that . . ." or "Is it fair to define your argument as . . ." and finish with an emotionally charged phrase implying that the argument was based on the individual's feelings or faulty sources. My classmate's questions were designed to leave his opponent with no choice but to provide answers that burned their argument down.

The scribes and Pharisees tried to trap Jesus in the same way. However, Jesus does not fall into traps (see John 8:9, below). Answer honestly: Have you ever tried to trap Jesus with a question? Will you accept His answers? —M. E.

6-7a. This they said, tempting him, that they might have to accuse him. But Jesus stooped down, and with his finger wrote on the ground, as though he heard them not. So when they continued asking him.

Tempting him in this instance should be understood as testing Jesus—fitting, given the teaching setting. Their motive was to discredit *Jesus.* If they were successful at discrediting Him, they would, in turn, be able to bring a charge against Him. This was not the first time Jesus' opponents asked Him seemingly innocent questions to have reason *to accuse him*. In those instances, Jesus always had a ready response (examples: Matthew 19:3-9; 22:23-46). When He *stooped down, and with his finger wrote on the ground,* the scribes and Pharisees might have believed they finally had Him stumped! Jesus, for once, seemed to be speechless.

What Jesus wrote or why He acted *as though he heard them not* is unclear (see John 8:7b-8, below). We could speculate based on the context and Jesus' character and ministry up to this point. His pause, however, did nothing to deter the men from continuing to question Him.

What Do You Think?

What would be the best way for you to respond when someone asks a question to trap you?

Digging Deeper

How can you control your emotions to give a wise response in such a situation?

7b-8. He lifted up himself, and said unto them, He that is without sin among you, let him first cast a stone at her. And again he stooped down, and wrote on the ground.

Rather than address the issue the scribes and Pharisees presented, Jesus went to the very heart of the matter. Whether the woman deserved to die for her sins faded to the background; Jesus' challenge was whether any of these men was *without sin.* Later Paul—an educated Pharisee himself—asserted that "all have sinned, and come short of the glory of God" (Romans 3:23), and further: "the wages of sin is death" (6:23). Surely these legal minds also knew that every person was a sinner.

Jesus' statement was a pointed reminder that even those who studied the law and sought to obey its every word were still guilty of breaking it (James 2:10-11). And because of that, all of them—not just the woman—faced a death sentence. This should prevent any honest person from initiating the execution.

9. And they which heard it, being convicted by their own conscience, went out one by one, beginning at the eldest, even unto the last: and Jesus was left alone, and the woman standing in the midst.

Heartfelt conviction of *conscience* leads to repentance (example: Acts 2:37). Far from insisting that they were correct, Jesus' challengers accepted this humbling turn of events and *went out one by one*. This movement started with the *eldest* accuser until Jesus was the only one left, suggesting something about wisdom that can come with age. Ironically, those who came to discredit Jesus and catch Him in a trap were caught in their own trap and left without a sound.

The men who left were also the only witnesses to this crime. Without witnesses, no one was left in the crowd who was able to initiate punishment (Deuteronomy 13:9; 17:7). Thus, the question of whether Jesus would break Roman law for the sake of Jewish law was rendered void (see John 8:5, above). *In the midst* reminds us of the learners who were still present, observing Jesus' interaction with the religious leaders and now with *the woman*.

C. Life-Changing Lesson (vv. 10-11)

10-11a. When Jesus had lifted up himself, and saw none but the woman, he said unto her, Woman, where are those thine accusers? hath no man condemned thee? She said, No man, Lord.

Jesus' response began with a pair of clarifying questions. Addressing the *woman* for the first time, Jesus' rhetorical questions were intended to confirm that the accusers were gone. Her address *Lord* stands in contrast to "Master" (John 8:4, above). We note that this use of *Lord* did not suggest insight into Jesus' character and could appropriately be translated "sir," as it is in Matthew 13:27. While the previous title *Master* was used less than genuinely, the woman spoke to Jesus with respect.

11b. And Jesus said unto her, Neither do I condemn thee: go, and sin no more.

Jesus knew this woman's sin, whether this particular accusation was true or not (example: John 4:16-19). Just like her accusers, the woman's sin made her subject to death (see 8:7b-8, above). And being the Son of God, Jesus was entitled to enforce the death penalty, if He so chose (consider Hebrews 10:28-31). But Jesus gave the woman another option. He desired her to repent and thus *sin no more*. In this act, we see an example of the choice between death in sin and life offered in Christ.

No further information is given regarding the woman's repentance. But based on other, similar interactions Jesus had, we might surmise that the woman did indeed find her heart changed by this interaction with the Lord (compare John 5:1-14).

> **What Do You Think?**
> How have you seen acts of mercy attract people to Jesus?
>
> **Digging Deeper**
> In what current situation(s) could your merciful intervention also be a call to repentance?

Learning from Experience

I sheepishly walked into work five minutes late. A coworker glared at me and pointed out my untimely arrival to our manager. My coworker was understandably frustrated; my tardiness caused her to take her break late. But my manager just laughed. A few coworkers were around, so my manager asked them if they had ever been late. Every single one had, so she told them no one had any right to criticize me. As my boss, and someone who is always early, she could have chosen to discipline me or just allow the comment to stand unaddressed. She offered me grace instead. She also declared that I should not be late again because that would be taking advantage of her kindness.

The Pharisees, like my coworkers, were not blameless. But Jesus *was* without sin, so He could have condemned the woman. Instead, He offered her grace conditioned on repentance. Have you accepted Jesus' offer of grace? Does it show in your habitual conduct? —M. E.

II. Abraham's Cause to Rejoice

(John 8:56-59)

A. Jesus' Day (vv. 56-58)

56. Your father Abraham rejoiced to see my day: and he saw it, and was glad.

Given that Jesus just asserted that the crowd's

actions showed them to be children of the devil, calling *Abraham* their *father* implies that, if they were really his children, they would react as Abraham did. The man had received the promise from God that his own family would bless the whole world (Genesis 12:1-3). This promise is fulfilled in Christ (Galatians 3:16), giving Abraham reason to rejoice that Jesus' day had finally come. By faith Abraham believed this would be so. Because of his hope in God's promise, Abraham *saw it, and was glad* even without living in Jesus' time (Hebrews 11:8-12).

57. Then said the Jews unto him, Thou art not yet fifty years old, and hast thou seen Abraham?

Given the antagonistic character of the conversation up to this point, it's no surprise that the Jews misunderstood what Jesus was saying. They knew Jesus was not even *fifty years old* in this time (compare Luke 3:23). He would need to be generations older than 50 to have *seen Abraham*! For context, Abraham was born about 2167 BC, which places his death at 1992 BC (Genesis 25:7). But readers of John's Gospel are well-aware that Jesus was not exaggerating His knowledge of Abraham—Jesus is from the beginning (John 1:1).

58. Jesus said unto them, Verily, verily, I say unto you, Before Abraham was, I am.

Verily, verily draws attention to the truth of what Jesus was about to declare. Not only did He know *Abraham*; Jesus predated the man (compare John 1:1-5)! His claim here is weighty indeed. "I am" is God's formula for self-identification (Exodus 3:14; Isaiah 43:10; 45:18; etc.). For anyone to use this formula in the same way was blasphemy (47:4-11; Zephaniah 2:15). With this statement, Jesus' audience heard Him claim to be God.

In the Gospel of John, we notice Jesus making frequent statements about himself that involve God's sacred name, I Am. For the sake of convenience, we can call these "the 'I am' sayings." These sayings take two forms. The first form occurs when Jesus simply applied God's divine name, I Am, directly to himself. He did this to stress His complete union with the Father (John 8:24, 28, 58; 13:19).

B. Not Jesus' Time (v. 59)

59. Then took they up stones to cast at him: but Jesus hid himself, and went out of the temple, going through the midst of them, and so passed by.

Leviticus 24:16 states that anyone who blasphemes the name of the Lord must be put to death by stoning. Their reaction confirms that they understood Jesus' "I am" to be a claim of equality with God (John 8:58, above). But the crowd was unsuccessful in the moment because *Jesus hid himself . . . and so passed by.* The larger picture, however, makes clear that they were unable to stone Jesus because His time had not yet come (John 7:6-8).

Conclusion

A. Following I Am

Jesus was completely within His rights to condemn the adulterous woman, but He chose to offer mercy with His call to repentance. Jesus could have refrained from revealing himself as I am, but He chose instead to make himself known. We certainly benefit from Jesus' self-revelation and His merciful call to turn to Him. Considering who Christ is and who He calls you to be, what repentance is necessary in your life? What "stonings" will you divert because of your love for Jesus? What rejoicing will you spread?

What Do You Think?

What is most challenging to you about Jesus' teaching and actions in today's lesson?

Digging Deeper

What is most comforting to you about His teaching and actions?

B. Prayer

Lord, we all have sinned and fallen short of Your ways. Lay our hearts bare so that we might repent and sin no more. In Jesus' name we pray. Amen.

C. Thought to Remember

What cause has Jesus given *you* to rejoice?

Involvement Learning

Enhance your lesson with KJV Bible Student *(from your curriculum supplier) and the reproducible activity page (at www.standardlesson.com or in the back of the* KJV Standard Lesson Commentary Deluxe Edition*).*

Into the Lesson

Ask learners to share examples from childhood, school, work, etc., in which they or someone they knew broke the rules but did not experience the consequences of their wrongdoing. Then ask participants to compare how they felt when they were not punished versus when others were not punished. Consider whether the severity of an offense makes any difference in how the learners felt about themselves or others not experiencing consequences. For instance, does it matter if someone was physically harmed as well as emotionally harmed?

Alternative. Distribute copies of the "When Can You Break the Speed Limit?" exercise from the activity page, which you can download. Have learners work in small groups to discuss as indicated. *Option.* Allow learners to use their mobile devices to check your state's traffic laws.

After either activity, work as a whole group to create definitions of *forgiveness* and *condemnation.* Write the definitions on the board for reference later in the lesson. Ask: What is the difference between "forgiving" and "not condemning"?

Make a transition by saying, "There are many circumstances in which we and others choose to break the law. We expect understanding and forgiveness for ourselves, but do we extend it to others? Today we are going to study a passage of Scripture in which Jesus is asked to condemn a woman who has broken the law. What will He do?"

Into the Word

Invite a volunteer to read John 8:1-11, 56-59 aloud. As a group, decide how the Pharisees might define *forgiveness* versus *condemnation.* Write these definitions below those that the class brainstormed earlier. Compare and contrast the definitions, then ask: How do these definitions show the hypocrisy of leaders who accuse others while breaking the law themselves? Ask the whole group to brainstorm ways the Jewish leaders broke not only the letter of the law, but the spirit of it. Share information from the commentary to add to the discussion. Invite learners to look at Matthew 23 for additional ideas on keeping the spirit of the law.

Invite a volunteer to reread John 8:56-59. Discuss in small groups: 1–What is Jesus publicly claiming in these verses? 2–How do Jesus' identity and actions contrast with the attitudes and actions of the religious leaders? 3–What challenge does Jesus give to people who are forgiven?

Into Life

Have the whole class focus on John 8:15 to discuss Jesus' challenge to the woman. Lead a brainstorming session for modern examples that show how one can extend forgiveness while at the same time urging people to repent. Be sure to encourage sensitivity as the groups talk through ways to do this in love and with an understanding of the person.

To conclude the lesson, distribute index cards and pens to participants. Ask learners to fill one side of their cards with examples of sins and mistakes for which God and other people have forgiven them. They can also include any laws of the land they have broken and not been punished for. Give learners one minute to repent of any ongoing sins for which Jesus has forgiven them.

Alternative. Distribute copies of the "Behavior and Motivations" activity from the activity page. Have learners complete it individually in a minute or less before discussing conclusions with a partner.

Read John 3:16-17. On the other side of the cards, ask learners to write a prayer of gratitude for escaping condemnation in Christ. Challenge learners to spend time during the week reflecting on their actions.

Inward and Outward

Devotional Reading: Ezekiel 36:25-30
Background Scripture: Romans 2:1-29

Romans 2:12-24, 28-29

12 For as many as have sinned without law shall also perish without law: and as many as have sinned in the law shall be judged by the law;

13 (For not the hearers of the law are just before God, but the doers of the law shall be justified.

14 For when the Gentiles, which have not the law, do by nature the things contained in the law, these, having not the law, are a law unto themselves:

15 Which shew the work of the law written in their hearts, their conscience also bearing witness, and their thoughts the mean while accusing or else excusing one another;)

16 In the day when God shall judge the secrets of men by Jesus Christ according to my gospel.

17 Behold, thou art called a Jew, and restest in the law, and makest thy boast of God,

18 And knowest his will, and approvest the things that are more excellent, being instructed out of the law;

19 And art confident that thou thyself art a guide of the blind, a light of them which are in darkness,

20 An instructor of the foolish, a teacher of babes, which hast the form of knowledge and of the truth in the law.

21 Thou therefore which teachest another, teachest thou not thyself? thou that preachest a man should not steal, dost thou steal?

22 Thou that sayest a man should not commit adultery, dost thou commit adultery? thou that abhorrest idols, dost thou commit sacrilege?

23 Thou that makest thy boast of the law, through breaking the law dishonourest thou God?

24 For the name of God is blasphemed among the Gentiles through you, as it is written.

---

28 For he is not a Jew, which is one outwardly; neither is that circumcision, which is outward in the flesh:

29 But he is a Jew, which is one inwardly; and circumcision is that of the heart, in the spirit, and not in the letter; whose praise is not of men, but of God.

Key Text

He is a Jew, which is one inwardly; and circumcision is that of the heart, in the spirit, and not in the letter; whose praise is not of men, but of God. —**Romans 2:29**

God's Law
Is Love

Unit 2: Faith Triumphs, Law Fails

Lessons 5–9

Lesson Aims

After participating in this lesson, each learner will be able to:

1. Restate what makes a person "a Jew."
2. Explain the importance of circumcision of the heart.
3. Make a plan to ensure that his or her actions serve as teaching examples.

Lesson Outline

Introduction
- A. Heart Surgery
- B. Lesson Context

I. Just Judgment (Romans 2:12-16)
- A. With or Without the Law? (v. 12)
- B. Hearers or Doers? (vv. 13-15)
  - *Categorize Yourself?*
- C. Secret or Public Violators? (v. 16)

II. False Faithfulness (Romans 2:17-24)
- A. Boastful Credentials (vv. 17-20)
  - *To See Ourselves as Others See Us*
- B. Blasphemous Hypocrisy (vv. 21-24)

III. True Identity (Romans 2:28-29)
- A. Outward Appearances (v. 28)
- B. Inner Convictions (v. 29)

Conclusion
- A. Circumcised Heart
- B. Prayer
- C. Thought to Remember

Introduction

A. Heart Surgery

A dear woman in a church where I ministered went into the hospital for heart surgery. When I made a post-surgical visit, I was surprised when her husband told me the surgeon had replaced a defective valve in her heart with a valve from a pig's heart. This use of a "porcine valve" in a human heart has now been practiced for over thirty years. It is known as "receiving xenographic tissue," meaning from a non-human source.

Once rare and dangerous, various types of heart surgery are now common. Included are "minimally invasive" or "keyhole" procedures, where small incisions are made and repairs involve tiny cameras and robot-assisted tools. The ultimate heart surgery is the heart transplant.

In Paul's day, the necessity of the heart for human survival was recognized, but surgical repairs to a heart were unknown. It is ironic, then, that Paul unknowingly anticipated some of the wonders of modern medicine when he wrote of a spiritual heart surgery, what he calls the "circumcision of the heart." This lesson explores what Paul means by this curious choice of words.

B. Lesson Context

Paul wrote the letter to the church in Rome in about AD 58, near the end of his third missionary journey. He had not visited Rome but hoped to do so in the near future (Romans 1:10). Despite this lack of firsthand familiarity, Paul was quite knowledgeable about issues causing dissention in the church of Rome. Conflict between Christians of Jewish and Gentile backgrounds was one of these issues. This may have been sharpened by the expulsion of all Jews from the city through an edict issued by Emperor Claudius in AD 49 (see Acts 18:2).

By the time Paul wrote, Claudius was dead, and Jews had returned to Rome. They included Jewish Christians. Gentile Christians had necessarily assumed leading roles in the church at Rome while the Jewish Christians were gone. We speculate that Paul knew that some of the returnees had attempted to assert their previous authority. In so doing, they may have elevated Jewish Christians above Gentile Christians. Circumcision, a sign of the old covenant, may have become a flash point in this conflict.

For the Hebrew people, circumcision began with Abraham (Genesis 17) as a sign of the covenant between God and Abraham. That was in about 2000 BC. About 550 years later, circumcision of male babies was established (codified) to occur when the baby was eight days old (Leviticus 12:3). This tradition began with Abraham and his son Isaac (Genesis 21:4). The God-given instructions to Abraham seem to have presumed that the man knew what circumcision was, thus implying that circumcision was practiced by others before him. The antiquity of circumcision outside of Judaism was confirmed in 2021 when scientists "digitally unwrapped" the intact mummy of Pharaoh Amenhotep I (reigned about 1525–1504 BC), discovering that he had been circumcised.

In Paul's day of the first century AD, neither the Romans nor the Greeks practiced circumcision. Greeks viewed circumcision as an intentional marring or mutilation of the ideal body. Prohibition of the practice had been a notable factor in the Maccabean Revolt, which began in 167 BC (see the nonbiblical 1 Maccabees 1:60-61; 2:45-46; 2 Maccabees 6:7-10). Paul addressed the implications of the circumcision issue at length in the book of Galatians. But he also did so in Romans 2—today's lesson.

I. Just Judgment

(Romans 2:12-16)

A. With or Without the Law? (v. 12)

12. For as many as have sinned without law shall also perish without law: and as many as have sinned in the law shall be judged by the law.

A way to express the distinction between Jews and Gentiles in Paul's day was to say that Jews were *in the law* while Gentiles were *without law*. The law that Paul had in mind was given by God through Moses for the nation of Israel: the Law of Moses. The first five books of the Old Testament, often called the Pentateuch, embody this law.

The Jews knew their law well. It was the basis for their faith, having been studied and practiced for centuries. Yet they had knowingly broken that law, and they could not avoid being *judged* according to those violations.

The Gentiles, for their part, had not been given this special revelation of law from God. Even so, Romans 1:18-21 establishes that Gentiles could not escape judgment by pleading ignorance.

What Do You Think?

Knowing that the Old Testament law cannot bring salvation, what value can Christians experience from studying it?

Digging Deeper

Does your answer change when you expand the question to include the entire Old Testament? Why or why not?

B. Hearers or Doers? (vv. 13-15)

13. (For not the hearers of the law are just before God, but the doers of the law shall be justified.

For this verse and the next two, Paul breaks the flow of his argument to give an aside. In so doing, he adds background to his criticism of Jews who boasted of their possession of the law. Faithful keeping of the law was more than merely having and being acquainted with it, which would amount to being nothing more than *hearers of the law*. Justification came from being *doers of the law* (but see also Romans 3:9-20).

To understand what Paul means by being *justified* is central to the book of Romans, where the underlying Greek verb occurs 15 times. In its noun form it occurs many more times than that! These terms come from the legal arena—the world of courtrooms and laws. To be justified in this sense means to be free from penalty for breaking the law. The Bible sees the Lord as the always-righteous judge and humans as always-unrighteous and guilty of sin, thereby incurring the wrath of God (Romans 2:8; 3:23). We are declared righteous because Christ has paid the penalty for our sin (3:21-26; 4:25; 5:18).

14. For when the Gentiles, which have not

the law, do by nature the things contained in the law, these, having not the law, are a law unto themselves.

The other side of the coin is the situation where a Gentile (a non-Jewish person) who is ignorant of the Law of Moses behaves in accordance with its precepts nonetheless. For example, if a Gentile believed strongly that adultery was a bad thing and lived faithfully in a monogamous marriage, he or she would unwittingly be keeping the commandment "thou shalt not commit adultery" (Exodus 20:14).

In so doing, *Gentiles* are keeping the Law of Moses by nature. *The laws* of God as given to the nation of Israel were not the imposition of unnatural, unreasonable, or unnecessary requirements for living. Rather, God's laws gave instructions for living according to His created plan. Sin has distorted and thwarted this divine blueprint for holy living.

Categorize Yourself?

I heard a flight attendant voice the following during the COVID-19 pandemic:

> You must wear a mask while on this flight, covering both your nose and mouth. If you do not intend to do this, please let us know now so that we can remove you from the plane. You will be free to make other arrangements to reach your destination. But be forewarned: you will not be allowed on any commercial airline in this country.

Such a stern warning resulted from insults and even assaults on flight attendants by opponents of mandatory masking. Rather than obey government rules on health and safety, some people believed that their personal rights allowed them to make their own rules.

Jews in Paul's days prided themselves for having a comprehensive set of rules (laws) that guided behavior. They believed that keeping these rules made them righteous and better than the Gentiles who did not have Jewish law. Yet Paul affirmed that neither Jews with the Law of Moses nor the Gentiles without that law were truly righteous. All were sinners, even if they denied it.

What category are you in? Are you a proud rule-breaker, one who believes in personal sovereignty? If so, read Romans 11:17-21; 13:1-5. Or are you one who keeps the rules and feels smugly superior in that regard? If so, read Romans 3:9-20 and James 2:10. Do you sincerely believe that neither group is righteous apart from faith in Jesus Christ?

—M. S. K.

15. Which shew the work of the law written in their hearts, their conscience also bearing witness, and their thoughts the mean while accusing or else excusing one another.)

This verse is sometimes seen as opening the door for the possibility of a Gentile achieving a state of righteousness without knowing the Law of Moses as Paul introduces the concept of *conscience*. Paul uses some form of this word 21 times in his epistles. Sometimes this word implies "to know" or "to be aware of" something (examples: Acts 23:1; 1 Corinthians 4:4); at other times, it refers to moral sensitivity. The latter is the meaning here. Even without having the Law of Moses, everyone has a built-in sense of right and wrong—a moral compass. But this guide can be suppressed (1 Timothy 4:2; Titus 1:15-16). And indeed it has been suppressed (compare Romans 1:18).

What Do You Think?

What role does conscience play in following the Spirit's leading?

Digging Deeper

How do you guard against a "seared" conscience that follows deceptive teaching (1 Timothy 4:1-2)?

C. Secret or Public Violators? (v. 16)

16. In the day when God shall judge the secrets of men by Jesus Christ according to my gospel.

Both Jews with the Law of Moses and Gentiles with the law written on their hearts will stand as guilty on *the day when God shall judge the secrets of men*. People may get away with hidden acts of sin under human judicial systems, but that is not so with God (also 1 Corinthians 4:5). The function of eternal judgment is entrusted to the Son, *Jesus Christ* (John 5:22; 9:39; Acts 17:31; 2 Corinthians 5:10). God knows what we believe to be hidden

(Psalm 139:1-3; Matthew 6:4). He is the omniscient (all-knowing) judge who never lacks evidence.

The phrase *my gospel* used here and other places (Romans 16:25, 2 Timothy 2:8) shows a personal attachment between Paul and the message of Christ. Paul had been taught the gospel message by none other than Jesus Christ himself (Galatians 1:11-12).

II. False Faithfulness

(Romans 2:17-24)

A. Boastful Credentials (vv. 17-20)

17-18. Behold, thou art called a Jew, and restest in the law, and makest thy boast of God, and knowest his will, and approvest the things that are more excellent, being instructed out of the law.

Paul turned his attention to readers of Jewish background. His propositions that begin in this verse are of the conditional "if . . . then" type. Such arguments feature one or more hypotheses (if-statements) followed by a logical conclusion; here, the word if is implied; compare Galatians 3:21, 29, where "if" is explicit.

The hypotheses take the form of what we might call a "résumé of righteousness"—a listing of things the Christians of Jewish background might smugly cite as evidence of their superiority to Christians of Gentile background. The Jews of Paul's day claimed to know the divine plan and desires of the Creator. They were confident that the law expressed God's enduring pattern for life in all aspects. These standards were seen as timeless and absolute.

19-20. And art confident that thou thyself art a guide of the blind, a light of them which are in darkness, an instructor of the foolish, a teacher of babes, which hast the form of knowledge and of the truth in the law.

Before reaching the conclusion of the argument, Paul adds more hypotheses. These two verses describe the ancient Jewish attitude toward Gentiles. As *a guide of the blind*, the Jew had spiritual insights that the Gentile lacked (see Isaiah 35:5). Combined with the image of being *a light of them which are in darkness*, the situation describes spiritual blindness—the Gentile inability to know and follow God's will fully (compare and contrast Isaiah 9:1-2 [quoted in Matthew 4:15-16]; Isaiah 42:6 and 49:6 [in Luke 2:32 and Acts 13:47]). The Jews living by God's law were to be a model of righteousness that condemned sin (Isaiah 51:4) while drawing people to God and His glory (60:3). Consequently, Jews believed themselves to be instructors and teachers in that regard.

What Do You Think?

In what circumstances are you a teacher?

Digging Deeper

How can you remain confident that what you do and say are teaching the same lesson to your "students"?

To See Ourselves as Others See Us

Denial and unawareness are part of the very definition of spiritual blindness. That's because if the one who was spiritually blind could and would admit to it, then he or she would correct the situation and wouldn't be spiritually blind!

At one time, Paul needed to be struck physically blind in order to have his spiritual blindness corrected (Acts 9:1-22). That correction qualified him to recognize spiritual blindness in his fellow Jews who saw themselves as spiritual guides yet suffered from spiritual blindness themselves. They had become as the blind guides whom Jesus described in Matthew 15:14; 23:16-24.

Many people today suffer from spiritual blindness, unable to see Jesus for who He really is. They need our help! But that help won't be effective unless we first correct our own areas of spiritual blindness. And *that* correction won't happen until a spiritually mature person makes us aware of our deficiencies in this regard. Whom will you invite to be your spiritual mentor? —R. L. N.

B. Blasphemous Hypocrisy (vv. 21-24)

21a. Thou therefore which teachest another, teachest thou not thyself?

Paul moves from if-statements to his concluding then-statements. These surely reflect the actual situation within the Roman church, where Christians of Jewish background had regained positions of leadership and teaching, lording over those of Gentile background. Paul's solution is to begin by questioning the consistency and sincerity of the teachers. Failure in this area results in being hypocrites—a condemnation on the lips of Jesus more than a dozen times in the Gospel of Matthew (see especially chapter 23).

21b-22. Thou that preachest a man should not steal, dost thou steal? Thou that sayest a man should not commit adultery, dost thou commit adultery? thou that abhorrest idols, dost thou commit sacrilege?

Paul now dives deeper, into the very heart of the law itself as he refers to behavior forbidden by the eighth, seventh, and first (and/or second) commandments, respectively (Exodus 20:3-4, 14-15; Deuteronomy 5:7-8, 18-19). Since Paul had never visited the church in Rome (see Lesson Context), it is unlikely that he knew of specific violations of Jewish law by these teachers. But we should remember Paul's background: he had been a student of the renown Gamaliel (Acts 22:3), and Paul had been raised as a Pharisee, a sect with fanatical devotion to strict interpretation and observance of the commandments (23:6; 26:5; Philippians 3:5). As an "insider," he had surely seen famous teachers whose private lives did not live up to their teaching.

Even if that was not the case among the Christians of Jewish background in Rome, the warning itself was valid. It was all too easy to skirt the commandments by rationalizing (see Mark 7:9-13).

The Greek word translated *sacrilege* is difficult; this is the only place in the New Testament where it appears. The Greek word does appear in the nonbiblical 2 Maccabees 9:2, where it refers to robbing the temple. That is likely the sense here. One theory is that Paul was referring to the possibility that some of his Jewish readers had sullied themselves by dishonorable contact with pagan temples, perhaps by shady business dealings with pagan priests.

23-24. Thou that makest thy boast of the law, through breaking the law dishonourest thou God? For the name of God is blasphemed among the Gentiles through you, as it is written.

The squeaky-clean moral image the Jews wished to project to the Gentile world was filled with hypocrisy (again, Matthew 23). Their pride in the Law of Moses was dishonored by their failure to keep that law. The Jews through their hypocritical behavior among the Gentiles were dishonoring the name of God. This was not a new problem in the first century AD, given that the phrase *as it is written* likely refers to the same problem of blasphemy in Isaiah 52:5 and Ezekiel 36:20-22. *For the name of God* to be *blasphemed* by pagans is bad enough; how much worse it was when such blasphemy came about *among the Gentiles* through God's covenant people of the Old Testament era! Paul did not countenance any sort of "Do as I say, not as I do" behavior (1 Timothy 3:7; etc.).

What Do You Think?

When you consider the state of the world, what would you consider to be the greatest sin problem "out there"?

Digging Deeper

How do you avoid the hypocrisy of contributing to this sin by your action or inaction (James 4:17)?

III. True Identity

(Romans 2:28-29)

A. Outward Appearances (v. 28)

28. For he is not a Jew, which is one outwardly; neither is that circumcision, which is outward in the flesh.

Paul began this section by appealing to those who proudly call themselves Jews (Romans 2:17). He now defines what *a Jew* is *not* in the ideal sense. Jewish identity is neither an issue of outward appearance in general nor the covenant sign of physical circumcision (or lack of it) in particular. Those are mere considerations of *the flesh*.

B. Inner Convictions (v. 29)

29. But he is a Jew, which is one inwardly; and circumcision is that of the heart, in the spirit, and not in the letter; whose praise is not of men, but of God.

Being *a Jew* in the ideal sense is an issue *of the heart, in the spirit,* not that of the flesh, which focuses on *the letter* of the Law of Moses. Therefore being a Jew in this sense is neither a matter of biological ancestry nor of adherence to the Law of Moses. In offering this proposition, Paul lifts the discussion above physical realities to that of spiritual realities. But that wasn't really anything new! God had always desired circumcision of the heart (Deuteronomy 10:16; 30:6; Jeremiah 4:4). To have a circumcised heart was to relinquish stubborn disobedience and be free to love God without limits. For Christians, it is to say with Jesus, "Not my will, but thine, be done" (Luke 22:42).

Truly following God is a matter of the heart, the inner being, not a surgical procedure on the physical body. Demands for strict, even slavish adherence to the Law of Moses may have elicited praise from men and women, but not necessarily the approval of God (Matthew 23:23-24; etc.). God knows our hearts, and He knows both Jews and Gentiles are sinners without excuse.

Many places in the Bible teach us that God looks upon our hearts (example: Psalm 44:21) and sees us as we truly are. Indeed, the Lord made David the King of Israel because God knew what was in David's heart (1 Samuel 16:7; Acts 13:22). Paul elsewhere drew on this idea of spiritual circumcision to identify the new people of God (Philippians 3:3; Colossians 2:11-12). Physical circumcision or uncircumcision is ultimately a nonissue; it's spiritual circumcision that accompanies faith in Christ that matters (Galatians 5:6).

What Do You Think?

What habits reveal the earnest conviction of your heart?

Digging Deeper

What habit would you like to break or develop to live in a way that reinforces your desire for God's praise over people's?

Conclusion

A. Circumcised Heart

The idea of the circumcised heart was powerful for Moses and Paul, and must be for us today. Can we humble ourselves and leave behind our tendencies to be stiff-necked? Can we trust fully in Christ for our salvation, not our own good works?

Visual for Lesson 5. *Allow learners one minute of silent reflection on this question before considering the questions associated with verse 29.*

Paul's exposition for the rest of the book of Romans required both Jews and Gentiles realize their need for God's salvation because all are under the power of sin (Romans 3:9). For both groups, hope comes not from keeping the law, whether it be the law of the conscience or the Law of Moses. It comes from faith in Christ.

B. Prayer

Heavenly Father, may our hearts turn away from pride and sin and toward You in faith and hope. May our trust be only in Your Son, Jesus. We pray in His name. Amen.

C. Thought to Remember

God wants a humble, obedient heart.

How to Say It

Amenhotep	Uh-men-*ho*-tep.
Claudius	*Claw*-dee-us.
Gamaliel	Guh-*may*-lih-ul or Guh-*may*-lee-al.
Maccabean	Mack-uh-*be*-un.
omniscient	ahm-*nish*-unt.
Pentateuch	*Pen*-ta-teuk.
xenographic	*zee*-nuh-graf-ik.

Involvement Learning

Enhance your lesson with KJV Bible Student *(from your curriculum supplier) and the reproducible activity page (at www.standardlesson.com or in the back of the* KJV Standard Lesson Commentary Deluxe Edition*).*

Into the Lesson

Write on the board *Good Living* as a heading. Divide learners into pairs. Invite pairs to each share an example of a living family member, friend, or acquaintance who is not a follower of Jesus yet whose life shows good moral qualities. Ask pairs to answer: How does this person act in ways that are compatible with Christian morality?

Alternative. Distribute copies of the "Right and Wrong Around the World" exercise from the activity page, which you can download. Students can work in pairs to complete as indicated.

Following either activity, gather the pairs together. As a whole group discuss what the world might conclude from the fact that people from various religious faiths or no faith at all seem to live generally moral lives. What might society say when those people appear more righteous than Christians?

Segue by saying, "Even though some people seem good, Paul teaches that being good just isn't good enough. Let's see what the lesson teaches, not just about other people, but about ourselves too."

Into the Word

Invite volunteers to read Romans 2:12-24, 28-29 aloud. As a group, create a list on the board of what Paul teaches about judging others. Include references from Romans and Paul's other letters. Do not erase the list, as it will be referred to in the Into Life section. (*Option.* Create a separate header for biblical teachings on or examples of judgment that are not found in Paul's writings.)

Use the list to help discuss: 1–why judgment should be left to God; and 2–why it was problematic for Paul's audience that their actions differed from what was required by God's law.

Ask a volunteer to reread Romans 2:29 aloud. Divide the class into small groups to talk about what Paul means by "circumcision of the heart." Distribute a handout (you create) with the following questions: 1–What did circumcision in the Old Testament symbolize? 2–Does circumcision of the heart differ from God's intention for circumcision in Israel? Why or why not? Share information from the commentary to help answer questions brought up in the discussions.

Into Life

Considering the list created in Into the Word, discuss as a class 1–What problems that Paul pointed out among the early Christians that are also problems among Christians today; and 2–What difference circumcision of the heart makes in showing God's love to others.

Divide the class in half for a debate on the resolution: *Do as I say, not as I do.* Allow time for the groups to formulate an opening statement, as many arguments as possible in favor of their position, and a concluding statement. Encourage these groups to include biblical examples of why it is or is not appropriate to ask others to do as you say, not as you do. Close the debate by talking together about which stance is in keeping with Paul's teaching and what nuance, if any, the other side of the conversation has to offer. Then give learners one minute to individually make a plan that ensures his or her actions serve as teaching examples, demonstrating integrity between what is said and what is done.

Option. Distribute copies of the "Repaired with Gold" exercise from the activity page. Have learners complete it individually in a minute or less before sharing with a partner.

Conclude the lesson with a prayer that learners would have open hearts that lead their actions throughout the week. Encourage them to watch for opportunities to teach in both word and deed and come to class next week prepared to report on their experiences.

October 8
Lesson 6 (KJV)

Old and New

Devotional Reading: Jeremiah 7:1-15
Background Scripture: Romans 7:1-25

Romans 7:1-12

1 Know ye not, brethren, (for I speak to them that know the law,) how that the law hath dominion over a man as long as he liveth?

2 For the woman which hath an husband is bound by the law to her husband so long as he liveth; but if the husband be dead, she is loosed from the law of her husband.

3 So then if, while her husband liveth, she be married to another man, she shall be called an adulteress: but if her husband be dead, she is free from that law; so that she is no adulteress, though she be married to another man.

4 Wherefore, my brethren, ye also are become dead to the law by the body of Christ; that ye should be married to another, even to him who is raised from the dead, that we should bring forth fruit unto God.

5 For when we were in the flesh, the motions of sins, which were by the law, did work in our members to bring forth fruit unto death.

6 But now we are delivered from the law, that being dead wherein we were held; that we should serve in newness of spirit, and not in the oldness of the letter.

7 What shall we say then? Is the law sin? God forbid. Nay, I had not known sin, but by the law: for I had not known lust, except the law had said, Thou shalt not covet.

8 But sin, taking occasion by the commandment, wrought in me all manner of concupiscence. For without the law sin was dead.

9 For I was alive without the law once: but when the commandment came, sin revived, and I died.

10 And the commandment, which was ordained to life, I found to be unto death.

11 For sin, taking occasion by the commandment, deceived me, and by it slew me.

12 Wherefore the law is holy, and the commandment holy, and just, and good.

Key Text

Now we are delivered from the law, that being dead wherein we were held; that we should serve in newness of spirit, and not in the oldness of the letter. —**Romans 7:6**

God's Law

Is Love

Unit 2: Faith Triumphs, Law Fails

Lessons 5–9

Lesson Aims

After participating in this lesson, each learner will be able to:

1. Identify what made Paul know what sin was.

2. Define "flesh" as Paul uses the term in the lesson's passage.

3. State a way to guard against a wrong view of the Old Testament law that he or she has heard expressed.

Lesson Outline

Introduction

A. The Ten Commandments

B. Lesson Context

I. Bondage of the Law (Romans 7:1-6)

A. Released by Death (vv. 1-3)

B. Released by the Spirit (vv. 4-6)

"Either/Or," Not "Both/And"

Don't Touch

II. Bondage of Sin (Romans 7:7-12)

A. Sin Defined by Law (vv. 7-8)

B. Death by Sin's Deception (vv. 9-12)

Conclusion

A. The Law Today?

B. Prayer

C. Thought to Remember

Introduction

A. The Ten Commandments

While teaching at a college, I became aware of a local controversy with national significance. Beginning in the 1950s, a fraternal organization began donating monuments of the Ten Commandments to state and local governments. This project gained traction when endorsed by film director Cecil B. DeMille as publicity for his movie *The Ten Commandments*. The number of these impressive granite slabs is not known but estimated to be over 150.

One of these was donated in 1959 to the city where I lived decades later. It stands on the street corner outside of the downtown police station. A lengthy court battle to remove this monument ensued, citing violation of the separation of church and state. That was resolved in 2005: the monument could stay. When I worked in that city, it was a block from my office. Overgrown shrubbery partially blocked sight of it, and few passersby even noticed its presence.

Does this reflect the attitude of Christians to the Law of Moses, of which the Ten Commandments form the core? Is that body of law merely a relic from a long-ago past? Does freedom from that law mean we can ignore it?

B. Lesson Context

Paul addresses the above questions in Romans 7, a deep dive into the purpose and applicability of the Old Testament law to Christians. Tension between Christians of Jewish and Gentile backgrounds is a context of the book of Romans—something that is no longer an issue in the church today. Even so, the question of the place of the Law of Moses as regulations for human behavior is still debated. Therefore, while understanding Paul's ongoing argument in Romans can be challenging, diligent study of this book is essential for the practice of biblical Christianity. The book of Romans is the fullest expression of Paul's teaching—what he calls "my gospel" (Romans 2:16; 16:25). Paul refers to his teaching this way as he draws frequently on his Jewish heritage. By one count, Romans features more than 50 direct quotes from the Old Testament.

In Romans 5, 6, and 7, Paul identifies three great tyrants of humankind: *sin, death,* and *the law.* Each of these has had a role in oppressing men and women and robbing them of the possibility of a reconciled relationship with the Lord. Each of these three has had "dominion" (Romans 6:9, 14; 7:1), the language of tyranny. Death has reigned in terror since the sin of Adam (5:14). Sin has reigned in the lives of men and women (6:12), leading to the consequences of judgment. Law (whether Mosaic or secular) exists as the authority to define and punish wrong behavior (6:15-23). In Romans 7, Paul returned to a discussion of the rightful place of the law in God's plan.

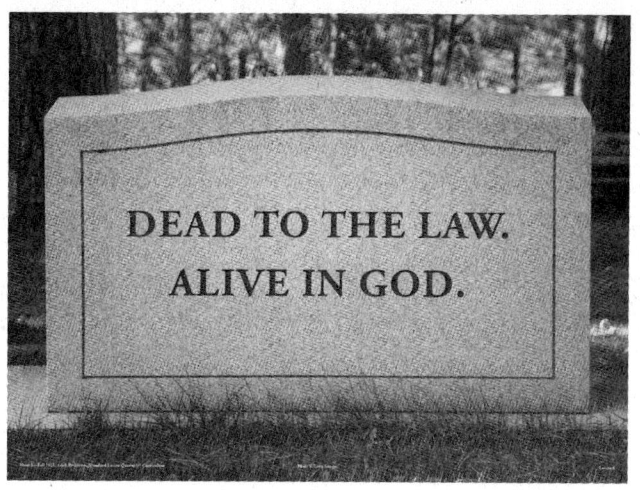

Visual for Lesson 6. *Allow one minute for reflection on this fact at the beginning of class and again at the end.*

I. Bondage of the Law

(Romans 7:1-6)

A. Released by Death (vv. 1-3)

1. Know ye not, brethren, (for I speak to them that know the law,) how that the law hath dominion over a man as long as he liveth?

For Paul to *speak to them that know the law* probably indicates the intended audience to have been those Christians who were of Jewish background. His presentation at this point is characteristic of the intricate argumentation of a learned rabbi of his day. It is a style that was both appealing and persuasive to Jewish readers. But Paul was certainly aware that Christians of Gentile background would be listening, too, and that some of them were well acquainted with the Jewish law.

Paul begins with a basic legal principle, one that is not confined to the Law of Moses: laws don't apply to dead people. A corpse cannot be charged and convicted of theft, even if the dead body belonged to a person who was a thief before dying. In that sense, death nullifies any *dominion* a law might have over a person.

2. For the woman which hath an husband is bound by the law to her husband so long as he liveth; but if the husband be dead, she is loosed from the law of her husband.

To illustrate this, Paul uses the customs of marriage. We should be careful how we apply this, for he is not teaching about marriage here. Rather, he is teaching about the applicability of law regarding death; in so doing, he uses marriage as an example.

Paul's point is that in a marriage the wife is bound by the law to her husband. This recognizes a reality of both Roman and Jewish society of the day. A man might divorce a wife, but among the old-covenant Jews there was no such thing as divorce initiated by a wife (compare Deuteronomy 24:1-4; contrast 1 Corinthians 7:11-13).

We should take care to not be distracted at this point by pondering how the modern legal system is superior in this regard. Paul is not defending the divorce law of his day. Rather, he's using that law as an example to make a point: marriage is a lifelong commitment, but the commitment would terminate if the husband were to die (compare 1 Corinthians 7:39).

3. So then if, while her husband liveth, she be married to another man, she shall be called an adulteress: but if her husband be dead, she is free from that law; so that she is no adulteress, though she be married to another man.

Paul introduces into his example a hypothetical situation (compare and contrast Matthew 19:9; Luke 16:18). The situation is not one of bigamy but of adultery. The bond of the woman's initial marriage had not been broken by death of the first husband. Therefore she would rightly *be called an adulteress*—someone who had violated the seventh commandment (Exodus 20:14; compare Leviticus 20:10).

But *if her husband be dead,* the situation is different. She is free from lawful requirements toward her deceased husband. She is legally able to marry another man without being an adulteress. But let's not miss Paul's main point: it's not merely that death frees the woman from marital obligations to her first husband, but also that she is permitted to remarry without breaking the law. This is because the situation with her previous husband no longer applies after his death.

B. Released by the Spirit (vv. 4-6)

4. Wherefore, my brethren, ye also are become dead to the law by the body of Christ; that ye should be married to another, even to him who is raised from the dead, that we should bring forth fruit unto God.

Paul now turns the marriage analogy toward its spiritual parallel. In the previous chapter, he had presented the fact of Christians' being "dead to sin" (Romans 6:2) as concurrent with beginning a new life in Christ (6:3-4). It is not that the law itself had died, but that Christians are *dead to the law.* "The law of her husband" (7:2, above) still stands whether the husband lives or dies. But if he dies, it no longer applies to the surviving wife. As believers who have died to sin—and therefore the law, since the law defines what sin is (5:13; 7:7-8)—we can be *married to another.* This is a union with *him who is raised from the dead,* Jesus Christ. There is no unfaithfulness to our first "husband" (the law) due to the fact that we are no longer under its control. The result is that we begin to live in ways that *bring forth fruit unto God.* This is the new life in Christ (see also 6:6; 8:2; Galatians 2:19-20; 3:23-25; 4:31; 5:1).

What Do You Think?

How does dying to sin and being set free from the law help us become more fruitful for God?

Digging Deeper

Which of the fruit of the Spirit in Galatians 5:22-23 could be even more abundant in your life if you had a deeper sense of freedom in Christ?

"Either/Or," Not "Both/And"

My wife felt the engine clunk. The steering wheel wouldn't turn. She managed to get off the busy road and breathed a sigh of relief. She glanced in the rearview mirror at the worried faces of our children.

I left work to go get them. A glance under the hood revealed that the alternator belt had come off. Our 15-year-old van had served us well, but that would be the fourth time in a month that I had to take it to a mechanic. I had known for a couple of years that we needed a new(er) van—one with a wheelchair ramp and unlikely to leave family members stranded.

But as long as I mentally clung to the old van, the new(er) one wouldn't happen. My psychological attachment to the old would only be released when it was no more. I was comfortable having it paid off, hesitant to commit to a replacement. But it had to be either "either/or," not "both/and."

The same is true of Christianity. It's a life of law *or* grace (Romans 5:20; 6:14-15; Galatians 5:4). Is there something in your life that needs to die? Think about this carefully: it's not that the law (which condemns your sin) has died; rather, it's the attraction to sin itself that has to die so that you are not condemned as a lawbreaker. —N. G.

5. For when we were in the flesh, the motions of sins, which were by the law, did work in our members to bring forth fruit unto death.

Paul now introduces a different way of expressing the pre-Christian life: as that of being *in the flesh.* The Greek word being translated "flesh" occurs 147 times in the New Testament, and more than 60 percent of those occurrences are in the writings of Paul. The word is flexible, and it must be understood in different ways, depending on context. Paul uses the Greek word translated "flesh" in at least six ways:

- of creatures generally (1 Corinthians 15:39)
- of our bodies specifically (1 Corinthians 6:16)
- of the human race generally (Galatians 2:16)
- that which is morally neutral (Romans 1:3)
- that which is morally negative (Galatians 6:12)
- of rebellious human nature (Romans 8:3-12)

The word *flesh* as used here matches the last of these six: our physical existence as opposed to the spiritual. This fleshly existence is characterized by the *motions* (or "affections," as the same word is translated in Galatians 5:24) *of sin*. Our material existence is weak, even prone to sin (see Romans 6:19). Our physical desires are gateways to violations of law.

Thus, sin's dominion over us uses our own body's impulses to control us. We produce fruit, but this is the fruit of sin that leads to *death*, spiritual death (compare Galatians 5:17-21). Sinful behavior wreaks havoc on us personally, on our marriages, on our families, and in our communities. It can have deadly consequences in our churches. Paul may have in mind the admonition from the law itself that the Lord continues the iniquities of fathers to the third and even the fourth generations (see Numbers 14:18). It is not so much that God continues to punish our children and grandchildren for our sins (Ezekiel 18:20), but that sin has a lasting effect, a persistence of *fruit unto death*, that affects more than just the one who commits it.

What Do You Think?

Thinking back to your pre-salvation self, what are some examples of deadly fruit that were evident in your life?

Digging Deeper

If some of that deadly fruit is still present in your life, what can you do about it? Would James 5:16 be a practical first step for you?

6. But now we are delivered from the law, that being dead wherein we were held; that we should serve in newness of spirit, and not in the oldness of the letter.

Our new existence allows us to be free from sin and, therefore, *delivered from the law*. This does not mean we are delivered into a state of permissible lawlessness. Paul has already made the point that freedom from sin is not a license to sin (Romans 6:1-2).

Instead, the focus of our new life in Christ is no longer to be "the flesh," reveling in the passions of our body. The focus and driver of our new life is the opposite of material existence: it is *newness of spirit*. Serving God is not simply a matter of keeping rules, obsessing over *the letter* of the law. We no longer behave in a right manner out of fear or in the hope of being rewarded. Rather, we obey Christ's commandments out of love for God and for others (see John 14:15; Galatians 5:14, 1 John 5:2). This yields the fruit of the Spirit as life transcends restrictions of the law (2 Corinthians 3:6; Galatians 5:22-23).

What Do You Think?

When do you experience tension between obeying the Lord out of love versus out of fear?

Digging Deeper

Does fear have any role to play when following the Lord from a loving motivation? Back up your answer with scriptures.

Don't Touch

"Don't touch the hot oil. It will burn you."

The little girl looked up at her dad's face, and her eyes hardened. She plunged her finger into the skillet.

Crying out in pain, she thrust her finger into her mouth.

"I told you, honey, that hot oil will burn you."

Her tear-filled eyes hardened again, and she plunged her finger back into the skillet. The oil wasn't hot enough to blister her, but her tears ran freely as she pulled her finger back the second time.

Her dad shook his head as he went to get the first aid kit. He said one last time, "That oil is hot. Don't touch it."

So she did it again.

My coworker told this story about his daughter, who had been a strong-willed child. His thrice-voiced warning was a good one, but it resulted in her rebellious spirit's burning her finger three times. He decided not to tell her a fourth time!

Has your church, your parents, or other authorities given you a warning that you ignore or a rule that you rebel against? Are you harming yourself or others by ignoring them?

P.S. That little girl is now grown and serving as a missionary. There is hope for us all through the gospel of Jesus! —N. G.

II. Bondage of Sin

(Romans 7:7-12)

A. Sin Defined by Law (vv. 7-8)

7. What shall we say then? Is the law sin? God forbid. Nay, I had not known sin, but by the law: for I had not known lust, except the law had said, Thou shalt not covet.

If death to sin frees us from the dominion of the law, then what is the purpose and value of the law? This is a concern often debated in the history of the church and even today. It can be framed more broadly as questioning the value and applicability of the Old Testament to the Christian and the church.

Paul often drives his teachings with rhetorical questions. These are questions he asks for which the answer is obvious. By having the readers answer these questions as they read, they follow Paul's line of thinking in the direction he desires. In this case, Paul anticipated that his readers would ask themselves *Is the law sin?* He has drawn many parallels between sin and the law. Both have been described as having enslaving dominion over humankind. So it is important to recognize that there is no sin without the law's definition.

We might further say that there would be no need for law if there were no sin. The connection is so strong that some might see an equivalency, such that the law wears sin as its clothing. So Paul answers his own question with a strong statement, *God forbid.* To conclude that the Law of Moses—Paul's area of expertise—was just sin in another form would be both ridiculous and insulting.

So then, what is the connection between sin and the law? Paul has addressed this issue before (see Romans 3:20; 5:13), and now offers a personal example. He chooses the tenth commandment, the prohibition against coveting (Exodus 20:17; Deuteronomy 5:21). Coveting is the desire to have something possessed by another person and to which we have no right. Coveting is characterized by *lust*, but this refers to more than sexual desires; it includes all sorts of greed, jealousy, and obsession.

If coveting is a natural impulse of our self-centered, material nature (the desire to have the best for ourselves), then why is it sinful? Paul's answer is simple: the law forbids it. The Lord, in giving the command against coveting, knows what is best for us as individuals and as larger society. Coveting is sin.

8. But sin, taking occasion by the commandment, wrought in me all manner of concupiscence. For without the law sin was dead.

Paul had experienced covetousness, but he had been able to control it. The intense word translated *concupiscence* is exactly the same word translated "lust" in Romans 7:7, above. Again, this refers to more than just unholy sexual impulses. The phrase *all manner of* casts a broad net over many kinds of undue desires.

Knowing of the tenth commandment had made Paul aware of all sorts of wrong desires harbored in his heart. Lust is a by-product of our material existence, the "flesh" (compare Romans 13:14; Ephesians 2:3). The point is that *without the law,* we would be unaware of God's desires. We would just experience the destructive effects of covetousness and inflict it on others without thought of its being inherently wrong or sinful.

B. Death by Sin's Deception (vv. 9-12)

9-10. For I was alive without the law once: but when the commandment came, sin revived, and I died. And the commandment, which was ordained to life, I found to be unto death.

Paul seems to broaden the discussion to include the larger human experience. Without the law, Paul had been *alive,* oblivious to the definition and consequences of sin. This could describe the behavior of a child, who may have no guilty feelings about selfishly taking a toy away from another child. But it also describes the pagan world of Paul's day, where ambitious self-gratification was often encouraged and celebrated, even in laws.

When such a "pre-law" person is confronted by *the commandment*, then *sin* takes on a new life. The result might seem like harmless greediness, but its toll is much higher: spiritual *death.* One cannot know of God's commandments, spurn them, and be in relationship with Him. Therefore, Paul's ironic conclusion is that even though the law was given for our benefit, our violation of it leads to death.

11. For sin, taking occasion by the commandment, deceived me, and by it slew me.

Here we become aware of a dangerous deception as it plays out in modern culture: whatever happens between consenting adults is proclaimed to be nobody's concern but their own. We want to be allowed to follow our desires as valued by today's world. Yet this is a fraudulent approach to life. Our lusts and desires are too often fed by self-centered sin. We think we find the rich life by following our passions. But the end of our pursuits is death.

12. Wherefore the law is holy, and the commandment holy, and just, and good.

To leave no doubt, Paul expands on his answer to the question of verse 7, "Is the law sin?" The Law of Moses is neither sin nor sinful. It is not the cause sin, but the definition of it. *The law is holy* because it defines, and is the definition, of moral purity. It is *just* (or righteous) because it promotes justice. It is *good* because it was given by the Lord for people's benefit.

While Christians may disagree over certain aspects of the applicability of the Old Testament law to today, we should agree as to its value and place for study. We will never understand sin and its dire consequences if we ignore the law and its teachings. It is still holy. It is still just. And, most of all, it is still good.

> **What Do You Think?**
> What value have you experienced because of your own study of the Old Testament?
>
> **Digging Deeper**
> What attitudes or practices could you change to enhance the benefit of this study?

Conclusion

A. The Law Today?

First Peter 1:16, quoting Leviticus 11:44-45, says "Be ye holy; for I am holy." We may disagree on which aspects of the Law of Moses still apply in the New Testament era and which don't, but this is one area where there is no doubt. We press further when we wonder *how* to be holy as God is holy. That is a profoundly important question, and as we wrestle with it, we must commit to growing in holiness throughout our lives.

To be holy requires a distinction from that which is unholy—and God is the one who makes that distinction known in His laws. Same thing with being loving versus being unloving (see Galatians 5:14, quoting Leviticus 19:18). If there is no God, no lawgiver, then there can be no absolute laws with regard to being holy, loving, etc. But God does exist, and He has given laws for the good of humankind. The philosophies of the world deceive us into thinking that selfish living is a full, authentic life when it is actually death. The way to counteract this influence is to study the ways God intends as presented throughout our Bibles.

> **What Do You Think?**
> What do you find most challenging about today's lesson?
>
> **Digging Deeper**
> What change in thought, word, or behavior will you make based on that challenge?

B. Prayer

Lord God, may we never despise Your laws! May You guard us from the deception of the world which claims that sin is good and satisfying. May Your Spirit continue to form us to become more and more like Your Son, Jesus, the one without sin. We pray these things in His name. Amen.

C. Thought to Remember

The law is necessary to teach us what is sinful.

How to Say It

concupiscence	con-**kyu**-puh-*cents*.
Gentiles	*Jen*-tiles.
Mosaic	Mo-*zay*-ik.
rabbi	*rab*-eye.

Involvement Learning

Enhance your lesson with KJV Bible Student *(from your curriculum supplier) and the reproducible activity page (at www.standardlesson.com or in the back of the* KJV Standard Lesson Commentary Deluxe Edition*).*

Into the Lesson

Ask the class how they think people would react if all laws, good and bad, great and small, were strictly enforced. Examples to focus on might be outdated or oddly specific laws. (*Option.* Research examples in your city or state of these kinds of laws, or allow the class five minutes to do the research themselves.) Ask whether people would become better because rules were strictly enforced, or seek out more devious ways to circumvent the law, or something else entirely?

Alternative. Distribute copies of the "Still on the Books" exercise from the activity page, which you can download. Have students work in pairs to complete as indicated. Then discuss the activity as a whole class.

Transition to the Bible study by introducing Paul's discussion of the law's nature and impact on people.

Into the Word

Begin by asking the class what they consider the role of the law. They should keep this concept in mind throughout the lesson to see how their definition of role of law compares and contrasts with Paul's own.

Invite a volunteer to read Romans 7:1-3 aloud. In pairs, have learners read Revelation 21 together. Ask these pairs to write down how the bride's status depended on being released from the law, as in Paul's analogy. After several minutes, bring the class back together to talk about what they found.

Alternative. Distribute copies of the "World-Record Marriages" activity from the activity page. Have learners discuss conclusions in small groups. Be sensitive to those members of the class who may have experienced loss of a spouse or divorce and remarriage.

Ask a volunteer to read Romans 7:4-6 aloud. In the same pairs, have learners read Galatians 5:19-21. What do these examples of "fruit unto death" (Romans 7:5) and the law have to do with one another?

Ask a volunteer to read Romans 7:7-12 aloud. Based on learners' answers to the Into the Lesson activity, how do these verses either confirm or refute their previous responses? Divide the class in half. One half will discuss how Romans 7:1-12 supports or modifies the aphorism "knowledge is power." The other half will do the same with the phrase "ignorance is bliss." (*Option.* Distribute a handout (you create) with both phrases printed on it so that pairs or small groups can consider both phrases at once.) After about 10 minutes, bring the groups together for a whole-class discussion on how these two phrases relate to Paul's teaching on the law's role and value.

Into Life

Ask a volunteer to reread Romans 7:7-12 aloud. How might learners' previous definitions of the role of the law be tweaked or overhauled in light of Paul's explanation? Ask how law is necessary as a tool to teach right from wrong. Encourage learners to provide both biblical and personal examples.

Distribute note cards and pens to learners. Ask class members to write down one wrong idea they have heard or believed about the Old Testament law. On the reverse side, ask learners to copy or paraphrase a verse from today's lesson that refutes that wrong idea. In pairs, have the learners talk about why it matters to think correctly about the role of the Old Testament law. Reasons might include: understanding the lives of the New Testament men and women better; learning to value the law without giving up freedom in Christ; etc. Encourage them to refer to this card throughout the week and jot down in the margins any new insights that occur in that time.

Close class with a prayer of thanks for what the law has taught us and for the freedom we experience in Christ.

October 15
Lesson 7 (KJV)

Works and Faith

Devotional Reading: Galatians 2:1-10
Background Scripture: Galatians 2:11-21

Galatians 2:11-21

11 But when Peter was come to Antioch, I withstood him to the face, because he was to be blamed.

12 For before that certain came from James, he did eat with the Gentiles: but when they were come, he withdrew and separated himself, fearing them which were of the circumcision.

13 And the other Jews dissembled likewise with him; insomuch that Barnabas also was carried away with their dissimulation.

14 But when I saw that they walked not uprightly according to the truth of the gospel, I said unto Peter before them all, If thou, being a Jew, livest after the manner of Gentiles, and not as do the Jews, why compellest thou the Gentiles to live as do the Jews?

15 We who are Jews by nature, and not sinners of the Gentiles,

16 Knowing that a man is not justified by the works of the law, but by the faith of Jesus Christ, even we have believed in Jesus Christ, that we might be justified by the faith of Christ, and not by the works of the law: for by the works of the law shall no flesh be justified.

17 But if, while we seek to be justified by Christ, we ourselves also are found sinners, is therefore Christ the minister of sin? God forbid.

18 For if I build again the things which I destroyed, I make myself a transgressor.

19 For I through the law am dead to the law, that I might live unto God.

20 I am crucified with Christ: nevertheless I live; yet not I, but Christ liveth in me: and the life which I now live in the flesh I live by the faith of the Son of God, who loved me, and gave himself for me.

21 I do not frustrate the grace of God: for if righteousness come by the law, then Christ is dead in vain.

Key Text

The life which I now live in the flesh I live by the faith of the Son of God, who loved me, and gave himself for me. —Galatians 2:20b

God's Law

Is Love

Unit 2: Faith Triumphs, Law Fails

Lessons 5–9

Lesson Aims

After participating in this lesson, each learner will be able to:

1. Identify how a person *is* and *is not* justified.
2. Summarize Peter's error.
3. Identify a parallel error today and commit to avoiding it.

Lesson Outline

Introduction
- A. More Than Doctrine
- B. Lesson Context

I. Dissonance (Galatians 2:11-14)
- A. Acting in Fear (vv. 11-12)
- B. Leading Others Astray (vv. 13-14)
  Carried Away

II. Gospel (Galatians 2:15-21)
- A. Justified by Faith (vv. 15-16)
- B. Accepting God's Grace (vv. 17-21)
  Already Dead

Conclusion
- A. Life in Christ
- B. Prayer
- C. Thought to Remember

Introduction

A. More Than Doctrine

Like many 18-year-olds, I thought I knew everything. I was a first-year Bible college student with a group of young, zealous, and like-minded guys who were dedicated to our doctrines, and anyone who disagreed with us was simply wrong. With a sense of superiority, we would often debate others in the dorms about their understandings of the particulars of Christian doctrines. Our statements and actions belittled anyone who came from a different Christian tradition. They were not like us, so we marginalized them.

At lunch one day, a friend of mine was nettling one of our opponents. A professor of ours stepped in. With firmness and truth, our professor told my friend that he was not representing Christ. I stood there in fear and humility, knowing that I too was receiving this correction. Our arguments over doctrines did not further the gospel in this case; they served as a dividing line between us and them. Our lesson today cuts to heart of a similar issue faced by Peter and Paul.

B. Lesson Context

Unlike many of his letters, Paul did not address the book of Galatians to the church in a particular city. Galatia was a Roman province in the central highlands area of modern Turkey. Paul and Barnabas had evangelized this area on the first missionary journey, including the cities of Pisidian Antioch, Iconium, Lystra, and Derbe (Acts 13–14). These cities were the recipients of the book, which was intended to be circulated among them and read to all the churches (Galatians 1:2).

Galatians very likely was written several years after the Jerusalem Council of Acts 15, which took place around AD 51. Many scholars believe that Galatians 2:1-10 is Paul's account of what happened when he attended that council. In this passage, Paul was careful to say that he did not need permission from anyone in Jerusalem to preach to the Gentiles, but he still welcomed their sanction and tacit agreement not to oppose his message. He noted that those church leaders had nothing to add to his message (2:6) and that God had ordained Paul to preach to Gentiles as Peter was chosen to preach to Jews (2:7).

Not everyone was on board with this arrangement. Some Judaizers had infiltrated the churches founded by Paul. They taught the members that they were required to follow the Jewish law (Galatians 2:4). Despite the decision of the Jerusalem Council, this Judaizing had continued. The churches were confused. Was the Law of Moses still in effect? Paul's exposition of this matter is the heart of the book of Galatians.

I. Dissonance

(Galatians 2:11-14)

A. Acting in Fear (vv. 11-12)

11. But when Peter was come to Antioch, I withstood him to the face, because he was to be blamed.

Antioch was the capital city of Syria in Paul's day. (This should not be confused with Pisidian Antioch, a smaller city in south central Asia Minor; see Acts 13:14.) After the stoning of Stephen and the following persecution, some believers settled in Antioch, resulting in the gospel being preached to both Jews and Gentiles. These believers were the first to be called "Christians" (11:19-26). This group of believers sent Paul and Barnabas on their first missionary journey; Paul traveled back to Antioch to report how God had worked through their ministry (13:1-3; 14:26-28).

We don't know why *Peter* made the journey of about 330 miles from Jerusalem to Antioch. He likely had some intention of meeting with the believers there. Why Paul *withstood him* and what Peter was *to be blamed* for are clarified in the following verses.

What Do You Think?

How do you decide whether to confront someone directly about his or her behavior?

Digging Deeper

In what situations might a less direct approach be more beneficial to the misbehaving person?

12. For before that certain came from James, he did eat with the Gentiles: but when they were come, he withdrew and separated himself, fearing them which were of the circumcision.

No command exists in the Old Testament that Israelites (later called Jews, a shortened form of "Judaeans") could not eat with Gentiles. The commands concerned unclean foods, not unclean people, as seen when God's people rejected these foods without mention of their table fellows (examples: Ezekiel 4:13-14; Daniel 1:9-14; compare and contrast Genesis 43:32). But a weighty tradition of sharing meals only with other Jews grew out of a desire to keep the law and avoid adopting the abhorrent practices of other nations (Leviticus 18:25-28; 20:23-24; Deuteronomy 8:20; etc.; see Acts 10:28). This was meant to ensure fidelity to God by avoiding idolatrous contamination from outsiders. But from the Gentile perspective, this practice probably betrayed an unacceptable elitism. Maintaining division between Jews and Gentiles called into question equal access to salvation of the two groups (Galatians 3:26-29).

The *certain* men who *came from James* apparently were associated with a Judaizing faction within the budding Christian faith. Though the issue of *circumcision* officially was resolved at the Jerusalem Council (Acts 15; see lesson 10), the Judaizing party was still active. James's association with these men contradicts his prior judgment not to trouble those "among the Gentiles [who] are turned to God," especially concerning certain ritual laws (15:19-20).

The movement from Peter's eating with *the Gentiles* to withdrawing and separating from them represented a retreat from the fullness of the gospel for both Jews and Gentiles, contradicting his own testimony before the council. His actions were blatant hypocrisy. Exactly why Peter feared this delegation is not stated. But his failure to live up to his earlier commitments reveals a double-mindedness regarding Gentiles, or at least a weakness of follow-through on what he believed to be true. We can contrast Peter's actions here with his own report of his ministry concerning the household of Cornelius, a Gentile. There, too, the criticism regarded eating with Gentiles (Acts 11:2-3).

But at that time, Peter rightly defended his fellowship with Gentiles as being the will of God (11:17).

B. Leading Others Astray (vv. 13-14)

13. And the other Jews dissembled likewise with him; insomuch that Barnabas also was carried away with their dissimulation.

Paul's language is particularly harsh! The term behind *dissembled* carries the sense "to be together as hypocrites." The pervasiveness of the hypocrisy is shown when Paul mentions that even *Barnabas* had become involved. This "son of consolation" (Acts 4:36; compare 11:22-24) found the peer pressure to avoid the Gentile believers too much to withstand. With his moment of weakness, we are left to think that Paul stood as the sole Jew willing to have complete fellowship with these Gentile Christians!

> **What Do You Think?**
> In what situations do you feel intimidated? How do you change the way you speak and act at those times?
> **Digging Deeper**
> When you feel pressure to change for others, what helps you take an authentic approach that is consistent with your values?

Carried Away

The guest speaker was famous, at least in my Christian circles. He'd written popular books, and he taught law at a large university. I sat up straight as he walked to the microphone during my college's morning chapel. He started with a joke. A dirty joke. Not so offensive that administrators would immediately boot him off the stage, but inappropriate. Several thousand students paused, then laughter began to roll around the auditorium. I didn't like the joke, but I smiled awkwardly to try to fit in.

"That's exactly the same response I get at secular universities," the speaker announced. He scolded us for not being different from the world. I didn't like his method, but I *still* remember the lesson. When everyone around me acted a certain way, including a respected leader, I found myself carried away with the crowd, much like Barnabas and Peter. Are you also blending in with people around you, even when you know better? What can you do differently? —N. G.

14. But when I saw that they walked not uprightly according to the truth of the gospel, I said unto Peter before them all, If thou, being a Jew, livest after the manner of Gentiles, and not as do the Jews, why compellest thou the Gentiles to live as do the Jews?

Paul's confrontation with Peter was not a small issue of favoritism and social practice. This matter cuts to *the truth of the gospel* of Jesus Christ. To be Christlike is to treat others the way Christ treats us. God makes no distinction between Jews and Gentiles when it comes to the offer of salvation (see Acts 10:34-35; 15:9; Romans 2:11). If God makes no distinction, neither should we. Therefore, Paul could write a little later, "There is neither Jew nor Greek, . . . ye are all one in Christ Jesus" (Galatians 3:28; see lesson 9).

It is easy to imagine that this was an intense, public confrontation (*before them all*). The Judaizers essentially said to Gentiles, "You don't have to be circumcised, but you have no part in us or this faith if you aren't" (compare Acts 15:5, lesson 10). The Gentiles' full acceptance by God would not be demonstrated by full partnership in Christ's body with the Jews.

> **What Do You Think?**
> How does your congregation demonstrate your welcome of people from all nationalities?
> **Digging Deeper**
> In what areas could this welcome be made more apparent?

II. Gospel
(Galatians 2:15-21)

A. Justified by Faith (vv. 15-16)

15. We who are Jews by nature, and not sinners of the Gentiles.

Jews were not alone in considering their teachings to be morally superior to others that were prevalent throughout the Roman Empire. Many things that were considered immoral by Jews were perfectly acceptable for non-Jews in the Greco-Roman environment. This was particularly true regarding sexual promiscuity, drunkenness, and idolatry. The benefit of Jewish moral teaching is why God-fearers—Gentiles who maintained elements of Jewish faith without converting (through circumcision)—existed even before Jesus' ministry (examples: Acts 10:2, 22; 13:26; 17:4, 17). These God-fearers rejected the permissive attitudes of other religious teachings and sought instead the higher call of God's standards. Based on this morally lax, albeit generalized, Gentile background, Paul could set up a dichotomy between Jews and *sinners of the Gentiles*. But read on, for Paul does not stop here.

16. Knowing that a man is not justified by the works of the law, but by the faith of Jesus Christ, even we have believed in Jesus Christ, that we might be justified by the faith of Christ, and not by the works of the law: for by the works of the law shall no flesh be justified.

Paul set up a dichotomy between Jews and Gentiles in verse 15, but here he tears it down. The key word for our understanding of this passage is *justified*, used three times in this verse alone. While we may be familiar with the religious implications of this word, its background is in the legal world. To be justified in a legal sense is to be declared innocent by a judge. In the context of our relationship with the divine judge, to be justified means that God does not intend to give us the deserved punishment for our sins.

The ultimate weakness of the Judaizing approach was its reliance on how faithfully a person could obey *the law*. Law-keeping itself was often commendable, but it was not a means for justification. After all, a person who kept the law 99.9 percent of the time was still guilty (James 2:10). Such a person fell short of righteous standing before God (see Romans 3:23).

The only possible way to be justified is through *the faith of Jesus Christ*. Some variation of this phrase occurs three times in this verse. Christians are justified in the eyes of God because they have placed their faith in Christ. This passage is ground zero for the doctrine of justification by faith as opposed to *works*—one of the foundational tenets of Christianity.

There are not two ways of salvation, one for Jews and one for Gentiles (see Romans 3:9). Jews may decide to keep the law for various valid reasons, but law-observance as a means to salvation is futile. Paul was an accomplished, educated Jew, with deep knowledge of the law and the technicalities of its observance (see Philippians 3:4-6). If anyone could be justified by the law, it would be Paul! But he taught the impossibility of this approach. In so doing, he undermined the credibility of the Judaizers who had been preaching another gospel to the Galatians (see Galatians 1:7-8).

B. Accepting God's Grace (vv. 17-21)

17. But if, while we seek to be justified by Christ, we ourselves also are found sinners, is therefore Christ the minister of sin? God forbid.

The Judaizers' question might look like this: If keeping the law is not a requirement for Christians, do we not open a door for all the sinful vices of the Gentile world? In other words, if we reduce the law's power, are we not saying that anything goes?

Paul addressed the same question from a different perspective in Romans 6:1: "Shall we continue in sin, that grace may abound?" In both cases, he used an argument we call *reduction to the absurd*. Paul pressed a mistaken notion to its logical extreme so that the consequences of the error became obvious. In Romans, it is absurd to think that sinning is a good thing if it allows additional grace to be given to us.

In Galatians, it is absurd to think that *Christ* is a *minister of sin*. The Judaizers feared that permissiveness regarding Gentiles' need to keep the law

How to Say It

Derbe	*Der*-be.
Galatia	Guh-*lay*-shuh.
Iconium	Eye-*ko*-nee-um.
Judaizers	Joo-duh-*ize*-ers.
Lystra	*Liss*-truh.
Pisidian	Pih-*sid*-ee-un.

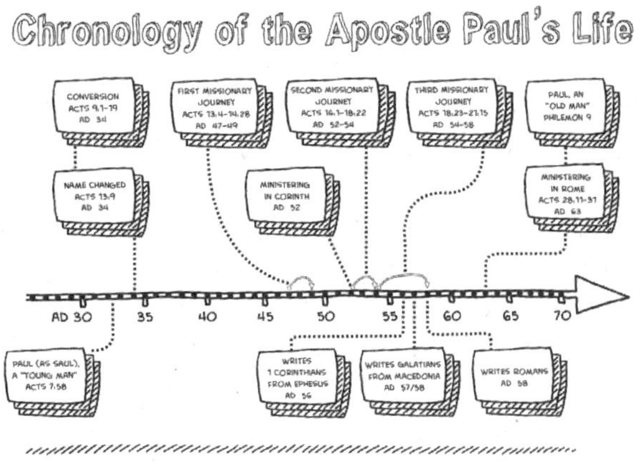

Chronology of the Apostle Paul's Life

Visual for Lesson 7. *Go over this time line of Paul's life while discussing the lesson context and leave it posted for reference through lessons 8-9.*

would end in immorality. And so, allowing Jews to fellowship with Gentiles apparently without concern for the law must also end in immorality. Though the Judaizers' concern for upright living was commendable, the content of their concern revealed a fundamental misunderstanding of Christ and His work. Could Christ ever be described as a minister of sin, as though what He encouraged His followers to do would lead to sin? If Christ and Paul promote this fellowship, are they promoting sin? In Paul's own words: *God forbid* (see Romans 6:2)!

18. For if I build again the things which I destroyed, I make myself a transgressor.

For Paul, the great sin is not in following the Law of Moses but in believing and teaching that it is a necessary part of being a Christian believer. If Paul were to fall into this trap, he would make himself *a transgressor.* This word has the sense of a "nonkeeper" of the law. Ironically, then, Paul would be violating the spirit of the law if he required Gentiles to keep it!

19. For I through the law am dead to the law, that I might live unto God.

It is not through *the law* that one finds life. Paul explained this similarly in Romans 7, where he wrote that his attempts to keep the law sometimes served only to inflame his passions for sin, thereby putting him on the road of death. Paul's experience with the law taught him that the law is a *dead* end. No one can be saved by the law because no one can keep it fully and perfectly.

But Jesus' death and resurrection have given us the means to *live unto God.* If our focus is on keeping rules rather than serving God, we will be unsuccessful. We will find that our attempts are imperfect and bear only the "fruit unto death" (Romans 7:5). But when a person is born of the Spirit, he or she has a new life (John 3:6).

20. I am crucified with Christ: nevertheless I live; yet not I, but Christ liveth in me: and the life which I now live in the flesh I live by the faith of the Son of God, who loved me, and gave himself for me.

Being *crucified with Christ* is an action that began in the past and has continuing effects in the present and future. It is not merely imitating Christ but rather being conformed to the sufferings of Christ (compare Romans 8:18; Philippians 3:10-11; Colossians 2:12-14). In Romans, Paul used the symbolism of Christian baptism to illustrate this parallel dying between the believer and Christ: we "were baptized into his death" (Romans 6:3). When we accept Jesus Christ as the Lord of our lives and trust Him for salvation, we are freed from enslavement to sin (6:6), which before we mistook as living any way we pleased. The old self was controlled by lust, by sinful passions (Ephesians 4:22). The new life is controlled by Christ, for He lives in us. By uniting with Christ through faith, we have a renewal that leads to becoming the man or woman God created us to be, a person in God's image (see Colossians 3:10). We are "dead indeed unto sin" (Romans 6:11), and the pursuit of sinful desires is no longer the controlling factor of our lives.

When we reach this point, the Judaizers' questions about law and sin begin to seem trivial. The Christian life is not a matter of how well we keep the rules. It is a matter of ongoing submission to the will of God, serving Him with all we do and say. Christ, then, is the Christian's master and Lord. Like Paul, we live for Christ, but Christ does not control us by threats or rules kept with legalistic fervor. We are controlled and motivated by the love of Christ as demonstrated on the cross (2 Corinthians 5:14).

There is nothing more important to Paul than God's demonstration of love through Christ's death. This is why Paul characterized his preaching as "Christ crucified" (1 Corinthians 1:23), which Paul acknowledged to be a "stumbling-block" (offense) to the Jews. It couldn't be that simple, could it? What about all these rules you need to keep? Is it possible that we can have decent behavior and true, rich fellowship based on our mutual love and faith in Christ? For Paul, the answer is yes.

What Do You Think?

What evidence do you see that Christ lives in you?

Digging Deeper

In what areas do you see the Spirit at work recreating you in Christ's image?

Already Dead

Four masked gunmen burst into our prayer gathering. They shouted at us to get down. They paced around us, making threats. One of the men stopped and pointed his gun at me. He asked, "Do you want to die?"

I felt peace as I answered, "I already have."

The gunman's eyes softened, and for a moment I saw the Christian under the actor who had also died with Christ to live a new life. Up to that moment, the simulation felt real. My youth group had gathered in a small room to imitate a hidden church living in a region hostile to Christianity. We were quietly praying and singing together when the gunmen actors burst in.

We have died with Christ, and we live in Him. What can you face with confidence, knowing that you have already died? —N. G.

21. I do not frustrate the grace of God: for if righteousness come by the law, then Christ is dead in vain.

If it were possible to be justified and obtain *righteousness* through *the law,* there would have been no reason for *Christ* to die on the cross. If the Judaizers were right, then the central message of the gospel was rendered ineffective. If we go the path of legalism, believing rule-keeping makes one righteous, then we have destroyed the gospel by nullifying the death of Christ. We are saying, "Jesus, You didn't really need to die for me. I'll just clean up my act and justify myself. Self-righteousness is the better way."

May we never come to the point of despising the death of Christ in this way! To yield to the Judaizing heresy would have been to *frustrate the grace of God,* meaning to reject God's gracious offer of salvation through Jesus Christ. If we seek to be saved by good works—by our attempts at self-righteousness—then we must realize we are still in our sins and have no promise of life.

What Do You Think?

How can you bear witness to the gospel to a nonbeliever who is generally regarded to be a "good person"?

Digging Deeper

Who in your life would benefit from this witness?

Conclusion

A. Life in Christ

Today, we should consider our own conversion. We must remember what Christ did for us in dying to pay sin's price and thereby treat others with the same grace that He has given to us (Matthew 18:23-35). Our lives should not be guided by fear of others or a need for prestige, nor by the customs that defined our old, sinful lives. Our life is found in Christ. Our faith is lived out in surrender, trust, and obedience to the will of Jesus, who gave His life for us. This is the motivating factor that changes how we see others. It informs how we react to pressures from others; it frees us from the false doctrine that any self-effort can lead to salvation.

Let us continue in God's grace, demonstrating the truth of the gospel through our love for our brothers and sisters in Christ (John 13:35).

B. Prayer

Father, help us live consistently for You so that Your gospel might be seen in and through us. In Jesus' name we pray. Amen.

C. Thought to Remember

Christ's love moves us to welcome all the faithful to the table.

Involvement Learning

Enhance your lesson with KJV Bible Student *(from your curriculum supplier) and the reproducible activity page (at www.standardlesson.com or in the back of the* KJV Standard Lesson Commentary Deluxe Edition*).*

Into the Lesson

Before students arrive, write the names of well-known celebrities on slips of paper. (You will need one slip for each pair of learners.) Divide learners into pairs, then ask them to plan a dinner party for friends. They should be as detailed as possible, including where the dinner party will happen, dress code, menu, and so on. After a few minutes, give each pair a slip of paper and challenge them to replan their dinner party based on inviting their assigned celebrity. After a few minutes more, gather the groups together. Have a whole-class discussion on how their plans changed when a celebrity was invited to dinner, including whether original guests were excluded. What factors led to these changes? What conditions could lead a person to rightly accuse the host of hypocrisy for changing the event? Examples include: catering from a fancy restaurant instead of serving a home-cooked meal in order to be more impressive; uninviting people who have inelegant manners; etc.

Alternative. Distribute copies of the "A Recipe for Winning Arguments" exercise from the activity page, which you can download. Have learners work in pairs to complete as indicated.

Connect this activity with today's lesson by saying, "Sometimes the arrival of someone new can be an unwelcome disruption. Let's learn how Paul addresses a situation like this in his letter to the Galatians."

Into the Word

Divide the class in two groups. Ask one group to research Peter's life while the other group researches Paul's life. Have both groups identify the relationship between their assigned apostle and both James and Barnabas. Provide biblical concordances or other research tools for the learners, and supplement with information from the Lesson Context and commentary as needed.

While the pairs work, draw a Venn diagram on the board and label one side *Peter* and the other *Paul*. After about 10 minutes, bring the class together and use the diagram to compare and contrast Peter and Paul's lives. Ask what notable similarities or differences the learners see.

In the same groups as before, have learners read Galatians 2:11-21, then analyze how Peter, Paul, the Jews, and the Gentiles acted in the Scripture passage. Ask them how the histories of these two individuals and of the groups of people they represent help explain the conflict and hypocrisy Paul pointed out.

Ask a volunteer to reread Galatians 2:15-21. Then lead a class discussion about how Christ brings these factions to himself and what this reveals/reinforces about the gospel.

Into Life

As a whole class, discuss how to navigate conflict in a way that nurtures both faith and relationship. Consider examples from home, work, or church. What about Paul's approach would be appropriate for today? After a few minutes, ask the class specifically how the gospel as laid out in today's text informs how they approach conflict.

Discuss how your congregation models dealing with conflict. What principles of the gospel is this model based on? Allow time after this discussion for prayer regarding any conflict the congregation is experiencing and/or giving thanks for leaders who follow Paul's example of confronting un-Christlike behavior.

Alternative. Distribute copies of the "Call and Response Prayer" exercise from the activity page. Complete as a whole class. Encourage learners to refer to this exercise throughout the upcoming week.

After either activity, close class with a time of prayer, asking the Father to reveal any hypocrisies so that they can be repented of and discarded.

Spirit and Flesh

Devotional Reading: Ephesians 1:3-14
Background Scripture: Galatians 3:1-18

Galatians 3:1-14

**1 O foolish Galatians, who hath bewitched
you, that ye should not obey the truth, before
whose eyes Jesus Christ hath been evidently set
forth, crucified among you?
2 This only would I learn of you, Received
ye the Spirit by the works of the law, or by the
hearing of faith?
3 Are ye so foolish? having begun in the
Spirit, are ye now made perfect by the flesh?
4 Have ye suffered so many things in vain?
if it be yet in vain.
5 He therefore that ministereth to you the
Spirit, and worketh miracles among you, doeth
he it by the works of the law, or by the hearing of faith?
6 Even as Abraham believed God, and it was
accounted to him for righteousness.
7 Know ye therefore that they which are of
faith, the same are the children of Abraham.
8 And the scripture, foreseeing that God
would justify the heathen through faith,
preached before the gospel unto Abraham, saying, In thee shall all nations be blessed.
9 So then they which be of faith are blessed
with faithful Abraham.
10 For as many as are of the works of the law
are under the curse: for it is written, Cursed
is every one that continueth not in all things
which are written in the book of the law to do
them.
11 But that no man is justified by the law
in the sight of God, it is evident: for, The just
shall live by faith.
12 And the law is not of faith: but, The man
that doeth them shall live in them.
13 Christ hath redeemed us from the curse of
the law, being made a curse for us: for it is written, Cursed is every one that hangeth on a tree:
14 That the blessing of Abraham might
come on the Gentiles through Jesus Christ;
that we might receive the promise of the Spirit
through faith.**

Key Text

Received ye the Spirit by the works of the law, or by the hearing of faith? **—Galatians 3:2b**

God's Law Is Love

Unit 2: Faith Triumphs, Law Fails

Lessons 5–9

Lesson Aims

After participating in this lesson, each learner will be able to:

1. State why Paul referred to the Galatians as foolish.

2. Contrast the nature and motives of the Spirit with those of the flesh.

3. Make a plan to apply the lessons of the contrast to his or her service in Christ.

Lesson Outline

Introduction

A. Not Our Works

B. Lesson Context

I. After the Law (Galatians 3:1-5)

A. Foolishness (v. 1)

April Is for Fools

B. Receiving the Spirit (v. 2)

C. Continuing in the Flesh (vv. 3-5)

II. Before the Law (Galatians 3:6-9)

A. Abraham's Faith (v. 6)

B. Abraham's Family (vv. 7-9)

My Father's Daughter

III. Cursed Under the Law (Galatians 3:10-14)

A. Evidence from Scripture (vv. 10-13)

B. Blessing Through Abraham (v. 14)

Conclusion

A. Christ Is Enough

B. Prayer

C. Thought to Remember

Introduction

A. Not Our Works

After taking my undergraduate course on God's grace and our response, a student followed me to my office to express a concern. She told me that she believed that Jesus is God and that through Him, we can go to heaven. She explained that she had messed up a lot of her life and felt that Christ could not forgive her for all of it. She continued to tell me that before she surrendered herself in baptism, she wanted to get everything in her life right first. I did my best to explain that whether our works have been mostly decent or full of evil, we all come to Christ the same way—in need of a Savior.

The Galatians might have related to her story as well. Faith is well and good, they might have said, but what of the Law of Moses?

B. Lesson Context

Paul's letter to the Galatians arose from a real-life crisis. He was confronting a menace to the churches he had planted in the province of Galatia. This danger was the false teaching that it was necessary to keep the Jewish law to be saved.

Paul's argument against this heresy necessarily involved exposition of Scripture. The effect of Paul's masterful and inspired use of Old Testament passages demonstrated that the gospel was not a radical departure from the Old Testament. Properly understood, the Old Testament also teaches a relationship to God based on faith rather than works.

We must keep in mind that the Jews in Paul's time had a very different understanding of the word *law* than we do. We tend to think of law as including civil rules and regulations—prescriptions that govern our conduct. While there was an element of that within Old Testament laws, that system was primarily meant to maintain a right relationship with God. To the Jews, these laws consisted of not only regulations concerning relationships but also ceremonial regulations covering such matters as worship and diet. Moral and ethical living was only a part of what the Jews thought of when they used the word *law*.

I. After the Law

(Galatians 3:1-5)

A. Foolishness (v. 1)

1. O foolish Galatians, who hath bewitched you, that ye should not obey the truth, before whose eyes Jesus Christ hath been evidently set forth, crucified among you?

In Galatians 1:11, Paul addressed the members of these churches as "brethren," and in Galatians 4:19, "my little children." But here, Paul addressed them very differently. The Greek word translated *foolish* does not mean uninformed or ignorant. Instead it implies that the *Galatians* knew *the truth* but were not acting on it (compare 1 Timothy 6:9; Titus 3:3). Paul loved these people and was gravely concerned about their error.

The Greek verb translated *bewitched* is found only in Galatians 3:1 in all the New Testament. Its root is the Greek word from which we get our word *fascinate*. This word has a deeper meaning than the sense of "enthralled" or "entertained," though. It meant to cast an evil spell on someone. There was no doubt among the people of Paul's world that magicians and witches were able to do just this (see Acts 8:9; 13:6; 19:19). But Paul's question about bewitching is not intended to be taken literally. He used the word to describe the effect that lofty rhetoric and arguments were having on the Galatians. Rather than magicians, sorcerers, or witches, the people were being mesmerized by false teachers.

For Paul, the heart of this truth is *Jesus Christ . . . crucified* (see 1 Corinthians 1:23; 2:2). Paul presented the crucified Christ so vividly that it was as if the cross was displayed directly before his audience. The word translated *set forth* was normally used to refer to a placard that was set up in a public place. Jesus' crucifixion was clearly, unmistakably set before the Galatians through the preaching of the gospel. Other commentators believe that this verse simply describes how Jesus himself was put on public display when He was crucified. In either case, the Galatian error was not in misunderstanding the truth, but in abandoning it.

How to Say It

Abraham	*Ay*-bruh-ham.
Galatia	Guh-*lay*-shuh.
Galatians	Guh-*lay*-shunz.
Gentiles	*Jen*-tiles.
Habakkuk	Huh-*back*-kuk.
heresy	*hair*-uh-see.
Judah	*Joo*-duh.
Judaizers	Joo-duh-*ize*-ers.
Moses	*Mo*-zes or *Mo*-zez.

What Do You Think?

Why is Jesus' crucifixion a good summary of the gospel?

Digging Deeper

What errors have you seen introduced to faith when Jesus' crucifixion is forgotten or disregarded?

April Is for Fools

Ever wondered about where that most prank-filled day of the year comes from? Several explanations have been posited, but the precise origin of April Fools' Day is uncertain. Perhaps the best explanation derives from the year 1582. A change in the French calendar resulted in the new year beginning on January 1.

You can imagine that news of such a momentous change took a while to travel! Those who celebrated at the traditional spring equinox around April 1 were considered fools for not knowing that the year was already three months old. It really wasn't fair to hold a nation responsible for this knowledge, given the seemingly arbitrary move of the year's start from the beginning of spring to early winter.

This example could not be further from the situation Paul faced with the Galatians. They *were* responsible for the gospel truth. Acting like fools who did not know the truth was dangerous. The Galatians needed to keep the truth in the forefront of their minds. What will you do to keep the truth before you and not fall for any schemes that will make *you* the fool?

—J. K.

B. Receiving the Spirit (v. 2)

2. This only would I learn of you, Received ye the Spirit by the works of the law, or by the hearing of faith?

This second rhetorical question contrasts *works of the law*—obedience to the Law of Moses—with *the hearing of faith*. One of the major distinctions between the Old Testament people of God and the New Testament people of God is the presence of the Holy Spirit. It is true that mention of the Holy Spirit can be found in the pages of the Old Testament, but the actual phrase *Holy Spirit* occurs only three times there: Psalm 51:11; Isaiah 63:10, 11. And only in Psalm 51:11 is there a sense of the Holy Spirit indwelling a believer (in that instance, King David). While the Spirit of God is often present (see Genesis 1:2), there is no description of the Holy Spirit being given to the people of Israel individually in the "indwelling" sense of the New Testament.

Paul's point is that the Old Testament laws do not promise anything like the Spirit. It is not "keep the Sabbath and you will receive the gift of the Holy Spirit." The gift of the Holy Spirit, experienced by the Galatian believers, is a part of the new covenant. This gift is seen only prophetically in the Old Testament (see Ezekiel 37:14). One does not receive the Holy Spirit through his or her own righteous efforts at obedience (see commentary on Galatians 3:3, 11, 14, below). Considering the conversion experience of the Galatians, this second question can only be truthfully answered one way. They *received . . . the Spirit* because of their faith, not their works. The thought is similar to that found in Romans 10:17: "So then faith cometh by hearing, and hearing by the word of God."

C. Continuing in the Flesh (vv. 3-5)

3. Are ye so foolish? having begun in the Spirit, are ye now made perfect by the flesh?

Paul's use of the phrase "the flesh" can be understood in six distinct ways, as determined by context (see also in lesson 6):

- of creatures generally (1 Corinthians 15:39)
- of our bodies specifically (1 Corinthians 6:16)
- of the human race generally (Galatians 2:16)
- that which is morally neutral (Romans 1:3)
- that which is morally negative (Galatians 6:12)
- of rebellious human nature (Romans 8:3-12)

The fourth definition is in view here. Paul asked, *Are ye so foolish?* using the same word as in verse 1. If the Galatians' Christian lives began by receiving *the Spirit* through faith, how could growth be maintained by striving to live Christ's life in *the flesh*?

Our Christian life starts with, is maintained by, and comes into completion only through surrender to Jesus and dependence on the Holy Spirit. To revert to the old covenant is to disregard and endanger this precious gift. It is to buy the lie that we can be *made perfect* by our own efforts apart from faith.

What Do You Think?

What makes living by the law seem easier or better than living by the Spirit?

Digging Deeper

What are some helpful habits you practice that remind you that the Spirit's work is not the result of your own effort?

4. Have ye suffered so many things in vain? if it be yet in vain.

The churches in Galatia had witnessed and experienced persecution (Acts 14:1-25; compare Galatians 6:12), as well as suffering common to all people. Rejection of the law as a means to salvation was not without consequences. But if there was a return to law-keeping by Jewish or Gentile Christians, this suffering would have been *in vain*, both for the Galatians and for Paul himself (see 4:11).

5. He therefore that ministereth to you the Spirit, and worketh miracles among you, doeth he it by the works of the law, or by the hearing of faith?

This verse echoes the question of Galatians 3:2 (above). God both gives *the Spirit* and works *miracles* (Hebrews 2:4)—these things are taken as fact. But those miracles (examples: Acts 14:10, 19-20) did not come from those who were teaching that believers must follow *the law*. Whatever spiritual blessings the Galatians experienced came as a result of their faith in Christ rather than through legalistic observances.

II. Before the Law

(Galatians 3:6-9)

A. Abraham's Faith (v. 6)

6. Even as Abraham believed God, and it was accounted to him for righteousness.

The substance of this verse is a quotation of Genesis 15:6 (see also Romans 4:3). If the Galatians required further evidence that faith pleases *God*, they needed to look no further than *Abraham* (see commentary on Galatians 3:7-9, 14, below; see 3:16, 18, 29; 4:22, not in our printed text). Abraham lived centuries before Moses, who gave the law to Israel. Therefore no one could assert that Abraham was counted as righteous because he followed the Law of Moses (see Romans 4:9-11).

Abraham's example of faith in action remains an example for us all (see Genesis 22; Hebrews 11:17-19), not least the Galatian believers. Abraham's obedient works were not motivated by wanting to earn a reward but by his confidence in God. Thus, to hold up Abraham as the main example of a person blessed and justified by God necessarily excludes circumcision from the discussion—and this was the linchpin of the Judaizers' demands.

B. Abraham's Family (vv. 7-9)

7. Know ye therefore that they which are of faith, the same are the children of Abraham.

Abraham's *faith* was his defining trait. Those *which are of faith* act as his *children* when they, too, are defined by their faith (compare John 8:37-47). This does not mean that salvation is only for those of a physical descent of Abraham; the promise made to Abraham is primarily spiritual (see commentary on Galatians 3:8, below). Allowing works of the law to interfere with this identity was like claiming their father had not taught them about the life of faith.

My Father's Daughter

I am my father's daughter. Anyone who knows Dad's side of the family says I'm the spitting image of his middle sister. I absorbed his love of reading and tendency to overstuff my bookshelves. My enjoyment of both playing and watching sports of many varieties can be directly traced to father-daughter days at the ballfield or ice rink. We share a sharp sense of humor reinforced by a shared taste in comedies. Neither of us will ever be described as morning birds.

And we share our faith. Dad was the preacher in my congregation during my teenage years, when so much of my faith took shape. Because of this faith, I can also claim that I am my father Abraham's daughter. So could the Galatians, and so can *you*. So we can ask ourselves: What habits might prevent us from being recognized as our father Abraham's—and ultimately *the* Father's—faithful children? —J. K.

8. And the scripture, foreseeing that God would justify the heathen through faith, preached before the gospel unto Abraham, saying, In thee shall all nations be blessed.

We might forget that the Old Testament (Paul's *scripture*) reveals that God would *justify the heathen through faith*, instead confusing God's focus on Israel with a supposed concern for Israel alone. But before *the gospel*—before the good news of salvation based on faith in Jesus—God had made it clear *unto Abraham* that *in thee shall all nations be blessed* (Genesis 12:1-3). And

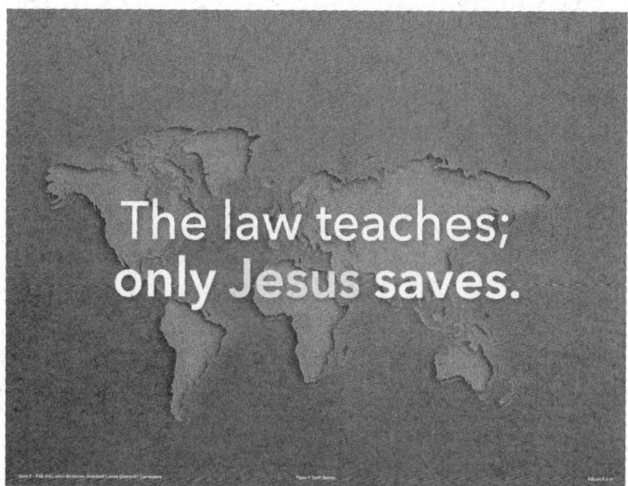
The law teaches;
only Jesus saves.

Visual for Lessons 8 & 9. *Encourage learners to keep this truth in mind during the week ahead in anticipation of studying lesson 9.*

this, Paul asserted, was in essence the gospel. Justification through faith opened the door to any person, regardless of association with Israel. Since this promise, too, came long before any practice of circumcision or the Law of Moses, Paul interpreted it as a promise based on faith. Thus, Paul was not preaching some new or misguided gospel but the oldest and truest gospel message of all.

9. So then they which be of faith are blessed with faithful Abraham.

This represents a summary of Paul's argument so far. Anyone, whether Jew or Gentile, who is faithful to Christ is *blessed*. Far from being a departure from what the Scripture revealed, this puts the faithful in the same company with *faithful Abraham*.

> **What Do You Think?**
> What benefit have you experienced because of study of faithful people in the Old Testament (examples: Hebrews 11)?
>
> **Digging Deeper**
> What blessings do you experience that they were still looking forward to?

III. Cursed Under the Law

(Galatians 3:10-14)

A. Evidence from Scripture (vv. 10-13)

10. For as many as are of the works of the law are under the curse: for it is written, Cursed is every one that continueth not in all things which are written in the book of the law to do them.

For it is written introduces a paraphrase of Deuteronomy 27:26, which is part of a list of accursed lawbreaking behavior (27:15-26). Everyone who broke *the law* on any count was *under the curse* (compare Romans 3:19-20). If the Galatian believers submitted themselves to *the works of* the law (in this case, exemplified by circumcision; see Galatians 2:12, lesson 7), they would be subject to the curse. The only escape was accepting the gospel based on faith, not works.

11. But that no man is justified by the law in the sight of God, it is evident: for, The just shall live by faith.

Paul quoted Habakkuk 2:4 to further bolster his assertion that *the just shall live by faith* (see Galatians 2:16, lesson 7). Habakkuk is unique among the prophets for his presentation of dialogue with God (some call it arguing). Habakkuk ministered in about 605 BC—a time when evil, selfish men controlled the southern kingdom of Judah. Their dishonesty and injustice seemed to go unpunished (example: Habakkuk 1:2-4). When Habakkuk complained about this, God told him that He was sending the Babylonians to wipe out the nation of Judah for this evil (1:6). Habakkuk objected to this in strong terms. He did not think it fair for God to use a "more" evil nation like Babylon to punish his own "less" evil nation (1:13).

God's answer to Habakkuk was that it was not for that prophet to know or understand all of God's dealings, particularly on the international level. Habakkuk's job was to trust God. In the end, it was the prophet's faith that would save him (Habakkuk 3:16-19).

12. And the law is not of faith: but, The man that doeth them shall live in them.

Paul returned to the theme of the law as condemning rather than saving. The law has a valuable function, and that is to define what actions constitute sin (see Romans 7:7). The law was not given to those who were already matured in their faith or had the Spirit of God to guide them. Using the example of little children, Paul later explained that the law was given as a tutor to lead them to Christ so that they might be justified (Galatians 3:23-25; 4:1-7; see lesson 9).

If one commits to following the law, one must carefully follow all laws. This can never work, however. It didn't work for Abraham or Paul. And it didn't for the Galatians or us. Life from the law is found only in perfection, as Paul's quotation from Leviticus 18:5 shows, and none of us can attain perfection. Under a law system, our righteousness before God becomes a transaction, a payment for good deeds. Because of our sin, our just reward is death (see Romans 6:23). There is no middle ground between law-keeping and faith-living as means for salvation. Thus, Paul's stark statement: *the law is not of faith.*

13. Christ hath redeemed us from the curse of the law, being made a curse for us: for it is written, Cursed is every one that hangeth on a tree.

"The wages of sin is death" (Romans 6:23); this is *the curse of the law.* We are made aware of our sins but unable to will ourselves into perfection. Therefore, we have all earned a death sentence.

But praise God! Our redemption came through Christ. Our sinless Savior was made a curse for us through His death *on a tree* (the cross). To be killed in this manner was reserved for the vilest of criminals. The law teaches that this manner of death is used to shame the one being executed (compare Deuteronomy 21:22-23; Acts 5:20; 10:39). Jesus was born under the law and endured the curse that falls on lawbreakers. But Jesus was no criminal. And because He was sinless, He was able to do what no one else could do: He perfectly satisfied the justice of God by absorbing the curse (Romans 3:21-26) in accordance with God's purpose and foreknowledge (Acts 2:23).

What Do You Think?

How would you counsel a Christian who feels like his or her life is still under the curse?

Digging Deeper

What Scriptures inform your answer?

B. Blessing Through Abraham (v. 14)

14. That the blessing of Abraham might come on the Gentiles through Jesus Christ; that we might receive the promise of the Spirit through faith.

Paul tied it all together in the final verse for this section. Through the atoning death of *Jesus Christ*, the promised *blessing of Abraham* is realized. Even *the Gentiles* can receive this blessing, best seen in the gift of *the Spirit.* All of this is based on *faith* rather than law-keeping. The arguments and teachings of the Judaizers were put to rest, and Paul did this by using Scriptures from the law itself.

What Do You Think?

What Scriptures give you confidence that the Spirit is at work in your life?

Digging Deeper

In what seemingly irredeemable circumstances can remembering the Spirit's work nurture hope?

Conclusion

A. Christ Is Enough

Who among us does not remember a parent, a teacher, or some other authority figure chiding us saying, "You know better"? Paul addressed the churches with the same lingering concern parents everywhere feel for their children. The Galatian churches were in danger of forgetting the truth of the gospel and embracing a works-oriented striving for salvation.

Sometimes our wrong thinking causes us to rely on law or works to please God. But this is not where salvation is found. We cannot gain salvation, forgiveness, or right standing before God by our works. These things are accomplished only through the work of Jesus and the grace of God (Romans 3:23-26). We receive the Spirit because of Jesus' gift following our faith response, not because we cleaned up our lives or obeyed all the right rules. As we reflect on this passage, we do well to ask whether our lives betray a continued striving for salvation rather than a joyful acceptance of it. Do we live and act based on the truth that Christ's work on our behalf is enough?

B. Prayer

Father, forgive us for the times when we have fallen back to our old ways of trying to earn what You have freely given. Help us instead to live our faith in action as a loving response to Christ's work for us. In His name we pray. Amen.

C. Thought to Remember

Our faith is in Christ alone.

Involvement Learning

Enhance your lesson with KJV Bible Student *(from your curriculum supplier) and the reproducible activity page (at www.standardlesson.com or in the back of the* KJV Standard Lesson Commentary Deluxe Edition*).*

Into the Lesson

Write *righteousness* on the board. As a whole class, create a definition of the word with supporting Bible verses. Check this definition against a dictionary and make any desired revisions. Ask each learner to think of one person whom he or she knows personally and considers righteous. Without giving names, invite participants to share words or phrases that describe how these people speak or act in ways that show they are righteous. Write these responses on the board under the definition. (Keep the words on the board to refer to later in the lesson.)

Transition to the Bible study by saying, "As we study today's passage of Scripture, pay attention to God's standard of righteousness."

Into the Word

Ask a volunteer to read aloud Galatians 3:1-5. Have learners use concordances to find examples of foolish behavior throughout the Bible. What actions or speech patterns are associated with fools? Examples include "[saying] there is no God" and doing evil (Psalm 14:1), "[despising] wisdom and instruction" (Proverbs 1:7), and disregarding Jesus' teaching (Matthew 7:26). Compare these examples to the definition and examples of righteousness that were developed in the Into the Lesson activity. Are there any similarities? What key differences do the learners see?

As a class, answer these questions: 1–Why is Paul calling the Galatians "foolish"? 2–How do the examples we found match the behavior Paul is condemning? 3–How do Paul's questions help the Galatian believers to identify their error and to understand and know what is true?

Ask another volunteer to read aloud Galatians 3:6-9. In pairs, have learners find examples of promises made to Abraham and of Abraham's faith. Verses to consider should include (but not be limited to) Genesis 12:1-9; 15:1-18; 17:1-22; 18:18-19; 22:1-19. Come back together as a class to discuss how the promises made to Abraham pointed to the gospel of Jesus.

Alternative. Distribute copies of the "Gospel to Abraham" exercise from the activity page, which you can download. Instruct partners to work together to complete as indicated. After a few minutes, ask the partners to present their findings for whole-class discussion.

Ask a volunteer to read aloud Galatians 3:10-14. Then have small groups look up Old Testament references Paul included—Leviticus 18:5; Deuteronomy 21:23, 27:26; Habakkuk 2:4—as well as Matthew 5:17-20. Ask, "How do Jesus' words connect the Old Testament verses with the verses in Galatians 3?" Allow time for group members to discuss before sharing their insights with the whole group. (Possible response: Jesus fulfills the law, so through Him we are made righteous.)

Into Life

Say, "Consider the people who came to your mind in the first activity. Do their lives reflect God's standard of righteousness through faith?" Refer to the words that were listed on the board. As a whole group, label the phrases that happen through the law or through faith. Then consider how God's promises have already been fulfilled and what remains to be fulfilled.

Alternative. Distribute copies of the "One in Christ" exercise from the activity page. Have learners complete as indicated.

Give learners one minute to write down one way they continue to be motivated by the flesh instead of by the Spirit. Then ask them to brainstorm with a partner how to be open to the Spirit's presence and leading in the week ahead as they seek opportunities to serve Christ. Have partners pray for each other in these efforts. Encourage them to come to class next week prepared to tell their partner about their experiences in the Spirit.

October 29
Lesson 9 (KJV)

Freedom as an Heir

Devotional Reading: Genesis 12:1-9
Background Scripture: Galatians 3:19–4:7

Galatians 3:23–4:7

23 But before faith came, we were kept under the law, shut up unto the faith which should afterwards be revealed.

24 Wherefore the law was our schoolmaster to bring us unto Christ, that we might be justified by faith.

25 But after that faith is come, we are no longer under a schoolmaster.

26 For ye are all the children of God by faith in Christ Jesus.

27 For as many of you as have been baptized into Christ have put on Christ.

28 There is neither Jew nor Greek, there is neither bond nor free, there is neither male nor female: for ye are all one in Christ Jesus.

29 And if ye be Christ's, then are ye Abraham's seed, and heirs according to the promise.

4:1 Now I say, That the heir, as long as he is a child, differeth nothing from a servant, though he be lord of all;

2 But is under tutors and governors until the time appointed of the father.

3 Even so we, when we were children, were in bondage under the elements of the world:

4 But when the fulness of the time was come, God sent forth his Son, made of a woman, made under the law,

5 To redeem them that were under the law, that we might receive the adoption of sons.

6 And because ye are sons, God hath sent forth the Spirit of his Son into your hearts, crying, Abba, Father.

7 Wherefore thou art no more a servant, but a son; and if a son, then an heir of God through Christ.

Key Text

Ye are all the children of God by faith in Christ Jesus. —**Galatians 3:26**

Photo © Getty Images

God's Law
Is Love

Unit 2: Faith Triumphs, Law Fails

Lessons 5–9

Lesson Aims

After participating in this lesson, each learner will be able to:

1. Restate the task of the law.

2. Compare and contrast conditions under the law with conditions in Christ Jesus.

3. State one way to express the reality of Galatians 4:7 to an unbeliever.

Lesson Outline

Introduction
- A. From a Slave . . .
- B. Lesson Context

I. Abraham's Seed (Galatians 3:23-29)
- A. Before Faith (vv. 23-24)
  - *Destination in View*
- B. Faith in Christ (vv. 25-29)

II. God's Children (Galatians 4:1-7)
- A. Underage Heirs (vv. 1-3)
- B. Grown Heirs (vv. 4-7)
  - *A Selfless Act*

Conclusion
- A. . . . To a Son
- B. Prayer
- C. Thought to Remember

Introduction

A. From a Slave . . .

Until I was in high school, I believed that God relished the prospect of disciplining me and sending me to hell for my sins. Because of this wrong view of God, I tried to manage my works with a list of dos and don'ts. I wasn't practicing a healthy rejection of evil, led by the Spirit; I was a slave to my own attempts to earn my salvation. This was my only relationship with God.

Paul's words in today's lesson had something to say to my young heart, and they yet speak to all of us as he puts the law in its proper context.

B. Lesson Context

In today's printed text, Paul continued his efforts to instruct the Galatian Christians about the correct relationship between law and grace. Because of some false teachers called Judaizers, the churches in the province of Galatia were adding works of the law to the gospel of Christ (Galatians 1:6-10). Paul reflected on his own "exceedingly zealous" experience in Judaism (1:14) as he highlighted his inability to follow the law to the point of justification (2:15-21; see lesson 7). Through Christ, the promise of salvation had been revealed to the whole world (3:6-9; see lesson 8). Paul went on to show the unifying nature of that salvation for all who would believe in Christ.

Because of Paul's preaching of the gospel of grace, some of his opponents accused him of acting in contradiction to the Old Testament (example: Acts 18:12-13). While Paul presented the new message of grace without apology, he also readily acknowledged that there was a purpose for the old Law of Moses. He strenuously maintained that the new is superior, but that the old had a vital purpose in God's plan.

Galatians 3:15-22 (immediately preceding our printed text) focuses on the illustration of Abraham's (singular) seed. It is in Christ alone that God fulfilled the law. And this fulfillment did not do away with the promises God made; far from it! Instead, Jesus was the means by which God made good on the promises to Abraham and his descendants. In 3:21-22, Paul focused on the limitation of the law, namely that it could not impart righteousness or life.

I. Abraham's Seed

(Galatians 3:23-29)

A. Before Faith (vv. 23-24)

23. But before faith came, we were kept under the law, shut up unto the faith which should afterwards be revealed.

Unto has the sense of "until," as in Ephesians 1:14. The Greek word translated *kept* is best understood here as guarding or shielding (compare Philippians 4:7; 1 Peter 1:5). Though it could refer to being held in custody against one's will (compare 2 Corinthians 11:22), Paul uses a different word entirely to discuss his imprisonments (6:5; compare Hebrews 11:36; 1 Peter 3:19). This might imply that the law served as a restraint, showing the extent of sin through Scripture (see Galatians 3:22, not in our printed text). We are so constrained because we are in fact guilty of sin. Every human being has been confined to a place on death row (Romans 5:12).

The faith (an appropriate translation for both instances of "faith" here) refers to a body of doctrine to be believed (see Ephesians 4:13; Philippians 1:27; 1 Timothy 6:21; Titus 1:13; Jude 3). More than a personal response, this is the set of truths that constitute the gospel. Believers were kept safe *under the law,* waiting for the gospel *which should afterwards be revealed.*

24. Wherefore the law was our schoolmaster to bring us unto Christ, that we might be justified by faith.

A *schoolmaster* was a man put in charge of a young boy by his parents. The man's role can be described as that of a tutor and mentor, like a coach looking to form the young boy from about age 6 into a wise, knowledgeable young man of about 16. This schoolmaster oversaw the boy's development primarily outside of the classroom, ensuring that tasks related to both schooling and household chores were accomplished properly. This position was frequently filled by a trusted slave.

This illustrates how *the law* played a key role in the development of God's people, and it was a time-limited role. No one could be *justified* under the Law of Moses (Acts 13:39). The law's purpose was never to save anyone; it was to show the need for the one who can save everyone. Because the law could do only so much, God sent His Son to fulfill the requirements of the law (see Romans 8:1-4). The work of *Christ* was the culmination of God's plan for our salvation; placing our faith in Him is the success of the schoolmaster. Now that Christ has come, we do not look to the law as a way to be in right standing before God; rather, we look to Christ as "the end of the law for righteousness" (10:4).

Destination in View

In 1856, William Rand opened a printing shop in Chicago. Two years later, he hired an Irish immigrant named Andrew McNally, who later became his business partner. The first Rand McNally® railroad guide was published in 1869, followed by a highway map in 1904.

I remember Rand McNally maps from road trips with my grandparents. Every year they would take me, my brother, and our cousins on our annual trip. My grandma sat in the front passenger seat with the Rand McNally book occupying all the space between her and the dash. As Grandpa drove, she prepared him for every lane change and exit necessary to get us to our Tennessee mountain destination.

The Rand McNally map that guided our route on family vacations has now been superseded by the GPS features in our cars. Either might be likened to how the law was intended to guide people to the Messiah. Now that we have reached our destination in Jesus, what role does that "map" play in your faith? What role should it play? —J. M.

B. Faith in Christ (vv. 25-29)

25. But after that faith is come, we are no longer under a schoolmaster.

Paul's Galatian audience held that justification was a "both/and" construct. Their understanding of justification required both following the law and expressing faith in Christ. To correct that error, Paul highlighted the superiority and finality of *faith* in bringing justification. Now that Christ has come, the *schoolmaster*—the law—is *no longer* required. It is "out of work" once we come to Christ and discover the freedom that He alone can provide. At that point, we have "matured" to where we are part of God's family.

What Do You Think?

What rules from your childhood have you discarded as an adult?

Digging Deeper

What did you learn from those rules? What lasting value have those lessons had in your life?

26. For ye are all the children of God by faith in Christ Jesus.

The false teachers in Galatia would have strenuously opposed Paul's statement here. It was one thing to say that Gentiles did not need to follow the law, the Judaizers' first point of contention. But to say Jews also need not obey the law would be heretical to the teachers.

Jews believed that *children of God* was a designation that belonged to them alone as they were God's chosen people who followed the law (example: Deuteronomy 14:1-2). And to be fair, the term never had applied to Gentiles before. But God's promises were always intended to come through Israel to the world, not stop with this one group of people (Galatians 3:8). Through *faith in Christ Jesus all* can equally be called children of God (John 1:12; Romans 8:14-16).

Paul had much more to say about faith as it relates to salvation. But right now, the summary statement we see here is sufficient for the line of argument he is establishing.

27. For as many of you as have been baptized into Christ have put on Christ.

Baptism is the ritual of being dipped in water, first practiced by John the Baptist. In the Jewish culture of the day, people purified themselves ceremonially by dipping themselves in water. John's actions, however, were different in procedure and significance. Regarding procedure, the person receiving baptism did not dip herself or himself. Rather, another performed the dipping action on the recipient. Regarding significance, John's baptism was one "of repentance for the remission of sins" (Mark 1:4). By contrast, Christian baptism was administered in the name of Jesus for receiving the Holy Spirit (Acts 19:1-6). We see these elements in Peter's exhortation on the Day of Pentecost that followed Jesus' resurrection: "Repent, and be baptized every one of you in the name of Jesus Christ for the remission of sins, and ye shall receive the gift of the Holy Ghost" (2:38; compare Matthew 28:19).

Circumcision had previously been the physical marker of whether a man was included in Israel's covenant relationship with God. Baptism levelled the playing field not only between Jewish and Gentile men, but women as well (see commentary on Galatians 3:28, below). It is the common experience of all believers (compare Acts 2:38; Romans 6:3-4). Baptism thus is a powerful expression of the equality and unity of Christ's followers. None are able to cleanse themselves, even those who had grown up following God's law. All rely utterly on Christ's cleansing. None can look to previous Israelite identity as credentials for inheriting eternal life. Rather, all must look to Christ's death and resurrection.

To *put on Christ* is to be clothed in Him. Jesus' "robe of righteousness" (Isaiah 61:10) has replaced our "filthy rags" (64:6). As we grow in the Christian life, we should become more and more like Christ and more comfortable wearing His wardrobe (compare Romans 13:14). Christians are not defined by ancestral heritage or former practices but by Christ's gracious forgiveness and gift of new life. Though we may look and act differently from one another, we all wear the same spiritual clothing. It is the uniform of the gospel that speaks of Christ alone (compare Isaiah 61:10).

In Christ, barriers are broken down. Together we are a new creation, transformed through the work of the Holy Spirit (2 Corinthians 5:17; Colossians 3:10-11). Lines of division regarding access

How to Say It

Abba	*Ab*-buh.
Judaizers	Joo-duh-*ize*-ers.
Mosaic	Mo-*zay*-ik.

to salvation are dissolved in Christ, and Paul used three important examples to emphasis this.

What Do You Think?

What helps you remember every day that you are clothed in Christ?

Digging Deeper

What is one article of spiritual clothing you still wear that doesn't "go" with the outfit of Christ?

28a. There is neither Jew nor Greek.

First, Paul addressed concerns of ethnic and cultural divisions as centered on the Law of Moses. Of main concern for a *Jew* was adherence to the law, notably the law's prescriptions for circumcision and the Judaizers' intent to bind Gentiles (Greeks) to it (see Acts 15:1). But in the Christian era, physical circumcision as a covenant sign is no longer applicable for God's people (Romans 3:30; 1 Corinthians 7:18-19; Galatians 5:6; 6:15).

28b. There is neither bond nor free.

Second, the structure of the Roman Empire required an economy of slavery. In the structure of God's economy of salvation, though, the servant in bondage and the *free* person have equal access; both can find eternal life in Christ Jesus. Under Christ, a bondservant was to be counted as "a brother beloved" (Philemon 16).

28c. There is neither male nor female.

Paul's third statement was not meant to disregard obvious gender differences or address varied beliefs on the roles of men and women. Rather, Paul addressed the issue of equal access to salvation, given the context of the passage at hand (see more on Galatians 3:29, below). In many cultures, the vulnerability of women becomes a basis for men to take positions of privilege. Such inequality of access includes the customs of inheritance: women typically did not inherit property in the Greco-Roman world of the first century AD. The fact that there *is neither male nor female* means that everyone has the same opportunity of an eternal inheritance (Acts 20:32).

28d. For ye are all one in Christ Jesus.

Divisions that result from living in a fallen world, including those that vex us yet today, are overcome by the gospel. Oneness *in Christ Jesus* means we treat each other with absolute love and respect as equal heirs of salvation. Our differences have no bearing on one's access to or standing in Christ. We serve as one body (Romans 12:4-8; 1 Corinthians 12:12-27).

What Do You Think?

Over the years, how has the Holy Spirit changed your heart regarding divisions that exist between people within the body of Christ?

Digging Deeper

Does that change of heart extend beyond the church? Why or why not?

29. And if ye be Christ's, then are ye Abraham's seed, and heirs according to the promise.

The word *ye* addresses all the baptized believers who are united in Christ. *Abraham's seed* previously referred only to his physical, Jewish descendants (compare Matthew 3:9; Luke 3:8). But union with Christ has made all believers *heirs according to* God's *promise* (Genesis 12:2-3; Romans 4; 8:16-17). Being in Christ implies having full access to the promise of His blessing.

What Do You Think?

If you met Abraham today, how would you describe your experience of the blessings that God promised would come to Abraham's seed?

Digging Deeper

How do you extend the invitation to experience God's blessings to people who are not currently Abraham's heirs?

II. God's Children

(Galatians 4:1-7)

A. Underage Heirs (vv. 1-3)

1-2. Now I say, That the heir, as long as he is a child, differeth nothing from a servant, though he be lord of all; but is under tutors and governors until the time appointed of the father.

These verses take up the analogy from

Galatians 3:24-25, above, to further illustrate the nature of God's plan. Paul did so by picturing an underage *child* who will eventually inherit the father's property. The underage person is treated as *a servant* although at the same time *he be lord of all*, having already been designated as the heir who will control the property. In Roman custom, an heir lacked control over family property until he reached the age of majority, around 25. The *tutors and governors*—like the "schoolmaster" of Galatians 3:24—exercised authority until then.

3. Even so we, when we were children, were in bondage under the elements of the world.

Paul now made the comparison: like those who are underage, the Galatian Christians had lived not as heirs, but *in bondage under the elements of the world*. What exactly Paul is referring to as he uses that phrase is difficult to determine; see also Galatians 4:9 and Colossians 2:8, 20, where Paul uses the same Greek word that is translated here as "elements." We derive the English word stochastic (meaning "random") from this word, but that doesn't really help determine what Paul means. Some students think that the word *elements* refers to the supernatural powers or forces regarded as having control over the events of this world, considering Paul's uses of this word in passages just noted.

Others think that the word *elements* in this particular context means "something that is basic or elementary," such as learning one's ABCs. In the specific context of Judaizers in Galatia, these elementary things would refer to the teachings of the Law of Moses. The past tense *were* implies that this bondage should be over (see commentary on Galatians 4:4, below).

B. Grown Heirs (vv. 4-7)

4. But when the fulness of the time was come, God sent forth his Son, made of a woman, made under the law.

The word *but* introduces a contrast as *the fulness of time was* reached—the time for Old Testament prophecies to be fulfilled (see Genesis 12:3; 2 Samuel 7:16; Isaiah 9:6-7; Mark 1:15; Ephesians 1:10). The contrast is with the era of childhood, described above. Because the Galatian believers were living when God had fulfilled His purposes with the Law of Moses, its regulations were of the past. There was no reason for Christians—whether of Jewish or Gentile background—to listen to those who insisted on submission to its distinctives in order to receive salvation in Christ (compare Mark 7:19; Colossians 2:16-23; etc.).

The *Son* is divine, eternal, and had been *sent* with purpose (John 1:1, 14; 3:16-19; 1 Corinthians 8:6; Galatians 1:16; Philippians 2:6-8; Colossians 1:15-18). *Made under the law* affirms that Jesus was subject to the Mosaic law (example: Luke 2:22-24).

5. To redeem them that were under the law, that we might receive the adoption of sons.

To redeem means "to buy back" (see Leviticus 25:25-55). In that regard, Jesus' ministry was twofold. First, He rescued us from the tyranny of *the law*, under which we stood condemned because of our sin. But He did not do that merely to send us out on our own; He has also adopted us into His family. We were once outside of the special relationship with God and its blessings, but now we stand to inherit the promises and their blessings as His children (Romans 8:15, 23). The use of the word *sons* does not exclude women from the family of God since male and female are one in Christ (Galatians 3:28; also 4:6-7, below).

What Do You Think?

What practical difference has being adopted into God's family made in your life?

Digging Deeper

How does your adoption into God's family affect how you interact with your earthly family?

A Selfless Act

My midwestern family learned that native Alaskan culture emphasizes respecting one's elders and living off the land. Both of these cultural values are demonstrated when a boy enters manhood. The boy would have learned to hunt and fish at a young age. So when the father decides his son is old enough, Dad takes him out to shoot his first moose. The son, now grown, gives all the meat away to an elder in his village or town. In this way, the son demonstrates his maturity through a selfless and generous act. The underlying principle is that "boys think of themselves, and men think of others."

Through His Son, God the Father gave us something far superior to a freezer full of moose meat. In the greatest of all selfless acts, Jesus came to redeem us by paying the sin price on our behalf. What selfless acts does our Father desire of us as we enter adulthood in His family? —J. M.

6. And because ye are sons, God hath sent forth the Spirit of his Son into your hearts, crying, Abba, Father.

The same language of sending *his Son* in Galatians 4:4 (above) is used of sending *forth the Spirit*. To Paul and other biblical writers, the heart is where our will resides, as well as our emotions (Mark 7:20-23; etc.). The work of *the Spirit of his Son* in our *hearts* is to transform us into Christ's image by reshaping our very desires (Romans 8:9-10).

The efficacy of our adoption is seen in the intimate language of *crying* to the *Father*. *Abba* is the warm, familial word used in the household for a father. It is a term of endearment and closeness (compare Mark 14:36). As children of God, we can go to God with such endearing language.

7. Wherefore thou art no more a servant, but a son; and if a son, then an heir of God through Christ.

Paul summarized everything he has said so far, and he applied it to each individual who is in *Christ*. Anyone who is redeemed in Christ and has His Spirit is redeemed from a state like that of *a servant* to that of, not only *a son*, but *an heir* to the Father's glorious inheritance. We are recipients of God's promises now and through eternity.

Conclusion

A. . . . To a Son

In my freshman year of high school, I went to a camp that described Jesus in a new way. This teaching depicted God—my Father—as one who loved me very much. This God would forgive me and never abandon me. This teaching was good news! When I surrendered to Jesus, I realized I had been a slave to a works-based salvation, a slave to sin, a slave to fear, and a slave to "trying hard, but never sure."

The law teaches;
only Jesus saves.

Visual for Lessons 8 & 9. *As class concludes, ask learners to give specific examples from the lessons in Galatians that back up this summary.*

But the situation is not hopeless. A pardon has been provided through the death of Jesus. In Christ, I am free from this anguish. And you, my brothers and sisters in Christ, enjoy the same status I do. We are loved; we are our Father's children. Our new status is a result of this relationship. The Spirit lives in our hearts to confirm this. God had a plan from the beginning, and regardless of who you once were, in Christ you are made right with God. You have been bought with a price and adopted as His child. We are not to be slaves to law, traditions, cultural norms, or other restrictions; we are free through faith in Jesus Christ to live fully as the heirs of God's promise.

B. Prayer

Father, forgive us for the times where we act as if You are not enough. Thank You for the new identity that You give us by loving us and making us Your children. Help us to live in the promise that You give us through faith. In Jesus' name we pray. Amen.

C. Thought to Remember

Whoever we are, wherever we come from, we can be children of God through Christ.

Involvement Learning

Enhance your lesson with KJV Bible Student *(from your curriculum supplier) and the reproducible activity page (at www.standardlesson.com or in the back of the* KJV Standard Lesson Commentary Deluxe Edition*).*

Into the Lesson

Write three questions on the board: *1–What expectations do people in authority have of you? 2–What restrictions do you have? 3–What freedoms or advantages can you enjoy in your position?* Then divide learners into three groups: **Young Children in School**, **Adult Members of a Political Dynasty**, and **Employees of a Powerful CEO**. Give the groups a few minutes to discuss and answer these questions based on their assigned demographic. Then invite them to share their responses with the whole group.

Alternative. Distribute copies of the "What Is Freedom? Part 1" exercise from the activity pages, which you can download. Have learners complete it individually in a minute or less before discussing answers with a partner.

After either alternative say, "We experience freedom in different ways, depending on who has authority and our relationship to them. In today's lesson, notice who has true freedom and how that freedom is defined."

Into the Word

Ask a volunteer to read aloud Galatians 3:23-29 while the learners follow along. Write on the board *Before Faith* and *Faith Has Come* as the headers of two columns. Divide the class in half, designating one half as the **Before Faith Group** and the other half as the **Faith Has Come Group**. Record answers as the activity progresses. Invite the **Before Faith Group** to recall one thing Paul mentioned about life before faith (without looking at the text). If that answer is correct, ask the **Faith Has Come Group** to recall one thing in the text about life after faith came. Continue to alternate back and forth between the groups. If a group cannot think of something to say, or gives an incorrect response, the other group gets a chance to answer. If neither group can answer, give both groups a chance to look over the text again. The first group to respond correctly gets the credit. (Answers may include: **Before Faith**—held in custody under the law, law was our guardian, before Christ came, divided; **Faith Has Come**—no longer under the law, children of God, baptized in Christ, all one in Christ.) When neither team can think of any more answers, count their responses; whichever team has more answers on the board wins.

Alternative. Distribute the "What Is Freedom? Part 2" exercise from the activity page. Have learners work in pairs to complete as indicated.

Have a volunteer read aloud Galatians 4:1-7. Have learners go back to the three groups from earlier in the lesson. Assign verses to the three groups: **Underage Heir Group**, verses 1-3; **Adopted Son Group**, verses 4-5; **Abba's Children Group**, verses 6-7. Instruct the groups to research what Paul is talking about in their assigned verses. Use the commentary to help clarify the research. Then have the groups report back and share any new insights they may have gained.

Into Life

Ask a volunteer to reread aloud Galatians 3:28-29. Ask the group how these distinctions still hold up today or how they might update the groups to better reflect their own context. Then discuss how the unity found in Christ is demonstrated in your congregation. Brainstorm one or two opportunities in your congregation to better demonstrate believers' unity because of shared faith in Christ. Discuss how visible unity as children of God furthers the spread of the gospel. Then state one way to express the reality of Galatians 4:7 to an unbeliever, keeping in mind the change in identity found in Christ.

Alternative. Distribute copies of the "What Is Freedom? Part 2" exercise from the activity page. Have learners work in pairs to complete as indicated.

Close in prayer, asking for opportunities to witness to unity in Christ and His gospel.

November 5
Lesson 10 (KJV)

Freedom from Expectations

Devotional Reading: Acts 17:22-34
Background Scripture: Acts 15:1-21

Acts 15:1-11

1 And certain men which came down from Judaea taught the brethren, and said, Except ye be circumcised after the manner of Moses, ye cannot be saved.

2 When therefore Paul and Barnabas had no small dissension and disputation with them, they determined that Paul and Barnabas, and certain other of them, should go up to Jerusalem unto the apostles and elders about this question.

3 And being brought on their way by the church, they passed through Phenice and Samaria, declaring the conversion of the Gentiles: and they caused great joy unto all the brethren.

4 And when they were come to Jerusalem, they were received of the church, and of the apostles and elders, and they declared all things that God had done with them.

5 But there rose up certain of the sect of the Pharisees which believed, saying, That it was needful to circumcise them, and to command them to keep the law of Moses.

6 And the apostles and elders came together for to consider of this matter.

7 And when there had been much disputing, Peter rose up, and said unto them, Men and brethren, ye know how that a good while ago God made choice among us, that the Gentiles by my mouth should hear the word of the gospel, and believe.

8 And God, which knoweth the hearts, bare them witness, giving them the Holy Ghost, even as he did unto us;

9 And put no difference between us and them, purifying their hearts by faith.

10 Now therefore why tempt ye God, to put a yoke upon the neck of the disciples, which neither our fathers nor we were able to bear?

11 But we believe that through the grace of the Lord Jesus Christ we shall be saved, even as they.

Key Text

God, which knoweth the hearts, bare them witness, giving them the Holy Ghost, even as he did unto us; and put no difference between us and them, purifying their hearts by faith. **—Acts 15:8-9**

God's Law Is Love

Unit 3: Christ Frees, Law Enslaves

Lessons 10–13

Lesson Aims

After participating in this lesson, each learner will be able to:

1. Summarize the viewpoint disputed by Paul and Barnabas.

2. Outline Peter's refutation of that viewpoint.

3. Describe how he or she will interrogate personal practices based on what is core to the gospel message.

Lesson Outline

Introduction

A. Steps to Resolve Disputes
B. Lesson Context: First-Century Judaism
C. Lesson Context: The Jerusalem Council

I. Conflict Described (Acts 15:1-3)

A. The Belief (vv. 1-2a)
B. The Parties (vv. 2b-3)

II. Conflict Debated (Acts 15:4-6)

A. Receiving (v. 4)
B. Reminding (vv. 5-6)

III. Conflict Resolved (Acts 15:7-11)

A. God's Work (vv. 7-9)
Level Ground
B. Our Response (vv. 10-11)
Accepting Healing

Conclusion

A. Seeking Resolution
B. Prayer
C. Thought to Remember

Introduction

A. Steps to Resolve Disputes

Conflict management is not a new practice. Sometimes people resolve conflict through conversation, debate, and allowances. Resorting to stonewalling, avoidance, or even advancing the conflict to a court of law can do little to reconcile those who find themselves in dispute.

One method (of many) to resolve conflict involves three steps. First, the parties in dispute are to be identified. Second, both sides must clearly understand the nature of their conflict. Third, the involved parties' shared values or common ground should be recognized. When mediators address these steps, an agreement that serves the interests of all conflicting parties can be reached.

Today's Scripture involves a conflict between parties of the first-century church. The Christian movement was just beginning, and believers had to work out conflicting perspectives on certain doctrines. The resolution in Acts 15 sets an important precedent for the church and the identity of the people of God.

B. Lesson Context: First-Century Judaism

Most of Jesus' earliest followers were Jewish, and they still participated in many of the practices of Judaism. For example, until the destruction of the Jerusalem temple in AD 70, Jewish followers of Jesus participated in some of the temple's ceremonies (examples: Acts 3:1; 21:26). Additionally, throughout the Roman Empire, Jewish believers continued to participate in the synagogues (example: 17:1-2). Jews gathered in these buildings for worship and teaching from the Scriptures.

Some Gentiles had become highly regarded within their local Jewish communities, partly because of their support of synagogues (example: Luke 7:1-10). The book of Acts mentions one such individual: Cornelius, a Gentile who "feared God" (Acts 10:1-2, 22). There is no indication that these Gentiles took up the requirements of Judaism. As a result, they were not considered "children of the stock of Abraham" (13:26).

There were, however, some Gentiles who chose to convert fully to Judaism. These converts were called "proselytes" (see Acts 13:43; compare 6:5). Male proselytes were required to be circumcised—a painful, even dangerous, surgical procedure in the days of rudimentary anesthetics and no antibiotics. Circumcision was the sign of the covenant between God and Abraham (see Genesis 17:9-14; compare Exodus 12:48). During the first century AD, some individuals had been teaching that Gentile followers of Jesus needed to be circumcised according to the Law of Moses (see Galatians 6:12-13). The reasoning for this position was that Israel had always been the distinct people of God. It was to Israel that God had revealed himself, given His law, and specified circumcision as the sign of His covenant. This group assumed that if God were making himself known to the nations, then the nations should be circumcised according to the Law of Moses.

C. Lesson Context: The Jerusalem Council

The book of Acts was written by Luke. Acts is the second of a two-volume work by Luke addressed to Theophilus (Acts 1:1; see Luke 1:1-4). See the Lesson Context from lessons 1 and 2 regarding details about the author, Luke.

Prior to the events in this lesson, Paul and Barnabas, leaders of the first-century church, had been traveling throughout Asia Minor (modern-day Turkey). These travels are identified as Paul's first missionary journey in AD 47–49 (Acts 13:4–14:28). The two visited various synagogues, where they taught from the Scriptures and preached the news of Jesus' resurrection (example: 13:32-33). They were not selective in choosing their audience; they preached to both Jews and Gentiles (see 14:1).

After their journeys, Paul and Barnabas returned to Antioch (Acts 14:26-27), a city in modern-day Syria (not to be confused with another Antioch located in Pisidia; see 13:14). Antioch in Syria was located approximately 330 miles north of Jerusalem.

The events of Acts 15:4-29 depict a meeting sometimes called the "Jerusalem Council." This meeting took place in approximately AD 51. The council was an early attempt to answer the vital question of how to incorporate Gentiles into the people of God. The church's future depended on how the council answered this question.

I. Conflict Described

(Acts 15:1-3)

A. The Belief (vv. 1-2a)

1. And certain men which came down from Judaea taught the brethren, and said, Except ye be circumcised after the manner of Moses, ye cannot be saved.

Judaea is the southern region of Israel. The area is mountainous; the largest city in the region, Jerusalem, is situated on a mountain top. A traveler *came down* in elevation when leaving Judaea.

The identity of these *certain men* is unknown. Their journey from Judaea took them to Antioch in Syria because it was there that Paul and Barnabas were ministering (see Acts 14:23-28). The visit to the believers (*the brethren*) in Antioch was seemingly unauthorized by the church leaders in Judaea (see 15:24). The visitors' message was direct: male Gentiles must *be circumcised* to identify as part of God's people. Because of this message, these visitors were likely either Jews or Gentile proselytes.

During the time between the Old and New Testaments, circumcision had become a boundary marker for Jewish identity. And the first-century church had not entirely abandoned the practice. For instance, the apostle Paul circumcised Timothy because of the context into which the two were traveling (see Acts 16:1-5). At another time, however, Paul did not require circumcision for his associate (see Galatians 2:3).

The issue at hand was not *if* Gentiles would be admitted into the people of God. The church had already celebrated God's work in Gentiles

How to Say It

Antioch	*An*-tee-ock.
Barnabas	*Bar*-nuh-bus.
Samaria	Suh-*mare*-ee-uh.
Pentecost	*Pent*-ih-kost.
Phenice	Fih-*nye*-see.
proselyte	*prahss*-uh-light.
Sidon	*Sigh*-dun.
Theophilus	Thee-*ahf*-ih-luss (*th* as in *thin*).
Tyre	Tire.

(example: Acts 11:1-18). Even the Old Testament prophets agreed that the incorporation of Gentiles into God's people would someday occur (examples: Isaiah 14:1; 56:6-7; Zechariah 8:23).

Instead, the issue was the *means* through which Gentiles entered the community of God's people. The visitors argued that for Gentiles to be counted as God's people, they would have to follow the law given to *Moses*. Their argument went as follows: since God provided the law, then all people—Gentiles included—must keep the law to *be saved*.

2a. When therefore Paul and Barnabas had no small dissension and disputation with them.

Paul—previously called "Saul" (Acts 13:9)—was from the tribe of Benjamin (see Romans 11:1). He was educated by a notable rabbi (see Acts 22:3) and trained as a Pharisee (see Philippians 3:4-6). Before meeting Christ, Paul approved of the persecution and killing of members of the first-century church (see Acts 7:59–8:3). After his conversion experience, Paul was accepted as a disciple of Jesus and was allowed to preach in the church (see 9:26-29). Following a season in the city of Tarsus (see 9:30), he returned to Antioch (see 11:25-28).

Barnabas was the first to introduce Paul to the other apostles (see Acts 9:27). The two men had traveled together on a missionary journey throughout Asia Minor (13:4–14:28; see Lesson Context). The two were identified as "apostles" (14:14) and, therefore, leaders in the first-century church.

That Paul and Barnabas expressed *dissension and disputation with* the visitors and their proclamation is unsurprising. The believers in Antioch had heard of the faith of Gentiles (see Acts 14:26-27). But the interlopers' message contradicted preaching from Paul and Barnabas regarding justification by faith and the limits of the Law of Moses (see 13:38-39).

B. The Parties (vv. 2b-3)

2b. They determined that Paul and Barnabas, and certain other of them, should go up to Jerusalem unto the apostles and elders about this question.

The decision to send *Paul and Barnabas* and a *certain other of them* reflects the respect held for the leaders in *Jerusalem*. Until *this question* of circumcision was answered, the believers in Antioch would withhold judgment—and their knives.

The apostles were the surviving members of the Twelve called by Jesus (see Luke 6:12-16; compare Matthew 27:5; Acts 12:1-2). *Elders* served in additional leadership positions in the church (see Acts 14:23; example: James 5:14). The council is one of the few places in Scripture where these two parties are listed together as church leaders (see Acts 15:4, 6, below; 15:22-23, not in our printed text; 16:4).

> **What Do You Think?**
> How should believers discern which doctrines are essential and which are nonessential?
> **Digging Deeper**
> How should believers handle disputes regarding nonessential doctrines?

3. And being brought on their way by the church, they passed through Phenice and Samaria, declaring the conversion of the Gentiles: and they caused great joy unto all the brethren.

Leaving *the church* in Antioch allowed Paul, Barnabas, and the others to visit churches en route to Jerusalem. The estimated 330 miles between the cities would have taken at least two weeks to travel on foot. Because of the trip's length, the travelers relied on the hospitality of other believers.

Phenice is the region of coastal plains located north of Galilee. It includes parts of the modern-day countries of Syria and Lebanon. City-states dotted the area in the first century AD, including Tyre (see Acts 21:2-3) and Sidon (see 27:3). Followers of Jesus scattered to this region after the persecution began in Jerusalem (see 11:19).

Further south, bordering the western banks of the Jordan River and extending to the Mediterranean Sea, was the region of *Samaria*. By the first century AD, Jews did not associate with Samaritans because of the former group's perceptions regarding the latter group's ritual cleanliness (see John 4:9). After Pentecost, however, the gospel infiltrated the region (see Acts 8:9-24) and led to the establishment of a growing church (9:31).

As the travelers proceeded through these

regions, they proclaimed the news that God had welcomed *Gentiles* into His people. This welcoming occurred when the Gentiles experienced a circumcision of the heart (see Ezekiel 44:9; compare Romans 2:28-29). *Conversion* is turning *away* from evil and *toward* God (see 1 Thessalonians 1:8-10). The conversion of Gentiles demonstrated that God had kept His promise to Abraham regarding the blessing to "all families of the earth" (Genesis 12:3).

II. Conflict Debated

(Acts 15:4-6)

A. Receiving (v. 4)

4. And when they were come to Jerusalem, they were received of the church, and of the apostles and elders, and they declared all things that God had done with them.

The message of Paul and Barnabas to the *Jerusalem* church focused on the work of *God* completed *with* the two of *them*. They likely reported on the conversion of Jews and Gentiles during their missionary journeys (see Acts 13:1–14:27). Through them, Jesus' command that His disciples be witnesses "in Jerusalem, and in all Judaea, and in Samaria, and unto the uttermost part of the earth" (1:8) was being fulfilled.

What Do You Think?

How will you tell the story of God's work in your life as an act of encouragement to other believers?

Digging Deeper

Who will you tell your story to in the upcoming week?

B. Reminding (vv. 5-6)

5. But there rose up certain of the sect of the Pharisees which believed, saying, That it was needful to circumcise them, and to command them to keep the law of Moses.

The *Pharisees* were a *sect* of first-century Judaism. They emphasized careful obedience to *the law of Moses* and its associated commentary and tradition (see Lesson Context, lesson 1). Their strict adherence to the Law of Moses and its interpretations made it understandable why these *certain* Christian Pharisees advocated for Gentile circumcision. Although the Gospels present the group as antagonistic toward Jesus (see lessons 1 and 2), some Pharisees (like Paul himself; see Philippians 3:4-11) had *believed* in Jesus.

6. And the apostles and elders came together for to consider of this matter.

This meeting to discuss the *matter* of circumcision appears to have been held in private, contrasting the initial church-wide reception of the believers from Antioch (Acts 15:4, above).

What Do You Think?

How should believers discern whether or not to bring in a mediator to help resolve a disagreement?

Digging Deeper

How would you respond to someone who says that believers should stifle disagreement altogether?

III. Conflict Resolved

(Acts 15:7-11)

A. God's Work (vv. 7-9)

7a. And when there had been much disputing, Peter rose up, and said unto them.

Simon *Peter* was one of the twelve apostles selected by Jesus. As a disciple, he experienced testing of his faith (see Matthew 14:22-32), and he denied having known Jesus (see Luke 22:54-62). However, Jesus reinstated Peter (see John 21:15-23). As a result, Peter became a leading figure in the church, just as Jesus promised (Matthew 16:17-19). The book of Acts describes how Peter led the apostles (Acts 1:15-26), preached the gospel (2:14-41; 8:14-25), and worked miracles (3:1-10; 9:32-35).

7b. Men and brethren, ye know how that a good while ago, God made choice among us, that the Gentiles by my mouth should hear the word of the gospel, and believe.

God had chosen Peter to proclaim *the gospel* message to "the circumcision" (Jews; Galatians 2:7-8) and *the Gentiles*. It was part of the long-promised plan of God to offer redemption to all people who would *believe* (see Romans 1:16).

What Do You Think?

How can believers discern God's call to serve as a cross-cultural missionary?

Digging Deeper

In what ways will you serve as a cross-cultural missionary to the various cultures in your neighborhood?

8. And God, which knoweth the hearts, bare them witness, giving them the Holy Ghost, even as he did unto us.

At this moment, perhaps Peter remembered his interactions with Cornelius, a Gentile who feared God (see Acts 10:1-2). After experiencing a vision (10:9-16), Peter went to the house of Cornelius and preached the message of Jesus' anointing and resurrection (see 10:23-43). The crux of Peter's declaration was that "God is no respecter of persons: but in every nation he that feareth him, and worketh righteousness, is accepted with him" (10:34-35). Every person—Jew or Gentile—who believed in Jesus would receive the forgiveness of sins (10:43). As Peter preached to these Gentiles, "the Holy Ghost fell on all them which heard the word" (10:44). This gift was evidence of the Gentiles receiving the gospel message and their responding in faith.

Although Peter preached the gospel, *God* alone *knoweth the hearts* of both Jews and Gentiles. The presence of *the Holy Ghost* in Gentiles served as evidence that their lives had turned toward God. This pouring out of the Spirit was *even as* God *did unto* Jesus' disciples at Pentecost (see Acts 2:1-5). The presence of God's Spirit on Gentiles gave *witness* to their inclusion into the people of God (example: 10:44-46; 11:15-18).

What Do You Think?

How will you continue living in a way that reflects the presence of God's Spirit?

Digging Deeper

What steps will you take to ensure that you are being attentive to the leading of God's Spirit?

9. And put no difference between us and them, purifying their hearts by faith.

Peter clinched his argument: the Gentiles' reception of God's Spirit was the sign of their acceptance into God's people. To God, there was *no difference between* Jews and Gentiles. Gentiles did not need to become circumcised. Instead, God cleans the *hearts* of all people who express faith in Christ (see Titus 3:5; Hebrews 10:22).

Faith is not merely a belief in a proposition. Rather, faith expresses trust and allegiance in Jesus as the Messiah and King. Such faith leads to a person being made right with God (see Romans 3:21-25; 5:1; Galatians 2:15-16; 5:4-6). Gentiles had received the Holy Spirit because of their faith in Christ. Through faith, "there is neither Jew nor Greek, . . . bond nor free, . . . male nor female: for ye are all one in Christ Jesus" (3:28; see lesson 9).

Level Ground

Indoor cycling classes are my favorite exercise. My coach motivates the class by setting difficult but attainable goals. While the coach is a professional, she still completes the same exercise as her students. Despite her experience and physical ability, she is held accountable to finish the same workout as the class. During class, we're all the same.

An adage states that "the ground is level at the cross." This statement speaks to the equality among believers. Regardless of a believer's life situation or spiritual history, all believers are part of the "one body" of Christ (see Romans 12:4-5). Do you draw distinctions between yourself and other believers, or do you look for ways to serve that "one body"? Does 1 Corinthians 12 offer any guidance in this regard? —M. E.

B. Our Response (vv. 10-11)

10. Now therefore why tempt ye God, to put a yoke upon the neck of the disciples, which neither our fathers nor we were able to bear?

The tendency of God's people to *tempt . . . God* had occurred in Israel's past. Such testing highlighted distrust of God and His plans (examples: Exodus 17:1-2; Numbers 14:20-25; Deuteronomy 6:16). Requiring Gentile circumcision amounted to testing God's will for His people. It was a faulty assumption that God's gift of the Spirit was mistakenly poured out to the Gentiles (see Acts 11:15-17).

A yoke is a wooden beam that pairs livestock together so they can work efficiently. The imagery of a yoke can have positive connotations, such as the yoke promised by Jesus (see Matthew 11:28-30). In Jewish teaching, the term *yoke* was used to describe the peoples' keeping of the Law of Moses. People's responsibility to the law guided and restrained them. To require law-adherence, especially circumcision, was equivalent to putting the burden of *a yoke upon the neck* of Gentiles (compare Galatians 5:1).

Neither Jesus (see Matthew 5:17) nor the apostle Paul (see Romans 3:31) desired to abolish the Law of Moses. The law was considered good (see 7:12; 1 Timothy 1:8) but inadequate for life and salvation (see Galatians 3:21). Such was not a new development in the first century. Certain limitations had marked the law since it had been received by Israel's ancestors—their *fathers* (see Romans 4). If Peter's peers and ancestors could not *bear* the requirements of the Law of Moses, why would the Gentiles be expected to do so?

11. But we believe that through the grace of the Lord Jesus Christ we shall be saved, even as they.

Peter ended with a reminder of the core of the gospel. Salvation comes only through one avenue: by *the grace of the Lord Jesus Christ.* No human work, including following the Law of Moses, could save a person (see Acts 13:38-39; Galatians 2:14-17).

Accepting Healing

As a high school freshman, I suffered my first concussion during an out-of-control game at youth group. As we played, I felt the sharp pain of someone's knee slamming into my head. Doctors advised me to avoid mental stimulation, which would slow the healing process.

I spent my recovery resting and avoiding basic activities. However, even rest had its limitations! I thought maybe I needed to push through the headaches and get accustomed to the pain. The recovery tested my patience. I wanted to do more to speed up the healing process. However, *nothing* is what was required of me.

Peter summarized the gospel message: salvation is through grace by faith. There is nothing we can do to better our chances of receiving salvation. We simply have to trust that God will heal our hearts. Do you believe that reality, or do you try to add requirements to God's gift? —M. E.

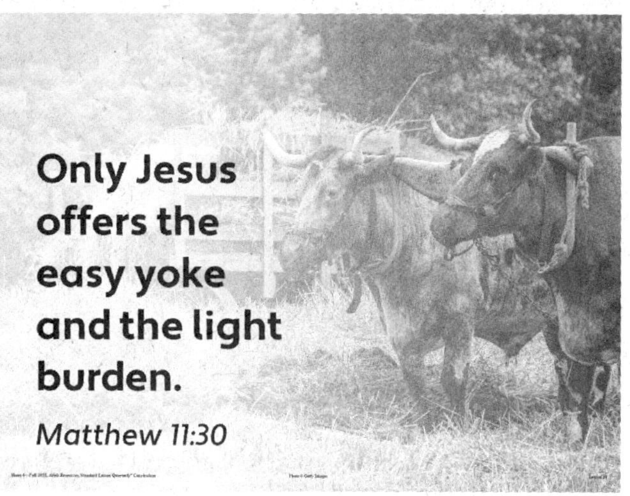

Only Jesus offers the easy yoke and the light burden.
Matthew 11:30

Visual for Lesson 10. *Point to this visual as you discuss the lesson commentary associated with Acts 15:10.*

Conclusion

A. Seeking Resolution

People try to hide conflict by avoiding or ignoring it altogether. Maintaining a facade of peace regardless of the underlying discord can be a severe failure. Evading problems usually makes the conflict worse.

The leaders of the first-century church did not dodge conflict regarding the question of Gentile circumcision. Instead, they resolved the dispute while staying faithful to the gospel. God's plan for salvation is beyond human expectations. We are saved through the grace of the Lord Jesus Christ and not through our heritage or achievements!

B. Prayer

God of salvation, thank You for showing Your mercy. Help us welcome as we have been welcomed and love as we have been loved. Show us how we can proclaim to others Your plan for salvation. In the name of Jesus. Amen.

C. Thought to Remember

Celebrate God's merciful gift of redemption!

Involvement Learning

Enhance your lesson with KJV Bible Student *(from your curriculum supplier) and the reproducible activity page (at www.standardlesson.com or in the back of the* KJV Standard Lesson Commentary Deluxe Edition*).*

Into the Lesson

Divide the class into two teams for a debate: **Team Pie** and **Team Cake**. Give teams five minutes to develop arguments for why their group's namesake is a better dessert. Each team will have two minutes to present their argument. Give time for each team to provide counterarguments and a defense.

Alternative. Distribute copies of the "Which Is Better?" exercise from the activity page, which you can download. Have learners complete it individually in a minute or less before discussing conclusions with a partner.

After either activity, say, "Believers have engaged in other debates that are more significant and harder to resolve. In today's lesson, let's consider the significance of an early debate of the first-century church and the implications of that debate for our faith."

Into the Word

Divide the class into three groups: **Circumcision Group, Paul and Barnabas Group**, and **Peter Group.** Distribute handouts (you create) of the questions below and allow 10 minutes for groups to answer the questions.

Circumcision Group: Read Acts 15:1-2, 5. 1–What was the viewpoint of the visitors and Pharisees regarding circumcision? 2–How do the events described in Acts 10:1–11:18 address that viewpoint? 3–What would be a modern-day equivalent to their viewpoint?

Paul and Barnabas Group: Read Acts 15:1-4. 1–Why did the viewpoint regarding circumcision cause Paul and Barnabas to have "no small dissension and disputation" (Acts 15:2)? 2–How does Paul's corrective to the church in Galatia (Galatians 5:1-12) apply to the situation described in Acts 15:1-11? 3–What would be a modern-day equivalent to Paul's corrective?

Peter Group: Read Acts 15:6-10. 1–How would you summarize the main points of Peter's speech? 2–How do these points and the events of Acts 10:1–11:18 refute the message of the visitors and the Pharisees? 3–How is Peter's speech applicable for modern-day believers?

Reconvene the class and ask a volunteer to read Acts 15:11 aloud. As a whole class, create a paraphrase of the verse. Write that paraphrase on the board. Allow time for learners to share new insights before working as an entire group to create a conclusion to settle the viewpoint from Acts 15:1.

Option. Ask a volunteer to read aloud Acts 15:5-11. Have the class reenact the story from Acts 10 that Peter likely referred to in Acts 15:7-9. Choose volunteers to play the roles of Cornelius, his messengers, the angels, Peter, God, and a narrator. The volunteers may improvise the story or read directly from Scripture. After reenactment, ask the following question for whole-class discussion: "What part of this story impacted you the most and why?"

Into Life

Write the following questions on the board:

1. How do believers strengthen their faith?
2. Why do we do these things?
3. Are these practices necessary to be a Christian?

Ask volunteers to give answers to each question, and write those responses on the board. Distribute paper and pens to learners. Ask learners to write down any personal faith practices that they do. Then ask learners to write down how they will interrogate these practices to determine which are core to the gospel message.

Alternative. Distribute copies of the "My Personal Practices" activity from the activity page. Have learners complete it as a take-home activity. Remind the class that they will have an opportunity to discuss their responses at the beginning of the next class.

November 12
Lesson 11 (KJV)

Freedom to Love

Devotional Reading: Matthew 22:34-40
Background Scripture: Romans 13:8-10; 1 Corinthians 13:8-13

Romans 13:8-10

8 Owe no man any thing, but to love one another: for he that loveth another hath fulfilled the law.

9 For this, Thou shalt not commit adultery, Thou shalt not kill, Thou shalt not steal, Thou shalt not bear false witness, Thou shalt not covet; and if there be any other commandment, it is briefly comprehended in this saying, namely, Thou shalt love thy neighbour as thyself.

10 Love worketh no ill to his neighbour: therefore love is the fulfilling of the law.

1 Corinthians 13:8-13

8 Charity never faileth: but whether there be prophecies, they shall fail; whether there be tongues, they shall cease; whether there be knowledge, it shall vanish away.

9 For we know in part, and we prophesy in part.

10 But when that which is perfect is come, then that which is in part shall be done away.

11 When I was a child, I spake as a child, I understood as a child, I thought as a child: but when I became a man, I put away childish things.

12 For now we see through a glass, darkly; but then face to face: now I know in part; but then shall I know even as also I am known.

13 And now abideth faith, hope, charity, these three; but the greatest of these is charity.

Key Text

Thou shalt not commit adultery, Thou shalt not kill, Thou shalt not steal, Thou shalt not bear false witness, Thou shalt not covet; and if there be any other commandment, it is briefly comprehended in this saying, namely, Thou shalt love thy neighbour as thyself. **—Romans 13:9**

God's Law
Is Love

Unit 3: Christ Frees, Law Enslaves

Lessons 10–13

Lesson Aims

After participating in this lesson, each learner will be able to:

1. Identify the greatest of the three things that remain or abide.

2. Summarize why it is the greatest of the three.

3. Commit to making that fact a personal reality in one specific way.

Lesson Outline

Introduction

A. Life Under Law and Love
B. Lesson Context: Romans
C. Lesson Context: 1 Corinthians

I. Love and the Law (Romans 13:8-10)

A. The Debt We Owe (v. 8)
B. The Imperatives to Obey (vv. 9-10)
The Abridged Version of the Law

II. Love and Spiritual Gifts (1 Corinthians 13:8-13)

A. That Which Is Temporary (v. 8)
B. That Which Is Incomplete (vv. 9-10)
C. That Which Is Expected (vv. 11-12)
D. That Which Is Supreme (v. 13)
Love Music

Conclusion

A. The Clarity of Love
B. Prayer
C. Thought to Remember

Introduction

A. Life Under Law and Love

A woman married a man who eventually was almost impossible to live with. He became very demanding, insisting that his meals be served at exactly the same time every day and prepared according to his specifications. He wanted every piece of his clothing to be ironed, every room in the house to be kept spotlessly clean, and all other requirements to be followed to the letter. If any of his high standards were not met, he stormed off in a rage, yelling at his wife at the top of his lungs. He made life miserable for her.

After about three years, the husband passed away unexpectedly. Eventually, the widow married a caring Christian man, who was the complete opposite of her first husband. She was so happy that she wanted to do all she could to show her gratitude for what she had never experienced with her first husband.

One day, it dawned on her that she was doing the very same things for her second husband that she had done for the first: fixing his meals the way he liked them, ironing his clothes, etc.—things that had at one time been demanded of her. Only this time, with her second husband, she was doing them out of love, not because someone was "laying down the law."

A person who lives primarily by law and a person who lives primarily by love both live obedient lives. But one of those approaches is much more satisfying—the subject of today's lesson.

B. Lesson Context: Romans

Thus far in the quarter, we have studied two lessons from Romans (lessons 5 and 6). Those lessons come from a section of the book that is more doctrinal (what we are to believe) in nature. Today's lesson moves us to a section that is more practical (what we are to do) in content as Paul shifts focus. Chapter 12 begins this section by challenging readers to offer themselves as "a living sacrifice" (Romans 12:1). What follows describes what that kind of life should look like in a Christian's daily conduct.

In the seven verses in Romans 13 that precede our first segment of text for this lesson, Paul examined a topic that should be of special interest to Christians of any century: our attitude toward civic authorities. The key concept here is one of obligation, which Paul uses to make a transition from how we are to relate to those authorities to how we are to relate to one another.

C. Lesson Context: 1 Corinthians

First Corinthians 13, the second of two segments of today's lesson, features Paul's timeless and matchless explanation of Christian love. The larger context of this chapter is Paul's discussion of spiritual gifts in chapters 12–14. Possession and use of spiritual gifts had become a source of great contention within the Corinthian church. Paul was concerned that undue focus on these gifts could distract the Corinthian believers from more crucial concerns. Should that happen, the result would be a fracturing of the unity in Christ that is to characterize followers of Jesus.

I. Love and the Law

(Romans 13:8-10)

A. The Debt We Owe (v. 8)

8a. Owe no man any thing, but to love one another.

The Greek verb translated *owe* is a reflection of the same word in its noun form in Romans 13:7 (not in today's lesson), there translated "dues." This continues the thought of *obligation* across these two verses (see also the Lesson Context). What's different now is that the object of the obligation has changed from being that of what we owe to civic authorities to what we owe to *one another.*

The first part of this half verse is certainly an approval of honoring one's commitments, be they in terms of money, property, etc. Some may question whether Paul is prohibiting the taking out of loans or mortgages. But approval or disapproval of monetary indebtedness is not the main point here. Rather, the phrasing sets up a contrast with the second part of this half verse regarding what should never be considered paid off: the obligation *to love.* Love among fellow believers is to be a primary characteristic of Christians (John 13:34-35; 1 John 3:14).

8b. For he that loveth another hath fulfilled the law.

What Paul states here he stresses in even stronger terms in Galatians 5:14: "all the law is fulfilled in one word, even in this; Thou shalt love thy neighbour as thyself."

> **What Do You Think?**
> What role do rules play in loving families with small children? adult children?
> **Digging Deeper**
> Do the rules in your family serve your love for one another? How might rules or obedience to them need to change in order to love one another best?

B. The Imperatives to Obey (vv. 9-10)

9. For this, Thou shalt not commit adultery, Thou shalt not kill, Thou shalt not steal, Thou shalt not bear false witness, Thou shalt not covet; and if there be any other commandment, it is briefly comprehended in this saying, namely, Thou shalt love thy neighbor as thyself.

The Ten Commandments (Decalogue) are found in Exodus 20:1-17 and Deuteronomy 5:6-21. Paul's citations from those indicate that what he has said about fulfilling "the law" in the previous verse refers to the Law of Moses rather than civic law.

We note that the positive command to *love thy neighbor as thyself* is framed in terms of several *thou shalt not* negative commands (compare Matthew 19:18). This implies that a foundation of neighbor-love is a commitment to do no harm.

How to Say It

Bethsaida	Beth-*say*-uh-duh.
Corinthians	Ko-*rin*-thee-unz (*th* as in *thin*).
Decalogue	*Dek*-uh-log.
Leviticus	Leh-*vit*-ih-kus.
Thessalonians	*Thess*-uh-lo-nee-unz (*th* as in *thin*).

Love your
neighbor
as yourself.
Visual for Lesson 11. *Point to this visual as learners spend one minute silently considering the Conclusion's questions before sharing with partners.*

But Christian love is not simply refusing to hurt someone else; it is also active as it works for the good of others, as included in the statement *if there be any other commandment.*

As we commit ourselves to such love, we will define neighbor-love as Jesus did in Luke 10:25-37: meeting the needs of those we encounter. Such love fulfills what Jesus called the second of the two greatest commandments, on which "hang all the law and the prophets" (Matthew 22:39-40; compare Leviticus 19:18). This is "the royal law according to the scripture" (James 2:8).

What Do You Think?

Whom do you love better: yourself or your neighbor?

Digging Deeper

What heart change is required to be able to bring these loves into proper balance?

The Abridged Version of the Law

I never liked studying geometry. Geometric proofs were uniquely challenging because problems not only had to be solved, they also had to be explained by way of complex statements and rules. I found it hard to remember all the rules, so I did not have much chance of correctly applying them.

But my problems with geometric rules pale in comparison to expectations according to the Law of Moses. That body of law features over 600 rules! I am so grateful that Jesus and Paul uncomplicated the law.

It's been said that the Old Testament is a collection of rules while the New Testament is a collection of principles. There's a lot of truth in that statement. But we should not let that general observation eclipse the fact that the New Testament itself has rules. Consider Jesus' statement in John 14:15: "If ye love me, keep my commandments." A primary one of those commandments is the imperative of love for neighbor. In what circumstances do you tend to act as if the rule of love does not apply? —M. E.

10. Love worketh no ill to his neighbor: therefore love is the fulfilling of the law.

Paul repeats what he has said previously. Therefore this verse serves as a kind of bookend to wrap up his line of thought before he makes a transition to another topic.

Even so, we can add the observation that Jesus himself came to fulfill the law (Matthew 5:17). He did so in His love for sinful humanity by taking on the Old Testament roles of prophet, priest, and king as He established the new covenant (Mark 6:4; John 12:15; Hebrews 7:11–8:13). He fulfilled the law by keeping it perfectly—He "knew no sin" (2 Corinthians 5:21). That qualified Him as the Son of God to be the perfect sacrifice that could take away and forgive the sins of humanity (1 Peter 1:18-19). There is no greater example of neighbor-love!

II. Love and Spiritual Gifts

(1 Corinthians 13:8-13)

A. That Which Is Temporary (v. 8)

8. Charity never faileth: but whether there be prophecies, they shall fail; whether there be tongues, they shall cease; whether there be knowledge, it shall vanish away.

The Greek word translated *charity* is exactly the same word translated "love" in Romans 13:10, above. Love is to be given priority in practice because it possesses much greater "staying power" than spiritual giftedness. Love *never faileth* in the sense of expiring or becoming unnecessary. This is the only place in Paul's letters where he uses the adverb translated here as "never," stressing the supremacy of love. By contrast, the time will come when the three gifts mentioned—*prophecies*, *tongues*, and *knowledge*—are no longer in use.

Paul has already mentioned those three gifts, among others, in this section of his letter (see 1 Corinthians 12:7-11). Perhaps disagreements regarding these three had been creating the greatest amount of tension within the Corinthian church. These gifts were rather "public" in nature, and thus those who possessed them tended to draw more attention to themselves (whether that was their motivation or not). Yet, as impressive as these gifts were, their impact was significantly lessened if the person exercising them did not do so out of love (compare 13:1-3).

B. That Which Is Incomplete (vv. 9-10)

9-10. For we know in part, and we prophesy in part. But when that which is perfect is come, then that which is in part shall be done away.

These two verses begin a deeper dive in examining why spiritual gifts are of lesser value than the imperative to love. The relative valuations are seen in the contrast between the phrases *in part* (thrice) and *that which is perfect*. There is no widespread agreement regarding what Paul is referring to by the latter phrase. One proposal is to see the contrast in terms of things that are temporary versus "perfect" things that are enduring, as the passage of time eventually reveals. This leads to the viewpoint that Paul is referring to life in the world to come after Jesus returns. What could be more perfect than that? At Jesus' second coming, the temporary things God provides for our spiritual growth now will no longer be necessary.

Another proposal is to see the contrast in terms of things that are incomplete in their contents versus things that are complete in that regard. Given the partial nature of the things that individuals may *know* and *prophesy* (see 1 Corinthians 8:1-3; 1 Peter 1:10-12), the proposed interpretation is that the term *that which* refers to the completion of the New Testament. In other words, the proposal is that certain spiritual gifts were no longer necessary after the first century AD after the exercise of those gifts had authenticated the new and perfect revelation of God's will within the new covenant.

Complicating the issue is the fact that the word translated *perfect* here can mean "mature." That idea is present in 1 Corinthians 14:20, where the same Greek word is used to contrast the immaturity of children with the maturity of adults. The idea of maturity is also present in the next two verses of today's lesson.

What Do You Think?

How have you seen love demonstrated when physical or mental abilities may be diminished?

Digging Deeper

What might these examples teach us about love, whatever our own physical or mental ability?

C. That Which Is Expected (vv. 11-12)

11. When I was a child, I spake as a child, I understood as a child, I thought as a child: but when I became a man, I put away childish things.

Clearly, there is a sense in which we are to remain childlike in our dependence on and trust in the Lord (Matthew 18:1-4). But remaining childish in terms of spiritual maturity is condemned (1 Corinthians 3:2; Hebrews 5:12-13). In the verse at hand, however, Paul is using the physical maturing process, when the interests and priorities of childhood fall away as we grow older, as his illustration. We take on new responsibilities and interests and put aside the childish things that once consumed much of our time and attention.

In the context of the discussion of love and spiritual gifts, the specifics represented by this child/adult contrast will vary according to one's view of the "perfect" in the previous verse. If perfection is understood in its absolute sense, then what occurs at the return of Christ is the issue (compare 1 Corinthians 15:51-52; Philippians 3:21). If "maturity" is more in view, then that is something that can happen in this present age as spiritual maturity results from having access to the completed New Testament (compare Romans 12:2; 2 Corinthians 3:18; 2 Timothy 2:15) rather than just fragmentary, incomplete prophecies.

What Do You Think?

In what sense(s) should we put childish things behind us?

Digging Deeper

In what sense(s) should we strive to remain childlike (example: Matthew 18:3)?

12. For now we see through a glass, darkly, but then face to face: now I know in part; but then shall I know even as also I am known.

The word *glass* refers to a mirror. We should not equate this with a silvered glass mirror, which was not invented until AD 1835. Mirrors of the first century AD were made of polished metal, yielding dim and distorted reflections. Paul uses this to illustrate what is known *in part*. This contrast, again, is with what he will eventually (*then*) know fully as dim reflection gives way to *face to face* clarity.

As above, there are two major lines of interpretation. One line understands "face to face" to be taken in a literal sense; therefore "that which is perfect" (1 Corinthians 13:10, above) would mean Jesus' second coming, when we "shall see his face" (Revelation 22:4; compare Psalm 17:15; 1 John 3:2).

The other line of interpretation takes "face to face" in a figurative sense of "clear communication" with God (Exodus 33:11; Numbers 12:8). This is seen to support the idea of the completion of the New Testament as God's definitive way of communicating His will as we mature in the faith.

D. That Which Is Supreme (v. 13)

13. And now abideth faith, hope, charity, these three; but the greatest of these is charity.

As with 1 Corinthians 13:8 (above), the Greek word translated *charity* is exactly the same word translated "love" in Romans 13:10 (also above). As Paul brings his discussion of Christian love to its conclusion, he emphasizes once more that which *abideth* (remains, endures) in an implied contrast to that which is temporary. *Faith, hope,* and *charity* (love) form a trio that sums up the crucial elements that are at the heart of Christian living (see also Ephesians 1:15-18; Colossians 1:3-5; and 1 Thessalonians 1:3; 5:8). Love is not only greater than spiritual gifts, but it is the greatest of Christian virtues.

But there is a relative ranking to these three in terms of endurance. Since "faith is the substance of things hoped for, the evidence of things not seen" (Hebrews 11:1), faith will no longer be necessary when Christ returns. In heaven, we will be walking by sight rather than by faith (2 Corinthians 4:18; 5:7).

Hope, too, is limited to our earthly lives only. What we hope for is eternal salvation (1 Thessalonians 5:8; Titus 3:7). And once we have it in its fullest sense, there is no more place for hope. After all, no one hopes for something that he or she already has (Romans 8:24)!

Love, however, towers over both faith and hope because love is eternally enduring. Love is a primary attribute of God (1 John 4:8, 16). For our part, "this is love, that we walk after his commandments" (2 John 6).

Regardless of the view of "that which is perfect" (1 Corinthians 13:10) one holds, we should not lose sight of what Paul was confronting and how. What the Corinthians needed more than anything in resolving conflicts over spiritual gifts was the attitude and practice of Christian love. Love was the starting point for addressing all the other issues mentioned in the letter—issues such as believers taking one another to court (6:1-8) and eating meat offered to idols (8:1-13). A lack of such love would stifle numeric and spiritual growth of the church. Love would move followers of Jesus—whether first century or twenty-first—beyond immature "me first" attitudes and behaviors and toward genuine Christlikeness.

Love Music

One thing about songwriting is enduringly true: the desire to give and receive love will sell music. I hadn't given that idea much thought until one day our professor led the class in a discussion of the impact of emotions by various kinds of music. It didn't matter whether the music genre was country, rock music, bluegrass, etc. In all cases, compositions centered on love led in popularity.

Even without "love music," the longing to love and be loved is universal, transcending time and distance. Consider the Bible itself, which features the word *love* more than 500 times! The contents of the Song of Solomon are enough to make one blush. Nothing has more potential to change a person than love.

Sadly, culture distorts the meaning and expression of love that God intends—a distortion often heard in music lyrics. Loving attitudes and actions are to characterize Christians. A quote attributed to US President Theodore Roosevelt (1858–1919) is most appropriate: "No one cares how much you know until they know how much you care." What changes do you need to make in that regard?

—M. E.

Conclusion

A. The Clarity of Love

I started wearing glasses in the seventh grade. My teacher had noticed how much I was squinting to see the blackboard (yes, it was that long ago), so she suggested to my parents that my eyes be examined. True, said the optometrist, I was going to need glasses. When I went to pick them up, the assistant told me to look across the street before I put them on. I did so without much thought. After I put the glasses on, she told me again to look across the street. I could not believe how much clearer everything looked! I was stunned to, literally, see how much I had been missing.

The actions and attitudes of Christian love improve our spiritual view in critical areas. Without it, we are somewhat like the man in the village of Bethsaida to whom Jesus gave sight in a two-stage miracle (Mark 8:22-26). After "stage one," Jesus asked him if he could see anything. The man replied, "I see men as trees, walking." After "stage two," the man could see clearly. Jesus was not content to leave the man's ability to see in stage one. Neither is Jesus content that our own spiritual vision remain partially obscured regarding whom we should or should not extend His love through our own attitudes and actions.

The process can be seen as two mutually reinforcing, upward-spiraling reciprocals. First, as the clarity of our spiritual vision improves, we will begin to see more and more opportunities to express the love of Christ to others; and as we express that love, the clarity of our spiritual vision will be improved.

Second, this improved vision will cause us to see that to minister to others in love is to serve God (Matthew 25:34-40); "If any man love God, the same is known of him" (1 Corinthians 8:3; compare and contrast Galatians 4:9; 1 John 4:19-21).

Because of Christ's love, we do not view people as the world does. We see them as those for whom Jesus gave His life and who need "the word of reconciliation" (2 Corinthians 5:19). The same love moves us to respond to those in need (1 John 3:16-18), the kind of "neighbor love" modeled by the Good Samaritan (Luke 10:33).

Those who have been baptized into Christ "have put on Christ." Given that fact, it is (or should be) only natural also to "put on" love as Paul told the Colossian Christians to do (Colossians 3:14).

What Do You Think?

What opportunities will you take to love Jesus' followers this week?

Digging Deeper

What will you do this week to love your neighbors—including your enemies?

B. Prayer

Father, we live in a time where love is perhaps more desperately sought after than ever before. Forgive us when we become callous to the needs around us. Help us to follow the example of Jesus and to see others as He sees them. In His name we pray. Amen.

C. Thought to Remember

Love remains the primary form of "ID" for the follower of Jesus.

Involvement Learning

Enhance your lesson with KJV Bible Student *(from your curriculum supplier) and the reproducible activity page (at www.standardlesson.com or in the back of the* KJV Standard Lesson Commentary Deluxe Edition*).*

Into the Lesson

Before class, create an environment for today's lesson by sharing some common cultural symbols of love: chocolate candies, red hearts, roses, etc. As learners enter, encourage them to share any experiences or responses they had to last week's class.

Ask each learner to list people who love him/her and a second list of people he/she loves. After one minute of writing, instruct learners to journal about a sacrifice someone made on his/her behalf that demonstrated love. Allow volunteers to share examples with the class.

Alternative 1. Before the session, ask group members about favorite hymns and pull them up with lyrics on a media device, or have a few ready to go on handouts. Choose and sing a few lines together from these hymns. Ask the class how the love celebrated in these songs differs from what they might hear on a secular radio station. Write themes and phrases on the board.

Alternative 2. Distribute copies of the "Love and Romance" exercise on the activity page, which you can download. Have learners complete as indicated.

After calling time, start a discussion by asking, "How is sacrifice a demonstration of love?" Encourage people to talk about a variety of relationships in this discussion. Transition to the Bible study by saying, "Paul writes to both the Romans and the Corinthians about God's sacrificial love. Let's discover how love makes a difference in the lives of those who follow Jesus."

Into the Word

Invite volunteers to read aloud Romans 13:8-10 and 1 Corinthians 13:8-13. If you used the first activity above, compare the list on the board with what Paul said about God's love. Discuss together the meaning of Paul's words "charity never faileth" (1 Corinthians 13:8). Supplement the discussion with information from the commentary as needed.

Alternative. Distribute copies of "The Bible on Love" exercise from the activity page. Have learners work in pairs to complete as indicated. After time is called, lead a discussion and write conclusions on the board.

Then draw two arrows pointing in opposite directions, parallel to one another with one line above the other, on a white board or chalkboard. Label the bottom line *Law* and the top *Love.* Discuss how law and love are related. Ask participants to name ways Christians follow God's law. Draw a large dot on the *Law* line along with a word or two to paraphrase each thought. Invite the group to refer to Romans 13:8. Then have the group name ways they love their neighbors. Draw large dots on the *Love* line and write those ideas near the dots.

Read aloud Romans 13:10. Ask: "What is fulfillment?" After a few minutes, have a volunteer with internet access look up and read definitions. Invite learners to discuss how fulfillment helps connect the two lines of law and love. Invite participants to add more ideas to the love line that demonstrate loving actions which fulfill the law. Erase the arrows on the ends that point in opposite directions.

Ask a volunteer to read aloud 1 Corinthians 13:13. Talk through any relationships between the previous discussion and the Bible verse. Point out that one way people show love for God is by loving others.

Into Life

Distribute index cards and pens to learners. Invite participants to write down the name of one person or group to whom they can show love during the coming week. Then ask them to write down one thing they will do to let that person or group know that they are loved. Challenge learners to accomplish what they wrote down in the upcoming week.

Freedom from the World

Devotional Reading: Leviticus 25:8-17
Background Scripture: Colossians 2:6-23

Colossians 2:16-23

**16 Let no man therefore judge you in meat,
or in drink, or in respect of an holyday, or of
the new moon, or of the sabbath days:
17 Which are a shadow of things to come;
but the body is of Christ.
18 Let no man beguile you of your reward
in a voluntary humility and worshipping of
angels, intruding into those things which he
hath not seen, vainly puffed up by his fleshly
mind,
19 And not holding the Head, from which
all the body by joints and bands having nourishment ministered, and knit together, increaseth with the increase of God.
20 Wherefore if ye be dead with Christ from
the rudiments of the world, why, as though living in the world, are ye subject to ordinances,
21 (Touch not; taste not; handle not;
22 Which all are to perish with the using;)
after the commandments and doctrines of
men?
23 Which things have indeed a shew of
wisdom in will worship, and humility, and
neglecting of the body; not in any honour to
the satisfying of the flesh.**

Key Text

As ye have therefore received Christ Jesus the Lord, so walk ye in him: rooted and built up in him, and stablished in the faith. **—Colossians 2:6-7a**

God's Law

Is Love

Unit 3: Christ Frees, Law Enslaves

Lessons 10–13

Lesson Aims

After participating in this lesson, each learner will be able to:

1. Identify "the head."

2. Describe the implications of being dead with Christ.

3. Recruit an accountability partner to make one such implication a personal reality.

Lesson Outline

Introduction

A. Simple vs. Complex

B. Lesson Context

I. Troubling Judgment (Colossians 2:16-19)

A. Shadowy Practices (vv. 16-17)

B. Misdirected Humility (v. 18)

C. Spiritual Decapitation (v. 19)

Staying Focused

II. Worldly Rules (Colossians 2:20-23)

A. Died with Christ (v. 20)

B. Temporary in Application (vv. 21-22)

C. Limited in Force (v. 23)

The Customer Service Manual

Conclusion

A. Seek the Head!

B. Prayer

C. Thought to Remember

Introduction

A. Simple vs. Complex

I once owned a Buick LeSabre with power windows. Because of bad design or poor construction, every window of that vehicle required repair at some point. Either the windows wouldn't lower, or they wouldn't raise. After completing the first repair, I longed for previous models' old-style, hand-crank windows. Those windows certainly didn't break as often—or so I remembered. These power windows should have made life simpler; instead, they had done the opposite. I experienced more difficulty and annoyance because of those windows.

In today's Scripture, false teachers in Colossae had been troubling Colossian believers by requiring additional practices for the people. These excessive requirements might have caused the Colossian believers difficulty in following Jesus. These false teachers weren't merely annoying the apostle Paul and the Colossian believers; their false teachings had eternal ramifications.

B. Lesson Context

The apostle Paul wrote the epistle of Colossians in the first half of the AD 60s. The recipients of the epistle were a community of believers in Colossae (see Colossians 1:1-2), a city in modern-day Turkey. When Paul composed this letter, he had not yet visited the area (see 1:4-7; 2:1). He likely penned the letter while under arrest (see 4:3) in Rome (see Acts 28:16, 30).

Whether or not Paul ever visited Colossae is unknown, but he had heard from others about the faith of the Colossian believers (see Colossians 1:4). He intended the letter to encourage the Colossians (2:2-3) and address false teachings that had infiltrated the church (see 2:4-5)

The exact nature of the false teaching in Colossae is unknown. Most of our modern-day understanding comes from reading the letter of Colossians and drawing informed conclusions based on the addressed topics. Taking this approach, we can assume that both Jewish and pagan teaching in Colossae threatened to lead the believers astray. This syncretistic belief system was comprised of various elements from different religious and philosophical traditions that were not rooted in the gospel of Jesus Christ.

The false teaching likely included aspects of Judaism. Paul provided correctives regarding lifestyle markers that distinguished Jews from Gentiles, such as circumcision (Colossians 2:11-15), dietary restrictions, and the observance of holy days (2:16). However, other aspects of the false teaching, such as angel worship (2:18) and misdirected fasting (2:23), mirrored pagan philosophies and cults. Paul proclaimed this belief system "philosophy and vain deceit, after the tradition of men" (2:8). This belief system concerned Paul because it added requirements for believers beyond God's work through Christ Jesus.

Colossians 1:15-22 and 2:6-15 feature Paul's corrective to the Colossians regarding Christ's preeminence. Christ has made believers complete (Colossians 2:9-10) and raised them to a new life (2:12-14). Further, He has triumphantly "spoiled principalities and powers" (2:15). These other philosophies, beliefs, and practices had taken the Colossians spiritually captive. If they continued to follow the false teachings, they would essentially deny the power of Christ's work.

I. Troubling Judgment

(Colossians 2:16-19)

A. Shadowy Practices (vv. 16-17)

16. Let no man therefore judge you in meat, or in drink, or in respect of an holyday, or of the new moon, or of the sabbath days.

The Law of Moses prohibited Jews from consuming particular meats (see Leviticus 11; Deuteronomy 14:2-20). These particular prohibitions would not have applied to Gentiles. However, first-century church leaders added prohibitions regarding the Gentiles' consumption of food (see Acts 15:20, 29; 21:25). Paul provided further guidance in this regard: believers can consume as long as it does not cause others to sin (see Romans 14:20-21; 1 Corinthians 8).

Alcoholic *drink* was standard in the first century AD (example: John 2:3-10). The Law of Moses did not prohibit consumption except for specific situations (examples: Leviticus 10:8-11; Numbers 6:1-4). Likely some believers in Colossae had consumed alcohol, leading others to *judge* the believers. However, merely eating certain foods or consuming certain drinks cannot cause spiritual uncleanliness (see Mark 7:14-19).

Religious celebrations and certain holy days held importance in Judaism (examples: Leviticus 23; 1 Chronicles 23:28-31; Ezekiel 45:17). The New Testament uses the underlying Greek word translated *holyday* when mentioning Jewish feasts (examples: Luke 2:41-42; John 6:4; 7:2). The Jewish religious calendar is partly based on the lunar cycle. Therefore, a *new moon* marked a new month and indicated the timing of certain celebrations (see Numbers 10:10; 28:11-15). Additionally, the Law of Moses required observance of *the sabbath days* for rest (see Exodus 20:8-11; Leviticus 23:3).

First-century churches in Rome and Galatia encountered conflict regarding similar regulations and observances (see Romans 14:1-10; Galatians 4:8-11). Paul rejected such regulations because they would cause division (4:17) and destruction (Romans 14:13-18). Believers should serve others with love, rather than chase appearances of holiness that disregard love. Out of this consideration and love for others, believers may limit their freedom to avoid causing other believers to sin (see 14:19-21; Galatians 5:13-15).

What Do You Think?

How do you evaluate the spiritual benefits of religious celebrations or observances?

Digging Deeper

How do you ensure that these events lead you closer to Christ and do not become an end to themselves?

17. Which are a shadow of things to come; but the body is of Christ.

By calling these practices *a shadow*, Paul may have used the wording of Greek philosophy of his day. Plato, a Greek philosopher who lived approximately three centuries before Paul, is one possible reference. Plato's work *Republic* described the physical world as a shadow of the ideal reality. Therefore, Paul used this philosophical language of his day to make a teaching point. The Law of Moses and its requirements were temporary and could not offer salvation (see Romans 3:19-20; Galatians 3:21-25). They are "a shadow of good things to come, and not the very image of the things" (Hebrews 10:1). Instead, these requirements would find fulfillment in a new era of salvation.

The *things to come* is one way that Paul describes salvation in and through Christ Jesus (compare Galatians 4:4-5). *Christ* is the culmination of all requirements for salvation (see Romans 10:4). "*The body* of his flesh through death" brings redemption to all people who believe in Him (Colossians 1:22). Salvation comes through faith in Christ's merciful and generous giving of himself (see Ephesians 2:8; Titus 3:5; etc.).

B. Misdirected Humility (v. 18)

18a. Let no man beguile you of your reward in a voluntary humility and worshiping of angels.

To *beguile* means "to deceive or lead astray through charm and persuasion." This instance is the only appearance of the Greek word in the New Testament. The Colossians were in danger of being deceived by false teaching. Their deception would result in losing the *reward* of a life submitted to God's rule.

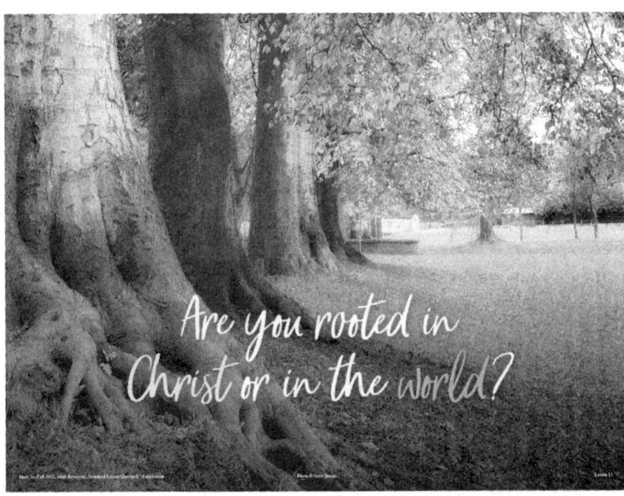

Visual for Lesson 12. *Allow the class to focus on this question for a few moments before closing with prayer.*

Paul commanded the Colossians to live with humility (see Colossians 3:12). However, the pagan teachers in Colossae had developed a false sense of *humility*. The nature of their displays of false humility is unknown. One possibility is that Paul was referring to *voluntary* practices of self-denial, such as fasting. Jesus had warned His followers regarding people who make a public spectacle of their fasting (see Matthew 6:16). These displays revealed an insincere or misdirected sense of humility. Rather than showing humility, these false teachers had become hypocritical and prideful through their actions (compare Colossians 2:18c, below).

The exact meaning of the phrase *worshipping of angels* is unknown. One interpretation is that the false teachers believed that angels would intercede to God on behalf of humans. However, worshipping a created being is a misdirected form of worship (see Revelation 22:8-9; see also Luke 4:7-8; Romans 1:25). Throughout the letter to the Colossians, Paul highlights the superiority of Christ over the created order (example: Colossians 1:16-17; 2:9-10). Because of Jesus' role as the "great high priest," believers confidently approach God without any other intercessor (Hebrews 4:14-16).

18b. Intruding into those things which he hath not seen.

Extreme practices of self-denial can sometimes result in a dramatic (and unhealthy) physical response, like a hallucination. Some false teachers in Colossae were likely experiencing such denial-induced hallucinations. These seemingly out-of-body experiences led them to see *those things which* they *hath not seen*.

God has revealed himself to people through visions (examples: Genesis 46:2-4; Acts 9:10-16). However, not all such occurrences come from God (examples: Ezekiel 13:6-7; Zechariah 10:2). The false teachers in Colossae led people astray by claiming their experiences as evidence of their supposedly heightened spirituality.

This verse includes the only appearance of the Greek word translated *intruding* in the New Testament. Its meaning in this verse is difficult to interpret for modern students. One interpretation teaches that the word refers to the false teachers' act of entering into great detail regarding their vision-like hallucinations..

18c. Vainly puffed up by his fleshly mind.

Paul's writings have at least six discernible uses of the word *flesh*. Among these uses are references to living creatures in general (see 1 Corinthians 15:39), the human body specifically (see 6:16), and rebellious human nature (see Romans 8:3-12). In this verse, Paul uses the adjective form of *flesh* to describe rebellious human behavior. This manner of flesh includes any human desires hostile to God (see Galatians 5:16-17, 19-21; compare Romans 13:13-14). The flesh and the *fleshly mind* are hostile to God and God's will. The false teachers in Colossae had reached a point of misdirected spiritual "wisdom." Instead of listening to God as the source of wisdom, they sought worldly wisdom that fed their fleshly desires. As a result, their so-called knowledge had *puffed* them up with pride (compare 1 Corinthians 8:1).

C. Spiritual Decapitation (v. 19)

19. And not holding the Head, from which all the body by joints and bands having nourishment ministered, and knit together, increaseth with the increase of God.

The comparison of the church to *the body* frequently occurs in Paul's writings (examples: Romans 12:4-5; 1 Corinthians 12:12-27; Ephesians 4:14-16). He had previously declared Christ as *the Head* of the church (Colossians 1:15-18; see Ephesians 1:22). If a body is cut off from the head, the body will die. The Colossian church was on the verge of perishing if it did not maintain a connection with Christ (compare John 15:1-7). Colossae's false teachers risked obstructing their students' connection to Christ. Spiritual death was certain if they were not rooted in Christ.

Each member of the church has a particular role and work, just as *joints and bands* have in a human body. The church will increase in strength as its members abide in Christ (example: Acts 2:42-47). Growth comes not from human works, as what was likely taught by the false teachers in Colossae. Instead, the church grows because *God* empowers it to do so (see 1 Corinthians 3:6).

What Do You Think?

What steps will you take to remove distractions and circumstances that detach you from a life with Christ?

Digging Deeper

How do your efforts contribute to your congregation's connection to Christ?

Staying Focused

Dancing with the Oldies videocassettes. P90X. Peloton. I've begun these fitness programs, only to put them aside after I did not achieve the desired results. After discarding one program, my wife reminded me why I failed to reach my goals: I had ignored the program's dietary plan. Just working out would not lead me to my desired results; my eating habits would also have to change.

The same thing can happen in our faith when we focus on our external practices but fail to maintain a connection to Christ. When we disregard Him, we fail to receive the life that He promises for His followers. The most important part of our "spiritual fitness" is our connection with Christ. Does your life bear fruit (see John 15:4) that demonstrates this connection? —J. M.

II. Worldly Rules
(Colossians 2:20-23)

A. Died with Christ (v. 20)

20. Wherefore if ye be dead with Christ from the rudiments of the world, why, as though living in the world, are ye subject to ordinances.

The *rudiments of the world* are the forces—visible and invisible—that hold power in the world. These could include demonic forces, pagan philosophies, or rules of vanity regarding the consumption of food and drink. These forces are the "principalities and powers" (Colossians 2:15) that lead people to follow "philosophy and vain deceit, after the tradition of men, after the rudiments of the world" (2:8).

Although the Colossian believers lived *in the world*, they were not to partake in its behavior. This manner of *living* described their old life. However, they were *dead* to that way of life. Instead, they had been raised into a new life *with Christ* through His death and resurrection (see Colossians 2:11-13). As a result of their new life, they would reorient their hearts toward heavenly things (see 3:1-3) and live as "the elect of God" (3:12-17).

What Do You Think?

In what ways do you reorient your life due to your being "dead with Christ"?

Digging Deeper

How do you ensure that you are seeking the Spirit's guidance and not relying on your own efforts?

B. Temporary in Application (vv. 21-22)

21. (Touch not; taste not; handle not.

Paul summarized the ordinances and commands of the false teachers. To *taste not* likely refers to their judgment regarding the consumption of food and drink (see Colossians 2:16, above). The meaning behind their commands to *touch not* and *handle not* is unclear. The Law of Moses prohibited people from handling certain items (example: Leviticus 5:2-3). However, the false teachers might have expanded those prohibitions beyond the scope of the Law of Moses.

The generality of these commands might also indicate a particular perspective from the false teachers regarding the physical world. They might have taught that people should withdraw from the world. This perspective is contrary to the behavior expected of followers of Jesus. Believers are not to separate themselves from the world. Instead, they must remain in the world but be sanctified from it (see John 17:15-21; Romans 12:2).

22. Which all are to perish with the using;) after the commandments and doctrines of men?

Human *commandments and doctrines* cannot provide eternal value. These things would eventually *perish* and no longer apply (compare 1 Corinthians 6:13). Human commandments and practices are not always worthless. Some can lead to growth and maturity in a person's spiritual health. However, adherence to these practices does not reliably indicate the status of a person's heart toward God (see Isaiah 29:13; Matthew 15:1-9).

What Do You Think?

How do you decide whether or not to observe a human tradition in order to keep a relationship with another person?

Digging Deeper

How do the actions of Paul in Acts 16:1-4 and 21:17-26 inform your response to the previous question?

C. Limited in Force (v. 23)

23a. Which things have indeed a shew of wisdom in will worship, and humility, and neglecting of the body.

The false teachers in Colossae had taught that following human commands and doctrines would bring unique wisdom from God. However, these *things* could never bring wisdom from God. Instead, they led to worldly *wisdom* and foolishness (see Romans 1:21-23; 1 Corinthians 3:19-20).

Paul unpacks three aspects of their commands and teachings. First were their requirements for *worship*. They focused on the human *will* to worship the created and not the Creator. Second, such worship led to "voluntary *humility*" (Colossians 2:18a, above). Such displays of misdirected humility likely included practices of self-denial.

Third, these requirements and displays of humility can lead a person to neglect *the body* (see Colossians 2:16, 21, above). Practices of self-denial are not always harmful. Scripture commands believers to "glorify God" with their bodies (1 Corinthians 6:20). Therefore, denying certain physical pleasures can help shape a believer's faith and trust in God. These practices, however, are not required to have a right relationship with God. The false teachers were more concerned with demonstrating self-denial than spiritual maturation.

True wisdom comes from knowledge of God's will rather than through misdirected worship and practices (see Colossians 1:9). God gifts this wisdom to His people (Ecclesiastes 2:26; James 1:5) and wants His people to share this wisdom with others (see Colossians 3:16).

23b. Not in any honour to the satisfying of the flesh.

The attempts of the false teachers to control *the flesh* through misdirected worship and self-denying practices had failed (see Colossians 3:5-8). Only people who demonstrate faith in Christ and receive God's Spirit can confront the flesh. Such people have life made new in Christ (see 3:9-10). Even if these self-denying practices and expressions of worship were of *some* value, such things could not completely prevent sinful desires.

What Do You Think?

How will you glorify God with your body (see 1 Corinthians 6:20)?

Digging Deeper

Who will you recruit as an accountability partner in this regard?

The Customer Service Manual

As a customer service lead for a major airline, I frequently read the customer service manual (CSM). This resource provided hundreds of pages of regulations regarding my response for almost every possible customer-service situation.

One time, the airline debuted an initiative to improve customer service. The plan empowered employees to make the best (and safest) decision for the customer, regardless of CSM's directives. However, not all employees appreciated the new-found freedom. Some employees held firmly to the CSM, refusing to make decisions that seemed to go against the CSM.

Some people in Colossae had submitted to ineffective human rules and religious regulations as the final authority. Paul reminded these people that these things could not restrain human desires. It only *seemed* wise for the people to follow such rules. Instead, believers have freedom from these rules because of Christ. What human rules and regulations seem full of wisdom but fail to bring you closer to Christ? —J. M.

Conclusion

A. Seek the Head!

Some false teachers in Colossae had made the Christian life more complicated than what was required by God. They had added obligations beyond God's to the Colossian believers. We do not know why these teachers presented the Colossians with these things. The false teachers had forgotten or altogether disregarded the importance of a connection to Christ, the head of the church. Instead of seeking life in Christ, they vainly sought wisdom through human regulations.

It can be tempting to believe that we don't add anything extra to our faith. Yet, the reality is that we often do. Sometimes, we set explicit or implicit rules on ourselves and, by extension, on other believers. Our observance of these rules or guidelines does not mean that our hearts are automatically more or less holy. But issues arise if we raise these rules to the same level as God's Word. We or other believers may be spiritually harmed.

We should carefully examine our behavior regarding such regulations. Ensure that you first maintain a relationship with Christ, the head of the church. What, after all, can be added to the gospel of salvation through Christ? What more do we need? Only when we accept that Christ's work has accomplished what we needed for reconciliation can we be filled with His wisdom. Ask for the Spirit's guidance to discern whether you are following the world's wisdom or God's wisdom. At the Spirit's leading, we will be free to engage in practices that lead to the glory of God and the edification of other believers. Seek the Head! And heed the Spirit.

B. Prayer

Heavenly Father, we want wisdom that only You can give. Soften our hearts so we can be attentive to the work of Your Spirit. Guide us to follow Your will. May we, as the body, always remain attached to Christ. In Jesus' name. Amen.

C. Thought to Remember

Spiritual life comes from Christ Jesus, the head.

How to Say It

Colossae	Ko-*lahss*-ee.
Colossians	Kuh-*losh*-unz.
Galatia	Guh-*lay*-shuh.

Involvement Learning

Enhance your lesson with KJV Bible Student *(from your curriculum supplier) and the reproducible activity page (at www.standardlesson.com or in the back of the* KJV Standard Lesson Commentary Deluxe Edition*).*

Into the Lesson

Have paper and pens available for learners to grab as they enter the room. Invite them to write down religious or secular practices and traditions that they once followed. (Examples: following a specific secular philosophy or adhering to the practices of a trendy diet plan)

After one minute, ask learners to evaluate their lists by considering how much energy they put into following those practices or adhering to those traditions.

Ask the following questions for whole-class discussion: 1–In what ways did these practices or traditions complicate your life? 2–What did these practices or traditions promise that made them appealing? 3–What made you realize these practices or traditions couldn't fulfill their promises?

Alternative. Distribute copies of the "Real or Fake?" exercise from the activity page, which you can download. Have learners complete it individually in a minute or less before discussing conclusions with a partner.

After calling time for either activity, lead into Scripture study by saying, "Today's lesson will examine Paul's message to the Colossians regarding wrong assumptions that added to the gospel message."

Into the Word

Before class time, ask a volunteer to prepare a five-minute presentation on the lesson context. The volunteer can use online resources, Bible commentaries, and even the Lesson Context portion of the commentary to teach the class about the diverse elements of the heresy faced in Colossae.

Divide learners into pairs. Distribute handouts (you create) with these prompts and questions for pairs to discuss: Read Colossians 2:16-19. 1–Based on the Scripture reading and Lesson Context, what possible rituals or traditions was Paul addressing? 2–What are one or two modern-day rituals or traditions that challenge our faithfulness to Christ? Read Colossians 2:20-23. 3–What are the results of believers being "dead with Christ"? 4–How does freedom in Christ allow people to break free from worldly norms? After 10 minutes, have pairs gather with other pairs to review their answers.

Into Life

Ask a volunteer to read Colossians 2:6-15 aloud. Ask the following question for whole-class discussion: "How does a believer's receiving Christ Jesus as Lord empower a person to break free of the desires of the flesh?"

Distribute an index card and pen to each learner. In the same pairs as previously divided, have learners discuss the implications of being considered "dead with Christ." Have learners write down those implications on one side of the index card.

Say, "It's one thing to *know* what it means to be 'dead with Christ,' but it's another thing to apply that meaning." Have learners flip over the index card and write a sentence about how to make the implications of being "dead with Christ" a personal reality.

Say, "As Paul alluded to in Colossians 2:19, believers are all part of one body, with Christ Jesus as its head. Therefore, growing in faith is not a solo work, but it is done with the support of other believers." Have learners write the name of an accountability partner for whom learners can ask for support regarding the previous point. Encourage learners to reach out to their accountability partners and discuss accountability regarding the written-down implications.

Alternative. Distribute copies of the "Stay Connected" exercise from the activity page. Have learners work in pairs to complete as indicated. Welcome the sharing of the word clouds at the end of this class or the beginning of the next one.

November 26
Lesson 13 (KJV)

Freedom to Edify

Devotional Reading: James 1:19-27
Background Scripture: 1 Corinthians 8; 10:23–11:1

1 Corinthians 10:23–11:1

23 All things are lawful for me, but all things are not expedient: all things are lawful for me, but all things edify not.

24 Let no man seek his own, but every man another's wealth.

25 Whatsoever is sold in the shambles, that eat, asking no question for conscience sake:

26 For the earth is the Lord's, and the fulness thereof.

27 If any of them that believe not bid you to a feast, and ye be disposed to go; whatsoever is set before you, eat, asking no question for conscience sake.

28 But if any man say unto you, This is offered in sacrifice unto idols, eat not for his sake that shewed it, and for conscience sake: for the earth is the Lord's, and the fulness thereof:

29 Conscience, I say, not thine own, but of the other: for why is my liberty judged of another man's conscience?

30 For if I by grace be a partaker, why am I evil spoken of for that for which I give thanks?

31 Whether therefore ye eat, or drink, or whatsoever ye do, do all to the glory of God.

32 Give none offence, neither to the Jews, nor to the Gentiles, nor to the church of God:

33 Even as I please all men in all things, not seeking mine own profit, but the profit of many, that they may be saved.

11:1 Be ye followers of me, even as I also am of Christ.

Key Text

All things are lawful for me, but all things edify not. **—1 Corinthians 10:23b**

God's Law
Is Love

Unit 3: Christ Frees, Law Enslaves
Lessons 10–13

Lesson Aims

After participating in this lesson, each learner will be able to:

1. Identify the text quoted in 1 Corinthians 10:26.

2. Explain Paul's understanding of the role of one's conscience.

3. Make a plan to eliminate one personal practice that has a high chance causing a fellow Christian to stumble.

Lesson Outline

Introduction
- A. No Place for Selfies
- B. Lesson Context: The City
- C. Lesson Context: The Church

I. Exercising Freedom (1 Corinthians 10:23-30)
- A. Self-Centered Behavior (v. 23)
  - *Your Self-Imposed Limits?*
- B. Others-Centered Behavior (v. 24)
- C. Principles Illustrated (vv. 25-30)
  - *Conscientious Eating*

II. Exercising Responsibility (1 Corinthians 10:31–11:1)
- A. To Glorify God (v. 31)
- B. To Help Others (vv. 32-33)
- C. To Follow Jesus (11:1)

Conclusion
- A. "He Made Us Better"
- B. Prayer
- C. Thought to Remember

Introduction

A. No Place for Selfies

By definition, a "selfie" is a photo that includes the person taking the picture. Selfies have become routine in modern life, but some claim that the first selfie was actually taken in the year 1839! That was the year when Robert Cornelius, an amateur chemist and photographer, took a picture of himself in the back of his family's chandelier store. The word *selfie* was not used back then, not appearing in print until 2002. Gaining in popular usage, the word was chosen as "Word of the Year" by the Oxford English Dictionary in 2013.

Selfies flirt with the concept of self-centeredness since by nature they always include—and often focus on—the person taking the picture. And one does not need a smartphone camera to engage in self-centered behavior. That fact has been evident ever since the serpent successfully tempted Eve into thinking that eating from the tree of the knowledge of good and evil would benefit her, putting her on the level of divinity (Genesis 3:5). Self-centered thinking and behavior inevitably result in sin (James 1:14-15).

When the apostle Paul describes characteristics of life in "the last days," he includes among them the fact that people will be "lovers of their own selves" (2 Timothy 3:1-2). Self-centeredness in the Corinthian church had resulted in the abuse of Christian freedom to the detriment of many. That was just one of many problems that Paul had to address in his first letter to that church—self-centeredness may even have been the basis of those other problems.

B. Lesson Context: The City

The city of Corinth was one of the great centers of commerce in the Mediterranean world of the first century AD. It was located near a narrow strip of land (an isthmus) that connected two major land masses. The city had a harbor for the Saronic Gulf and Aegean Sea to the east (at Cenchrea; see Acts 18:18) and another harbor for the Gulf of Corinth and Adriatic Sea to the west (at Lechaion). Maritime traffic between Asia and Rome had a choice of routes: either the dangerous and longer route around the Peloponnesian Peninsula or the shortcut of a four-mile limestone trackway between Corinth's two harbors. Merchants choosing the latter would pay to have their ships hauled in their entirety from one harbor to the other on this road.

Like many seaport cities, Corinth was quite worldly and eclectic in nature. Pagan temples and the idolatry they represented characterized the city (compare Acts 17:16 regarding Athens, some 50 miles to the east). The contents of 1 Corinthians indicate that many in the church there had struggled to overcome practices of their former pagan lifestyles (see 1 Corinthians 6:9-11).

C. Lesson Context: The Church

Having planted the church in Corinth on his second missionary journey (about AD 52; see Acts 18:1-17), Paul found it necessary to write to its members while he was in Ephesus on his third journey (AD 56; Acts 19:1–20:38; 1 Corinthians 16:8, 19). Paul was headed toward Corinth at the time (Acts 20:1-3), but Ephesus was several days away by sea travel, and the situation couldn't wait for a personal visit. Reports had come to Paul regarding needed correctives and clarifications in Corinth (1 Corinthians 1:11; 7:1; see also lesson 11).

In 1 Corinthians 8, Paul had introduced the difficult issue (for that time) of eating meat that had been offered on pagan altars to idols. Meat that was left over from a pagan sacrifice, initiated by a worshipper who had brought the sacrificial animal, was at the disposal of the officiating priests. What they couldn't eat personally they would sell in the marketplace. Such meat would be less expensive than other meat because the pagan priests didn't have any investment to recover. Some Christians wondered about the propriety of buying such meat. In doing so, were they participating in pagan worship and thus compromising their witness for Christ?

In this regard, Paul emphasizes two points in 1 Corinthians 8. The first is the awareness that an idol is "nothing" (8:4); therefore those who are mature in knowledge on this point were free to eat such meat. Paul's second point counterbalances the first: "But take heed lest by any means this liberty of yours become a stumblingblock to them that are weak" (8:9). This stresses the importance of demonstrating concern for those having a weak conscience. Such a person might witness a fellow believer eating meat that had been offered to idols and thereby be drawn back into idolatry. Paul had more to say on this issue, and that is today's text.

I. Exercising Freedom

(1 Corinthians 10:23-30)

A. Self-Centered Behavior (v. 23)

23a. All things are lawful for me, but all things are not expedient:

The two statements in this half-verse are almost an exact repeat in the Greek of what Paul previously stated in 1 Corinthians 6:12a. The statement *all things are lawful for me* appears to have been something of a proverb among the Corinthian believers. Perhaps they created it to justify certain behaviors in light of their freedom in Christ.

In response, Paul points out something the Corinthians apparently had not considered: the issue of what is legally permissible should be considered alongside the issue of what is *expedient*. The word being translated occurs in contexts that address things that are advantageous (compare Acts 20:20; 2 Corinthians 8:10; 12:1).

23b. All things are lawful for me, but all things edify not.

The first of these two statements is almost identical to 1 Corinthians 6:12b. Again, Paul does not outright challenge the truthfulness of the statement. Instead, he sets alongside it another important consideration as he calls on the idea of *edify* (see also three uses in 1 Corinthians 14:4, 17).

As in 1 Corinthians 8, Christian freedom must not be exercised in a manner that considers only

How to Say It

Adriatic	Ay-dree-*at*-ic.
Aegean	A-*jee*-un.
Cenchrea	*Sen*-kree-uh.
isthmus	*i*-smes.
Peloponnesian	*Pell*-uh-puh-**ne**-shen.

what is legally allowable (see the Lesson Context). There is a bigger issue at stake: the impact of one's actions on others.

> **What Do You Think?**
> What is the first example that comes to mind of something you are free to do but do not do because it is not expedient?
>
> **Digging Deeper**
> Are you more motivated by your own edification or others'? What difference might you see in your behavior if you considered the ***opposite*** first?

Your Self-Imposed Limits?

"What's your verse?" my friend snarled. "Where in the Bible does it say that it's wrong for me to sleep next to my girlfriend as long as we're celibate?"

My wife and I had asked our guests to sleep in different beds because they were unmarried. Our guest room is right next to the bedroom of our young children, who were learning what to believe about relationships and marriage. (In retrospect, I could have made my expectation clear in advance, but I did not anticipate that they intended to share a bed.)

In response, I didn't quote any Scripture to him, though we had a two-hour conversation and prayed together. It seemed to end well, but he grew angry again and left for a hotel at 1:00 a.m.

Later as I pondered his question "What's your verse?", 1 Corinthians 10:23 came to mind. Our hearts can go to great lengths to justify our actions in terms of the freedoms we enjoy in Christ. But to consider what effect our actions could have on others requires spiritual maturity.

Here's a quick self-check: When an opportunity arises to do something, go somewhere, etc., is your primary thought about what you desire for yourself or about how your choice may influence others? —N. G.

B. Others-Centered Behavior (v. 24)

24. Let no man seek his own, but every man another's wealth.

You may notice that the word *wealth* is italicized in the *King James Version*. That means there's no word in the Greek text being translated, but the translators needed to supply a word for smooth reading. Wealth in this context implies the spiritual enrichment of another person. The principle that Paul sets forth here is entirely consistent with his instruction to other churches (examples: Romans 15:2; Philippians 2:4).

> **What Do You Think?**
> What fears prevent you from considering others' benefit before your own?
>
> **Digging Deeper**
> What examples of God's care (from the Bible and your own experience) help you to overcome these fears?

C. Principles Illustrated (vv. 25-30)

25-26. Whatsoever is sold in the shambles, that eat, asking no question for conscience' sake: for the earth is the Lord's, and the fulness thereof.

Paul continues to affirm Christian freedom regarding an issue of his day (see also Lesson Context). The word *shambles* carries for modern readers a negative image of a place that is rundown and in a state of disrepair. At one time, the word designated a place of slaughter or bloodshed, and it came to be used of places where animals were butchered and the meat sold. See the Lesson Context regarding how the meat being *sold* could be recognized as being associated with a pagan sacrifice.

As we read the two verses before us, we may be inclined to think in terms of the clean/unclean issue regarding food in Mark 7:19 and Acts 10:15 as setting aside the dietary restrictions of Leviticus 11 (compare Romans 14:14). But that's not the point here. Rather, Paul is reaffirming the reality of a Christian's freedom to buy and *eat* marketplace food, regardless of its association with paganism. Psalm 24:1 is quoted in support of this reality.

27. If any of them that believe not bid you to a feast, and ye be disposed to go; whatsoever is set before you, eat, asking no question for conscience' sake.

Paul then sets forth a hypothetical scenario in which an unbeliever invites a Christian *to a feast.* Whether such a feast takes place "in the idol's temple" (1 Corinthians 8:10) or elsewhere isn't Paul's stress at the moment. Rather, he is stressing that this could be considered an "open door" that presents an opportunity to share the gospel. This may be compared to the times when Jesus was invited to dine with those considered "sinners" (Luke 5:29-30). Again, one's freedom in Christ allows eating *whatever is set before* him or her.

Conscientious Eating

"It's called *taulo,*" my host said as he handed me a plate of noodle-like medallions. "From cow intestines."

I took the plate, thanked him, and sat in the shade of a tree. The medallions were chewy and fibrous, not unlike the texture of a towel. But I ate them without offending my host in southeast Tanzania. I had a harder time with pots of okra slime in North Africa. Even today I gag at the memory of the taste and texture.

Let's make sure, however, that we distinguish matters of *conscience* from matters of *taste.* The above two foods weren't to my taste, but I ate them anyway to avoid insulting my hosts. What Paul is talking about, however, is what should not be allowed to bother our moral center in Christ. If we allow something to bother us that should not be consider immoral, then we risk losing a chance for a gospel-interaction with unbelievers.

There are plenty of culture-specific ideas "out there" that are foreign to both you and me. The question is, Which ones are bothersome to my conscience, but not to God? —N. G.

28-29a. But if any man say unto you, This is offered in sacrifice unto idols, eat not for his sake that showed it, and for conscience' sake: for the earth is the Lord's, and the fulness thereof: Conscience, I say, not thine own, but of the other.

Paul briefly departs from his main line of thought to deal with a related issue: another person's *conscience.* Suppose the host at a meal informed his Christian guest that the meat being served had been part of a pagan sacrificial offering. In that case, the believer is to refrain from eating. Given the host's statement, to eat of this meat could be seen by the host as an acknowledgement of the idol by the Christian. Thus the host is potentially led astray (see especially 1 Corinthians 8:7).

The earliest manuscripts of the New Testament do not have the phrase *for the earth is the Lord's, and the fulness thereof,* which is from Psalm 24:1. But since there is no doubt that it is indeed quoted at 1 Corinthians 10:26, above, we are certain it is part of Paul's thought.

What Do You Think?

In what circumstances do you defer to another person's sense of conscience?

Digging Deeper

What parameters help you determine whether to defer to another or instead to defend your freedom to choose differently?

29b-30. For why is my liberty judged of another man's conscience? For if I by grace be a partaker, why am I evil spoken of for that for which I give thanks?

Sorting out the complexities of Paul's statements is a matter of some debate among many students. One proposal is that Paul is now resuming his main line of thought after the parenthetical verse-and-a-half just considered. In so doing, the apostle restates his freedom to eat his own choice of food and not be paranoid about what others think. Thus there's a certain tension between freedom and restraint. We saw this tension earlier in the first verse of this lesson (1 Corinthians 10:23). At the point of 10:29, where we are now, Paul seems to be leaning a bit more toward the freedom side of the two actions because of freedom's evangelistic potential.

II. Exercising Responsibility

(1 Corinthians 10:31-33–11:1)

A. To Glorify God (v. 31)

31. Whether therefore ye eat, or drink, or whatsoever ye do, do all to the glory of God.

Our last section maintains the tension between freedom and restraint. But now a vital context is presented: that of doing *all to the glory of God.* Christians today are rarely, if ever, faced with the issue of eating meat offered to idols. But there are modern parallels. And no matter what difficult (and easy) choices we face, we must honor this imperative.

The privilege and duty of all creation to glorify God is a theme that permeates Scripture (examples: Psalm 19:1-6; Romans 11:36; 2 Corinthians 1:20; 4:15). This requirement transcends all times, places, and cultures. Sharing meals was one way the first-century believers brought glory to God (Acts 2:42; contrast 1 Corinthians 11:20-22), and it can be so today as well. Paradoxically, we are the freest when we think least of ourselves in our desire to please the one who is our Creator, Ruler, and Redeemer (1 Thessalonians 4:1; Hebrews 11:6). In so doing, we follow the example of Jesus who "pleased not himself" (Romans 15:3), but who humbled himself in an unparalleled way (Philippians 2:5-8, 11).

What Do You Think?

How can your mealtimes remind you to give glory to God in *all* situations?

Digging Deeper

How can other mundane tasks become reminders to glorify God?

B. To Help Others (vv. 32-33)

32a. Give none offense.

Here we see another vital imperative regarding conduct. In contrast to the positive imperative of the previous verse, this one is stated as a negative—what not to do.

To grasp the full meaning, we must consider the nature of the phrase *give none offense.* The Greek word being translated is rarely found in literature of the era. It occurs in the New Testament also in Acts 24:16 and Philippians 1:10 In all cases the foundational idea is that of neither causing offense (in terms of not causing to stumble) nor taking offense (meaning to have a clear conscience). A closely related word, spelled nearly the same, is found in John 11:9, 10; Romans 9:32; 14:21; 2 Corinthians 6:3; and 1 Peter 2:8. All these occurrences refer to stumbling in a spiritual sense. These passages as seen in their respective contexts indicate that the word *offense* is not to be understood as merely an insult or affront; Paul uses different words for that action.

32b-33. Neither to the Jews, nor to the Gentiles, nor to the church of God: Even as I please all men in all things, not seeking mine own profit, but the profit of many, that they may be saved.

The imperative is all-inclusive, and the reason is clear: Paul wants to be able to have the widest hearing possible for the gospel. Given his desire that everyone—Jew and Gentile alike—*be saved,* Paul states later in this letter that "I am made all things to all *men*, that I might by all means save some" (1 Corinthians 9:22). Were he to focus on his *own profit,* he would be no better than the false prophets of the day. He was determined not to be a stumbling block (2 Corinthians 6:3). This is what he means by not seeking his own profit (Romans 14:1-7; 1 Corinthians 8:13).

Paul points to himself as an example of the kind of conduct he desired the Corinthians to imitate. This was not egotism on his part, simply an honest, straightforward assessment of the kind of man he was. Elsewhere he refers to himself as having served the Lord "with all humility of mind" (Acts 20:19). A cynic would characterize that self-assessment as Paul's having developed a sense of humility he could be proud of. But Paul's actions match his words (next verse).

C. To Follow Jesus (11:1)

1. Be ye followers of me, even as I also am of Christ.

Paul never desired to build a following for himself, as he made clear at the beginning of this epistle (1 Corinthians 1:12-17). He was interested only in building disciples of Jesus—people who shared his passion for knowing Jesus and proclaiming His gospel of grace to others. He lived out the lifestyle he was encouraging his readers to follow: a life that glorified God in every way possible, including the need to edify others. To do that is to embrace the freedom that Jesus promised to all who choose to follow Him (John 8:36; Romans 8:21).

What Do You Think?

Who is the most Christlike role model in your life? What do you see in that person that reminds you of Jesus?

Digging Deeper

How can you follow his or her example even if that role model is not present with you?

Conclusion

A. "He Made Us Better"

A certain Christian publication featured a series of tributes to a Christian leader who had gone to be with the Lord. That this man's life and ministry had an impact on countless numbers of people was clear from the words written about him. Among the tributes included was one statement that caught my attention: "He made us better."

To make others better is part of what it means to edify others—the key word in our lesson title. Sadly, we are surrounded by influences that make us anything but better. The behavior on display in media of many kinds often features and even glorifies the worst in human conduct. These won't make us better except possibly as cautionary tales. As followers of Jesus in a fallen world, we will not win every person with whom we share our faith in Jesus. But we can, as salt and light, seek to make the people we encounter better, or at least add some brightness to their lives, because we brought something of the spirit and character of Jesus into their lives.

Paul's primary concern in our lesson text is making the edification of others a priority within the body of Christ. The example he gives of eating meat offered to idols is not an issue for most believers today. Modern equivalents might be those places and things that observers come to associate with us when they see us—places and things that work against holiness. Do we have Christian freedom to attend movies that are rated other than "G"? Yes, indeed. But how will doing so affect the openness to receive the gospel of those who see us at such movies?

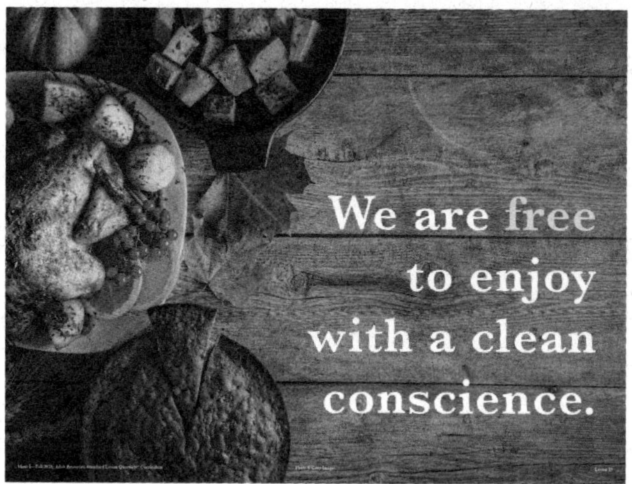

We are free
to enjoy
with a clean
conscience.

Visual for Lesson 13. *Use this visual as a jumping off point to discuss the questions associated with verses 28-29a.*

This is, of course, an all-the-time challenge. It involves our lives out in the public arena, which must be lived with a sense of duty both to glorify God and as a witness to others (believers and unbelievers). It involves the kind of freedom that is anchored in personal holiness (1 Peter 1:15-16), without legalism or hypocrisy (Matthew 23:16-26). It involves foregoing our "rights," as Paul did (1 Corinthians 8:9; 9:15, 18), for the good of others.

Think of the person who introduced you to Christ. That person wasn't perfect, and neither will you be. But that doesn't mean the standard of Matthew 5:48 should be lowered! Resolve to be like the one above who "made us better" as if eternal destinies are at stake—because they are!

As we ponder these things in our hearts, may it be said of us as Paul said of himself near the close of his life, "I endure all things for the elect's sakes, that they may also obtain the salvation which is in Christ Jesus with eternal glory" (2 Timothy 2:10).

B. Prayer

Father, thank You for the freedom in Jesus that liberates people from slavery to sin. In this world where freedom is often misunderstood and abused, help us to represent our freedom in Jesus in a way that honors You and edifies others. In Jesus' name we pray. Amen.

C. Thought to Remember

To edify others is one way to glorify God.

Involvement Learning

Enhance your lesson with KJV Bible Student *(from your curriculum supplier) and the reproducible activity page (at www.standardlesson.com or in the back of the* KJV Standard Lesson Commentary Deluxe Edition*).*

Into the Lesson

Have volunteers share about a time they participated in an activity simply because they could do so. This could be as small as running a 5k or as complicated as taking an extended vacation across the world. Ask them to reflect on what impact—good, bad, or indifferent—their actions had on others, including family, friends, strangers, etc.

Continue by writing the headers *Lawful* and *Builds Up* on the board and discussing the similarities and differences between actions in these two lists. Ask: In valuing personal freedoms, how are we challenged to overemphasize that which is lawful for the individual but perhaps harmful to ourselves or others? If needed, have a personal example ready to start the conversation. Encourage learners to think about their own challenges. Talk about how that relates to the heading on the board.

Alternative. Distribute copies of the "Just Because You Can" exercise from the activity page, which you can download. Have learners work in pairs to complete as indicated. After time is called, allow time for group discussion.

Explain that today's Bible study examines how Paul's message to the Corinthians roots this message in our faith, including our call to be salt and light to others.

Into the Word

Ask a volunteer to read 1 Corinthians 10:23–11:1 out loud. Divide the class in half. Distribute handouts (you create) of these questions for in-group discussion: 1–How does Paul contrast self-centeredness with other-centered thinking (1 Corinthians 10:23-24)? 2–How can one create a balance between exercising one's freedom in Christ and not hindering another person's growth in Christ?

Ask one half of the class to research the morality of Corinth and its inhabitants at the time of Paul. Ask the other half to research the Corinthians' practice of selling meat in the open market that came from animals sacrificed in pagan temples. Supplement their research with information from the lesson commentary. Then invite someone to read aloud 1 Corinthians 10:25-30. Lead a discussion to answer these questions: 1–Why was this meat practice a problem for some Christians and not for others? 2–What would have been the telltale signs of crossing from a celebratory feast into a gluttonous one?

Alternative. Distribute copies of the "How Shall We Act?" exercise on the activity page. Have learners work in pairs or groups of three to complete as indicated.

Ask a volunteer to read 1 Corinthians 10:31–11:1. Discuss what it means to do whatever you do to the glory of God. Have learners give examples from the Bible of glorifying God.

Into Life

Draw parallels between first-century Corinth and our culture today. Brainstorm together a list of social practices that may cause others to stumble or question either your faith or their own. If applicable, refer to the list created at the beginning of the lesson. Be careful that this doesn't become a discussion of what is right or wrong.

Distribute note cards and pens to participants. Allow a minute for learners to write down a personal practice that causes fellow Christians to stumble or question their faith. Then allow a few minutes for participants to write a plan to stop that practice.

Close with a prayer time asking for God's guidance in implementing those plans. Include prayers for understanding and tolerance when encountering others who do not always share their convictions about what is beneficial in the Christian life.

Faith That Pleases God

Special Features

Lessons

Unit 1: Profiles in Faith

Unit 2: Learning About Faith

Unit 3: The Righteous Live by Faith

Quarterly Quiz

Use these questions as a pretest or as a review. The answers are on page iv of This Quarter in the Word.

Lesson 1

1. Naomi said that she was too _____ to have a husband. *Ruth 1:12*

2. Naomi and Ruth arrived in Bethlehem at the end of the barley harvest. T/F. *Ruth 1:22*

Lesson 2

1. David fought which animals? (Choose two: boar, bear, lion, snake) *1 Samuel 17:34*

2. The Philistine came to David with a sword, a spear, and a _________. *1 Samuel 17:45*

Lesson 3

1. Jesus is "the son of David, the son of _________." *Matthew 1:1*

2. Matthew's genealogy is grouped into three sets of fourteen generations. T/F. *Matthew 1:17*

Lesson 4

1. After the baby leaped in Elisabeth's womb, who or what filled her? (wisdom, peace, the Holy Ghost) *Luke 1:41*

2. Mary stayed with Elisabeth for six months before returning home. T/F. *Luke 1:56*

Lesson 5

1. Jesus was born when ______ was king. *Matthew 2:1*

2. When the wise men saw the star, they were filled with fear. T/F. *Matthew 2:10*

Lesson 6

1. Who offered "a more excellent sacrifice" to God? (Abraham, Cain, Abel) *Hebrews 11:4*

2. Who gave deathbed instructions regarding his bones? (Isaac, Jacob, Joseph) *Hebrews 11:22*

Lesson 7

1. The son is commanded to bind what around his neck? (Choose two: grace, peace, mercy, truth) *Proverbs 3:3*

2. The son is commanded to "trust in the Lord" with all his strength. T/F. *Proverbs 3:5*

Lesson 8

1. The people of Judah were reminded that "the ________ is not yours, but God's." *2 Chronicles 20:15*

2. Levites stood up and praised the Lord with a loud _________. *2 Chronicles 20:19*

Lesson 9

1. Members of the body do not have the same "office." T/F. *Romans 12:4*

2. Believers have different gifts according to the ________ that is given. *Romans 12:6*

Lesson 10

1. What is another given title for "the everlasting God, the Lord"? (Creator, Sustainer, Provider) *Isaiah 40:28*

2. Those who wait on the Lord will be renewed. T/F. *Isaiah 40:31*

Lesson 11

1. Nebuchadnezzar ordered that the furnace be heated how many times hotter than normal? (three, seven, fourteen) *Daniel 3:19*

2. Nebuchadnezzar described the fourth man in the fire as appearing like an angel. T/F. *Daniel 3:25*

Lesson 12

1. Daniel kneeled and prayed four times a day. T/F. *Daniel 6:10*

2. Daniel told the king that God had sent "his _______" to shut the lions' mouths. *Daniel 6:22*

Lesson 13

1. Habakkuk will stand watch on the _________. *Habakkuk 2:1*

2. The just person will live by his _________. *Habakkuk 2:4*

Quarter at a Glance

by Jon Miller

This quarter's lessons examine how individuals from Scripture lived faithful lives that pleased God. Their stories reveal how we can honor God through our lives of faith. Without faith, our attempts to please God will fall short (see Hebrews 11:6).

Profiles in Faith

This quarter begins by exploring the faith of various people from Scripture. One person who demonstrated unwavering faith is Ruth the Moabite. Because of her faith, she had confidence that the Lord would be with her and her mother-in-law, even in desperate circumstances (see Ruth 1:16-17, lesson 1).

Demonstrating faith is not easy; sometimes faith requires that people stand alone. The young shepherd David faced this reality as he confronted the Philistine (see 1 Samuel 17:45, lesson 2). In doing so, David went against the expectations of his people and his king (see 17:31-33).

Likewise, it was not easy for Mary, a young, unwed pregnant woman in the first century AD. After receiving a word from God, she joined her pregnant relative Elisabeth. Together the women expressed faith in God's plan and His promises (see Luke 1:39-45, lesson 4). Similarly, certain wise men faced threats to their lives as they followed God's directives (see Matthew 2:1-12, lesson 5). Living with faith requires boldness to act and a trust that God will sustain.

Faith and Confidence

Faith is "the substance of things hoped for, the evidence of things not seen" (Hebrews 11:1, lesson 6). Faith demands that we trust the Lord rather than ourselves (see Proverbs 3:5, lesson 7). King Jehoshaphat demonstrates one example of confident faith. Enemies had come against Judah, resulting in the people's fear. However, the Spirit of the Lord came upon Jahaziel the Levite, who reminded King Jehoshaphat that the battle belonged to the Lord and the Lord alone (see 2 Chronicles 20:15, lesson 8).

Christians have another reason to be confident: despite life's challenges, we do not live that life alone. The apostle Paul taught that through faith, Christians become "one body" with other believers (Romans 12:5, lesson 9). As members of that body, we receive spiritual gifts that we can use to serve and encourage the whole body (12:6-8).

Living by Faith

The final unit highlights the role of faith in challenging situations. The prophet Isaiah encouraged Israel to consider how creation reveals God's power (Isaiah 40:26, lesson 10). The all-powerful God who created everything is worthy of receiving our trust, even when we may feel insignificant.

Faith demands that we trust the Lord rather than ourselves.

Living with faith does not mean we will never face trials. Instead, living with faith means trusting that the God of creation will never leave us. After Shadrach, Meshach, and Abednego refused the king's command to worship an image of gold, they were thrown into the flaming furnace (see Daniel 3:19-23, lesson 11). They had confidence that God would be faithful to them, even if He chose not to save them. In the same way, Daniel demonstrated a life of faith as he continued in prayer, even though doing so might have significantly cost him (see 6:10-11, lesson 12). He trusted in God's power, even when grave consequences seemed inevitable.

When life's hardships overwhelm us or when we can't make sense of the world, Scripture tells us that "the just shall live by . . . faith" (Habakkuk 2:4, lesson 13). God's people are marked by their faith, even in situations that seem entirely out of control.

Get the Setting

by Jon Miller

Travel woes have always beset people. Though we have many innovations today that make travel easier than ever before, travelers still face abundant frustrations. Bad weather, canceled flights, mechanical problems, poor roads, closed gas stations—any number of factors make travel more interesting than we would prefer.

Our modern problems pale in comparison to the difficulty and danger of travel in the ancient world. We can broadly consider travel before the Roman Empire (times recorded in the Old Testament) and then in the time of the Empire (times recorded in the New Testament). The influence of Greek culture and Roman ingenuity changed travel. Comparing the two can help us better understand the preparation and effort people had to make even to complete a short trip.

Travel in the Old Testament

Travelers in the Old Testament faced many challenges, so people did not venture far from home without good reason. One primary reason for travel was finding land for livestock to graze. Joseph's brothers traveled about 60 miles to Shechem and later to Dothan to find pastures for their father's flock (Genesis 37:12-17). Another motivation for travel was a natural disaster or famine at home, such as what drove Joseph's brothers to Egypt (Genesis 42). People also traveled for religious reasons (Psalm 122). Longer trade journeys grew in the Bronze Age, and Solomon brought the Israelites into international commerce (1 Kings 10:20-29).

For those who could afford them, several beasts of burden could make travel easier. Donkeys were used to transport provisions (example: Genesis 22:3). Oxen would pull carts or wagons (example: Numbers 7:3-8), though most roads were not suitable for heavy traffic. Camels were also a great benefit (examples: Genesis 24:61; 30:43; 31:17).

A trip in ancient times required much planning and preparation (example: Judges 19:19). The Bible mentions lodging, but it was usually out of the way for travelers and insufficient for large groups of people and animals (example: Exodus 4:24). Thus, travelers often were at the mercy of the people residing in the towns and villages they passed through (examples: 2 Samuel 17:27-29; Isaiah 21:14-15). One part of Job's defense of his righteousness was his practice of hospitality for travelers (Job 31:32). Besides these difficulties, travelers were in danger of thieves (whether in a strange town or on their way) and wild beasts (consider Genesis 19:1-11; Judges 9:25; Isaiah 30:6).

Travel in the New Testament

Rome changed the ancient Near Eastern world, including travel. With the rule of law and improved roads in Rome, travel became much safer, and people traveled long distances. Modes of transportation came to include horses, chariots, and ships in addition to the camels and donkeys of before (Matthew 21:2; Acts 8:25-38; 23:23-24; 2 Corinthians 11:25-26). Ordinary people still traveled by foot.

Business and commerce were the primary reasons for traveling in the New Testament. People might also travel great distances for religious reasons, as seen at Pentecost (Acts 2:5-11).

Given what we now know about travel from the Old and New Testaments, we can read differently the passages in this quarter that approach travel. We still travel for many of the same reasons that we read about in the Bible. However, a great gulf separates our present-day world from theirs. Their travel took longer, required fastidious preparation and trust in the hospitality of strangers, and was very frequently dangerous. When we read that someone in the Bible traveled from one place to another, it was a decision not made on a whim. They traveled with purpose!

Mon, Feb. 12	**Fear God, Not Pharaoh**	Exodus 1:8-21
Tue, Feb. 13	**Why Are You Afraid?**	Matthew 8:18-27
Wed, Feb. 14	**Do Not Let Your Hearts Be Troubled**	John 14:1-11
Thu, Feb. 15	**Earthly and Heavenly Authority**	John 19:1-11
Fri, Feb. 16	**God Cares for the Flock**	1 Peter 5
Sat, Feb. 17	**Unfazed by a Blasphemous Law**	Daniel 6:1-15
Sun, Feb. 18	**Delivered from the Lions**	Daniel 6:10-11, 14, 16, 19-23, 26-27
Mon, Feb. 19	**God's Plan for Welfare and Hope**	Jeremiah 29:8-14
Tue, Feb. 20	**In Christ, All Things Were Created**	Colossians 1:13-20
Wed, Feb. 21	**God Will Complete God's Work**	Philippians 1:3-11
Thu, Feb. 22	**God Works for Our Good**	Romans 8:19-28
Fri, Feb. 23	**God Plans Our Steps**	Proverbs 16:1-9
Sat, Feb. 24	**God's Consuming Judgment**	Habakkuk 1:5-17
Sun, Feb. 25	**Living by Faith**	Habakkuk 2:1-5

Answers to the Quarterly Quiz on page 114

Lesson 1—1. old. 2. False. **Lesson 2**—1. shield. 2. lion, bear. **Lesson 3**—1. Abraham. 2. True. **Lesson 4**—1. Holy Ghost. 2. False. **Lesson 5**—1. Herod. 2. False. **Lesson 6**—1. Abel. 2. Joseph. **Lesson 7**—1. mercy, truth. 2. False. **Lesson 8**—1. battle. 2. voice. **Lesson 9**—1. True. 2. grace. **Lesson 10**—1. Creator. 2. True. **Lesson 11**—1. seven. 2. False. **Lesson 12**—1. False. 2. angel. **Lesson 13**—1. tower. 2. faith.

This Quarter in the Word

Mon, Nov. 27	**A Faithful Friendship**	Proverbs 17:17-22
Tue, Nov. 28	**Peter's Test of Faith**	Matthew 26:31-35
Wed, Nov. 29	**Hear God's Voice**	Hebrews 3:7-19
Thu, Nov. 30	**Faith in Action**	Leviticus 19:30-37
Fri, Dec. 1	**God Honors Genuine Faith**	Acts 10:34-48
Sat, Dec. 2	**Naomi Becomes a Grandmother**	Ruth 4:13-22
Sun, Dec. 3	**Ruth's Compassionate Faith**	Ruth 1:6-18, 22
Mon, Dec. 4	**Faith and Courage**	Joshua 1:1-9
Tue, Dec. 5	**The Son of Man Came to Serve**	Matthew 20:25-34
Wed, Dec. 6	**Ask in Faith**	Matthew 21:18-22
Thu, Dec. 7	**The Faithful Will Wait on the Lord**	Psalm 27
Fri, Dec. 8	**Rekindle God's Gift and Stand Firm**	2 Timothy 1:3-14
Sat, Dec. 9	**Israel's Wavering Faith**	1 Samuel 17:1, 3-4, 8, 20-30
Sun, Dec. 10	**Faith That God Will Act**	1 Samuel 17:31-37, 45, 48-50
Mon, Dec. 11	**Risk-taking Faith**	Genesis 38:6-11, 13-18, 24-26
Tue, Dec. 12	**Rahab's Faith**	Joshua 2:1-6, 8-16
Wed, Dec. 13	**Patient Faith**	James 5:1-11
Thu, Dec. 14	**God's Grace Overflowed**	1 Timothy 1:12-17
Fri, Dec. 15	**Bathsheba's Challenged Faith**	2 Samuel 11:1-5, 26–12:1, 4-7a,15-16, 24
Sat, Dec. 16	**The Stronghold for the Oppressed**	Psalm 9:1-14
Sun, Dec. 17	**A Family Tree of Faith**	Matthew 1:1-17

Mon, Dec. 18	**Contentment in Every Situation**	Philippians 4:10-19
Tue, Dec. 19	**God Is My Refuge**	Psalm 91:1-16
Wed, Dec. 20	**The Lord Has Done Great Things!**	Joel 2:18-27
Thu, Dec. 21	**The Announcement to a Priest**	Luke 1:5-17
Fri, Dec. 22	**Doubt and Rejoicing**	Luke 1:18-25
Sat, Dec. 23	**Believe!**	John 20:19, 24-29
Sun, Dec. 24	**Women Express Faith**	Luke 1:36-45, 56
Mon, Dec. 25	**Christ the Savior Is Born**	Matthew 1:18-25
Tue, Dec. 26	**Mary's Exultant Faith**	Luke 1:46-55
Wed, Dec. 27	**Reject Imitations of Faith**	Deuteronomy 18:9-14
Thu, Dec. 28	**Make Disciples in Faith**	Matthew 28:16-20
Fri, Dec. 29	**God's Salvation for All the Earth**	Isaiah 49:1-6
Sat, Dec. 30	**Arise, Shine; Your Light Has Come**	Isaiah 60:1-6
Sun, Dec. 31	**Worship the King of the Jews**	Matthew 2:1-12
Mon, Jan. 1	**The Lord Is Our King**	Isaiah 33:15-22
Tue, Jan. 2	**Show Favor to Your People**	Psalm 106:1-12
Wed, Jan. 3	**The Faith of Israel's Ancestors**	Hebrews 11:20-29
Thu, Jan. 4	**The Victory of Faith**	Hebrews 11:32-40
Fri, Jan. 5	**God's Covenant Prevails**	Psalm 106:13, 26-27, 42-48
Sat, Jan. 6	**Righteousness Through Jesus Christ**	Romans 5:12-21
Sun, Jan. 7	**Assurance and Conviction Through Faith**	Hebrews 11:1-4a, 7a, 8, 17-18, 20-23, 32, 39-40
Mon, Jan. 8	**God's Word Lights My Path**	Psalm 119:97-112
Tue, Jan. 9	**Rest to the Weary**	Matthew 11:25-30
Wed, Jan. 10	**I Put My Trust in God**	Psalm 56
Thu, Jan. 11	**Trust in the Unchanging Lord**	Hebrews 13:5-16
Fri, Jan. 12	**I Will Not Leave You Orphaned**	John 14:18-27
Sat, Jan. 13	**God's Surpassing Wisdom**	1 Corinthians 2:6-16
Sun, Jan. 14	**A Father's Teaching**	Proverbs 3:1-12

Mon, Jan. 15	**Praise the God Who Comforts**	2 Corinthians 1:3-11
Tue, Jan. 16	**God Delivers Me from My Fears**	Psalm 34:1-10
Wed, Jan. 17	**God's Eyes Are on the Righteous**	Psalm 34:11-22
Thu, Jan. 18	**Encourage One Another**	1 Thessalonians 5:1-15
Fri, Jan. 19	**Rejoice, Pray, and Give Thanks**	1 Thessalonians 5:16-28
Sat, Jan. 20	**Remember God's Power and Might**	2 Chronicles 20:5-12
Sun, Jan. 21	**Do Not Be Dismayed**	2 Chronicles 20:13-20
Mon, Jan. 22	**A New Spirit and Heart**	Ezekiel 11:17-21
Tue, Jan. 23	**A Transforming Testimony**	John 9:17-25
Wed, Jan. 24	**Be Holy, for God Is Holy**	Leviticus 20:22-26
Thu, Jan. 25	**A Prayer for Transformation**	Psalm 51:1-15
Fri, Jan. 26	**God Breathes New Life**	Ezekiel 37:1-14
Sat, Jan. 27	**From Death to Life**	1 John 3:14-24
Sun, Jan. 28	**God Gives Different Gifts**	Romans 12:3-8
Mon, Jan. 29	**Christ Dwells in Your Heart**	Ephesians 3:14-21
Tue, Jan. 30	**Sing of God's Might**	Psalm 89:1-13
Wed, Jan. 31	**Rely on God**	1 Chronicles 16:8-22
Thu, Feb. 1	**God Reigns in Power**	Revelation 11:14-19
Fri, Feb. 2	**The Power of God for Salvation**	Romans 1:8-17
Sat, Feb. 3	**Be Strong in the Lord**	Ephesians 6:10-18
Sun, Feb. 4	**Wait on God, Who Gives Strength**	Isaiah 40:12-13, 25-31
Mon, Feb. 5	**Misdirected Worship**	Daniel 3:1-7
Tue, Feb. 6	**Defying an Immoral Command**	Daniel 3:8-18
Wed, Feb. 7	**Works That Proclaim Truth**	John 10:24-38
Thu, Feb. 8	**When Faith Comes Under Fire**	Acts 4:7-20
Fri, Feb. 9	**We Must Obey God Alone**	Acts 5:17-29
Sat, Feb. 10	**You Will Not Be Burned**	Isaiah 43:1-7
Sun, Feb. 11	**Delivered from the Flames**	Daniel 3:19-28a

Chart Feature

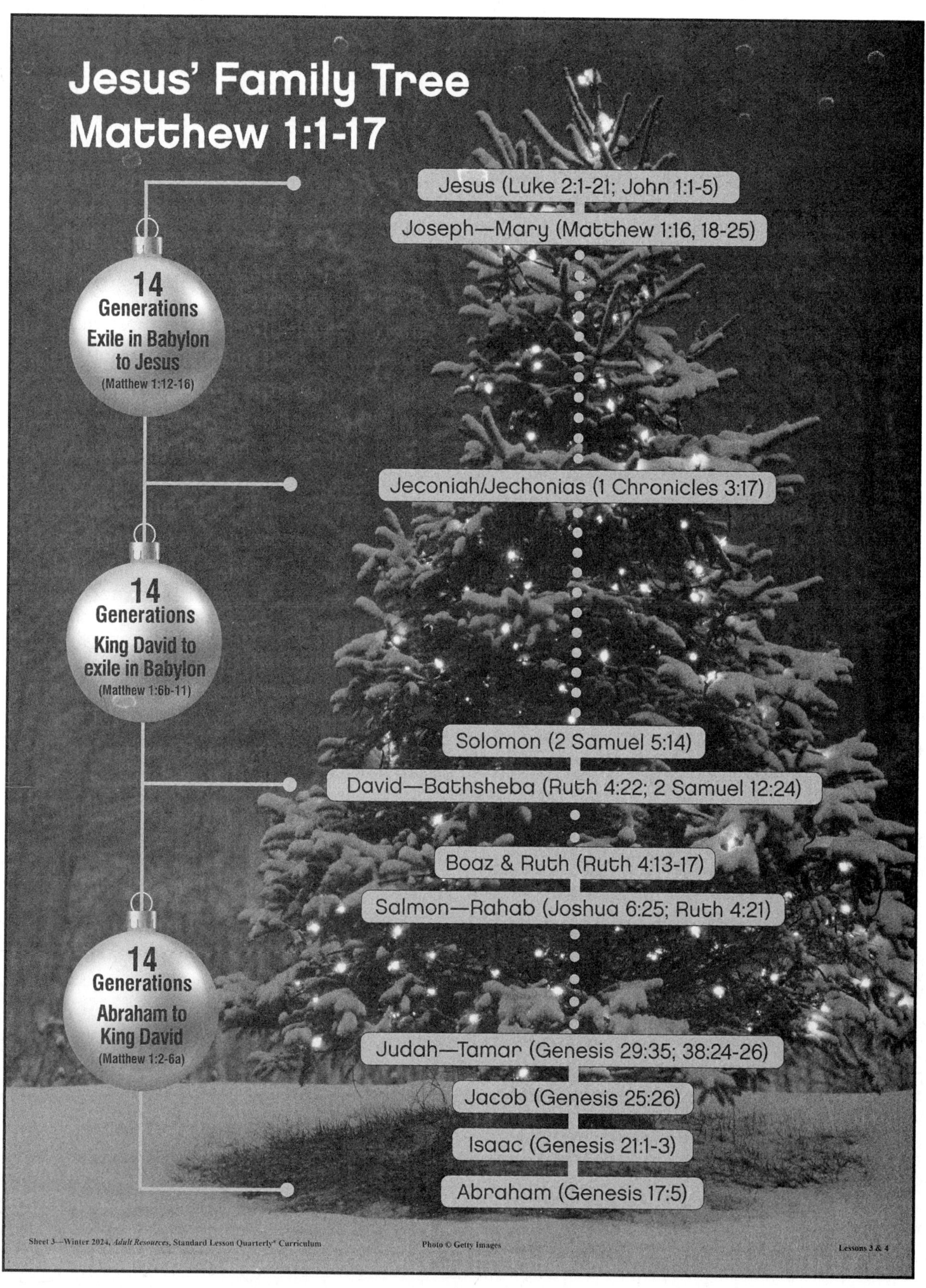
Jesus' Family Tree
Matthew 1:1-17
14
Generations
Exile in Babylon to Jesus
(Matthew 1:12-16)
14
Generations
King David to exile in Babylon
(Matthew 1:6b-11)
14
Generations
Abraham to King David
(Matthew 1:2-6a)
Jesus (Luke 2:1-21; John 1:1-5)
Joseph—Mary (Matthew 1:16, 18-25)
Jeconiah/Jechonias (1 Chronicles 3:17)
Solomon (2 Samuel 5:14)
David—Bathsheba (Ruth 4:22; 2 Samuel 12:24)
Boaz & Ruth (Ruth 4:13-17)
Salmon—Rahab (Joshua 6:25; Ruth 4:21)
Judah—Tamar (Genesis 29:35; 38:24-26)
Jacob (Genesis 25:26)
Isaac (Genesis 21:1-3)
Abraham (Genesis 17:5)
Sheet 3—Winter 2024, *Adult Resources*, Standard Lesson Quarterly® Curriculum
Photo © Getty Images
Lessons 3 & 4

Flexible You?

Teacher Tips by Ronald L. Nickelson

Under what circumstances, if any, should teachers of the Bible be flexible in their teaching? This question can be answered differently depending on whether we're asking about the ***content*** or the ***form*** of our lessons. A cup of coffee illustrates the distinction: the word *content* speaks of what's in the cup—the coffee beverage itself; the word *form* deals with the nature of the cup—its size, shape, etc.

Lesson Content

The content of our lessons is always the same: it's the Bible as to its proper meaning and significance. In this regard, our teaching is to be inflexible. The general command here is from Jesus himself in the passage known as the Great Commission:

> Go ye therefore, and teach all nations. . . . Teaching them to observe all things whatsoever I have commanded. —Matthew 28:19-20

The most densely packed instructions on the specifics of things to be taught and not taught are found in the pastoral epistles of 1 Timothy, 2 Timothy, and Titus.

Unlike the contents of a cup of coffee, however, our flexibility in teaching Bible content is limited by the fact that we are neither to add to nor take away from that content (Revelation 22:18-19). Even so, there must be a bit of flexibility within this inflexibility when we consider the nature of our audience. If our learners are already Christians, we focus on passages that promote spiritual growth (see Ephesians 4:1-16), and the level of their growth will determine whether we focus our teaching on the "milk" or "meat" of the Bible (1 Corinthians 3:2; Hebrews 5:12). But if our learners are unbelievers, the teaching focus would be on evangelistic passages (Acts 2:36-39; etc.).

An example of flexibility in content-focus is the apostle Paul. He taught directly from Scriptures to those who already believed them (Acts 17:2). But to pagan philosophers, he taught on various Scripture themes in a way that did not presume that his audience accepted the reliability (or even existence) of those Scriptures (Acts 17:22-31).

Lesson Form

There are various forms (methods) for teaching Bible content. The *Standard Lesson Commentary* offers three such possibilities in every lesson: lecture, discussion questions, and learning activities. Offering examples of flexibility in this regard are the teaching methods of Jesus. He often used a lecture format; examples are Matthew 5:1-12 and Mark 12:38-40. Examples of a discussion-question method are seen in Matthew 17:25-26; Luke 9:18-20; and John 14:9; 21:15-19. Examples of learning activities are Matthew 14:28-33 and Luke 10:1-17.

At this point, we should pause to consider four cautions. First, we should realize limitations in using Jesus as a model; His being the Son of God means that He was able to do things we cannot. Second, the examples offered above all involve interacting with people who were favorable or at least neutral toward Him; we are not considering methods He used when interacting with opponents. Third, the teaching methods under consideration are not "either/or" but "both/and," as we see elements of two (or all three) methods together in some examples. Fourth, others have analyzed Jesus' teaching methods differently, seeing as few as two and as many as nine methods.

Flexible You?

Are you frozen in one teaching method? Or are you willing and able to adjust your method as situations call for? Flexibility must be part of being "apt to teach" (2 Timothy 2:24). Consider:

> Those who are victorious plan effectively and change decisively. They are like a great river that maintains its course but adjusts its flow. . . . They are skilled in both planning and adapting. —Sun Tzu

The Faith of Ruth

Devotional Reading: Acts 10:34-38
Background Scripture: Ruth 1; 4:13-22

Ruth 1:6-18, 22

6 Then she arose with her daughters in law, that she might return from the country of Moab: for she had heard in the country of Moab how that the LORD had visited his people in giving them bread.

7 Wherefore she went forth out of the place where she was, and her two daughters in law with her; and they went on the way to return unto the land of Judah.

8 And Naomi said unto her two daughters in law, Go, return each to her mother's house: the LORD deal kindly with you, as ye have dealt with the dead, and with me.

9 The LORD grant you that ye may find rest, each of you in the house of her husband. Then she kissed them; and they lifted up their voice, and wept.

10 And they said unto her, Surely we will return with thee unto thy people.

11 And Naomi said, Turn again, my daughters: why will ye go with me? are there yet any more sons in my womb, that they may be your husbands?

12 Turn again, my daughters, go your way; for I am too old to have an husband. If I should say, I have hope, if I should have an husband also to night, and should also bear sons;

13 Would ye tarry for them till they were grown? would ye stay for them from having husbands? nay, my daughters; for it grieveth me much for your sakes that the hand of the LORD is gone out against me.

14 And they lifted up their voice, and wept again: and Orpah kissed her mother in law; but Ruth clave unto her.

15 And she said, Behold, thy sister in law is gone back unto her people, and unto her gods: return thou after thy sister in law.

16 And Ruth said, Intreat me not to leave thee, or to return from following after thee: for whither thou goest, I will go; and where thou lodgest, I will lodge: thy people shall be my people, and thy God my God:

17 Where thou diest, will I die, and there will I be buried: the LORD do so to me, and more also, if ought but death part thee and me.

18 When she saw that she was stedfastly minded to go with her, then she left speaking unto her.

---

22 So Naomi returned, and Ruth the Moabitess, her daughter in law, with her, which returned out of the country of Moab: and they came to Bethlehem in the beginning of barley harvest.

Key Text

Ruth said, Intreat me not to leave thee, or to return from following after thee: for whither thou goest, I will go; and where thou lodgest, I will lodge: thy people shall be my people, and thy God my God. **—Ruth 1:16**

Faith That

Pleases God

Unit 1: Profiles in Faith

Lessons 1–5

Lesson Aims

After participating in this lesson, each learner will be able to:

1. Identify the three named people in the text.
2. Summarize their situation in light of the period of the judges.
3. State a way that he or she can imitate Ruth's model of courage and faithfulness.

Lesson Outline

Introduction

- A. Before and After
- B. Lesson Context

I. First Exchange (Ruth 1:6-10)

- A. Naomi Reasons (vv. 6-9a)
- B. Daughters-in-Law Respond (vv. 9b-10)

II. Second Exchange (Ruth 1:11-14)

- A. Mother Pleads (vv. 11-13)
  - *Dressed in Christ*
- B. Daughters Diverge (v. 14)

III. Third Exchange (Ruth 1:15-18, 22)

- A. Naomi's Final Plea (v. 15)
- B. Ruth's Promise (vv. 16-18)
- C. Outcome (v. 22)
  - *Catching the Vision*

Conclusion

- A. Walk with One Another
- B. Prayer
- C. Thought to Remember

Introduction

A. Before and After

Tragedy creates a "before" and an "after"—before the job loss, the accident, the fight; after the break-up, the death, etc. When tragedy strikes, we might question God's sovereignty or fear that He is using His strength to punish us through our pain. No matter how strong our faith, tragedy can leave us raw and feeling that we are merely surviving.

Reading the stories of tragedy found within the Bible can offer comfort. When we see examples of how others remained faithful to God, we are inspired to persevere. And even more, when we see how God demonstrated His faithfulness to others, we can regain confidence in His provision no matter our current circumstance. We don't need easy answers in pain; we need God's love, often expressed through the love of other believers. Ruth's story is one biblical example of love expressed in the after time of tragedy.

B. Lesson Context

The author of the book of Ruth is unknown. The date of composition has been proposed as early as King Solomon's reign (approximately 970–930 BC) to as late as 250 BC, long after the return from Babylonian exile. This huge range speaks to the many factors one might point to as evidence of an earlier or later date as well as the text's own ambivalence concerning these questions.

The setting of the events within Ruth are comparatively much better defined as occurring during the time of the judges (Ruth 1:1), that is, sometime between 1373 and 1043 BC. The conquest of Canaan was completed with the Israelite tribes settled in the land (Joshua 23). But the Israelites experienced oppression from outside nations, Moab occasionally being one of them (example: Judges 3:12-31). The Moabites were descended from Abraham's nephew Lot (Genesis 19:33-37). Conflict with Moab was already ancient by the time the time of the judges in Israel (Numbers 22–25). Unsurprisingly, perhaps, the Moabites were banned from entering the assembly of the Lord (Deuteronomy 2:26-30; 23:3-6), though marriage to Moabites was not banned specifically (contrast 7:1-3).

Despite these deep antipathies, a persistent famine in Israel motivated a certain Naomi's Israelite family to leave Bethlehem and settle in Moab (Ruth 1:1; see commentary on 1:6, 22, below). Ten years are covered quickly in the text, apparently beginning with the death of Naomi's husband, Elimelech, and ending with the death of her sons (1:3, 5). In the meantime, these two sons had married Moabite women, Ruth and Orpah, before leaving them childless with their untimely deaths.

What Do You Think?

What circumstances could entice you to start your life over away from home?

Digging Deeper

What faith challenges and opportunities for growth could you anticipate experiencing?

Widowhood was an especially precarious state for women. In the ancient Near East, including both Moab and Israel, men had far more economic power than women. A woman left without male relatives to care for her could be reduced to abject poverty, and prostitution might result. Fathers or sons were the best lines of defense to protect widows; in the case of younger widows, this protection lasted until new husbands could be found (compare Genesis 38:11; Leviticus 22:13). God had given Israel specific instructions for caring for widows, both within the family and the larger community (examples: Deuteronomy 14:28-29; 24:17; see commentary on Ruth 1:11, below).

I. First Exchange

(Ruth 1:6-10)

A. Naomi Reasons (vv. 6-9a)

6. Then she arose with her daughters in law, that she might return from the country of Moab: for she had heard in the country of Moab how that the LORD had visited his people in giving them bread.

Regarding the journey *from the country of Moab* to Bethlehem, see commentary on Ruth 1:22 (below). Returning to her people was Naomi's best option to be cared for in her widowed state. And God's renewed provision in her homeland meant that her family's legal obligations to care for her (see Lesson Context) would not burden an already famished community. The inclusion of *her* (Moabite) *daughters in law* might surprise us, as their families of origin would be expected to care for them in their widowhood. This tension drives the action to come.

7. Wherefore she went forth out of the place where she was, and her two daughters in law with her; and they went on the way to return unto the land of Judah.

There is no clear indication regarding how soon after her sons' deaths Naomi received news that the famine in Judah had ended (Ruth 1:6, above). For Naomi, the journey *unto the land of Judah* was a return to her family and the safety net they represented. But using the same rationale of familial obligation and care, Naomi's *two daughters in law* would have been expected to stay in their homeland, Moab.

That the Moabite women began this journey with their mother-in-law speaks to the depth of their love for and devotion to her (compare Ruth 1:11-13, below). Traveling with Naomi potentially put her well-being over the younger widows' own future prospects for marriage and family. Following her initially may also indicate that the daughters-in-law were not thinking clearly, stricken as they were by grief at the tremendous loss they had suffered with Naomi (contrast 1:14, below).

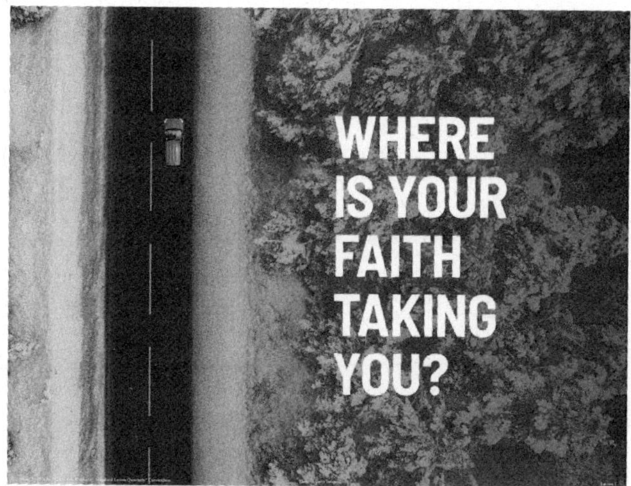

Visual for Lesson 1. *Ask the class to consider this question with the first pair of discussion questions and again before closing the class with prayer.*

8a. And Naomi said unto her two daughters in law, Go, return each to her mother's house.

We might have expected Naomi to urge the young widows back to their fathers' homes (see Lesson Context). But returning *each to her mother's house* might mark a subtle shift in focus from the material benefit of marriage to the relational (Genesis 24:28-38, 67; Song of Solomon 3:4; 8:2). Or it may be a tacit acknowledgement of polygamy. In this case, the mother's house would be a separate dwelling from the father's primary residence.

More than these options, though, the language suggests that Naomi was relinquishing her rights to any support *her two daughters in law* might offer her. She was not their mother, and because of that, they were not obligated to share in the difficulties that widowhood would represent for Naomi.

8b-9a. The Lord deal kindly with you, as ye have dealt with the dead, and with me. The Lord grant you that ye may find rest, each of you in the house of her husband. Then she kissed them.

As Moabite widows, Ruth and Orpah would be incredibly vulnerable in Israel (see Lesson Context). Naomi's words *deal kindly with you* have a ring of covenant language. She intended to leave the women in the Lord's care even though she also intended to leave them in the land of Moab. Naomi did not explicitly say but clearly believed that *the Lord* was not only able but also willing to bless the younger widows, even outside of Israel. As is true throughout the book, the Lord's kindness would be experienced through human relationships (example: Ruth 2:4-12). *Rest* for the widows was expected to be found in their mothers' homes before moving on to new families in the houses of new husbands.

Naomi's future was far from assured (compare Ruth 1:11-13, below); the gift she felt she could give her daughters-in-law was to free them to find more likely sources of stability than she could offer. In a typical farewell gesture, Naomi sealed her hopes for them with a kiss. It signified her love in what she expected to be her final act of care for them (compare 1:14, below).

B. Daughters-in-Law Respond (vv. 9b-10)

9b-10. And they lifted up their voice, and wept. And they said unto her, Surely we will return with thee unto thy people.

They lifted up their voice, and wept is clearly lament language. In context it could be for the general position in which they all found themselves—husbandless and with uncertain futures—or it could specifically have been in response to the pain these two younger women felt at the thought of separating from Naomi. *Surely we will return with thee unto thy people* does not constitute a binding oath but does communicate great devotion to Naomi. It was not a pragmatic response or a thought-out plan; it was the pleading of two daughters-in-law who didn't want to see their mother-in-law leave.

II. Second Exchange
(Ruth 1:11-14)

A. Mother Pleads (vv. 11-13)

11. And Naomi said, Turn again, my daughters: why will ye go with me? are there any more sons in my womb, that they may be your husbands?

Naomi asked her *daughters* (a subtle change from the "daughters in law" designation up to this point) literally to turn from their current course and return to their mothers' homes.

Naomi emphasized the darker, more painful truth about her motivation to send them away: she could not bear *any more sons* to grow up and care for her dead sons' wives. This concern was in keeping with a provision within the Law of Moses concerning care for widows. The brother of the widow's deceased husband was required to marry the widow in a levirate marriage (Deuteronomy 25:5-10; example: Genesis 38:6-14). This not only ensured care for the widow but also allowed her

How to Say It

Chemosh	*Kee*-mosh.
Elimelech	Ee-*lim*-eh-leck.
Moabites	*Mo*-ub-ites.
Orpah	*Or*-pah.

dead husband's lineage to continue. Due to Naomi's own widowhood and age, she knew that her *womb* would not provide new *husbands* for Orpah and Ruth. Naomi saw clearly (if erroneously; see Ruth 4:16-17) the end of her family line.

12-13a. Turn again, my daughters, go your way; for I am too old to have a husband. If I should say, I have hope, if I should have a husband also to night, and should also bear sons; would ye tarry for them till they were grown? would ye stay for them from having husbands?

The phrase *I am too old to have a husband* continued the "reality check" for the two daughters. Naomi's childbearing years were behind her, such that no man of her times would be inclined to marry her. And even if she had hope that she could remarry that very day and conceive *sons* that night, how could the widows be expected to wait years for those sons to be old enough to marry? These hypothetical sons wouldn't be ready for marriage until their early 20s, likely putting Ruth and Orpah somewhere in their 40s. Even today, a pregnancy is considered geriatric after the age of 35. Back then as now, pregnancy at that age and beyond was increasingly unlikely and dangerous.

Turn again emphasizes the benefit of Ruth and Orpah's returning to their families of origin in Moab (see commentary on Ruth 1:11, above). Remarriage in Moab was thus the best option for Ruth and Orpah's flourishing after being widowed. Their families were invested in their well-being and could arrange marriage contracts for their widowed daughters. Naomi's own care would be more easily obtained if she did not come home with two grown female dependents (compare Ruth 4:1-6).

13b. Nay, my daughters; for it grieveth me much for your sakes that the hand of the LORD is gone out against me.

The hand of the Lord can refer to God's blessing, guidance, and protection (examples: Ezra 7:6, 9; Nehemiah 2:8). But His hand conversely can refer to curse, discipline, and judgment (examples: Exodus 9:3; Judges 2:15). *Gone out against me* illustrates Naomi's feeling that God had not so much abandoned her; rather, He was judging her. The writer doesn't outright confirm or deny Naomi's feeling. But when she returned home, Naomi asked to be called *Mara* (which means "bitter"), "for the Almighty hath dealt very bitterly with me" (Ruth 1:20, not in our printed text). We can make too much of the fact that the writer never called Naomi *Mara*. But it subtly suggests that the writer didn't accept that Naomi's life was bitter, or at least that it wasn't irretrievably bitter.

Ascribing motivations to God is a dangerous business—we need only read Job to be reminded of this. But in the middle of so much grief, one way of arriving at meaning, either legitimately or illegitimately, is to find God's judgment in pain. We do well to remember that we cannot know why God allows hard circumstances in our lives (Job 42:1-6). We are wise to remember that His ways are not ours and His thoughts are above ours (Isaiah 55:9). And we can rest in the hope that God uses all things to our benefit if we place our hope in Him, regardless of our circumstances (Romans 8:28-35).

What Do You Think?

When have you interpreted God's hand in your life as punishment?

Digging Deeper

Have circumstances since then changed your mind about God's intentions for you? How, or why not?

Dressed in Christ

At the end of our street, my trick-or-treating children and I met an elderly woman sitting in a lawn chair, a bowl of candy in her lap. "Trick or treat!" the children called. Unexpectedly, the woman began to cry. "Oh, what's wrong?" I asked. She replied, "My husband passed away. This is my first time passing out treats without him. He loved seeing the children in their costumes." My children spontaneously hugged the woman, and we prayed for her.

I had been reluctant to allow my children to go trick-or-treating. But even in costumes, we were all dressed in Christ to meet our new friend. Who in their distress needs to experience Christ through you?

—A. W.

B. Daughters Diverge (v. 14)

14. And they lifted up their voice and wept again: and Orpah kissed her mother in law; but Ruth clave unto her.

At first *Orpah* and *Ruth* had responded in unified lament following Naomi's goodbye kiss (Ruth 1:9a-10, above). But then Orpah *kissed* Naomi. As with Naomi's previous gesture, this was a kiss goodbye (see 1:15, below). We might be tempted to conclude that Orpah acted faithlessly toward Naomi. But the text does not indicate here or elsewhere that Orpah made a poor decision. She acted in keeping with the wisdom of her time and with Naomi's greatest hopes for Orpah's future thriving.

By contrast, Ruth would not be swayed by any argument Naomi could make. Ruth *clave unto her* and would not change her mind.

What Do You Think?

How do you discern whether to move forward with a risky plan or fall back on a more conventionally wise action?

Digging Deeper

What biblical examples can you find of both moving forward and retreating as faithful action?

III. Third Exchange

(Ruth 1:15-18, 22)

A. Naomi's Final Plea (v. 15)

15. And she said, Behold, thy sister in law is gone back unto her people, and unto her gods: return thou after thy sister in law.

Naomi made one last plea to Ruth to turn back. Returning *unto her people* would be a comfortable cultural fit for Ruth, complete with a return to worship of Moabite gods. In the ancient world, gods were often associated not only with certain spheres of activity (agriculture, military, etc.) but also with geographic regions (see commentary on Ruth 1:8b-9a, above). The principle deity worshipped in Moab was the detestable Chemosh (Numbers 21:29; 1 Kings 11:7, 33). The Israelites were meant to be distinct from their neighbors by rejecting all gods other than the Lord—never worshipping a pantheon of multiple deities (Exodus 20:1-6). Ruth's choice was between what she had known before and what she had come to know in her husband's household.

B. Ruth's Promise (vv. 16-18)

16-17a. And Ruth said, Intreat me not to leave thee, or to return from following after thee: for whither thou goest, I will go; and where thou lodgest, I will lodge: thy people shall be my people, and thy God my God: where thou diest, will I die, and there will I be buried.

The introductory statement is an emphatic statement of Ruth's immovable will to follow Naomi, strengthened by Ruth's listing her commitments to Naomi. Ruth's response reflected Naomi's hopes for Ruth but unexpectedly anticipated their fulfillment to be found in a future that included the two women together. The commitment to Naomi's people and God directly tied back to Naomi's plea for Ruth to follow Orpah's example (see Ruth 1:15). The commitments to *go* and *lodge* with Naomi tied Ruth's future to Naomi's. Whatever provision Naomi would find among her people, Ruth would accept as well. Naomi would expect to die well before Ruth. Yet Ruth's commitment was to *die* in Judah and *be buried* there (compare and contrast Genesis 50:1-6). In these ways, Ruth declared Naomi to be her mother and outlined the devotion that she would demonstrate as Naomi's true child.

What Do You Think?

What did you leave behind when you made the decision to follow God?

Digging Deeper

What habits from your old life still need to be broken?

17b-18. The Lord do so to me, and more also, if ought but death part thee and me. When she saw that she was stedfastly minded to go with her, then she left speaking unto her.

Unlike Orpah and Ruth's spontaneous declaration in Ruth 1:10 (above), this is the most solemn of vows (compare 1 Samuel 3:17; 20:13). Ruth had carefully considered the cost of going with Naomi (compare Luke 14:26-33). Realizing this, Naomi stopped trying to convince Ruth to take a different journey.

What Do You Think?

How easy do you find it to accept God's provision that comes through other believers' care for you?

Digging Deeper

What attitudes or circumstances might be preventing you from experiencing God's care through His people?

C. Outcome (v. 22)

22. So Naomi returned, and Ruth the Moabitess, her daughter in law, with her, which returned out of the country of Moab: and they came to Bethlehem in the beginning of barley harvest.

Bethlehem (in Judah; Ruth 1:1) can be literally translated as "house of bread," giving an ironic cast to the famine that had occurred there. Drought was a likely cause of the famine, as rain clouds would sometimes pass straight over Bethlehem and climb to higher elevations—such as in *Moab*—before bursting. The women's westward journey from Moab around the northern shore of the Dead Sea apparently passed without incident.

The mention of the *barley harvest* confirmed that the famine was broken (Ruth 1:6, above). The beginning of that harvest took place sometime in mid-March to mid-April. In later Jewish tradition, the book of Ruth was read at the feast of weeks in celebration of God's provision of the harvest (compare Leviticus 23:15-22).

Catching the Vision

Janice and Wendy met in a widows' support group and became friends instantly. Janice had not been active in her faith for many years until Wendy started inviting her to church events. Together they joined a women's Bible study and served on their church's missions team. There, they started to catch a vision for world missions.

A visiting missionary who had served many years in Turkey began sharing with them how many widows and orphans had migrated from Syria and Iraq as a result of the civil wars. Neither of the women had formal training as missionaries or in the Bible. But they could give smiles and hugs and share tears with women who had been through losses similar to their own. Janice and Wendy departed for Turkey and began learning the language and culture. They bonded with dozens of women who had endured severe hardship.

God fulfills His promise to set "the solitary in families" (Psalm 68:6). Are you in a position now to be brought into a family or to invite others into yours? Ask the Lord for eyes to see the harvest He has set before you (John 4:35). —A. W.

Conclusion

A. Walk with One Another

We are created to be in community with God and with others. Ruth's faithfulness to the Lord and to Naomi is an example to all of what living and loving in community might require of us. Ruth's words and actions demonstrated true commitment to carrying Naomi's burdens (compare Galatians 6:2). Showing up in the midst of pain and anguish is difficult, especially if we are dealing with our own feelings of loss. How we respond to tragedy will determine whether we are following Ruth's example as she followed Christ's example without even knowing her many-times great grandson (see lesson 3; 1 Corinthians 11:1).

B. Prayer

Lord, help us to demonstrate Your love in our relationships and in our communities, that we may be active in Your plan to bless others. In Jesus' name we pray. Amen.

C. Thought to Remember

Remain steadfast in your love for the Lord and His people.

Visuals FOR THESE LESSONS

The visual pictured in each lesson (example: page 123) is a small reproduction of a large, full-color poster included in the *Adult Resources* packet for the Winter Quarter. Order No. 9780784739631 from your supplier.

Involvement Learning

Enhance your lesson with KJV Bible Student *(from your curriculum supplier) and the reproducible activity page (at www.standardlesson.com or in the back of the* KJV Standard Lesson Commentary Deluxe Edition*).*

Into the Lesson

Ask three or more volunteers to use a whiteboard or large pad of paper and markers to play a "Major Life Changes" drawing charades game. Have a volunteer draw a clue while the class guesses the event. Some clue suggestions are baptism, graduation, moving, marriage, parenthood, death, or divorce. Following the activity, give the class the opportunity to share memories of relevant personal life events. Be prepared to ask questions to encourage students to speak about their feelings and how their lives changed from the events.

Alternative. Distribute copies of the "How Do You Shop?" exercise from the activity page, which you can download. Have learners work in pairs to complete the exercise as indicated before discussing conclusions as a whole group.

After either activity, say, "Today we're going to look at the life of Ruth and how love motivated her to take a leap of faith."

Into the Word

Set the stage for today's lesson by sharing some background on Naomi's family using the Lesson Context. Recruit participants to act out Ruth 1:6-14 in reader's theater style. Be sure to cover the roles of a narrator, Naomi, Orpah, and Ruth. Encourage the use of drama and vocal inflection to help the Scripture come to life. Ask the class to discuss the motivations of the women to this point before continuing the activity with Ruth 1:15-18, 22.

Distribute handouts (you create) of the following questions for in-group discussions. Divide the class into two groups: **Naomi's Perspective** and **Ruth's Perspective**. Each group should answer the questions from their assigned perspective: 1–What motivated you to leave Moab? 2–What concerns did you have for the woman you were traveling with? 3–How did your experience of God's care influence your decision-making? 4–What hope and future possibilities did you have in Moab? 5–How did your hope and future possibilities change for the better or worse in Judah?

Bring the class back together to share their viewpoints. Be prepared to emphasize the following points if the discussion doesn't bring them out: Naomi was traveling *toward* her community, where she could expect to be cared for, even in the face of what she believed was God's punishment. Ruth was traveling *away* from her community, against conventional wisdom, thus lessening her prospects of starting her own family.

Option. Distribute copies of the "What Would You Give Up?" exercise from the activity page. Have learners complete it individually in a minute or less before discussing conclusions with the class.

After either activity, talk through how Ruth's courage and faithfulness helped both her and Naomi deal with their situation.

Into Life

Distribute index cards to the learners and ask them to write *Naomi* at the top of one side. Challenge participants to write down the biggest and most fearsome challenge they, or someone close to them, are facing. On the other side, ask them to write *Ruth* at the top of the card and list at least three reasons for hope in this situation. They might think of past similar experiences God has led them through, abilities and resources God has provided, or others in their lives who love them. Then ask them to conclude with one courageous action they can take in response to their reasons for hope. Challenge learners to concentrate on the "Ruth" side of the card during the week.

Lead the class in a closing prayer thanking God for the people He has placed in our lives to remind us of our hope in Him and to carry our burdens with us.

December 10
Lesson 2 (KJV)

The Faith of David

Devotional Reading: Psalm 27
Background Scripture: 1 Samuel 17:1-58

1 Samuel 17:31-37, 45, 48-50

31 And when the words were heard which David spake, they rehearsed them before Saul: and he sent for him.

32 And David said to Saul, Let no man's heart fail because of him; thy servant will go and fight with this Philistine.

33 And Saul said to David, Thou art not able to go against this Philistine to fight with him: for thou art but a youth, and he a man of war from his youth.

34 And David said unto Saul, Thy servant kept his father's sheep, and there came a lion, and a bear, and took a lamb out of the flock:

35 And I went out after him, and smote him, and delivered it out of his mouth: and when he arose against me, I caught him by his beard, and smote him, and slew him.

36 Thy servant slew both the lion and the bear: and this uncircumcised Philistine shall be as one of them, seeing he hath defied the armies of the living God.

37 David said moreover, The LORD that delivered me out of the paw of the lion, and out of the paw of the bear, he will deliver me out of the hand of this Philistine. And Saul said unto David, Go, and the LORD be with thee.

45 Then said David to the Philistine, Thou comest to me with a sword, and with a spear, and with a shield: but I come to thee in the name of the LORD of hosts, the God of the armies of Israel, whom thou hast defied.

48 And it came to pass, when the Philistine arose, and came and drew nigh to meet David, that David hasted, and ran toward the army to meet the Philistine.

49 And David put his hand in his bag, and took thence a stone, and slang it, and smote the Philistine in his forehead, that the stone sunk into his forehead; and he fell upon his face to the earth.

50 So David prevailed over the Philistine with a sling and with a stone, and smote the Philistine, and slew him; but there was no sword in the hand of David.

Key Text

David said moreover, The LORD that delivered me out of the paw of the lion, and out of the paw of the bear, he will deliver me out of the hand of this Philistine. **—1 Samuel 17:37a**

Faith That

Pleases God

Unit 1: Profiles in Faith

Lessons 1–5

Lesson Aims

After participating in this lesson, each learner will be able to:

1. Give the reason for David's confidence.
2. Explain the most important parts of David's initiative.
3. State one or more ways to have the courage of David when facing the figurative Goliaths of life.

Lesson Outline

Introduction
- A. Courage Without Risk?
- B. Lesson Context

I. David's Initiative (1 Samuel 17:31-37)
- A. Bold Volunteer (vv. 31-32)
- B. Skeptical King (v. 33)
  - *Weak Believer, Strong God*
- C. Confident Rejoinder (vv. 34-37)

II. Battle's Outcome (1 Samuel 17:45, 48-50)
- A. David's Taunt (v. 45)
  - *The Christian's Source of Courage*
- B. Combatants' Movements (v. 48)
- C. David's Victory (vv. 49-50)

Conclusion
- A. Faith and Responsibility
- B. Prayer
- C. Thought to Remember

Introduction

A. Courage Without Risk?

Many individuals in history are known for their courage. One such person is Rosa Parks (1913–2005), a Black woman who lived in the segregated South. On December 1, 1955, she challenged segregation laws by refusing to take a different seat on a city bus after the seat she was sitting in was redesignated from "Black" to "White." This turned out to be a key incident in the American Civil Rights Movement.

Rosa believed in having the courage to do what is right. Courage by definition is exercised at the risk of something—a person's freedom or even one's very life. If there's no risk involved, then there's no courage involved.

B. Lesson Context

The events of today's text occur sometime before 1010 BC, the year that Israel's kingship transitioned from Saul to David. Prior to the events of this lesson's text, the prophet Samuel had anointed David to be Saul's successor as king of Israel (1 Samuel 16:1-13). Having been rejected by the Lord, Saul's days as king were numbered (see 1 Samuel 15). Even so, Saul looked on David with favor and employed him in personal service (16:14-23)—at least for a time.

David entered the army encampment in 1 Samuel 17 as part of an episode of an Israelite war with the Philistines. David was a late arrival due to the fact that he had been left to tend sheep while his older brothers went off to war (1 Samuel 17:13-14). After several weeks, the war degenerated into something of a stalemate. But the Israelite army seemed ready to break due to low morale (17:11, 24). The reason was the relentless taunts of a Philistine named Goliath,

How to Say It

Philistines	Fuh-*liss*-teenz or *Fill*-us-teenz.
Goliath	Go-*lye*-uth.
terminus ad quem (Latin)	*tur*-muh-nus ehd **kwem**.
Sabaoth (Hebrew)	*Sab*-a-oth.

who stood about 9'9" tall (17:4-10). As our text begins, David had heard the taunt (17:23) as well as the promise of reward for defeating Goliath (17:25-27). David had also just borne the criticism of his oldest brother for an apparent neglect of duty to attend to sheep left in David's care (17:28).

I. David's Initiative

(1 Samuel 17:31-37)

A. Bold Volunteer (vv. 31-32)

31. And when the words were heard which David spake, they rehearsed them before Saul: and he sent for him.

The words . . . which David spake seem to be that of his volunteering to accept Goliath's challenge to a one-on-one duel (1 Samuel 17:8-10). King *Saul* had been looking for just such a volunteer (17:25), and David's inquiry was promptly passed up the chain of command to the king himself. Saul, for his part, seemed to waste no time in sending for David.

32. And David said to Saul, Let no man's heart fail because of him; thy servant will go and fight with this Philistine.

This verse is linked to 1 Samuel 17:11, 24, which reveal the emotional state of the army. History is witness to many instances where low morale was the decisive element in an army's defeat (compare Deuteronomy 20:3; 1 Samuel 14:15). Low morale leads to (and results from) fear, fear leads to panic, and panic leads to rout. David, a shepherd and a musician, was also "a man of war" (16:18). As such, he instinctively knew all this, thus the direct and immediate offer we see from him in the verse at hand.

B. Skeptical King (v. 33)

33. And Saul said to David, Thou art not able to go against this Philistine to fight with him: for thou art but a youth, and he a man of war from his youth.

This was not the first time that King *Saul* had encountered *David*. The two were actually well acquainted, given David's service in the king's court heretofore (1 Samuel 16:14-23). Saul's reference to David's *youth* may indicate that the young man was under the age of 20, thus ineligible to be in the army (Numbers 1:3; 26:2). We know that David was age 30 when he became king (2 Samuel 5:4); this fact establishes what is called a *terminus ad quem*, which is a final limiting point in time. But David's ascension to the throne is at least several years away at this point in the text. This lends credence to the "under age 20" proposal.

King Saul could only see the contrast between David as a weak youth and the Philistine as *a man of war from his youth*. But David stepped forward with a confidence that seemed to defy this logic.

What Do You Think?

What current situation requires you to show brave leadership?

Digging Deeper

Can you choose to grow in courage? How, or why not?

Weak Believer, Strong God

Janna identified as a "young Christian." She began to profess belief in Jesus just a few years ago, so when an idea popped into her head to start a Bible study with her non-Christian friend Sammie, she suppressed it. Sammie, who had been a friend since their freshman year in college, noticed a change in Janna. Aware of Janna's weekly church attendance, Sammie would occasionally ask questions about her friend's faith.

Janna had been praying for the courage to dive deeper with Sammie and others regarding Christianity. But leading a Bible study sounded like a job for . . . well . . . *leaders*. Janna had never taught anyone anything before.

Saul's feedback to David on his chance of defeating Goliath echoed Janna's self-talk. David was young in years; Janna was young in Christianity. But their weaknesses are infinitely less relevant than God's strength. As the apostle Paul noted centuries after the life of David, God's power is made perfect in human weakness (2 Corinthians 12:9). When have you experienced this personally—if ever?

—D. D.

C. Confident Rejoinder (vv. 34-37)

34. And David said unto Saul, Thy servant kept his father's sheep, and there came a lion, and a bear, and took a lamb out of the flock.

David's salutation *thy servant* reveals self-awareness of his status as being subservient to King *Saul*. David maintained this respectful attitude consistently, even when being hunted down later by an increasingly irrational and paranoid Saul (see 1 Samuel 24; 26). Even so, the statement in the verse at hand indicates a pushback against Saul's skepticism. Those who think that it's safer to tend sheep rather than being in the front line of battle should think again (17:13-15)!

35. And I went out after him, and smote him, and delivered it out of his mouth: and when he arose against me, I caught him by his beard, and smote him, and slew him.

David established his capabilities by explaining encounters with predators that are often more dangerous than human adversaries. The sequence of events is noteworthy in being *smote/delivered/slew*, not *smote/slew/delivered.* The actual sequence indicates David's focus had been to deliver the victim lamb from the jaws of a predator that he had only wounded, which increased the danger to David. The *smote/slew/delivered* sequence would have indicated an intent to ensure the predator was dead first; the additional time this would have required before the rescue of the lamb put the lamb at greater risk while decreasing the risk to David. His choice reveals something about his character (compare John 10:11-13).

36a. Thy servant slew both the lion and the bear: and this uncircumcised Philistine shall be as one of them.

David believed his work as a shepherd warding off predators had prepared him to act quickly, skillfully, and decisively, more than qualifying him for battle. The phrase *uncircumcised Philistine* is thoroughly derogatory and dismissive (see also Judges 14:3; 1 Samuel 17:26; 2 Samuel 1:20).

36b. Seeing he hath defied the armies of the living God.

The phrase *the living God* is a favorite of biblical writers, appearing more than two dozen times across both Old and New Testaments. It stands in direct contrast to lifeless idols representing fictitious gods (Leviticus 26:30; Psalm 106:28; Jeremiah 10:14; 16:18; 51:17; Habakkuk 2:19). There is only one God, and the Philistines in general and Goliath in particular oppose Him. How foolish!

Joshua had declared hundreds of years previously that the Israelites would know that the living God was among them when He drove out their enemies (Joshua 3:10). Hundreds of years after David, the prophet Jeremiah equated "the living God" with "the true God" (Jeremiah 10:10). David was within this stream of faith, confident of the Lord's present, powerful, and ongoing involvement in history.

37a. David said moreover, The LORD that delivered me out of the paw of the lion, and out of the paw of the bear, he will deliver me out of the hand of this Philistine.

Here, David can be said to be using a "from the greater to the lesser" type of argument. Lions and bears are often more dangerous than human opponents, especially in an era before gunpowder. A lion may weigh between 265 and 550 pounds; bears may weigh about the same. Their paws conceal deadly claws. Both predators are well equipped for and inclined toward paws-on combat. Biblical writers sometimes compare God's wrath to the tactics of lions and bears (Lamentations 3:10-11; Hosea 13:7-8). Other passages use bear-and-lion imagery to make vital and radical points (Proverbs 28:15; Amos 5:19; Revelation 13:2). Since *the Lord* had *delivered* David from these more dangerous foes that specialize in ambush, would the Lord also not do so regarding a non-ambush situation with *this Philistine*?

The situation at hand involved a change of tactics by the Philistines from their previous war against King Saul and the Israelites. Rather than being characterized by relative sizes of forces (1 Samuel 13:2, 5, 15; 14:2), maneuvers (13:3, 16-18), and quality of weapons (13:19-22), the outcome of the current war was to be decided by a one-on-one combat (see 17:8-10). Victory in a previous war against the Philistines had been set in motion by two Israelites defeating at least 20 Philistines (14:6-14). The Lord had been behind that victory (14:15), and David expected Him to be behind the victory to come as well.

What Do You Think?

What situations from your past give you confidence in your own abilities?

Digging Deeper

How do you balance confidence in yourself and in the Lord so that it doesn't become arrogance or yield dependence on yourself?

37b. And Saul said unto David, Go, and the Lord be with thee.

King *Saul* didn't attempt to challenge David's logic and passionate belief. Although Saul realized that he himself no longer had the favor of *the Lord* (1 Samuel 15:10, 26; 16:14), his entreaty on David's behalf seems genuine. The expressed desire is therefore a reaffirmation of what Saul had previously been told regarding David's favor with the Lord (16:18; compare 20:13). This prayer expression gives us insight into Saul's belief that the Lord would still act on Israel's behalf. Later, the Lord's favor toward David and disfavor toward Saul will become a source of fear for the king (18:12).

What Do You Think?

How can you encourage young people to exercise wise leadership?

Digging Deeper

What cautions need to be considered when empowering a leader of any age?

II. Battle's Outcome

(1 Samuel 17:45, 48-50)

A. David's Taunt (v. 45)

45. Then said David to the Philistine, Thou comest to me with a sword, and with a spear, and with a shield: but I come to thee in the name of the Lord of hosts, the God of the armies of Israel, whom thou hast defied.

In the intervening verses not part of our lesson text, *David* rejected wearing battle gear; instead, he chose to take his staff, stones, and sling (1 Samuel 17:38-40).

David's identification of each combatant's support is insightful. For David to *come . . . in the name of the Lord of hosts, the God of the armies of Israel* indicates reliance on protection from a divine source. Note that David did not say, "I come to you with a sling and a stone!" By contrast, mention of Goliath's *sword, spear,* and *shield* indicate that man's reliance on his own skills. The nature and dimensions of his weapons as described in 1 Samuel 17:5-7 do not seem to have intimidated David in the least.

The title *the God of the armies of Israel* is unique to this passage in the pages of the Old Testament. *The name of the Lord of hosts* is also military language. The underlying word translated "hosts" is *Sabaoth,* which you might recognize from the second stanza of the hymn "A Mighty Fortress Is Our God":

> You ask who that may be?
> Christ Jesus, it is he;
> Lord Sabaoth his name,
> from age to age the same;
> and he must win the battle.

The Hebrew word *Sabaoth* occurs hundreds of times in the Old Testament. Used as a verb, it occurs in contexts of fighting or doing battle. Used as a noun, it often refers to elements of an army (divisions, etc.). The word is also part of the phrase "the host of heaven" in Deuteronomy 4:19 to refer to literal stars in the sky (similar are 2 Kings 17:16; 21:3, 5; Isaiah 40:26; etc.). Some passages seem to use the word *host* to refer to angelic beings (examples: 2 Chronicles 18:18; Psalms 103:20-21; 148:2-3).

Whichever sense is intended here, the one true God is highest in the chain of command over them. David had great assurance in the fact that His Lord, the God of Israel, was the God over all things and beings. This is the same God whom Goliath had blasphemed, as evident in the phrase *whom thou hast defied.* This isn't David's conclusion; Goliath himself had said he was defying "the armies of Israel" (1 Samuel 17:10). To do so was tantamount to defying the God to whom those armies belonged (compare 2 Kings 18:28-35 with 19:4-6, 22-23).

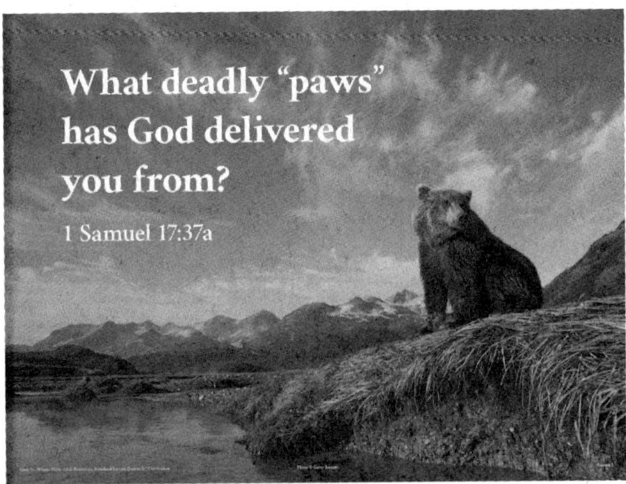

What deadly "paws" has God delivered you from?
1 Samuel 17:37a

Visual for Lesson 2. *Pose this question as the class discusses today's key verse, 1 Samuel 17:37a.*

The Christian's Source of Courage

Only an inch of playground separated the two second-grade boys at recess. Stepping furiously into Lucas's personal bubble was Jackson. Moments earlier, Lucas had shoved him to the ground during a game of tag. And it wasn't the first time.

"Stop touching me," Jackson growled.

Jackson—all 3'6", 45 pounds of him—made his threat looking up at his much taller, stronger classmate. Lucas appeared taken aback by Jackson's boldness. "Wait until my cousin sees you after school," Jackson continued.

The confusion on Lucas's face turned to anger, but he backed away. Jackson's cousin starred on the fifth-grade football team. For the rest of recess, no one tagged Jackson roughly.

Where did Jackson's confidence lie? Certainly not in his own ability to protect himself. He still had trouble opening heavy doors. He knew someone, however, whose strength was superior to his enemy's. Jackson looked not inside, but outside of himself for confidence—to a protector who just so happened to be family.

Christians in the trials of life do not work up courage by looking in the mirror. They look to the Lord Almighty, the God of the armies of Heaven (Matthew 26:53; Revelation 19:14). When a threat arises, where do you look to first for deliverance—to your own abilities or to God? Before you answer, read 2 Kings 6:15-17 carefully! —D. D.

B. Combatants' Movements (v. 48)

48. And it came to pass, when the Philistine arose, and came and drew nigh to meet David, that David hasted, and ran toward the army to meet the Philistine.

The nature of the weaponry (1 Samuel 17:6, 40, 45) and the contents of the combatants' "trash talk" (17:44-46) indicate that a relatively close-range battle was to come. No archery would be involved (contrast 2 Kings 9:23-24). So each combatant moved to close the distance, presumably to reach the optimum range for their respective weapons. Goliath's sword would be useful only within arms' length; but both the sword and his arm were quite long! He might have been able to throw his spear a few yards.

David's sling, by contrast, was a type of artillery, able to launch a projectile. Under certain circumstances, a sling could out-range a bow and arrow, but only if the stone was slung in a high trajectory. This tactic (known as "indirect fire") would be suitable against a group of enemies who were close together in a tight formation; accuracy would be relatively unimportant—the stone was likely to hit *someone*. The effective range of a sling launching a stone on a low-trajectory range ("direct fire") depended on many factors but was perhaps between 50 and 100 yards.

David therefore may have seemed to have an advantage over Goliath because David's weapon had greater range. He could start to fight from further away than Goliath was able. But that advantage could be negated by Goliath's armor (1 Samuel 17:5-6). But in the final analysis the ultimate advantage was with David—the Lord was on his side.

C. David's Victory (vv. 49-50)

49. And David put his hand in his bag, and took thence a stone, and slang it, and smote the Philistine in his forehead, that the stone sunk into his forehead; and he fell upon his face to the earth.

David's tremendous courage is matched by his skill with a sling. To hit a forehead—which is only a few square inches—with a sling involves incredible marksmanship! Expert slingers would come to be seen as the snipers on ancient battlefields.

The weapon is deadly when slinging a stone with enough force, as here (compare Judges 20:16). Before Goliath even knew what was happening, the stone hit the very spot that his armor didn't cover. He had received the penalty due for his blasphemy (Leviticus 24:16).

With David's skill and courage duly noted, the battle was ultimately between the one, true God of Israel and the fictitious gods of the Philistines; we take special note of how each combatant saw it this way (1 Samuel 17:43, 45-46). Goliath's falling *upon his face to the earth* is somewhat mirrored in an earlier incident where the Philistines' idol Dagon fell on its face (twice!) in the presence of the ark of God (5:1-4).

50. So David prevailed over the Philistine with a sling and with a stone, and smote the Philistine, and slew him; but there was no sword in the hand of David.

This passage again notes the minimal weaponry of *David*. As the encounter had begun, David had predicted that he would cut off Goliath's head (1 Samuel 17:46), *but there was no sword in the hand of David*. This meant that for David to cut off the head of *the Philistine*, he would have to use Goliath's sword to do so. And that's exactly what happened (17:51).

This battle validated David's anointing as the king to replace Saul (1 Samuel 16:1-13). And it would not be the last time David would use Goliath's sword (21:9-10).

> **What Do You Think?**
>
> What are some spiritual weapons Christians have that the world might consider weak or ineffective (consider 2 Corinthians 10:4)?
>
> **Digging Deeper**
>
> What Bible verses inform your answer?

Conclusion

A. Faith and Responsibility

Faith and responsibility are key aspects of walking with God. Faith is our decision to follow the Lord, and responsibility is how we live out our faith on this earth. If we step out in confidence to bring the living God to others, we love as the Lord loves us.

My own faith and responsibility shined bright when I was a life skills educator for teenage mothers. I worked with teen moms to prepare them for life, school, and work. The mothers were often judged for being pregnant, and many people did not see their potential.

My role was not an easy one because of their lack of self-confidence and support. However, I brought my love of the Lord to work every day to show them that God's love for them was mine as well. Many times the love I demonstrated led to conversations about God's loving them. The young mothers opened up to me and appreciated my company, which I attributed to the presence of the living God in my life.

What made the job harder was the fact that many teen moms were foster children or had been sent to us by the court system. They had experienced many childhood traumas; they didn't trust adults. But that was all the more reason to show them the love of God. That was my fundamental reason for coming to work every day. I wanted them to know whom I was following as I served as His hands and feet. And that is the key factor of the violent encounter of today's text: there was no doubt whom David served and whom Goliath served. Can the same be said of you?

> **What Do You Think?**
>
> Consider the cautions discussed with verse 37b (above). What situation(s) might call for throwing caution to the wind?
>
> **Digging Deeper**
>
> How can you discern when caution is the less faithful choice?

B. Prayer

Lord, may we grow in courage in our faith. May people see the love of Jesus as He guides our steps through the Holy Spirit. In Jesus' name we pray. Amen.

C. Thought to Remember

Make sure others know whom you serve.

Involvement Learning

Enhance your lesson with KJV Bible Student *(from your curriculum supplier) and the reproducible activity page (at www.standardlesson.com or in the back of the* KJV Standard Lesson Commentary Deluxe Edition*).*

Into the Lesson

Poll your class regarding which animals they think they could fight off bare-handed: a rat, a house cat, a goose, an eagle, a large dog, a king cobra, a crocodile, a lion, a grizzly bear. Jot notes on the board as you go. Ask volunteers to share why they feel confident about defeating one animal but not another. Then compare their responses to the results of a 2021 poll that asked a group of Americans the same question: a rat (72%), a house cat (69%), a goose (61%), an eagle (30%), a large dog (23%), a king cobra (15%), a crocodile (9%), a lion (8%), a grizzly bear (6%). Which results surprised the class? Where did the class differ significantly from these other polling results?

Alternative. Distribute copies of the "Lions, Tigers, and Bears?" exercise from the activity page, which you can download. Have learners complete it as indicated.

Next, say, "David, as a shepherd boy, was able to expertly fight animals that threatened his flock. Let's see how he brought down a giant with just one stone."

Into the Word

Ask a volunteer to read today's Scripture aloud. Following the reading, divide the class into thirds, designating one group as the **David Group**, the second as the **Saul Group**, and the third as the **Goliath Group**. Have each group read 1 Samuel 17:1-37 among themselves. Distribute handouts (you create) of the following questions for in-group discussion based on the information found regarding their assigned person. Some questions might require research beyond the assigned Scripture: 1–How would you describe this man's character overall? 2–Does this man command respect? Why, or why not? 3–What accomplishments can this man brag about? 4–What made this man feel confident or insecure? Ask the groups to give a summary of their assigned characters based on their discussion.

Then have the same groups read 1 Samuel 17:38-50 and consider whether their answers changed based on the events recounted there.

Option. Distribute copies of the "David and Goliath Acrostic" exercise from the activity page. Give groups time to complete as indicated before discussing their conclusions as a whole class.

Ask learners to recall examples from Scripture 1–of situations in which people trusted in God in the face of seemingly insurmountable difficulty and 2–of similarly difficult situations in which people did not trust God. Did faith or lack thereof make a difference in the outcome? *Option.* Point readers to Hebrews 11 as a starting point, using a concordance to find these examples in their original context; examples of faithlessness are likely also found nearby in these Old Testament texts.

Into Life

Ask the class for examples of times when faithfulness (or a lack of faith) has made a difference in their own lives. Though this could include miracles, encourage the class to highlight seemingly more ordinary ways God shows His care for His children. With partners, have learners discuss how these times have encouraged them in their own skills and in their trust in God's plans and care.

Distribute a note card and pencil to each learner. Give learners one minute to write down at least one personal "Goliath" they can anticipate facing during the coming year. Then ask each learner to write down personal experience(s) they can recall to reinforce why they can trust God with those situations. Explain to learners that they will not be required to share these answers.

Allow time for participants to write a prayer to use during the week that encourages them to face their Goliaths with faith and trust in the Lord. Ask a volunteer to end the class in prayer that each member would have the courage of David's faith while facing their Goliaths.

December 17
Lesson 3 (KJV)

The Family of Faith

Devotional Reading: Psalm 9:1-14
Background Scripture: Genesis 38; Joshua 2; 6:22-25; 2 Samuel 12:24; Ruth 4:13-22; Matthew 1:1-17

Matthew 1:1-17

1 The book of the generation of Jesus Christ, the son of David, the son of Abraham.

2 Abraham begat Isaac; and Isaac begat Jacob; and Jacob begat Judas and his brethren;

3 And Judas begat Phares and Zara of Thamar; and Phares begat Esrom; and Esrom begat Aram;

4 And Aram begat Aminadab; and Aminadab begat Naasson; and Naasson begat Salmon;

5 And Salmon begat Booz of Rachab; and Booz begat Obed of Ruth; and Obed begat Jesse;

6 Jesse begat David the king; and David the king begat Solomon of her that had been the wife of Urias;

7 And Solomon begat Roboam; and Roboam begat Abia; and Abia begat Asa;

8 And Asa begat Josaphat; and Josaphat begat Joram; and Joram begat Ozias;

9 And Ozias begat Joatham; and Joatham begat Achaz; and Achaz begat Ezekias;

10 And Ezekias begat Manasses; and Manasses begat Amon; and Amon begat Josias;

11 And Josias begat Jechonias and his brethren, about the time they were carried away to Babylon:

12 And after they were brought to Babylon, Jechonias begat Salathiel; and Salathiel begat Zorobabel;

13 And Zorobabel begat Abiud; and Abiud begat Eliakim; and Eliakim begat Azor;

14 And Azor begat Sadoc; and Sadoc begat Achim; and Achim begat Eliud;

15 And Eliud begat Eleazar; and Eleazar begat Matthan; and Matthan begat Jacob;

16 And Jacob begat Joseph the husband of Mary, of whom was born Jesus, who is called Christ.

17 So all the generations from Abraham to David are fourteen generations; and from David until the carrying away into Babylon are fourteen generations; and from the carrying away into Babylon unto Christ are fourteen generations.

Key Text

The book of the generation of Jesus Christ, the son of David, the son of Abraham. **—Matthew 1:1**

Faith That

Pleases God

Unit 1: Profiles in Faith

Lessons 1–5

Lesson Aims

After participating in this lesson, each learner will be able to:

1. Identify the "three 14s" of the text.
2. Explain the purpose of documenting Jesus' lineage.
3. State a way to value personally his or her own genealogy in Christ while avoiding the danger noted in 1 Timothy 1:4 and Titus 3:9.

Lesson Outline

Introduction
- A. The Big Business of Genealogy
- B. Lesson Context

I. From Abraham to David (Matthew 1:1-6a)
- A. Introduction to Jesus (v. 1)
- B. Pre-Nation of Israel (v. 2)
- C. Pre-Monarchy of Israel (vv. 3-6a)
  - *What a Mess!*

II. From David to the Exile (Matthew 1:6b-11)
- A. Unified Kingdom (vv. 6b-7a)
- B. Kingdom of Judah (vv. 7b-11)

III. From the Exile to Christ (Matthew 1:12-17)
- A. In Babylon (v. 12)
- B. In Judah (vv. 13-16)
  - *Family Legacy*
- C. Generational Summary (v. 17)

Conclusion
- A. Jesus' Family
- B. Prayer
- C. Thought to Remember

Introduction

A. The Big Business of Genealogy

Genealogical research has become big business worldwide. Tools for genetic testing can identify anyone's unique DNA sequencing. These tools, combined with vast computing power, have allowed for the compilation of an ever-growing database of millions of individuals' genetic information. The digitization of massive amounts of genealogical records going back many centuries allows individuals to trace family traits. One leader in this area claims to have billions of records in its database to help with any given search. For a price, individuals can learn details of their ancestors that were inaccessible even a few decades ago.

B. Lesson Context

Biblical genealogies are not necessarily lists of ancestors in exhaustive detail. Differences within two accounts of the same family tree are born not out of error but instead of the writer's intention. We need only consider that Luke's genealogy of Jesus (Luke 3:23-38) contains 56 generations between Abraham and Jesus compared to Matthew's 42 generations (see Matthew 1:2-17, below) to understand that something other than precise family history is intended in these lists.

The chronology of the two (in reverse order of one another) further affirms that each writer had priorities beyond mere recitation of family facts. Differences between Matthew and Luke's genealogies of Jesus could be explored. But we will remain focused on Matthew's genealogy, keeping in mind that Matthew had valid reasons for organizing Jesus' genealogy as he did.

Considering who is included in Matthew's genealogy prepares the careful reader for important themes that recur throughout that Gospel (see commentary on Matthew 1:1-2, 6, below). The curious inclusion of four women (plus Mary; see 1:3, 5-6, 16, below) introduces two other themes that will be found in Matthew's Gospel (examples: 9:18-25; 15:21-28; 28:16-20). Furthermore, the episodes associated with these women (and others) highlight God's continued willingness to work through sinful people and imperfect circumstances (examples: 4:18-22; 16:13-23; 26:69-75; 28:16-20).

I. From Abraham to David

(Matthew 1:1-6a)

A. Introduction to Jesus (v. 1)

1. The book of the generation of Jesus Christ, the son of David, the son of Abraham.

Right away we can sense Matthew's primary reason for writing this Gospel: to reveal who *Jesus Christ* is and why His life is significant. The Hebrew word for *messiah* and its Greek equivalent, *Christ*, mean "anointed one." *Messiah* also referred at various times to both priests and kings (examples: Exodus 28:41; 1 Chronicles 29:22). Sometime after the fall of David's royal line, the phrase came to more explicitly refer to an anticipated savior of the Jewish people (example: Isaiah 61:1). This hope grew out of the expectation that God continued to care for Israel and would reverse the nation's painful circumstances (compare Matthew 1:20-22, not in our printed text). All of the New Testament expands on what it means for Jesus to be the Christ (Philippians 2:5-11; Hebrews 9:11-14; 1 Peter 2:21; Revelation 1:5-6; etc.).

As *the son of David, the son of Abraham*, we anticipate that Jesus is important to the nation of Israel (see Matthew 1:2a, 6a, below). Matthew's original readers (likely Christian Jews who were still active in their synagogues) knew of promises made to Abraham and David. Jesus fulfilled these promises, though how He did so will take the rest of the Gospel to answer (example: 21:5, 9). One subtle way Matthew emphasizes this point is by referring to Jesus as "son of David" 10 times, more than all the other Gospels combined.

B. Pre-Nation of Israel (v. 2)

2a. Abraham begat Isaac; and Isaac begat Jacob.

Matthew 1:2-6a is the first third of the genealogy, covering approximately 1,100 years. The three men listed here are Israel's patriarchs and the subjects of Genesis 12–50. They represent the time following God's choosing of *Abraham* to God's creating the new nation of Israel. Perhaps most notable for themes found in Matthew, Abraham received the promise from God that "in thee shall all families of the earth be blessed" (Genesis 12:3; see Galatians 3:8).

Isaac was a miracle baby, born to Abraham and Sarah in their old age when it seemed they would not have a family through which to establish God's promise (Genesis 21:1-3). Unexpectedly, the promise was carried out through Isaac's second son, *Jacob* (25:23). Jacob was renamed *Israel*, a designation meaning "struggles with God," because "as a prince hast thou power with God and with men, and hast prevailed" (32:28). This made Israel the namesake of the nation from which Jesus came.

2b. And Jacob begat Judas and his brethren.

The "founding fathers" of Israel were the 12 sons of *Jacob*, here presented as *Judas* (Judah; Genesis 29:35) and *his brethren* (46:8-24). These brothers became the ancestors of the tribes of Israel (35:22-26; Deuteronomy 27:12-13).

C. Pre-Monarchy of Israel (vv. 3-6a)

3a. And Judas begat Phares and Zara of Thamar.

Despite not being the oldest brother, a descendant of *Judas* would fulfill the words Jacob spoke: "the sceptre shall not depart from Judah, nor a lawgiver from between his feet" (Genesis 49:10; see Matthew 1:6, below).

We note Matthew's first deviation of the pattern from male to male (so far, father to son). *Thamar* (Tamar) was Judah's daughter-in-law, assumed to be a Canaanite given Judah's own marriage and his physical location when Tamar married into the family (Genesis 38:1-6). She was left a childless widow when her husband, Er, died

How to Say It

Esrom	*Hezz*-rom.
Jechonias	*Jek*-o-nye-us.
Joatham	*Jo*-thum.
Josaphat	*Jos*-uh-fat.
Naasson	*Nah*-shahn.
Roboam	Ruh-*boe*-um.
Salathiel	Sa-la-*tee*-el.
Zorobabel	Zeh-*rub*-uh-bul.

and his brother, Onan, refused to fulfill his duty according to what would come to be known as Levirate marriage (38:7-8; Deuteronomy 25:5-10; see lesson 1). When Judah proved unwilling to care for his daughter-in-law, Tamar devised a plan to become pregnant by Judah himself (Genesis 38:11-18). The result was twin boys, *Phares* (Pharez; 38:29) and *Zara* (Zarah; 38:30).

From this spotlight, we can anticipate two themes in Matthew: God's concern for Gentiles (any non-Israelite) and for women. This hints at the hope of salvation beyond Israel, as well as the need for a more robust understanding of salvation than mere political independence (see Matthew 1:5-6, below; compare Acts 15:7-11). Furthermore, we see God's care and concern in the mess of this real human family. The juxtaposition between the Christ and His family cannot be missed. Nor can we miss God's willingness to work through sinful people to fulfill His promises.

What a Mess!

Why does the genealogy of Jesus emphasize the fact that He is descended from Pharez, born after Tamar posed as a prostitute to entrap her father-in-law (Genesis 38)? Several possibilities come to mind, all indicative of God's love. No matter how serious our sins, or how they compound with one choice after another, God can redeem those situations and offer grace. None of us are doomed to follow our parents' flawed paths, nor guaranteed that we will follow their faithful examples. And we can find comfort in the pain of our own messy families because Jesus' family was also a mess—and look what God did through them!

When you read about Tamar and Judah and the other messes up and down Jesus' family tree, what encouragement do you experience? Who else will benefit from that encouragement and meeting Jesus in the middle of His messy family? —A. W.

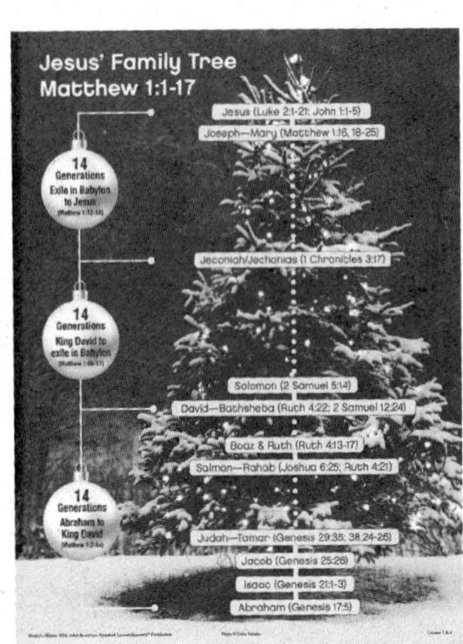

Visual for Lessons 3 & 4

Allow students to refer to this image as they reacquaint themselves with Jesus' family tree.

3b. And Phares begat Esrom; and Esrom begat Aram.

Phares and *Esrom* (Hezron) journeyed to Egypt during the famine in Canaan (Genesis 46:12). Their father's complicity in the sin of selling his own brother Joseph into slavery (37:12-36) was redeemed through Joseph's God-given work of mitigating the effects of a transnational famine (45:4-8).

4. And Aram begat Aminadab; and Aminadab begat Naasson; and Naasson begat Salmon.

Aram and *Aminadab* (Amminadab) represent generations born in Egypt who experienced part of the 430 years there, culminating in the exodus from slavery in 1447 BC (see Exodus 12:40). Amminadab is further associated with the 40-year wandering in the wilderness, as is *Naasson* (Nahshon; see Numbers 1:7; 7:12; 10:14). *Salmon* represents the first generation that was tasked with conquering Canaan in the days of Joshua, about 1400 BC (Joshua 1; see Matthew 1:5a).

5a. And Salmon begat Booz of Rachab.

Rachab (Rahab) is the second Gentile woman to be named. Specifically, she was the Canaanite prostitute who became a heroine in Israel's conquest of Jericho (Joshua 2; 6:25; compare Hebrews 11:31). Her inclusion reinforces the reality of sinfulness in Jesus' family tree as well as God's continued redemptive work through this less-than-ideal family.

5b. And Booz begat Obed of Ruth, and Obed begat Jesse.

The story of *Booz* (Boaz) and *Ruth* comprises the four chapters of the biblical book named after this Moabite heroine (see lesson 1). She is the third Gentile to be named in this genealogy. The birth of her son, *Obed*, relieved her mother-in-law of her great sorrow (Ruth 4:13-17).

6a. And Jesse begat David the king.

Jesse originally offered his older sons as candidates for kingship. But the Lord chose Jesse's youngest son, *David,* instead (1 Samuel 16:7, 11-13; see lesson 2 for more on David).

Referring to David as *the king* and emphasizing his position in Jesus' family tree (see Matthew 1:1, 16) calls to mind promises God made to David. Chief among these promises was that David's throne would be established forever (2 Samuel 7:5-15; 1 Kings 2:45; Psalm 89:35-37; see commentary on Matthew 1:11, below).

What Do You Think?

How might a family's faith be enriched by the perspective of believers from other cultures?

Digging Deeper

What opportunities exist in your community to experience enrichment from different groups of Christian believers?

II. From David to the Exile

(Matthew 1:6b-11)

A. Unified Kingdom (vv. 6b-7a)

6b. And David the king begat Solomon of her that had been the wife of Urias.

Matthew 1:6b-11 represents the second third of the genealogy, covering about 400 years, from 1000 to 586 BC. We can hazard some educated guesses as to why Bathsheba is referred as *the wife of Urias* (Uriah; 2 Samuel 11:3) instead of by name. Given that the other women in this list were Gentiles, it's possible that giving this title to Bathsheba highlights that she was likely a Hittite as was Uriah. And the designation emphasizes her first marriage that was destroyed after David called her to his house (11:4-27). Reminding the reader of David's grave sins serves to temper any hero worship that the king's status—especially having been hand-picked by God and received incredible blessings from Him (see Matthew 1:6a, above)—might otherwise inspire.

7a. And Solomon begat Roboam.

David had several wives and many children (1 Chronicles 3:1-9); at his death, *Solomon* became king (1 Kings 1:31-34). He was the last king of the united monarchy of Israel, due in large part to his own faithlessness later in his reign (see 11:9-13). His son *Roboam* (Rehoboam; 11:43) acted foolishly by listening to his friends instead of wise advisors (a warning to us all!). This precipitated the division of the kingdom that the Lord decreed following Solomon's faithlessness. Even so, God left a remnant to David's family in light of God's promise to that man (12:1-24).

What Do You Think?

What takeaway should believers have from Solomon's life of early faith and late apostasy?

Digging Deeper

What other biblical texts affirm or challenge that takeaway?

B. Kingdom of Judah (vv. 7b-11)

7b-8. And Roboam begat Abia; and Abia begat Asa. And Asa begat Josaphat; and Josaphat begat Joram; and Joram begat Ozias.

This verse and a half lists the names of King *Roboam* and his successors who ruled over the southern kingdom of Judah in Jerusalem from 931 to 740 BC, following the revolt of Israel's 10 northern tribes. *Abia* was not a righteous king (Abijah; 1 Kings 15:1-3). But his son *Asa* and grandson *Josaphat* were righteous (Jehoshaphat; 15:11; 22:42-43). *Joram* stepped out of his father and grandfather's footsteps and "wrought that which was evil" (Jehoram; 2 Chronicles 21:5-7). *Ozias* (Uzziah) was again characterized as doing "that which was right in the sight of the Lord" (26:1-4; contrast 26:16-21). Matthew skipped three kings and a queen between Jehoram and Uzziah.

9-10. And Ozias begat Joatham; and Joatham begat Achaz; and Achaz begat Ezekias; and Ezekias begat Manasses; and Manasses begat Amon; and Amon begat Josias.

The kings listed here represent some of Judah's best—*Joatham* (Jotham; 2 Kings 15:32-34); *Ezekias* (Hezekiah; 18:1-4); and *Josias* (Josiah; 22:1-2). Assyria conquered Israel during the reign of

Hezekiah (722 BC). Judah's survival of that crisis is attributed in part to Hezekiah's continued faithfulness to the Lord (19:14-36). Later, Josiah was credited with reinstituting the worship of the Lord and teaching the book of the law (probably a copy of Deuteronomy; see 2 Chronicles 34:15).

These kings also represent some of Judah's worst—*Achaz* (Ahaz; 2 Kings 16:1-4); *Manasses* (Manasseh; 21:1-9); and *Amon* (21:19-22). The prophet Jeremiah attributed the eventual fall of Jerusalem in part to the disastrous reign of Manasseh (Jeremiah 15:4).

What Do You Think?

Why isn't a God-fearing parent like Hezekiah guaranteed to have a God-fearing child (consider wicked Manasseh)?

Digging Deeper

What support can you offer parents whose children have rejected godly living?

11. And Josias begat Jechonias and his brethren, about the time they were carried away to Babylon.

Josiah's wicked (grand)son *Jechonias* (Jehoiachin; 2 Kings 24:8-9) *and his brethren* were exiled in the first wave of captives (24:15-16). Jerusalem and the temple were destroyed in the final Babylonian siege in 586 BC (25:8-12). Many residents were killed; most survivors *were carried away to Babylon*. The exile marks the end of the second set of 14 generations (see Matthew 1:17b, below).

III. From the Exile to Christ

(Matthew 1:12-17)

A. In Babylon (v. 12)

12. And after they were brought to Babylon, Jechonias begat Salathiel; and Salathiel begat Zorobabel.

Matthew 1:12-16 is the final third of the genealogy, covering just under 600 years. *Babylon* was the low point of Jewish history. The people had been forcibly removed from the promised land by God's own plan (Jeremiah 20:4-5; etc.). And the throne was never reestablished in Jerusalem.

This time also gave rise to the messianic expectations of a Davidic king to come, which Jesus fulfilled in unexpected ways (see lesson 5 on the importance of prophetic fulfillment in Matthew). *Jehoiachin*, *Salathiel* (Shealtiel; 1 Chronicles 3:17), and *Zorobabel* (Zerubbabel; 3:19) represent the 70 years of Babylonian exile. After Babylon was conquered by the Persians, King Cyrus allowed the people of Judah to return to Jerusalem in 538 BC (Ezra 1:1-4). Zerubbabel was instrumental in rebuilding the Jerusalem temple (3:2; 5:2; 6:13-18), completed about 516 BC.

What Do You Think?

In what ways does remembering family history, including successes and failures, help younger generations?

Digging Deeper

Why might shared history of trauma (like exile) be especially important or instructive?

B. In Judah (vv. 13-16)

13. And Zorobabel begat Abiud; and Abiud begat Eliakim; and Eliakim begat Azor.

With *Zorobabel*, the Old Testament account of the kingly line ends. Matthew includes nine names in verses 13-15 that come from a source unknown to us.

14-15. And Azor begat Sadoc; and Sadoc begat Achim; and Achim begat Eliud; and Eliud begat Eleazar; and Eleazar begat Matthan; and Matthan begat Jacob.

Again, nothing is available in the biblical record about these men, whose lives cover the time from the rebuilding of the temple (see Matthew 1:12, above) to Jesus' own adoptive paternal grandfather, *Jacob*.

Family Legacy

Photos from the past help us remember tidbits about family we never met. Maybe Great-Grandpa Sam had a silver dollar collection, or Great-Great-Aunt Lucy was the first woman to leave the family farm for a job in town. An Uncle Deet (short for Dietrich) and his first wife (whose name was forgotten) passed down the German Bible they brought when they immigrated.

We may forget the details of their lives, but no doubt our ancestors' influence continues in our families. If you can leave only one legacy for your descendants when you are only a photograph, what do you hope it to be? How can you live today so that this hope can come to be? —A. W.

16. And Jacob begat Joseph the husband of Mary, of whom was born Jesus, who is called Christ.

The final entries in the genealogy are carefully worded. Matthew breaks his pattern of "begetting" with *Joseph*. He is *the husband of Mary*, not a biological relative of Jesus (Matthew 1:18, not in our printed text). Jesus' belonging in Joseph's family was a matter of choice, like adoption, instead of natural heritage.

Mary is the fifth and final woman in the genealogy. Unlike the others, she was not a Gentile and was a virgin when she conceived. Mary accepted God's plan for her with faith and humility (Luke 1:26-38; see lesson 4), demonstrating why He chose her to raise Jesus. Calling Jesus *Christ* bookends the genealogy (see commentary on Matthew 1:1, above).

C. Generational Summary (v. 17)

17. So all the generations from Abraham to David are fourteen generations; and from David until the carrying away into Babylon are fourteen generations; and from the carrying away into Babylon unto Christ are fourteen generations.

Numbering *fourteen generations* between *Abraham* and *David*, David and *the carrying away into Babylon*, and the Babylonian exile to Jesus is an organizational tool that emphasizes the roles of Abraham, David, and the exile as formative people/events in Israel's history.

This summary serves to emphasize the fulfillment of God's promises. Abraham received the first promises specific to the nation of Israel and blessing through the nation for the world (see Matthew 1:2a, above). David received promises for a kingly line in Israel (see 1:6a). *The carrying away into Babylon* marked the end of kingship in Judah and seemingly of the nation itself, thus throwing into question God's continued intention to fulfill His promises, especially toward David (Psalm 89:46-52). But only 14 generations later *Christ* was born!

Conclusion

A. Jesus' Family

Some of us learn very early, others later on, that it is challenging, sometimes heartbreaking, to belong in a family. For all of us, being reminded of the mix of righteous people (like David) along with those who famously fell in sin (also like David) in Jesus' own family line is a word of comfort: no matter who we come from, we can look for God's hand at work in our families.

More than this, Jesus' genealogy is a word of comfort because it is a word about our Lord Jesus Christ. In Him, God fulfilled promises He made (by Matthew's count) as early as 42 generations prior! The lineage of Jesus shows how God moved beyond people's sin and selfishness to use them in His plan for His Messiah. This genealogy is the first evidence Matthew presents of Jesus' Messiahship, and certainly not the last (example: Matthew 16:16).

What Do You Think?

Who in Matthew's genealogy of Jesus do you most identify with?

Digging Deeper

What comfort do you find in God's working through that person for His promises to be fulfilled in Christ?

B. Prayer

Lord God, may we be reminded that You use all sorts of people to accomplish Your will. May You use us, in spite of our sins and weaknesses. In Jesus' name we pray. Amen.

C. Thought to Remember

God uses imperfect people to accomplish His perfect plans.

Involvement Learning

Enhance your lesson with KJV Bible Student *(from your curriculum supplier) and the reproducible activity page (at www.standardlesson.com or in the back of the* KJV Standard Lesson Commentary Deluxe Edition*).*

Into the Lesson

Engage the class in a discussion of genealogy. Possible questions to ask are: 1–How have you researched your family heritage? 2–What ancestors are you most proud of? Why? 3–Which ancestors would you rather forget? Why? 4–What family legacy has been handed down to you from your ancestors? Guide the group to consider not only material inheritance but also family traditions, customs, values, educational legacies, occupations, and faith heritage that have been woven into the fabric of the family for generations.

Alternative. Distribute copies of the "Surprising Ancestors" exercise from the activity page, which you can download. Have learners work individually on the exercise as indicated for a minute or less before discussing conclusions as a whole group. *Option.* Read the exercise aloud and have the class vote on each statement.

Next, say, "Jesus' genealogy includes a lot of characters who might surprise us—if we forget that God works through surprising people. Let's see what we can learn from Jesus' ancestry and how we can be encouraged by it."

Into the Word

Distribute a handout (you create) of Matthew 1:1-17. After reading verse 1 aloud to the class, ask three volunteers to read the three genealogical divisions (vv. 2-6a, 6b-11, 12-16); close by reading verse 17 yourself. As you and the volunteers read, have the rest of the class circle names they recognize, write question marks by names they don't recognize, and put stars by people they are surprised are named. Allow one minute for learners silently to reread the genealogy to complete their mark-up. Ask the class what themes they can identify from the genealogy that are present throughout Matthew's Gospel. See the Lesson Context for possible answers.

Alternative. Invite the class to pick out any familiar names they know from the genealogy and tell biblical stories they remember about these characters. They may want to use their phones or the concordances or glossaries in the back of their Bibles to find some details. What good and bad qualities did Jesus' ancestors have?

Divide the group into three groups: **Father Abraham** (Matthew 1:2-6a), **King David** (1:6b-11), and **Exile in Babylon** (1:12-16). Allow 10 minutes for the groups to explore the importance of their respective person or event in Israel's history, as well as any names within their verses they identified in the previous exercise. Use the lesson commentary to find starting points for learning more about the men and women listed. When the class comes back together, ask each group to summarize their main character/event and disclose one surprising or eye-opening fact they discovered. Ask whether this exercise yielded any new insight regarding themes in Matthew.

Alternative. Distribute copies of the "Genealogy Puzzle" exercise from the activity page. Have learners complete it as directed in groups of three.

Conclude with a discussion about why Matthew started his Gospel with the genealogy of Jesus. What is Matthew claiming in 1:1 and again in 1:17? Why is that important? Refer to the commentary as desired.

Into Life

In pairs, have learners share themes in their own genealogies that show God's work in their families. Then have each learner share ideas about how to value his or her own genealogy in Christ. After a few minutes, bring the class back together and ask one volunteer to read 1 Timothy 1:4 and another to read Titus 3:9. Discuss how to avoid the dangers noted in these two verses.

Close the class in prayer, praising God for making us part of His family lineage.

Expectant Mothers' Faith

Devotional Reading: Philippians 4:10-19
Background Scripture: Luke 1:1-25, 39-45, 56-60

Luke 1:36-45, 56

36 And, behold, thy cousin Elisabeth, she hath also conceived a son in her old age: and this is the sixth month with her, who was called barren.

37 For with God nothing shall be impossible.

38 And Mary said, Behold the handmaid of the Lord; be it unto me according to thy word. And the angel departed from her.

39 And Mary arose in those days, and went into the hill country with haste, into a city of Juda;

40 And entered into the house of Zacharias, and saluted Elisabeth.

41 And it came to pass, that, when Elisabeth heard the salutation of Mary, the babe leaped in her womb; and Elisabeth was filled with the Holy Ghost:

42 And she spake out with a loud voice, and said, Blessed art thou among women, and blessed is the fruit of thy womb.

43 And whence is this to me, that the mother of my Lord should come to me?

44 For, lo, as soon as the voice of thy salutation sounded in mine ears, the babe leaped in my womb for joy.

45 And blessed is she that believed: for there shall be a performance of those things which were told her from the Lord.

56 And Mary abode with her about three months, and returned to her own house.

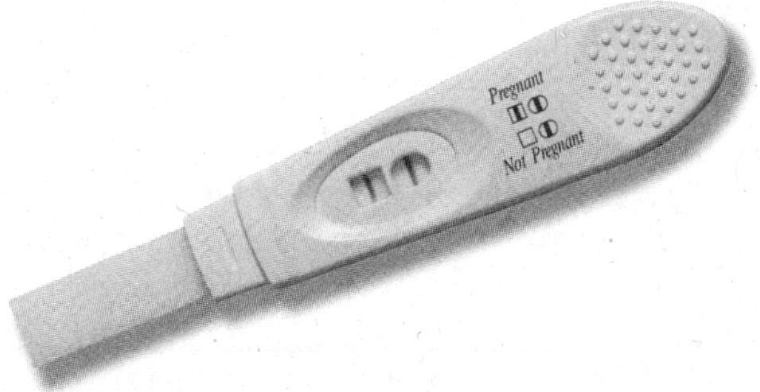

Key Text

And it came to pass, that, when Elisabeth heard the salutation of Mary, the babe leaped in her womb; and Elisabeth was filled with the Holy Ghost: and she spake out with a loud voice, and said, Blessed art thou among women. **—Luke 1:41-42a**

Faith That

Pleases God

Unit 1: Profiles in Faith

Lessons 1–5

Lesson Aims

After participating in this lesson, each learner will be able to:

1. Identify the relationship between the two expectant mothers.

2. Explain the significance of Elisabeth's greeting.

3. Suggest one way that he or she can move closer to having a faith as one or both expectant mothers had.

Lesson Outline

Introduction

A. Infectious Joy

B. Lesson Context

I. Acceptance of the Message (Luke 1:36-38)

A. Encouragement to Believe (vv. 36-37)

B. Belief and Submission (v. 38)

II. Joyous Meeting (Luke 1:39-45, 56)

A. Hope-Filled Journey (vv. 39-40)

B. Blessed Be the Mother (vv. 41-44)

When the King Comes to Us

C. Blessed Be Your Faith (vv. 45, 56)

The Greater Blessed

Conclusion

A. Two Models, Two Paths

B. Prayer

C. Thought to Remember

Introduction

A. Infectious Joy

Early in our marriage, my wife was not certain whether she ever wanted children. That was something I had to work through because I was certain that I *did* want children to be part of our family. I ultimately decided that I hadn't married her for her ability to have children, and I had to leave the question in God's hands. However, she was interested in birthing as a profession, and she completed her training to become a *doula* (a Greek word meaning "female servant"), which is a labor and birth support worker. This means she was with women having babies a lot.

My wife's job had her working both with new parents and parents who were having their fifth or sixth child. In both cases, she witnessed a lot of pain but also the boundless joy of the parents as their babies were born. Her reluctance about having children changed, and now we have three. She desires more, saying that she would happily have six children if she could. This has even led us into looking at adoption. All of this happened because the joy of other parents was infectious.

In this lesson, we will see how joy can be infectious, from the unborn John the Baptist to his mother Elisabeth, to even the shared joy between Elisabeth and Mary.

B. Lesson Context

Early church tradition unanimously identified Luke, a physician and traveling companion of Paul, as the writer of the third Gospel and the book of Acts (Colossians 4:11-14). While the evidence is slim, there is a chance that Luke was the only Gentile author in the New Testament. Some scholars put the date of writing at around AD 60. This most likely occurred while Paul was imprisoned at Caesarea Maritima (as recorded in Acts 23:33; 24:27), which would have freed up Luke to interview the eyewitnesses of Jesus' earthly ministry (Luke 1:1-3). The accuracy of the resulting research puts Luke in the company of the very best ancient Greek historians.

One of the eyewitnesses that Luke could have

interviewed was Mary, the mother of Jesus. Such an interview would not be surprising, for the Gospel of Luke has more material regarding women than either of the other synoptic Gospels, Matthew and Mark. One example of this material unique to Luke's Gospel is Jesus' interaction with Mary and Martha in Luke 10:38-42. Another example is today's text. As the text opens, the birth of the person who came to be known as John the Baptist has been foretold (Luke 1:5-25), as has been the birth of Jesus (1:26-35)—both by angelic visitation.

I. Acceptance of the Message

(Luke 1:36-38)

A. Encouragement to Believe (vv. 36-37)

36. And, behold, thy cousin Elisabeth, she hath also conceived a son in her old age: and this is the sixth month with her, who was called barren.

The one speaking is the angel Gabriel, and the one being spoken to is Mary (Luke 1:26-27). Exactly how Elisabeth and Mary were related is not certain since the Greek word translated *cousin* simply means "female relative." Although the birth of Elisabeth's son, John the Baptist, had already been foretold, the news apparently didn't reach Mary until this point, six months after the conception (compare 1:24). That conception was miraculous, given that Elisabeth had been through menopause (1:7, 18). She and her husband had been childless to this point, given the *barren* state of Elisabeth (compare and contrast Genesis 11:30; 25:21; 29:31; Judges 13:2-3; 1 Samuel 1:2).

There is uncertainty as to exactly how old John's parents were. His father, Zacharias, was a priest, and priests were from the tribe of Levi. Levites had to retire at age 50 (Numbers 8:25; compare 4:46-47), but no specific age limit is found for priests. (All priests were Levites, but not all Levites were priests.) Thus we should not be surprised that Zacharias was still serving in his priestly role (Luke 1:8-9). Additionally, the high priest typically served for life (see Joshua 20:6).

This information about Elisabeth's pregnancy would have strengthened Mary's faith. It confirmed what the angel Gabriel had just said about the child Mary would be bearing.

37. For with God nothing shall be impossible.

This verse would have reminded the original reader of Abraham and Sarah's struggle with infertility, for it is an allusion to Genesis 18:14: "Is any thing too hard for the Lord?" (See also Matthew 19:26; Mark 10:27.)

> **What Do You Think?**
> How does Luke 1:37 encourage your trust in God's Word?
>
> **Digging Deeper**
> How does Jesus' interpretation of Scripture in Matthew 4:1-11 inform your response?

B. Belief and Submission (v. 38)

38. And Mary said, Behold the handmaid of the Lord; be it unto me according to thy word. And the angel departed from her.

Both the elderly priest Zacharias and the young virgin *Mary* asked the question, "How?" (Luke 1:18, 34). However, Gabriel's responses to each of them differ. Zacharias asked skeptically for a sign—an inappropriate response from a person of his status. God responded with a sign, though probably not the kind Zacharias had

How to Say It

Caesarea Maritima	Sess-uh-*ree*-uh Mar-uh-*tee*-muh.
eulogy	*you*-luh-jee.
Gabriel	*Gay*-bree-ul.
Galilee	*Gal*-uh-lee.
Hebron	*Hee*-brun or *Heb*-run.
Levi	*Lee*-vye.
Levites	*Lee*-vites.
Nazareth	*Naz*-uh-reth.
synoptic	sih-nawp-tihk.
Thessalonians	*Thess*-uh-**lo**-nee-unz (*th* as in *thin*).
Zacharias	Zack-uh-*rye*-us.

expected (see 1:19-20). Mary's reaction, on the other hand, was one of innocent inquiry, given her subsequent humility, as seen in the verse before us. She was willing to do whatever service that God would require of her. Young Mary's faith surpassed that of an old priest! Mary's faith can be compared and contrasted with Hannah's (1 Samuel 1:10-20).

There is nothing in Gabriel's response to suggest that God's plan was contingent on Mary's agreement with it. Even so, her statement of submission is important. In describing herself as a *handmaid*, Mary used a term that refers to servants (the same Greek word noted in the Introduction, above; also in Luke 1:48 and Acts 2:18). In so doing, so she expressed her intended obedience to the Lord.

II. Joyous Meeting

(Luke 1:39-45, 56)

A. Hope-Filled Journey (vv. 39-40)

39. And Mary arose in those days, and went into the hill country with haste, into a city of Juda.

Mary lived in "a city of Galilee, named Nazareth" (Luke 1:26), while Elisabeth and her husband, Zacharias, lived in an unnamed *city of Juda*. The exact location of their home is unknown, but *the hill country* would have included the city of Hebron, which was given to the priests (see Joshua 21:11). A journey from one to the other would have been about 100 miles. The two villages were located in different areas that later would have different rulers (see Matthew 2:22; Luke 3:1). But, in the time of the event depicted in this verse, Herod the Great ruled both (see 1:5).

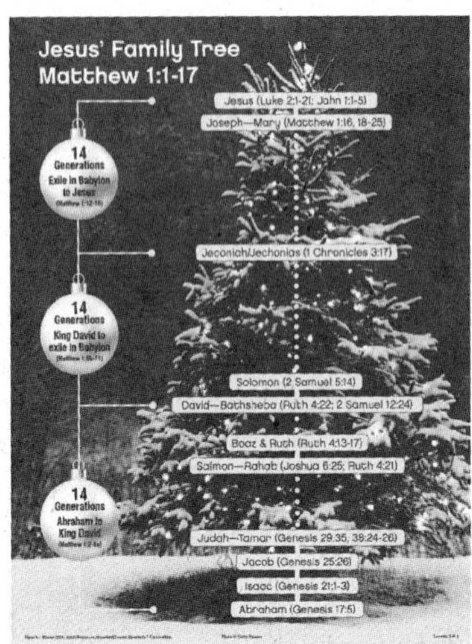

Visual for Lessons 3 & 4

Encourage learners to pray for God to work through their families this holiday season.

Hilly Juda is the district that included Jerusalem. If Hebron was not the unnamed city, then the trip would still be at least 35 miles, assuming that the city is at the northern tip of Judean territory. Either way, it's a long trip by foot! Mary most likely made the trip with a caravan or a companion for safety. Luke indicates that Mary traveled to see Elizabeth with a sense of urgency that may reflect that difficult travels are more manageable in the early stages of pregnancy. The haste in which she did so seems to reflect her eager desire to see this wonder that the angel told her of.

> **What Do You Think?**
> What steps will you take to be a relative who your family can turn to during confusion, crisis, or need?
>
> **Digging Deeper**
> How will you improve your margin with time and money so that you can better help family members?

40. And entered into the house of Zacharias, and saluted Elisabeth.

Luke made no mention either of distance or exhaustion. Instead, he focused on the interactions of those present. On entering *the house*, Mary began a normal exchange of greetings with *Elisabeth*; the word translated *saluted* occurs elsewhere in terms of normal greetings (examples: Romans 16:3, 6, 8, 11). There were several common greetings from that period, such as, "The blessing of Yahweh be upon thee," or, "Be thou blessed of Yahweh," or, "May peace be yours" (compare Luke 24:36; John 20:19-26). We don't know which of these salutations Mary used, if any. Greetings in antiquity often included some type of kiss (examples: Exodus 18:7; 1 Thessalonians 5:26).

B. Blessed Be the Mother (vv. 41-44)

41. And it came to pass, that, when Elisabeth heard the salutation of Mary, the babe leaped in her womb; and Elisabeth was filled with the Holy Ghost.

While no details are given as to exactly when *Mary* became pregnant, time factors indicate that she was not far enough along to be showing. Even so, *Elisabeth* realized that her younger relative was with child when the two met, provoking a startling reaction!

There is nothing inherently unusual about a baby moving about in the *womb*, of course. But the timing of that reaction here is significant in view of the relationship that later emerges between Jesus (Mary's child) and John the Baptist (Elisabeth's child). The latter was to be "filled with the Holy Ghost, even from his mother's womb" as empowerment "to make ready a people prepared for the Lord" (Luke 1:15-17). Even before his birth, John began to fulfill his role by signaling to his mother that the anticipated Christ, himself yet unborn, was present. At the same time, *Elisabeth was filled* with the Spirit to confirm the message Mary had received from the angel (next verse).

The Holy Ghost is a key figure throughout the Scriptures written by Luke. His Gospel and the book of Acts combined feature about 60 percent of the New Testament's usages of this designation.

42. And she spake out with a loud voice, and said, Blessed art thou among women, and blessed is the fruit of thy womb.

While Mary possibly would not have been showing as pregnant yet, her state was revealed to Elisabeth by the Holy Spirit. Not only that, but the identity of the child was also revealed to her. Elisabeth could not be silent concerning the events that were transpiring. She may have been in seclusion concerning her own pregnancy, but when the mother of the Lord shows up on her doorstep, Elisabeth became a *loud* proclaimer of the truth.

The word *blessed* occurs three times in today's text: twice here and once in verse 45. However, different Greek words are behind the translations. The word behind the two instances of "blessed" in the verse at hand is also our English word *eulogy*. As we use that word today, we refer to statements in honor of someone who has died. But we should not take the modern way we use this word and "read it back" into the Bible! There it means "to speak well of," "to celebrate with praises," or "to extol" someone, but not just at funerals. Elisabeth was speaking well of Mary while the latter was still very much alive!

Given the importance of this verse in certain religious circles, it is essential to note that these two statements do not speak to why Mary is blessed (but see Luke 1:45, below). We can note at this point that doubled expressions of blessing have precedent in the Old Testament (see Deuteronomy 28:3, 6; Judges 5:24).

What Do You Think?

What is one action you can take in the upcoming week so that others feel blessed when they are with you?

Digging Deeper

How does Galatians 5:22-23 affect your response?

43. And whence is this to me, that the mother of my Lord should come to me?

Elisabeth was the first person to acknowledge Jesus as *Lord*, even though Jesus was still in Mary's womb. In Scripture, the designation *my Lord* is used for both God and Jesus and is preferred by Luke. For comparative purposes, Mark uses the phrase *my Lord* 6 times, and Luke uses the designation 27 times! While it is uncertain precisely what Elisabeth understood by this address, the fact that she used it highlights her great faith that God was intervening in history. Elisabeth's question is one of great humility as well as divinely given insight.

When the King Comes to Us

A king paid a surprise visit to the house of his servant and—to no surprise—left the servant befuddled.

"Sir," stammered the servant, "What are you doing here?"

The servant's question and confusion were

understandable. Why would a royal leader show up at the home of a lowly hireling? Was the servant in trouble? Did he do something wrong?

"I wanted to get to know your situation firsthand and see what needs of yours I can meet," replied the king.

For several minutes, the servant experienced a tidal wave of various emotions—inadequacy, gratitude, relief, joy, etc. Realizing his utter unworthiness to host the king humbled him.

Do you, Christian, experience a similar range of emotions when you reflect on the fact that the Son of God put on flesh to meet us on our own turf? Are you no less amazed than Elisabeth at the arrival of God's grace to us in Christ? If not, what deficit do you need to address in this regard?

—D. D.

44. For, lo, as soon as the voice of thy salutation sounded in mine ears, the babe leaped in my womb for joy.

This verse repeats information from verse 41, above, and adds *for joy.* John the Baptist's prenatal reaction seems somehow to have reflected his sense of anticipation of the coming of the one who would give meaning to John's mission.

Since Elisabeth was six months along in her pregnancy, the child in her womb was developed enough for Elisabeth to feel movement—and John *the babe* really moved! As John the Baptist would reflect on rejoicing at the hearing of the bridegroom Jesus' voice some 30 years hence (Luke 3:23; John 3:29), so here John rejoiced at the hearing of Mary's voice as she carried the unborn Jesus. And Elisabeth herself had some insight to discern that John's movement was not arbitrary.

It is likely that the Spirit informed the unborn John who this was, and John leaped for joy. The whole reason for John's existence was now here before him. The filling of Elisabeth by the Holy Spirit is what allowed her to discern what John's sudden movement meant. She gave voice to the joy that the baby inside her felt.

John 1:29-34 reveals that it wasn't anything about John himself that caused him to recognize Jesus. Instead, God informed him of Jesus' identity, and the same must be true here.

C. Blessed Be Your Faith (vv. 45, 56)

45. And blessed is she that believed: for there shall be a performance of those things which were told her from the Lord.

Elisabeth stated that Mary was blessed first, not because of Mary's identity, but because of with whom Mary was pregnant. This is very much the same sort of salutation that Gabriel gave to Mary when he first appeared to her (Luke 1:28).

The Greek word translated *blessed* here and three verses later is not the same word translated that way in Luke 1:42, above. The word under consideration here, occurring 50 times in the New Testament, will be the one that Jesus used later in pronouncing the Beatitudes (Matthew 5:3-11). It carries the sense of "enjoying favorable circumstances" (compare its translation as "happier" in 1 Corinthians 7:40).

While the blessing of Luke 1:42 was based on the fact that Mary was to bear the Messiah, the blessing pronounced here is based on her faith (*she that believed*). Mary's belief starkly contrasts the unbelief of the elderly priest Zacharias, father of John the Baptist (see Luke 1:5-20). Use of the word translated *blessed* usually includes a reason or explanation for someone to be regarded as blessed. We see such a reason here. Mary was blessed because she believed that *there shall be a performance of those things which were told her from the Lord.*

What Do You Think?

What steps can you take to imitate Mary's belief?

Digging Deeper

What distractions do you need to remove in order to do so?

The Greater Blessed

Jackie married her high school sweetheart, received an offer for her dream job, bought her dream house, and became pregnant in the same year. Every conversation she had with her friends resulted in the response: "You are so blessed!" Her sister, Jasmine, did not hear the same pronouncement nearly as often. Jasmine remained single and made less than half as much money as Jackie.

But Jasmine was a Christian and a member of a church, while sister Jackie was not. Which of these two women was the greater blessed?

The answer to that depends on which lens you use in viewing their situations. Viewed strictly through a worldly lens, Jackie was the greater blessed; but viewed through the heavenly lens of eternity, the greater blessed is Jasmine.

Which lens do you use to view your own status and situation?

Have you forgotten how blessed you are to believe in Christ? It's easy to do in a world that casts God to the side and enthrones His gifts as gods themselves. But let Elisabeth's pronouncements of blessing remind you of the true nature of blessedness. —D. D.

56. And Mary abode with her about three months, and returned to her own house.

The *three months* spent with Elisabeth were undoubtedly an additional blessing for *Mary*. Here was a safe place for this young woman to adapt to her changed situation as Elisabeth provided support. Mary also was undoubtedly a blessing to Elisabeth in return, as the older woman in the latter stage of her pregnancy probably needed the help of a younger person.

Since the six months of Luke 1:26, 36 plus the three months of the verse before us equals nine months, Mary would have left just before John's birth or just after it. Relatives were at the naming ceremony (see Luke 1:58), and these could have included Mary. But ultimately, this is speculation—the text does not say.

What Do You Think?

What are some ways you can provide hospitality and support to expectant mothers?

Digging Deeper

How is James 1:27 relevant here?

Conclusion

A. Two Models, Two Paths

When it comes to belief and faith, I have often wondered whether I am more in the mold of Zacharias, with his doubts, than I am in the role of Mary, with her faith and acceptance. As I write this, there are multiple degrees in biblical studies hanging on my office wall, and I have 20 years of teaching experience at a Bible college under my belt. As a seasoned priest, Zacharias was similarly well-educated in the things of God. You would expect him to have the greater faith. But the greater faith is found with Mary.

Now I genuinely believe my education is a blessing and helps my faith. Yet there are times when I wonder whether my education distracts me from having faith like Mary's. Perhaps we trust in our learning and understanding to figure things out rather than trusting God, and in so doing violate Proverbs 3:5-6: "Trust in the Lord with all thine heart; and lean not unto thine own understanding. In all thy ways acknowledge him, and he shall direct thy paths." Mary wasn't as formally educated as the learned priest. Yet, her belief was genuine. What Mary was asked to accept was not an easy thing, and God understood this. In encouraging Mary's faith, the angel pointed her both backward to the story of Abraham and Sarah and forward to what was happening to Elisabeth. God may call you to a role similar to that of the angel as you point another person backward to a champion of faith and forward to an example of how God is now working.

The joy experienced by John the Baptist and Elisabeth resulted from Mary's faith, at least in part. The ripple effect of this joy is also seen in passages such as Matthew 2:10 and Luke 2:10, 21-38 (contrast Matthew 2:3). That ripple effect reaches us here in the twenty-first century—or at least it should!

B. Prayer

Lord, thank You for the example of Mary's trusting belief. Show us how Mary's example can inform our own faith. Help us move ever more toward belief and faith! Thank You for the encouragement of Your faithful people of the past as recorded in Your Word. We pray in Jesus' name. Amen.

C. Thought to Remember

Faith with obedience leads to great joy.

Involvement Learning

Enhance your lesson with KJV Bible Student *(from your curriculum supplier) and the reproducible activity page (at www.standardlesson.com or in the back of the* KJV Standard Lesson Commentary Deluxe Edition*).*

Into the Lesson

Ask volunteers to give examples of ways that children have unique insight. You may want to write responses on the board.

Transition to another topic by asking, "What are some of the funny or clever things you have heard children say?"

Transition to a third topic by inviting any parents to share about times when their baby kicked in the womb more than usual or reacted to particular sounds or experiences. Ask, "What might the baby have been communicating to the mother?"

Option: Before class, do an online search for insights by kids. Share with the class the results of your search.

Alternative. Distribute copies of the "Baby Talk Translator" exercise from the activity page, which you can download. Have learners complete it individually in a minute or less before discussing conclusions with a partner.

After either activity, say, "When Mary visited her relative Elisabeth, the unborn baby of Elisabeth reacted when hearing Mary's voice. In today's lesson, we will explore the significance of Elisabeth's response."

Into the Word

Ask three volunteers to play the parts of the angel, Mary, and Elisabeth. Have another volunteer read aloud Luke 1:36-45, 56 and have the three volunteers reenact the events depicted in the Scripture. After reading, pause for a time of prayer to thank God for the miracle of the birth of Jesus.

Divide the class into two groups: **Mary Group** and **Elisabeth Group**. Ask each group to use the Scripture reading to develop a profile of the faith of their group's namesake. Write these questions on the board to guide the groups:

1. What was the role of the Holy Spirit in each mother's reactions?
2. How did each woman's age affect her response?
3. What gave the women courage to accept and share their joy?
4. In what ways would the women have felt encouragement by having a relative who was also pregnant?
5. In what ways did the women respond with faith and courage to the call that God placed on their lives?
6. In one word, how would you describe the faith of Mary? of Elisabeth?

After 10 minutes, reconvene groups to share their profiles with the whole class.

Into Life

Ask learners to spend one minute in silent consideration regarding how they might respond in courage and faith to a call that God has given each of them.

Say, "One way that we can move closer to the kind of faith that both women had is through praising God in all circumstances, no matter how unusual or uncertain those circumstances may be." Divide learners into pairs. Allow time for each learner to share with his or her partner three reasons for praising God despite any challenging circumstances that learners may be experiencing.

Alternative. Distribute copies of the "Write Your Own Song" activity from the activity page. Have learners complete it individually in a minute or less before sharing their prayers of praise with a partner.

Conclude class with a time of worship and praise. Play Christmas songs that are related to today's Scripture and meaningful to your congregation. Display the song lyrics for students to sing or read along as they choose.

Option. If learners wrote their own songs in the previous activity, ask volunteers to read what they wrote as prayers of praise to God.

December 31
Lesson 5 (KJV)

The Faith of the Wise Men

Devotional Reading: Isaiah 49:1-6
Background Scripture: Micah 5:2-4; Matthew 2:1-12

Matthew 2:1-12

**1 Now when Jesus was born in Bethle-
hem of Judaea in the days of Herod the king,
behold, there came wise men from the east to
Jerusalem,
2 Saying, Where is he that is born King of
the Jews? for we have seen his star in the east,
and are come to worship him.
3 When Herod the king had heard these
things, he was troubled, and all Jerusalem with
him.
4 And when he had gathered all the chief
priests and scribes of the people together, he
demanded of them where Christ should be
born.
5 And they said unto him, In Bethlehem of
Judaea: for thus it is written by the prophet,
6 And thou Bethlehem, in the land of Juda,
art not the least among the princes of Juda: for
out of thee shall come a Governor, that shall
rule my people Israel.
7 Then Herod, when he had privily called
the wise men, enquired of them diligently what
time the star appeared.
8 And he sent them to Bethlehem, and said,
Go and search diligently for the young child;
and when ye have found him, bring me word
again, that I may come and worship him also.
9 When they had heard the king, they
departed; and, lo, the star, which they saw in
the east, went before them, till it came and
stood over where the young child was.
10 When they saw the star, they rejoiced
with exceeding great joy.
11 And when they were come into the
house, they saw the young child with Mary his
mother, and fell down, and worshipped him:
and when they had opened their treasures, they
presented unto him gifts; gold, and frankincense, and myrrh.
12 And being warned of God in a dream
that they should not return to Herod, they
departed into their own country another way.**

Key Text

Where is he that is born King of the Jews? for we have seen his star in the east, and are come to worship him. **—Matthew 2:2**

Faith That
Pleases God

Unit 1: Profiles in Faith

Lessons 1–5

Lesson Aims

After participating in this lesson, each learner will be able to:

1. Describe the historical setting of the encounter between Herod and the wise men.

2. Contrast God's guidance of the wise men on their mission with His guidance of Christians today.

3. Identify one area of ministry where God is leading him or her and discuss with a church leader the best way to follow that path faithfully.

Lesson Outline

Introduction
- A. Still Seeking Jesus?
- B. Lesson Context

I. The New King Is Born (Matthew 2:1-2)
- A. Coming to Jerusalem (v. 1)
- B. Seeking the King (v. 2)
  - *"The Star"*

II. The Old King Is Troubled (Matthew 2:3-8)
- A. Consulting the Scholars (vv. 3-4)
- B. Pinpointing Bethlehem (vv. 5-6)
- C. Plotting Murder (vv. 7-8)
  - *The Great and the Terrible*

III. The Child Is Worshipped (Matthew 2:9-12)
- A. Following the Star (vv. 9-10)
- B. Presenting Treasures (v. 11)
- C. Exiting Another Way (v. 12)

Conclusion
- A. Offer Thy Heart
- B. Prayer
- C. Thought to Remember

Introduction

A. Still Seeking Jesus?

The Christmas season reveals many sayings that try to encapsulate the meaning of the holiday in just a few words. Near my neighborhood, one house always displays a banner that reads, "Christ is the reason for the season." Another neighbor annually displays a sign proclaiming, "Let's put Christ back in Christmas." These sayings are self-explanatory. After all, why have a season bearing the name of Christ without consideration of Christ himself?

Even asking that question shows the absurdity of some secular Christmas traditions. Should Christmas remind us of cola-drinking polar bears in red mufflers? Clydesdales hauling a beer wagon? A snowman come to life? Or is there something more important?

Another saying requires a bit of knowledge of the biblical Christmas story to make sense: "Wise men still seek him." This saying is based on the account in today's text.

B. Lesson Context

Our text for study involves a mysterious star. This invites a consideration of the distinction between astronomy and astrology. In modern times, we make a clear-cut distinction between those two areas of inquiry. But the two were blended together in the ancient world. *Astronomy* is the scientific study of the sun, moon, stars, planets, etc.; *astrology* combines that study with the belief that the so-called gods orchestrate the appearance, positions, and movements of heavenly phenomena and, therefore, reveal information about divine plans for the future (omens). Astrology is practiced today in the form of horoscopes associated with the zodiac.

In the Old Testament, astrologers are mentioned most notably in the book of Daniel (Daniel 2:2, 10; 4:7; 5:7, 11; see also Isaiah 47:13). The people of Israel were warned about pagan occult practices; astrology, being a type of divination, was one of those (Deuteronomy 18:10-11; Jeremiah 10:2). And moving from consulting the stars to worshipping the stars was an all-too-easy step to take (Deuteronomy 4:19; 17:2-5; Jeremiah 8:2).

The ancient Greek translation of the book of Daniel designates such men as *magoi*, from which we derive our modern word *magician*. But words change meaning over time, and how ancient people viewed *magoi* is not to be equated with the contemporary role of a magician who uses sleight of hand to entertain audiences. Instead, this word describes men of wisdom; we surmise they were astrologer-scholars. This same Greek word *magoi* is behind the English translation "wise men" in Matthew 2:1, 7, 16. It occurs also in Acts 13:6, 8, translated there as "sorcerer."

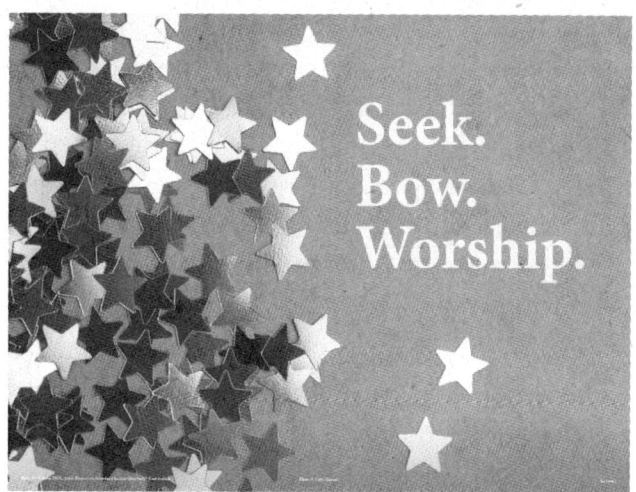

Visual for Lesson 5. *Point to the visual after reading verse 2b and ask volunteers to share how they seek, bow, and worship.*

I. The New King Is Born

(Matthew 2:1-2)

A. Coming to Jerusalem (v. 1)

1a. Now when Jesus was born in Bethlehem of Judaea.

Matthew gives fewer details about the actual birth of Jesus than does Luke. Instead, Matthew relates the nativity story with simplicity: *Jesus was born in Bethlehem.* A few details are added, tying his account to the geography and history of Palestine. *Bethlehem* (meaning "house of bread") *of Judaea* was a village located a few miles south-southwest of Jerusalem. It is not to be confused with Bethlehem of Zebulun (Joshua 19:15). The Bethlehem noted in today's text was the birthplace of King David (1 Samuel 20:6).

1b. In the days of Herod the king.

The phrase *the days of Herod the king* sets the context of a specific ruler in an identifiable time frame. This is the king known as Herod the Great, who ruled 37–4 BC as the first Roman puppet-king of Judea. The name *Herod* occurs in the New Testament about 40 times, often referring to different people—it's a challenge not to get them confused! According to our best records, the Herod in view here died in 4 BC. Therefore, the events in today's text take place shortly before that (compare Matthew 2:19).

Herod the Great was not an ethnic Jew but an Idumean (related to modern Arabs). He is designated "the Great" because of his extensive building projects. The grandest of these was the rebuilding of the temple in Jerusalem, a project he began about 20 BC and that was unfinished at the time of his death (compare John 2:20).

1c. Behold, there came wise men from the east to Jerusalem.

Many legends have arisen in Christian tradition about these *wise men*. These include speculations regarding their occupations (kings?), their number (three?), their names (Melchior, Caspar, and Balthazar?), and their place of origin (Babylon? Persia?). Matthew's account doesn't answer such questions. See the Lesson Context for background observations regarding the word *magoi*, translated as "wise men."

We should understand *from the east* as describing their point of origin, not their route; it's "wise men from the east," not "came from the east." This origin reminds us of the lands of Babylon and Persia, which lie 600 miles or more from Jerusalem in a straight line that crosses the Syrian Desert. But it is highly unlikely that the wise men traveled across that intervening desert. Instead, they would have come *to Jerusalem* by following the Euphrates River valley to Syria and then south through Damascus. This was a well-traveled trade route through a region known as the Fertile Crescent. Such a route would have been over a thousand miles, making a grand geographic arc from the Middle East to Palestine. To walk this distance would have taken four months (compare Ezra 7:8-9).

That there are at least two wise men is certain because the term is plural. But beyond that, we don't know how many there were. (The tradition that there were three wise men seems based on the fact they offer three gifts to Jesus in Matthew 2:11, below.) They likely would have been in a large, well-funded entourage, perhaps a couple of dozen men altogether (compare 1 Kings 10:1-2). These details paint a picture of determination on their part.

B. Seeking the King (v. 2)

2a. Saying, Where is he that is born King of the Jews?

Verse 7, below, indicates that the wise men were granted a personal audience with Herod at some point. But we aren't sure that was the case, as the wise men posed the question in the verse before us. An immediate audience would indicate that they were not a rag-tag group of nobodies! They either had diplomatic letters of introduction, could offer generous bribes, or presented such a regal appearance that Herod agreed to see them sooner rather than later. This access to Herod has led some to speculate the visitors were "kings" in their own right. However, Matthew does not mention this, and it is not implied in their designation as "wise men" or *magoi*.

2b. For we have seen his star in the east, and are come to worship him.

The reason for the wise men's question is threefold. First, the fact that a particular *star* caught their attention points to their vocation as learned stargazers. These were astrologers who spent many hours attempting to interpret astral movements as omens from deities. (See the Lesson Context for a deeper dive here.) While the Old Testament connects divination with pagan idolatry (Deuteronomy 18:10; 2 Kings 17:17; Jeremiah 14:14), we should not rule out God's use of a specially prepared star to signal the birth of Jesus.

Second, the wise men's departure point *in the east* yields the possibility that they were Jews from the large Jewish community that remained in Babylon after the exile ended around 538 BC. But that possibility seems unlikely, given their astrological orientation.

Third, the wise men interpreted the new star as a sign that the newly arrived King of the Jews was important enough to be worthy of their *worship*. Although not specified by Matthew, this is often seen as a fulfillment of the "Star out of Jacob" prophecy of Numbers 24:17. Whether these men were Jews or not, this realization had touched them profoundly—so much so that they were willing to come to Jerusalem at enormous cost and considerable danger.

What Do You Think?

In what ways can seeing creation lead you to worshipping God?

Digging Deeper

How would you respond in worship in this regard?

"The Star"

As I was channel-surfing one day, I chanced upon a science-fiction tale. It was a TV adaptation of a short story titled "The Star," written by Arthur C. Clarke in 1954.

The plot involved a spaceship that was exploring the Phoenix Nebula, the remnant of a star that had exploded as a supernova. Aboard the spacecraft was a Roman Catholic priest highly skilled in astrophysics. As the exploration progressed, a horrific truth dawned on him: this supernova had been the star of Bethlehem. The viewer was drawn to the conclusion that an entire civilization that was "disturbingly human" had been exterminated by this supernova. The result for the priest was a crisis of faith.

How to Say It

Damascus	Duh-*mass*-kus.
Euphrates	You-*fray*-teez.
frankincense	*frank*-in-sense.
Herod	*Hair*-ud.
Idumean	Id-you-*me*-un.
Judaea	Joo-*dee*-uh.
magoi (Greek)	*mah*-joy.
myrrh	mur.
Persia	*Per*-zhuh.
Sadducees	*Sad*-you-seez.
Zebulun	*Zeb*-you-lun.

Such stories can engage the imagination in profound ways, but the imaginative elements are (or should be) easily recognized. When it comes to pondering rightly God's provisions for humanity, it's vital to avoid speculations and to stick with established facts: (1) the wise men were guided by a phenomenon provided by God, and (2) the "how" of that phenomenon is not provided. When you are pondering how God may be guiding you, how much effort do you devote to separating fact from imaginative thinking? —R. L. N.

II. The Old King Is Troubled

(Matthew 2:3-8)

A. Consulting the Scholars (vv. 3-4)

3. When Herod the king had heard these things, he was troubled, and all Jerusalem with him.

The wise men's inquiry did not sit well with the paranoid *Herod the king.* He was an old man who had sons and wives put to death when seen as threats to his throne. So Matthew, in grand understatement, says Herod *was troubled.* This was not mild irritation! The old family saying is "When Momma's not happy, nobody's happy," and it applies here. In *Jerusalem,* when Herod wasn't happy, no one in Jerusalem was happy, fearing another murderous rampage. The people of the city would be willing to do about anything to placate the king.

4. And when he had gathered all the chief priests and scribes of the people together, he demanded of them where Christ should be born.

The chief priests ruled Jerusalem's temple. They had an uneasy alliance with Herod that had enriched them greatly as the party of the Sadducees (Acts 5:17). The *scribes* were the experts in the Jewish Scriptures, often called upon to interpret fine points of the Law of Moses.

Herod was no expert on things such as prophecies concerning coming kings. Even so, he was apparently aware that the Jews believed a *Christ* was coming, the chosen Messiah of the Lord. (*Christ* and *Messiah* both mean "anointed one"; John 4:25.) Herod connected these prophecies with the inquiry of the wise men. Therefore, he *demanded* the religious leaders to reveal the birthplace of the Messiah, believing it must be specified in the writings of the prophets. While this would give an answer to the wise men, Herod had a more devious motive in learning the location, as we shall see.

B. Pinpointing Bethlehem (vv. 5-6)

5-6. And they said unto him, In Bethlehem of Judaea: for thus it is written by the prophet, And thou Bethlehem, in the land of Juda, art not the least among the princes of Juda: for out of thee shall come a Governor, that shall rule my people Israel.

In response, the religious leaders quoted Micah 5:2. On the precise designation *Bethlehem of Judaea,* see commentary on Matthew 2:1a, above. The prophet Micah worked in the eighth century BC, during the time of the prophet Isaiah. So this prophecy was already 700 years old at the time of Herod.

The Gospel of Matthew shows great interest in fulfilled prophecy, so this verse is a highlight. Micah's prophecy checks many boxes. It recognizes the relative insignificance of Bethlehem, still valid in Herod's day. It foretells the raising up of a new *Governor* or ruler from this city. And it indicates this person would not be a mere city ruler or district supervisor. Instead, the prophesied Messiah would *rule my people Israel.*

What Do You Think?

How might your congregation's influence in your community remind people of Jesus?

Digging Deeper

How will your congregation glorify the Lord locally? nationally? globally?

C. Plotting Murder (vv. 7-8)

7. Then Herod, when he had privily called the wise men, enquired of them diligently what time the star appeared.

The word *privily* indicates that *Herod* had dismissed the religious leaders in order to meet with *the wise men* alone. He set aside his rage in favor of putting on his happy face for this meeting. Ancient astrology was based on keeping precise records, so the wise men would have known the *time the star appeared*. The response of the wise men is not given. But we know the answer must have been at least four months prior to this meeting since that's the time required for the wise men to have walked to Jerusalem. The wise men's response was important to Herod because it determined the time window of his murderous decision in Matthew 2:16.

8. And he sent them to Bethlehem, and said, Go and search diligently for the young child; and when ye have found him, bring me word again, that I may come and worship him also.

Since we know Herod's real intent and how things turned out (see Matthew 2:13-18), the story becomes downright sinister at this point. His expressed desire to *worship him also* is a flat-out lie. But since Herod had been helpful to the wise men, they had no reason to suspect ulterior motives. So they took his words at face value.

> **What Do You Think?**
> How do believers discern whether to obey or disobey government leaders?
>
> **Digging Deeper**
> How do Daniel 3; Romans 13:1-14; Titus 3:1-2; and 1 Peter 2:13-17 inform your answer?

The Great and the Terrible

Ivan IV was born into the royal family of Russia in the year 1530. At 16, Ivan was crowned "tsar and grand prince of all Russia" by the Russian Orthodox Church and became the undisputed leader of feudal Russia.

Ivan was convinced that he was God's representative on earth. Therefore Ivan saw extending the power of "Holy Russia" over neighboring countries as his duty. Moreover, he thought it was his right and responsibility to punish the sins of his rivals with unspeakable tortures that were fashioned after medieval ideas of hell. Increasingly mentally unstable, he killed his eldest son and heir to the throne in a fit of rage. By his death at age 53, he had thoroughly earned his reputation as "Ivan the Terrible."

Political leaders such as Herod and Ivan aren't the only ones susceptible to seeing themselves as God's infallible representatives. Many others have fallen (or jumped) into that trap (examples: Numbers 12:2; Ezekiel 22:28). Ordinary people still use the name of Jesus to advance their agendas. As the modern saying goes, "Hands are the window to the intent." However, Jesus had this idea first (see Matthew 7:16-20). To know who follows Jesus, we must look at what they do. And when we look at them, let's make sure to look at ourselves as well.—A. W.

III. The Child Is Worshipped
(Matthew 2:9-12)

A. Following the Star (vv. 9-10)

9-10. When they had heard the king, they departed; and, lo, the star, which they saw in the east, went before them, till it came and stood over where the young child was. When they saw the star, they rejoiced with exceeding great joy.

The wise men would have exited Jerusalem from a gate near Herod's palace on the city's western side. We don't know what time of day it was. But to travel near or after sunset in a pre-electricity era simply didn't happen. The *exceeding great joy* the men experienced is thus understandable if the reappearance of *the star, which they saw in the east* happened as (or if) darkness settles. The wording indicates that the star moved in the same way as the pillar of fire guided the Hebrew people through the wilderness (see Exodus 13:20-22). The wise men could walk to Bethlehem in the dark, reaching *the young child* Jesus without waiting until sunrise.

B. Presenting Treasures (v. 11)

11. And when they were come into the house, they saw the young child with Mary his mother, and fell down, and worshipped him: and when they had opened their treasures, they presented unto him gifts; gold, and frankincense, and myrrh.

The location of *the young child with Mary his mother* was no longer the manger of Luke's account (Luke 2:16) but a *house*. Therefore, we may assume that the time spent by Mary and Joseph in the place of the manger was short before they found adequate shelter.

The wise men were not empty-handed in their worship of *the young child*. They presented Him with costly gifts fit for a king (see Isaiah 60:6). We easily understand the value of a gift of *gold*. While Matthew does not specify the form of this precious metal, it was likely coins. These were a vital resource for the family's subsequent flight to Egypt and return to Nazareth (Matthew 2:13-23).

Frankincense was considered the finest incense in the ancient world (see Exodus 30:34; Revelation 18:13). The word comes from Old French and means "pure incense." Made from the resin of the Boswellia tree and imported from southern Arabia and Africa, it was prized for its use in religious ceremonies and as a costly sacrificial offering.

Myrrh is an aromatic resin of the Commiphora tree. It was (and remains) valued as an ingredient in perfume; it was also used for anointing and in preparing a body for burial (John 19:39). It also had medicinal uses, both as a type of antiseptic for wounds and as a type of pain reducer (see Mark 15:23). Both frankincense and myrrh were extremely valuable and served as a compact treasure for Joseph and Mary, providing further resources beyond the gold.

> **What Do You Think?**
> How will you bring your best gifts to Jesus?
> **Digging Deeper**
> Who will you share those gifts with as an act of worshipping God?

C. Exiting Another Way (v. 12)

12. And being warned of God in a dream that they should not return to Herod, they departed into their own country another way.

The wise men, unsuspecting of Herod's treachery, needed to be *warned of God in a dream* not to report back to that tyrant. This warning served to protect not only the child Jesus but also Mary, Joseph, and the wise men. Herod's intent all along was to have this potential king killed, and the others could have very well ended up feeling the despot's wrath as well (compare Matthew 2:16).

The wise men left Bethlehem by *another way*, a road that would not take them through Jerusalem. For Matthew, this further confirmed that God was orchestrating the birth and protection of the Messiah.

> **What Do You Think?**
> How can a believer discern whether a dream is from the Lord or not?
> **Digging Deeper**
> What Scriptures inform your response?

Conclusion

A. Offer Thy Heart

A favorite Christmas carol of mine about the wise men is the nineteenth-century composition "The Three Kings" by Peter Cornelius. True, it has many of the legendary aspects of their story in presuming that they were kings, that they came from Persia, etc. The lesson of the carol is still powerful, though, and speaks to us today as one stanza implores the audience to travel with the kings to Bethlehem and offers hearts to the infant King of kings.

Most of us don't have much gold to offer Jesus. And if we even had any frankincense or myrrh, how would we offer those? But we can offer Him sincere hearts in worship. He is the Son of God, the true Messiah. At this time of year when we remember and celebrate the birth of our Lord in Bethlehem, may we offer our most precious gift: our hearts.

B. Prayer

Father, help us to emulate the faith of the wise men! As they let nothing stop them from reaching Jesus, may we do so as well. May the faith that allowed them to thwart the plans of a powerful opponent be ours as well. May we offer Your Son, Jesus, no empty-handed worship. We pray this in Jesus' name. Amen.

C. Thought to Remember

Wise men and women seek to worship King Jesus only and fully.

Involvement Learning

Enhance your lesson with KJV Bible Student *(from your curriculum supplier) and the reproducible activity page (at www.standardlesson.com or in the back of the* KJV Standard Lesson Commentary Deluxe Edition*).*

Into the Lesson

Invite volunteers to recall the most exciting baby announcement they ever received. Prompt them to share more by asking: 1–What circumstances made this announcement particularly special? 2–What hopes and dreams did you have for the coming child?

Alternative. Distribute the "Baby Gifts" exercise from the activity pages, which you can download. Have learners complete it individually in a minute or less before discussing conclusions as a whole class.

Say, "As we study today's lesson, consider how the baby announcement and gifts reveal the child's importance to the gift-givers and gift-receivers."

Into the Word

Ask a volunteer to read aloud Matthew 2:1-4. Divide learners into two groups: **Wise Men Group** and **King Herod Group**. Instruct groups to study these verses from the perspective of their group's namesake. Write the following questions on the board for groups to answer: 1–How did they get the "baby announcement"? 2–What was their response to the news? 3–Why did they want to know the location of the child? 4–What are one or two additional details about your character(s) based on Matthew 2:1-4?

Write the following headers on the board: *Wise Men* and *King Herod*. Invite volunteers from the groups to list their answers in the appropriate columns. Ask for volunteers to compare and contrast the information in the columns.

Ask a volunteer to read aloud Matthew 2:5-8. Have the **Wise Men Group** read Isaiah 9:2-7, and have the **King Herod Group** read Micah 5:2-5. Instruct groups to study these verses from the perspective of their group's namesake. Write the following questions on the board for groups to answer: 1–How does this prophecy connect to your group's namesake? 2–How might they have believed these prophecies would be fulfilled compared with how they were? Have a volunteer from each group share their responses. Invite each group to add their responses to the columns on the board.

Ask a volunteer to read aloud Matthew 2:9-12. Direct the **Wise Men Group** to discuss why they were able to accomplish their goal, then ask the **King Herod Group** to discuss why Herod's goal was foiled. Again, ask volunteers to write their group's conclusions on the board under the appropriate header.

Ask the class to look at the board and draw conclusions about God's guidance in this Scripture passage. Ask volunteers to discuss other examples from the Bible, history, or their own lives when good triumphed over evil plans.

Into Life

Say, "The wise men lived in faith and showed obedience to God by following the star and believing His guidance." Divide the class into small groups of three learners. Encourage learners to think about a church ministry to which God is leading him or her to volunteer. Ask: "How can you show faith and obedience this week in that ministry?" Invite learners to identify one area of ministry where God might be leading him or her to serve, and have them share these ideas with their small group. Encourage small groups to spend time praying for each other to follow God's leading faithfully.

Alternative. Distribute copies of the "Faith in Action" activity from the activity page. Have learners complete it individually in a minute or less before discussing conclusions in small groups. Challenge them to complete the first step of the activity during class, then complete the rest of the activity throughout the upcoming week. Give individuals the opportunity to share about this experience at the beginning of the next class time.

January 7
Lesson 6 (KJV)

Faith and Righteousness

Devotional Reading: Romans 5:12-21
Background Scripture: Hebrews 11

Hebrews 11:1-4a, 7a, 8, 17-18, 20-23, 32, 39-40

1 Now faith is the substance of things hoped for, the evidence of things not seen.

2 For by it the elders obtained a good report.

3 Through faith we understand that the worlds were framed by the word of God, so that things which are seen were not made of things which do appear.

4a By faith Abel offered unto God a more excellent sacrifice than Cain.

7a By faith Noah, being warned of God of things not seen as yet, moved with fear, prepared an ark to the saving of his house.

---

8 By faith Abraham, when he was called to go out into a place which he should after receive for an inheritance, obeyed; and he went out, not knowing whither he went.

---

17 By faith Abraham, when he was tried, offered up Isaac: and he that had received the promises offered up his only begotten son,

18 Of whom it was said, That in Isaac shall thy seed be called.

---

20 By faith Isaac blessed Jacob and Esau concerning things to come.

21 By faith Jacob, when he was a dying, blessed both the sons of Joseph; and worshipped, leaning upon the top of his staff.

22 By faith Joseph, when he died, made mention of the departing of the children of Israel; and gave commandment concerning his bones.

23 By faith Moses, when he was born, was hid three months of his parents, because they saw he was a proper child; and they were not afraid of the king's commandment.

---

32 And what shall I more say? for the time would fail me to tell of Gedeon, and of Barak, and of Samson, and of Jephthae; of David also, and Samuel, and of the prophets:

---

39 And these all, having obtained a good report through faith, received not the promise:

40 God having provided some better thing for us, that they without us should not be made perfect.

Key Text

Now faith is the substance of things hoped for, the evidence of things not seen. **—Hebrews 11:1**

Faith That

Pleases God

Unit 2: Learning About Faith

Lessons 6–9

Lesson Aims

After participating in this lesson, each learner will be able to:

1. State the definition of faith.

2. Explain the meaning and significance of the key verse.

3. List one change each in the categories of thought, behavior, and speech by which he or she will become more of a stranger to the world.

Lesson Outline

Introduction

A. Listening to the Trustworthy Voice

B. Lesson Context

I. Faith Explained (Hebrews 11:1-4a)

A. Definition (vv. 1-2)

B. Foundations (vv. 3-4a)

II. Faith Lived Out (Hebrews 11:7a, 8, 17-18, 20-23, 32)

A. Noah (v. 7a)

The Value of Fear

B. Abraham (vv. 8, 17-18)

C. Isaac (v. 20)

D. Jacob (v. 21)

E. Joseph (v. 22)

F. Amram and Jochebed (v. 23)

G. Others (v. 32)

Faith in a Blessed Future

III. Promises Because of Faith (Hebrews 11:39-40)

A. Not Received (v. 39)

B. Something Perfect (v. 40)

Conclusion

A. The Faith of Imperfect People

B. Prayer

C. Thought to Remember

Introduction

A. Listening to the Trustworthy Voice

I remember a particular game we played during youth group. Someone would be blindfolded and assigned specific tasks to accomplish; another person would be designated as a guide but was allowed only to speak instructions to the one who was blindfolded. The job of other people in the room was to cause distractions by shouting, making noise, giving wrong instructions, etc. The blindfolded person had to have faith in the guide and listen to only the guide.

God functions much like the guide in that game, and He has proven himself trustworthy. We may desire to do something that our limited vision tells us is edifying and appropriate. But if we are listening to our guide and trusting His voice above all else, we may discover otherwise.

B. Lesson Context

When reading a text, it's always a good idea to know the purpose for which it was written. The natural approach is to look for a clear purpose statement, such as in Luke 1:3-4 and John 20:30-31. The book of Hebrews, however, has no such statement. So the book's purpose must be inferred from its contents. The extended comparisons and contrasts of Jesus with Old Testament personalities, the Levitical priesthood, angels, etc., signify the purpose being to encourage wavering and persecuted Christians of Jewish background to stand firm in Christ and not retreat into Judaism. Beyond this relatively certain conclusion, there is no consensus regarding the authorship and date of Hebrews.

At the very end of the book, the 1611 edition of the *King James Version* has this footnote: "Written to the Hebrews from Italy by Timothy." But whether this is original to the text or the conclusion of the translators is debated.

Regarding the date of writing, we have some certainty that the book cannot have been written after AD 96 because Clement of Rome seems to quote from it up to four times while writing his epistle to the Corinthian church. The book of Hebrews also discusses the worship within the temple as though such a structure were still in existence, so a date prior to the temple's destruction in AD 70 is likely.

Questions of authorship, date, and provenance aside, what is clear from the contents of Hebrews is that the addressees were in danger of giving up due to their suffering for having faith in Christ (Hebrews 10:32-39). Today's study begins immediately after that danger is addressed.

I. Faith Explained

(Hebrews 11:1-4a)

A. Definition (vv. 1-2)

1. Now faith is the substance of things hoped for, the evidence of things not seen.

Ancient Greek words translated as *faith*, *faithful*, and *faithfulness* occur some 316 times in ancient New Testament manuscripts. The 37 occurrences of these words in the book of Hebrews comprise almost 12 percent of the 316. However, Hebrews constitutes only about 3.6 percent of the New Testament. Clearly, the subject of faith is vital to the author, thus his offer of the definition we see here.

The concept of faith is complex, not reducible to a single definition. For example, the phrase "the faith" used in Jude 3 refers to a body of doctrine to be believed. But that is not the sense in the text before us now. A key to understanding what the writer of Hebrews intends is the word translated *substance*. This word is translated elsewhere as "confidence" or "confident" (2 Corinthians 9:4; 11:17; Hebrews 3:14), and that is the sense here. The author does not say that faith creates reality. Instead, the writer emphasizes faith as the answer to the eternal rewards God has promised. Hope and confidence are also connected in Hebrews 3:6.

The writer emphasizes this in the phrase that follows, using terms that enhance the two ideas in the first half of this verse. One enhancement is the movement from the word *faith* to the word *evidence*; the latter word is to be understood in the sense of "verification" or "certain persuasion." Another enhancement is the movement from the phrase *things hoped for* to the phrase *things not seen*; the latter more precisely describes the desired result of hope. The Christian's ultimate hope is not in anything in the present, visible world (John 17:16; James 4:4; 1 John 2:15). Rather, our hope is in the unseen eternal reality yet to come (2 Corinthians 4:18).

Belief and faith are closely related, but faith is the stronger of the two concepts (compare James 2:19). The writer is setting the stage for the numerous illustrations of this fact.

What Do You Think?

How will you live in faith that God will be present with you in the upcoming week?

Digging Deeper

How does the definition of *faith* in Hebrews 11:1 assist you in facing daily circumstances?

2. For by it the elders obtained a good report.

The elders are the Old Testament faithful, and the word *it* refers to their faith as just defined in the previous verse. God is the one who gave them *a good report* (the same word is translated "witness" in Hebrews 11:4b, not in our printed text). With this observation, the writer both begins and ends (see 11:39) what has come to be called the "Hall of Faith."

B. Foundations (vv. 3-4a)

3. Through faith we understand that the worlds were framed by the word of God, so that things which are seen were not made of things which do appear.

Faith is necessary to understand things that are real but cannot be observed, such as God's creating *the worlds*. This faith is not "blind faith," which is a belief in something without evidence to support that belief. Instead, what we're talking about is faith based on evidence. Since the evidence of God's holy character and limitless power have been established many times over, we can trust that His account of the creation of the cosmos—unseen by humans—is true. That's faith based on evidence, not blind faith (compare John 20:30-31).

4a. By faith Abel offered unto God a more excellent sacrifice than Cain.

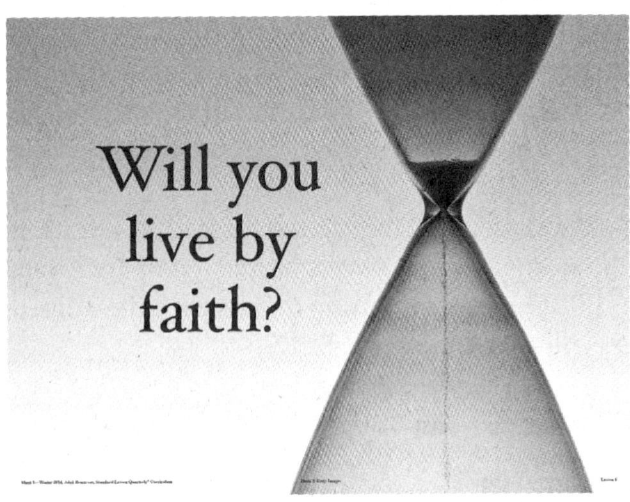

Visual for Lesson 6. *While reading Hebrews 11:40, have this posted and ask for specific examples of circumstances that require us to live by faith.*

This account is found in Genesis 4. Abel *offered* the best of his flock, while Cain "brought of the fruit of the ground" (4:3). The different types of offerings were in accordance with the brothers' respective occupations per Genesis 4:2. God's favor on Abel and not Cain was because Abel brought his best, not keeping it for himself. As a result, he is known as "righteous Abel" (Matthew 23:35), while Cain—who murdered his brother (Genesis 4:8)—is infamous as a negative example (1 John 3:12; Jude 11).

II. Faith Lived Out

(Hebrews 11:7a, 8, 17-18, 20-23, 32)

A. Noah (v. 7a)

7a. By faith Noah, being warned of God of things not seen as yet, moved with fear, prepared an ark to the saving of his house.

Noah's account is found in Genesis 6–9. Building the *ark* was no small exercise in faith! The expression of *things not seen as yet* is connected with the beginning of Hebrews 11:1. Thus, Noah's *faith* was based on the word of God concerning the flood, which Noah was not yet able to see.

The Value of Fear

Jason felt increasingly isolated at his high school as more and more of his friends began dabbling in recreational drugs, underage drinking, and premarital sex. As Jason resisted those temptations, his friendships dwindled.

One thing kept Jason from following their path: fear. Jason's dad repeatedly warned him of the consequences of substance abuse and sexual immorality. Jason feared for his physical health and dreaded the thought of disappointing his father.

The spiritual consequences can be more devastating, however. God sees everything we do, hears everything we say, and knows every thought we think. The Bible speaks of "fearing God," "fearing the Lord," etc., at least 80 times. A holy fear of God that directs our actions, speech, and thoughts is as appropriate today as it was for Noah. As Jesus said, "Fear him, which after he hath killed hath power to cast into hell; yea, I say unto you, Fear him" (Luke 12:5). How do we keep from domesticating God so that we give no thought to fearing Him? —D. D.

B. Abraham (vv. 8, 17-18)

8. By faith Abraham, when he was called to go out into a place which he should after receive for an inheritance, obeyed; and he went out, not knowing whither he went.

The call of *Abraham* is found in Genesis 12:1-3, with the man's walk of faith recorded from 12:4 through 25:11 (compare Acts 7:1-7). Abraham had to trust the unseen, invisible God rather than the visible, fictitious gods (idols) of his culture. And he did so as he departed for an unknown land several hundred miles distant. Considering that Abraham was the man who "believed in the Lord; and he counted it to him for righteousness" (Genesis 15:6), it is certainly fitting that he is included on this list.

But that doesn't mean Abraham never sinned (see Genesis 16:3-4; 12:12-13; 20:2). As we consider the faith-walk of several members of the Hall of Faith, we will remind ourselves that they were not without flaws.

17-18. By faith Abraham, when he was tried, offered up Isaac: and he that had received the promises offered up his only begotten son, Of whom it was said, That in Isaac shall thy seed be called.

This account of the near-sacrifice of *Isaac* by *Abraham* is detailed in Genesis 22; a much-abridged version is found in James 2:21. Both passages focus on how the man's faith was evidenced by action. When God commanded him to sacrifice his son, Abraham arose early in the morning in obedience (Genesis 22:3)—no delay. Abraham reasoned that God could raise Isaac from the dead (Hebrews 11:19). While there are certainly resurrections predicted and recorded in the Old Testament, none are noted as occurring as far back as in the time of Abraham, who lived about 2000 BC (see 1 Kings 17:17-23; 2 Kings 4:18-37; 13:21; Isaiah 26:19; Daniel 12:2). Perhaps Abraham believed that God was willing and able to do something that Abraham had never seen or heard of. The last line of the text at hand quotes Genesis 21:12.

What Do You Think?

How can you manage the emotions of disappointment, grief, or anger that may arise when God's will doesn't make sense?

Digging Deeper

Who can you turn to for wise counsel when God's will doesn't make sense?

C. Isaac (v. 20)

20. By faith Isaac blessed Jacob and Esau concerning things to come.

After *Isaac* was born in about 2067 BC, he grew up to become the father of *Jacob and Esau*, twins born in about 2007 BC. Isaac, like his father Abraham, was something of a mixed bag of character traits. Isaac obeyed God *by faith* (see Genesis 26:1-6), but Isaac also adopted his father's practice of deception (26:7). He was also guilty of the parental error of favoritism (25:28). God sometimes uses people in His service despite themselves.

Jacob and Esau were born to Isaac and Rebekah. This family wrestled with the sins of deceit and favoritism (see Genesis 25:28; 26:7). However, when it appeared that God's plan might be in danger as a result of these situations, the author of Hebrews reminds us that God was still at work. Isaac blessed his sons, looking forward to how God used them in His plan (27:27-40). Some scholars believe that Jacob is mentioned before Esau because it was through the lineage of Jacob that the promise would be fulfilled in Christ.

D. Jacob (v. 21)

21. By faith Jacob, when he was dying, blessed both the sons of Joseph; and worshipped, leaning upon the top of his staff.

This verse is a quotation from Genesis 47:31. The quotation here may not fully match up with 47:31 in your Bible because the writer is quoting from the Septuagint, the ancient Greek version of the Old Testament. When *Jacob* blessed both of Joseph's *sons*, he essentially adopted them as his own. As a result, 2 of the 12 "landed" tribes of Israel descend from them: the tribes of Ephraim and Manasseh (Joshua 14:4). Jacob's *faith* is evidenced by his worship of God, which he continued to his deathbed. His sins involved deception (Genesis 27:18-24), manipulation (25:29-33; 30:37-43), and favoritism (37:3-4)—but the Lord used him in service nevertheless!

E. Joseph (v. 22)

22. By faith Joseph, when he died, made mention of the departing of the children of Israel; and gave commandment concerning his bones.

This verse reiterates Genesis 50:24-26. In about 1899 BC, Joseph's brothers sold him to Ishmeelites when he was 17 years old; in turn,

How to Say It

Amram	*Am*-ram.
Barak	*Bair*-uk.
Canaan	*Kay*-nun.
Ephraim	*Ee*-fray-im.
Gedeon	*Gid*-e-un (*G* as in *get*).
Ishmeelites	*Ish*-me-el-ites.
Jephthae	*Jef*-the (*th* as in *thin*).
Jochebed	*Jock*-eh-bed.
Manasseh	Muh-*nass*-uh.

the Ishmeelites sold him into Egyptian slavery (37:2, 28). At age 30, Joseph had been appointed second-in-command in Egypt (41:46), facing numerous challenges to his *faith* in the intervening years.

As we see the phrase *the children of Israel*, we may immediately think of Israel as the organized nation it would become 430 years later, after the exodus (Exodus 12:40-41). But we should not lose sight of the fact that the word *Israel* in this context refers specifically to Joseph's father, Jacob, who had his name changed to Israel (Genesis 32:28; 35:10; 46:8).

Joseph's directive *concerning his bones* was that they not be left in Egypt when the exodus occurred (Genesis 50:24-25). This directive was rooted in God's promise made to his father Jacob, grandfather Isaac, and great-grandfather Abraham concerning possession of the land of Canaan (15:7; 48:3-4; Exodus 6:8; etc.).

> **What Do You Think?**
> How can you be a blessing and encourage a younger person this week?
>
> **Digging Deeper**
> What role does sharing our faith have in blessing those around us according to Galatians 3:9?

F. Amram and Jochebed (v. 23)

23. By faith Moses, when he was born, was hid three months of his parents, because they saw he was a proper child; and they were not afraid of the king's commandment.

This passage treats the lives of Abraham and *Moses* as journeys of faith. Thus they are the prominent figures presented in today's lesson. The extended version of the fact noted by the writer of Hebrews is found in Exodus 2. We note that the *faith* of Moses' *parents* is at issue here, not the faith of Moses himself. According to Exodus 6:20, the parents' names are Amram and Jochebed.

The phrase *proper child* is a complex expression. Some think it means "beautiful." It may carry the sense that Moses' parents had an awareness that the child would grow to be someone special. The Hebrew word behind this phrase in Exodus 2:2 is merely the typical word for "good."

The *commandment* of the "new king over Egypt, which knew not Joseph" (Exodus 1:8) initially stated that all newborn Hebrew boys were to be killed (1:16). When this directive was disobeyed, the king tried again by requiring that "every son that is born ye shall cast into the river" (1:22). Since baby Moses was put into a waterproof ark before being cast into the Nile River, the parents had obeyed this command—technically speaking!

> **What Do You Think?**
> How do you trust God even when you can't immediately see the results of His plans?
>
> **Digging Deeper**
> How do the examples of Hall of Faith encourage you in that regard?

G. Others (v. 32)

32. And what shall I more say? For time would fail me to tell of Gedeon, and of Barak, and of Samson, and of Jephthae; of David also, and Samuel, and of the prophets.

The Hall of Faith continues, as the writer ensures that readers don't think the importance of faith ended with Moses. Instead, exercises of faith continued through the centuries. The story of *Gedeon* (Gideon) is found in Judges 6–8. He served as a judge from 1192 BC to 1152 BC. He's most notable for his 300-man force defeating the Midianite army. *Barak*—a contemporary of Deborah, who judged from 1239 BC to 1199 BC—raised an army to defeat the Canaanites, according to Judges 4. *Samson* served as judge from 1075 BC to 1055 BC; his opposition to the Philistines is found in Judges 13–16. The leadership of *Jephthae* (Jephthah) against the Ammonites is recorded in Judges 11–12; his judgeship extended from 1086 BC to 1080 BC.

The extensive record of *David* (reigned 1010–970 BC) runs from 1 Samuel 16 through 1 Kings 2. The ministry of *Samuel*—who is pivotal for being the last of the judges and the first *of the prophets*—is found in 1 Samuel 1–25. These individuals of faith were not faultless, however.

Faith in a Blessed Future

Sheila didn't say much anymore. An 80-square-foot room in the local nursing home had become her dwelling. The 93-year-old woman had outlived her husband and two sons, so she didn't have many visitors. Sheila's failing eyesight and memory made Bible-reading increasingly difficult. Her circumstances seemed to be some of the saddest in the nursing home.

Yet Sheila had developed a surprising reputation among the nursing-home staff. In the few times daily that she did speak, she would communicate joy with her soft voice, weathered by life.

"I waited 18 years to marry my husband," she would say. "I won't have to wait that long to see my Shepherd."

Sheila has since joined the great "cloud of witnesses" of Hebrews 12:1, a group whose lives were informed by a future they couldn't see. How does your faith compare with Sheila's? —D. D.

III. Promises Because of Faith

(Hebrews 11:39-40)

A. Not Received (v. 39)

39. And these all, having obtained a good report through faith, received not the promise.

The writer repeats the thoughts of Hebrews 11:13 (not in today's lesson text) but in a condensed form. The word translated *having obtained a good report* is the same as that in Hebrews 11:2, above; it carries the idea of "having been witnessed" doing something *through faith*. Since the faith of those being considered looked ahead to the arrival of Jesus, which did not come about in their lifetimes, they *received not the promise* (contrast Matthew 13:16-17). But they had faith nonetheless.

B. Something Perfect (v. 40)

40. God having provided some better thing for us, that they without us should not be made perfect.

The *better thing* is the promise fulfilled in the earthly mission of Christ. Both we and *they* are *made perfect* in His suffering (Hebrews 2:10; 5:8-9; 7:28). In combining such facts with the conjunction "wherefore" that begins the next verse, Hebrews 12:1, the author prepares the readers to relate the Old Testament Hall of Faith to themselves.

What Do You Think?

What are some examples of knowledge and resources we have today that the heroes of the past could have never imagined?

Digging Deeper

How do you think God would like you to use these blessings?

Conclusion

A. The Faith of Imperfect People

The writer of Hebrews selected some very faithful people as examples, people who also had some significant imperfections.

We are to walk faith and not by sight (2 Corinthians 5:7), and this should be easier for us than for the Old Testament luminaries. They lived with only a promise and a hope, while we live with the cross and resurrection as accomplished facts (1 Peter 1:12). But although we are privileged to see much more of God's plan fulfilled, some promises remain to be fulfilled—a resurrection body, a new heavens, a new earth, etc. Many times we must make decisions without being able to see their results. A faith-based decision is based on believing the promises of God and determining to do what God has called you to do, regardless of how it might look in your eyes or the eyes of others. May the Holy Spirit empower us to do so!

B. Prayer

Heavenly Father, we thank You for these faithful servants of Yours whose deeds inspire us in our faith. May we prove to be at least as faithful as they were. In Jesus' name we pray. Amen.

C. Thought to Remember

Faith overrides imperfections!

Involvement Learning

Enhance your lesson with KJV Bible Student *(from your curriculum supplier) and the reproducible activity page (at www.standardlesson.com or in the back of the* KJV Standard Lesson Commentary Deluxe Edition*).*

Into the Lesson

Place learners in pairs, blindfold one person in each pair, and station pairs around the room. Set a container of candies on a table. Instruct the "seeing" partners to verbally guide their blindfolded partners to the container to pick out two pieces of candy and return to their seats. (*Option.* If learners have mobility limitations, set pairs at a table before they are blindfolded. Then put out containers of candy within reach of the blindfolded person.)

Alternative. Distribute a blank piece of paper and copies of the "What Is Unseen" exercise from the activity page, which you can download, to half of the class. Instruct them to find a partner that did not receive the exercise and complete it as indicated. Tell learners who received the exercise to read the instructions carefully without showing the page to their partners.

After either activity, say, "Sometimes it is hard to do things before we have all the information or know how it will end. In today's lesson, notice how each person's actions were evidence of faith."

Into the Word

Read Hebrews 11:1 aloud. As a class, use the verse to create a definition of *faith.* Write the definition on the board. Ask a volunteer to read aloud Hebrews 11:1-4a, 7a. Divide participants into three groups: **God's Command Group** (v. 3), **Abel Group** (v. 4), and **Noah Group** (v. 7a). Challenge the groups to study their verse and determine how the definition of faith from Hebrews 11:1 relates to their example verse. Reconvene the class and ask the following question for whole-class discussion: "Which of these three acts of faith would you personally find most difficult to do, and why?"

Alternative 1. Distribute copies of "The Hall of Faith" activity from the activity page. Have learners complete the first column with a partner before discussing conclusions in small groups.

Write four headers on the board: *He Knew, He Didn't Know, He Wanted to Know,* and *He Learned.* Divide learners into four groups and assign one header to each group. Have groups study Hebrews 11:8, 17-18, and create two to three responses to each heading on the board. Have groups refer to Genesis 12:1-9; 22:1-14 for more details.

Alternative 2. Have pairs complete the second column of the "The Hall of Faith" activity.

Ask a volunteer to read aloud Hebrews 11:20-23. Say, "These verses depict an inheritance of faith passed down from generation to generation." Divide learners into small groups and have each group discuss the following questions: 1–How was each person mentioned in these verses faithful to God? 2–What was the result of their faith?

Alternative 3. Have pairs complete the third and final column of "The Hall of Faith" exercise.

Ask a volunteer to read aloud Hebrews 11:32, 39-40. Divide participants into six groups and assign the Scripture passage associated with their character: **Gideon Group** (Judges 7), **Barak Group** (Judges 4), **Samson Group** (Judges 16), **Jephthah Group** (Judges 11), **David Group** (1 Samuel 17), and **Samuel Group** (1 Samuel 15:10-16:13). Give each group five minutes to read their assigned passage and give a summary of their group's namesake to the whole class. Ask each group to answer the following question: "How did your character demonstrate faith and a lack of faith?"

Into Life

Write the following categories as headers on the board: *Thought, Behavior,* and *Speech.* Distribute an index card to each learner. Allow one minute for learners to reflect on the definition of *faith* from Hebrews 11:1 and write one way they can each change something in each of the above categories to develop a life of deeper faith and be reminded of our stranger status in this world. End class with prayer.

January 14
Lesson 7 (KJV)

Faith and Trust

Devotional Reading: Psalm 56
Background Scripture: Proverbs 3:1-12

Proverbs 3:1-8

1 My son, forget not my law; but let thine heart keep my commandments:

2 For length of days, and long life, and peace, shall they add to thee.

3 Let not mercy and truth forsake thee: bind them about thy neck; write them upon the table of thine heart:

4 So shalt thou find favour and good understanding in the sight of God and man.

5 Trust in the LORD with all thine heart; and lean not unto thine own understanding.

6 In all thy ways acknowledge him, and he shall direct thy paths.

7 Be not wise in thine own eyes: fear the LORD, and depart from evil.

8 It shall be health to thy navel, and marrow to thy bones.

Key Text

Trust in the LORD with all thine heart; and lean not unto thine own understanding. **—Proverbs 3:5**

Faith That

Pleases God

Unit 2: Learning About Faith

Lessons 6–9

Lesson Aims

After participating in this lesson, each learner will be able to:

1. Identify principles that lead to a blessed life.
2. Explain why fear of the Lord is foundational to other proverbial principles.
3. Make a plan to identify and change an area of life to align more closely with the Lord's will by application of a proverbial principle.

Lesson Outline

Introduction
- A. Whose Influence?
- B. Lesson Context

I. One Law (Proverbs 3:1-2)
- A. Remembering Commands (v. 1)
  - *Do Not Forget*
- B. Promise of Life (v. 2)

II. Two Virtues (Proverbs 3:3-4)
- A. Bind and Write (v. 3)
- B. Promise of Favor (v. 4)

III. One Trust (Proverbs 3:5-6)
- A. Relying on the Lord (v. 5)
- B. Promise of Direction (v. 6)

IV. Two Actions (Proverbs 3:7-8)
- A. Fear and Avoidance (v. 7)
  - *Wise in My Own Eyes*
- B. Promises of Wholeness (v. 8)

Conclusion
- A. Voices of Authority
- B. Prayer
- C. Thought to Remember

Introduction

A. Whose Influence?

Who do you regard as an authoritative voice? Perhaps you consider a particular writer, podcast host, or teacher as such an influence. When I think about the voices that influence me, I immediately think of my professors from Bible college. After graduation, I kept and organized all my notes from their classes for future reference. These notes even went with me during my time as an overseas missionary! I trusted the expertise and wisdom of those professors and wanted to ensure that I would not forget their teachings.

One of the earliest authoritative voices in a person's life is a parent. Most parents want to see their children flourish. Therefore, they will teach their children to become kind, thoughtful, and intelligent people. Parents who follow Jesus will also desire that their children seek God's wisdom and experience a personal relationship with Jesus.

The book of Proverbs invites us to hear the teachings of a father to his son. Regardless of whether or not our parents have taught us God's wisdom, we can learn from this father figure and apply his wisdom to our lives.

B. Lesson Context

The book of Proverbs is generally attributed to King Solomon (see Proverbs 1:1). His wisdom was renowned (examples: 1 Kings 4:30-31; 10:24), and over 3,000 proverbs originated with him (4:32), so he was an ideal person to write this book of wisdom literature. Additionally, the text attributes two other sections to Agur (Proverbs 30:1) and King Lemuel (31:1). However, we know nothing about these two men.

The text does not indicate when these texts were consolidated into the form of Proverbs that we read today. Further, the text does not have a direct recipient. The significance of Proverbs is not found in its original writers, date of composition, or original audience. Instead, its importance is in how it communicates what makes up a life of wisdom. All people can learn and apply the wisdom taught in the book of Proverbs.

For some readers, the book of Proverbs reads

like disjointed sets of oracles without any connection. However, five sections divide the book: an introduction to wisdom (Proverbs 1–9), the proverbs of Solomon (10:1–22:16; 25:1–29:27), the words of the wise (22:17–24:34), the words of Agur (Proverbs 30), and the words of King Lemuel (Proverbs 31).

The first section begins with an explanation of the importance of wisdom (see Proverbs 1:1-7). After the introduction, most of that section is written from the perspective of a father advising his son on the importance of seeking wisdom from the Lord.

With one exception (see Proverbs 3:5), the poetic order of each pair of verses in today's Scripture follows the same pattern. First, the father gives his son a negative command (example: 3:1a). Second, the father gives a positive command (example: 3:1b). Finally, the father concludes that section with a promise for the son (example: 3:2).

I. One Law
(Proverbs 3:1-2)

A. Remembering Commands (v. 1)

1a. My son, forget not my law.

Although the text leaves the speaker unidentified, we assume that a father is instructing his *son* (see Proverbs 4:1). The book of Proverbs presents wisdom from God as a quality that can be passed from generation to generation through teaching (4:3-7). The commands of a father and the law of a mother are understood to be one of the most influential voices for a child in this regard (see 6:20).

Frequently in the Old Testament, the "law" refers to that given by God to His people (examples: Exodus 24:12; 2 Kings 17:34-37). However, the qualifier *my* indicates that this particular *law* consists of a father's instruction to his son. Such instruction is a prominent theme in the first section of Proverbs (see Proverbs 1:8; 4:2; 6:20; 7:2).

The son is told to *forget not* his father's law because of possible risks that such forgetfulness might incur (compare Proverbs 4:5). Similarly, the Israelites were warned the same regarding God's law and His covenant with them (see Deuteronomy 4:23).

What Do You Think?

How do you ensure you do not forget the wisdom others have given you?

Digging Deeper

What steps will you take to pass along wisdom to younger generations?

Do Not Forget

"It's always something. It's never simple. It's always late."

When I was a child, my dad constantly repeated these maxims in moments when I felt exasperated by life's challenges. At the time, I couldn't understand what he meant by these sayings. However, after several decades of life experience, my father's wisdom now makes sense. His point was that life is filled with complications and challenges. He wanted me to expect these challenges rather than become frustrated and angered by them. These days, I share that same wisdom with my children and students. They frequently disregard my counsel because they consider it inapplicable or untimely. But perhaps someday—maybe decades later—they'll remember what I've told them.

God has surrounded you with wise people—some older than you and some younger than you. What instruction from them do you need to remember, even if you don't fully understand its importance in the current moment? —N. G.

1b. But let thine heart keep my commandments.

Most modern-day perspectives consider the heart the emotional center of a person. Such views believe this emotional center lacks the capacity for rational guidance or direction. In the Old Testament, however, the *heart* refers to a person's inner being. Among other aspects, this inner being

How to Say It

Deuteronomy	Due-ter-*ahn*-uh-me.
omnipotent	ahm-*nih*-poh-tent.
omnipresent	ahm-*nih*-prez-ent.
omniscient	ahm-*nish*-unt.
Septuagint	Sep-*too*-ih-jent.

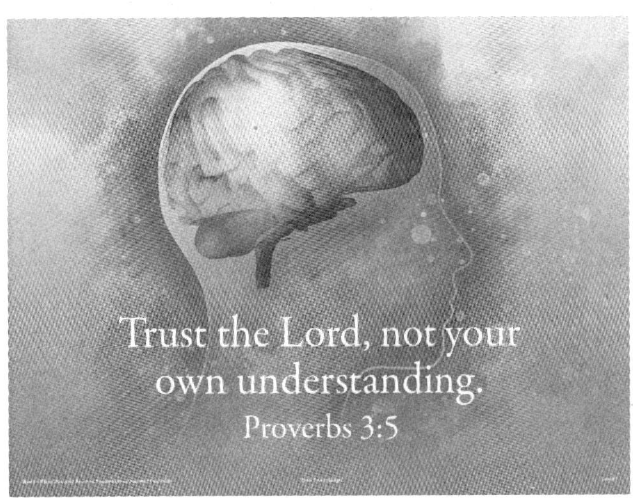

Trust the Lord, not your
own understanding.
Proverbs 3:5

Visual for Lesson 7. *Display this visual as you discuss the commentary and discussion questions associated with Proverbs 3:5.*

includes a person's volition (examples: Genesis 6:5; Exodus 25:2; Proverbs 16:9), emotions (examples: Isaiah 30:29; Nehemiah 2:2), and knowledge (example: 1 Kings 3:9, 12). The centrality of the heart led the father in Proverbs to warn his son regarding its safe keeping (see Proverbs 4:23). The son must be willing and able to receive his father's exhortations and apply them to his life.

One way that the son could *keep* his father's *commandments* would be to commit them to memory and obey them (compare Psalm 119:11). The Law of Moses commanded parents to teach their children about God's law (see Deuteronomy 6:4-9). Parents honor God when they train their children to follow God. Further, children obey God and receive a blessing when they give honor to their parents and follow their commands (see next verse; see also Ephesians 6:1-3; Colossians 3:20). Remembrance of the law and commands is the foundation of a life strengthened by God (see Psalm 119:93).

B. Promise of Life (v. 2)

2. For length of days, and long life, and peace, shall they add to thee.

When a child honors his or her parents, the days of that child "may be long upon the land which the Lord thy God giveth thee" (Exodus 20:12). The promise of a *long life* stands in contrast to the promise that whoever "pursueth evil pursueth it to . . . death" (Proverbs 11:19). The wicked person does not follow the commands of God. Such a person "shall not inhabit the earth" (10:30). As a child follows and honors his or her parents, that child is entering a life of wisdom. Later, the father describes wisdom as a woman who holds "length of days . . . in her right hand" (3:16, not in our printed text). While a long life is not inevitable, a flourishing life begins with seeking wisdom from godly parents.

The Hebrew understanding of peace sometimes does imply an absence of conflict (example: 1 Samuel 7:14). However, the Hebrew word for *peace* can also encompass ideas of flourishing (see Jeremiah 29:7), relational harmony (Isaiah 57:18-19), or the completeness of God's work (54:10; Nahum 1:15). It is the first two aspects that this father is most concerned about for his son.

II. Two Virtues

(Proverbs 3:3-4)

A. Bind and Write (v. 3)

3a. Let not mercy and truth forsake thee.

Mercy and *truth* are key words in the Old Testament, especially regarding the attributes of God. *Mercy* frequently refers to God's loyalty and commitment toward His people (example: Psalm 136). God's mercy is rooted in His faithfulness and promises (see Deuteronomy 7:9, 12; 1 Kings 8:23; Psalm 26:3). His mercy seeks redemption and safety for God's people (example: Exodus 15:13). *Truth* conveys the idea of reliability (examples: 71:22; Isaiah 61:8).

The father's concern is not only his son's behavior; the father also desires to see the son's heart transformed. A transformed heart will result in changed behavior (see Matthew 15:19). A life that appears righteous but lacks a rightly ordered heart is full of hypocrisy and sin (see 23:28). The heart's deception will someday be exposed (Proverbs 26:24-26). The father wants his son to do good actions—actions that come from a heart transformed and oriented toward the virtues of mercy and truth.

A heart filled with mercy and truth should be the foundation for the son's behavior. A life seeking God's wisdom results in that life developing mercy and truth that will bear fruit through righteous and wise actions. These attributes are part of

God's character, so they should be part of the character of His people (compare Proverbs 16:6; 20:28).

3b. Bind them about thy neck; write them upon the table of thine heart.

In biblical times, necklaces were signs of honor or rank (examples: Genesis 41:42; Daniel 5:29). To *bind* something around one's *neck* revealed the importance and significance of that item to the wearer. The figurative language in this verse highlights the extent that the son should go to develop a life of mercy and truth. The opposite of a life with these virtues would be considered "stiff-necked"—rebellious and disobedient (examples: Exodus 32:9; Jeremiah 17:23; Acts 7:51).

The command to *write* mercy and truth *upon the table of* the *heart* is another example of figurative language. This verse also alludes to Deuteronomy 6:6-8. In those verses, God commanded the people of Israel to internalize His law and apply it to all areas of life. Such virtues are not to be hidden from the world. Instead, a wisdom-filled life will develop these virtues in the heart. Such lives are "declared to be the epistle of Christ" through God's Spirit (see 2 Corinthians 3:3).

What Do You Think?

How will you continue to "write" these virtues "on your heart"?

Digging Deeper

What steps do you take to ensure you are attentive to the Spirit's leading in this regard?

B. Promise of Favor (v. 4)

4. So shalt thou find favour and good understanding in the sight of God and man.

To *find favour* in a person means to hold that person in high regard (example: Daniel 1:9). Even children, when they follow God, can receive favor from other people and God (example: 1 Samuel 2:26). To have a *good understanding* signifies character and integrity of insight that leads a person to act righteously. This character develops when a person seeks the wisdom of the Lord and lives in obedience to Him (see Psalm 111:10).

A life of character will not only be pleasing *in the sight of God,* but other people will also recognize it (compare Luke 2:52). The apostle Peter admonished believers to live in a way that would lead unbelievers to glorify God (see 1 Peter 2:12; compare Matthew 5:16; 1 Timothy 3:7). A good name and good reputation take time to develop. Not only do these things provide a personal benefit, but they are also avenues to honor God and reveal God to other people.

III. One Trust

(Proverbs 3:5-6)

A. Relying on the Lord (v. 5)

5a. Trust in the LORD with all thine heart.

We tend to place trust in things and people other than God (examples: Psalm 52:7; Isaiah 42:17; Jeremiah 17:5). At best, this misplaced trust can lead to futility. At worst, however, it can lead to destruction (see 13:24-27; 49:4-5). Misplaced trust does not lead to any lasting and eternal wisdom.

However, the father's efforts were intended to result in his son's developing *trust in the Lord* (compare Proverbs 22:19). The Lord is worthy to be trusted because, among other things, He is the source of salvation (see Isaiah 12:2). When people trust the Lord, they experience blessing from Him (see Psalm 37:3-7; Jeremiah 17:7-8).

To display trust *with all thine heart* implies a total commitment. As with showing love and devotion to the Lord (see Deuteronomy 6:5; 10:12), this kind of trust is an all-encompassing act; it requires the totality of a person's being, beginning with one's inner being (see commentary on Proverbs 3:1, above).

5b. And lean not unto thine own understanding.

The book of Proverbs contains numerous warnings against pride (examples: Proverbs 8:13; 11:2; 16:5, 18). The reminder to *lean not unto thine understanding* is another warning in that regard. Only foolish people trust themselves more than the wisdom of the Lord (see 28:26). Their downfall is inevitable (see 18:12). When people consider themselves to be wise in the eyes of the world, their so-called wisdom amounts to foolishness in the eyes of God (see 1 Corinthians 3:18-19).

What Do You Think?

What steps do you take to ensure you trust the Lord with *all* your heart?

Digging Deeper

How do you establish personal guardrails when you want to lean on your own knowledge and expertise?

B. Promise of Direction (v. 6)

6. In all thy ways acknowledge him, and he shall direct thy paths.

To *acknowledge* God means to know Him and give Him proper recognition for His activity in a person's life (compare Proverbs 2:1-5). It involves intimate knowledge of God and a willingness to submit to His will. When people submit to God, they do not forge ahead as though God does not exist. Instead, they recognize God's power and presence (see Philippians 3:7-11).

Those who submit to God can be assured that He will *direct* their *paths* of life (compare Jeremiah 10:23). God is all-knowing (omniscient), all-present (omnipresent), and all-powerful (omnipotent). Therefore, we can trust that He will provide His people with a wise and righteous path (see Psalm 16:11; Proverbs 2:8). This is not a promise of an easy life—trials are inevitable (see James 1:2-3; 1 Peter 4:12). However, God has provided us with an avenue of peace through Christ Jesus (see John 16:33). Through Christ Jesus, we can trust that God will guide and deliver us, no matter the nature of that path.

What Do You Think?

How do you overcome obstacles that prevent you from fully submitting to God?

Digging Deeper

Who will you recruit as an accountability partner in this regard?

IV. Two Actions

(Proverbs 3:7-8)

A. Fear and Avoidance (v. 7)

7a. Be not wise in thine own eyes.

The opposite of trusting in and submitting to God is to consider one's wisdom as the final say. To be *wise in thine own eyes* is to be sure that one's own wisdom is superior and ultimate. When people depend on their own wisdom and do what seems right to them, they are no better than fools (see Proverbs 18:2)—or worse (see 26:12).

God is the source of wisdom (see Proverbs 2:6) and desires to give His people wisdom through His Spirit (see 1 Corinthians 2:6-16; James 1:5). As a result, God's people should avoid lives of pride and arrogance (see Romans 12:16) and seek out wisdom from God (see James 3:13-16).

The example of King Solomon provides us with a warning based on this verse. He received wisdom from God (1 Kings 3:5-14). However, he failed to follow God's wisdom (11:1-8). As a result, he experienced heartache and the promise of consequences that would extend past his lifetime (11:9-13).

Wise in My Own Eyes

I was one of a few high school freshmen who lettered in track; the hurdles were my specialty. One day, three guest coaches came to work with my team. The coaches adjusted familiar drills to force us to change our approach to training. For example, they placed the hurdles farther apart than usual. So, instead of taking three steps between hurdles, the drill forced us to take five or more steps.

I wanted to show off my power and strength. On my turn to complete the drill, I stretched out and only took three steps between hurdles. After the exercise, one of the coaches said that he liked my power and strength but that my form was also essential to develop. Hearing only what I wanted to hear, I drank in his praise, and my ego swelled. The next time my teammates ran the drill, I offered them unprompted advice for their improvement. Eventually, one of my teammates proclaimed an honest-but-harsh opinion about my new attitude. My ballooning ego popped.

In retrospect, I hadn't heard all that the coach had told me. I had ignored the coach's directives regarding my form. I only listened to the coach's praise and considered myself skilled and wise. Is your self-determined wisdom causing you to be unable to hear the wisdom of others? —N. G.

7b. Fear the LORD, and depart from evil.

Scripture provides instances when people were afraid of the Lord and His power (example: Genesis 3:10). In this verse, however, to *fear the Lord* involves having an attitude of reverence, awe, wonder, faith, and trust in the Lord. It is impossible to be wise in one's own eyes and, simultaneously, fear the Lord. Instead, an attitude of humility is required (see Proverbs 22:4). Those who fear the Lord come to have true wisdom (see 1:7), which leads to an avoidance of evil (14:16). God delights in those who show humility and fear Him (see Psalm 147:11). Christians are commanded to live in a way that reflects their fear of the Lord (1 Peter 2:17; example: Acts 9:31).

Fearing God and loving evil are incompatible (see Exodus 20:20; example: Job 1:1). Fearing the Lord requires actively turning from evil (see Psalm 34:11-14). To *depart from evil* involves an attitude of repentance—turning away from sin and turning to God in faith and obedience.

B. Promise of Wholeness (v. 8)

8. It shall be health to thy navel, and marrow to thy bones.

This verse begins with a Hebrew idiom that provides difficulty to translators. The translation of *navel* is accurate to the Hebrew text. However, the Septuagint (the ancient Greek translation) has the word for *body* instead. Perhaps the Hebrew text is an example of a literary practice of using a part of the whole to represent the whole. In this case, the *health* of the *navel* is representative of the health of the entire body.

Marrow is the life-giving tissue located in the cavities of most *bones*. This substance creates blood cells and provides energy for the body. However, the author of Proverbs would have likely been unaware of this fact. A nourished body contains marrow and strength in its bones (see Job 21:24).

A life of humility, fear of the Lord, and obedience to Him results in the complete wholeness of a person. The son is promised health and vitality when he follows his father's teachings (see Proverbs 4:20-22). We know, however, that a person's status in life does not correlate to the quality of a person's heart. While people may experience wholeness and health in part while on earth, Scripture promises a time in the future when "God shall wipe away all tears . . . and there shall be no more death, neither sorrow, nor crying, neither shall there be any more pain" (Revelation 21:4).

> **What Do You Think?**
>
> How would you respond to the claim that this verse cannot be trusted because people "fear the Lord" but still experience ailments?
>
> **Digging Deeper**
>
> How do Psalms 103:14; 139:13-16; Isaiah 45:7; Luke 12:6-7; John 9:1-7; and 1 Peter 4:13 inform your response?

Conclusion

A. Voices of Authority

A 2022 study showed that most people spend about two and a half hours daily on social media platforms. While this may not seem like a lot of time, it is a significant increase from 10 years prior, when the average daily usage hovered around one hour per day. Social media has become a "voice of authority" for many people, regardless of the actual knowledge, expertise, or wisdom of that voice.

It is easy for believers to say that we are seeking the wisdom of God when in actuality, other voices influence our lives and shape our perspectives. If we're filling our lives with human ideas rather than the wisdom of God, which will have more influence?

B. Prayer

Heavenly Father, thank You for the inspired wisdom You have revealed to us in Scripture. Help us to listen and follow Your Word. Show us how we can be more attentive to the direction of Your Spirit so that we might have lives of wisdom. In Jesus' name. Amen.

C. Thought to Remember

God's children seek the wisdom
of their heavenly Father.

Involvement Learning

Enhance your lesson with KJV Bible Student *(from your curriculum supplier) and the reproducible activity page (at www.standardlesson.com or in the back of the* KJV Standard Lesson Commentary Deluxe Edition*).*

Into the Lesson

Invite learners to share their favorite "word of wisdom" or proverb (example: "Don't look a gift horse in the mouth"). Ask learners where they first heard the proverb. As a whole class, discuss the meaning of these "words of wisdom" or proverbs and how people have applied them to their lives.

Alternative. Distribute copies of the "Words of Wisdom" exercise from the activity page, which you can download. Have learners complete it individually in one minute or less before comparing responses with a partner.

Say, "Most proverbs help us make good decisions and point us to having positive relationships. Today, as we study the proverbs of Scripture, consider how we can apply their wisdom to our lives of faith and trust in God."

Into the Word

Ask a volunteer to read aloud Proverbs 3:1-2. Divide learners into seven equal groups. Distribute a sheet of paper, a stack of index cards, and pens to each group. Ask, "How do you remember to complete important tasks?" Have each group answer by making a list of common strategies (examples: writing the task on a sticky note, setting a cellphone alarm, using mnemonic devices). Challenge groups to write down at least two commands from Scripture and discuss how to apply their memory strategies to remember to follow the commands.

Alternative. Distribute the "World's Way vs. God's Way" activity from the activity page. Have learners work in small groups to complete row one as indicated.

Ask a volunteer to read aloud Proverbs 3:3-4. Write *Psalm 15:1-3*; *Matthew 9:12-13*; and *1 Corinthians 13:4-7* on the board. Invite the small groups to look up the references and discuss how those Scriptures relate to Proverbs 3:3-4.

Alternative. Instruct groups to complete row two of the "World's Way vs. God's Way" exercise.

Invite another volunteer to read aloud Proverbs 3:5-6. Assign one of the following Scriptures to each small group: Psalm 18:2; Jeremiah 29:11; Romans 11:33; Ephesians 1:11-12; Hebrews 13:8; and James 1:17. Allow five minutes for groups to read their assigned Scripture and discuss how it relates to Proverbs 3:5-6.

Write the following phrase on the board:

We can trust the Lord because He is . . .

With the help of the assigned Scripture, have each group think of one adjective that describes God. Invite a volunteer from each group to share their group's adjective and write it on the board to complete the phrase.

Alternative. Instruct groups to complete row three of the "World's Way vs. God's Way" exercise.

Ask a final volunteer to read aloud Proverbs 3:7-8. Have groups answer the following questions in small-group discussion: 1–What does "fear of the Lord" mean? 2–How is "fear of the Lord" foundational for today's Scripture? 3–As described in these verses, what are possible steps for a healthy life?

Challenge small groups to come up with one example for how to follow the imperatives in Proverbs 3:7 (example: A person might be not wise in their own eyes by asking for advice from a more mature and knowledgeable person).

Alternative. Instruct groups to complete row four of the "World's Way vs. God's Way" activity.

Into Life

Distribute an index card and pen to each learner. Place learners into pairs and allow five minutes for them to identify an area of their life that they can change by applying one of the principles from Proverbs. Ask learners to write down that change on their index card. Have learners share their plan for change with their partners. Encourage learners to place the index card in a visible location where they can see it in the upcoming week.

January 21
Lesson 8 (KJV)

Faith and Encouragement

Devotional Reading: 1 Thessalonians 5:1-15
Background Scripture: 2 Chronicles 20:5-20

2 Chronicles 20:13-20

13 And all Judah stood before the LORD,
with their little ones, their wives, and their
children.
14 Then upon Jahaziel the son of Zechariah, the son of Benaiah, the son of Jeiel, the
son of Mattaniah, a Levite of the sons of Asaph,
came the Spirit of the LORD in the midst of the
congregation;
15 And he said, Hearken ye, all Judah, and
ye inhabitants of Jerusalem, and thou king
Jehoshaphat, Thus saith the LORD unto you, Be
not afraid nor dismayed by reason of this great
multitude; for the battle is not yours, but God's.
16 To morrow go ye down against them:
behold, they come up by the cliff of Ziz; and ye
shall find them at the end of the brook, before
the wilderness of Jeruel.
17 Ye shall not need to fight in this battle:
set yourselves, stand ye still, and see the salvation of the LORD with you, O Judah and Jerusalem: fear not, nor be dismayed; to morrow
go out against them: for the LORD will be with
you.
18 And Jehoshaphat bowed his head with
his face to the ground: and all Judah and the
inhabitants of Jerusalem fell before the LORD,
worshipping the LORD.
19 And the Levites, of the children of the
Kohathites, and of the children of the Korhites,
stood up to praise the LORD God of Israel with
a loud voice on high.
20 And they rose early in the morning, and
went forth into the wilderness of Tekoa: and as
they went forth, Jehoshaphat stood and said,
Hear me, O Judah, and ye inhabitants of Jerusalem; Believe in the LORD your God, so shall
ye be established; believe his prophets, so shall
ye prosper.

Key Text

Believe in the LORD your God, so shall ye be established; believe his prophets, so shall ye prosper.

—2 Chronicles 20:20b

Faith That

Pleases God

Unit 2: Learning About Faith

Lessons 6–9

Lesson Aims

After participating in this lesson, each learner will be able to:

1. Summarize the faith actions that led to Jehoshaphat's victory.

2. Evaluate the cause-and-effect tenor of the key text.

3. Notice God's presence and help in facing his or her fears.

Lesson Outline

Introduction

A. Encouragement Passed Along

B. Lesson Context

I. Facing a Crisis (2 Chronicles 20:13-17)

A. Solemn Gathering (v. 13)

Families Together?

B. Inspired Messenger (v. 14)

C. Reassuring Message (vv. 15-17)

II. "Faith-ing" a Crisis (2 Chronicles 20:18-20)

A. By Worshiping the Lord (vv. 18-19)

Genuine Worship

B. By Trusting the Lord (v. 20)

Conclusion

A. When Uplook Changes Outlook

B. Prayer

C. Thought to Remember

Introduction

A. Encouragement Passed Along

On April 15, 1947, Jackie Robinson became the first African American to take the field for a major league baseball team in the modern era when he started in a game for the Brooklyn Dodgers. Breaking the color barrier was a milestone in moving toward an end to discrimination in baseball and in America as a whole. But it was an uphill battle to reach that point, and encouragement from others helped Robinson contribute to overcoming the racial bias of post-World War II America (with more progress yet needed today).

Robinson's success in baseball and later as an activist in the Civil Rights Movement became, in turn, an encouragement for others to succeed by overcoming prejudice and other obstacles. To offer "you can do it" words of encouragement is good as far as it goes. But to be an example of one who has been through the fire of adversity is encouragement on a whole other level! Encouragement is one of the most positive ways to use words and actions, especially when those who need to be encouraged face times of great uncertainty and challenge.

B. Lesson Context

The book of 2 Chronicles covers the time period 970 BC to 536 BC. This period spans from Solomon, the last king of Israel as a united monarchy, to Cyrus, the king of Persia who ended the Babylonian exile. Readers of the Bible may wonder why the books of 1–2 Chronicles are useful, since their content often mirrors that of 2 Samuel and 1–2 Kings. A clue is found in the titles of 1 and 2 Chronicles as appearing in the Greek version of the Old Testament, known as the Septuagint. There the titles translate into English as "Things Omitted." That is certainly appropriate regarding the text of today's lesson, which focuses on events during the reign of Jehoshaphat, king of Judah (the southern kingdom of divided Israel) from about 872 BC to 848 BC. The text of 2 Chronicles 17:1–21:3 has much more information about him than is recorded in 1 Kings 15:24; 22:1-50.

Uncertainty exists regarding the author of

Chronicles. As a result that person is often referred to merely as "the chronicler." The priest and scribe Ezra, who led the return from exile in 458 BC, is our best guess for being the author. This is because 2 Chronicles 36:22-23 is virtually identical, letter for letter, to Ezra 1:1-3 in the Hebrew.

Some students propose that Ezra (if indeed he was the author) wrote 1–2 Chronicles to teach God's people to avoid sin, lest they suffer anew the consequences that led to exile in the first place. A special focus on the importance of faithfulness to the Lord can be detected in 1 Chronicles 22:13; 2 Chronicles 17:3-6; 24:20; 29:6-9; 31:20, 21; 36:15-21—texts with no parallel in 2 Samuel or 1–2 Kings. Ezra would have agreed with the often-quoted statement that "Those who cannot remember the past are condemned to repeat it" (George Santayana, 1863–1952).

Jehoshaphat reigned during the period of the divided monarchy in Israelite history. He was one of the more godly kings of Judah (see 2 Chronicles 17:3-4). He is noted for his efforts to rid Judah of idol worship and to promote the teaching of God's law throughout the land (17:1-9). Also noteworthy is the respect held by surrounding people and the attention he gave to various building projects and to administrative reforms (17:10-19).

On the downside, however, Jehoshaphat entered into an ill-advised alliance with ungodly Ahab, king of northern Israel, who enlisted Jehoshaphat's aid in retaking some territory from the Syrians. At Ahab's behest, Jehoshaphat wore his royal robes into battle against the Syrians while Ahab disguised himself in an effort to keep the prophet Micaiah's prediction of his death from being fulfilled (2 Chronicles 18:1-31a). The move nearly cost Jehoshaphat his life, but "the Lord helped him" (18:31b), and he was spared.

After hearing of God's displeasure with that alliance (2 Chronicles 19:1-3), Jehoshaphat reorganized his government both physically and spiritually (19:4-11). At an unspecified time later, a coalition of enemy forces began to march toward Judah (20:1-2). This resulted in the king and country becoming unified in fasting and public prayer—prayer that confessed utter reliance on the Lord to defeat this threat (20:3-12). The Lord's response came next.

I. Facing a Crisis

(2 Chronicles 20:13-17)

A. Solemn Gathering (v. 13)

13. And all Judah stood before the LORD, with their little ones, their wives, and their children.

The phrase *all Judah stood before the Lord* reflects 2 Chronicles 20:4, which records that people "out of all the cities of Judah" came to seek the Lord's help during the crisis at hand (see Lesson Context for details). The place where they gathered was "the house of the Lord" (20:5), meaning the temple in Jerusalem. It seems that representatives from every town were present. The crisis was so severe that it was not only men gathered, but whole families. Having just heard their king's prayer (see Lesson Context), they awaited God's response.

Second Chronicles 20:5 states that the king stood "in the house of the Lord, before the new court." This "court" was likely a new courtyard, perhaps a renovation undertaken during the reigns of either Asa (Jehoshaphat's father) or Jehoshaphat himself, both of whom are commended for their exemplary devotion to the Lord (2 Chronicles

How to Say It

Ahab	*Ay*-hab.
Asa	*Ay*-zuh.
Asaph	*Ay*-saff.
Azariah	Az-uh-*rye*-uh.
Benaiah	Be-*nay*-juh.
Cyrus	*Sigh*-russ.
En-Gedi	En-*gee*-dye.
Jahaziel	Juh-*hay*-zuh-el.
Jehoshaphat	Jeh-*hosh*-uh-fat.
Joash	*Jo*-ash.
Kohathites	*Ko*-hath-ites.
Korhites	*Kor*-hites.
Mattaniah	Mat-uh-*nye*-uh.
Tekoa	Tih-*ko*-uh.
Uzziah	Uh-*zye*-uh.

14:2-6; 15:17; 17:3-6). Here is where the assembly (including families and their little ones) stood before the Lord following Jehoshaphat's fervent prayer for the Lord's help against the invading forces. Jehoshaphat had closed his prayer with words expressing his and the people's complete dependence upon the Lord.

What Do You Think?

How do you prioritize prayer and worship time within your family?

Digging Deeper

In what ways can you invite your friends and neighbors to join your family in prayer and worship?

Families Together?

When our children were small, my wife and I made an effort to keep them with us as much as possible when we attended church. We wanted to get them involved in worship service, listening to the sermon, and talking with them about both afterward. This paid off in some unexpected ways. My youngest daughter decided she liked worship songs, even the old hymns, and asked me to sing them to her at bedtime. My son watched the worship band intently, developed a love for drumming and is well on his way to becoming a world-class percussionist. My oldest daughter became enamored with missions and is going to Bible college to become a missionary to Germany. Worshipping together as a family is not the only reason they made these choices, but it's a part of a foundation of faith we tried to lay in their lives.

Seeking the Lord through worship, prayer, etc., happens both individually and collectively. For instance, the apostle Paul wrote letters to both individuals and churches. It's important not to let one aspect eclipse the other. Do you? —A. W.

B. Inspired Messenger (v. 14)

14a. Then upon Jahaziel the son of Zechariah, the son of Benaiah, the son of Jeiel, the son of Mattaniah, a Levite of the sons of Asaph.

What an avalanche of names! Consternation multiplies when we discover that the 6 names are rather common, designating altogether some 67 people with one of those names in the Old Testament (compare 1 Chronicles 1–9). The chronicler has gone to a lot of work to record these *the son of* connections. Being able to prove one's lineage was important to the ancient Jew (compare Ezra 2:59-62; Nehemiah 7:61-64), as it is in establishing the line of Jesus in the New Testament era (Matthew 1:1-17, lesson 3; Luke 3:23-38). Genealogies have their place, but they can be overemphasized (Matthew 3:9; 1 Timothy 1:4; Titus 3:9). In any case, for *Jahaziel* to have his pedigree traced back to the *Asaph* of King David's era some three centuries previous is noteworthy (see 2 Chronicles 5:12; Nehemiah 11:17).

14b. Came the Spirit of the Lord in the midst of the congregation.

The declaration of the Holy Spirit's "coming upon" someone in the Old Testament era is associated predominantly with the books of Judges and 1 Samuel. In 2 Chronicles, the occurrence is associated with King Azariah (Uzziah), who spoke a message of both encouragement and warning to King Asa (2 Chronicles 15:1-7). Later "the Spirit of God" came upon a different Zechariah, who rebuked King Joash for turning away from the Lord and leading Judah and Jerusalem into idolatry (24:20).

These instances in the Old Testament era seem to have been of limited durations for specific individuals regarding specific tasks and events. On the other hand, the gift of the Holy Spirit for the era of the New Testament is present in all Christians (1 Corinthians 6:19; Ephesians 1:13).

What Do You Think?

What does it look like for believers to be empowered by the Holy Spirit? Consider Ephesians 5:18-20 in your answer.

Digging Deeper

How will you continue being attentive to the ways that the Holy Spirit works in and through you?

C. Reassuring Message (vv. 15-17)

15. And he said, Hearken ye, all Judah, and ye inhabitants of Jerusalem, and thou king

Jehoshaphat, Thus saith the Lord unto you, Be not afraid nor dismayed by reason of this great multitude; for the battle is not yours, but God's.

The message was not directed to all 12 tribes of divided Israel, but only to the southern kingdom of *Judah,* where *Jerusalem* was located. God intended that everyone receive His message. Therefore, it is addressed to all the people of Judah and Jerusalem, with the king referred to last. Since northern Israel was ruled by ungodly kings (see Lesson Context), the content of the message being delivered was not appropriate for them.

The phrase *thus saith the Lord* occurs over 400 times in the Old Testament. Whether the message that follows is initially targeted toward an individual (Jeremiah 27:2) or a group (4:3), the expected outcome will concern the bigger picture. That is the case here, as Jahaziel directed his words to *all* the people who were assembled (the phrase *unto you* is also plural). Interestingly, the negative phrase *be not afraid nor dismayed* also appears in 2 Chronicles 32:7, where it is preceded by the positive phrase "be strong and courageous" with regard to a different enemy (compare 1 Chronicles 22:13).

King Jehoshaphat, as leader of God's people, especially needed to hear these words. The *great multitude* of the enemy coalition was already at En-Gedi, located on the western shore of the Dead Sea southeast of Jerusalem (2 Chronicles 20:2). The distance from En-Gedi to Jerusalem was about 25 straight-line miles. However, since road distances varied, the practical distance between the locations was a bit farther. An army marching at a rate of two miles per hour would be at the gates of Jerusalem in less than three days!

When in a crisis situation, there's always the perceived need to do something as people begin to panic. Yet Jehoshaphat did not need to concern himself with how he and his people would overcome the enemy army, for he was not the real commander-in-chief: *The battle is not yours, but God's* (compare 1 Samuel 17:47; 2 Kings 6:15-17).

16. To morrow go ye down against them: behold, they come up by the cliff of Ziz; and ye shall find them at the end of the brook, before the wilderness of Jeruel.

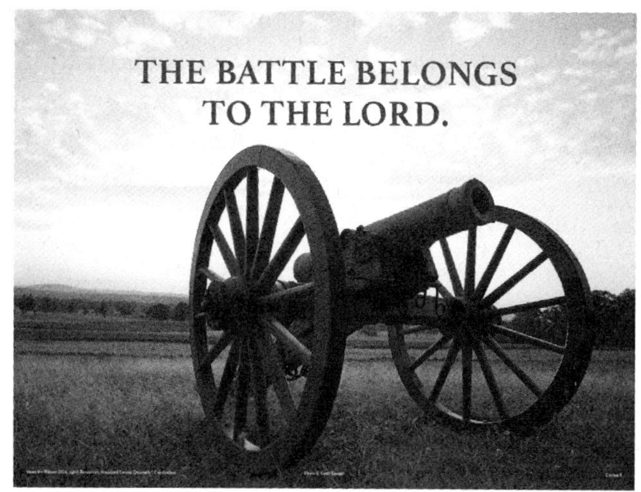

Visual for Lesson 8. *Point to this visual after reading verse 17 and ask for examples of ways that the Lord fights for us today.*

The enemy army's location *by the cliff of Ziz* means that those troops had marched about seven miles to the north from En-Gedi (again, 2 Chronicles 20:2), along the road bordering the western shore of the Dead Sea. This puts that army less than 20 miles from Jerusalem. The *wilderness of Jeruel* was in this vicinity (20:20). Exactly how King Jehoshaphat was to proceed at that point is specified in the next verse.

17. Ye shall not need to fight in this battle: set yourselves, stand ye still, and see the salvation of the Lord with you, O Judah and Jerusalem: fear not, nor be dismayed; to morrow go out against them: for the Lord will be with you.

This verse essentially repeats the message of 2 Chronicles 20:15, above. The Scriptures witness to the Lord's defeating enemy armies in various ways (examples: Exodus 14; Deuteronomy 3:1-11; Joshua 8; Judges 4, 7; 2 Kings 19). Sometimes the Lord works through human intermediaries in this regard, and sometimes not. The promise *ye shall not need to fight in this battle* is a strong hint that this time it will be the latter.

The commands *stand ye still, and see the salvation of the Lord with you* and *fear not . . . for the Lord will be with you* are remarkably similar to Moses' instructions in Exodus 14:13-14 to the Israelites when being pursued by the Egyptian army during the exodus many centuries earlier: "Fear ye not, stand still, and see the salvation of the Lord. . . . The Lord shall fight for you." The assurance of the Lord's presence is found in numerous places (examples: Genesis 31:3; Deuteronomy 31:6; Isaiah 41:10).

What Do You Think?

How can each element of the armor of God (see Ephesians 6:10-18) help you stand firm in the contexts in which God has placed you?

Digging Deeper

How will you discern whether "battle strategies" are necessary in your context of serving the Lord?

II. "Faith-ing" a Crisis

(2 Chronicles 20:18-20)

A. By Worshipping the Lord (vv. 18-19)

18. And Jehoshaphat bowed his head with his face to the ground: and all Judah and the inhabitants of Jerusalem fell before the LORD, worshipping the LORD.

Clearly, the Lord had heard the king's prayer! Worship was the only proper response. The king set the example, and the people joined him. He had declared that "our eyes are upon thee" (2 Chronicles 20:12); now he and those same eyes were turned to the ground in reverence. They had been standing "before the Lord" (20:13); they then *fell before the Lord*.

19. And the Levites, of the children of the Kohathites, and of the children of the Korhites, stood up to praise the LORD God of Israel with a loud voice on high.

The *Kohathites* took their name from Kohath, the second of the three sons of Levi (Genesis 46:11). From the Kohathites came the priestly family of Aaron (1 Chronicles 6:1-3). *The Levites* were responsible for "keeping the charge of the sanctuary" (Numbers 3:28).

The *Korhites* refer to the sons of Korah, another Levite from the clan of Kohath, whose father was Izhar, the brother of Amram, Moses and Aaron's father (Exodus 6:18, 21). Korah is infamous for organizing a rebellion against the authority of Moses and Aaron during Israel's wanderings in the wilderness. Korah and those who joined him in his defiance were swallowed up by the earth in a terrifying demonstration of God's wrath (Numbers 16:25-35). There were, however, descendants of Korah who did not join him in his action, and those mentioned in our passage would be descendants of those individuals. Certainly the difference in attitude between these who *stood up* to join Jehoshaphat in *praise* and worship and their forefathers who "rose up" to defy Moses (16:2) is worth noting. As time moved on and the tabernacle gave way to the temple, the Korhites became gatekeepers (1 Chronicles 6:22; 9:17-19).

What Do You Think?

In what ways can you worship God without fear of being distracting or disturbing others?

Digging Deeper

How is your public witness strengthened when you publicly worship God?

Genuine Worship

What does genuine, authentic worship look like? In Italy, day and night at regular hours of prayer, monks gather in robes and chant ancient hymns in a Gothic cathedral. In Iowa, on the stage of a tiny country church, a shaggy-headed guitarist rocks out to heavy metal before a sea of tattooed and pierced motorcycle enthusiasts, singing along to lyrics of devotion to Jesus. In India, an elderly woman prays and worships at a niche in her living room wall that once held pictures and statues of Hindu gods but now features only a cross. In Oklahoma, a well-dressed couple sit in the theater seating of a megachurch and watch a well-rehearsed drama, laughing and thinking soberly about God's gentle, persistent call in their lives.

Around the world, worship of God is as diverse as God's people. Love for Jesus can be expressed in any language, as well as by all sorts of music, art, and body language. Regardless of how amateurish various worship expressions might look, two things matter most: (1) that it is offered from a sincere heart of devotion and (2) that it is offered only to the true God, who sent His Son to die on our behalf (John 4:23). To worship with the first without the second is idolatry; to worship with the second without the first is hypocrisy. Which way might you tend most to err? —A. W.

B. By Trusting the Lord (v. 20)

20. And they rose early in the morning, and went forth into the wilderness of Tekoa: and as they went forth, Jehoshaphat stood and said, Hear me, O Judah, and ye inhabitants of Jerusalem; Believe in the LORD your God, so shall ye be established; believe his prophets, so shall ye prosper.

Rising *early in the morning* indicates the king and the people's anticipation to see how the Lord would work on their behalf. It's an 18-mile walk, and they need to get to *the wilderness of Tekoa* before nightfall (see 2 Chronicles 20:16, above). King *Jehoshaphat* took the lead in encouraging his people to demonstrate faith in the Lord—a key theme of Jahaziel's message the day before. (Perhaps Jahaziel accompanied the people as they went forth, but we are not told.) As Jehoshaphat challenged the people to *believe in the Lord* and in His messengers, the *prophets,* it appears the king accepted Jahaziel's message as prophetic.

The link between trusting the Lord and trusting His prophets should not be overlooked. If God's covenant people desired to obey Him, then they must accept the words spoken by His inspired messengers, the prophets. When God's people ignored and even mocked these Heaven-sent messengers, a Heaven-sent judgment came upon them (see 2 Kings 17; etc.).

For the time being, King Jehoshaphat and the people of Judah had chosen to heed the words spoken to them. When they raised their voices in praise to the Lord, the Lord indeed came to their rescue and brought about a miraculous deliverance that allowed the people to plunder the possessions of their enemies (2 Chronicles 20:21-25). So the king and the people then returned to Jerusalem as they had left it—in triumphant praise and worship of the Lord (20:26-28).

What Do You Think?

What most challenges you about today's passage?

Digging Deeper

What will you do to respond to that challenge?

Conclusion

A. When Uplook Changes Outlook

King Jehoshaphat had offered a passionate plea to the Lord for help, admitting that neither the king nor his people had any strategy or resources to confront the oncoming threat. Perhaps as his prayer progressed, his voice grew louder, possibly even trembling as he reached the end and declared his utter dependence upon God: "Neither know we what to do: but our eyes are upon thee" (2 Chronicles 20:12). Then came Jahaziel's Spirit-empowered words. The people's uplook changed their outlook.

All of us can probably recall a time when a passage of God's Word was especially reassuring and helped get us through difficult circumstances. We may not have felt as desperate as Jehoshaphat did, but we experienced the energy that comes with God's encouragement. We may not be like Jahaziel, who encouraged a king and his nation when the Spirit of God came upon him. But perhaps during the course of a day, someone will come to mind that we should share a Scripture passage with by a phone call, text message, email, or postcard.

Who might that be?

B. Prayer

Father, our culture and our world are often characterized by speech and actions that oppose Your truth. Keep our eyes on You daily, that we may escape their influence! Thank You for those who have encouraged us over the years through Your promises. May we seek to pass that blessing on to others. In Jesus' name we pray. Amen.

C. Thought to Remember

Let your uplook change your outlook.

Involvement Learning

Enhance your lesson with KJV Bible Student *(from your curriculum supplier) and the reproducible activity page (at www.standardlesson.com or in the back of the* KJV Standard Lesson Commentary Deluxe Edition*).*

Into the Lesson

Invite learners to list famous battles in world history. Write the list on the board and refer to the list as you ask the following questions for whole-class discussion: 1–What was the context of the battle? 2–Who is considered to have "won" the battle? 3–What resulted from the conflict?

Option. Bring a checkerboard and arrange the pieces with one piece of one color in a corner and three "kinged" pieces of another color surrounding it. Explain how this layout demonstrates one-to-three (1:3) odds. Challenge learners to develop a strategy for the one to overcome the three and win.

Say, "It is easy for us to feel overwhelmed, discouraged, and defeated when we feel the odds are stacked against us. That is how King Jehoshaphat and the people of Judah felt in today's Scripture. As we study, pay attention to what God told them and how their response reflected their faith."

Into the Word

Prepare for today's Scripture reading by sharing the Lesson Context from the commentary. Ask a volunteer to read aloud 2 Chronicles 20:13-14. Divide the class in half. Ask one half to list the listeners mentioned in verse 13 and discuss why it was important for each listed group to hear the word of the Lord on that day. Ask the other half to record the lineage of Jahaziel based on verse 14 and discuss why he had the authority to speak. Give the two groups time to discuss and then ask for volunteers to share their group's conclusions.

Ask a volunteer to read aloud 2 Chronicles 20:15-17. Divide participants into pairs or triads. Distribute a sheet of paper and pens to each group. Ask each group to sketch the plan God instructed the people of Judah to follow. Invite groups to use their "sanctified imagination" to fill in the gaps in their sketches regarding strategic battle instructions and other related details. After 10 minutes, ask a volunteer from each group to share their drawing with the whole class. Discuss any conclusions and insights that groups discovered.

Ask a volunteer to read aloud 2 Chronicles 20:18-20. Ask three or more volunteers to act out these verses before the whole class. Choose volunteers to play the roles of King Jehoshaphat, people of Judah, and Levite(s). After the performance, invite the class to discuss what behaviors demonstrated the characters' faith in what God had told them. Ask the following questions for whole-class discussion: 1–What is significant about the people worshipping God before the battle? 2–How did Jehoshaphat and the people of Judah show their faith? 3–How does v. 20 apply to us? 4–How would you respond if God told you directly that He would fight for you?

Option. Allow one minute for learners to complete the "Asaph's Psalm" exercise from the activity page, which you can download. Then ask learners to pair up to discuss their results.

Into Life

Ask participants to choose a partner. Write the following three questions on the board:

1. What things in your life cause you to experience fear or worry?
2. How does today's Scripture text encourage you and strengthen your faith?
3. What will you do this week to be attentive to God's presence in facing your fears and worries?

Allow time for the pairs to discuss their fears and worries and then pray for each other. Reconvene the class and spend the remainder of class time praying and praising God, declaring He is greater than our fear and worry.

Alternative. Distribute the "Your Song" exercise from the activity page to be completed individually. Encourage learners to refer to their song or poem throughout the week to remember God's deliverance and faithfulness.

January 28
Lesson 9 (KJV)

Faith and Transformation

Devotional Reading: Ezekiel 11:17-21
Background Scripture: Romans 12:3-8

Romans 12:3-8

3 For I say, through the grace given unto me, to every man that is among you, not to think of himself more highly than he ought to think; but to think soberly, according as God hath dealt to every man the measure of faith.

4 For as we have many members in one body, and all members have not the same office:

5 So we, being many, are one body in Christ, and every one members one of another.

6 Having then gifts differing according to the grace that is given to us, whether prophecy, let us prophesy according to the proportion of faith;

7 Or ministry, let us wait on our ministering: or he that teacheth, on teaching;

8 Or he that exhorteth, on exhortation: he that giveth, let him do it with simplicity; he that ruleth, with diligence; he that sheweth mercy, with cheerfulness.

Key Text

Having then gifts differing according to the grace that is given to us. **—Romans 12:6a**

Faith That

Pleases God

Unit 2: Learning About Faith

Lessons 6–9

Lesson Aims

After participating in this lesson, each learner will be able to:

1. List several spiritual gifts.
2. Compare and contrast the printed text with the gift lists in 1 Corinthians 12 and Ephesians 4.
3. Create a plan to use a spiritual gift more effectively.

Lesson Outline

Introduction

A. Where's My X-ray?
B. Lesson Context

I. How to Think (Romans 12:3-5)

A. About Self (v. 3)
B. About Others (vv. 4-5)
Team Moon

II. How to Serve (Romans 12:6-8)

A. With Well-Defined Gifts (vv. 6-8a)
B. With Less-Defined Gifts (v. 8b-8d)
Striking Mercy

Conclusion

A. All Gifts Matter
B. Your Gift(s)?
C. Prayer
D. Thought to Remember

Introduction

A. Where's My X-ray?

My four-year-old son, Valor, is fascinated by the human body. His favorite book to have me read is about the human body and its different parts. He loves opening the little tabs in the book to reveal the internal organs and bones of the "body." A local medical clinic recently provided free medical exams, and Valor was excited. He listened carefully as the doctor's assistant explained how the spine and nerves fit together. He got very excited about getting an X-ray, and that's where things got difficult. He wasn't old enough for an X-ray, but his sister and brother were.

That upset him. He wanted the picture of how his body fit together! For much of the trip home, he begged us to go back to get his X-ray picture taken.

It's too bad that Christians don't concern themselves this much with how the body of Christ fits together. Maybe if we did, we would have healthier churches as members appreciated each other more.

B. Lesson Context

The book of Romans was written by Paul in about AD 58, probably toward the end of his third missionary journey. At that point, Paul had not yet been to Rome, but greatly wished to visit (Romans 1:11-15; 15:23-24). He would do so, but in chains as a prisoner, as Acts 27–28 records.

He made it to Rome by about AD 61 but remained under house arrest, unable to move about the city as he might have wished (Acts 28:16, 20, 23, 30). Paul wrote his letter to the church at Rome to introduce himself and his teaching prior to a personal visit there. The church likely had been established not long after the day of Pentecost, some three decades earlier (2:1). Some of the Jews who heard Peter's sermon that day were from Rome (2:10), and it's easy to imagine that they were the ones who started the church after returning home to Rome. There can be little doubt that the Roman church had heard of Paul (28:15) and looked forward to meeting him.

One of the great debates concerning the context of the book of Romans is the demographic composition of the Roman church when Paul wrote. Were the members primarily of Jewish background, of Gentile background, or evenly split? Although it is highly likely that the church was founded by believers of Jewish background, Paul seems to suggest that the church was composed primarily of Gentiles (see Romans 1:5-6, 13). The Roman emperor Claudius expelled Jews from Rome about AD 49 (Acts 18:2), which would have resulted in believers of Gentile background coming into greater prominence.

But by the time that Paul wrote this letter, Claudius had died and the expulsion order was rescinded, allowing Jews to return to Rome. How many believers of Jewish background constituted the Roman church is uncertain, but Paul does spend Romans 9:1–11:12 speaking about the nation of Israel. Even so, that section depicts a direct address to Gentiles in 11:13. The weight of the evidence therefore points to a Gentile majority in the church in Rome.

The book of Romans falls into two major sections. The first part, Romans 1–11, features some of the most doctrinally heavy thoughts in all of Scripture. A shift comes with Romans 12–16, which addresses how Christians should then live in light of the truth of those doctrines. Today's lesson comes from this second section.

I. How to Think

(Romans 12:3-5)

A. About Self (v. 3)

3a. For I say, through the grace given unto me, to every man that is among you, not to think of himself more highly than he ought to think.

This verse starts with a conjunction by which Paul introduces the logical explanation for what he has already said. The ability to discern the "good, and acceptable, and perfect, will of God" (Romans 12:2) begins with the correct thought of ourselves. The word *for* seems to introduce the way people should think of themselves in the appropriate manner: by being "renewed in the spirit of your mind" (Ephesians 4:23). Paul is able to offer this imperative because of *the grace given* to him—an expression he never tires of using (see Romans 15:15; 1 Corinthians 15:10; Galatians 2:9; Ephesians 3:7; 4:7). That phrase establishes his authority as coming from God.

3b. But to think soberly, according as God hath dealt to every man the measure of faith.

For a person *to think soberly* is to think rationally and appropriately (compare Mark 5:15; 2 Corinthians 5:13). Paul introduced the common standard of measurement by which to evaluate oneself: it is *the measure of faith.* But there is debate over what kind of faith Paul had in mind. The two main possibilities are the "common faith" that every Christian has (see Titus 1:4) and "distributed" faith, which is given for differing capacities for service (see 2 Corinthians 10:13). There are strong arguments both ways. But notice that in either case, the measure is not that of one person compared to another person—the natural and unhealthy tendency.

> **What Do You Think?**
>
> How do you determine whether you think too highly of yourself or underestimate yourself?
>
> **Digging Deeper**
>
> How will you use an accountability partner to help consider yourself with sober judgment?

B. About Others (vv. 4-5)

4. For as we have many members in one body, and all members have not the same office.

Paul uses this analogy to the human *body* also in 1 Corinthians 12:12-14 and Ephesians 4:16. It should be obvious that not all parts of the *body* perform the same function. A hand does not function as an ear and vice versa. We note that the word *office* is not referring to the offices of elder, deacon, etc. The Greek underneath this word is also translated "deeds" in Romans 8:13 and Colossians 3:9, and that is the sense here.

5. So we, being many, as one body in Christ, and every one members one of another.

Paul desired his readers to think in terms of *one* as a collective singular of *many*. As Christians cannot serve effectively apart from other Christians, so also *one body* cannot operate independently of the head, who is *Christ*. These themes are so important that Paul repeats them in several places (see 1 Corinthians 12:27; Ephesians 1:22-23; 4:12, 25; Colossians 1:18, 24).

What Do You Think?

How do you discern your function within the body of Christ that is the church?

Digging Deeper

How do Ephesians 4:11-16 and 1 Peter 4:10-11 inform your process of discernment?

Team Moon

Trivia question: How many people landed *Apollo 11* on the moon in 1969? According to Catherine Thimmesh, the answer is 400,000!

In her book *Team Moon*, Thimmesh highlights the diverse roles that were essential to the mission. Seamstresses stitched 22 layers of fabric on each spacesuit. Engineers designed an array of systems, which were then built by skilled technicians. Safety inspectors, physicians, mission-control personnel, and others made the mission possible and successful. But as people gathered around their television sets to watch the drama unfold, they saw only three astronauts in space and only two of them land on the lunar surface.

My wife and I used to be missionaries in rural Africa, which in some ways felt like being an astronaut in an unknown world. We also stood in the spotlight as we reported to churches. But when our daughter was born with severe cerebral palsy, our roles changed—we became part of the support team based in the United States.

I'm ashamed to admit that I once thought the overseas missionary role felt more important than the roles of the support team. The accountants, trainers, fundraisers, administrators, and media creators are all members of the same body; if they weren't essential, they wouldn't be on the team. Also members of the team are the thousands who pray and donate funds. Which mistake are you more likely to make: overrating your role in the body of Christ or underrating it?

—N. G.

II. How to Serve

(Romans 12:6-8)

A. With Well-Defined Gifts (vv. 6-8a)

6. Having then gifts differing according to the grace that is given to us, whether prophecy, let us prophesy according to the proportion of faith.

The echo of 1 Corinthians 12:4-11 is quite strong here and in the two verses that follow (compare 1 Peter 4:10-11). With the word *prophecy*, Paul begins a list of seven *gifts differing*, which fall into a group of four and a group of three. The gift of prophecy is also found in 1 Corinthians 12:28 and Ephesians 4:11. Paul prized the appropriate display of this gift (see 1 Corinthians 14).

When we see the word *prophecy*, we often think of predicting the future (as in Acts 11:28; 21:10-12). But that is not its main impulse in the New Testament era; rather, prophecy more often involves proclaiming information divinely revealed for the church's edification (compare 1 Corinthians 14:3, 24-25, 30). Moreover, the message of a prophet was evaluated by others having the same gift (14:29-32).

We pause here for a caution: as Paul begins his listing of spiritual gifts, it is tempting to jump in hastily and compile a list of such gifts according to

How to Say It

Beatitudes	Bee-*a*-tuh-toods (*a* as in *mat*).
caveat emptor (Latin)	ka-vee-ought em-tor.
Claudius	*Claw*-dee-us.
Colossians	Kuh-*losh*-unz.
Corinthians	Ko-*rin*-thee-unz (*th* as in *thin*).
Ephesians	Ee-*fee*-zhunz.
Galatians	Guh-*lay*-shunz.
Gentile	*Jen*-tile.
Pentecost	*Pent*-ih-kost.
Titus	*Ty*-tus.

this text and others. But to do so runs the risk of missing the bigger picture. That bigger picture is that spiritual gifts serve as an example of a church that is united in its diversity. Spiritual gifts are not given merely to bless the person receiving the gift, but to build up the church as a whole (Ephesians 4:11-12). Most of all, these gifts are intended to be displays of love between believers (see 1 Corinthians 13).

What Do You Think?

What steps will you take to either (1) discern your spiritual gift or (2) discern how to use your gift for the church?

Digging Deeper

Who will you ask for insight and guidance in this regard?

7a. Or ministry, let us wait on our ministering.

We move to the second gift in Paul's grouping of four. The word translated *ministry* and *ministering* is also translated "serve" in Romans 15:31, and that is the sense here. "Service" was the usual way to describe the work that Christians did on behalf of others. As Paul uses this word, he can refer to various types of service:

- Christian ministry in general (Romans 15:25; Philemon 13);
- The ministry of Christ (Romans 15:8; Galatians 2:17);
- Specific Christian ministries (Romans 11:13; 2 Corinthians 9:12-13);
- Ministry of the office of deacon (Philippians 1:1; 1 Timothy 3:8-13);
- Ministry of a secular authority (Romans 13:4).

Since the other gifts Paul names in our text involve specific functions, he was likely thinking of a specific gift of service that qualified a person to be in the office of deacon.

7b. Or he that teacheth, on teaching.

The gift of *teaching* is also noted in 1 Corinthians 12:28-29 and Ephesians 4:11. In the text before us, Paul is focusing on *he that teacheth* rather the gift of teaching as such. Why he makes this switch is unclear. What is clear, however, is

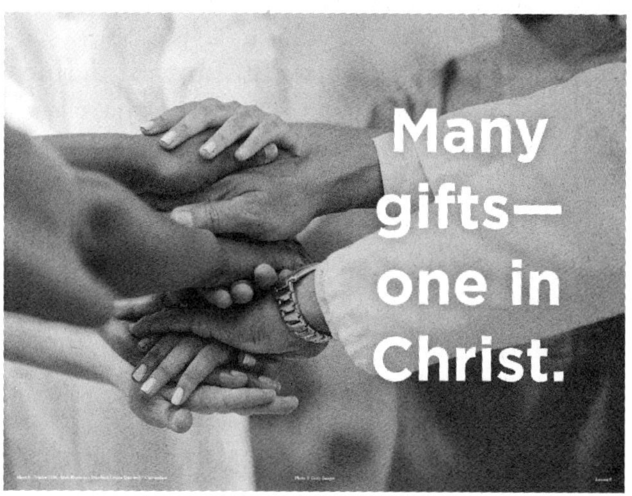

Visual for Lesson 9. *Point to this visual and ask for volunteers to share how their spiritual gifts can be used to serve the church.*

that teaching is distinct from prophesying. Prophecy is based on revealing the information that God has placed in the prophet's mouth; teaching, on the other hand, involves communicating the truth of the gospel (see 2 Timothy 2:2; 3:10).

Teaching was critical for the first-century church, where many people were not formally educated. They learned from auditory instruction rather than reading. Therefore, it was and is a primary task of the eldership (1 Timothy 3:2; 5:17).

8a. Or he that exhorteth, on exhortation.

We come to the fourth gift in Paul's subgrouping of four well-defined spiritual gifts. He uses the verb translated *exhorteth* and the noun translated *exhortation* a total of 80 times across his letters. The ways he uses the verb in 60 occurrences are translated "comfort(eth)" (example: twice in 2 Corinthians 1:4), "beseech" (example: 2:8), or "exhort" (as here). The 20 times he uses the noun are translated "comfort" (example: 1:4), "consolation" (example: Romans 15:5), or "exhortation" (as in this verse).

Putting this all together, we get the idea that Paul is challenging those with this gift to use it in terms of being a bit stronger than merely "requesting" something of someone else but a bit less strong than "commanding" that person.

B. With Less-Defined Gifts (v. 8b-8d)

8b. He that giveth, let him do it with simplicity.

We come now to the first in a subgrouping of three spiritual gifts—gifts that are less-defined than the previous four. To give is to share with another or the church what one has. This is an expectation of all believers (1 Corinthians 16:2). The word translated *simplicity* occurs eight times in the New Testament, always in Paul's letters. Its translations in other passages are "liberal(ity)" (2 Corinthians 8:2; 9:13), "bountifulness" (9:11), and "singleness" of heart (Ephesians 6:5; Colossians 3:22). Understanding "simplicity" to reflect "singleness of purpose" seems to be the idea. There are to be no ulterior motives for giving (contrast Acts 5:1-4).

What Do You Think?

In what ways can a believer utilize the gift of giving without always focusing on financial giving?

Digging Deeper

Who can be the recipient of your non-financial giving?

8c. He that ruleth, with diligence.

As with the word translated *simplicity* (Romans 12:8b, above), the Greek word translated *ruleth* occurs eight times in the New Testament, always in Paul's letters. It is used of church leadership (1 Thessalonians 5:12; 1 Timothy 5:17), family leadership or household management (3:4, 5, 12), and self-management (Titus 3:8, 14). The overall idea is that of "one who presides." To be such a person is to be in control in a godly sense.

8d. He that sheweth mercy, with cheerfulness.

To show *mercy* requires both action and a proper attitude. As such, showing mercy involves more than merely offering lip-service sympathy (compare 1 John 3:17-18) or forgiveness. In the Beatitudes, Jesus stated, "Blessed are the merciful: for they shall obtain mercy" (Matthew 5:7).

No specific ways of being merciful are listed in the text before us, and Paul seems intentionally to want the general sense. As one who had received mercy, the importance of being merciful was quite personal to him (1 Timothy 1:13, 16). Indeed, the mercy we ourselves have received from God is the basis for our own acts of mercy, as Jesus' parable of the unmerciful servant makes clear (Matthew 18:21-35). We see the *cheerfulness* aspect of showing mercy also reflected in giving (2 Corinthians 9:7), such giving being a specific kind of merciful act.

At this point, this list of spiritual gifts ends. But the very next verse (Romans 12:9) relates love to spiritual gifts in much the same way 1 Corinthians 12–14 does. Love is the touchstone for how any spiritual gift is used.

As we wrap up our consideration of this subgrouping of three gifts, we should consider a possible implication regarding these gifts being less-defined than other gifts. That implication is that these three are expected of *all* Christians. Think about it: Shouldn't everyone give with sincerity (2 Corinthians 9:7)? Shouldn't everyone rule or manage at least his or her own life to keep from being unproductive (2 Peter 1:5-8)? Shouldn't everyone be merciful (James 2:13)?

What Do You Think?

How might you demonstrate the gift of mercy in the upcoming week?

Digging Deeper

What might prevent believers from wanting to show mercy, even if they have the gift for doing so?

Striking Mercy

One of the earliest displays of mercy that I remember came during recess in the sixth grade. As the group played soccer, two kids ran up to the soccer ball and kicked it at the same time. One child lost his balance mid-kick and fell down to the ground. It was truly an accident—and comical at that. But the embarrassed child did not think so. It seemed that he thought that the other child had committed a grievous error. As soon as the child got off the ground, he stormed to the other child and struck him in the face.

However, the hit child didn't retaliate; he didn't show any anger or fear. Instead, he just picked up his glasses and kept playing soccer. No fight would occur that day. The coach saw the incident and pulled the other kid off the field to address his behavior. What did that youngster need in that moment: correction or mercy? Maybe he needed both! (Compare and contrast Acts 15:36-40.)

Are you in a position of being able to extend mercy to someone else? If so, do so cheerfully!

—N. G.

Conclusion

A. All Gifts Matter

We understand that all spiritual gifts are important. But at the same time, we know that not all such gifts are equal (see 1 Corinthians 12:31; 14:1) and that not all believers are equally gifted (see Matthew 25:14-15).

As a result, our natural tendency is to pay more attention to the gifts that are more visible, more "out front" to the public. The highly visible preacher of the church usually gets paid more than the less visible custodian who cleans the church. But here's where Paul's illustration of body members working together (unity in diversity) comes in per Romans 12:4-5: I don't think you would want to go to dirty and smelly church any more than you would want to go to a church with a horrible preacher! The functions of one's hands are much more varied, useful, and visible than are the functions of one's elbow. But a nonfunctioning elbow will severely limit how the hand can function (compare 1 Corinthians 12:12-27).

Pride is a danger to those having the more visible gifts (see Proverbs 16:18). Also a danger is that those who have the less visible gifts won't use them, perhaps figuratively "burying" them (Matthew 25:25). But just as no human body functions to its highest potential unless all of its parts work together, so also the church—the body of Christ—does not function at full potential until all of its members use their spiritual gifts. The cure (or preventative) for both pride of gifts and non-use of gifts is Luke 17:10: "So likewise ye, when ye shall have done all those things which are commanded you, say, We are unprofitable servants: we have done that which was our duty to do."

B. Your Gift(s)?

A popular tool that churches and ministries have turned to since at least the 1980s is a spiritual-gifts assessment inventory. I took several of these inventories (or "tests") during my time as a student in Bible college and seminary. Most of the time, they told me what I suspected already: that teaching was one of my spiritual gifts.

Occasionally, an inventory would indicate that I had a secondary gift that I didn't realize. One such result was that I had the gift of administration. I found that to be exceptionally funny, given the reality of the piles of books, articles, and papers piled on my desk, floor, and couch!

This goes to show that these inventories aren't perfect—they can even be misleading. The axiom *caveat emptor* ("let the buyer beware") applies in more ways than one!

An assumption behind those inventories is that helping people identify what their giftings are will mean that those who have been thus enlightened will automatically start using those gifts. But that is not always so. People will need encouragement to use and otherwise develop their spiritual gifts. Sometimes, people need the wisdom and insight of others to help discern which giftings are present.

Another assumption is that such inventories are even needed for people to be able to identify their areas of spiritual giftedness. A more accurate indicator may be personal experience. What types of Christian service do your personal experiences tell you that you have been best at? Where have you fallen flat?

C. Prayer

Father, You have called all of Your servants to serve. Help us to realize our gifts and give us the courage to develop and use them for Your glory. Help us to remember that no matter what our gifts are, we are all members of one body, and that no one is unimportant to Your church and to You. We pray in Jesus' name. Amen.

D. Thought to Remember

Know your spiritual gifts and use them with humility.

Involvement Learning

Enhance your lesson with KJV Bible Student *(from your curriculum supplier) and the reproducible activity page (at www.standardlesson.com or in the back of the* KJV Standard Lesson Commentary Deluxe Edition*).*

Into the Lesson

Bring to class time a game or toy in multiple pieces, such as a jigsaw puzzle, a disassembled toy, or a small model kit. Distribute pieces to each learner so that everyone has at least one component. Instruct the class to work together to assemble the pieces into a complete product. After no more than 10 minutes, lead a whole-class discussion regarding the ease or difficulty of putting together the object with many people involved.

Alternative. Divide participants into groups of three. Distribute copies of the "Common Goal" exercise from the activity page, which you can download. Have groups work together to complete the activity as indicated before bringing the groups together to talk about their experiences.

Say, "God has given us value and purpose, but He has also designed us to need each other. In today's lesson, think about how this truth is especially relevant in the church, among the body of believers."

Into the Word

Option. Divide learners into pairs to play a game of "10 Questions." Invite each learner to think of a way for a person to serve in the church (examples: play an instrument, teach a class, etc.). Tell learners to keep their examples to themselves. Partners will go back and forth, asking each other yes-or-no questions to determine the service thought of by their partner. Each learner will ask up to 10 questions until one learner can correctly guess. Conclude by challenging learners to identify one thing they can do to serve other church members.

Ask a volunteer to read aloud Romans 12:3-5. Ask the following questions for whole-class discussion: 1–In what ways is the human body a fitting comparison to the church? 2–Why is it essential to recognize what we can do well? 3–What is significant about acknowledging the things we cannot do well?

Ask a volunteer to read aloud Romans 12:6-8. Divide learners into seven small groups and assign each group one of the following spiritual gifts to discuss: (1) prophesying, (2) ministering/serving, (3) teaching, (4) exhorting/encouraging, (5) giving, (6) leading, (7) showing mercy. Ask groups to discuss the following questions in their group: 1–What might the church be like without the presence of this gift? 2–What might the church be like if this were the only gift present? 3–How might the church encourage people with this gift? 4–How do 1 Corinthians 12:12-31 and Ephesians 4:1-16 help inform the use of this gift? After 10 minutes, have a volunteer from each group share their conclusions with the whole class.

Into Life

Divide learners into groups of three. Distribute index cards and pens to learners. Ask each group member to list spiritual gifts that they recognize in the other members of their group and write examples of those gifts in action in that person. Ask each learner to write down the spiritual gifts others identified he or she has. Give the groups five minutes to brainstorm different ways each group member can use his or her gifts within the church. Challenge learners to consider one gift identified in them and think of a way they can practice that gift more effectively in the coming week. Close class with group members praying for encouragement for their group to use their gifts in service to God in the upcoming week. (*Option.* Set aside time at the beginning of next week's lesson for learners to share how their plans worked.)

Alternative. Distribute copies of the "Badge of Gifts" exercise from the activity page. Have learners complete the activity as indicated. Allow time after the pages have been completed for partners to pray for each other. Start next week's lesson with participants sharing about how they are sharing their gifts to help the church.

Faith in the Power of God

Devotional Reading: Romans 4:9-22
Background Scripture: Isaiah 40:12-31

Isaiah 40:12-13, 25-31

12 Who hath measured the waters in the hollow of his hand, and meted out heaven with the span, and comprehended the dust of the earth in a measure, and weighed the mountains in scales, and the hills in a balance?

13 Who hath directed the Spirit of the LORD, or being his counsellor hath taught him?

---

25 To whom then will ye liken me, or shall I be equal? saith the Holy One.

26 Lift up your eyes on high, and behold who hath created these things, that bringeth out their host by number: he calleth them all by names by the greatness of his might, for that he is strong in power; not one faileth.

27 Why sayest thou, O Jacob, and speakest, O Israel, My way is hid from the LORD, and my judgment is passed over from my God?

28 Hast thou not known? hast thou not heard, that the everlasting God, the LORD, the Creator of the ends of the earth, fainteth not, neither is weary? there is no searching of his understanding.

29 He giveth power to the faint; and to them that have no might he increaseth strength.

30 Even the youths shall faint and be weary, and the young men shall utterly fall:

31 But they that wait upon the LORD shall renew their strength; they shall mount up with wings as eagles; they shall run, and not be weary; and they shall walk, and not faint.

Key Text

He giveth power to the faint; and to them that have no might he increaseth strength. **—Isaiah 40:29**

Faith That
Pleases God

Unit 3: The Righteous Live by Faith
Lessons 10–13

Lesson Aims

After participating in this lesson, each learner will be able to:

1. List some characteristics of the Creator that are uniquely His.

2. Explain the implications of those characteristics.

3. Suggest ideas for a plan a worship service that focuses on God as Creator.

Lesson Outline

Introduction
- A. Taking God to Court
- B. Lesson Context

I. Supreme Ruler (Isaiah 40:12-13)
- A. Overseeing Creation (v. 12)
- B. Possessing Full Knowledge (v. 13)

II. Sustaining Ruler (Isaiah 40:25-31)
- A. Regarding His Identity (v. 25)
- B. Regarding His Abilities (vv. 26-28)
  - *Creation Sights, Creator Insights*
- C. Regarding Our Need (vv. 29-31)
  - *On Being Worn Out*

Conclusion
- A. No Shortage Here!
- B. Prayer
- C. Thought to Remember

Introduction

A. Taking God to Court

Back in 2007, Nebraska state senator Ernie Chambers filed a lawsuit against God. Chambers was seeking a permanent injunction against God, whom Chambers blamed for causing various natural disasters. The lawsuit further accused God of the crime of failing to stop "terroristic threats." Chambers stated that he had tried to contact God about these matters on multiple occasions, but without success.

This man knew that he had no hope of winning a lawsuit against the Almighty. He filed the lawsuit in an attempt to make a broader point about the wastefulness of frivolous lawsuits.

The Bible offers us various word pictures of God's heavenly courtroom. Certain passages are narratives regarding the individuals who are present: one or more of judge, jury, prosecutor, victim, defendant, etc. (examples: Job 16:19-21; Psalm 89:37; Matthew 19:28; Revelation 11:18; 19:19–21:8). Also suggested are locations in the courtroom: a judgment seat, a witness stand, etc. (examples: Job 40:2; Romans 14:10; 2 Corinthians 5:10). These serve as warnings regarding who is susceptible to judgment and who is not.

B. Lesson Context

Today's lesson comes from the writings of the Old Testament prophet Isaiah. His text is the first in a group of five referred to as the Major Prophets; those five are the books known as Isaiah, Jeremiah, Lamentations, Ezekiel, and Daniel.

We may wonder what value the Old Testament books of the prophets still have in the New Testament era. After all, the days of those prophets are long gone, and we're under the new covenant, not the old (Colossians 2:14). The value of the prophets today is firmly established in how many times they are cited by Jesus and the authors of the New Testament. One clue to their value today is to be aware of how often these books are quoted in the New Testament. By one count, the tallies are Isaiah (67 times), Jeremiah (5 times), Lamentations (0 times), Ezekiel (2 times), and Daniel (5 times).

These figures reveal the continuing relevance

of the book of Isaiah. It has been called "the fifth Gospel" because of its numerous prophecies declared as fulfilled in the messianic era of the New Testament (examples: Isaiah 6:9-10 in Matthew 13:14-15 and Mark 4:12; Isaiah 53:7-8 in Acts 8:32-33).

Isaiah prophesied during some very dismal times for God's people. His prophetic call came "in the year that king Uzziah died" (Isaiah 6:1; compare 2 Chronicles 26:22), which would have been 740 BC (see 2 Chronicles 26; Uzziah is also known as Azariah in 2 Kings 15:1-7). The final historical event recorded by the prophet is the death of Sennacherib, which occurred in 681 BC (Isaiah 37:38). That makes for a lengthy period of ministry!

The text under consideration in our lesson follows a prophecy that warns King Hezekiah of Judah regarding a time when Babylon would carry away Judah's wealth and people to Babylon (Isaiah 39:5-7); more than 100 years would pass before that happened, but it indeed *did* happen. This was a punishment from the Lord for the people's sins, followed by "comfort" in declaring that that punishment would eventually end (40:1-2). The predictions that immediately follow in Isaiah 40:3-5 shift forward more than five centuries for fulfillment, quoted in Matthew 3:3; Mark 1:3; Luke 3:4-6; and John 1:23.

The passage of time from pronouncement to fulfillment of these prophecies makes for valuable study. But the study in today's lesson takes us beyond time-bound prophecies in considering the timeless nature of God himself.

I. Supreme Ruler

(Isaiah 40:12-13)

A. Overseeing Creation (v. 12)

12a. Who hath measured the waters in the hollow of his hand, and meted out heaven with the span?

Today's text comes to us in the form of Hebrew poetry. This style often involves balanced lines known as *parallelism*. This means expressing the same thoughts across different lines using different words (synonyms).

Visual for Lesson 10. *After reading verse 12a, use this visual and ask for specific examples of other things in nature that point to the power of God.*

We see that parallelism here regarding the verbs *measured* and *meted out.* Both expressions deal with calculating something. See Isaiah 65:7, where the word translated *meted out* is translated "measure." Additional parallelism occurs with the phrases *hollow of his hand* and *the span.* The latter refers to the distance from the end of the thumb to that of the little finger when these are extended—in other words, about nine inches (compare 1 Samuel 17:4).

The words translated *waters* and *heaven* occur together about three dozen times in the Old Testament; most closely aligned with their usage here are Genesis 1:20; Proverbs 30:4; and Amos 9:6. Isaiah uses this imagery to call attention to things God can do that humans cannot. The rhetorical questions being posed are similar to those that the Lord confronted Job with (see Job 38–41). Of particular interest in light of the half-verse under consideration is Job 38:5. Modern science allows us to make educated guesses regarding the volume of water in the oceans and the vastness of space in light years. But whatever the unit of measure, no human device can determine those things with exactness. Only their Creator can do that.

Through rhetorical questions, the prophet provides his reader with the proper perspective of God. The human mind cannot fathom the amount of water in the ocean or the distance of one galaxy to another. However, the Creator can measure the distance using His hand. In this verse, Isaiah declares the greatness of God and lays down the basis of the criteria by which the Israelites may compare their God to the gods of other nations.

12b. And comprehended the dust of the earth in a measure, and weighed the mountains in scales, and the hills in a balance?

Isaiah's question has an answer so obvious that it should not have to be stated. The verb translated *comprehended* implies something like "hold" or "contain" (compare its translation in Jeremiah 2:13 concerning "broken cisterns, that can hold no water"). Parallelism continues between *mountains* and *hills* as well as *scales* and *balance* (compare Job 38:18).

What Do You Think?

In what ways can you be more attentive to God's power and creativity in the natural environment surrounding you?

Digging Deeper

In what ways can your caring for creation be an act of worship to God?

B. Possessing Full Knowledge (v. 13)

13. Who hath directed the Spirit of the Lord, or being his counsellor hath taught him?

The Hebrew word translated *Spirit* has a range of meanings. It can mean "wind" (Isaiah 7:2), "breath" (11:4), or what might be called "attitude" (4:4), among other meanings. Context determines what the writer means at any given point.

The importance of this verse for the New Testament era is seen in the fact that the apostle Paul quotes it twice (see Romans 11:34 and 1 Corinthians 2:16). Paul uses the word *mind* rather than *Spirit* because he is quoting from the Greek version known as the Septuagint. Even so, his understanding of what the passage says about God is entirely consistent with Isaiah's: God has never had to learn anything from anyone. God is omniscient, meaning "all-knowing."

Isaiah 40:14-24, which comes between the two segments of our lesson text, continues the prophet's confrontational questions. These include declarations of the Lord's superiority to the nations (Isaiah 40:15-17), idols (40:18-20), and earthly rulers (40:23-24).

II. Sustaining Ruler

(Isaiah 40:25-31)

A. Regarding His Identity (v. 25)

25. To whom then will ye liken me, or shall I be equal? saith the Holy One.

The prophet raised this question earlier, in Isaiah 40:18. It reminds us that we should be extremely cautious with statements that start with "God is like . . ." because the next word will result in the Creator's being compared to something He has created.

Even so, Isaiah's question *To whom then will ye liken me* does not forbid certain figurative language from being used as illustrations of God's various roles. These roles include His being a shepherd (Psalm 23:1), a rock (2 Samuel 22:32), a shield and a sword (Deuteronomy 33:29), a fortress (Psalm 18:2), and even that of a winged and feathered creature (91:4). These are not saying that God's essence is similar or *equal* to any of those; rather, such texts illustrate various functions that God exercises.

The designation *Holy One* is used especially by the prophet Isaiah (30 of its 42 occurrences in the Old Testament). This frequency may be linked to the impression that Isaiah's prophetic call made upon him. In that commissioning ceremony, he saw the Lord "high and lifted up" and heard the seraphim cry, "Holy, holy, holy, is the Lord of hosts" (Isaiah 6:1-3).

What Do You Think?

How can you prevent past experiences with authority from negatively influencing the way you view God?

Digging Deeper

What steps will you take to transform any misguided and distorted perceptions of God?

B. Regarding His Abilities (vv. 26-28)

26a. Lift up your eyes on high, and behold who hath created these things, that bringeth out their host by number.

Isaiah calls attention to the heavens as he did previously in Isaiah 40:12 and will do again in

51:6. The *host by number* refers to the stars. Worship of these was explicitly forbidden (Deuteronomy 4:19), but it happened anyway (2 Kings 17:16; 23:5), with promised punishment that followed (Jeremiah 8:2). Avoiding such idolatry begins with realizing that there's a Creator behind these stars (Nehemiah 9:6). To worship created things rather than the Creator is to invite the death penalty (Romans 1:18-25, 32).

Creation Sights, Creator Insights

Our family enjoys traveling and seeing the creation of God. The mountains are always on our list of favorite places. My love of facts sometimes hinders my enjoying the fantastic view; while family members absorb the sight of the mountain, I am busy searching on my phone for facts to proclaim about the mountain.

We live 114 miles from Denali, the highest mountain in North America. You can see the 20,310-foot mountain from 150 miles away in clear weather. The prophet Isaiah's directives imply that in pondering the majesty of creation, one learns more about the Creator. Pondering creation allows us to come to a proper conclusion regarding our place in it and our relationship to the Creator. Both involve "looking up" (compare Psalm 19). How long has it been since you did so?

—J. M.

26b. He calleth them all by names by the greatness of his might, for that he is strong in power; not one faileth.

Elsewhere, the Bible records the *names* of some stars and their constellations (Job 9:9; 38:31-32; Amos 5:8). Whether covered by clouds are not, they are in the night sky every night without fail. Modern astronomy sometimes lets us predict with general accuracy the very rarely seen explosion of a supernova (see lesson 5 regarding the difference between astronomy and astrology). By one count, there have been only seven such explosions visible to the naked eye throughout history.

And even these may have involved stars invisible to the naked eye before their demise; thus, the ancients would not have perceived any stars that failed to appear.

27. Why sayest thou, O Jacob, and speakest, O Israel, My way is hid from the Lord, and my judgment is passed over from my God?

Again we have the parallelism that typifies Hebrew poetry: the verbs *sayest* and *speakest* parallel one another, as do the proper names *Jacob* and *Israel* (see Genesis 32:28; 35:10; 46:2). The parallelism continues with the phrase *my way is hid* mirroring *my judgment is passed over*; then the phrase *from the Lord* echoes *from my God.* Thus one overall thought is expressed, not two. Nothing is hidden from God's sight (Jeremiah 16:17; 23:24; Hebrews 4:13).

What Do You Think?

How should we respond when people say that God doesn't care about them and their problems?

Digging Deeper

What Scriptures comes to mind to address this concern?

28. Hast thou not known? hast thou not heard, that the everlasting God, the Lord, the Creator of the ends of the earth, fainteth not, neither is weary? there is no searching of his understanding.

Hast thou not known? hast thou not heard are favorite expressions of the prophet Isaiah (see Isaiah 37:26; 40:21). In this case, they respond to the rhetorical questions of the verse previous to this one. The implication is that nothing is ever concealed from God. It's inconceivable that the reader should plead ignorance to the facts that follow. Even without having the benefit of Scripture, God's characteristics are discernible from nature itself (compare Romans 1:20). Thus, Isaiah should not have to remind the people of truths with which they are already familiar.

The writer offers a rare collection of terms in using different Hebrew words for *God, Lord,* and *Creator.* This collection is the only place in the Old Testament where the three words are seen together as nouns; it seems that the writer wants no mistake to be made regarding the identity of the subject! God is not susceptible to human limitations. He does not tire; He never becomes exhausted; He neither slumbers nor sleeps (Psalm 121:4). That God rested on the seventh day following the six days of creation (Genesis 2:2-3) does not imply that He became *weary*; it simply means that He ceased His creative activity.

At this point, we should take special note of how Scripture uses the word *weary* in different contexts. In the text at hand, that word is used with reference to God's "running out of energy"—which doesn't happen. In Isaiah 1:14, on the other hand, the prophet uses the word in the sense of God's "being fed up"—which definitely *does* happen (also Isaiah 43:24; Malachi 2:17).

These truths expressed in this passage and throughout the Scriptures concerning the Lord and His uniqueness are why prophets such as Isaiah speak so passionately against the sin of idolatry (example: Isaiah 40:18-20). Idol worshipers do no harm whatsoever to God, who remains the same *everlasting* God described by Isaiah. They harm only themselves by following such delusions.

C. Regarding Our Need (vv. 29-31)

29. He giveth power to the faint; and to them that have no might he increaseth strength.

The promise of *strength* from the Lord, especially during times of human frailty and weakness, resonates throughout Isaiah (Isaiah 12:2; 25:4; 26:4; 41:10; 45:24; 49:5) and is found in numerous passages of the psalter (Psalms 18:32; 22:19; 28:7-8; etc.). The issue is one of trust since God has His own timetable for replacing our weakness with His strength. Trust requires waiting (Isaiah 8:17; 25:9; 33:2; 40:31 [below]; 49:23; 64:4).

Few have experienced more acutely the need for—and receiving of—strength from the Lord as did the apostle Paul (2 Corinthians 1:8-11; 6:3-10; etc.). His declaration, "I can do all things through Christ which strengtheneth me" (Philippians 4:13) rings true for us today.

> **What Do You Think?**
> How do you seek strength from the Lord when you feel most weary?
>
> **Digging Deeper**
> Who has God placed in your life to whom you can be a source of encouragement in the upcoming week?

30. Even the youths shall faint and be weary, and the young men shall utterly fall.

Youth is often associated with vigor and endurance, something that diminishes with age. But certain situations arise that leave even *youths* disheartened and fearful of what lies ahead. Physical strength is an asset that can prove useful in numerous situations. The ability to do more than expected can last only as long as the adrenaline does. But inner spiritual strength from the Lord is what provides the endurance to resist the temptations frequently encountered in a world broken by sin. Thus could Paul boldly declare, "We faint not; but though our outward man perish, yet the inward man is renewed day by day" (2 Corinthians 4:16).

31. But they that wait upon the LORD shall renew their strength; they shall mount up with wings as eagles; they shall run, and not be weary; and they shall walk, and not faint.

We now come to some of the most well-known declarations in all of Scripture. We see them displayed artistically on coffee mugs, tapestries, desk mementos, etc. The need to *wait upon the Lord* is found in many places (examples: Psalms 37:9; 123:2; Isaiah 8:13; Romans 8:25). To *wait* implies trust in the *Lord*. An example of impatience and failure to wait is Abraham in Genesis 16. When

How to Say It

Azariah	Az-uh-*rye*-uh.
Babylon	*Bab*-uh-lun.
Hezekiah	Hez-ih-*kye*-uh.
Isaiah	Eye-*zay*-uh.
Judah	*Joo*-duh.
Messianic	Mess-ee-*an*-ick.
omniscient	ahm-*nish*-unt.
Psalter	*Sawl*-ter.
Sennacherib	Sen-*nack*-er-ib.
Septuagint	Sep-*too*-ih-jent.
Uzziah	Uh-*zye*-uh.

we wait, we keep faith that He will work His purpose in our circumstances, even when—or especially when!—the way forward is not obvious to us. But waiting does not come easily in our fast-paced society that often demands instant results. Our tendency all too frequently is to act on our own timing and by our own judgment; we want to keep things moving!

The imagery of mounting up *with wings as eagles* pictures an ability to soar into the sky, oblivious to any potential distractions below. The Lord used that same imagery when He established His covenant with the nation of Israel. He contrasted what He did to the Egyptians with "how I bare you on eagles' wings, and brought you unto myself" (Exodus 19:4). Later, Moses used similar imagery to remind the people of God's special care (Deuteronomy 32:11-12). Isaiah's words yet apply today.

The concluding *they shall run, and not be weary; and they shall walk, and not faint* offers yet more instances of parallelism in expression.

What Do You Think?

In what ways can you practice waiting on the Lord so that you can be attentive to God's Spirit renewing you?

Digging Deeper

In what ways does your waiting on the Lord go against your culture's expectations regarding waiting?

On Being Worn Out

We recently discovered why God allowed us to have our children only when we were younger. It happened after we agreed to watch our grandson as his parents took a vacation. The two-year-old wore us out, mentally and physically! We love our grandchildren and cherish the time we spend with them. But whenever we're on "grandchild duty," we take a rest day from the gym—dealing with the youngsters is enough of a workout!

God challenges us to remember Him as the one who never tires and never needs to sleep. The creator of the universe holds the record for days without sleep! And He grants energy and knowledge to those who need strength and power when they are at the point of fainting. When you are low on energy, where is the first place you look to for a recharge? —J. M.

Conclusion

A. No Shortage Here!

When the impact of the coronavirus pandemic began to be felt during the spring of 2020, one result was shortages in various commodities. Issues with business closings and logistical limitations meant that goods were not as readily available as before. Stores simply ran out of certain items, even after limiting purchases per customer. Many consumers found themselves frustrated at being unable to purchase the things they wanted (or outright *needed*) with the convenience to which they were accustomed.

Our passage for today reminds us that the God we worship and serve has never been subject to any kind of weakness, attrition, or scarcity in His resources. The prophet's affirmations of God's incomparable sustaining power and of His promise to provide strength to those who grow tired or weary have no expiration date. God's power and strength are indeed available to us today! But here, a caution must be interjected concerning what the Chronicler records: "The Lord is with you, while ye be with him; and if ye seek him, he will be found of you; but if ye forsake him, he will forsake you" (2 Chronicles 15:2). The only restriction regarding our access to God's resources is our own sin and unwillingness to trust Him.

B. Prayer

Father, we thank You for the record left to us by the prophet Isaiah! May we realize fully that, with the New Testament, we now have immeasurably more insight into Your nature than Isaiah did! Help us to take neither You nor Your Word for granted. Renew our strength as only You are able to do. In Jesus' name we pray. Amen.

C. Thought to Remember

There is never any power shortage with God.

Involvement Learning

Enhance your lesson with KJV Bible Student *(from your curriculum supplier) and the reproducible activity page (at www.standardlesson.com or in the back of the* KJV Standard Lesson Commentary Deluxe Edition*).*

Into the Lesson

Write the following open-ended sentence on the board for learners to see as they arrive:

If I could spend more time in nature,
I'd want to be in . . .

Divide the learners into pairs and allow three minutes for them to share their answers and the reasoning behind them with their partners. Ask volunteers to share their responses.

Alternative. Display photos of beautiful nature scenes. (Find pictures online by searching for free stock photos.) Distribute slips of paper to each learner and ask them to write their reactions to the images. Collect the slips and read them back to the whole class. Lead a discussion by asking: "What can nature teach us about God? about ourselves? about the past and future?"

Say, "Throughout history, people have experienced God through the marvelous sights, sounds, and smells found in the world. Today's Scripture is an example of such an occurrence. As we study, consider how the prophet uses nature to point his listeners to the trustworthiness of God."

Into the Word

Option. Before class, choose a volunteer to give a brief presentation on this Scripture's historical and cultural background. The volunteer can use other commentaries and the Lesson Context in preparation. Allow five minutes at the start of class for the presentation.

Distribute a worksheet (you create) with the headings *Who God Is, What God Has Done, Questions God Asks,* and *What God Promises.* Divide the class into groups of four. Invite the groups to study Isaiah 40:12-13, 25-31 and write words or phrases from the Scripture that would go under each heading. Remind groups to provide verse references.

Option. Distribute copies of "The Warning and the Comfort" exercise from the activity page, which you can download. Have learners work together in groups to complete as indicated. After five minutes, ask for volunteers from each group to share what their group discovered.

Ask the following questions for whole-class discussion: 1–How do you think Isaiah's prophecy comforted the original audience? 2–What promises and prophecies of God give you the most comfort? 3–What keeps us from hearing or receiving that comfort?

Into Life

Divide learners into four groups to brainstorm ideas for a worship service that would focus on praising God for His creativity, especially as seen in the beauty of His creation. Questions are provided to assist each group's brainstorming efforts.

Visual Arts. 1–How could the visual arts be used in worship to praise God for His remarkable creativity? 2–What resources or tools would you need in this regard?

Music. 1–How could music be used in a unique way to worship and praise God for His remarkable creativity? 2–What ways can music be used beyond corporate singing?

Spoken Word. 1–How could poetry or short stories be used to worship God and praise Him for His remarkable creativity? 2–How do the Psalms provide an example in this regard?

Your Choice. 1–What other worship components fit your congregation? 2–What skills and talents are needed?

After allowing 10 minutes for planning, ask the groups to share their ideas. Ask, "How would these elements encourage worshippers to remain faithful despite their circumstances?"

Option. Distribute copies of the "This Is My Father's World" activity from the activity page. Ask learners to complete the activity as a take-home. To encourage completion, allow time at the beginning of the next class for learners to share insights.

Faith in the Fiery Furnace

Devotional Reading: Isaiah 43:1-7
Background Scripture: Daniel 3:1-30

Daniel 3:19-28

19 Then was Nebuchadnezzar full of fury, and the form of his visage was changed against Shadrach, Meshach, and Abednego: therefore he spake, and commanded that they should heat the furnace one seven times more than it was wont to be heated.

20 And he commanded the most mighty men that were in his army to bind Shadrach, Meshach, and Abednego, and to cast them into the burning fiery furnace.

21 Then these men were bound in their coats, their hosen, and their hats, and their other garments, and were cast into the midst of the burning fiery furnace.

22 Therefore because the king's commandment was urgent, and the furnace exceeding hot, the flame of the fire slew those men that took up Shadrach, Meshach, and Abednego.

23 And these three men, Shadrach, Meshach, and Abednego, fell down bound into the midst of the burning fiery furnace.

24 Then Nebuchadnezzar the king was astonied, and rose up in haste, and spake, and said unto his counsellors, Did not we cast three men bound into the midst of the fire? They answered and said unto the king, True, O king.

25 He answered and said, Lo, I see four men loose, walking in the midst of the fire, and they have no hurt; and the form of the fourth is like the Son of God.

26 Then Nebuchadnezzar came near to the mouth of the burning fiery furnace, and spake, and said, Shadrach, Meshach, and Abednego, ye servants of the most high God, come forth, and come hither. Then Shadrach, Meshach, and Abednego, came forth of the midst of the fire.

27 And the princes, governors, and captains, and the king's counsellors, being gathered together, saw these men, upon whose bodies the fire had no power, nor was an hair of their head singed, neither were their coats changed, nor the smell of fire had passed on them.

28 Then Nebuchadnezzar spake, and said, Blessed be the God of Shadrach, Meshach, and Abednego, who hath sent his angel, and delivered his servants that trusted in him, and have changed the king's word, and yielded their bodies, that they might not serve nor worship any god, except their own God.

Key Text

Then Nebuchadnezzar spake, and said, Blessed be the God of Shadrach, Meshach, and Abednego, who hath sent his angel, and delivered his servants that trusted in him, and have changed the king's word, and yielded their bodies, that they might not serve nor worship any god, except their own God. —**Daniel 3:28**

Faith That

Pleases God

Unit 3: The Righteous Live by Faith

Lessons 10–13

Lesson Aims

After participating in this lesson, each learner will be able to:

1. Recall the names of the three whom God rescued from the fiery furnace.

2. Summarize the reasons for Nebuchadnezzar's changes in attitude.

3. Commit to bearing faithful witness to God in facing a personal "fiery furnace."

Lesson Outline

Introduction

A. The Power of Witness

B. Lesson Context

I. Royal Anger (Daniel 3:19-23)

A. Heated Response (vv. 19-21)

B. Urgent Command (vv. 22-23)

II. Divine Presence (Daniel 3:24-28)

A. The King's Astonishment (vv. 24-25)

Never Alone

B. The King's Directive (vv. 26-27)

C. The King's Worship (v. 28)

A Noticed Fearlessness

Conclusion

A. Faith and Courage

B. Prayer

C. Thought to Remember

Introduction

A. The Power of Witness

Salvadorians remember Óscar Romero (1917–1980) as a hero who advocated for the needs of the people in El Salvador. During his time as the Roman Catholic archbishop of San Salvador, he worked against the unjust treatment of his impoverished compatriots. This work included calling out the frequently violent intimidation tactics by the government and guerrilla groups. His belief that the church should show preferential treatment to the poor served as the basis for his work with Salvadorians. His witness was only as effective as his commitment to loving and following God.

However, his commitment ultimately cost him; he was assassinated by extremist groups while observing Mass. Before his assassination, Romero reflected on the risks he faced as a Christian who advocated for the needs of others. He accepted these risks and expressed hope in the promised bodily resurrection of believers.

Christian history recounts numerous stories of people who stood for their faith. Such people committed to live with complete devotion to God. When we commit to trusting in Him, we will inevitably have our faith tested. Today's Scripture recounts the ultimate example of such testing. How would three Jewish men respond to threats from the most powerful individual in their world?

B. Lesson Context

By telling the stories of the prophet Daniel and his associates, the book of Daniel depicts Jewish life in a foreign land. A series of deportations from Judah by the Babylonians began in 605 BC (see Daniel 1:1-2). These continued until Judah fell in 586 BC (see 2 Kings 25). Among the deported were talented young men selected for their fitness for service to the Babylonian king (see Daniel 1:3-4). Daniel and his associates were taken to Babylon during this time, in approximately 605 BC. The book describes the wisdom of Daniel and his friends as they lived and served in Babylon (example: 2:17-24). Their positions required that they demonstrate some loyalty to the Babylonian king, evident in their name change (see 1:6-7). This book's events occur from the time of their arrival in Babylon until at least 537 BC, "the third year of Cyrus king of Persia" (10:1).

Part of the book of Daniel is preserved in Hebrew (Daniel 1:1–2:4a; 8:1–12:13), while another part is preserved in Aramaic (2:4b–7:28). The use of two languages indicated the different cultures depicted in the book: Hebrew for the Jews and Aramaic for the Gentile empires (2 Kings 18:26; Ezra 4:7). Today's Scripture comes from the part of Daniel preserved in Aramaic.

Today's lesson Scripture is the second part of the narrative that begins at Daniel 3:1. Nebuchadnezzar, the king of Babylon (reigned 605–562 BC), had erected a large image of gold at "the plain of Dura" (Daniel 3:1). This location is suggested to have been several miles south of the city of Babylon. Royal subjects, advisors, and kingdom officials arrived for the image's dedication ceremony and to worship it (3:2-5). Refusing to worship the image would result in inevitable death in a "burning fiery furnace" (3:6). But Shadrach, Meshach, and Abednego—men the king had placed in a leadership position (see 2:49)—refused. They had confidence that the Lord would be with them (3:17-18).

I. Royal Anger
(Daniel 3:19-23)

A. Heated Response (vv. 19-21)

19. Then was Nebuchadnezzar full of fury, and the form of his visage was changed against Shadrach, Meshach, and Abednego: therefore he spake, and commanded that they should heat the furnace one seven times more than it was wont to be heated.

The *fury* of *Nebuchadnezzar* becomes a central point in the early chapters of the book of Daniel. He became angry when his wise men could not interpret his dreams (see Daniel 2:10-13). The refusal of the three Jewish men to bow before the golden image led the king to "rage and fury" (3:13). The king's anger continued. Whatever goodwill *Shadrach, Meshach, and Abednego* had experienced from the king (examples: 1:19-20; 2:48-49) was lost. The king had once demonstrated some sense of worship of the God of Israel (see 2:46-47). However, when the worship of the true God prevented Nebuchadnezzar from receiving worship, the king resorted to anger and wrath.

The king's command that *the furnace* be heated *seven times more* than usual is a hyperbolic figure of speech. A mention of the number *seven* in Scripture typically indicates fullness, totality, or completion (examples: Leviticus 26:18, 21, 24; Proverbs 24:16; Matthew 18:21-22). There was likely no way to accurately measure the furnace's temperature to know whether it was seven times hotter. The command intended to communicate that the furnace should be heated to the maximum temperature it could reach.

20. And he commanded the most mighty men that were in his army to bind Shadrach, Meshach, and Abednego, and to cast them into the burning fiery furnace.

Nothing in the narrative indicates why Nebuchadnezzar chose *the most mighty men* of *his army*. These soldiers would have been the best of the best in the king's military. They were likely an elite fighting force valued for their physical strength and power. Perhaps the king anticipated that the Jewish men would put up a fight when they realized their destination.

Furnaces in the ancient Near East were usually made of clay bricks or stone. Their layout consisted of at least two chambers (the main chamber and a fire chamber) and a flue. Large furnaces smelted metals, refined precious metals, or fired ceramics. Simpler furnaces, made of one

How to Say It

Abednego	Uh-*bed*-nee-go.
Aramaic	*Air*-uh-**may**-ik.
Cyrus	*Sigh*-russ.
Deuteronomy	Due-ter-*ahn*-uh-me.
Meshach	*Me*-shack.
Nebuchadnezzar	*Neb*-yuh-kud-**nez**-er.
Shadrach	*Shay*-drack or *Shad*-rack.

compartment like a modern-day pizza oven, were used for baking. A large *furnace* to hold *Shadrach, Meshach, and Abednego* reveals the Babylonian empire's vast construction and military needs. The text does not say, but perhaps this furnace refined the gold for the king's image!

What Do You Think?

Who in your life best exemplifies faith while in the "fiery furnace"?

Digging Deeper

What qualities do they have that you can emulate?

21. Then these men were bound in their coats, their hosen, and their hats, and their other garments, and were cast into the midst of the burning fiery furnace.

The exact *garments* worn by the three Jewish *men* are unknown because the underlying Aramaic words are relatively rare. Their clothes were likely more in the style of Persia rather than that of Israel. This detail reveals that the king had the men *bound* as they wore flammable clothing. Such wearable "fuel" would have ignited when the king's toughest men *cast* the three Jewish men *into* the superheated *furnace*.

B. Urgent Command (vv. 22-23)

22. Therefore because the king's commandment was urgent, and the furnace exceeding hot, the flame of the fire slew those men that took up Shadrach, Meshach, and Abednego.

Angry outbursts followed by acts of haste and harshness were typical for Nebuchadnezzar. After the king heard that his wise men could not interpret his dreams, he angrily ordered their execution (see Daniel 2:10-13). When hearing of the king's directive regarding his wise men, Daniel questioned why such a "hasty" decree had been issued (2:14-15).

In this verse, Nebuchadnezzar's *urgent* command toward the three Jewish men again revealed his brutality. The king's *commandment* affected the three Jewish men and led to the death of the "most mighty *men*" (3:20, above).

23. And these three men, Shadrach, Meshach, and Abednego, fell down bound into the midst of the burning fiery furnace.

The narrative repeats two details already known: the names of *these three men* and the intensity of the *fiery furnace*. That these three men *fell down bound into* the furnace was not the result of an unfortunate accident. They had refused to follow the directive to "fall down" and worship Nebuchadnezzar's image of gold (Daniel 3:5). Now, the king forced the three men to "fall down" to a *burning* death—or so he thought.

II. Divine Presence

(Daniel 3:24-28)

A. The King's Astonishment (vv. 24-25)

24. Then Nebuchadnezzar the king was astonied, and rose up in haste, and spake, and said unto his counsellors, Did not we cast three men bound into the midst of the fire? They answered and said unto the king, True, O king.

Throughout the book of Daniel, the leaders in Babylon reacted with fear and amazement when God demonstrated miraculous power (examples: Daniel 2:46-47; 5:1-8; 6:19-23; see lesson 12). Nebuchadnezzar's response before us continued that trend. *Nebuchadnezzar* intended to execute the three Jewish men. However, something unique and miraculous caused *the king* to be *astonied*. As in the other examples, this occurrence was something only God could bring about.

The king's *counsellors* consulted with the king on various kingdom matters. The book of Daniel lists this group alongside other regional rulers of Babylon (example: Daniel 3:27). It is unlikely that they held positions of political power. Instead, they consulted and advised the king, in the same way that cabinet members might consult a head of state (see also 6:7). In this instance, their consultation simply confirmed what the king already knew regarding the *three men bound* (compare 3:23, above).

25. He answered and said, Lo, I see four men loose, walking in the midst of the fire, and they have no hurt; and the form of the fourth is like the Son of God.

The identity of the *fourth* figure *in the midst*

of the fire has long been a subject of discussion among students. The capitalization of the title *Son of God* indicates one possibility: this fourth person was the preincarnate Christ. However, this option provides interpretive difficulty and more questions than answers. For example, it leads us to question what Nebuchadnezzar did to merit this unique vision of the preincarnate Christ. Although we cannot rule out this possibility, this option is challenging to hold.

It is notable, however, that the title comes from the lips of the Babylonian king and not from one of the Jews. Nebuchadnezzar worshipped many pagan gods (example: Daniel 3:14). He likely did not recognize that this figure was the one true God. From his perspective, this figure was a member of the pantheon of pagan gods that he worshipped.

The phrase "son(s) of God" can refer to angels (examples: Job 1:6; 2:1; 38:7) or presumed deities (example: Genesis 6:2, 4). This option explains the likely identification of this mysterious figure (see Daniel 3:28, below). This angelic presence protected the three men amid their fiery trial (compare Exodus 23:20; see also Psalms 34:7; 91:11). The Babylonian king received a sign. The God who sent this angelic presence protected His people from being *hurt*.

What Do You Think?

How has God made His presence known to you in times of danger or distress?

Digging Deeper

How can you witness about God's presence either during trials or following them?

Never Alone

Pandemic-related restrictions would prevent Elise's husband from being present at the birth of their next child. When Elise heard this news, she began researching other countries where she could give birth.

"Canada? No . . . France? No . . . What am I going to do?" she thought.

Elise's husband always held her hand, sang to her, reminded her to breathe, and advocated for her needs. She couldn't imagine enduring the pain of labor and delivery alone. Who would bring her delicious meals so she wouldn't have to eat the bland cafeteria food?

"What do you think about a home birth, honey?" she asked her husband.

Shadrach, Meshach, and Abednego did not experience the trials of the fiery furnace alone. God showed His faithfulness to them by rescuing them from the fire.

Jesus promised His followers that they would never be alone (Matthew 28:20). No matter our circumstances, we can confidently echo the psalmist's prayer: "Thou has holden me by my right hand" (Psalm 73:23).

But here's a question: Do you face trials confidently, knowing that you're not alone? —D. D.

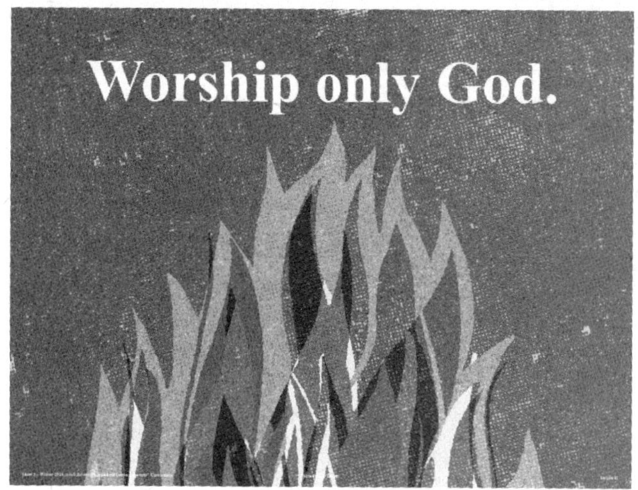

Visual for Lesson 11. *Refer to this visual as the class discusses the questions associated with verse 28.*

B. The King's Directive (vv. 26-27)

26. Then Nebuchadnezzar came near to the mouth of the burning fiery furnace, and spake, and said, Shadrach, Meshach, and Abednego, ye servants of the most high God, come forth, and come hither. Then Shadrach, Meshach, and Abednego came forth of the midst of the fire.

A furnace of this size would have likely had multiple openings. These may explain how *Nebuchadnezzar* could go *near* the *mouth* of the *furnace* and not be killed (compare Daniel 3:22, above).

Upon seeing the fourth figure, the king experienced a change of heart. His rage (see Daniel 3:13) diminished, and he addressed the men by their (Babylonian) names. Although they received these names from the king, their ultimate allegiances lay beyond Nebuchadnezzar. Instead, they were *servants* of God (compare 3:20). In this proclamation, Nebuchadnezzar admitted the folly of his previous statement regarding the power of God (see 3:15).

The title *most high* refers to the God of Israel (examples: Daniel 4:17, 32, 34; 5:18, 21; 7:25). Surrounding nations may have used the title to refer to the primary god of their pantheon of gods. However, the people of Israel applied the title to the one true God, knowing there was no other God. The same title refers to God's power (see Genesis 14:18-22; Psalm 83:18) and transcendence (see Acts 7:48). The title is also used when referring to God's work (example: Deuteronomy 32:8) or as a reference to the Son of God (see Mark 5:7; see also Luke 1:32).

Nebuchadnezzar's announcement of this title indicates some level of acknowledgment of the superiority of the God of Israel. However, the king had an imperfect understanding of the Lord's power. The king's admission that the Lord was "most high" still allowed him to accept other pagan gods (compare Daniel 2:47). It would take a humbling experience before Nebuchadnezzar gave praise and honor to the one true God of Israel (see Daniel 4).

What Do You Think?

If you could not verbally proclaim your faith, what evidence could others provide that you are a servant of the Most High God?

Digging Deeper

In what situations can your faithful actions speak louder than your words?

27. And the princes, governors, and captains, and the king's counsellors, being gathered together, saw these men, upon whose bodies the fire had no power, nor was an hair of their head singed, neither were their coats changed, nor the smell of fire had passed on them.

While the furnace had killed the king's strongest men, the three Jewish *men* showed no evidence of exposure to fire or smoke. The *princes, governors, captains,* and *counsellors* had bowed before the king's image (see Daniel 3:2-3). But they ended up seeing the limits of the king's power and the miraculous act of deliverance by the God of Israel.

C. The King's Worship (v. 28)

28. Then Nebuchadnezzar spake, and said, Blessed be the God of Shadrach, Meshach, and Abednego, who hath sent his angel, and delivered his servants that trusted in him, and have changed the king's word, and yielded their bodies, that they might not serve nor worship any god, except their own God.

The stories of Daniel 1–6 reveal a pattern to the ways that Babylon's royalty regarded the work of God. First, Babylon's king experienced a miraculous work of the God of Israel (Daniel 2:45b; 4:28-34a; 5:1-6; 6:19-22). Second, the king acknowledged the work as coming from the God of Israel. Third, in most instances, the king proclaimed the supremacy of Israel's God (2:47; 4:34b-37; 6:25-27; contrast 5:26-31).

This verse reveals that the same pattern occurred in today's Scripture. Nebuchadnezzar saw God's miraculous work of deliverance (Daniel 3:24-27). As a result, the king proclaimed that God be *blessed*. The king *changed* his *word* and acknowledged that God's power to save was unparalleled (3:29, not in our printed text). However, the text does not indicate that the king believed *the God of Shadrach, Meshach, and Abednego* to be one, true, only God. Total and complete worship by the king to the one true God would eventually come (see 4:34-37).

The king's confession of worship resulted from the character and faithfulness of Shadrach, Meshach, and Abednego. They refused to bow before the king's image, even if their decision led to martyrdom, because of their commitment to the one true God. Their commitment to trust God was anchored in their rightly held belief in God's faithfulness (see Daniel 3:16-18). The Lord had promised to be with His people (example:

Leviticus 26:12-13), and that promise came to fruition for these three Jewish men. The promises made to the prophet Isaiah applied to the three men: "When thou walkest through the fire, thou shalt not be burned; neither shall the flame kindle upon thee. For I am the Lord thy God, the Holy One of Israel, thy Saviour" (Isaiah 43:2-3; compare Psalm 66:12).

What Do You Think?

What false gods does our society expect us to worship?

Digging Deeper

What are some specific ways you demonstrate that you will not worship these idols?

A Noticed Fearlessness

Marissa's boss, Jack, called her into his office.

"You can close the door," he said, waiting until it shut before adding, "Our biggest client needs a favor."

He explained how their accounting firm needed to ignore a client's unpleasant financial numbers so the firm could appease stockholders. If Marissa complied with the request, nothing would stand between her and a long-awaited promotion.

However, Jack had asked the wrong accountant. He should've known Marissa was a believer whose allegiance lay with Christ alone.

"Risking my promotion and receiving some cold shoulders will be hard," Marissa told her Bible study group. She asked the group to pray that she would continue trusting God, even if she experienced harassment or pressure. Most of all, Marissa wanted her boss and coworkers to notice her commitment to behaving as the gospel requires. She prayed that they would see how she lived differently and ask her about the reason for her behavior.

After seeing God's deliverance of the three Jewish men, Nebuchadnezzar noticed the commitment of the men and praised God in response. How do you need to live so that others see your behavior and look to God? —D. D.

Conclusion

A. Faith and Courage

Two options face believers when we experience the testing of our faith. One possibility is that we succumb to the testing and quite possibly commit apostasy. The other option is to maintain faithfulness to God, despite the testing. Even when faced with death, the men in today's Scripture chose the latter option. They refused to bend their faith and go along with the king's demands for worship. Their faith in God—rooted in His long history of faithfulness—provided the courage they needed to withstand the testing and resist committing evil.

Although we may never experience the same testing these men faced, all believers will likely experience some amount of testing of our faith. However, we can be encouraged. Our victory has already been established (see 1 John 5:4). Even though our enemy seeks to devour, we can stand firm in our faith. God is faithful to His people, even when they are tested. When we face these experiences, we can have trust and respond with faithfulness to Him (1 Corinthians 10:13).

What Do You Think?

How do you react to global reports of the persecution of Christians?

Digging Deeper

What does the faith of persecuted Christians inspire you to do?

B. Prayer

Most High God, You are the one true God. You are faithful to Your people, and You continue to show your faithfulness to us. Through Your Spirit, fortify our faith and trust so we can resist the temptation to worship other "gods"—large and small. Show us how we might support other believers in their trials of faith. Give us encouragement and strength no matter where You have called us. In the name of Jesus. Amen.

C. Thought to Remember

Because of God's faithfulness,
we can be faithful to Him.

Involvement Learning

Enhance your lesson with KJV Bible Student *(from your curriculum supplier) and the reproducible activity page (at www.standardlesson.com or in the back of the* KJV Standard Lesson Commentary Deluxe Edition*).*

Into the Lesson

Ask pairs of learners to brainstorm historical instances of dramatic changes in fortune. Encourage them to think of both positive and negative examples. Then have each pair focus on one example they came up with and go into as much detail as possible regarding how relationships, social standing, finances, faith, etc., were transformed as a result of the change. Bring the class together and ask for volunteers to share briefly their examples.

Tell learners, "Everyone has problems, but none of us has faced a trial like the one we'll read about in today's text. Let's examine it to discover how faith in God made the difference for three men in this story."

Into the Word

Remind class members of the background for today's text by preparing a short lecture on Daniel 3:1-18. Consult the Lesson Context as desired for more information.

Alternative. Provide Bible concordances to look up any names or terms found in these verses with which learners are unfamiliar.

Option. Distribute copies of the "Keys to Context" exercise from the activity page, which you can download. Have learners work in pairs or groups to complete as indicated. Have learners add concepts or notes to the exercise as you discuss the lesson.

Distribute a handout (you create) with each of the following statements. Ask students in pairs to decide whether each is true or false based on Daniel 3:19-28a. Beside each, they should write the verse reference to support their conclusion. (Note: Each of these statements is false.)

1. Nebuchadnezzar was forced by his advisors to throw Shadrach, Meshach, and Abednego into the furnace.
2. Nebuchadnezzar cooled the furnace down to prevent any fatalities.
3. One of Nebuchadnezzar's advisors went into the furnace with the Jewish men to help them.
4. Nebuchadnezzar's most mighty men had a hot tale to tell their families that night!
5. No one acknowledged that anything unusual happened in the furnace.
6. Shadrach, Meshach, and Abednego came out of the furnace smelling smoky, with scorched clothes.
7. Nebuchadnezzar dismissed the whole affair as some sort of joke or magic trick.

After calling time, ensure that the groups found all these statements to be false.

Into Life

Brainstorm answers to this question with the class: "What trials do people face today?" Write as many suggestions as possible in one minute on the board. With the class, decide on three to five trials that are the hardest to bear. Have a second brainstorming session, this time talking about ways to be a faithful witness to God both as a person facing that trial and as a person giving support to the sufferer.

Alternative. Distribute copies of the "Advice for Those Facing Trials" exercise from the activity page. Have learners complete it in pairs before discussing conclusions with the whole group.

Following either activity, divide the class into pairs. Distribute note cards and pens to each person. Give learners one minute to write down a personal "fiery furnace" they are currently facing. Then, with the help of his or her partner, have each learner write down one or two ways to be a faithful witness to God while dealing with the difficulty. Encourage the partners to close class by praying for one another that each will be able to act faithfully in the middle of the fiery furnace.

February 18
Lesson 12 (KJV)

Faith in Times of Trouble

Devotional Reading: Matthew 8:18-27
Background Scripture: Daniel 6:1-28

Daniel 6:10-11, 14, 16, 19-23, 26-27

10 Now when Daniel knew that the writing was signed, he went into his house; and his windows being open in his chamber toward Jerusalem, he kneeled upon his knees three times a day, and prayed, and gave thanks before his God, as he did aforetime.

11 Then these men assembled, and found Daniel praying and making supplication before his God.

---

14 Then the king, when he heard these words, was sore displeased with himself, and set his heart on Daniel to deliver him: and he laboured till the going down of the sun to deliver him.

---

16 Then the king commanded, and they brought Daniel, and cast him into the den of lions. Now the king spake and said unto Daniel, Thy God whom thou servest continually, he will deliver thee.

---

19 Then the king arose very early in the morning, and went in haste unto the den of lions.

20 And when he came to the den, he cried with a lamentable voice unto Daniel: and the king spake and said to Daniel, O Daniel, servant of the living God, is thy God, whom thou servest continually, able to deliver thee from the lions?

21 Then said Daniel unto the king, O king, live for ever.

22 My God hath sent his angel, and hath shut the lions' mouths, that they have not hurt me: forasmuch as before him innocency was found in me; and also before thee, O king, have I done no hurt.

23 Then was the king exceeding glad for him, and commanded that they should take Daniel up out of the den. So Daniel was taken up out of the den, and no manner of hurt was found upon him, because he believed in his God.

---

26 I make a decree, That in every dominion of my kingdom men tremble and fear before the God of Daniel: for he is the living God, and stedfast for ever, and his kingdom that which shall not be destroyed, and his dominion shall be even unto the end.

27 He delivereth and rescueth, and he worketh signs and wonders in heaven and in earth, who hath delivered Daniel from the power of the lions.

Key Text

My God hath sent his angel, and hath shut the lions' mouths, that they have not hurt me: forasmuch as before him innocency was found in me; and also before thee, O king, have I done no hurt. **—Daniel 6:22**

Faith That Pleases God

Unit 3: The Righteous Live by Faith

Lessons 10–13

Lesson Aims

After participating in this lesson, each learner will be able to:

1. Summarize Daniel's personal conviction of faith in God in the midst of injustice.

2. Compare and contrast Daniel's faith-expression with those of his three colleagues in last week's lesson.

3. Commit to bearing faithful witness to God in facing a personal "lions' den."

Lesson Outline

Introduction

A. Authentic Prayer

B. Lesson Context

I. Violation and Consequence (Daniel 6:10-11, 14, 16)

A. Daniel's Prayer (vv. 10-11)

Consistency

B. Darius's Problem (v. 14)

C. Den's Predators (v. 16)

II. Release and Vindication (Daniel 6:19-23, 26-27)

A. The Question (vv. 19-20)

Flooded with Faithfulness

B. The Innocent (vv. 21-23)

C. The Decree (vv. 26-27)

Conclusion

A. Confession as Celebration

B. Prayer

C. Thought to Remember

Introduction

A. Authentic Prayer

Would you feel comfortable "correcting" someone who was praying in a way that seemed wrong? My guess is that a majority of Christians would instantly respond *No! Prayer is personal between God and the person praying! Who am I to criticize or correct the prayer of another?* Alongside that reaction, however, we can place Scripture passages that *do* direct the form, content, and motives of our prayers. See, for example, Matthew 6:5-13; Luke 11:1-13; 18:1-14; and James 4:3.

Personal motives that stand behind prayer practices vary widely. Prayer has been used as a tool to gain political clout, as a public act of remembrance, or as a habitual nicety before meals. These kinds of prayers are often little more than exercises in ceremonial theism. Such "window dressing" prayer may achieve the desired earthly outcome, as it motivates people to act. The danger of such prayer is that it treats God as a kind of cosmic vending machine: insert the right words, get the right publicity, and receive the vended outcome. We know better in that regard, but do we *do* better?

A first step in doing better with regard to prayer is to remind ourselves that God is already aware of our needs (Matthew 6:32)—we can't tell Him something He doesn't already know. The foundational part of prayer, rather, is that it orients us to God's faithfulness and ability to provide and protect. In prayer, we address the God who loved us enough to give His Son for our sins. And He wants to hear from us!

B. Lesson Context

The context for this lesson is generally the same as for lesson 11. However, several years had passed between the events of Daniel 3 (see lesson 11) and today's Scripture. The most notable is that a new empire replaced the Babylonians: the Persians (2 Chronicles 36:15-20).

After a hand wrote a message of warning to Babylonian king Belshazzar, the king died (see Daniel 5:1-30). Scripture does not reveal exactly how he died, only that it occurred and that the

62-year-old "Darius the Median" (5:31), "son of Ahasuerus" (9:1), replaced him in power. Outside of Scripture, there is no mention of this particular "Darius," and it was a common name; therefore identifying him is nearly impossible. He is likely not the same as the Persian king Darius I (also known as Darius the Great) (reigned 522–486 BC) mentioned in Ezra 4–6; Haggai 1–2; Zechariah 1, 7; and perhaps in Nehemiah 12:22. One proposal identifies our "Darius" as a regional governor of Babylon, installed under the oversight of Cyrus. Another proposal hypothesizes that "Darius" was another name for a Persian commander who led the Persian army into Babylon.

Today's study has as its backdrop the appointment of 120 "princes" under the oversight of three "presidents" that included Daniel (see Daniel 6:1-2). Daniel's reputation with previous kings influenced Darius. The king "preferred" Daniel over all the other princes and presidents and "sought to set [Daniel] over the whole realm" (6:3). However, the king's high regard for Daniel led Daniel's peers to scheme against him. Although they tried to find fault with Daniel, they could not find grounds to file charges against him (6:4-5). Instead, they developed a trap that Darius could not overturn.

Their plan encouraged Darius to establish a statute that whoever should pray to any deity or man, except the king, for 30 days would be thrown into the den of lions (see Daniel 6:7). Prayer *for* a monarch was standard in the ancient Near East. But prayer *to* a monarch was exceptional. Further, the officials maneuvered the king to issue the decree "according to the law of the Medes and Persians, which altereth not" (6:8). There would be little Darius could do to prevent the enforcement of the statute after it he "signed the writing and the decree" (6:9).

I. Violation and Consequence

(Daniel 6:10-11, 14, 16)

A. Daniel's Prayer (vv. 10-11)

10. Now when Daniel knew that the writing was signed, he went into his house; and his windows being open in his chamber toward Jerusalem, he kneeled upon his knees three times a day, and prayed, and gave thanks before his God, as he did aforetime.

Daniel experienced a high level of privilege (and wealth) as an official of the king (Daniel 6:1-3). Houses in ancient Babylon would have had a flat rooftop that functioned as another room or patio. Frequently, these rooftop patios would have included walls and windows for privacy. However, for a man in Daniel's position, his prayers could not have remained secret, even if he desired (compare Matthew 6:5-6).

The Law of Moses includes general commands regarding the people's daily remembrance of God's commands (example: Numbers 15:37-41). However, it did not command kneeling and praying *three times a day.*

At the dedication of Solomon's temple, the Lord commanded the people to pray toward *Jerusalem* and the temple at various times of distress (see 1 Kings 8:35-38, 44-45, 48-49). Kneeling and bowing are mentioned together in Psalm 95:6 as parallel postures of worship.

What Do You Think?

In what ways can a consistent daily prayer time be beneficial to your relationship with God?

Digging Deeper

How can you guard against this practice becoming only a dry ritual?

Consistency

When I think of the word *consistency*, a deacon in a church where I ministered immediately comes to mind. Numerous crises had affected his life, including the death of his wife and his cancer diagnosis. Despite these tragedies, he kept a calm demeanor and a faithful presence in our congregation. His commitment to our community revealed his consistency in character and his consistency in his love for God and others.

That man was our church's Daniel. How do you practice consistency in the ways that you follow God? You might never know whose faith you

No power can stand against the Lord's purposes.

Visual for Lesson 12. *Ask learners to reflect on the king's question in verse 20 and whether they question God's ability to save in certain situations.*

strengthen as they watch the character of your faith! —J. M.

11. Then these men assembled, and found Daniel praying and making supplication before his God.

These men were those who had pushed Darius to pass the decree that only the king was to be worshipped (see Lesson Context). Daniel's open windows made catching him in the act quite simple (see Daniel 6:10, above). He was *praying and making supplication* as was his habit without regard for any danger it posed (compare 9:2-3).

B. Darius's Problem (v. 14)

14. Then the king, when he heard these words, was sore displeased with himself, and set his heart on Daniel to deliver him: and he laboured till the going down of the sun to deliver him.

The phrase *these words* refers to Daniel 6:12-13 (not in our printed text), in which the king's officials reminded Darius of his decree and then revealed Daniel's disobedience to it. After hearing this, Darius realized how his officials had manipulated him for their selfish gain. They had used deception and Darius's naivete to launch their plan. He had inadvertently been a pawn in their scheme against Daniel. Rather than direct his displeasure toward Daniel, the king was *displeased* with his own behavior. The king had failed to see the underlying reason for the officials' request for the decree.

The king exerted himself in order to find grounds *to deliver* Daniel from the consequences of breaking the decree. "The law[s] of the Medes and Persians" are only mentioned in this narrative (Daniel 6:8, 15, not in our printed text) and in the book of Esther (Esther 1:19). The exact stipulations of these laws are unknown because there is no nonbiblical reference to them. Simply revoking the decree was out of the question (see Daniel 6:15; compare Esther 8:8). For the king to provide a way out for Daniel seemed impossible.

What Do You Think?

How does hoping for God's deliverance from harm differ from expecting a worldly authority to help?

Digging Deeper

How do you balance expecting God's deliverance with acknowledging that He might have other plans?

C. Den's Predators (v. 16)

16a. Then the king commanded, and they brought Daniel, and cast him into the den of lions.

The officials had forced the king's response, and he could not revoke the decree that initiated this chain of events. If Darius had responded in any way other than to approve the punishment, he would have revealed a disrespect for his culture and law. So he *commanded* that the previously determined consequences were to be leveled against Daniel.

The Lion Hunt of Ashurbanipal, an excavated Assyrian relief from the seventh century BC, depicts the sport of hunting lions and its importance for the Assyrian royals. The *den* was a place to hold trapped *lions* for use in a royal lion hunt. Lions remained there until the appropriate time when they would be released into an arena for the king to "hunt" and kill.

16b. Now the king spake and said unto Daniel, Thy God whom thou servest continually, he will deliver thee.

Darius likely practiced a form of polytheism—

the belief in many gods. As a result, if he believed in the same *God* that Daniel served, it was not a belief in God as the only true God. The text is unclear whether we should interpret the word as a form of skeptical sarcasm or a genuine prayer, though the latter is more likely.

Darius's response should prompt comparisons to Nebuchadnezzar's reaction when the three Jewish men refused to bow before the golden image (see Daniel 3, lesson 11). In that example, Nebuchadnezzar doubted that any god could rescue the three men (see 3:15). Only after seeing how God saved them did the king proclaim that "there is no other God that can deliver after this sort" (3:29). Darius, however, believed that God could *deliver* Daniel, even without him having evidence.

> **What Do You Think?**
> How do you encourage others as they wait for God's deliverance?
> **Digging Deeper**
> What verses encourage you when you are waiting on the Lord?

II. Release and Vindication

(Daniel 6:19-23, 26-27)

A. The Question (vv. 19-20)

19. Then the king arose very early in the morning, and went in haste unto the den of lions.

The king's rising *very early* the next *morning* reveals his urgency and distress regarding Daniel's fate. Darius's anxiety regarding what he had done to Daniel led to a restless night (see Daniel 6:18, not in our printed text). Additionally, *the den* had been sealed with the royal signet and the signets of the other officials (see 6:17). No one would dare break the seal and save Daniel. The only way for Daniel to have survived the night with the *lions* would have been if God had intervened.

20. And when he came to the den, he cried with a lamentable voice unto Daniel; and the king spake and said to Daniel, O Daniel, servant of the living God, is thy God, whom thou servest continually, able to deliver thee from the lions?

A night without sleep or food would have escalated the king's anxiety regarding the life of one of his most trusted presidents. As Darius approached the sealed den, he called out *with a lamentable voice*, assuming the worst possible outcome.

The king's address *to Daniel* revealed his deepening understanding of the one true God. The pagan gods, idols, and images of Babylon (example: Daniel 3:1; 5:4) were lifeless (see Psalm 135:15-18). They were incapable of giving life to their worshippers. In contrast to these so-called gods, Darius recognized that the God of Daniel was *the living God* (also Daniel 6:26). Scripture uses this title regarding possible doubt (examples: Deuteronomy 5:26; 1 Samuel 17:26, 36; Isaiah 37:4; Matthew 16:16; John 5:26) or regarding God's provision (cxample: Psalm 84:2) and power (example: Jeremiah 10:10). The people of Israel survived because the living God was in their midst (see Joshua 3:9-10) and He made them His people (see Hosea 1:10). When the other nations trusted in their idols, the Israelites could trust the living God, the Lord who was their help and their protection (see Psalm 115:1-11).

Daniel's faithfulness to God was evident. The presidents and princes acknowledged that Daniel was free from fault and was entirely trustworthy (see Daniel 3:4). He behaved as a *servant* of the living God by showing honor and respect as a servant of the king.

Flooded with Faithfulness

My wife and I decided we would serve as foster parents. After completing the state's screening process, which included an inspection of our rental house, we were approved to foster. As we waited for the arrival of the children, a rainstorm flooded our house. Although we had no control over the flooding, we were evicted and told that we had caused the flooding.

Our dreams of being foster parents seemed dashed. However, after an extensive search, we found a new rental house. Much to our relief, it passed the state inspection. We were again approved to be foster parents! God's plan for our lives continued, despite us experiencing an apparent injustice.

Everything was outside Daniel's control, but it wasn't outside God's control. The next time you experience injustice, will you respond so that people call you a "servant of the living God"?

—J. M.

B. The Innocent (vv. 21-23)

21. Then said Daniel unto the king, O king, live for ever.

The king's advisors, direct reports, and even the queen wished for the king's good health and long life (Daniel 2:4; 3:9; 5:10; 6:6). However, this is the first and only time in the book that an Israelite greeted the *king* in this manner. Even though Daniel's situation came about because of the king's lack of insight, *Daniel* still greeted him with respect and honor.

22. My God hath sent his angel, and hath shut the lions' mouths, that they have not hurt me; forasmuch as before him innocency was found in me; and also before thee, O king, have I done no hurt.

Daniel first attributed his survival to the intervention of an *angel* from *God* (see also Daniel 3:28). Angels are heavenly beings who serve God and follow His commands (see Psalm 103:20). Their ministry includes serving God's people (see Hebrews 1:13-14; example: Numbers 20:16), including protection (see Psalm 34:7; example: Acts 12:11). This angel miraculously *shut the lions' mouths*, though precisely how is unknown (see also Hebrews 11:32-33).

Second, Daniel noted that he survived because he was innocent before God and the *king*. Innocence does not mean that Daniel lived perfectly. Later, he confessed before God the ways that he had been a part of the sin of his people (Daniel 9:1-19). Instead, Daniel could claim innocence in this matter because he had followed God and was faithful to God's law.

23. Then was the king exceeding glad for him, and commanded that they should take Daniel up out of the den. So Daniel was taken up out of the den, and no manner of hurt was found upon him, because he believed in his God.

The king's distress changed to joy and gladness upon seeing God's deliverance at work (compare Isaiah 25:9). Daniel escaped his ordeal without being *hurt* or wounded (compare Daniel 3:27). Although God saved Daniel, Scripture is clear that faithfulness does not obligate God to save believers from death by martyrdom. For some believers, martyrdom is possible (see Luke 21:16; examples: Acts 7:54-60; Hebrews 11:35-38). Anyone who remains faithful to God in the midst of suffering has been promised eternal rewards (see Revelation 2:10). Public displays of faithfulness will have a transforming influence on the community. This transformation can occur individually, such as how Darius became exceedingly *glad* for Daniel. However, it can also occur for a whole kingdom, as the following verses indicate.

C. The Decree (vv. 26-27)

26a. I make a decree, That in every dominion of my kingdom men tremble and fear before the God of Daniel.

After hearing from Daniel and observing how God had saved him from the lions, Darius proceeded with two actions. First, he commanded that the officials who had accused Daniel face the same punishment they had intended for him (see Daniel 6:24, not in our printed text). Second, Darius wrote *a decree* to "all people, nations, and languages, that dwell in all the earth" (6:25). Such wide-reaching language suggested the scope of *every dominion* of the *kingdom* (see also 3:4).

Babylonian king Nebuchadnezzar had decreed that no one speak against the God of Shadrach, Meshach, and Abednego (Daniel 3:28-29). Darius's decree went further—it legislated that all people *fear* the *God of Daniel.* Coming from the mouth of a pagan king, this kind of fear could include being afraid of the consequences of God's righteousness (see Genesis 3:10; Isaiah 33:14; Luke 12:4-5; Hebrews 10:31). It could also refer to a respectful sense of worship to God (see Deuteronomy 6:2-3; 1 Samuel 12:24; Psalms 2:11; 147:11).

26b. For he is the living God, and stedfast for ever, and his kingdom that which shall not be destroyed, and his dominion shall be even unto the end.

The decree provided several reasons why the

king's subjects should fear Daniel's God. First, Daniel's God is *the living God,* and He alone can give life and sustenance to all who would receive it (see commentary on Daniel 6:20, above). Second, God's kingdom would never be destroyed and would never end (see Psalm 145:13). Earthly kingdoms, like the Babylonians, will end. However, God is the eternal king, and His kingdom will be eternal (see Exodus 15:18; Isaiah 9:7; Daniel 2:44; 7:14, 27; Luke 1:29-33; etc.).

> **What Do You Think?**
> How do you refute the idea that God is not active in His creation?
> **Digging Deeper**
> Do you have any habits that might suggest God is not active in creation? If so, what change will you make to acknowledge His continued work?

27. He delivereth and rescueth, and he worketh signs and wonders in heaven and in earth, who hath delivered Daniel from the power of the lions.

The decree also emphasized how God had done miraculous work for His people. God showed His power to His people by delivering and rescuing them (examples: Exodus 20:2; Psalm 34:4; Daniel 3:26-29; Jeremiah 15:11). When God rescued His people, He frequently did so through miraculous *signs and wonders* (see Exodus 14:13-30; Jeremiah 32:19-22). The way God *delivered Daniel* was no exception.

Conclusion

A. Confession as Celebration

Public confessions model something meaningful for today's Christians. It's easy to think of "confession" as an admission of sin, especially in a lurid, tell-all fashion. But that is not what the word means when describing the texts in Daniel. Here, the confession tells good news. The Lord chose to deliver Daniel, which resulted in the king's surprising new edict. Daniel's confessing what happened with the lions and the king's reaction reoriented both the characters in the story and those reading about them to a larger truth. God's reign is both eternal and full of goodness. God's loyalty to His people reflects His divine character and the large-scale divine plan to redeem humanity. Daniel knew that, and eventually, so did Darius.

So do we. The church continues to confess its sins but also God's redemption. Our life of celebration begins where Darius ended his learning experience. By repeatedly confessing God's goodness, we bring those outside within hearing distance of the gospel itself. Daniel did so by his faithfulness in this story, and we do so too when we confess the gospel of our salvation.

> **What Do You Think?**
> What would you say is the greatest "wonder" God has worked in your life?
> **Digging Deeper**
> How will you confess this wonder in order to edify both believers and unbelievers?

B. Prayer

Living God, You care for Your people and have promised to be with us no matter what we face. Give us the courage to face adversity and maintain faithfulness to You. Help us behave with mercy to those who have sought to harm us. Show us how to follow You in a manner that brings other people closer to You. In the name of Jesus. Amen.

C. Thought to Remember

Our faithfulness to God has personal and public implications.

How to Say It

Ahasuerus	Uh-haz-you-*ee*-rus.
Ashurbanipal	*As*-shure-**bah**-nee-pahl.
Babylon	*Bab*-uh-lun.
Belshazzar	Bel-*shazz*-er.
Hosea	Ho-*zay*-uh.
Medes	Meeds.
Nebuchadnezzar	*Neb*-yuh-kud-**nez**-er.

Involvement Learning

Enhance your lesson with KJV Bible Student *(from your curriculum supplier) and the reproducible activity page (at www.standardlesson.com or in the back of the* KJV Standard Lesson Commentary Deluxe Edition*).*

Into the Lesson

Divide learners into groups of four. Challenge each group to compile a list of deep convictions that a person may have about a particular assigned issue. Depending on the temperament of your class, you might choose trivial categories (the best TV show of all time, the best place to vacation or what to do on vacation, etc.) or more serious topics (best strategies for managing money, importance of education, etc.). *Option.* Write several categories on the board and facilitate a whole-class brainstorming session to list convictions under each heading. Remind learners that they don't have to agree with the convictions.

After five minutes, ask each group to report on convictions they discussed as well as what factors play into those convictions (for instance, a TV show might be best because of the story line, strength of acting, number of seasons it was produced, etc.). Ask the whole class to brainstorm a list of factors that prompt people to abandon their convictions, either temporarily or permanently. Ask the class to agree on the top two or three factors.

Alternative. Distribute copies of "My Daily Habits" exercise from the activity page, which you can download. Have individuals complete it as indicated.

After either activity, lead into the Bible study by saying, "Today we'll look at a story about a faithful follower of God who would not renege on his convictions or his faithful habits, even though this refusal threatened his very life."

Into the Word

Before class, prepare a summary of the sections of Daniel 6 not included in today's printed text. Be ready to answer these questions: 1–Where were the Jews living and why? 2–Who was the king? 3–What happened between last week's lesson (in Daniel 3) and today's lesson regarding government? *Option.* Assign this task to one or several learners. Then present the whole story of Daniel in the lions' den by alternating between the volunteer summaries and reading aloud the printed text (Daniel 6:10-11, 14, 16, 19-23, 26-27).

Alternative. Divide learners into groups of four to read Daniel 6 and to outline and summarize the chapter. After five minutes, compare the groups' answers.

Divide the class into small groups. Distribute handouts (you create) with the following questions for in-group discussion: 1–What is surprising about Daniel's reaction to the king's decree? 2–What other choices might Daniel have made? How could these other decisions have been justified? 3–How does Daniel's situation compare with that of Shadrach, Meshach, and Abednego? 4–How did the king feel about Daniel, and why? After several minutes, have groups present their findings. Then discuss what impact Daniel's faithfulness may have had on the other exiled Jews.

Into Life

Divide learners into pairs. Have them share with each other an obstacle, fear, or pressure that feels as strong as a lion. Invite them to share the following: 1–How is that "lion" threatening your faith today? 2–What encouragement do you receive from today's story to help you resist it?

After a few minutes of sharing time, call the pairs together. Invite volunteers to share about their "lions" and how Daniel's story helps them face the difficulties. *Alternative.* Distribute copies of the "Daniel's Example and New Testament Teaching" activity from the activity page. Have learners work in groups to discuss.

Ask individuals to pray for the needs revealed in this discussion. Take time for a series of prayers, mentioning specific problems that learners are comfortable sharing. Close with a prayer of thanksgiving for the example of Daniel and the opportunity to stand up for God today.

February 25
Lesson 13 (KJV)

Faith in God's Purpose

Devotional Reading: Jeremiah 29:8-14
Background Scripture: Habakkuk 1:5–2:5

Habakkuk 2:1-5

1 I will stand upon my watch, and set me upon the tower, and will watch to see what he will say unto me, and what I shall answer when I am reproved.

2 And the LORD answered me, and said, Write the vision, and make it plain upon tables, that he may run that readeth it.

3 For the vision is yet for an appointed time, but at the end it shall speak, and not lie: though it tarry, wait for it; because it will surely come, it will not tarry.

4 Behold, his soul which is lifted up is not upright in him: but the just shall live by his faith.

5 Yea also, because he transgresseth by wine, he is a proud man, neither keepeth at home, who enlargeth his desire as hell, and is as death, and cannot be satisfied, but gathereth unto him all nations, and heapeth unto him all people.

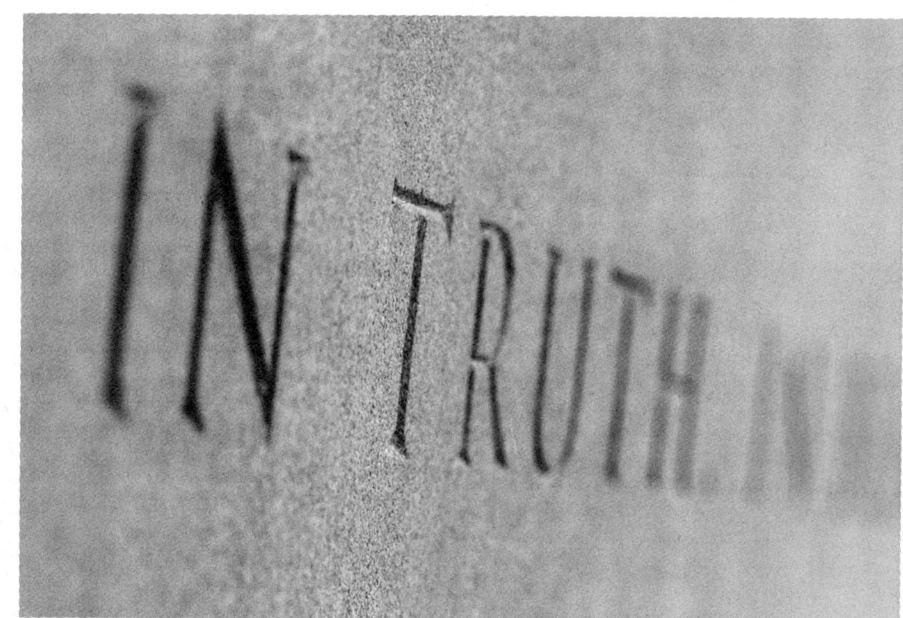

Key Text

For the vision is yet for an appointed time, but at the end it shall speak, and not lie: though it tarry, wait for it; because it will surely come, it will not tarry. **—Habakkuk 2:3**

Faith That

Pleases God

Unit 3: The Righteous Live by Faith

Lessons 10–13

Lesson Aims

After participating in this lesson, each learner will be able to:

1. Describe the dialogue between Habakkuk and God.

2. Contrast the first half of Habakkuk 2:4 with the second half of that verse in light of Romans 1:17; Galatians 3:11; and Hebrews 10:37-38.

3. State a commitment of "yet I will rejoice in the Lord" in spite of some lingering and personal negative situations.

Lesson Outline

Introduction

A. "Can You Hear Me Now?"
B. Lesson Context: The Man and His Times
C. Lesson Context: The Book

I. One Conversation (Habakkuk 2:1-3)

A. The Prophet Waits (v. 1)
B. The Lord Responds (vv. 2-3)
Make It Plain
Breakup

II. Two People (Habakkuk 2:4-5)

A. The Prideful, Part 1 (v. 4a)
B. The Faithful (v. 4b)
C. The Prideful, Part 2 (v. 5)

Conclusion

A. Questioning God
B. Prayer
C. Thought to Remember

Introduction

A. "Can You Hear Me Now?"

No one likes spotty cell phone service. When a phone call seems to drop out, you ask, "Can you hear me now?" hoping that the other party will respond. In the early 2000s, a wireless network provider used that question as the foundation for a series of ubiquitous television commercials. The advertisements were intended to conjure a sense of trust from the audience toward this particular wireless network provider. The commercial implied there was no need to ask *that* question with *this* wireless provider.

Faced with the unjust behavior of Judah's enemies, the prophet Habakkuk questioned the Lord. Habakkuk wondered whether the Lord heard his questions or if the Lord had left the conversation altogether. The prophet asked his own version of the question, "Can you hear me now?" The Lord responded, but would His answer be the message Habakkuk wanted to hear?

B. Lesson Context: The Man and His Times

The book of Habakkuk gives us virtually no personal information regarding "Habakkuk the prophet" (Habakkuk 1:1). His name occurs only one other time after the first chapter (see 3:1). Even then, the text provides no further information about the man. Compared to other Old Testament prophets (examples: Isaiah 1:1; Jeremiah 1:1-3), we know nothing regarding the exact details of the life of Habakkuk.

However, some clues in the text of Habakkuk inform our educated guesses regarding the man and his times. Early in the book, the Lord promised to raise "the Chaldeans" (another name for the Babylonians) to punish the kingdom of Judah (Habakkuk 1:6). Using the then-future Babylonian exile of 586 BC as a historical marker, Habakkuk likely served sometime during the last decade of the seventh century BC; that would have been during the reign of evil King Jehoiakim (609–598 BC).

Following the split of Israel into two kingdoms in about 931 BC (1 Kings 11:43–12:24), things went pretty much downhill for both. The kingdoms of "Israel" (10 tribes to the north) and

"Judah" (2 tribes to the south) glared at each other for about 200 years until the Assyrians conquered and exiled the northern tribes in 722 BC (2 Kings 17). The southern kingdom of Judah narrowly escaped the same fate (18:13–19:36), even though they were also guilty of the same behavior that led to the destruction of their northern kin (17:18-20).

About a century later, the Babylonian Empire became the regional superpower after defeating the Assyrians and Egyptians at the battle of Carchemish in 605 BC (Jeremiah 46:2). King Josiah of Judah unwisely interfered, contributing to the Babylonian victory; Josiah's action also cost him his life (2 Chronicles 35:20-27). Just as Habakkuk 1:6 promised, Babylonian forces invaded Judah and overthrew its king (see 36:5-8).

For a few years, Judah's kings served as vassals to the Babylonians. However, this arrangement didn't last. During the final year of the reign of King Zedekiah (586 BC), Jerusalem and the kingdom of Judah fell to the Babylonians after about a decade of conflict (see 2 Kings 25).

There was a series of deportations from Judah by the Babylonians—one each in 605, 594, and 586 BC. Habakkuk likely served prior to the first of those, given the future tense of Habakkuk 1:6. This places Habakkuk as a contemporary of the prophet Jeremiah. Both prophets received a warning that the people of Jerusalem would face dire consequences because of sinful behavior.

C. Lesson Context: The Book

An outline of the book of Habakkuk reveals a conversation between the prophet and the Lord. Two sections of the book consist of the prophet's questions to the Lord (Habakkuk 1:2-4; 1:12–2:1). Following each round of inquiry, the Lord responded (1:5-11; 2:2-20). In Habakkuk's first section of questioning, he expressed discontent that the Lord had seemingly not heard the prophet's call for correction of sin. In his complaint, the prophet's conclusion for this uncorrected state of affairs was that "the law is slacked, and judgment doth never go forth" (1:4). The Lord answered that He was going to use the Babylonians to punish Judah and Jerusalem (1:5-11).

This response left Habakkuk even more confused. In his lengthy rejoinder, the prophet asked why the Lord would use a less-righteous nation to punish a more-righteous nation (Habakkuk 1:12–2:1). Today's text picks up at the very end of Habakkuk's second complaint.

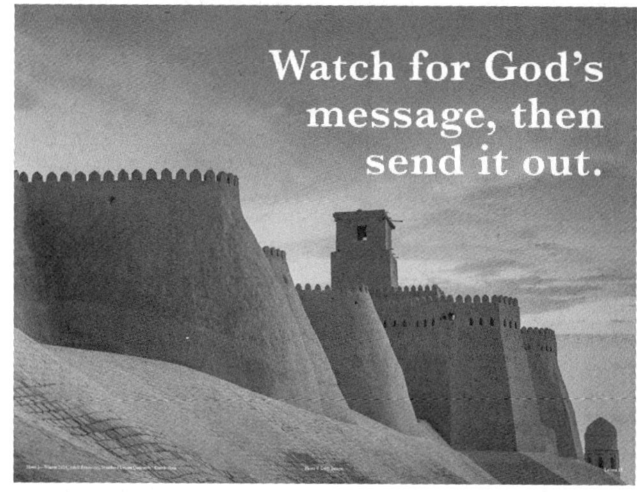

Visual for Lesson 13. *Point to this visual as you ask how learners can watch for God's message and ensure that it is sent out into the world.*

I. One Conversation

(Habakkuk 2:1-3)

A. The Prophet Waits (v. 1)

1. I will stand upon my watch, and set me upon the tower, and will watch to see what he will say unto me, and what I shall answer when I am reproved.

This verse completes Habakkuk's second section of questioning that began at Habakkuk 1:12 (see Lesson Context). In the verse before us, the prophet shifts from questioning the Lord to waiting for the Lord's response. When people call out to the Lord, the timing of His response is always perfect, but it is not always as fast as we desire. Habakkuk himself has been impatient in this regard (Habakkuk 1:2).

Habakkuk had no idea how long it would take—if ever—for the Lord to answer his second question. But he wasn't willing merely to toss his prayer to Heaven and then go about his daily tasks. Instead, we see a determination to stay focused as he waited for a response. In this determined concentration, the prophet envisioned himself as a lookout who would *stand upon* his *watch* as he performed the duty of a person responsible for sounding an early warning of something that was approaching.

In describing the task of a lookout, the phrases *I will stand upon my watch* and *set me upon the tower* are similar to Isaiah 21:8: "I stand continually upon the watchtower in the daytime, and I am set in my ward whole nights." In Habakkuk's day, lookouts were stationed at vantage points such as high towers. From such vantage points, lookouts were in a position to see things that others could not yet see. Thus, they warned of approaching enemies (example: 2 Kings 9:17-20) or visitors (example: 2 Samuel 18:24-28).

The Old Testament prophets were spiritual lookouts for the people they served. The prophets were to proclaim the arrival of the Lord's reign (example: Isaiah 52:8-10) and warn the people of the consequences of their disobedience (example: Ezekiel 3:16-17). In most cases, the people failed to heed the warning of these prophetic watchmen (example: Jeremiah 6:17). But if their failure to heed was due to the prophet's failure to warn, then the prophet would be accountable (Ezekiel 3:20).

The distressed prophet was obviously concerned for the welfare of his people. However, he also acknowledged that he might be rebuked (as the word *reproved* is translated in Proverbs 27:5) by the Lord.

What Do You Think?

In what ways can a believer "stand watch" to receive God's word?

Digging Deeper

How do the directives of Colossians 3:15-17 inform your answer in this regard?

B. The Lord Responds (vv. 2-3)

2. And the Lord answered me, and said, Write the vision, and make it plain upon tables, that he may run that readeth it.

As Habakkuk anticipated, *the Lord answered* the prophet's complaints. The content and form of this *vision* the prophet experienced are uncertain.

When prophets wrote messages from the Lord, they frequently did so on rolls (scrolls) of papyrus (see Isaiah 8:1; Jeremiah 36:2-4, 28). However, the *tables* commanded of Habakkuk were likely made of stone, similar to the "tables of stone" on which the law was divinely etched and given to Moses (Exodus 31:18; 32:15-16; Deuteronomy 4:13). The content of this vision, etched plain and legible in stone, was, therefore, an almost-permanent medium for the message. Ancient scrolls were fragile and could be burned (Jeremiah 36:22-23); the same cannot be said of stone.

The Lord sometimes commanded that His prophets write down His message as a witness for the people (examples: Exodus 34:27; Isaiah 30:8; Jeremiah 36:2-3). At other times, however, the Lord sealed His message until its fulfillment (examples: Daniel 8:26; 12:4). Because the Lord did not seal this particular message, the people of Judah would have immediate knowledge of its content and implications.

In ancient times, a messenger might *run* to proclaim the content of vital, time-sensitive messages (Joshua 7:22). Without modern-day wireless communication, running messengers were the quickest way to convey information over distance. The speed with which the message needed to travel highlighted its importance.

What Do You Think?

How could the practice of writing in a journal provide insights into the ways that God has answered your prayers?

Digging Deeper

What steps do you need to take to begin this practice?

Make It Plain

I had just begun serving as a preacher when a more experienced preacher approached me with counsel: strong sermons are short, simple, and straightforward. A preacher should be able to communicate the sermon's main point in one clear, concise sentence.

This advice also applies to other communicators, not just preachers. Consider Martin Luther King Jr.'s "I Have a Dream" speech, given from the steps of the Lincoln Memorial. One line can summarize the 17-minute address: "I have a dream that my four little children will one day live in a nation where they will not be judged by the color of their skin but by the content of their character." This one line reflects the speech's clarity of vision.

The Lord had an urgent message to give Habakkuk and the people of Judah. The urgency of that message required that it be clear and easily communicated. Even today, the Lord's message to us is urgent and sharp (see Hebrews 4:12). What steps are you taking so that you might communicate that message? —J. M.

3. For the vision is yet for an appointed time, but at the end it shall speak, and not lie: though it tarry, wait for it; because it will surely come, it will not tarry.

Habakkuk had waited for the Lord (Habakkuk 1:2; 2:1), and now part of the waiting concluded as the prophet received the Lord's response. But there was more waiting to come for Habakkuk to see the fulfillment of *the vision* at *an appointed time*. God's promises would eventually be fulfilled, but not on a timetable that Habakkuk desired.

We frequently become impatient when we have to wait. Rather than wait for God to act, we may take steps to expedite God's promises (examples: Genesis 16:1-4; see also Psalm 106:13). Rather than see God as longsuffering (see Romans 2:4; 2 Peter 3:8-9), we interpret God's silence as His refusal to act or hear (compare Lamentations 3:8, 44). Habakkuk needed to trust that the Lord would respond to wickedness in the Lord's own time and manner (see Nahum 1:3).

What Do You Think?

How can you practice patience regarding the Lord's answers to your prayers?

Digging Deeper

How might the Holy Spirit use other people in your life to help you develop patience?

Breakup

To an Alaskan, the word *breakup* implies the unofficial start to summer. Breakup is the day when the river ice breaks up and begins moving downstream to the sea. After breakup day, the river opens for various summer activities, but not before multiple celebrations commemorate the day.

After the celebrations, rural Alaskans begin to wait for the day when the river will again freeze over. For these Alaskans, a frozen river provides improved access to remote villages. Late-summer weather in Alaska can be unpredictable, and the specific date of the river freeze can span weeks. A waiting season precedes that day, just like the weeks before breakup day.

Waiting can seem at best like a waste of time. But the breakup day will be when it will be. There are times when we must wait for the river ice to melt and times when we must wait for the Lord.

While we're at it, let's look at things the other way around: How often has God had to wait for you to produce the kingdom fruit expected of you? —J. M.

II. Two People
(Habakkuk 2:4-5)

A. The Prideful, Part 1 (v. 4a)

4a. Behold, his soul which is lifted up is not upright in him.

The Lord's message distinguishes two types of people. The first type is the person whose *soul* is *lifted up* with self-assured pride and arrogance. Such a perspective was indicative of Judah's enemies during this time. The military strength of the Babylonians was undeniable, leading them to count their power as a god (Habakkuk 1:11). Babylonian King Nebuchadnezzar saw the expanse of the kingdom as the result of his power (see Daniel 4:28-30). Even as the Lord raised the Babylonians to conquer Judah, He acknowledged their pride (see Habakkuk 1:7). Similarly, when the unnamed king of Assyria looked out over his conquest, he proclaimed the strength of his hand (see Isaiah 10:12-13).

Even the kingdoms of Judah and Israel were guilty of arrogance (see Jeremiah 13:9; Hosea 5:4-5; 7:10; Amos 6:8). This behavior was part of the reason that enemies conquered them. The Lord detests those whose thoughts and behavior are grounded in pride (Proverbs 16:5). Such people will inevitably face dramatic consequences (see Leviticus 26:19; Luke 18:14).

B. The Faithful (v. 4b)

4b. But the just shall live by his faith.

This half-verse offers an immediate contrast between two types of people. One type—the prideful—has just been discussed. The second type—*the just*—lives with an entirely different outlook, an outlook of *faith*. Their lives are grounded in righteousness. Such a person follows God's standards regarding their relationships with God and others. This person lives with integrity and without blame for wrongdoing (see Proverbs 20:7).

Psalm 15, attributed to King David, depicts the mindset and behavior of a righteous person. This type of person speaks well of others (Psalm 15:2-3), keeps a trustworthy word (15:4), and treats others fairly (15:5). God expresses great pleasure when His people live justly and righteously (see Hebrews 11:7). This is because His nature is righteousness (Ezra 9:15; Psalm 116:5), and His rule over creation is one of justice (see Hebrews 1:8).

The Hebrew word translated *faith* is also translated as "truth" in Jeremiah 5:1, 3; 7:28; 9:3. To be a person of faith goes hand in hand with being a person of truth. Unfaithful people depart from the truth (2 Timothy 2:17-18; 3:8-9). In the book of Habakkuk, God calls His people to have faith in the truth of His plans, even when those plans seemed unbelievable (Habakkuk 1:5). Although the Babylonians would prosper for a time by placing faith in themselves, the people of Judah were to depend on the Lord. The apostle Paul connected the concepts of truth and faithfulness in applying them to his ministry as an apostle (1 Timothy 2:7; Titus 1:1). We must proclaim truth and live with faithfulness as we follow God and trust Him.

How to Say It

Assyria	Uh-*sear*-ee-uh.
Assyrians	Uh-*sear*-e-unz.
Carchemish	*Kar*-key-mish.
Ecclesiastes	Ik-*leez*-ee-**as**-teez.
Galatians	Guh-*lay*-shunz.
Habakkuk	Huh-*back*-kuk.

Elsewhere, Paul quoted Habakkuk 2:4b in explaining the nature of the gospel with regard to righteousness, which is a characteristic of God that is to be ours as well (Romans 1:16-17). In a preliminary sense, to be righteous is to do what is right in God's eyes. But having a right standing with God can't be based on mere good behavior because, as Paul later noted, "There is none righteous, no, not one" (3:10, drawing on Psalms 14:1-3; 53:1-3; and Ecclesiastes 7:20). Instead, a right standing before God is imputed on the basis of faith (Romans 3:21-26). This basis is reaffirmed in Galatians 3:11-14, where Paul quotes Habakkuk 2:4b again.

In a section of Hebrews that teaches the importance of the perseverance of faith, the author also quotes from a portion of Habakkuk 2:3: "For yet a little while, and he that shall come will come, and will not tarry. Now the just shall live by faith" (Hebrews 10:37-38a). We live by faith because we can trust that God will also be faithful to His promises.

> **What Do You Think?**
> In what ways can you live by faith in the upcoming week?
>
> **Digging Deeper**
> How does the Hall of Faith passage in Hebrews 11:1–12:3 inform your answer in this regard?

C. The Prideful, Part 2 (v. 5)

5a. Yea also, because he transgresseth by wine, he is a proud man, neither keepeth at home, who enlargeth his desire as hell, and is as death, and cannot be satisfied.

In a continuation of Habakkuk 2:4a, above, the Lord's message returns to the behavior of the *proud* person. Becoming drunk, perhaps on *wine*, might follow a successful military campaign (example: 1 Samuel 30:16). Babylon's military successes were intoxicating, leading the nation to desire more through military conquest. Babylon was incapable of staying at rest in her homelands (compare and contrast the behavior of the "Babylon" depicted in Revelation 14:8; 17:3-6; 18:3).

The Hebrew word translated *hell* is a vague

word that occurs dozens of times in the Old Testament. In contexts involving *death*, it is translated as "hell" about half the time and "grave" about half the time. As such, it may not refer to hell as the New Testament uses that word in Matthew 5:22, 29-30; James 3:6; and elsewhere. The word in the original language has a similar spelling to the Hebrew word for *ask*. This association brings to mind a place that is always asking for more but is never satisfied. Similarly, the desires of the proud and arrogant never cease; they never say, "Now I have enough" (compare Proverbs 30:15-16; Ecclesiastes 5:10; Luke 12:15-21).

The Bible addresses the danger of pride and arrogance more than 200 times. By proportion, the greatest concentrations of these are found in the texts of Psalms and Proverbs. Arrogant, prideful people always incur God's disfavor (examples: Psalms 18:27; 31:23; Proverbs 15:25; 16:5).

5b. But gathereth unto him all nations, and heapeth unto him all people.

One way that the proud expand their power is through military conquest. As a planter gathers fruit at harvest, prideful rulers gather *all nations* under their authority and conquest (compare Habakkuk 1:15-17). During these campaigns, enemies took captives into exile and slavery (see 2 Kings 15:29; 17:6; Jeremiah 50:33).

However, such prideful behavior will not go unpunished. God will reverse selfish ambition. In response to the arrogant and destructive behavior of Judah's enemies, the Lord predicts punishment in terms of five sets of "woe" (Habakkuk 2:6-19, not in today's text). Although Judah was to suffer for its arrogant disobedience, its prideful and arrogant enemies would also experience a downfall equally devastating, if not more so (see Jeremiah 51:6-8).

Conclusion

A. Questioning God

Is it OK to question God's (apparent) actions or inactions? The dependable answer is, "It depends." We see God tolerating, even welcoming, questions in numerous places (examples: Judges 20:18; James 1:5; 4:2). One thing God does not tolerate, however, are inquiries that question His justice (see Job 40:8; Ezekiel 18:25-29; Jeremiah 2:29). The prophet Habakkuk came close to doing that. Consider the following thumbnail sketch of the book:

Question 1: Why do you, O God, tolerate the sins of Your people?
Response 1: Don't worry about it—I'm sending the Babylonians to punish them.
Question 2: How is it fair to use the less-righteous to punish the more-righteous?
Response 2: Don't worry about it—the Babylonians will get theirs too.
God's ending of the discussion: Be quiet!

When our suffering does not seem "fair," there are a lot of questions we might naturally ask. God was under no obligation to answer Habakkuk's questions, and He is not obligated to answer ours. Habakkuk needed faith to trust the Lord's plans, regardless of whether or not those plans made human sense.

God reminded Habakkuk that a life of faithfulness was most important. And the faith we are talking about isn't "blind faith"—a faith where one merely believes. Instead, the faith we are talking about is a faith based on evidence. God has a long track record of faithfulness to His promises. Upon that track record is where our faith is based. Such faith trusts God's control in all circumstances. As a result, we can be secure in Him, regardless of whether or not we understand His plans.

What Do You Think?

What do you find most challenging about today's lesson?

Digging Deeper

What change in thought, word, or behavior will you make based on that challenge?

B. Prayer

God, as we face life's hardships and want to question You, help us have the confidence of faith. In Jesus' name we pray. Amen.

C. Thought to Remember

The righteous will live by faith.

Involvement Learning

Enhance your lesson with KJV Bible Student *(from your curriculum supplier) and the reproducible activity page (at www.standardlesson.com or in the back of the* KJV Standard Lesson Commentary Deluxe Edition*).*

Into the Lesson

Begin today's session by writing *WAIT* vertically down the center of the board. Ask the class to create an acrostic based on the word to express commonly held feelings about waiting.

Ask the following questions for whole-class discussion: 1–Why is waiting difficult? 2–When was a time that you were unhappy because you had to wait? 3–When was a time when waiting resulted in something good?

Say, "Today, we will consider what Scripture says about waiting on the Lord. Let's learn how the book of Habakkuk can inform our waiting in faith and trusting in God's timing."

Into the Word

Before class, choose a volunteer to give a brief presentation on the historical background of the book of Habakkuk. The volunteer can use other commentaries and the Lesson Context in preparation. Before the presentation, write the following questions on the board: 1–When did Habakkuk live? 2–Who was the audience of his prophetic ministry? 3–What was happening in their lives? Allow five minutes at the start of class for the presentation and an additional five minutes for a whole-class discussion of the above questions.

Divide the class into three groups: **Habakkuk Group, Old Testament Group,** and **New Testament Group.** Distribute handouts (you create) of the assignments below and allow 10 minutes for groups to answer the questions.

Habakkuk Group: Read Habakkuk 1:2–2:5. 1–What was Habakkuk's first complaint? 2–How did God respond? 3–What was Habakkuk's second complaint? 4–How did God respond?

Old Testament Group: Read Habakkuk 2:1-5. 1–Compare and contrast this Scripture with Psalms 27; 37. 2–Compare and contrast this Scripture with Lamentations 3. 3–Compare and contrast this Scripture with Isaiah 40:27-31; 64:4-7. 4–What messages are common to all these Scriptures?

New Testament Group: Read Habakkuk 2:1-5. 1–Compare and contrast this Scripture with Romans 1:14-20. 2–Compare and contrast this Scripture with Galatians 3:1-14. 3–Compare and contrast this Scripture with Hebrews 10:19-39. 4–What messages are common to all these Scriptures?

After 10 minutes of in-group discussion, reconvene the class and ask a volunteer from each group to discuss their group's findings.

Into Life

Write these phrases on your board:

Wait on the Lord.
The righteous will live by faith.

Ask the following questions for whole-class discussion: 1–Why do we need faith when we're waiting on God? 2–Is waiting on God easier or more difficult than the situations we discussed during Into the Lesson? 3–What does it mean that the righteous will live by faith?

Divide learners into pairs and ask each person to share with their partner about a current situation where they feel they are waiting on God. Then have each person brainstorm how they can continue to practice commitment and faithfulness to the Lord in light of this negative situation.

Alternative. Distribute copies of the "Praying, but Still Suffering" exercise from the activity page, which you can download. Have learners work in pairs to complete as indicated.

Write *FAITH* vertically down the middle of the board. Challenge pairs to create a new acrostic that expresses the truths discussed in today's lesson.

Option. Distribute copies of the "Personal Prayer from One Who Waits" exercise from the activity page. Have learners complete it individually in a minute or less. Give them one minute to jot down thoughts under each of the two headings.

Examining Our Faith

Special Features

Lessons

Unit 1: Faithful vs. Faithless

Unit 2: The Measure of Faith

Unit 3: Standing in the Faith

Quarterly Quiz

Use these questions as a pretest or as a review. The answers are on page iv of This Quarter in the Word.

Lesson 1

1. Jude tells his audience to remember what had been spoken by the apostles. T/F. *Jude 17.*

2. Jude says to save others by pulling them from what? (fire, pit, persecution) *Jude 23*

Lesson 2

1. Believers should examine themselves to see whether they are in what? (the right, the faith, the church) *2 Corinthians 13:5*

2. Paul commands believers to "live in __________." *2 Corinthians 13:11*

Lesson 3

1. Responding to certain evils with an equal amount of evil is appropriate. T/F. *1 Peter 3:9*

2. Always be prepared to give an answer regarding the reason for your _________. *1 Peter 3:15*

Lesson 4

1. The false witnesses claimed that Stephen spoke blaspheme against what things? (Choose two: the Sadducees, this holy place, the law, Elijah) *Acts 6:13*

2. The face of Stephen appeared like "the face of an __________." *Acts 6:15*

Lesson 5

1. Peter had gone with the women to the tomb to help them roll away the stone. T/F. *Mark 16:3*

2. The women were told that Jesus was going to what region? (Judea, Galilee, Samaria) *Mark 16:7*

Lesson 6

1. Jesus forgave the man's sins before the man stood up. T/F. *Luke 5:20*

2. The Son of Man has ________ to forgive sins. *Luke 5:24*

Lesson 7

1. The centurion sent soldiers to Jesus to ask for healing for the centurion's servant. T/F. *Luke 7:3*

2. The centurion demonstrated a great __________ not found in Israel. *Luke 7:9*

Lesson 8

1. The ointment was stored in a container made of what material? (amethyst, agate, alabaster) *Luke 7:37*

2. The woman refused to pour perfume on Jesus' feet. T/F. *Luke 7:46*

Lesson 9

1. The woman called Jesus the "Son of ________." *Matthew 15:22*

2. Jesus told the woman that she demonstrated great _________. *Matthew 15:28*

Lesson 10

1. "For all have sinned, and come short of the _______ of God." *Romans 3:23*

2. A person is justified by faith and the requirements of the law. T/F. *Romans 3:28*

Lesson 11

1. Where there is no law, there is no what? (transgression, transfiguration, testimony) *Romans 4:15*

2. Christ was raised to life for "our _________." *Romans 4:25*

Lesson 12

1. Because of justification by faith, believers have ________ with God. *Romans 5:1*

2. At the right time, Christ died for the ________. *Romans 5:6*

Lesson 13

1. Christ is the end of the ____________. *Romans 10:4*

2. Paul quoted from an Old Testament passage that declared the beauty of what body part that proclaims good things? (feet, lips, hands) *Romans 10:15*

Quarter at a Glance

by Jon Miller

The Greek word for *faith* appears over two hundred times in the New Testament. Its usage can refer to at least two different but related concepts. This quarter will explore the significance of faith and how the people of God live with faith.

Community Faith

The expression "the faith" refers to the beliefs and paradigms distinct to followers of Jesus (examples: Acts 6:7; 1 Corinthians 16:13; 2 Corinthians 13:5; 1 Timothy 3:9; Titus 1:13; Jude 3). The most central belief and the key to the faith itself is the resurrection of Jesus Christ (see Mark 16:1-8, lesson 5). Without Jesus' death and resurrection, our faith would be in vain.

Following "the faith" consists of being filled with Christ and indwelt by God's Spirit. The apostle Paul encourages believers to practice self-examination regarding the presence of Christ in their lives and whether or not they are "in the faith" (2 Corinthians 13:5, lesson 2). The point of this self-examination is not to win an argument or to fill oneself with pride. Instead, it aims to build up the body of Christ, which is the church (13:10-11).

Believers in the faith are likely to face trials and persecutions. Followers of Jesus have experienced these things since the birth of the church (example: Acts 6:7-15, lesson 4).

Additionally, believers are likely to come across the influence of false teachings. Therefore, the writers of Scripture frequently teach how a believer might defend the faith. Jude guards the "most holy faith" against destruction (Jude 17-20, lesson 1). Peter presents the faith as the foundation of the Christian life, worthy of defense (1 Peter 3:8-16, lesson 3). These writers encourage believers to contend for the faith.

Individual Faith

Scripture's second use of the word *faith* consists of belief in Christ and trust in God. One way a person's faith is revealed is through their decisions and behavior. The Gospels provide numerous examples of people who demonstrate faith through their actions. The faith of several men led them to seek healing for their friend (Luke 5:17-26, lesson 6). The faith of a centurion led him to ask Jesus for the long-distance healing of his servant (7:1-10, lesson 7). The faith of a certain woman demonstrated that she believed that Jesus could forgive sins (7:36-39, 44-50; lesson 8). Even a Gentile woman showed faith that Jesus could heal her daughter (Matthew 15:21-28, lesson 9).

The Benefits of Faith

The quarter's final unit investigates the spiritual benefits of having faith in Christ. Some of the recipients of Paul's New Testament letters were of Jewish heritage. For this reason, his writings frequently contrast a person's keeping the Law of Moses with a person's faith in Christ.

> *By our faith, we have received the ultimate benefit: becoming children of God.*

Paul argues that people do not receive justification through keeping the Law of Moses. Instead, justification and righteousness come through faith (Romans 3:21-28, lesson 10). As an example, it was Abraham's faith, not his actions, that were counted to him as righteousness (4:13-25, lesson 11).

A person expresses faith after they hear the good news of Christ (Romans 10:14-17, lesson 13). Believers enter the community of God's people by confessing sin and believing that Jesus is Lord. As a result, believers can rejoice! Because of our faith in Christ, we celebrate a relationship of peace with God (5:1-5, lesson 12). We were once adversaries of God, but by our faith, we have received the ultimate benefit: becoming children of God. This new identity is good news for all who would believe.

Get the Setting

by Jon Miller

During Jesus' ministry, He interacted with Jews and Gentiles. One shocking thing in the Gospels is how many stories highlight people outside of Jewish ancestry exercising faith in Christ. Jesus even told a centurion that his faith was greater than any faith Jesus found in Israel (Matthew 8:10)!

Jews and Gentiles came from very different cultural and religious backgrounds. However, the first-century church evolved from a world under Roman rule and included people shaped by Roman, Greek, and Jewish thinking. Thus, it is beneficial for us to look at how these people groups understood faith with respect to their religious and cultural heritage.

Greco-Roman

Classic Greek religion greatly influenced practice in the Roman Empire as people became interested in the worship of power. This gave rise to an appeal of magic, astrology, and the cult of the emperor. These beliefs led people to think of the least powerful gods as demons and to believe in fate and superstition.

In Greco-Roman culture, the worship of divinities was not exclusive. Even when someone gave devotion to a pagan god, they did not deny the existence of other gods. For example, to ensure no god was lacking adoration, certain people in Athens built an altar for "the unknown god" (Acts 17:23). The apostle Paul took advantage of the open door and introduced the people to the God they didn't know (17:22-28).

Religion was a part of daily life and did not have a separation from the government in Greco-Roman society. Temples to the gods and goddesses were built from public funds, and every city had at least one patron deity (Acts 19:26-28). Religion as the personal issue of one's belief and practice was unheard of in their society. Similarly, morality was not something that people aside from Judaism and Christianity associated with religious belief.

Judaism

Although the Greeks and Romans were hostile toward the Jewish people, the Jews enjoyed a privileged position in the empire. Because the Jewish people had offered help to the Roman rulers during the Maccabean period (second century BC), they received a pass to practice their religion without worshipping the divinities of Rome. Moreover, they were exempted from military service and allowed to live according to their laws within their communities, including the observance of the Sabbath.

"When in Rome" the Jewish people did not "do as the Romans do." Instead, they remained strictly monotheistic, adhering to the Law of Moses, practicing circumcision, and maintaining other rites of ritual purity. They also continued to offer sacrifices in the temple. To Jewish people, faith was based on the covenantal relationship they had as a people through Abraham.

Christianity

Christianity formed around a set of beliefs about Jesus' death, burial, and resurrection. Initially, Christianity was considered a sect of Judaism and enjoyed the same privileges as Jews in the free exercise of their faith. The appeal of the Christian faith was rational worship, high moral norms, monotheism, strong community, and respect for the Old Testament. This pleased some Gentiles because, unlike Judaism, it did not associate with one nationality or insist on the rite of circumcision or the observance of the Sabbath for inclusion.

These differences quickly established a line between the Christian faith and all other religions, including Judaism. In the Christian community, faith could refer to adherence to an established belief regarding Jesus (Philippians 1:27). Faith was also trusting in the covenantal relationship between God and humanity.

Mon, May 13	**Trusting in God Brings Perfect Peace**	Isaiah 26:1-11
Tue, May 14	**Good News of the Coming Lord**	Isaiah 40:1-11
Wed, May 15	**God's Spirit Poured Out**	Acts 2:1-4, 14, 16-24, 36
Thu, May 16	**The Firstfruits of Reconciliation**	Acts 2:37-47
Fri, May 17	**Brothers Reconciled**	Genesis 33:1-15
Sat, May 18	**May God Bless Us with Peace**	Psalm 29
Sun, May 19	**Peace with God Through Jesus Christ**	Romans 5:1-11
Mon, May 20	**Call on God and Be Saved**	Joel 2:28-32
Tue, May 21	**Striving on the Basis of Faith**	Romans 9:14-16, 25-33
Wed, May 22	**All Israel Will Be Saved**	Romans 11:1-4, 17-27
Thu, May 23	**God's Word Is Very Near**	Deuteronomy 30:11-20
Fri, May 24	**Do Not Fear, Only Believe**	Mark 5:35-43
Sat, May 25	**A Beautiful Announcement**	Isaiah 52
Sun, May 26	**Confession and Belief Lead to Salvation**	Romans 10:1-17

Answers to the Quarterly Quiz on page 226

Lesson 1—1. True. 2. fire. **Lesson 2**—1. the faith. 2. peace. **Lesson 3**—1. False. 2. hope. **Lesson 4**—1. the holy place, the law. 2. angel. **Lesson 5**—1. False. 2. Galilee. **Lesson 6**—1. True. 2. power. **Lesson 7**—1. False. 2. faith. **Lesson 8**—1. alabaster. 2. False. **Lesson 9**—1. David. 2. faith. **Lesson 10**—1. glory. 2. False. **Lesson 11**—1. transgression. 2. justification. **Lesson 12**—1. peace. 2. ungodly. **Lesson 13**—1. law. 2. feet.

This Quarter in the Word

Mon, Feb. 26	**The Faith in Which We Stand**	1 Corinthians 15:1-11
Tue, Feb. 27	**Turn Away from the Wicked**	Numbers 16:12-13, 23-34
Wed, Feb. 28	**Flee from Sin**	Genesis 18:20-22; 19:1-5, 15-17, 22-25
Thu, Feb. 29	**Always Do the Right Thing**	1 Peter 2:13-25
Fri, Mar. 1	**Walk with God**	Genesis 5:18-24
Sat, Mar. 2	**Contend for the Unchanging Faith**	Jude 3-16
Sun, Mar. 3	**Remain in God's Love**	Jude 17-25
Mon, Mar. 4	**Testing Produces Endurance**	James 1:2-12
Tue, Mar. 5	**The Sources of Temptations**	James 1:13-18
Wed, Mar. 6	**God Has Searched Us**	Psalm 139:1-12
Thu, Mar. 7	**God Knows All Things**	Psalm 139:13-18, 23-24
Fri, Mar. 8	**God's People Boast in Weakness**	2 Corinthians 11:22-33
Sat, Mar. 9	**Strength Through Christ Alone**	2 Corinthians 12:1-10
Sun, Mar. 10	**Live by God's Power**	2 Corinthians 13:1-10
Mon, Mar. 11	**Proclaim God's Message**	2 Timothy 4:1-8
Tue, Mar. 12	**Let All the People Praise God**	Psalm 67
Wed, Mar. 13	**Proclaim What Jesus Has Done**	Mark 5:1-2, 6-7, 11-20
Thu, Mar. 14	**A Powerful Defense of the Faith**	Acts 9:10-22
Fri, Mar. 15	**Come, Let Us Argue It Out**	Isaiah 1:16-20
Sat, Mar. 16	**Live Honorably Among Unbelievers**	1 Peter 2:4-12
Sun, Mar. 17	**Be Ready to Speak for Christ**	1 Peter 3:8-17

Mon, Mar. 18	**Blessings of Walking in God's Ways**	Deuteronomy 28:1-14
Tue, Mar. 19	**Let Your Life Match Your Words**	Titus 2:1-8
Wed, Mar. 20	**Fear God and Gain Knowledge**	Proverbs 1:1-9
Thu, Mar. 21	**A Promise for the Future**	2 Corinthians 5:1-11
Fri, Mar. 22	**Vessels Prepared for Every Good Work**	2 Timothy 2:8-21
Sat, Mar. 23	**The Ministry of Caring for Others**	Acts 6:1-6
Sun, Mar. 24	**A Spirit-Empowered Witness**	Acts 6:7-15
Mon, Mar. 25	**Faith Revealed Through Extravagant Love**	Mark 14:1-9
Tue, Mar. 26	**Faith in God's Deliverance**	Exodus 14:10-20
Wed, Mar. 27	**Faith in God's Protection**	Exodus 14:21-31
Thu, Mar. 28	**Faith Challenged and Encouraged**	Mark 14:17-26
Fri, Mar. 29	**An Unexpected Confession of Faith**	Mark 15:25-39
Sat, Mar. 30	**Faith Despite Pain and Loss**	Psalm 22:1-11, 28-31
Sun, Mar. 31	**Faith in the Risen Christ**	Mark 16:1-8
Mon, Apr. 1	**Come and See**	John 1:37-42
Tue, Apr. 2	**Heal Me and Save Me**	Jeremiah 17:12-17
Wed, Apr. 3	**Jesus Provides Living Water**	John 4:4-18
Thu, Apr. 4	**Worship God in Spirit and Truth**	John 4:19-29, 39-42
Fri, Apr. 5	**Tell What God Has Done**	Psalm 66:1-5, 13-20
Sat, Apr. 6	**Here Am I; Send Me**	Isaiah 6:1-8
Sun, Apr. 7	**Jesus Heals and Forgives**	Luke 5:17-26
Mon, Apr. 8	**Accept What God Has Made Clean**	Acts 10:1-15
Tue, Apr. 9	**God's Servant Enlightens the Nations**	Isaiah 42:1-12
Wed, Apr. 10	**God Is Praised Among the Nations**	Malachi 1:10-14
Thu, Apr. 11	**Christ Is All and in All**	Colossians 3:1-11
Fri, Apr. 12	**Nations Shall Seek the Lord**	Zechariah 8:18-23
Sat, Apr. 13	**All Shall See God's Salvation**	Luke 3:1-14
Sun, Apr. 14	**Jesus Helps a Righteous Gentile**	Luke 7:1-10

Mon, Apr. 15	**Jesus' Compassion for the Grieving**	Luke 7:11-18
Tue, Apr. 16	**Sing Praises to God's Name**	Psalm 92
Wed, Apr. 17	**Confession, Prayer, and Healing**	James 5:12-20
Thu, Apr. 18	**God Pardons Iniquity and Transgression**	Micah 7:7-20
Fri, Apr. 19	**God Is Good and Forgiving**	Psalm 86:1-7, 11-17
Sat, Apr. 20	**No Condemnation in Christ**	Romans 8:1-16
Sun, Apr. 21	**Jesus Forgives a Sinful Woman**	Luke 7:36-50
Mon, Apr. 22	**God Provides for a Gentile Woman**	1 Kings 17:8-16
Tue, Apr. 23	**God's Authority over Life and Death**	1 Kings 17:17-24
Wed, Apr. 24	**God Blesses Whomever God Wills**	Luke 4:24-30
Thu, Apr. 25	**Hear My Cry, O God**	Psalm 61
Fri, Apr. 26	**May God Grant Your Heart's Desire**	Psalm 20
Sat, Apr. 27	**God Gives Grace to the Humble**	James 4:1-10
Sun, Apr. 28	**A Woman of Great Faith**	Matthew 15:21-28
Mon, Apr. 29	**Vindicate Me, O Lord My God**	Psalm 35:1-7, 22-28
Tue, Apr. 30	**Blessed Are They Who Fear God**	Psalm 112
Wed, May 1	**Repent and Turn to God**	Acts 3:12-26
Thu, May 2	**God So Loved the World**	John 3:1-8, 13-17
Fri, May 3	**Lord, Lead Me in Your Righteousness**	Psalm 5
Sat, May 4	**Christ, Our Atoning Sacrifice**	1 John 1:1–2:2
Sun, May 5	**Atonement by Christ's Blood**	Romans 3:21-30
Mon, May 6	**God Is Generous to the Unworthy**	Matthew 20:1-16
Tue, May 7	**A Great and Blessed Nation**	Genesis 13:14-18
Wed, May 8	**A Promise of Countless Heirs**	Genesis 15:1-6
Thu, May 9	**Your Sins Are Forgiven**	1 John 2:12-17
Fri, May 10	**God's Abundant Forgiveness**	Psalm 32
Sat, May 11	**Trust God, Who Justified the Ungodly**	Romans 4:1-12
Sun, May 12	**Our Justification, Christ's Resurrection**	Romans 4:13-25

Chart Feature

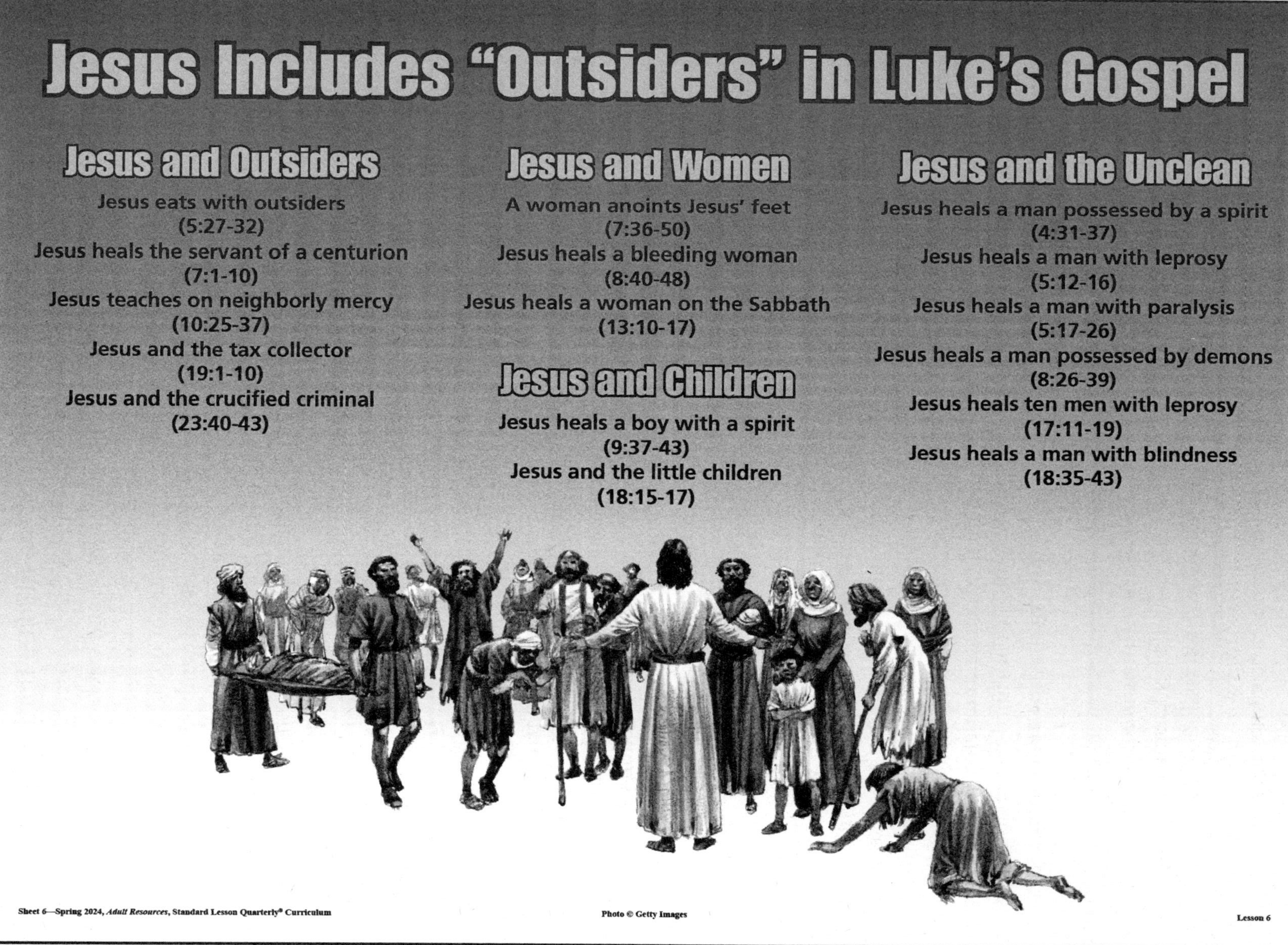

Jesus Includes “Outsiders” in Luke's Gospel
Jesus and Outsiders
Jesus eats with outsiders
(5:27-32)
Jesus heals the servant of a centurion
(7:1-10)
Jesus teaches on neighborly mercy
(10:25-37)
Jesus and the tax collector
(19:1-10)
Jesus and the crucified criminal
(23:40-43)
Jesus and Women
A woman anoints Jesus' feet
(7:36-50)
Jesus heals a bleeding woman
(8:40-48)
Jesus heals a woman on the Sabbath
(13:10-17)
Jesus and Children
Jesus heals a boy with a spirit
(9:37-43)
Jesus and the little children
(18:15-17)
Jesus and the Unclean
Jesus heals a man possessed by a spirit
(4:31-37)
Jesus heals a man with leprosy
(5:12-16)
Jesus heals a man with paralysis
(5:17-26)
Jesus heals a man possessed by demons
(8:26-39)
Jesus heals ten men with leprosy
(17:11-19)
Jesus heals a man with blindness
(18:35-43)
Sheet 6—Spring 2024, Adult Resources, Standard Lesson Quarterly® Curriculum
Photo © Getty Images
Lesson 6

"Discussion Leaders"?

Teacher Tips by Ronald L. Nickelson

Years ago, I overheard a conversation at a church that made me quite uncomfortable. A church leader was trying to recruit a teacher for an adult Bible class. When the leader offered the assignment to a particular individual, the man replied that he didn't feel qualified to be a teacher. However, he was willing to be a "discussion leader." I breathed a sigh of relief when the offer was gently declined.

I appreciated the man's honesty in recognizing his unqualified status. More than that, I appreciated the leader's decision to keep looking!

The Vital Difference(s)

Secular education theory recognizes some important differences between *teachers* and *discussion leaders*—the latter are usually called *facilitators.* A frequently seen summary of their functions is that a teacher is a "sage on the stage," while a facilitator is a "guide on the side."

Much research exists that compares and contrasts the two functions of teacher and facilitator. Although both roles are valued, those who analyze such things in secular contexts tend to conclude that *facilitators* usually produce better results. In the shaded box below are some of some typical assumptions or discoveries.

It is not our task here to explore whether or not such observations are valid in secular contexts. But we certainly should evaluate those conclusions to see where (if anywhere) those distinctions apply in Christian contexts of learning God's Word and putting that learning into practice.

The Biblical Distinction(s)

It's easy to discover what the Bible says about teachers and teaching, both positively and negatively. A quick way to do so is to search for those terms in an online or hard-copy concordance. The massive number of "hits" will leave no doubt about what God expects from teachers and their teaching. Some vital New Testament passages in that regard are Matthew 5:19; 28:19-20; Romans 12:6-7; 1 Corinthians 12:28-29; Ephesians 4:11; 1 Timothy 1:3-11; 2:12; 2 Timothy 2:2, 24; 4:3; Titus 1:10-14; James 3:1; and 2 Peter 2:1.

Regarding facilitators (discussion leaders), we may initially conclude that the Bible does not discuss that role since the terminology seems absent. But a bit of digging leads us to consider Jesus' parables. Jesus used parables because He wanted listeners to connect His teaching with their experiences regarding weeds, fishing, etc. Outside the parables, Jesus' interaction with Peter in Matthew 17:24-27 is also an example of Jesus' expertise as a facilitator.

We end up drawing this firm conclusion: *A facilitator or discussion leader must first and foremost be a teacher as a subject-matter expert.* To take on the role of facilitator while being unqualified as a teacher will surely result in the blind leading the blind (Luke 6:39). Class sessions are likely to end up being only "what it means to me" sharing. Helping your learners apply Scripture to life is vital, of course. But determining a given passage's meaning, as intended by the original writer, must be the basis for that application.

Teachers . . .

- are (or should be) subject-matter experts
- control the session
- prioritize content and concepts
- add new knowledge

Facilitators (Discussion Leaders) . . .

- are (or should be) learning-process experts
- coordinate the session
- prioritize experiences
- help connect new knowledge with experience

Sustaining Our Faith

Devotional Reading: 1 Corinthians 15:1-11
Background Scripture: Jude

Jude 17-25

**17 But, beloved, remember ye the words
which were spoken before of the apostles of our
Lord Jesus Christ;
18 How that they told you there should be
mockers in the last time, who should walk after
their own ungodly lusts.
19 These be they who separate themselves,
sensual, having not the Spirit.
20 But ye, beloved, building up yourselves
on your most holy faith, praying in the Holy
Ghost,
21 Keep yourselves in the love of God, looking
for the mercy of our Lord Jesus Christ unto
eternal life.
22 And of some have compassion, making
a difference:
23 And others save with fear, pulling them
out of the fire; hating even the garment spotted
by the flesh.
24 Now unto him that is able to keep you
from falling, and to present you faultless before
the presence of his glory with exceeding joy,
25 To the only wise God our Saviour, be
glory and majesty, dominion and power, both
now and ever. Amen.**

Key Text

But ye, beloved, building up yourselves on your most holy faith, praying in the Holy Ghost, keep yourselves in the love of God, looking for the mercy of our Lord Jesus Christ unto eternal life. **—Jude 20-21**

Examining

Our Faith

Unit I: Faithful vs. Faithless

Lessons 1–5

Lesson Aims

After participating in this lesson, each learner will be able to:

1. Identify the doxology in the text.
2. Distinguish between what God promises to do and what He expects us to do regarding personal holiness.
3. Create a plan to implement the imperatives of the Key Text.

Lesson Outline

Introduction

A. Anxious Times

B. Lesson Context

I. Remembrance (Jude 17-19)

A. Remembering the Apostolic Word (v. 17)

B. Revisiting the Warning (v. 18)

C. Recognizing False Teachers (v. 19)

In a Flash Flood

II. Perseverance (Jude 20-23)

A. Remain in God's Love (vv. 20-21)

B. Reflect God's Love (vv. 22-23)

Leading by Example

III. Praise God (Jude 24-25)

A. God's Work for Us (v. 24)

B. God's Glory (v. 25)

Conclusion

A. The Love of God and Loving Others

B. Prayer

C. Thought to Remember

Introduction

A. Anxious Times

We live in anxious times. Many believers live with doubt. Many often feel like people are mocking their faith from both inside and outside the church. Historic beliefs are under attack. The gospel itself is under attack. Skeptics deny the resurrection of Jesus from the dead and His ultimate return. Within the church, abuse and immorality are becoming more known. Some leaders have destroyed their congregations through their own ambition and pride. Social media and newspapers are filled with these kinds of stories. The church has lost its moral credibility and its authority to speak truth in the eyes of many people. While the church and its ministers at one time were ranked high in trustworthiness, that ranking has fallen over the past 30 years. These are perilous times for the Christian faith.

B. Lesson Context

Jude is a brief letter, and it reflects a perilous time similar to our circumstances. Some ambitious and prideful people had attached themselves to congregations, presented themselves as leaders, and practiced an immoral lifestyle. Jude calls them "ungodly" people who turn the "grace of our God into lasciviousness" (Jude 4). These intruders exploited their welcome by promoting immorality (v. 4). They mocked the judgment of God and behaved as if God would not hold them accountable for their actions and immoral ethics. They despised authority, spoke evil of others, and sought wealth in their greed (vv. 8, 11). Jude called them "spots in your feasts of charity" who had nothing true or valuable to offer; they were like clouds "without water" and fruitless trees (v. 12). They walked "after their own lusts," and though they influenced many, their words were filled with their own ambition (v. 16). This was a dangerous time for the churches, and Jude addresses the situation directly with both warning and hope.

Jude, the author of this letter, was the brother of James, and James was one of the elders and leaders of the church in Jerusalem (Acts 12:17; 15:13; 21:18; Galatians 1:19; 2:9). Since James was a brother of

Jesus, this means Jude was as well. Though both opposed Jesus during His ministry before His death, both became committed believers after the resurrection of Jesus (1 Corinthians 15:7; Jude 1).

What we know as the book of Jude was probably a sermon that circulated among several congregations as an open letter. Jude addressed a number of congregations at one time, and they were all endangered by ungodly intruders and leaders. Jude clearly stated his main interest. He encouraged believers to "contend for the faith" that had been delivered to them (Jude 3). He identified the troublemakers, warned that their destiny is the same as that of Sodom and Gomorrah (v. 7) and the devil (v. 9), and promised God would execute judgment against the "ungodly" for their "ungodly deeds" (v. 15).

But what are believers to do? How do they "contend for the faith" (Jude 3)? How do believers live out their faith in such perilous times? Jude ends his letter with a call to persevere in the faith. That call is our lesson text for today.

I. Remembrance
(Jude 17-19)

A. Remembering the Apostolic Word (v. 17)

17. But, beloved, remember ye the words which were spoken before of the apostles of our Lord Jesus Christ.

Remember! That is the main point (compare Jude 5). After describing the characteristics of these false leaders and the judgment that awaits them, Jude reminded his readers that this was not unexpected. *The apostles* warned about the rise of ungodly people who would disturb the church and seek to gain their own followers. For example, the apostle Paul warned the elders of the church at Ephesus that wolves would arise from among their own leadership (Acts 20:29). Consequently, the situation should not have surprised them. The apostles told them it was going to happen.

By reminding them of this apostolic warning, Jude highlighted the importance of the apostolic voice in the early church. The apostolic word, or teaching, both guides and warns the church. According to Acts 2:42, the disciples of Jesus devoted themselves to the teaching of the apostles. The church listens to the apostles of *our Lord Jesus Christ*, heeds their direction and warnings, and follows them as they follow Jesus. Their teaching, along with the prophets, is the church's foundation, with Jesus Christ as the cornerstone (Ephesians 2:20). Jesus sent the apostles with His authority, and the apostles spoke for Jesus.

In the middle of this perilous time, Jude not only reminds his readers of the apostolic warning but also reminds them who they are. They are *beloved*, and Jude called them as such three times (Jude 3, 17, 20). While we need reminders about the dangers of any situation, we also need reminders that we are loved by God and loved by our leaders. Jude, for example, was a leader who wrote forcefully against false teachers but compassionately for those whom those ungodly leaders endangered. Believers have been called by God and kept safe in Jesus Christ (v. 1). Despite the dire circumstances and uncertainties of the times, they are secure in Jesus and loved by God.

What Do You Think?

How do you encourage other believers to remember they are beloved by God?

Digging Deeper

How can those same practices help you remember that you are beloved?

B. Revisiting the Warning (v. 18)

18. How that they told you there should be mockers in the last time, who should walk after their own ungodly lusts.

What did the apostles say to the church? A time was coming and had already arrived when *mockers* and scoffers would arise within churches, and their only concern would be pursuing their own *ungodly* interests.

When Jude used the language of *the last time* or "last times," he was not referring to something in the distant future, though it includes that. Rather, he reminded his readers about this warning because it was already happening in their congregations. Often "last time" or "last days" (Acts 2:17; Hebrews 1:2; 2 Peter 3:3) refers to the last era of God's redemptive work in the world. This is the final era because after this comes the judgment of God and the salvation of God's people. It was important to hear the apostolic warning not only applying to some final moment in the world's future but also to Jude's readers and the whole history of the church. Mockers and scoffers have always been part of the story of the church, and the warning is for all believers throughout the life span of the church. This is a constant danger rather than a unique one.

What drives these false leaders? They mock God's judgment and scoff at any notion of personal accountability. They did not believe God's judgment applied to them, or perhaps that there was any coming judgment at all. Rather, they followed their own desires. They had their own agenda, and they were only interested in indulging their own cravings. Jude emphasized that their motivations were ungodly (see also Jude 4, 15). They were only interested in themselves, whether that greed or ambition was about wealth, power, or sex, among other possible lusts.

The apostles warned that people would come who had no interest in authentic faith. Rather, they would ridicule accountability before God and pursue their interests for their own gain.

What Do You Think?

When have you needed to resist a person who was trying to manipulate faith for their own selfish gains?

Digging Deeper

What steps do you take to guard against any impure motives in your own faith walk?

C. Recognizing False Teachers (v. 19)

19. These be they who separate themselves, sensual, having not the Spirit.

Jude described these ungodly people in three ways. They (1) are divisive, (2) are worldly, and (3) lack *the Spirit* of God. In essence, Jude identified this ungodly presence by their works or their effect on the congregation. They lacked the fruit of the Spirit. There was no evidence of the Spirit in their lives. They created divisions as they separated themselves and created their own followers. They lived by the seat of their pants. In other words, they lived by their natural urges and impulses rather than by the mind of Christ. Their interests were rooted in their sensuality and the works of the flesh. They were not led by the Spirit but by their *sensual* compulsions driven by their ungodly agenda.

What Do You Think?

What characteristics suggest that a person does not have the Spirit? Offer supporting verses for your answer.

Digging Deeper

What other verses caution you about declaring this or that person not to have the Spirit?

In a Flash Flood

Stuart's wipers were going full speed, but he could barely see the road. The drumming rain drowned out the radio's warning of flash flooding. Ahead, an SUV inched into the turbulent water running across the road. The car behind Stuart blew its horn. He pressed the gas pedal and inched into the torrent, the water rising around his tires. The car lurched sideways and lost contact with the road! Then the tread found pavement, and Stuart could proceed. By the time he made it home, his heart was pounding, and he was drenched, not from rain but from sweat. Later he learned that two cars had been washed away at that same treacherous spot, with disastrous results.

How often do we follow the example of those who scoff at danger? Scripture's warnings of judgment seem distant, unlikely to affect us. But one day, the consequences could sweep us away. Where in your life do you need to stop and turn around before it's too late? —A. W.

II. Perseverance
(Jude 20-23)

A. Remain in God's Love (vv. 20-21)

20-21. But ye, beloved, building up yourselves on your most holy faith, praying in the

Holy Ghost, keep yourselves in the love of God, looking for the mercy of our Lord Jesus Christ unto eternal life.

Jude contrasted his readers with these ungodly mockers. While the ungodly mock the faith, believers build their lives on the faith. While the ungodly lack the Spirit, believers pray in the Spirit. While the ungodly scoff at the judgment that accompanies the coming of the *Lord Jesus Christ*, believers joyfully anticipate the mercy they will receive when Jesus comes again. Jude addressed these believers as *beloved*, and this belovedness was rooted in God's love for them. It was not simply Jude's love for his readers but also their relationship with God as people who are beloved *of God*. God loves them.

In the Greek text, the main verb—and the only imperative or command—is *keep yourselves in the love of God* (Jude 21). This was a call to action. Jude thought believers ought to respond to perilous times by persevering in God's love. In other words, as dangers mounted and seemed to overwhelm, believers need to continually ground themselves in God's love. Jude called believers to pursue godly living by remembering that they were beloved.

But what does that look like? Jude gave his readers three cues: (1) by building on the *most holy faith*, (2) by *praying in the Holy Ghost*, and (3) by looking forward to *the mercy of* Jesus. These three cues were means of grace or spiritual practices that could sustain faith during perilous times Jude's readers endured.

First, they can build on the foundation of the faith. The faith for which the Christian community was to contend (Jude 3) is also the foundation for remaining in the love of God. The *faith* refers to the work of God in Jesus by the Spirit to redeem and save the world from its ungodly lusts and practices. It is the gospel of Jesus Christ. Believers build on an authentic foundation secured by the love of God, the grace of Jesus, and the communion of the Holy Spirit rather than one imagined by the mockers who stirred up trouble among the churches.

Second, they should pray in the Spirit. This includes two important points. On the one hand, Jude thought prayer was a necessary response to perilous times. Prayer calls upon God to act and deliver. On the other hand, prayer was not simply wishful thinking but addressing God in the Spirit. To pray in the Spirit is probably a rather broad idea that includes almost anything that could be said about prayer. The full meaning of prayer includes not only the work of the Spirit in hearts but also the function of the Spirit in communicating the prayers. We pray in the Spirit when we pray in accordance with God's agenda, pray out of a heart sanctified by the Spirit, and pray by the power of the Spirit who unites us with God's own heart (compare Romans 8:26; 1 Corinthians 14:15).

Third, they should trust in the mercy of God. The faithful looked forward to the day when the fullness of God's mercy will be poured out on believers to usher them into eternal life with God. The second coming of Christ, though it involves judgment for the ungodly, is mercy for believers who build their lives on the most holy faith and pray in the Spirit.

Importantly, these verses refer to the God who is Father, Son, and Spirit. Jude recognized the Triune God by naming the love of God, the mercy of Jesus Christ, and the communion of the Holy Spirit. Jude's language is similar to the final benediction of Paul's second letter to the Corinthians (2 Corinthians 13:14).

What Do You Think?

What do you do to keep yourself in God's love?

Digging Deeper

What encouragement do you find regarding the fruit of imperfect effort in this endeavor?

B. Reflect God's Love (vv. 22-23)

22-23. And of some have compassion, making a difference: and others save with fear, pulling them out of the fire; hating even the garment spotted by the flesh.

Jude invited his readers to remain in the love of God, and then Jude turned his attention to how his readers ought to love others with that love. Remaining in the love of God means pouring out that love on others.

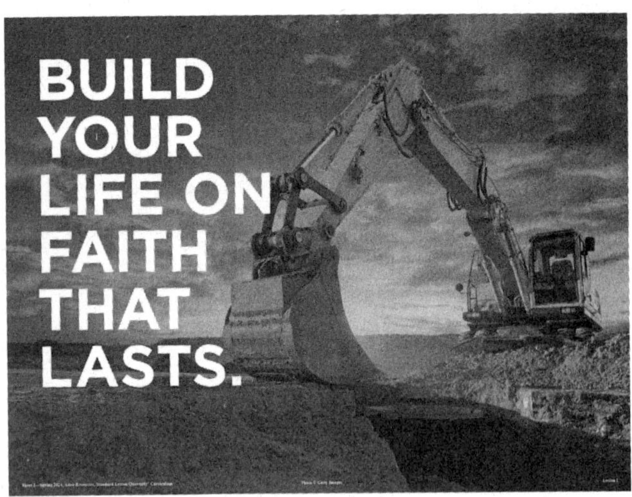
BUILD
YOUR
LIFE ON
FAITH
THAT
LASTS.

Visual for Lesson 1. *Discuss human effort and the Spirit's work that goes toward fulfilling this directive (based on Jude 20).*

We can imagine Jude's readers were angered by the disturbances within their churches. Indeed, ungodly mockers who divided a church for their own selfish gains deserved anger and exclusion, and they received Jude's condemnation. The damage these mockers left in their wake was probably devastating. It affected many people, and Jude does not forget them. Those who persevered in the love of God needed to love the people who had been damaged by these mockers. How does Jude want believers to love people in anxious times?

First, some were doubting due to the influence of the scoffers. The meaning of the Greek word behind the phrase *making a difference* is difficult to determine in this context. It may refer to a process of discernment, or it may refer to doubting or wavering. It seems the latter is more likely, but whichever is the case, Jude's main concern is the command to show mercy or *have compassion*. Jude commanded believers to have mercy on those who doubt or are evaluating. They should not be mocked or dismissed. On the contrary, just as the Lord Jesus will show mercy when He returns, so believers ought to show mercy and have compassion for those who are struggling with their faith.

How to Say It

apostolic	ap-uh-*stahl*-ick.
doxology	dawk-*saw*-leh-jee.
Triune	*Tri*-yoon.

The mercy Jesus gives to believers is the same mercy believers ought to show to doubters. Jude used the same word (*mercy* or *compassion*) in both verses 21-22.

Second, some needed rescuing from *the fire* stirred up by the mockers. Jude commanded believers to act in ways that would save others from the destructive mess created by the mockers. Rather than contribute to the fire by stoking it or neglecting those who are endangered by the fire, believers, according to Jude, ought to save them from the fire.

Third, some were so entangled in the ungodly patterns of the mockers that Jude commanded believers to act with mercy but also with fear. Again, the mercy of the Lord Jesus Christ is a quality Jude wanted shared with others. At the same time, it ought to be shared in a way that one does not become complicit in evil itself. The love of God means evil is hated. Even as mercy and compassion are given, Jude's language respects the danger of evil. The love of God rescues people from evil rather than joining them in their evil.

Jude commanded believers to keep themselves in the love of God, and Jude also commanded believers to show mercy to those caught up in the agenda of the mockers. The beloved are to love others because God has loved them.

Leading by Example

When the doctor diagnosed her as prediabetic, Jeannine wasn't convinced any lifestyle changes were possible for her. She was resigned to developing diabetes. But Jeannine's daughter Morgan knew not only what her mother needed to do but also how to convince her to do it. Morgan led by example. She invited her mother regularly for diabetic-friendly meals and shared the recipes. Morgan took Jeannine shopping to get her walking. Gradually, Jeannine started to make positive lifestyle changes.

A similar approach can help those who are resistant to the gospel. Christians can be merciful and understanding to those who doubt. We can walk alongside them and demonstrate the Christian life. Reaping a harvest takes time, care, and the work of the Spirit. If God is patient, we must be as well.

—A. W.

III. Praise God
(Jude 24-25)

A. God's Work for Us (v. 24)

24. Now unto him that is able to keep you from falling, and to present you faultless before the presence of his glory with exceeding joy.

Jude concluded his letter with a doxology, a praise to God. The doxology first identified what God is doing for us (Jude 24), and then it attributed to God what rightfully belongs to Him (v. 25).

While Jude stressed that believers are responsible for keeping themselves in the love of God, he also made it clear that it is God who empowers our perseverance in that love (Jude 1, 24). God keeps us, while believers are also accountable for their own faith as well. Ultimately, believers do not save themselves, nor do they generate their own assurance. Rather, God acts to keep us and causes us to stand in His *presence* without blemish. It is God's loving mercy through Jesus Christ in the power of the Spirit that redeems us and gives us a righteous and holy standing before the Triune God.

What Do You Think?

What practice could you begin or deepen to be more aware of God's helping you to stand faultless before Him?

Digging Deeper

How can this practice nurture the joy of being in God's presence?

B. God's Glory (v. 25)

25. To the only wise God our Saviour, be glory and majesty, dominion and power, both now and ever. Amen.

Because of God's gracious mercy, Jude praised God's eternal *glory*, *majesty*, *dominion*, and *power*. These characteristics or attributes describe God's relationship to the world and, consequently, God's own capacity both to keep us from falling and present us without blemish.

Since this doxology is offered to *God* through Jesus, it constitutes a prayer of praise. As Jude has already told us, believers pray in the Spirit. In effect, then, Jude offered a triune prayer. God is praised through the Son in the Spirit. That is the most holy faith. God poured out mercy through the Son by the gift of the Holy Spirit, and we joyfully return to God the Father our praise through the Son in the Spirit.

Conclusion

A. The Love of God and Loving Others

We live in perilous times, much like the church at the time when Jude was written. So we should recognize and identify the dangers. The church is called to exercise healthy discernment and heed the warnings of the apostles. We ignore them at our own peril.

At the same time, the church does not live in fear but in confidence. We root ourselves in God's love for us, and we pour that same love on those who have been damaged by these perilous times. We confidently live within the love of God as God's beloved, and we mercifully show that love to others in our community. Our response to this divine grace is deep joy and gratitude.

While we practice discernment and contend for the faith, we also show God's mercy to others as we minister to those who doubt, those ensnared in the fire, and those who have soiled their garments. Secured in the love of God by the foundation laid down by apostolic teaching, praying in the Spirit, and looking forward to the mercy of Christ's second coming, we help others and show them the love with which God has loved us.

B. Prayer

God, keep us secure in Your love and enable us to show mercy to others in need of Your love. In the name of Jesus. Amen.

C. Thought to Remember

Secure in God's love, we are able to love others.

Involvement Learning

Enhance your lesson with KJV Bible Student *(from your curriculum supplier) and the reproducible activity page (at www.standardlesson.com or in the back of the* KJV Standard Lesson Commentary Deluxe Edition*).*

Into the Lesson

Group learners in pairs and have them take turns sharing the best advice they ever received. Ask them to discuss whether or not they heeded that advice and what consequences resulted. Bring the class back together and ask for volunteers to share briefly the advice they received.

Then talk together about what factors help us decide whether we have received good advice or bad, and how we decide whether to heed that advice. What factors might cause us to disregard advice even when we believe it to be sound? What might convince us to take advice we think is questionable at best? Ask to what degree a positive or negative outcome might change one's mind about whether advice was good or not.

Alternative. Distribute copies of the "Beloved" exercise from the activity page, which you can download. Ask learners to pair up to finish as indicated. After about 10 minutes, bring the class back together to discuss their findings.

Lead into the lesson by saying, "It is good to be able to recognize when a good leader has our best interests at heart. Jude's words in our lesson today encourage us to remember what we know of God and to remain true to Him."

Into the Word

Ask a volunteer to read Jude 17-19. Have another read 2 Peter 3:3-7. Keeping these texts in mind, have pairs of learners find New Testament examples of mockers. *Option.* Get the class started with these examples: Acts 5:1-11; 1 Corinthians 5:1-5. The learners should explain who, if anyone, acted in keeping with Jude's advice before answering the following questions: 1–How were the mockers' actions opposed to God? 2–What harm did this do? Bring the class together to talk about the examples they identified.

Ask a volunteer to read Jude 20-23. Have the class identify the seven actions mentioned in these verses as you record them on the board. (Expected responses: build yourselves up in your most holy faith; pray in the Holy Ghost; keep yourselves in God's love; look for the mercy of Jesus; have compassion; save others from the fire; hate garments spotted by the flesh.)

Then divide the class into seven small groups and assign an action to each group. Give the groups a couple of minutes to discuss their action further and answer: 1– How does this action reflect the heart of God? 2–What New Testament examples show Jude's directives in action? 3–What were the results of acting in keeping with Jude's advice? After several minutes, invite groups to share their insights with the whole class. Take notes on the board as they discuss.

Ask a volunteer to read Jude 24-25. Talk about how these verses are an expression of praise. Have the same small groups from the previous activity review the points listed on the board considering these two verses and discuss: 1–How are believers able to resist living like the world? 2–How are believers able to live sustainably in faith and holiness? (Expected response: through the grace and mercy of Jesus.)

Into Life

Divide the class into pairs to discuss which of Jude's directives they feel most comfortable trying to carry out and which they feel least equipped to do. Have them talk about the examples brought up in previous exercises for any insights or encouragement as they seek to heed Jude's direction in the upcoming week. Encourage the pairs to conclude with a concrete plan to live out Jude 20-21. *Option.* Distribute the "Build Yourselves Up" exercise from the activity page to facilitate creating a plan for implementing Jude 20-21. Pray for the learners as you wrap up class time.

March 10
Lesson 2 (KJV)

Testing Our Faith

Devotional Reading: Psalm 139:13-18, 23-24
Background Scripture: 2 Corinthians 13:1-11

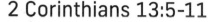

2 Corinthians 13:5-11

5 Examine yourselves, whether ye be in the
faith; prove your own selves. Know ye not your
own selves, how that Jesus Christ is in you,
except ye be reprobates?
6 But I trust that ye shall know that we are
not reprobates.
7 Now I pray to God that ye do no evil; not
that we should appear approved, but that ye
should do that which is honest, though we be
as reprobates.
8 For we can do nothing against the truth,
but for the truth.
9 For we are glad, when we are weak, and
ye are strong: and this also we wish, even your
perfection.
10 Therefore I write these things being
absent, lest being present I should use sharp-
ness, according to the power which the Lord
hath given me to edification, and not to
destruction.
11 Finally, brethren, farewell. Be perfect, be
of good comfort, be of one mind, live in peace;
and the God of love and peace shall be with
you.

Key Text

Examine yourselves, whether ye be in the faith; prove your own selves. **—2 Corinthians 13:5a**

Examining

Our Faith

Unit I: Faithful vs. Faithless

Lessons 1–5

Lesson Aims

After participating in this lesson, each learner will be able to:

1. Identify criteria for being "in the faith."
2. Explain how the imperatives of 2 Corinthians 13:11 are interrelated.
3. Create a test question that reflects Paul's challenge in the Key Text.

Lesson Outline

Introduction
- A. Self-Testing
- B. Lesson Context

I. Examination (2 Corinthians 13:5-6)
- A. Imperative (v. 5)
  - *Dangerous Spots*
- B. Result (v. 6)

II. Expectation (2 Corinthians 13:7-10)
- A. Paul's Request (v. 7)
- B. Paul's Values (vv. 8-9)
  - *The Value of Weakness*
- C. Paul's Purpose (v. 10)

III. Exhortation (2 Corinthians 13:11)
- A. Invitation to Community (v. 11a)
- B. Assurance of God's Presence (v. 11b)

Conclusion
- A. Taking Inventory
- B. Prayer
- C. Thought to Remember

Introduction

A. Self-Testing

Social media is filled with opportunities to test ourselves. We can test our knowledge of history, the Bible, government, and even our personalities and tastes. Self-testing is part of modern culture.

We test ourselves to gain insight into our capabilities. Such testing is sometimes quite valuable. At other times, however, we may focus on such tests narcissistically by interpreting personality defects as strengths. And some self-evaluations are designed to form or influence us as consumers.

Despite these potential problems, testing can often serve productive and valuable ends. We all take tests, need tests, and benefit from tests. This includes, as we will see, the benefits of Christians and churches testing themselves.

B. Lesson Context

Paul had established the church in Corinth during a personal visit to that city in about AD 52 (Acts 18:1-18). We are not certain how many letters he wrote to that church, but there were at least two—the ones we call *1 & 2 Corinthians.*

Paul wrote 2 Corinthians in preparation for a return visit (2 Corinthians 10:2; 12:20-21; 13:10). While the church in Corinth had, in general, responded favorably to Paul's previous letter (see chapter 7), he knew some problems remained (12:20-21).

At least part of the reason for those problems was that some doubted that Christ was speaking through Paul; they wanted proof (2 Corinthians 13:3). Was he a true apostle of the Lord Jesus, or was Paul a con artist? Some Corinthians thought that Paul's weaknesses—his weak presence and suffering-filled ministry—meant that the answer was *no.* But Paul proved earlier in the letter that such weakness and suffering proved the opposite (much of chapters 6, 10, and 11).

Weakness was how Jesus came into the world, and He suffered on the cross to display God's power (2 Corinthians 13:4). Paul's apostolic ministry had been (and was being) tested and verified through suffering rather than by avoiding it. The power of God seen in Paul's suffering was also seen in the life of Jesus. In like manner, through Paul's suffering and weakness, God's power gave life through Paul's ministry. Therefore, it wasn't Paul's credibility that was on the line. Instead, it was the credibility of the naysayers in the church at Corinth that was at issue.

I. Examination

(2 Corinthians 13:5-6)

A. Imperative (v. 5)

5a. Examine yourselves, whether ye be in the faith; prove your own selves.

This is the second time that Paul has challenged the believers in Corinth to *examine* and *prove* themselves (the first time was in 1 Corinthians 11:28). The challenge was for the readers to undergo a season of spiritual self-discernment. This self-examination required the readers to stop questioning Paul's credibility and instead look to their credibility as Christian believers.

We note how the word *faith* is used in this context. This word usually refers to one's personal belief (assent) in Christ (John 20:31; 2 Corinthians 4:13; etc.). Included in that understanding is the concept of trust. Therefore, the word *faith* in Scripture typically means belief plus trust (Psalms 78:22; 86:2; Romans 4:5; 2 Timothy 1:12). But that is not the sense here. Instead, the phrase *the faith* refers to the body of doctrine to be believed and practiced (compare Acts 6:7; Ephesians 4:13; Titus 1:13; Jude 3). Thus, Paul's challenge is not to examine oneself to determine how much faith (belief plus assent) his readers have in Jesus but rather to determine whether the readers accept his doctrinal teaching regarding the nature of the Christian faith. The stress on the importance of being *in the faith* is highlighted by the bookend phrase *examine yourselves* and *prove your own selves.*

How to Say It

apostolic	ap-uh-*stahl*-ick.
Corinth	*Kor*-inth.
Corinthians	Ko-*rin*-thee-unz (*th* as in *thin*).
epistle	ee-*pis*-ul.
Philippians	Fih-*lip*-ee-unz.
Thessalonians	*Thess*-uh-*lo*-nee-unz (*th* as in *thin*).

What Do You Think?

How can believers "examine" their beliefs and actions to ensure they are "in the faith"?

Digging Deeper

In what ways can an accountability partner or a small group help a believer complete this examination?

5b. Know ye not your own selves, how that Jesus Christ is in you, except ye be reprobates?

Testing, both self-imposed (Galatians 6:4) and imposed by others (James 1:12; 1 Peter 4:12-13; etc.), is necessary for evaluating one's status regarding whether *Jesus Christ is in* him or her. The test is not graded in terms of letter grades, such as an A– or a C+. Neither is it graded on a "curve." Instead, it's simply Pass/Fail. Either Jesus is in you, or He is not; there's no in-between. To fail in this regard is to *be reprobates.* As Paul uses the underlying Greek word elsewhere, it is translated "unjust" (1 Corinthians 6:1) and "unrighteous" (6:9).

While this pointed question challenged the church in Corinth, it seems intentionally focused on those who were dismissive of Paul and unconvinced of his authority. Thus, we detect a bit of "verbal judo" by Paul: those who find fault with him are revealing a fault of their own. They ought to test themselves rather than test Paul. They should be concerned about whether they had failed the test rather than whether Paul had failed it.

Paul's hope, of course, was that the readers would realize the seriousness of the issue. To fail the self-evaluation would be to reveal a life without Jesus.

Dangerous Spots

Recently I went to the doctor to have a strangely shaped mole examined. Peering closely at it, she said, "It's good you came in; this could be cancerous." She then proceeded to freeze it with liquid nitrogen (cryotherapy). Should the mole reassert itself, its removal by surgery would be needed.

The doctor went on to identify more than 20 spots on my skin that she decided to treat preventively. She explained, "Once I had a patient with a spot only a couple of millimeters across, really easy to miss. It was cancer, and if we hadn't caught it, he could have died within a year." Dangerous spots are easy to miss, especially if our attention is unduly distracted by spots that exist only in our imaginations. As the "problem people" in the church at Corinth were misdiagnosing Paul, he did them a great service by pointing out that (1) the spots they saw in him were imaginary and (2) they had very real spots of their own—spots they should have seen but could not due to their focus on him.

Jesus himself addressed this problem of wrong focus (Matthew 7:3-5). It's an issue of self-imposed spiritual blindness (23:16-34; etc.). We all tend to have one or more spiritual blind spots. Some such spots are more serious than others, but the goal is to eliminate them all (1 Timothy 6:13-15). Will you be proactive in searching for them and enlisting others to help? Or will you simply assume you don't have any? —A. W.

B. Result (v. 6)

6. But I trust that ye shall know that we are not reprobates.

Here, Paul does two things to the phrase "except ye be reprobates?" from the previous verse: (1) he changes the question to a statement, and (2) he changes "ye" to "we." These indicate that Paul was confident that his proposed self-examination on the part of the Corinthians would cause them to realize who had the presence of Christ (Paul himself and most members of the church at Corinth) and who did not (the minority of troublemakers in that church).

The key to reaching the correct conclusion was ensuring that the proper criteria were applied to the assessment. Paul sprinkles these criteria throughout this letter (examples: 2 Corinthians 10:2, 7, 12) and includes the general criteria noted in the next verse in our lesson.

II. Expectation

(2 Corinthians 13:7-10)

A. Paul's Request (v. 7)

7. Now I pray to God that ye do no evil; not that we should appear approved, but that ye should do that which is honest, though we be as reprobates.

As Paul prepared for his third visit to Corinth (2 Corinthians 13:1), he prayed *to God* regarding the state of the church there. The nature of the prayer, which we see in the verse at hand, is neither that of simple-minded wishful thinking nor one of mere psychological encouragement. Instead, Paul's prayer calls upon God to strengthen the readers against *evil*.

In this light, we keep in mind that a significant theme of this letter is a defense of Paul's ministry and apostolic authority. The two main pieces of evidence that validate that ministry and authority were God's power that shone through Paul's weakness (2 Corinthians 12:9; 13:4) and the moral transformation of the members of the church at Corinth (3:2-6). For those believers to *do no evil* would maintain their growth with regard to that transformation. Paul hastened to add that this was *not that we should appear approved* (that is, for the sake of his reputation), but *that ye should do that which is honest* (that is, for the reputation of his readers). Thus, Paul is principally concerned that his readers bear the fruit of their transformation and be less concerned with his credentials as an approved apostle.

B. Paul's Values (vv. 8-9)

8. For we can do nothing against the truth, but for the truth.

The epistle of 2 Corinthians has been called the least organized of Paul's writings. That's because he often seems to jump from topic to topic in a stream of consciousness. But here we detect an important and well-organized chain of thought: the confidence in 2 Corinthians 13:6 combined with the prayer in 13:7 leads to the certainty that gospel *truth* will prevail. Indeed, the importance of truth is a theme of this letter (see 4:2; 7:14; 11:10; 12:6). One truth was that Paul had not failed any test regarding the validity of his message and authority, though some Corinthians thought he had.

9a. For we are glad, when we are weak, and ye are strong.

Paul uses accusations from his critics (2 Corinthians 10:10) and transforms them into an asset.

Unlike the apostolic pretenders of 2 Corinthians 11:5 and 12:11-12, Paul had neither sought wealth nor had tried to deceive. He was not a manipulator but one who lived authentically and without guile (2 Corinthians 4:1-4). Paul conformed his ministry to the gospel, which included his willingness to suffer and place himself in a position of weakness for the sake of others. He was willing to suffer the hardships and persecutions of gospel ministry if it meant strengthening the faith of the Corinthians (6:3-10; 11:23-29). Paul willingly worked with his hands to be self-supporting so that the Corinthians would not be distracted by requests for financial support (11:7-9; 12:13-17; compare Acts 18:2-3). This was Paul's joy. He gladly lived in weakness so that the Corinthians might live in strength (2 Corinthians 12:19).

What Do You Think?

How can believers embrace their perceived weaknesses in order to encourage the spiritual growth of others?

Digging Deeper

How will you respond to the lie that believers must be "strong" in the eyes of the world?

9b. And this also we wish, even your perfection.

We may wonder what exactly is entailed in Paul's desire for the Corinthians' *perfection*. The Greek word being translated occurs in its noun form only here in the New Testament. But in its verb form, it appears five times in Paul's letters. In four of the five cases, it refers to movement from one state of being to a better one (1 Corinthians 1:10; 2 Corinthians 13:11; Galatians 6:1; 1 Thessalonians 3:10). In the remaining case, it refers to the opposite (Romans 9:22). Using the two passages from the Corinthian letters as touchstones, the idea is one of church unity that results from the repentance of rebellious believers.

Paul prayed that God would sufficiently equip them for life in the gospel. Paul prayed that God would move their hearts toward good and away from evil and fully equip them to participate in the ministry of reconciliation with Paul rather than

Visual for Lesson 2. *Ask students to silently contemplate this question before you pose the questions associated with verse 5a.*

oppose Paul. This is parallel to the kind of preparation Paul described in Ephesians 4:12 or what Scripture supplies to the people of God so that they are fully equipped for every good work (see 2 Timothy 3:17). The perfection described here is one where the people of God are sufficiently equipped to live out the gospel in their lives faithfully.

In essence, Paul prayed that the Corinthians would grow up in their faith. As they went about doing good and avoiding evil, God would equip them for greater participation in the ministry of the gospel as the church became ever more unified.

The Value of Weakness

Linda had been a missionary and church planter for 16 years when she and two female coworkers made their way to a remote tribe. That tribe was highly patriarchal, placing little importance on women. On the plus side, this meant female missionaries were not seen as a cultural threat in the way males would have been.

The arrival of these outsiders was a matter of significant curiosity to the tribe. When Linda began to tell stories of Jesus to the women and children, several men stood on the periphery to "supervise." They acted disinterested initially, but the men began listening intently as the days passed.

One day, a bold young warrior strode to the front and announced that men were in charge. Therefore, he would tell the story, not Linda. He repeated her most recent story, getting some details wrong. However, other men remembered the story better and corrected him. The whole tribe became interested and engaged.

Had this happened in her own culture, Linda may have been offended. But here, she saw this turn of events as a significant breakthrough: the gospel was being accepted and claimed by the "gatekeepers" of the tribal culture. In this situation, Linda had ministered in the role of one who was "weak" so that others might become "strong." When was the last time you did so as well? —A. W.

C. Paul's Purpose (v. 10)

10a. Therefore I write these things being absent, lest being present I should use sharpness.

The opening *therefore* introduces Paul's expanded explanation of why he wrote this letter rather than waiting to deliver the message in person. Paul wants the Corinthians to listen to the letter's sharp words so that he does not have to exercise his apostolic authority when he visits. The responsibility of those who occupy leadership positions in the church includes giving an account to God for the souls of those they served (see Hebrews 13:17). Sometimes, this responsibility requires reproving and rebuking those who oppose the truth (see 2 Timothy 4:2).

Spiritual health is essential, and some Corinthians had lost their sense of the gospel. Some continued their divisive practices, and others had not repented of their sexual immorality (2 Corinthians 12:20-21). If the church allowed such behavior to go unchallenged, the result would be a spreading spiritual cancer, as some would see such toleration as permission. Thus Paul's sharp tone.

What Do You Think?

How do believers discern whether or not a rebuke is necessary for the health of their congregation?

Digging Deeper

How do Scriptures like Matthew 18:15-17; Luke 17:3-4; Galatians 6:1; and 1 Timothy 5:20 inform believers' approach to carrying out a rebuke?

10b. According to the power which the Lord hath given me to edification, and not to destruction.

Even so, Paul's purpose was not to destroy the Corinthians but to edify them (compare 2 Corinthians 10:8). Again, he states the ultimate validation of his apostleship: *the power which the Lord hath given* him. God's goal was and is the making of disciples who grow in maturity (Matthew 28:19-20; 1 Corinthians 3:1-2; Hebrews 5:11–6:3). But when disobedience abounded, and the gospel was subverted, Paul intended to use his authority to tear down evil in the congregation. Yet, that was and is a last-ditch solution, and it was not the response that Paul desired. Therefore, he wrote this letter to prepare the Corinthians for his visit, call them to self-examination, and remind them of his desire for their growth in the gospel.

III. Exhortation

(2 Corinthians 13:11)

A. Invitation to Community (v. 11a)

11a. Finally, brethren, farewell. Be perfect, be of good comfort, be of one mind, live in peace.

Paul concluded by reaffirming his relationship with the Corinthian audience. They were his siblings (*brethren*) in Christ. He had not given up on them. On the contrary, he remained connected to them as part of the family of God. Paul loved the Corinthians not only as spiritual siblings but also as their spiritual father (1 Corinthians 4:15; 2 Corinthians 6:13; 12:14).

With such familial affection, Paul concluded this section with five brief and pointed challenges. The first of his challenges is found in the word translated *farewell.* The underlying Greek also occurs in its identical form in Philippians 3:1 and 4:4 (twice). There the translation is the imperative "rejoice," and that is the sense here.

The second challenge, to *be perfect,* translates the verb form of the noun translated "perfection" in 2 Corinthians 13:9, above. This command echoes Jesus' imperative to "Be ye therefore perfect, even as your Father which is in heaven is perfect" (Matthew 5:48), although a different word is translated there. We know, of course, that perfection in this life is unattainable since all have sinned (Romans 3:23). But that doesn't mean that the standard should be lowered!

The third command, *be of good comfort*, seems to be a condensed version of 2 Corinthians 1:4-6 (see also 2 Corinthians 2:7; 7:6-7). The fourth command, *be of one mind*, stresses the importance of church unity (also Philippians 2:2, 5; 4:2). This can speak to doctrinal unity, but also essential is a shared humility that lives worthy of the gospel. Such unity will achieve the fifth imperative: *live in peace* (see Mark 9:50; 1 Thessalonians 5:13).

What Do You Think?

How can believers eliminate hindrances that prevent life with "one mind" and "in peace" with other believers?

Digging Deeper

What Scriptures come to mind in this regard?

B. Assurance of God's Presence (v. 11b)

11b. And the God of love and peace shall be with you.

Paul writes of the God "of peace" several times in his letters (Romans 16:20; Philippians 4:9; 1 Thessalonians 5:23; 2 Thessalonians 3:16). But this is the only time he writes of *the God of love and peace.* The practice of the five imperatives would shape the Corinthian church along those two lines. God had not given up on the Corinthian church, nor had Paul. On the contrary, both were committed to the church.

Conclusion

A. Taking Inventory

Many congregations are in turmoil, and the times in which we live are perilous. Faith is under attack from within and from without. In such times it is important to take inventory and examine ourselves. The contents of Paul's prayer indicate the sort of life that passes the test. Avoiding evil is not enough in and of itself. Evil must be replaced with doing what is right. To avoid evil without replacing it with good is to leave one open to the situation described in Matthew 12:43-45. An unexamined faith, some have said, is not worth living. Paul calls us to submit to a process of discernment by which we try our hearts (compare Psalm 139:23-24). Are we seeking to do good? Are we seeking to avoid evil? Are we pursuing maturity in Christ? Are we seeking to be equipped to do good and participate in the ministry of reconciliation?

This process will be painful but will build us up, not destroy us. We pursue this self-examination with the confidence that we are loved by God and with the assurance that the gospel is true. God is for us rather than against us. We pursue love and peace because God is the God of love and peace. Some have called this goal "the ability to think God's thoughts after Him." God responds to the prayers that ask for the strength to do good, the courage to avoid evil, and the power to participate in the ministry of the gospel as fully equipped disciples of Jesus.

This necessary self-examination requires a familial bond, a desire for maturity, a striving toward perfection, mutual encouragement, a shared commitment to live out the meaning of the gospel, and peaceful practices. An examined faith can flourish in that kind of church. Without such a community, faith will suffer and perhaps die spiritually. The process begins by asking whether we know ourselves. Do we?

What Do You Think?

What aspect of spiritual self-examination seems the most difficult for you in your current season of life?

Digging Deeper

How will you remember that you are a beloved child of God as you take up the practice of spiritual self-examination?

B. Prayer

O God, we ask You for the courage to examine ourselves with unvarnished honesty so that we may discern Christ in us. In the name of Your Son, who gives resurrection life, we pray. Amen.

C. Thought to Remember

Testing yourself is not optional.

Involvement Learning

Enhance your lesson with KJV Bible Student *(from your curriculum supplier) and the reproducible activity page (at www.standardlesson.com or in the back of the* KJV Standard Lesson Commentary Deluxe Edition*).*

Into the Lesson

Create activities to test physical strength, focus, problem-solving abilities, and knowledge. Ensure that all activities are appropriate to the age and skills of the learners. (Examples: To test strength, place a weight, such as a whole bag of flour, on top of a seated volunteer's ankles and have them raise their feet until their legs are parallel to the floor. To test agility, put a 6-foot line of masking tape on the floor and have a volunteer walk down the line without deviation. To test problem-solving skills, give a volunteer a riddle or brain teaser. To test knowledge, ask volunteers to answer a trivia question.)

After every volunteer has the chance to test, ask the following question for whole-class discussion: "How does it feel testing your different abilities?

Lead into the Bible study by saying, "It is usually fun for us to test our abilities, but not as fun when we realize personal limits or weaknesses. In today's lesson, identify what is being tested, how it is being tested, and why that test is necessary."

Into the Word

Ask a volunteer to read aloud 2 Corinthians 13:5-6. Divide the class into four small groups: **Matthew 7:18-20 Group**, **John 13:35 Group**, **John 14:15 Group**, and **Romans 10:9 Group**. Instruct groups to read their Scripture passage and discuss how it informs self-examination regarding whether a person is "in the faith" (2 Corinthians 13:5). After three minutes, ask a volunteer from each group to share their group's insights.

Alternative. Distribute copies of the "Fruit of the Spirit Test" exercise from the activity page, which you can download. Have learners complete it individually in a minute or less before discussing conclusions in pairs.

Ask a volunteer to read aloud 2 Corinthians 13:7-9. Distribute a note card and pencil to each learner. Invite learners to write down the names of two or three influential spiritual mentors. Prompt learners to consider family members, church members, and community members of all ages. After one minute, have learners explain to their partner why that mentor has been influential. Have pairs pray for the growth and encouragement of their mentors.

Option. Distribute copies of the "My Prayer for You" activity from the activity page. Have learners complete it individually in one minute or less.

Ask a volunteer to read aloud 2 Corinthians 13:10-11. Divide the class into four small groups: **Perfect Wholeness Group**, **Comforting Encouragement Group**, **One Mind Group**, and **Living Peaceably Group**. Have the groups answer the following questions in small-group discussion: 1–How does 2 Corinthians 13:10-11 address the concept or attitude described in your group's name? 2–How does this concept or attitude build others up? 3–What do you need to do to develop this attitude?

Reconvene the class and have a volunteer from each group share their answers.

Into Life

Write this question on the board:

How did my actions and attitudes during the last week demonstrate my faith in Christ?

Ask the class how this question can help guide them throughout the week as they discover Christ in their lives and grow in faith.

Distribute three sheets of blank letter-size printer paper to each learner. Ask them to stack the sheets and fold them to make a pamphlet. Invite learners to write the question on the board at the top of the booklet's first page. On the bottom of that page, ask them to write down the lesson's Key Text: 2 Corinthians 13:5a. Challenge participants to set aside a daily time to examine their faith. Encourage learners to create a "test question" like the one above that reflects Paul's challenge in the Key Text. Before the next lesson, invite volunteers to share what they learned from this daily examination.

Defending Our Faith

Devotional Reading: 2 Timothy 4:1-8
Background Scripture: 1 Peter 3:8-17

1 Peter 3:8-17

8 Finally, be ye all of one mind, having compassion one of another, love as brethren, be pitiful, be courteous:

9 Not rendering evil for evil, or railing for railing: but contrariwise blessing; knowing that ye are thereunto called, that ye should inherit a blessing.

10 For he that will love life, and see good days, let him refrain his tongue from evil, and his lips that they speak no guile:

11 Let him eschew evil, and do good; let him seek peace, and ensue it.

12 For the eyes of the Lord are over the righteous, and his ears are open unto their prayers: but the face of the Lord is against them that do evil.

13 And who is he that will harm you, if ye be followers of that which is good?

14 But and if ye suffer for righteousness' sake, happy are ye: and be not afraid of their terror, neither be troubled;

15 But sanctify the Lord God in your hearts: and be ready always to give an answer to every man that asketh you a reason of the hope that is in you with meekness and fear:

16 Having a good conscience; that, whereas they speak evil of you, as of evildoers, they may be ashamed that falsely accuse your good conversation in Christ.

17 For it is better, if the will of God be so, that ye suffer for well doing, than for evil doing.

Key Text

For it is better, if the will of God be so, that ye suffer for well doing, than for evil doing. **—1 Peter 3:17**

Examining

Our Faith

Unit I: Faithful vs. Faithless

Lessons 1–5

Lesson Aims

After participating in this lesson, each learner will be able to:

1. Identify the Old Testament text quoted.
2. Compare and contrast the things he or she "must do" with what he or she "must not do."
3. State one "must do" and one "must not do" for personal focus in the week ahead.

Lesson Outline

Introduction

- A. Man's Search for Meaning?
- B. Lesson Context: Peter, the Apostle
- C. Lesson Context: Peter, the First Letter

I. Right Behavior (1 Peter 3:8-12)

- A. Be a Blessing (vv. 8-9)
  - *Which Route?*
- B. Pursue Peace (vv. 10-12)

II. Confident Believers (1 Peter 3:13-17)

- A. Do Not Fear (vv. 13-14)
- B. Give an Answer (vv. 15-17)
  - *Faith to the End*

Conclusion

- A. Finding Meaning
- B. Prayer
- C. Thought to Remember

Introduction

A. Man's Search for Meaning?

Why does God allow bad things to happen to good people? Shouldn't we "get even" with those who do us wrong? Anyone with life experience will inevitably ask these questions. We want to make sense of our suffering and find a way to deal with the resulting despair, if not eliminate it entirely.

Viktor E. Frankl's 1946 book *Man's Search for Meaning* details his attempts to find meaning and purpose in his experiences as a prisoner in a Nazi concentration camp. By the end of the book, Frankl acknowledges human evil and the capacity of suffering humans to find meaning in their experiences.

Many individuals described in Scripture suffered persecution. The various ways they reacted are timeless in their ability to instruct all future generations.

B. Lesson Context: Peter, the Apostle

Peter was one of Jesus' original 12 disciples (also known as "apostles"; Luke 6:13). Peter (also called Simon or Cephas; John 1:42) was known for being impulsive (examples: Matthew 14:22-28; 16:22; 26:35; Mark 9:5-6; John 18:10). In spite of that fact—or perhaps because of it—he seems to have held a special place among the Twelve. He is named first in all four listings of those Twelve (Matthew 10:2-4; Mark 3:16-19; Luke 6:14-16; Acts 1:13). Jesus conferred on him "the keys of the kingdom of heaven" (Matthew 16:19). After Jesus' ascension, Peter was a leader of the first-century church (see Acts 1:15-17; 2:14-40; 15:6-29). His ministry focused mainly on Jews (see Galatians 2:8). In that position, he experienced persecution (example: Acts 12:1-4), which informed his outlook regarding suffering and trials.

C. Lesson Context: Peter, the First Letter

First Peter 5:13 reveals the likely location of where the letter was written: the city of Rome. That verse says "Babylon," not "Rome," but there is widespread agreement that *Babylon* is a code word for *Rome.* Historic, literal Babylon had been the great oppressor of the Jews in the sixth century BC (2 Kings 24–25). This served as Peter's analogy to

Rome of the first century AD (compare Revelation 14:8; 16:19; 17:5; etc.), particularly under the evil Emperor Nero (reigned AD 54–68).

The letter's positive attitude toward government (1 Peter 2:13-17) may indicate that Nero's state-sponsored persecution had not yet reached full intensity (but see 4:12). In any case, Peter was not shy about confronting ruling authorities when necessary (Acts 4:19; 5:29). As one writer notes, 1 Peter is "one of the earliest Christian documents reflecting on the problem of the relation of the Christian to the state."

The letter of 1 Peter is one of two existing letters by that apostle (1 Peter 1:1; 2 Peter 1:1). The recipients of both letters were the various churches found in an area of northeastern Asia Minor, located in modern-day Turkey (1 Peter 1:1; 2 Peter 3:1). The first letter was likely intended to be circulated among the regions, perhaps by way of Silvanus, an assistant to Peter (1 Peter 5:12). Were the intended recipients primarily of Jewish background, primarily of Gentile background, or a roughly even split? The letter's dozen or so quotations from the Old Testament could indicate that the intended audience was primarily of Jewish background. A stronger case can be made, however, for seeing the audience as primarily Gentile in background as Peter addressed their former lives of "ignorance" (1 Peter 1:14; compare Paul's use of this same word in Ephesians 4:17-19 to refer to Gentiles).

The occasion for Peter's letter was primarily a response to the suffering of believers, particularly since more was yet to come (see 1 Peter 1:6-7; etc.). Peter could address whatever suffering his audience had or would experience because he had been "a witness of sufferings of Christ" (5:1); Peter himself had suffered for that name (Acts 12).

I. Right Behavior

(1 Peter 3:8-12)

A. Be a Blessing (vv. 8-9)

8a. Finally, be ye all of one mind.

Verse 8 as a whole is only nine words in the original language. Five of those nine words are adjectives that describe behavior fitting for believers facing a hostile world.

The first adjective, translated as *one mind*, describes the desired unity of believers. Unity is a gift from God (Romans 15:5-6). The frequency of New Testament references to unity speaks to its importance (John 10:16; 17:11, 21-22; 1 Corinthians 1:10-12; 2 Corinthians 13:11; Ephesians 4:3, 13; Philippians 2:1-4; 4:2).

What Do You Think?

Why might Christians not experience God's gift of unity?

Digging Deeper

What scriptural evidence gives you confidence in unity as a gift, even if believers seem divided?

8b. Having compassion one of another.

This is the translation of the second of the five adjectives. Were we to take the individual letters of the underlying Greek word and flip them to their sound-alike letters in the English alphabet, we would hear the word *sympathy*. The word appears in its verb form in Hebrews 4:15; 10:34.

8c. Love as brethren.

Repeating the procedure from verse 8b, converting the individual letters of the underlying Greek word to their sound-alike letters in English results in hearing the word *Philadelphia*—the city of brotherly *love*. Believers are described as part of God's household or family (Matthew 12:50; John 1:12; Galatians 6:10; Ephesians 2:19; 1 John 3:1-2). Therefore, the third adjective describes the love that family members are to have for one another.

8d. Be pitiful, be courteous.

This verse's fourth and fifth adjectives elaborate on how believers can live with love and compassion. The word translated *be pitiful* is also translated "tenderhearted" in Ephesians 4:32, and that is the sense here. To have heartfelt concern toward others is a crucial part of the life of a believer

How to Say It

anthropomorphism	an-thruh-pu-*more*-fih-zm.
Polycarp	Paw-lih-*karp*.
Silvanus	Sil-*vay*-nus.
Smyrna	*Smur*-nuh.

(compare Colossians 3:12). Its presence reflects a life transformed by God's love (see 1 John 3:17).

To *be courteous* is probably an umbrella term that includes deference, kindness, and thinking of others more highly than oneself (compare Romans 12:16; Philippians 2; 1 Peter 5:5).

9a. Not rendering evil for evil, or railing for railing.

The command regarding *not rendering evil for evil* can be found in several other passages (examples: Proverbs 20:22; 24:29; Matthew 5:39, 44; Romans 12:17, 19; 1 Thessalonians 5:15). An aspect of evil treatment the original readers had suffered or were suffering was *railing.* The idea is that of slander, reproach, or insult. Jesus himself had faced mocking and insults leading up to and during His crucifixion (Matthew 27:27-31; Mark 15:29-32; Luke 22:63-65). However, He did not respond to His abusers in the manner in which He was treated (see 1 Peter 2:23).

What Do You Think?

In which situations is it most difficult not to respond to verbal assaults?

Digging Deeper

In those situations, how can you lean on the Holy Spirit to guide your responses?

9b. But contrariwise blessing; knowing that ye are thereunto called, that ye should inherit a blessing.

It's not sufficient merely to refrain from rendering evil for evil. Rather, potential evil reactions are to be replaced with actual holy reactions (Matthew 5:44). This should not be confused with a salvation based on works, for Peter has already established salvation as God's work (1 Peter 1:3, 23). As a result of our salvation, we are to be conduits for God's blessing in the world.

Which Route?

He was a new Bible college professor. He knew his teaching skills needed much improvement, and negative student feedback wounded him deeply. In one feedback evaluation, a student said he should find a different line of work.

An especially painful incident occurred one day during the college's chapel service. A student had organized a skit in which the actors mocked a clueless professor who was obviously modeled after this man. After chapel, students watched as he went up to the stage to speak to the student who had instigated the mockery. Smiling, he shook the student's hand firmly and pulled him into a side-hug. Looking the student in the eyes, the professor said, "You're a brilliant actor, Jim. God's given you a great talent. I'm glad you're my student."

Jim managed to stammer a "thanks" and went back to moving stage props. Although the skit had been mortifying, the man was confident that he had chosen the route of Jesus—the route of love, compassion, and blessing. Had you been that professor, would you have done the same? —A. W.

B. Pursue Peace (vv. 10-12)

10. For he that will love life, and see good days, let him refrain his tongue from evil, and his lips that they speak no guile.

This verse begins with a quote from Psalm 34:12-16, supporting Peter's point regarding the right kind of behavior amid trials and difficulty. According to this psalm's superscription, David wrote this psalm during a time of personal suffering and trials, as recorded in 1 Samuel 21:10-15. Therefore, it was an appropriate psalm to cite to an audience of believers who themselves were undergoing trials (see Lesson Context: Peter, the First Letter). With this quote, Peter switches back to the negative, what-not-to-do imperatives but with greater specificity: *evil* as it comes from one's *tongue* (compare James 3:1-10).

The feature of Hebrew poetry known as *parallelism* is quite evident here. Note that the words *tongue* and *lips* are synonyms in the sense of being instruments of speech. The *evil* and *guile* they can produce are also parallel in meaning. The parallelism continues in the next verse.

11a. Let him eschew evil, and do good.

Perhaps you recall from previous lessons that when Hebrew parallelism is present, then only one idea is in view, not two. Thus to *eschew evil, and do good* are to be seen as a single action. The way to avoid evil is to replace those impulses with doing good as one action. To avoid evil without replacing it with doing good introduces the danger noted in Luke 11:24-26.

11b. Let him seek peace, and ensue it.

More Hebrew parallelism presents itself in this continuing quote from Psalm 34:14: to *seek peace* is the same thing as to *ensue it* (compare Matthew 5:9). God's people have peace with Him (Romans 5:1), and we are expected to seek peace in relationships with others (14:19). This is not peace "at any cost," but is peace "as much as lieth in you" (12:18). We don't yield or agree to unholy viewpoints merely to keep the peace (Matthew 10:34-36; Luke 12:51-53). God is indeed a "God of peace" (Romans 15:33; 16:20), but He also wages war (Revelation 2:16; 19:19; etc.).

12. For the eyes of the Lord are over the righteous, and his ears are open unto their prayers: but the face of the Lord is against them that do evil.

This verse features a literary tool called *anthropomorphism*, which is seeing God in terms of human characteristics and behavior. "God is a Spirit" (John 4:24) and, therefore, does not have a physical body. However, Peter describes the Lord figuratively as having *eyes*, *ears*, and a *face*. Peter does this to help his audience better understand the Lord's character. This technique is nothing new, being used dozens of times in both Old and New Testaments (examples: Genesis 6:8; Exodus 33:10, 20, 23; Amos 9:8; James 5:4).

II. Confident Believers

(1 Peter 3:13-17)

A. Do Not Fear (vv. 13-14)

13. And who is he that will harm you, if ye be followers of that which is good?

Another literary tool presents itself: that of the rhetorical question. Such questions are not intended to elicit an answer because the answer is obvious. The rhetorical question here contrasts an ideal situation with what was likely already being experienced by Peter's audience, per the next verse, below.

14a. But and if ye suffer for righteousness' sake, happy are ye.

While Peter hoped to see good behavior receive proper recognition (see 1 Peter 2:13-14), this would not always be the case. Oppression is not inevitable for believers, but it is a possibility that all believers must prepare themselves to face—and not be surprised when it does (4:12; 1 John 3:13).

The underlying Greek word for *happy* is elsewhere translated as "blessed" (Matthew 5:3-11; James 1:12; etc.). This clarifies that Peter was not suggesting those who suffer experience a masochistic enjoyment of their own pain. Blessing comes when people hear God's word and obey His commands (Luke 11:28). The ultimate blessing comes when a person receives forgiveness for sin through faith in Christ Jesus (see Romans 4:4-8).

What Do You Think?

What blessing have you experienced during or following suffering for righteousness' sake?

Digging Deeper

How can you communicate the hope of blessing while not ignoring the pain another is currently experiencing?

14b. And be not afraid of their terror, neither be troubled.

This half-verse alludes to Isaiah 8:12. That section of the book where it is located details a conflict between the southern kingdom of Judah and the northern kingdom of Israel. When Ahaz, king of Judah, was faced with the destruction of his kingdom, the Lord promised that Judah would be protected (Isaiah 7:3-9). Even though Ahaz and his people faced destruction, they were commanded not to be afraid. They were to fear the Lord rather than earthly opponents (8:12-15).

B. Give an Answer (vv. 15-17)

15a. But sanctify the Lord God in your hearts.

Again, the challenge was (and is) to replace what is not to be done with what should be done instead. To *sanctify* means to designate someone or something being set apart as holy (John 10:36). The underlying Greek word is also translated as "hallowed" in verses proclaiming the holiness of

God's name (Matthew 6:9; Luke 11:2). Given the imperative tone of the verb *sanctify* as used here, we may wonder how we mere humans can possibly *sanctify the Lord God* more than He already is sanctified! Indeed, this verb is used in its imperative tone only five times in the New Testament: here and in Matthew 6:9; Luke 11:12; John 17:17; Revelation 22:11.

The key to understanding all this is context. Words take on definite meanings only within the contexts used. Take, for instance, the word *fine.* By itself, it has no fewer than seven potential meanings! Which of the seven is intended is discovered only in the context of that word's use in a sentence and paragraph. The context of the imperative in the verse before us is found in these three words: *in your hearts.* Humans certainly do not sanctify God by literally making Him holier than He already is! What we are to change, rather, is how we view Him.

15b. And be ready always to give an answer to every man that asketh you a reason of the hope that is in you.

Colossians 4:6 says much the same thing as this verse. "Readiness" in a general New Testament sense has two aspects: we are to be ready to do good (Titus 3:1) even as we remain ready for the Son's return (Matthew 24:44; Luke 12:40). We err when we focus on either of those at the expense of the other. One error is reflected in the old description of someone who was "so heavenly minded that he was no earthly good." The other error lets a Christian's responsibility to be a change agent for social justice eclipse the need to evangelize for the life to come in eternity.

There are various areas in which Christians are to be ready. Peter specifies one of these: one's readiness *to give an answer to every man that asketh you a reason of the hope that is in you.* Notice that this isn't addressing what preachers and Bible teachers are to do on Sunday morning to people who are already saved by the blood! Rather, it applies to all Christians as they (we) interact with unbelievers in everyday life.

Notice also that Peter's imperative isn't dealing with a Christian's initiative in bringing up the subject of salvation in Jesus. Rather, the imperative here deals with how to react when an unbeliever asks about our hope. But before the unbeliever asks about our hope, he or she needs to see that hope reflected in how we talk and behave differently from the ways the world does (1 Peter 4:3-4).

15c. With meekness and fear.

Any response that believers provide will be as effective only as the attitude with which it is given. In that light, the phrase *with meekness and fear* speaks to a low-key response. Such a demeanor is to characterize followers of Jesus (see Matthew 5:5; Galatians 5:22-23; Ephesians 4:2; Colossians 3:12).

What Do You Think?

How do you remain ready to testify about the hope you have?

Digging Deeper

How would someone hearing you speak about your hope describe your attitude?

16. Having a good conscience; that, whereas they speak evil of you, as of evildoers, they may be ashamed that falsely accuse your good conversation in Christ.

The New Testament has much to say about the importance of one's *conscience* as it uses that word about 30 times. The conscience can be a marvelous guide to proper thought and behavior if it is properly informed in doing so (Acts 23:1; 24:16; Romans 9:1; etc.). When functioning as God intended, it is a moral alarm system (Romans 2:15). But one's conscience can be overridden by evil desires (Ephesians 4:19; 1 Timothy 4:2).

The word *conversation* requires a bit of attention because it does not mean today what it did when the *King James Version* was published in 1611. Today, we use that word in a narrow sense of people engaging in verbal communication. But in the *KJV* it refers more broadly to the way one lives, one's lifestyle (compare Ephesians 4:22).

17. For it is better, if the will of God be so, that ye suffer for well doing, than for evil doing.

Proper conduct (*well doing*) in all situations is an important theme in this letter (see 1 Peter 2:15, 20; 4:19). When believers *suffer* for such conduct, the result is a powerful witness for unbelievers.

The ultimate example of suffering in this regard is Christ (see 3:18, not today's lesson text).

This verse also reveals another aspect of believers' suffering: *the will of God*. We should approach this topic with much caution because *the will of God* in some contexts means that He *causes* something to happen, but in other contexts, it means that He *permits* it to happen. God exercises His sovereign control by permitting what He does not cause. Some relevant passages to help understand the difference are Job 1:12; 2:6; Lamentations 3:32-33; Acts 14:16; 16:7; 1 Corinthians 16:7; Hebrews 6:3; 12:4-11; James 1:13-15; 4:15.

In any case, God is able to bring good out of suffering—indeed, that is His intent (Romans 8:28). God does not enjoy seeing people suffer, but He does allow it (example: Exodus 3:7-9) at times. A believer's suffering leads to faithful endurance (Romans 5:3-4; James 1:3) and a deeper relationship with Christ (Philippians 3:8-10).

Faith to the End

According to church history, Polycarp was a disciple of the Apostle John. Polycarp became the leader of the church of Smyrna (compare Revelation 2:8-11). At age 86, he was put to death by the Roman government for refusing to pray to the emperor. Given the chance to save his own life by recanting his faith, Polycarp said, "86 years have I have served Him, and He has done me no wrong. How can I blaspheme my King and my Savior?" Polycarp was burned at the stake in AD 155.

Polycarp didn't do anything to deserve this death. And in facing it, he set apart Christ as his Lord to the very end. He died with a clear conscience. If those who took his life were not ashamed of their slander in this life, they will be at the final judgment. In your last days, will you have so clear a testimony of faithfulness to Christ? —A. W.

Conclusion

A. Finding Meaning

Few of us will experience the level of suffering endured by the martyrs of Christian history. However, that does not make Peter's directives any less applicable—quite the opposite! When faced with

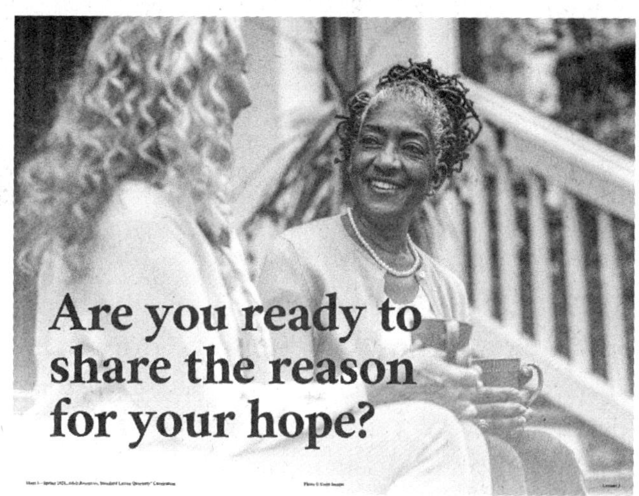

Visual for Lesson 3. *Allow learners to ponder this question before moving to those associated with verse 15c.*

suffering, we may search for meaning in that experience. The question asked relentlessly is, *Why?*

That question is natural and understandable. But it must also be temporary because ultimately the *Why?* needs to change to *What's next?* This is a way that our response to suffering can also serve as a way to point people to a life of faith in Jesus. God wants the best for people. When such suffering occurs, believers should remember to be unified in demonstrating trust in God.

What Do You Think?

What is your main takeaway from this lesson?

Digging Deeper

What will do you this week in response to that takeaway?

B. Prayer

Heavenly Father, we thank You for being with us in all situations. Help us be unified with other believers. Show us how we can be attentive to the working of Your Spirit. Fill us with peace and humility in all the trials that we might face. We trust that You will work through us to complete Your will in the world. In the name of Jesus. Amen.

C. Thought to Remember

Let suffering strengthen your faith.

Involvement Learning

Enhance your lesson with KJV Bible Student *(from your curriculum supplier) and the reproducible activity page (at www.standardlesson.com or in the back of the* KJV Standard Lesson Commentary Deluxe Edition*).*

Into the Lesson

Divide participants into three small groups: **Beach Group**, **Crowded Subway Group**, and **Movie Theater Group**. Based on their assigned locations, instruct groups to write two lists of appropriate behaviors and discouraged behaviors. Challenge them to include at least three do's and three don'ts.

After several minutes, ask the groups to write some guidelines for appropriate behavior in their setting, based on the behaviors they have already discussed. After a few more minutes, have the small groups share their rules with the whole group. Discuss what they discovered about rules and expectations.

Lead into the Bible study by saying, "Whether we realize it or not, everything we do is governed by rules or expectations. As we study the passage of Scripture today, consider what rules and expectations God has for His children."

Into the Word

Have participants return to their previous groups. Assign each group one of the following texts: Matthew 5:43-48; John 13:12-17; and John 17:20-26. Have groups compare their text with 1 Peter 3:8-9 and answer these questions:

1. What is the common theme between the two passages?
2. What did Jesus do in His ministry that shows this theme in action?
3. What "must do" and "must not do" actions did you find in the passages?

Allow time for small group discussion, then ask groups to share their insights with the whole class. Based on the group discussion, create a list of *Must Do* items on the board as well as a second list of *Must Not Do* items.

Alternative. Distribute copies of the "To Do and Not to Do" exercise from the activity page, which you can download. Have learners work in pairs to complete as indicated before coming together as a whole class to discuss.

Ask a volunteer to read 1 Peter 3:10-12. As a class, discuss what these verses reveal about why we ought to follow the commands of verses 8-9. Ask volunteers to read Psalm 34 out loud. Then assign the previous three small groups these sections: Psalm 34:1-7; 34:8-14; 34:15-22. Have each group make a list of all the reasons why believers should strive to live godly lives, as indicated in their verses and 1 Peter 3:10-12. After bringing the three groups back together, create a third list titled *Why* on the board. Have the groups provide answers to fill in this new list.

Ask a volunteer to read 1 Peter 3:13-17. Have participants pair up. Ask the pairs to share between them examples of when they have suffered in the past, and how God turned that suffering into a blessing.

Into Life

Review the lists written on the board earlier in the lesson. Challenge participants to choose one "must do" and one "must not do" from the verses, which they will put into practice in the week ahead. Distribute an index card and pencil to each person. Have participants write their chosen "must do" and "must not do" on the card. Invite participants to refer to their cards throughout the week. Ask participants to bring their cards and an assessment of their progress to share at the beginning of the next lesson. *Option.* If you used the alternative above, allow learners to work from their activity page.

Alternative. Distribute copies of the "With Meekness and Fear" exercise from the activity page. Allow learners one minute to complete as indicated before pairing up to give their answers.

Pray with learners before dismissing class.

March 24
Lesson 4 (KJV)

Living in Faith

Devotional Reading: Deuteronomy 28:1-14
Background Scripture: Acts 6

Acts 6:7-15

7 And the word of God increased; and the
number of the disciples multiplied in Jerusalem greatly; and a great company of the priests
were obedient to the faith.
8 And Stephen, full of faith and power, did
great wonders and miracles among the people.
9 Then there arose certain of the synagogue,
which is called the synagogue of the Libertines,
and Cyrenians, and Alexandrians, and of them
of Cilicia and of Asia, disputing with Stephen.
10 And they were not able to resist the wisdom and the spirit by which he spake.
11 Then they suborned men, which said,
We have heard him speak blasphemous words
against Moses, and against God.
12 And they stirred up the people, and
the elders, and the scribes, and came upon
him, and caught him, and brought him to the
council,
13 And set up false witnesses, which said,
This man ceaseth not to speak blasphemous
words against this holy place, and the law:
14 For we have heard him say, that this Jesus
of Nazareth shall destroy this place, and shall
change the customs which Moses delivered us.
15 And all that sat in the council, looking
stedfastly on him, saw his face as it had been
the face of an angel.

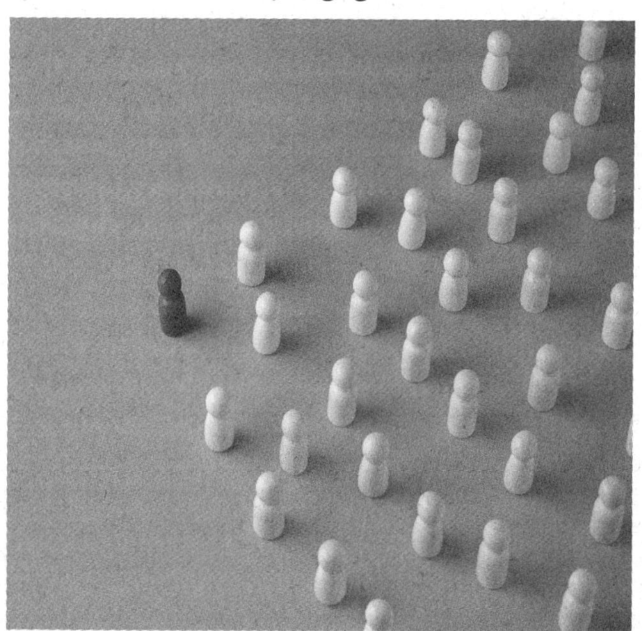

Key Text

Then there arose certain of the synagogue, which is called the synagogue of the Libertines, and Cyrenians, and Alexandrians, and of them of Cilicia and of Asia, disputing with Stephen. And they were not able to resist the wisdom and the spirit by which he spake. —**Acts 6:9-10**

Examining

Our Faith

Unit I: Faithful vs. Faithless

Lessons 1–5

Lesson Aims

After participating in this lesson, each learner will be able to:

1. State the charge against Stephen and its basis.
2. Critique the "ends justify the means" tactic used by Stephen's opponents.
3. Evaluate various ways of responding or reacting when he or she faces opposition to Jesus today.

Lesson Outline

Introduction
- A. Sacred Space
- B. Lesson Context: First-Century Church
- C. Lesson Context: The Jerusalem Temple

I. The Growing Church (Acts 6:7-10)
- A. Disciples and Priests (v. 7)
- B. Power and Wonders (v. 8)
  - *Full of Power*
- C. Wisdom and Spirit (vv. 9-10)
  - *A Grandma's Wisdom*

II. The Emboldened Opposition (Acts 6:11-15)
- A. The Conspiracy (vv. 11-12)
- B. The Witnesses (vv. 13-14)
- C. The Steadfast Man (v. 15)

Conclusion
- A. Divine Service
- B. Prayer
- C. Thought to Remember

Introduction

A. Sacred Space

In the building of my childhood church, there was a room that we called the "sanctuary." It contained pews, a high ceiling, a choir loft, a pulpit, and an organ. Each week, that room served as the location for worship services. While we infrequently used that space, certain behaviors were deemed unacceptable there. For example, holding a water balloon fight in the sanctuary was out of the question for our youth group!

The congregation established these expectations as a way to honor God. We knew, however, there was nothing holy about that room in and of itself. We believe that God dwells in His people (1 Corinthians 3:16), not buildings (Acts 17:24). But we wanted to set aside that room as a sacred space to honor and worship Him nonetheless.

Violation of the sacred space of the temple in Jerusalem was a severe matter to first-century Jewish leaders. An accusation of such a violation would lead to harsh consequences.

B. Lesson Context: First-Century Church

After Jesus' ascension, the number of believers increased and were "added" to the numbers in Jerusalem (Acts 2:47b; 5:14; 6:1). The expanding number of believers led them to develop habits for their gatherings and expectations for how they would treat each other (see 2:42-47a; 4:32-35).

During that time, almost all believers were ethnically Jewish. However, not all had the same cultural upbringing. Some had lived in the Greek-speaking (Hellenistic) portions of the Roman Empire, while others lived in Jewish regions of Palestine. The differences between these groups of first-century Jews led to conflict regarding the treatment of widows (Acts 6:1). As a result, the apostles faced challenges while trying to oversee the church (6:2).

To ease the load for the apostles, they selected seven men to handle specific tasks (see Acts 6:3-4). The book of Acts mentions two of these seven men in further detail: Philip (8:4-40) and Stephen (6:8–8:1). In some ways, the role of these seven men was analogous to the position of deacon (see 1 Timothy 3:8-13). The word *deacon* comes from the Greek noun *diakonos*, which is not used in Acts 6. However, a variation of that word does appear in Acts 6 and is translated as "ministry" (Acts 6:4). The term describes some aspects of the work of the apostles.

C. Lesson Context: The Jerusalem Temple

For first-century Judaism, the temple in Jerusalem served as the faith's physical and spiritual center. The temple complex was the focus of the people's worship and served as the headquarters for religious leadership.

Several versions of the Jewish temple existed. Construction on the first began in about 966 BC during the reign of Solomon (1 Kings 6:1). After 13 years, Solomon's Temple was completed (7:1) and dedicated (1 Kings 8). During his reign, the temple became a place to worship God and store valuable artifacts. As such, it was a notable place for enemy forces to plunder (example: 14:25-28).

In 597 BC, the Babylonians attacked Jerusalem, took the people into exile, and looted Solomon's Temple (2 Kings 24:10-14). In 586 BC, the Babylonians destroyed Solomon's Temple and took the remaining artifacts from the temple (25:8-17).

There would be attempts to rebuild this place of worship. In 538 BC, the Persian king Cyrus allowed Jewish exiles to return to Jerusalem and rebuild the temple (see Ezra 1:1-4; 6:1-12; 2 Chronicles 36:22-23). Under the oversight of Zerubbabel (see Ezra 3:2, 8; 4:2), construction faced delays. Eventually, it was finished, and the temple was dedicated in 515 BC (see 5:1–6:22). That temple—sometimes called Zerubbabel's Temple—was smaller and less impressive than the temple of Solomon's day (see Haggai 2:3).

Over time, Zerubbabel's Temple experienced harsh treatment. Greek king Antiochus IV, also known as Antiochus Epiphanes (reigned 175–164 BC), desecrated that temple and took its treasures (see nonbiblical 1 Maccabees 1:20-28). His actions led the people to revolt to free Jerusalem and the temple from foreign powers.

Their freedom was temporary. In 63 BC, Roman general Pompey desecrated the temple and its sacred artifacts. Although in shambles, the temple was not entirely demolished. It needed renovation and restoration.

The temple mentioned in the Gospels was the one renovated by Herod the Great (reigned 47–4 BC). Work on that temple began in around 20 BC (compare John 2:20). Construction on the temple complex was completed in about AD 64. The first-century Jewish leaders were not about to let anyone else again defile their holy place. They were especially not going to allow anyone to speak harshly against the building and its associated customs.

I. The Growing Church

(Acts 6:7-10)

A. Disciples and Priests (v. 7)

7. And the word of God increased; and the number of the disciples multiplied in Jerusalem greatly; and a great company of the priests were obedient to the faith.

This verse reveals two important aspects regarding the growth of the first-century church. First, the church's development was caused by the dramatic spread of *the word of God* (see also Acts 12:24; 19:20). As the influence of the gospel message *increased* among people, so did *the number of the disciples*. When the gospel falls on willing hearts, spiritual fruit will result, often in multiples (see Luke 8:8, 15).

Second, that their number *multiplied . . . greatly* implies that the *Jerusalem* church underwent rapid numerical growth. Comparing the number of

How to Say It

Alexandrians	Al-ex-*an*-dree-unz.
Antiochus	An-*tie*-oh-kus.
Cilicia	Sih-*lish*-i-uh.
Cyrenians	Sigh-*ree*-nee-unz.
diakonos (Greek)	dee-*ah*-ko-nawss.
Epiphanes	Ih-*piff*-a-neez.
Hellenistic	*Heh*-lah-nih-stik.
Herod	*Hair*-ud.
Josephus	Jo-*see*-fus.
Sadducees	*Sad*-you-seez.
Sanhedrin	*San*-huh-drun or San-*heed*-run.
Zerubbabel	Zeh-*rub*-uh-bul.

believers in the first chapters of the book of Acts reveals this expansion (see Acts 1:15; 2:41; 4:4).

Counted among these believers were *priests.* These men served in the temple when their lot was chosen (example: Luke 1:5, 8-10). They differed from the elite religious ruling class of the Sanhedrin. Instead, these priests would have been relatively poor. They would not have profited much from the wealth created by the temple.

The text does not indicate how many priests numbered in *a great company.* The first-century historian Josephus estimated that there were 20,000 priests at the time. We can assume that the number of believers among the priesthood numbered at least in the hundreds. Only a short time had passed since Jesus' ascension, but the gospel message found fertile soil for growth in Jerusalem.

What Do You Think?

How do you follow the Spirit's leading in helping make disciples in your neighborhood?

Digging Deeper

How can your congregation be a conduit for the spread of the gospel in your neighborhood and town?

B. Power and Wonders (v. 8)

8. And Stephen, full of faith and power, did great wonders and miracles among the people.

Great wonders and miracles had been attributed to Jesus (examples: John 2:11; 11:46-47; Acts 2:22) and the apostles (examples: 2:43; 5:12). When the apostles did these things, it confirmed the presence of God's grace and the empowerment of His servants (see 2 Corinthians 12:12).

The book of Acts does not reveal the kind of miraculous work that Stephen did *among the people.* The apostles healed and restored people suffering from both physical and spiritual ailments (examples: Acts 3:1-10; 5:14-16). Therefore, it is likely that Stephen did similarly. Although Stephen was not an apostle, he had been chosen by God to give witness to salvation (compare Hebrews 2:3-4). Stephen was "full of *faith* and of the Holy Ghost" (Acts 6:5). His life demonstrated the spiritual *power* that had been promised by Jesus (1:8).

What Do You Think?

In what ways can believers develop spiritual power?

Digging Deeper

How can mature believers leverage their power to encourage the spiritual growth of newer believers?

Full of Power

Bodybuilder Ethan Andrews triumphantly lifted his arms in celebration. He had broken his personal bench press record. A commentator proclaimed afterward, "Andrews is a man who is full of power." This power came through hard work and dedication to the sport. Andrews developed strength and power through grueling hours in the weight room.

The book of Acts describes Stephen as being full of power. However, his power differed from that of a bodybuilder. The athlete attains *physical* power through many hours in the weight room. Stephen, however, received *spiritual* power through his faith in Christ Jesus.

Because of God's grace, we are "full of power" to proclaim the gospel. Christ is the source of that power. We're simply "earthen vessels" to express it (2 Corinthians 4:7). Whose notoriety do you seek to enhance through an expression of your power?

—D. D.

C. Wisdom and Spirit (vv. 9-10)

9. Then there arose certain of the synagogue, which is called the synagogue of the Libertines, and Cyrenians, and Alexandrians, and of them of Cilicia and of Asia, disputing with Stephen.

After the exile that began in 586 BC, the need arose for synagogues among the Jewish people. These were locations for prayer and teaching of Scripture (examples: Matthew 4:23; Acts 13:14-15; 15:21). For more information on synagogues, see the commentary on Luke 7:4-5, lesson 7.

The underlying Greek text is unclear regarding the number of synagogues mentioned in this verse. One proposal is that this verse describes one *synagogue* attended by different groups of Jewish people.

Another option is that the verse describes multiple synagogues, each frequented by a different group. Paul tells of the existence of more than one synagogue in Jerusalem (Acts 24:11-12). Therefore, it is possible that the groups mentioned in this verse each attended different synagogues. They all, however, had a certain dispute with Stephen.

Libertines were Jewish people who had been liberated from slavery or who were descendants of those freed. These people were different from freeborn citizens of the Roman Empire who had never experienced enslavement. Other groups included *Cyrenians* from northern Africa, *Alexandrians* from Egypt, and people from *Cilicia* and *Asia*, both located in modern-day Turkey.

Stephen's teachings gave these groups a reason for *disputing*. If he had only performed miracles and served food (compare Acts 6:2-3), it is unlikely that these groups would have had any dispute. However, what led to conflict with the synagogue members were his words.

Stephen undoubtedly followed Peter and John in proclaiming God's salvation in Jesus the Messiah (compare Acts 3:12-26). However, the Jewish leadership in Jerusalem did not want anyone to preach that message (4:13-18). Jesus' promises to His followers regarding opposition (Luke 21:12-15) were coming true.

10. And they were not able to resist the wisdom and the spirit by which he spake.

That the synagogue members *were not able to resist* Stephen does not mean that they agreed with that message. Rather, they had no answer to his teachings. They had opposed the leading of God's Spirit. They were "stiffnecked and uncircumcised in heart and ears" (Acts 7:51).

Stephen had been chosen because he was "full of the Holy Ghost and *wisdom*" (Acts 6:3). His irrefutable words were a direct fulfillment of Jesus' promises to His disciples (Luke 21:15).

What Do You Think?

What steps will you take to ensure that your speech is filled with wisdom?

Digging Deeper

How do Proverbs 15:1-2; Ephesians 4:29-32; Colossians 4:5-6; and James 1:19; 3:13-18 inform your answer?

A Grandma's Wisdom

Eliana loved to sit in Grandma Sophia's living room and inquire about her grandma's life. The elder had 77 years' worth of entertaining and educating stories. She had been an active member of a local church congregation for her entire adult life. As Eliana grew and faced life's difficulties, she could always count on her grandma to offer biblical wisdom. Grandma Sophia's wisdom came because she had spent her whole life studying Scripture and seeking God.

It's no wonder that Stephen's opponents could not answer him. God's Spirit had filled Stephen with the wisdom of God. If the thought of speaking about Jesus makes you uncomfortable, be encouraged! The all-wise God can (and will) give you wisdom regarding how and when to speak as you have prepared yourself to do so. What progress are you making in that regard? —D. D.

II. The Emboldened Opposition

(Acts 6:11-15)

A. The Conspiracy (vv. 11-12)

11. Then they suborned men, which said, We have heard him speak blasphemous words against Moses, and against God.

Stephen's wisdom did not sit well with the religious leaders. Unable to win an argument with him, they took a different approach to quiet him. Certain *men* were secretly persuaded (*suborned*) to speak up against Stephen regarding his teachings.

The charge of *blasphemous words* came from their understanding of Stephen's teaching regarding the Law of *Moses*. Their accusation had severe consequences for Stephen. The Law of Moses prohibited blasphemous language *against God* and the leaders of Israel (Exodus 20:7; 22:28).

12. And they stirred up the people, and the elders, and the scribes, and came upon him, and caught him, and brought him to the council.

The council refers to the Sanhedrin, a 70-member "supreme court" for matters regarding Jewish law. The group consisted of chief priests, *elders*, and *scribes* (Mark 15:1). Members of the Sadducees and Pharisees were also likely part of the council to some extent (see Acts 23:6). The group carried

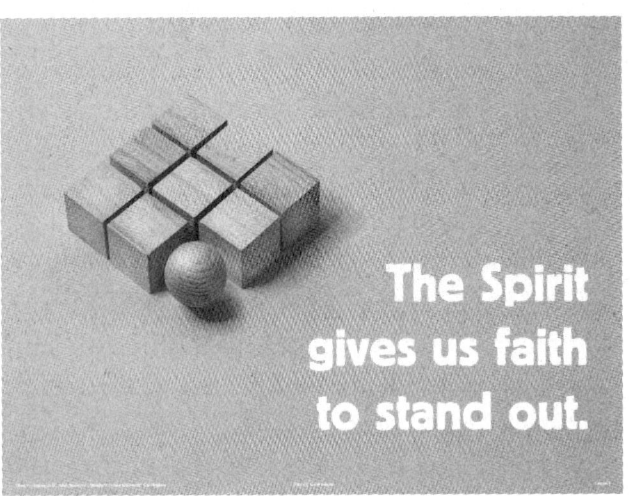
The Spirit
gives us faith
to stand out.

Visual for Lesson 4. *Point to this visual as you ask the class to consider how God's Spirit provides faith for them to stand out to the world.*

significant influence in first-century Judaism. They had the power to level consequences for offenders of the law (examples: John 9:22; Acts 15:17-40). Any claim that would have *stirred up the people* and the religious leaders would have been significant.

B. The Witnesses (vv. 13-14)

13. And set up false witnesses, which said, This man ceaseth not to speak blasphemous words against this holy place, and the law.

A *false* testimony would have been scandalous. The Law of Moses states, "Thou shalt not bear false witness against thy neighbour" (Exodus 20:16; compare Deuteronomy 19:16-18). Luke does not say whether the Sanhedrin encouraged these *witnesses*. If they had, the council would have been guilty of supporting the attacks on Stephen.

The Sanhedrin met in a chamber connected to the temple. The charge that they heard was that Stephen was preaching threats *against this holy place*. In the view of the Sanhedrin, this was a *blasphemous* act by Stephen. Blasphemy was a severe offense with serious consequences (see Leviticus 24:10-16). A similar accusation was brought against the prophet Jeremiah (Jeremiah 26:7-11).

14a. For we have heard him say, that this Jesus of Nazareth shall destroy this place.

Their claims had a grain of truth. *Jesus* had indeed prophesied regarding the destruction of *this place*, the temple (Luke 21:5-6). He had also proclaimed, "Destroy this temple, and in three days I will raise it up" (John 2:19). The apostle John, however, interpreted this statement as a metaphor for Jesus' body (2:21).

Jesus never claimed that He himself would be the one to destroy the temple. However, He had faced charges similar to the ones brought before Stephen (see Matthew 26:60-61; 27:40; Mark 14:57-58). The point of Jesus' teachings was to serve as prophetic reminders regarding the temporary nature of the temple (see Matthew 24:25-18). In AD 70, Jesus' prophecies regarding the temple were fulfilled when Roman commander Titus destroyed the temple.

14b. And shall change the customs which Moses delivered us.

Some of the *customs* described in the Law of *Moses* included circumcision (Leviticus 12:3) and dietary practices (see Leviticus 11; 17). These things were a way for the Jewish people to separate themselves from Gentiles. Therefore, any teachings regarding a *change* to these things would affect their unique identity as a people.

Jesus' teaching transformed or set aside these customs. One way is found in His teaching on food and spiritual defilement. The Law of Moses indicates that consuming certain foods makes a person unclean (Leviticus 11; 17). However, Jesus taught that what a person eats does not lead to defilement (Matthew 15:17-20; Mark 7:14-23).

Jesus did not seek to abolish the Law of Moses. Instead, His teachings and entire ministry fulfilled the law and the other writings of Scripture (Matthew 5:17). All parts of Hebrew Scripture—the writings of Moses, the prophets, the psalms, and the wisdom literature—served as guideposts that point people to Jesus. Rather than nullify these Scriptures, Jesus fulfilled them through His life, death, and resurrection (see Luke 24:27, 44).

The charges regarding Stephen's teachings (see Acts 6:14a-14b, above) were intended to unify the factions of the Sanhedrin against him. The temple was the primary economic engine of Jerusalem. It provided wealth for many people (example: Matthew 21:12). Because Sadducees were elite members of the priesthood, they benefited from the wealth created by the temple.

The Pharisees, however, were on board for different reasons. Their interpretations of the law depended on their traditions (example: Mark 7:3-4). The prospect of the temple's destruction and the law's annulment threatened the power and influence of these parties. This threat to vested interests was what motivated the arrest of Jesus as well (John 11:48).

C. The Steadfast Man (v. 15)

15. And all that sat in the council, looking stedfastly on him, saw his face as it had been the face of an angel.

The New Testament describes angels as appearing like men (examples: Luke 24:4; John 20:11-12). However, no other instances regarding the angelic countenance of a human are provided in the New Testament. The phrase *the face of an angel* highlights the supernatural nature of the expression on Stephen's face. His facial expression should have been a clue to the divine approval of his teachings.

The description also reveals the intimacy that Stephen had with God. Other people in Scripture experienced a change in their countenance after they had a personal experience with the glory of God (examples: Exodus 34:29; Luke 9:29).

Stephen began his speech to the Sanhedrin by referring to "the God of glory" (Acts 7:2). As he concluded, Stephen's first view of Heaven would be to see "the glory of God, and Jesus standing on the right hand of God" (7:55). That vision was the final straw for the Sanhedrin as he was stoned to death by mob action (7:56–8:1a).

> **What Do You Think?**
> How do your actions, attitudes, and expressions indicate to others that you are a follower of Christ?
>
> **Digging Deeper**
> What are the limitations to judging spiritual status based on outward markers?

Conclusion

A. Divine Service

What should the Christian's response be to attacks and insults to faith? Such attacks might include name-calling, harsh remarks, or judgment regarding our use of time, energy, and resources. These abuses might even come from coworkers, friends, or family members.

The verbal attacks on Stephen led to a physical attack that resulted in his death. It is unlikely that we will experience the same end as Stephen. However, his manner of living can inform our behavior —whether or not attacks on our faith result.

Stephen was a student of Scripture, demonstrated by his speech before the Sanhedrin (Acts 7:2-54). Not only did he know the *facts* of Scripture, but he also knew how Jesus *fulfilled* all of Scripture. This knowledge led him to display confidence and hope during his interaction with the Sanhedrin. He proclaimed the gospel with the hope that they would believe in Jesus as the long-awaited Messiah.

Most of all, Stephen faced his final crisis with peace and poise. He displayed a sense of peace that comes from a knowledge of God's will and power. The false accusations did not deter Stephen; he trusted that it was all a part of God's plan.

Consider the example of Stephen the next time you pray. Ask the Lord for wisdom, power, and peace. When we practice and display these attributes, we can better serve the Lord, especially in the face of criticism or attacks from the world.

> **What Do You Think?**
> How does today's lesson inform your thoughts and behaviors for the upcoming Holy Week?
>
> **Digging Deeper**
> What steps will you take to seek God's wisdom, power, and peace as you invite someone to Easter services?

B. Prayer

Lord, You are the God of wisdom, power, and peace. Give us the wisdom to know how to navigate a world that increasingly despises You. Show us the power of Your Spirit at work in and through us. Fill us with peace to face whatever circumstances we might face. We pray in the name of Jesus. Amen.

C. Thought to Remember

God's wisdom, power, and peace will overcome the harshest opponents.

Involvement Learning

Enhance your lesson with KJV Bible Student *(from your curriculum supplier) and the reproducible activity page (at www.standardlesson.com or in the back of the* KJV Standard Lesson Commentary Deluxe Edition*).*

Into the Lesson

Ask learners to suggest incidents about people falsely accused. Write a sentence on the board summarizing each incident. After volunteers share, ask the following questions in a whole-class discussion: 1–How did the accused respond to the accusation? 2–How did the accused respond when the accusation was revealed to be false?

Alternative. Distribute copies of the "Worst-Case Scenario" exercise from the activity page, which you can download. Have learners work in groups of three to complete as indicated.

Lead into the lesson by saying, "There may be times when we face a situation that seems unjust or unfair. Our response reveals the nature of our faith in the Lord. Consider Stephen's response to accusations and how you might have responded."

Into the Word

Before class, recruit a volunteer to present a three-minute presentation on Stephen's life, death, and ministry. Encourage the volunteer to read Acts 6:1–8:3. The volunteer can also use online resources in preparation. Ensure the presentation covers the following questions: 1–How was Stephen chosen for ministry? 2–What were the main points of his speech before the Sanhedrin? 3–What resulted from his death?

Announce a Bible-marking activity. Provide copies of Acts 6:7-15 for those who do not want to write in their Bibles. Provide handouts (you create) with these instructions:

- Underline any words or phrases that describe Stephen.
- Double underline the accusations brought against Stephen.
- Draw a question mark around any words or phrases you would like to study further.
- Draw a circle around any mention of or allusion to the Jerusalem Temple or the Law of Moses.

Slowly read the Scripture aloud (or ask volunteers to do so) at least twice and as many as four times. As the Scripture is read, class members should mark their copies in the ways noted.

After the final reading, divide the class into pairs to discuss the following questions: 1–What are some words or phrases that describe Stephen? 2–What were the main points of the accusations brought against him? 3–What elements of truth might have been in the accusations?

Option. Divide the class into four groups and have each group read the assigned Scripture text: **Joseph Group** (Genesis 39:1-20), **Daniel Group** (Daniel 6:1-24), **Mordecai Group** (Esther 3:1-14), **Jesus Group** (Mark 14:53-65). After each group reads the assigned Scripture, have each answer the following questions: 1–Who was the accused? 2–What was the accusation? 3–Who was the accuser? 4–What were the results of the accusation? 5–What does this story have in common with the account of Stephen?

Into Life

Divide learners into groups of three and have them answer the following questions: 1–Who are the people you will interact with in the upcoming week? 2–What opportunities will you have to boldly share the gospel with them? 3–What are possible worst-case scenarios that could result from your gospel presentation? 4–How would you respond to these results? 5–How should believers respond when facing opposition to the gospel?

Distribute an index card and pen to each learner and have them write their evaluation of their group's response to question 4. Encourage learners to consider biblical standards and examples in their evaluation. Conclude by having group members pray for courage and boldness to share the gospel.

Alternative. Distribute the "Responses and Reactions" activity from the activity page. Have learners complete it individually in a minute or less before discussing conclusions in small groups.

The Resurrection: Key to Faith

Devotional Reading: Exodus 14:10-14, 21-23, 26-31
Background Scripture: Mark 16

Mark 16:1-8

1 And when the sabbath was past, Mary
Magdalene, and Mary the mother of James,
and Salome, had bought sweet spices, that they
might come and anoint him.
2 And very early in the morning the first
day of the week, they came unto the sepulchre
at the rising of the sun.
3 And they said among themselves, Who
shall roll us away the stone from the door of
the sepulchre?
4 And when they looked, they saw that the
stone was rolled away: for it was very great.
5 And entering into the sepulchre, they saw
a young man sitting on the right side, clothed in
a long white garment; and they were affrighted.
6 And he saith unto them, Be not affrighted:
Ye seek Jesus of Nazareth, which was crucified: he is risen; he is not here: behold the place
where they laid him.
7 But go your way, tell his disciples and
Peter that he goeth before you into Galilee:
there shall ye see him, as he said unto you.
8 And they went out quickly, and fled from
the sepulchre; for they trembled and were
amazed: neither said they any thing to any
man; for they were afraid.

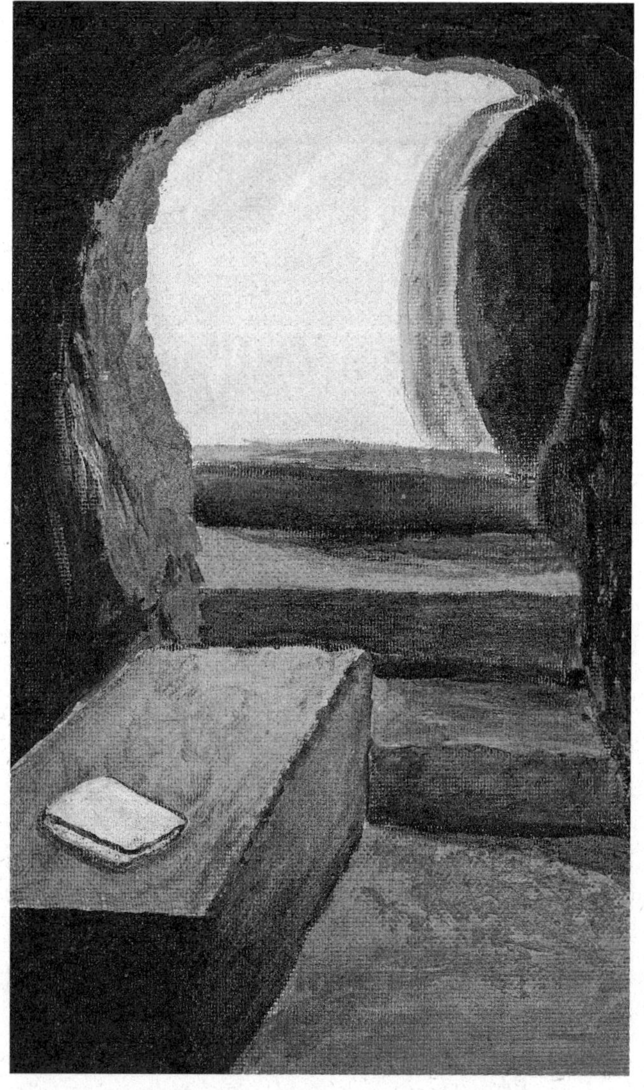

Key Text

He saith unto them, Be not affrighted: Ye seek Jesus of Nazareth, which was crucified: he is risen; he is not here: behold the place where they laid him. **—Mark 16:6**

Examining

Our Faith

Unit I: Faithful vs. Faithless

Lessons 1–5

Lesson Aims

After participating in this lesson, each learner will be able to:

1. Summarize the women's encounter with the man at Jesus' empty tomb.

2. Explain the significance of the time elements of the text.

3. Make a commitment not to allow fear to result in failure to speak up when doing so is necessary.

Lesson Outline

Introduction

A. Abrupt Endings

B. Lesson Context: Mark, the Man

C. Lesson Context: Mark, the Gospel

I. The Women (Mark 16:1-4)

A. Intention (v. 1)

B. Timing (v. 2)

C. Trouble (vv. 3-4)

II. The Messenger (Mark 16:5-8)

A. Angelic Appearance (v. 5)

B. Remarkable Report (vv. 6-7)

Great Expectations

C. Fearful Flight (v. 8)

Fleeing or Faith?

Conclusion

A. Singular Event

B. Vital Reality

C. Prayer

D. Thought to Remember

Introduction

A. Abrupt Endings

My wife had just finished reading Beatrix Potter's classic *The Tale of Peter Rabbit* to our children. Surprised by its ending, my wife exclaimed, "That's it? That's the end?!"

The book tells the story of Peter, a playful and disobedient young rabbit who decides to steal vegetables from the garden of Mr. McGregor. Peter is discovered but flees before Mr. McGregor can catch him. In Peter's hurry to escape, he leaves behind his jacket and shoes.

Once Peter returns home, he doesn't tell his mother about his escape. Instead, he goes straight to bed. Peter's mother wonders why her son lost his jacket and shoes. In the book's closing pages, the reader learns that Mr. McGregor used Peter's jacket and shoes to create a scarecrow, and the story ends at that point. The story's abrupt conclusion leaves the reader wondering whether Peter faced any consequences for his mischievous actions.

Abrupt endings can both frustrate and entice audiences. Clever storytellers use these endings to their advantage because audience members can be challenged to imagine the outcome. As you read today's Scripture, think about why the writer of this Gospel might have decided to end his account the way that he did.

B. Lesson Context: Mark, the Man

Tradition tells us that the Gospel of Mark was written by John Mark, an associate of Peter and Paul (see Acts 12:12; 1 Peter 5:13). This man was not an apostle. But he was a close relative of Barnabas (Colossians 4:10), who probably convinced Paul (Saul) to take John Mark on that apostle's first missionary journey (Acts 12:25). John Mark abandoned the trip before its conclusion (13:13). This put him in disfavor with Paul (15:36-39), although the two later reconciled (2 Timothy 4:11; Philemon 24). Students propose that Mark's Gospel account is based on Peter's firsthand experiences with the person and ministry of Jesus, given the closeness of Mark to Peter in light of Peter calling him "my son" (1 Peter 5:13).

C. Lesson Context: Mark, the Gospel

Although Mark's Gospel is the shortest of the four, its narrative packs a punch! Students frequently call it "the Gospel of action." This designation stems from the fact that Mark jumps quickly from scene to scene to chronicle Jesus' ministry.

The Gospel's description of the last week of Jesus' ministry highlights its inclination toward action. Of the nearly 700 verses of the Gospel, 241 of them—more than one-third of the Gospel—recount events from that week (Mark 11:1–16:8). In describing scenes from that week, the Gospel jumps quickly between scenes. Mark tells us how Jesus entered Jerusalem on that Sunday (11:1-11) and taught others regarding righteousness (11:12-25; 12:28-34). On that Thursday, He ate a final meal (14:12-31) before He was arrested (14:43-52) and tried (14:53-65; 15:1-15). Finally, on that Friday, He was crucified and killed at the hands of Roman soldiers (15:16-41).

Friday evening of that week, Joseph of Arimathaea, a member of the Sanhedrin, approached Pontius Pilate to ask for Jesus' body (Mark 15:43). Before granting the request, Pilate wanted confirmation that Jesus was truly dead (15:44-45). There was to be no doubt on the part of Pilate that Jesus was indeed dead. Once Pilate received this verification, Joseph took Jesus' body and prepared it for burial.

To begin the burial proceedings, Joseph wrapped Jesus' body in linen (Mark 15:46a). The Gospels do not indicate whether or not Jesus' body was washed as was customary at this time (example: Acts 9:37). Joseph then placed the body in a rock tomb sealed with a stone (Mark 15:46b). After the burial, two women observed the burial location (15:47). They would return after Sabbath to finish caring for Jesus' body.

Some students believe that the original ending to this Gospel came at Mark 16:8 and that Mark 16:9-20 was a later addition in the decades after Mark wrote. Much of the information in verses 9-20 is reflected in the other Gospels (Matthew 28:19-20; Luke 24:13-43, 50-51; John 20:14-18). In this lesson, we will engage in a *what-if.* What if Mark did end at verse 8? What could that abrupt ending teach us today?

I. The Women

(Mark 16:1-4)

A. Intention (v. 1)

1. And when the sabbath was past, Mary Magdalene, and Mary the mother of James, and Salome, had bought sweet spices, that they might come and anoint him.

Jesus died on a Friday, the day of preparation for the Sabbath (Mark 15:37-42). The Law of Moses prohibited work on the Sabbath (Exodus 20:8-11; Leviticus 23:3). Therefore, the burial process (see Lesson Context) would have to wait until *the sabbath was past.* The task of treating the body of Jesus would fall to the women, some of whom were at the crucifixion (Mark 15:40; John 19:25) and subsequently had seen the tomb's location (Mark 15:47; compare Matthew 27:61; Luke 23:55-56).

The name *Mary* was common in the first century AD. By one estimate, one in four women in Palestine was so named at that time. The Gospels mention several women named Mary, so it is easy to confuse them.

One of the women with that name was *Mary Magdalene,* who became a devoted follower of Jesus after He freed her from spiritual oppression (see Luke 8:1-2). The designation *Magdalene* was not a family name. Instead, it indicates that she likely came from the town of Magdala (compare Matthew 15:39).

The second *Mary* is unknown to us. One possibility is that she is "*the mother of James* the less and of Joses" (Mark 15:40, 47). Another possibility is that she was "the wife of Cleophas" (John 19:25).

Matthew's account of the burial mentions a woman who is "the mother of Zebedee's children" (Matthew 27:56). This woman could be *Salome,* thus making her the mother of James and John (compare 4:21; Mark 15:40).

Sweet spices combatted the stench of decaying flesh (compare John 11:39). These treatments were an essential part of the burial process (19:39-40). The women prepared these things before the Sabbath (Luke 23:55-56). They waited for the conclusion of that day of rest to return to the grave and *anoint* the remains of Jesus.

> **What Do You Think?**
> In what ways will you show devotion to the Lord, even if doing so requires personal discomfort?
> **Digging Deeper**
> How can you encourage that level of devotion among other believers?

B. Timing (v. 2)

2. And very early in the morning the first day of the week, they came unto the sepulchre at the rising of the sun.

The phrases *very early in the morning* and *at the rising of the sun* reveal the eagerness of the women to complete their tasks. We assume that they set out just before sunrise, in the dim, pre-dawn light (compare John 20:1). The women were confident of their destination, having been there two days earlier (see comments on Mark 16:1, above).

C. Trouble (vv. 3-4)

3. And they said among themselves, Who shall roll us away the stone from the door of the sepulchre?

What the women seemed to have forgotten up to this point is that a massive disk-shaped *stone* sealed the entrance to the grave (Matthew 27:60-61; Mark 15:46-47). Several strong individuals would be needed to *roll* it *away* from the entryway. The women's question reveals that they belatedly realized that they would not be able to move it.

The women's question also reveals the attitudes and behaviors of Jesus' followers. The disciples fled at Jesus' arrest (Mark 14:50). Peter, in particular, denied having known Jesus (John 18:15-18, 25-27). Others likely hid out of fear for what might happen to them (compare 20:19). Because of their grief, shame, or fear, some of Jesus' followers had distanced themselves from being associated with Him (contrast 19:38-42). They would not be of any help in removing *the stone from the door of the sepulchre.*

4. And when they looked, they saw that the stone was rolled away: for it was very great.

The Gospel accounts of Mark, Luke, and John do not reveal how *the stone was rolled away.* They only report that the stone was no longer blocking the tomb's entrance when the women arrived (here and Luke 24:2; John 20:1). Matthew, however, discloses that "the angel of the Lord descended from heaven, and came and rolled back the stone from the door" (Matthew 28:2). The massive nature of this *very great* stone is also noted in Matthew 27:60.

> **What Do You Think?**
> In what ways has your faith been strengthened by an experience during a funeral service or at a cemetery?
> **Digging Deeper**
> How can your acts of comforting a grieving person strengthen your faith?

II. The Messenger
(Mark 16:5-8)

A. Angelic Appearance (v. 5)

5. And entering into the sepulchre, they saw a young man sitting on the right side, clothed in a long white garment; and they were affrighted.

Mark's Gospel does not provide further identifying information regarding the *young man sitting* in *the sepulchre.* However, we can determine his nature from the other Gospel accounts.

Matthew 28:2 describes him as an "angel of the Lord." Luke identifies "two men . . . in shining garments" (Luke 24:4) who are "angels" (24:23); John 20:12 is similar. Scripture often describes heavenly beings in terms of the brightness of their garments (examples: Matthew 17:2; 28:3; Mark 9:3; Luke 9:29-30; Acts 1:10).

The women came to the tomb to care for the body of Jesus. Instead of seeing His body, they saw an unknown visitor. The sight of this mysterious person would have been a valid reason for the women to feel *affrighted.*

B. Remarkable Report (vv. 6-7)

6a. And he saith unto them, Be not affrighted: Ye seek Jesus of Nazareth, which was crucified.

Fear is a common reaction to seeing an angelic messenger (examples: Judges 13:21-22; Matthew 28:4; Acts 10:3-4) or a supernatural occurrence (examples: Mark 4:41; 5:15; 9:4-6). When this occurs, a form of the reminder to *be not affrighted* usually follows (examples: Judges 6:21-23; Daniel 10:10-12, 19; Luke 1:11-13, 30; 2:9-10).

The angel's designation *Jesus of Nazareth* referred to the location of Jesus' upbringing. The village of Nazareth was located about 70 miles north of Jerusalem in the hilly region west of the Sea of Galilee. Residents of that village were likely impoverished. As a result, others held them in low regard (see John 1:46). Jesus' parents were from Nazareth (Luke 2:4), and the family returned there after Jesus' birth (Matthew 2:21-23). Jesus remained in Nazareth until He began His public ministry (4:12-13).

6b. He is risen; he is not here: behold the place where they laid him.

The angel's proclamation that Jesus *is risen* does not mean that His spirit went to Heaven, leaving behind His dead body. The empty tomb reveals that His physical body was resurrected from the dead. His post-resurrection appearances provided further evidence of this reality (see Luke 24:37-39; John 20:27).

The resurrection should not have come as a surprise to His followers. Jesus had prophesied to them numerous times regarding His death and resurrection (examples: Mark 8:31; 9:9, 31; 10:33-34). However, His disciples rarely understood His teaching on this topic (see 9:10, 32).

Burial customs during Jesus' day began with washing the body (example: Acts 9:37). Then the body was wrapped with cloths, treated with fragrant spices and ointments, and *laid* upon a flat surface in the grave. The command to *behold* that *place where* Joseph had *laid Him* indicated that the tomb no longer contained the body of Jesus.

What Do You Think?

How would you respond to the claim that belief in the bodily resurrection of Jesus is nonessential for Christians?

Digging Deeper

How do John 20:24-25, 29; Acts 2:22-24; Romans 4:25; 1 Corinthians 15; and 1 Peter 1:3-4 inform your response?

Great Expectations

As one of the world's last remaining rainforests, the Amazon River Basin is home to an unparalleled diversity of plant and animal life. By one recent estimate, the region contains over 40,000 plant species, nearly 1,300 bird species, roughly 430 species of mammals, and approximately 2.5 million species of insects. And these numbers are only estimates; scientists discover new species each year!

When visitors to this region learn of this diversity, they expect to feel fear. A habitat with such a variety of species will indeed be overwhelming to the unfamiliar! While some threats do exist in the untamed rainforest, it is not complete chaos. Instead, the rainforest can be surprisingly peaceful. Most visitors leave the rainforest and remark on its serenity. It is a balanced and ordered ecosystem of interdependent plants and animals.

The women at the tomb expected to see Jesus' body. Their expectations changed when they were told that Jesus was no longer there. At that moment, the lives of these women began to change radically. How has your life changed because of your relationship with the risen Lord? What has not changed that should have? —O. P.

7. But go your way, tell his disciples and Peter that he goeth before you into Galilee: there shall ye see him, as he said unto you.

The command to *go* and *tell* of the risen Lord indicates a change in emphasis for Mark. In his Gospel, he frequently mentions times when Jesus urged others to be silent regarding His identity

How to Say It

Arimathaea	*Air*-uh-muh-***thee***-uh (*th* as in *thin*).
Barnabas	*Bar*-nuh-bus.
Cleophas	*Klee*-o-fus.
Magdala	*Mag*-duh-luh.
Magdalene	*Mag*-duh-leen or Mag-duh-*lee*-nee.
Pontius Pilate	*Pon*-shus or *Pon*-ti-us *Pie*-lut.
Salome	Suh-*lo*-me.
Zebedee	*Zeb*-eh-dee.

and work (Mark 3:11-12; 5:42-43; 7:36; 8:29-30; contrast 5:18-20). Now that Jesus' resurrection had occurred, His followers would not need to remain silent about Him (see 9:9).

Jesus' *disciples* had fled at His arrest (Mark 14:50). On that occasion, they were concerned for their safety. Rather than punish the disciples for leaving Jesus, the angel's message offered them a chance to reunite with their Lord.

The angel showed particular attention to *Peter* by naming him specifically. This apostle is known for his position of prominence, being named first in all listings of the apostles (Matthew 10:2-4; Mark 3:16-19; Luke 6:14-16; Acts 1:13-14) and for his impulsive behavior (examples: Mark 9:5-6; John 13:1-11). He had confidently proclaimed fidelity to Jesus, even if it led to death (Mark 14:29-31). Later that same night, however, Peter thrice denied knowing Jesus (14:66-72). Later, after Peter received the women's report, he still had to see the empty tomb for himself (Luke 24:11-12).

Before Jesus' arrest, He had prophesied that His disciples would be "offended" and "scattered" (Mark 14:27). In the same breath, however, He promised, "After that I am risen, I will go before you into *Galilee*" (14:28). The angel's message to the women indicated the pending fulfillment of Jesus' promises.

The selection of Galilee as the location of this promised reunion was made with intent. Jesus began His public ministry there (see Mark 1:9, 14). It was in that region that He called His first disciples (1:16-20). The angel's message sent the apostles back to where their relationship with Jesus began.

Visual for Lesson 5

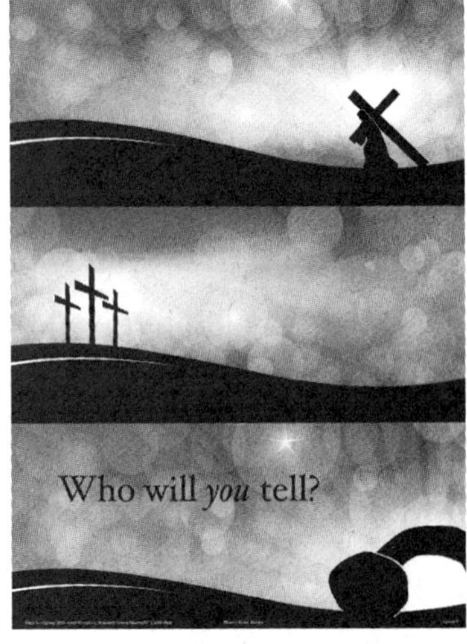

Before closing with prayer, encourage the class to reflect on this question throughout the week.

C. Fearful Flight (v. 8)

8. And they went out quickly, and fled from the sepulchre; for they trembled and were amazed: neither said they any thing to any man; for they were afraid.

Three strong emotions overwhelmed the women as they *went out quickly* and *fled from the sepulchre*. Their feelings were decidedly mixed; this is the only verse in the New Testament where the Greek words for *trembled*, *amazed*, and *afraid* occur together. The picture was one of uncertainty as the women found themselves in an in-between state: the empty tomb was initial evidence of a miraculous occurrence, but they had not yet seen the risen Jesus personally.

What Do You Think?

What is the significance of living in an "in-between" state when we have evidence of Jesus' resurrection but have not yet seen Him personally?

Digging Deeper

How does John 20:24-25, 29 inform your answer?

Fleeing or Faith?

A *cenote* is a limestone sinkhole that connects to pools of water underground. Many cenotes are so deep that their exploration requires scuba equipment and training. While serving as a missionary in Mexico, I visited one such cenote. Before arriving, our guide gave us very few details about the sinkhole. When we finally arrived, we were amazed by its magnitude and beauty. Smooth, shiny rock revealed a seemingly bottomless pool of water. As I approached the edge of the cenote, I became afraid and wanted to turn and leave.

After receiving the angel's message, the women were afraid and fled from the tomb. Does fear ever prevent you from serving the Lord? When that occurs, remember the words of our resurrected Lord: "Fear not; I am the first and the last: I am he that liveth, and was dead; and, behold, I am alive for evermore, Amen" (Revelation 1:17-18). Believe this and have great faith! —O. P.

Conclusion

A. Singular Event

Today's Scripture abruptly ends with a declaration of the women's fear. If this were all we knew of the story, we would wonder what happened next. Praise God that we know the conclusion to this story—a story that continued with Jesus' ascension to Heaven (Acts 1:1-9) and will culminate with His promised return to earth (Revelation 22:20).

The resurrection of Jesus is a singular event in history. It is distinct from other resurrections in the Bible (examples: 2 Kings 4:32-37; Luke 7:11-15; 8:49-56; John 11:38-44). Those were instances of the temporary restoration of physical life—temporary because all those people died again later. The resurrection of Jesus, by contrast, is permanent (Revelation 1:18a).

That permanence has vital implications. Death is God's penalty for sin (Genesis 2:16-17; Romans 5:12), but now the risen Jesus holds "the keys of hell and of death" (Revelation 1:18b).

Another characteristic that sets Jesus' resurrection apart from the others noted above is that His body was transformed, not merely resuscitated. After His resurrection, He appeared and disappeared in ways He had not done previously (Luke 24:31, 36, 51; John 20:19, 26), although He still had a physical body that other people could touch (Luke 24:37-43; John 20:27). The transformation of Jesus' body prefigures the promised transformation of those who belong to Him when we are raised on the last day (1 Corinthians 15:42-57).

B. Vital Reality

From our vantage point some 2,000 years later, the empty tomb is the universal image of Christ's victory over death. The women who found the open tomb that morning had prepared themselves to be confronted with death. Instead, they were confronted with the announcement of life.

The reality of death confronts all, and we make preparations for it. We help friends and family members with funeral planning. We purchase cemetery plots. But the best spiritual preparation is to let our thoughts dwell on resurrection life.

Jesus has promised that what was accomplished in Him on that third day will also be accomplished in us when He returns. The power of life over death that He demonstrated for himself is the same power that will instantly and forever transform us (see Philippians 3:21). Jesus is Lord over death, having conquered it. That makes Him Lord over eternal life—our eternal life.

Therefore, as we prepare for death, we keep in mind that "the last enemy that shall be destroyed is death" (1 Corinthians 15:26). Death is our enemy, but it is ultimately a defeated enemy. When Jesus returns, we all will be changed. In a moment, in the twinkling of an eye, death will be no more.

Consider the abrupt ending to verse 8 as an invitation to proclaim the good news of the resurrected Christ. The women at the tomb that morning ran in fear; our task today is to run in joy with the message of the empty tomb. May we ever proclaim Christ's victory over death; may we never lose sight of the fact that His victory is ours as well—for eternity. Death could not permanently silence Jesus or obstruct God's plan. Will fear silence you from sharing this good news?

What Do You Think?

How do you deal with feelings of fear that may arise when sharing the news of Jesus' resurrection?

Digging Deeper

Who can you recruit as an accountability partner to encourage your faith?

C. Prayer

God of resurrection, where there is death, You bring life. We hope for the day when we will experience resurrection and new life. In the meantime, encourage us when we feel we cannot proclaim this good news. When fear overtakes us, keep us from forgetting that You are the source of life. In Jesus' name we pray. Amen.

D. Thought to Remember

Fear not—Jesus has risen!

Involvement Learning

Enhance your lesson with KJV Bible Student *(from your curriculum supplier) and the reproducible activity page (at www.standardlesson.com or in the back of the* KJV Standard Lesson Commentary Deluxe Edition*).*

Into the Lesson

Ask the following question for whole-class discussion: "What's the best news you've heard this week?" Allow three minutes for volunteers to give their responses as you write them on the board. Evaluate the responses by asking the following questions: 1–Why are these things considered good news? 2–To whom did you tell this good news? 3–How did others respond to this good news?

Lead into Bible study by saying, "Today's Scripture recounts the best news the world has ever received. But this news was initially not received joyfully."

Into the Word

Ask a volunteer to read aloud Mark 16:1-8. Divide the class into equal groups. Distribute handouts with the following questions (you create) for in-group discussion: 1–Who went to the tomb? 2–Why did they go? 3–When did they go, and what was the reason for their timing? 4–How did they respond to the message they received?

Option 1. Before class, find a recording of the song "Was It a Morning Like This?" on an online streaming platform. After playing it for the class, ask them to list the song's lyrics that retell the events from Mark 16:1-8. Ask the following question for whole-class discussion: "How does the song help you understand this Scripture better?"

Option 2. Divide the class into four groups and give each group a handout (you create) with the following headers: *Question / Mark 16:1-8 / Luke 24:8-20.* Write numbers one through five vertically in the Question column. Have groups compare the two Scripture passages by writing their answers to the following questions next to the appropriate question number in column one: 1–What was the good news, and who delivered it? 2–What is surprising about who received the good news? 3–How did they react to receiving that news? 4–What did the recipients of the good news do with it? 5–How did the news change the lives of the people who received it?

Alternative. Distribute copies of the "Rest of the Story" exercise from the activity page, which you can download. Have learners work in pairs to complete as indicated before sharing conclusions with the whole class.

Into Life

Write the following prompt on the board:

Sometimes I'm afraid to talk with a nonbeliever about Jesus' resurrection because . . .

Distribute two slips of paper and a writing utensil to each learner. Have them anonymously complete the prompt on one of the slips. After one minute, collect the slips and redistribute them. Ask volunteers to read aloud responses.

Say, "Fear is one possible reason believers are afraid to talk about Jesus' resurrection. That's understandable; fear was a response of the first eyewitnesses to the empty tomb."

Ask the following questions for whole-class discussion: 1–What would have happened if the women remained silent regarding the empty tomb? 2–What happens when believers today remain silent regarding Jesus' resurrection? 3–Why do believers often fail to tell others about our resurrected Savior? 4–How can we overcome fear or apathy in this regard?

Write the following prompt on the board and have learners complete it on their second slip of paper:

In order not to allow fear to result in failure to speak up when doing so is necessary, I will . . .

After one minute, have volunteers share what they wrote.

Alternative. Distribute copies of the "Notes for a Letter" activity from the activity page. Have learners work in pairs to complete as indicated.

April 7
Lesson 6 (KJV)

Faith of the Persistent

Devotional Reading: John 4:4-18
Background Scripture: Luke 5:17-26

Luke 5:17-26

**17 And it came to pass on a certain day, as
he was teaching, that there were Pharisees and
doctors of the law sitting by, which were come
out of every town of Galilee, and Judaea, and
Jerusalem: and the power of the Lord was present to heal them.**
**18 And, behold, men brought in a bed a
man which was taken with a palsy: and they
sought means to bring him in, and to lay him
before him.**
**19 And when they could not find by what
way they might bring him in because of the
multitude, they went upon the housetop, and
let him down through the tiling with his couch
into the midst before Jesus.**
**20 And when he saw their faith, he said
unto him, Man, thy sins are forgiven thee.**
**21 And the scribes and the Pharisees began
to reason, saying, Who is this which speaketh
blasphemies? Who can forgive sins, but God
alone?**
**22 But when Jesus perceived their thoughts,
he answering said unto them, What reason ye
in your hearts?**
**23 Whether is easier, to say, Thy sins be for-
given thee; or to say, Rise up and walk?**
**24 But that ye may know that the Son of man
hath power upon earth to forgive sins, (he said
unto the sick of the palsy,) I say unto thee, Arise,
and take up thy couch, and go into thine house.**
**25 And immediately he rose up before them,
and took up that whereon he lay, and departed
to his own house, glorifying God.**
**26 And they were all amazed, and they glo-
rified God, and were filled with fear, saying,
We have seen strange things to day.**

Key Text

Behold, men brought in a bed a man which was taken with a palsy: and they sought means to bring him in, and to lay him before him. And when they could not find by what way they might bring him in because of the multitude, they went upon the housetop, and let him down through the tiling with his couch into the midst before Jesus. **—Luke 5:18-19**

Unit II: The Measure of Faith

Lessons 6–9

Lesson Aims

After participating in this lesson, each learner will be able to:

1. Identify the correct and incorrect conclusions of the scribes and Pharisees.

2. Explain the connection between the plural "their" and the singular "thy" in verse 20.

3. Brainstorm modern helping situations analogous to that of the text.

Lesson Outline

Introduction

A. Imposter Friends

Words and their definitions seem to change all the time. In recent years, discussions on blogs and opinion pieces have focused on defining the word *friend* in the age of social media. Is it possible for a person to have thousands of "friends"? Is it possible to be friends with someone you have never met in person? Many so-called friends on social media are criminals hiding behind fictitious names! They are imposters.

I have found a simple way to identify one's genuine friends: announce that you are moving and see who volunteers to help. My wife and I have moved more than 20 times during our 22 years of marriage. Surprisingly, we have had no more than five people who have helped us pack and load the trucks. By contrast, I have over 300 "friends" on social media. Today's lesson allows us a first-century look at the results of authentic, Christ-honoring friendship.

B. Lesson Context

The third Gospel and the book of Acts were written by a man named Luke. He was a traveling companion of the apostle Paul and a physician by profession (see Colossians 4:14; 2 Timothy 4:11; Philemon 24). Because Luke was not an eyewitness to the ministry of Jesus, he gathered his information from those who had been so he could write a detailed account (Luke 1:1-4). Most students believe that the Gospel of Mark was written first and, therefore, could have been one of the sources used by Luke. The scene in today's lesson is worded quite similarly to Mark 2:1-12 (but see Luke 5:17, below; compare Matthew 9:1-8).

Today's lesson locates Jesus in Galilee, early in His three-and-a-half-year ministry. His popularity was rising, and He was drawing crowds. The news of Jesus' teaching and miracles was spreading rapidly (Luke 4:37), and attempts to keep things under control in that regard didn't work (5:14-15). As a result, Jesus had to make a conscious effort to carve out some "alone time" for prayer with His heavenly Father (4:42; 5:16).

Luke 5:12 states that the healing miracle just prior to the one in today's text occurred "in a certain city" of Galilee. Mark 2:1 is more specific in indicating that the events of today's lesson took place in Capernaum. This town, located on the northwestern bank of the Sea of Galilee, became something of a headquarters for Jesus during His tours of Galilee (Matthew 4:13).

I. Faith That Seeks

(Luke 5:17-20a)

A. Teaching a Gathering (v. 17)

17a. And it came to pass on a certain day, as he was teaching, that there were Pharisees and doctors of the law sitting by, which were come out of every town of Galilee, and Judaea, and Jerusalem.

The phrase *on a certain day* indicates that the events that follow probably occur on a day other than a Sabbath. Recognizing that this supposition is an argument from silence, we note that there are no complaints from Jesus' opponents concerning a Sabbath violation, as we see in Luke 6:1-11 and 13:10-16.

This verse includes the first of 27 mentions of *Pharisees* in the Gospel of Luke. Two factors indicate their presence to have been an ominous turn of events. The first is that they were accompanied by *doctors of the law.* This rare designation (a Greek word of 14 letters) is found only here, in Acts 5:34 (applied to the renowned Gamaliel), and in 1 Timothy 1:7 (regarding misguided aspirations). Much more often, Pharisees are said to be accompanied by "scribes" (examples: Luke 5:30; 15:2), a different Greek word being translated. Pharisees opposed Jesus (examples: Luke 11:53-54; John 11:45-57), with a few exceptions (examples: 3:1; 19:39). On the distinctive beliefs and practices of the Pharisees, see Matthew 23:1-36; Mark 7:3-5; Luke 18:10-12; and Acts 23:8.

The second ominous factor is that these religious leaders are not merely "local yokels" *out of every town of Galilee.* Instead, they include individuals from *Judaea* and *Jerusalem.* It's a long walk from Jerusalem and its temple to Capernaum—approximately 80 miles! For these religious leaders to commit to such a trip reveals a determined intent that the person and work of Jesus required a thorough investigation.

17b. And the power of the Lord was present to heal them.

With this phrase, Luke unites this event with Isaiah 61:1-2, which Jesus had read concerning himself when He was in Nazareth a short time before (Luke 4:16-21). The healings, both physical and spiritual, fulfill messianic prophecy.

The reference to healing *them* raises a question of antecedent: Who does the pronoun "them" refer to? The problem lies in the fact that the word being translated differs slightly in spelling across some ancient manuscripts.

In any case, the focus is on the source of the power: *the Lord* (compare Micah 3:8; etc.).

B. Finding a Way (vv. 18-19)

18. And, behold, men brought in a bed a man which was taken with a palsy: and they sought means to bring him in, and to lay him before him.

The helping action of the friends of *a man which was taken with a palsy* is selfless and authentic. In their effort, the friends show what Jesus called the second greatest commandment: love your neighbor as yourself (Matthew 22:39; Mark 12:31). This account does not specify how many men are carrying the bed, but Mark 2:3 does: there are four. This makes sense when we imagine something like a medical stretcher with one person at each corner.

The Greek verb to describe the man's disease is in the tradition of other ancient medical writers, and Luke's books feature four of its five occurrences in the New Testament (here and in Luke 5:24; Acts 8:7; 9:33; compare to the fifth occurrence

How to Say It

Capernaum	Kuh-*per*-nay-um.
Galilee	*Gal*-uh-lee.
Messianic	Mess-ee-*an*-ick.
Nazareth	*Naz*-uh-reth.
Pharisees	*Fair*-ih-seez.
Synoptic	Sih-*nawp*-tihk.

in Hebrews 12:12, there translated "feeble"). If spoken in Greek, the word would sound very much like our English word *paralyzed.* The affliction made it impossible for the man to come to Jesus without assistance.

What Do You Think?

How will you demonstrate the second greatest commandment (see Matthew 22:39; Mark 12:31) toward a friend in need in the upcoming week?

Digging Deeper

Who might you recruit to help you in this regard?

19. And when they could not find by what way they might bring him in because of the multitude, they went upon the housetop, and let him down through the tiling with his couch into the midst before Jesus.

The religious leaders' determination to investigate Jesus (Luke 5:17a, above) was matched by the determination of four men to have the suffering man healed by Jesus. This verse reads quite similarly to its parallel in Mark 2:4, except for Luke's phrase *into the midst before Jesus,* which Mark did not include.

First-century Palestinian houses typically had flat roofs with exterior steps or a ladder providing access. Roofs were built with beams resting on the outer walls, with smaller posts crossing the beams and covered with thatch and mud. The rooftop was a place for household activities, drying laundry, and getting fresh air. It was also where people sometimes hid, conferred, mourned, and prayed (Joshua 2:6; 1 Samuel 9:25; Isaiah 15:3; Acts 10:9, respectively). Roofs were also places where bad things could happen (2 Samuel 11:2; 16:22; Deuteronomy 22:8; Jeremiah 19:13).

Even with outside access readily available, for the four men to climb the stairs or ladder while transporting the man was undoubtedly quite difficult—another sign of their faith and commitment. And lowering the man *down* would probably have required ropes, possibly an indication of advance preparation.

What Do You Think?

How can perceived physical or spiritual obstacles become an opportunity to demonstrate your faith and trust?

Digging Deeper

How is your faith strengthened by the examples from Scripture of people who faced and overcame obstacles to faith (example: Paul, 2 Corinthians 11:23-33)?

A Lesson in Persistence

I was a college student visiting Europe, foolish enough to wear a belt pouch with a single, inviting zipper. It attracted thieves like chum attracts sharks.

In Paris, a man held open a door for me while he tried to sneak the zipper open. In Rome, a trio of young women jangled bells in my face while they did likewise. In both cases, I clamped my hand over the zipper.

It was an older woman in Rome whose persistence paid off. She begged in a loud voice as she pushed a swaddled baby against me. A moment later, I felt her rummage in my belt pouch.

I stepped back. "Did you take something from me?"

The woman's failed burglary didn't faze her one bit. She pointed to the water bottle in my hand and cried out, "For the baby! For the baby!"

I gave it to her.

Lord, help us to seek You with that persistence as we do so with godly motives! —N. G.

C. Seeing Their Faith (v. 20a)

20a. And when he saw their faith, he said unto him.

The four Gospels mention *faith* a total of 24 times (in Greek), and Luke features 11 of those instances. The verse before us is the first (earliest) of those 11. Faith, being a mental and spiritual state, cannot literally be seen in and of itself by us ordinary humans. That limitation does not apply to the Son of God, however. He knows people's spiritual and mental states (see Luke 5:22, below). But even though we lack the divine ability to see the faith (or lack of faith) in someone's heart, we can certainly see evidence of faith in one's actions or inactions (James 2:17). What the crowd saw in the actions of the men Jesus *saw* in both heart and action.

We must not assume that the phrase *their faith* refers only to the man's friends to the exclusion of the paralyzed man. There is no indication that he opposed others' carrying him to Jesus. It's likely that he was more than willing to seek out Jesus.

> **What Do You Think?**
> In what ways do a believer's actions reveal his or her faith in God?
> **Digging Deeper**
> How do Hebrews 11:1–12:3 and James 2:14-26 inform you of the connection between faith and action?

II. Faith That Finds

(Luke 5:20b-26)

A. Man Is Forgiven (v. 20b)

20b. Man, thy sins are forgiven thee.

How Jesus addresses the man varies across the accounts of Matthew, Mark, and Luke (the synoptic Gospels). Luke uses the generic Greek word for *man*, while the other two Gospels use the Greek word that can be translated as "son" (Matthew 9:2; Mark 2:5).

B. Jesus Is Disparaged (vv. 21-22)

21. And the scribes and the Pharisees began to reason, saying, Who is this which speaketh blasphemies? Who can forgive sins, but God alone?

Not (yet) finding anything in Jesus' teaching to criticize, *the scribes and the Pharisees* focus their attention on His actions and implied identity. They are not correct in an absolute sense when they say that *God alone* can forgive sins—people are encouraged to forgive sins committed against one another (Matthew 6:14; 18:21-22; Luke 11:4; 17:3-4; Colossians 3:12-13). But the scribes and the Pharisees are correct in the sense of a person sinning against God (Exodus 34:6-7; Psalm 103:2-3; Isaiah 43:25; 1 John 1:8-9). According to Jewish writings in the period between the Old and New Testaments, the Jews expected a righteous Messiah to overthrow foreign invaders. They did not expect a Messiah who would be God-in-the-flesh, able to forgive sins.

This unspoken question of the religious experts goes to the heart of understanding the person and work of Jesus. The experts actually had a good grasp of what was happening: Jesus was speaking and acting in a manner reserved for God. For a mere human to forgive sins committed against God would indeed be blasphemy, which was punishable by death (Leviticus 24:16). Various forms of the word *blasphemy* occur dozens of times in the New Testament. Jesus eventually would be crucified on this very charge (Matthew 26:65-66; Mark 14:64; compare John 5:16-18; 10:31-33). The text establishes this instance as the first organized opposition to Jesus in the Gospel of Luke.

> **What Do You Think?**
> How can you prepare yourself for others' questions regarding the identity and authority of Jesus?
> **Digging Deeper**
> What steps do you need to take to be successful in this regard?

Part of the Solution or the Problem?

My wife and I have been reading Helen L. Taylor's *Little Pilgrim's Progress* to our kids each night. They love this adaptation of Bunyan's classic *Pilgrim's Progress,* published in 1678. They are fascinated by all the obstacles Little Christian encounters—giants, lions, and other children who mock him as he keeps moving along the King's Way toward the Celestial City.

The characters who oppose Little Christian are what might be called "threshold guardians," and they have names that reveal their nature. Characters named "Obstinate" and "Pliable" try to keep Little Christian from ever starting his journey of faith; "Worldly" tries to get him to go an easier way; "Self" attempts to enslave him, etc.

The Pharisees arose as threshold guardians against Jesus' ministry, but Jesus did not abandon His calling. When you think of the problem of spiritual threshold guardians, how do you ensure you're not part of the problem? —N. G.

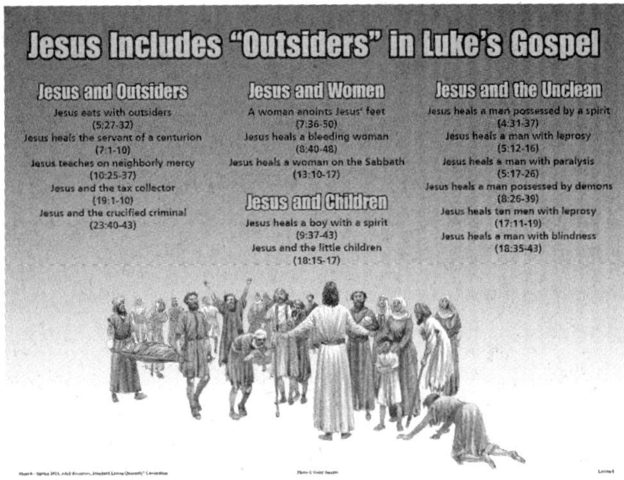
Jesus Includes "Outsiders" in Luke's Gospel
Jesus and Outsiders
Jesus eats with outsiders (5:27-32)
Jesus heals the servant of a centurion (7:1-10)
Jesus teaches on neighborly mercy (10:25-37)
Jesus and the tax collector (19:1-10)
Jesus and the crucified criminal (23:40-43)
Jesus and Women
A woman anoints Jesus' feet (7:36-50)
Jesus heals a bleeding woman (8:40-48)
Jesus heals a woman on the Sabbath (13:10-17)
Jesus and Children
Jesus heals a boy with a spirit (9:37-43)
Jesus and the little children (18:15-17)
Jesus and the Unclean
Jesus heals a man possessed by a spirit (4:31-37)
Jesus heals a man with leprosy (5:12-16)
Jesus heals a man with paralysis (5:17-26)
Jesus heals a man possessed by demons (8:26-39)
Jesus heals ten men with leprosy (17:11-19)
Jesus heals a man with blindness (18:35-43)

Visual for Lesson 6. *Point to this chart and ask, "What do Jesus' actions in the Gospel of Luke reveal about who or what Jesus finds most important?"*

22. But when Jesus perceived their thoughts, he answering said unto them, What reason ye in your hearts?

Everyone present could see the evidence of the faith of the man and his friends in their actions. Jesus, however, was able to see the doubt and lack of faith in the *hearts* of the religious leaders. The ability to know people's hearts and innermost thoughts is one of the divine characteristics of Jesus that Luke emphasizes (see Luke 6:8; 9:47; 24:38). With this ability, He was able to respond to their unspoken question with an audible question of His own. Although Jesus knew the thoughts of their hearts, He asked them a question, a method of teaching that He often used (2:49; 6:9, 39, 46; etc.).

C. Man Is Healed (vv. 23-25)

23. Whether is easier, to say, Thy sins be forgiven thee; or to say, Rise up and walk?

Not waiting for an answer to His question, Jesus immediately poses another one. Some students see this as a "greater to lesser" argument (technically known as *a maiore ad minus*). A simple example of this argument goes like this: "If a glass can hold eight ounces of water, then it can surely hold five ounces of water." Other students see it as the opposite—a "lesser to greater" argument (technically known as *a minore ad maius*). A simple example might be: "If it is illegal to shoot fireworks on the Fourth of July (a single day), then it is surely illegal to shoot them off on all other days."

In either case, Jesus' question gave the religious leaders something to think about. What was to be not doubted was Jesus' ability not just to say *rise up and walk* but actually to bring that action about, as the next verses demonstrate.

24. But that ye may know that the Son of man hath power upon earth to forgive sins, (he said unto the sick of the palsy,) I say unto thee, Arise, and take up thy couch, and go into thine house.

This verse—worded almost the same as Matthew 9:6 and Mark 2:10-11—stresses that Jesus healed the paralyzed man as evidence of Jesus' authority to forgive sins (compare John 5:8). In this way, Luke again connects what has happened here to Jesus' reading of the prophet Isaiah in the synagogue (see notes on Luke 5:17b, above). When John the Baptist wavered in his faith while imprisoned, Jesus confirmed His messiahship by mentioning signs such as this (7:22-23). Faith in Jesus is based on evidence!

This verse is the first of 25 occasions that Luke records Jesus' using the self-designation *Son of man*. Overall, this expression occurs across all four Gospels more than 80 times. In almost every case, it comes from the lips of Jesus and not as a description of Jesus by the Gospel writers. (Luke 24:7 and John 12:34 are the only two exceptions, both quoting Jesus.) The background of this designation comes from the Old Testament. The book of Ezekiel applies the title to that prophet more than 80 times, but without suggesting that he was divine (examples: Ezekiel 5:1; 6:2; 7:2). The two uses of the designation in the book of Daniel recognize the Son of Man as having divine attributes (Daniel 7:13-14; 8:17).

25. Immediately he rose up before them, and took up that whereon he lay, and departed to his own house, glorifying God.

Earlier, Luke established Jesus' authority and power to heal and drive out demons (Luke 4:33-36). And we remember that *authority* is "the right to do something," and *power* is "the ability to do something." Luke is the only writer of the four Gospels to use both words together (examples: 4:36; 9:1; 20:20). Although the text now under consideration does not explicitly use those words, both concepts are present in this verse.

The adverb *immediately* establishes that the healing happened instantly at the mere spoken words of Jesus. This particular adverb is a favorite of Luke's. The Greek word that is being translated occurs most often in the New Testament in the Gospel of Luke (examples: Luke 1:64; 8:44; 13:13; 18:43) and the book of Acts (examples: Acts 12:23; 13:11). The healing did not happen over a length of time. And there is no indication that Jesus' touch was involved, as healing miracles featured in other contexts (compare Mark 8:22-25; John 9:6-7).

The man's sudden ability to walk was (or should have been) evidence that Christ had both authority and power to forgive sins (see Luke 20:2-8). The statement *before them* is essential to this proof—everyone present saw the result. In biblical times two or three witnesses were required to prove the veracity of an event (Deuteronomy 17:6; 19:15; Matthew 18:16; John 8:13-18; 2 Corinthians 13:1). Thus, Luke confirms that a sufficient number of witnesses were present to verify the miracle.

What Do You Think?

How do you ensure that worship is your first response when you experience God's work?

Digging Deeper

How do you maintain an attitude of worship even when it seems God has not worked in the manner that you desired?

D. Crowd Is Amazed (v. 26)

26a. And they were all amazed, and they glorified God, and were filled with fear.

This is the only verse in the New Testament where amazement, glorifying *God*, and *fear* occur together as reactions of a crowd. The parallel verses of Matthew 9:8 and Mark 2:12a, by contrast, record only two of these three reactions each. We presume that the word *all* includes the religious leaders who were present. This was their first encounter with Jesus, as recorded in the Gospel of Luke, and it's not unreasonable to conclude that they shared in everyone's reactions. Like everyone else, those leaders needed time to process the evidence for Jesus' deity just seen. Soon enough, however, some people will reach the wrong conclusion (see Luke 11:14-16).

26b. Saying, We have seen strange things today.

This is the crowd's fourth reaction, as recorded by Luke. If spoken aloud, the Greek word translated *strange things* (which occurs only here in the New Testament) would sound like the English word *paradoxical.* This reaction, unlike that in Luke 4:28-29, is one of confused neutrality. It reaches no conclusion.

Conclusion

A. Authentic Friends

Social media has changed the world's concept of friendship. Only time will tell whether a new word is needed to distinguish between a virtual social-media friend and an authentic real-life friend. In the meantime, I will continue to post online as we prepare for our next move and patiently wait for my 300 so-called friends to show up.

The friends in today's lesson remind us of the nature of authentic friendship. We are unsure how long they had been carrying their friend around on this bed. We know that when Jesus came into the city, they believed He could help their friend. However, they did not stop at simply believing. They put their faith into action and brought their friend to Jesus, overcoming every obstacle on the way.

It was not an easy task to get their friend onto the roof, tear it apart, and lower him into the room. Undoubtedly, they could have spent their time on other matters that day. How can you dedicate your time and resources to assisting a friend in need?

B. Prayer

Father, we are grateful for the friends who have helped us on our faith journey. We pray that You will help us be the friend who carries the bed of another when needed, regardless of the obstacles in our path. We give You thanks for friends and the strength to be a friend in Jesus' name. Amen.

C. Thought to Remember

God enables us daily to be faithful friends!

Involvement Learning

Enhance your lesson with KJV Bible Student *(from your curriculum supplier) and the reproducible activity page (at www.standardlesson.com or in the back of the* KJV Standard Lesson Commentary Deluxe Edition*).*

Into the Lesson

Look up the definition of *friend* in a dictionary and write that definition on the board. Distribute index cards and pens to each learner and ask them to write down the first three words they think of when they hear the word *friend*.

After one minute, ask volunteers to share their three words as you write those words on the board. Lead a whole-class discussion using the following questions: 1–Which of the listed words are similar? 2–Which words stand out as unique? 3–How do these words match the definition? Keep these words and their definitions on the board for the entire class time.

After comparing the contributed words with the dictionary definition of *friend*, lead a discussion regarding how the meanings of words can change over time. Say, "For example, the word *friend* means something entirely different in the context of social media." Lead into Bible study by saying, "In today's lesson, Luke describes a faithful friendship. While reading the text, notice how the text uses active words to describe the actions of a friend."

Into the Word

Divide the class into three groups: **Jesus Group**, **Religious Leaders Group**, and **Friends Group**. Write the following headers on the board: *Jesus / Religious Leaders / Friends*. Introduce the activity by saying that the action verbs found in this section of Scripture help us understand the passage.

Distribute a sheet of paper and pen to each group. Ask each group to read Luke 5:17-26 and write down all the action verbs associated with their group's namesake. After five minutes, have a volunteer from each group write their group's words on the board under the appropriate header.

Lead a whole-class discussion using the following questions: 1–What do the lists of verbs reveal about the characters' motives? 2–What do these verbs reveal about the faith of the friends? 3–What do these verbs highlight about the disbelief of the religious leaders? 4–What do these verbs tell us about what is most important to Jesus? 5–What is the connection between the faith of the friends and Jesus' actions?

Option 1. Ask a volunteer to read aloud Matthew 17:14-20. Ask the following questions for whole-class discussion: 1–How does Matthew 17:14-20 pertain to today's lesson? 2–What is the connection between having authentic faith and our actions?

Option 2. Distribute copies of the "God's Definition of a Friend" exercise from the activity page, which you can download. Have the learners work in pairs to complete and discuss the activity page as indicated.

Into Life

Ask learners to work in small groups to create a definition of the word *friend* using only the ideas conveyed in Luke 5:17-26. Ask each group to write their definition on the board. In a whole-class discussion, ask how these definitions are similar to or different from the definition from Into the Lesson. Allow five minutes for this discussion.

Have learners work in their small groups to brainstorm real-life helping situations analogous to today's Scripture text. Ask, "How does each helping situation fulfill the role of a friend as described in your definition?" Then have groups come up with possible challenges they may face in acting on these helping situations. Distribute an index card to each learner and have them write the name of a person who can benefit from a helping situation in the upcoming week.

Alternative. Distribute copies of the "Remarkable Friendship" activity from the activity page. Have learners complete it as a take-home activity. To encourage completion, tell the class that you will set aside some time at the beginning of the next class to review the activity and its results.

April 14
Lesson 7 (KJV)

Faith of a Centurion

Devotional Reading: Zechariah 8:18-23
Background Scripture: Luke 7:1-10

Luke 7:1-10

1 Now when he had ended all his sayings in the audience of the people, he entered into Capernaum.

2 And a certain centurion's servant, who was dear unto him, was sick, and ready to die.

3 And when he heard of Jesus, he sent unto him the elders of the Jews, beseeching him that he would come and heal his servant.

4 And when they came to Jesus, they besought him instantly, saying, That he was worthy for whom he should do this:

5 For he loveth our nation, and he hath built us a synagogue.

6 Then Jesus went with them. And when he was now not far from the house, the centurion sent friends to him, saying unto him, Lord, trouble not thyself: for I am not worthy that thou shouldest enter under my roof:

7 Wherefore neither thought I myself worthy to come unto thee: but say in a word, and my servant shall be healed.

8 For I also am a man set under authority, having under me soldiers, and I say unto one, Go, and he goeth; and to another, Come, and he cometh; and to my servant, Do this, and he doeth it.

9 When Jesus heard these things, he marvelled at him, and turned him about, and said unto the people that followed him, I say unto you, I have not found so great faith, no, not in Israel.

10 And they that were sent, returning to the house, found the servant whole that had been sick.

Key Text

Wherefore neither thought I myself worthy to come unto thee: but say in a word, and my servant shall be healed. —**Luke 7:7**

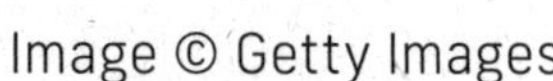

Examining

Our Faith

Unit II: The Measure of Faith

Lessons 6–9

Lesson Aims

After participating in this lesson, each learner will be able to:

1. Identify the reason for Jesus' amazement.

2. Explain the role of the town of Capernaum in Jesus' ministry.

3. Brainstorm ways to exhibit faith as analogous to that of the centurion.

Lesson Outline

Introduction

A. Remote Everything

B. Lesson Context

I. Desperate Need (Luke 7:1-5)

A. Situation in Capernaum (v. 1)

B. Request and Endorsement (vv. 2-3)

C. Insistent Elders (vv. 4-5)

Credit Check

II. Unmatched Faith (Luke 7:6-10)

A. Insightful Centurion (vv. 6-8)

First Resort or Last Resort?

B. Astonished Jesus (v. 9)

C. Remote Healing (v. 10)

Conclusion

A. Centurion Faith

B. Prayer

C. Thought to Remember

Introduction

A. Remote Everything

My first modem-equipped computer allowed me to purchase a small amount of usage time from an Internet service provider, connect to a phone line, and access distant servers. I marveled at what I could do. An exciting moment came when I was able to access the digital catalog of a university library in England, helping me identify a book I had needed for months.

Now we take the Internet for granted. My wife and I have weekly video calls with my grandson and his mother from 1,500 miles away. When I teach online, it is not uncommon for me to have students in several geographically separated areas "attend" class at once.

Physical distance was a challenge to communication in Jesus' day. Indeed, distance remained a challenge to rapid communication until the year 1844, when the first public telegraph went into operation. We easily see the challenge of distance in today's lesson. What is more difficult to see is the positive importance physical distance played in communicating with Jesus. We dare not miss it.

B. Lesson Context

The physical context of today's lesson is the village of Capernaum (see also the parallel account in Matthew 8:5-13). It was located on the northwest shore of the Sea of Galilee, a freshwater lake in northern Palestine. Bible students are accustomed to thinking of Jesus as being from Bethlehem (John 7:42; etc.) or from Nazareth (Matthew 2:23; etc.). But a case can also be made for the claim that He was "from Capernaum" because the village became something of a headquarters or base of operations for His preaching and teaching tours of Galilee (4:13; Mark 2:1); notice that Matthew 9:1 refers to Capernaum as Jesus' "own city."

The importance of Capernaum is seen in the fact that it is mentioned 16 times in the New Testament, in one instance quite negatively (Matthew 11:23 and parallel Luke 10:15). Five of Jesus' twelve disciples were residents of Capernaum when Jesus called them to follow Him: four fishermen (James, John, Peter, and Andrew; see Matthew 4:18-22) and one tax collector (Matthew, also known as Levi; see Mark 2:14).

Although Capernaum probably did not have more than a few hundred residents, it was a thriving regional hub for at least three reasons. First, the fishing industry provided steady income for many families. The lake was productive, with one account telling of a haul of 153 large fish (John 21:11). Fishing businesses like that of the Zebedee family (Mark 1:19-20) would have caught more fish than could be sold locally. So some fish were preserved with salt and sent to larger cities such as Jerusalem.

Second, Capernaum was situated on the main road from Damascus into the region. This location made it a good place for the Romans to set up points for tax collectors to assess tolls on goods passing into the area. Matthew worked for the Romans this way, maintaining a tax-collecting booth on this road (Luke 5:27). Jewish tax collectors from Jerusalem also operated out of Capernaum to collect the annual temple tax from the Jews of Galilee (Matthew 17:24).

Third, Capernaum was important enough to have had some Roman soldiers stationed there, as today's lesson reveals (compare Acts 10:1). The need to safeguard the tax money collected may have been the reason. It is possible they were under the authority of Herod Antipas, the Roman client "tetrarch" of the Galilee region from 4 BC to AD 39 (Luke 3:1).

Capernaum has been the site of some remarkable archaeological discoveries over the last hundred years. A lavish synagogue dating from the fourth century AD likely sat on a foundation floor from the time of Jesus. This place could be the location of the synagogue of Capernaum where Jesus taught (Mark 1:21). Also uncovered nearby is a large house that has become a Christian pilgrimage site. Evidence suggests this was the actual house of Simon Peter, a place where Jesus resided while in town (Luke 4:38).

I. Desperate Need

(Luke 7:1-5)

A. Situation in Capernaum (v. 1)

1. Now when he had ended all his sayings in the audience of the people, he entered into Capernaum.

We reach a transition point in the narrative. The teaching (*all his sayings*) and healing actions of the previous section (Luke 6:17-49) were concluded, so Jesus moved from one place to another. The location of where He moved from is only given as "the plain" (6:17), perhaps referring to a suitably level site on or at the base of the mountainside (6:12). For Jesus to have then *entered into Capernaum* was probably not a long walk, given His record of movements around that area at the time (see Lesson Context).

B. Request and Endorsement (vv. 2-3)

2. And a certain centurion's servant, who was dear unto him, was sick, and ready to die.

A centurion was a soldier who commanded a unit known as a "century" in a legion of a Roman army. A Roman legion ideally consisted of 59 centuries organized in 10 cohorts. The second through the tenth cohorts consisted of 6 centuries, each century having 80 men. A legion's first cohort was an exception. That cohort had only five centuries, but each of those, also commanded by a centurion, was at double strength. The math of all this adds up to 59 centurions in a legion of approximately 5,000 troops. Thus, the centurion in today's lesson was likely the most important and senior Roman official around Capernaum.

The *centurion's* domestic situation in the case at hand is indicated by his having at least one *servant* in his household. This servant was likely not a hired hand but an enslaved person owned by the centurion. Roman military campaigns often resulted in those people on the losing side being

How to Say It

Capernaum	Kuh-*per*-nay-um.
centurion	sen-*ture*-ee-un.
Damascus	Duh-*mass*-kus.
Herod Antipas	*Hair*-ud *An*-tih-pus.
Levi	*Lee*-vye.
Nazareth	*Naz*-uh-reth.
synagogue	*sin*-uh-gog.
tetrarch	*teh*-trark or *tee*-trark.

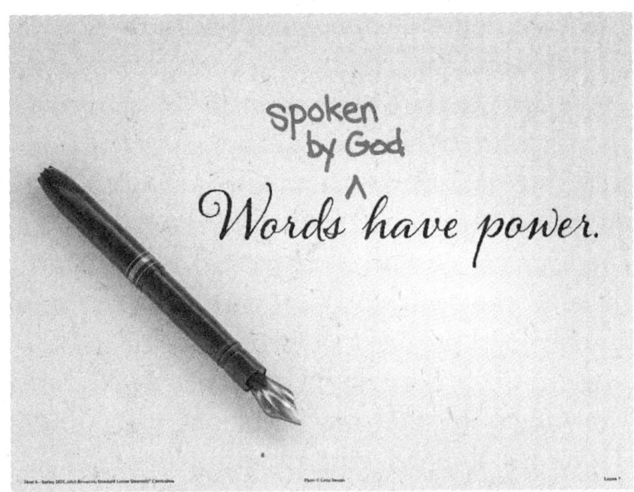
spoken
by God
Words have power.

Visual for Lesson 7. *Point to this visual and ask volunteers for other examples from Scripture when God's power was revealed through human words.*

taken into bondage. Also common during this period were children born into slavery as the offspring of women who were themselves enslaved. Legally, Roman slavery laws allowed the owner to use another man "like a piece of property or a domestic animal" (historian Dio Chrysostom; lived AD 40–120). But not all master/slave relationships were brutal or exploitative.

Slavery was not necessarily a lifetime situation among the Romans (compare 1 Corinthians 7:21). Ancient sources indicate that many were freed (manumitted) by age 30, thereby becoming "Libertines" (compare Acts 6:9, lesson 4). In depicting the deathly ill servant as *dear* to the centurion, Luke uses a word that expresses value and respect (compare the same word's translation as "precious" in 1 Peter 2:4, 6).

Luke, a physician, does not give us his specific diagnosis of the man's affliction; Luke gives us only the prognosis: he was *sick, and ready to die.* Matthew adds more information by noting that the servant was "sick of the palsy, grievously tormented" (Matthew 8:6). In contrast with the situation in Luke 5:18, the servant may have been too ill to be brought to Jesus. Although people in antiquity had a limited understanding of disease and its causes, they could recognize the signs of unlikely recovery and impending death.

3. And when he heard of Jesus, he sent unto him the elders of the Jews, beseeching him that he would come and heal his servant.

The centurion undoubtedly had heard of Jesus in two senses: through general word of mouth (Luke 4:14, 37) and specifically of His return to Capernaum. Perhaps the fact that the centurion sent his healing request via the elders of the Jews reflects an intentional strategy, reasoning that Jesus may respond more positively to fellow Jews than to a Gentile (compare Matthew 10:5-6; 15:21-24).

This verse paints a picture of an intelligent man who recognized and understood the cultural issues of Gentiles interacting with Jews (Acts 10:28; 11:1-3). Rather than risk being spurned in a public, face-to-face meeting with Jesus, the centurion turned to Jewish leaders with whom he had become a friend in the community.

C. Insistent Elders (vv. 4-5)

4-5. And when they came to Jesus, they besought him instantly, saying, That he was worthy for whom he should do this: For he loveth our nation, and he hath built us a synagogue.

The elders who *came to Jesus* were apparently leaders of the synagogue in Capernaum. They did not convey the centurion's message as reluctant lackeys—they earnestly pled his case.

For some unstated reason, the centurion loved the Jewish *nation*. The proof of that love is found in an astonishing detail: the centurion had *built* Capernaum's *synagogue*. The expense might have included not only funding for the structure itself but also the interior furnishings: (1) a place to store scrolls for preservation and convenient access (compare Luke 4:17), (2) an elevated platform from which someone reading the Scripture would be visible to all in attendance (compare Nehemiah 8:4-5), (3) lamps for illumination, and (4) adequate seating (Luke 4:20a). We don't know whether the centurion footed the bill for these, but it is possible.

Synagogues are not mentioned in the Old Testament, except for Psalm 74:8. However, the underlying Hebrew word is also translated "congregations" in that same psalm (Psalm 74:4). Elsewhere, the word occurs very frequently in conjunction with the tabernacle, which was the focus of assembly for worship before the temple was built (examples: Numbers 1:1; 2:2).

The need for synagogues as gathering places for

worship and instruction in Scripture arose during the Babylonian exile that began in 586 BC (2 Kings 25). With the temple in Jerusalem destroyed and Jews far from their homeland, the people needed places to congregate; the word *synagogue* is a Greek word that means "place of assembly." The return from exile probably modified the function of synagogues to being primarily places of Scripture teaching rather than worship. This transition was because worship in its fullest sense was to take place at the temple (compare 1 Kings 8:29-51; John 4:20; contrast 1 Kings 13:26-30), which had been rebuilt.

Some students believe that the centurion was a Gentile in the category of "one that feared God" (compare Acts 10:2, 22; 13:16, 26). Such Gentiles were not proselytes (converts) to Judaism (contrast Matthew 23:15; Acts 6:5; 13:43) but were devout nonetheless. Therefore, the centurion's funding of the synagogue was more than a public works project designed to curry favor. Instead, it was rooted in his deep respect for Judaism and its God.

What Do You Think?

In what ways can your congregation act as a go-between in connecting resources to those in need?

Digging Deeper

How can your congregation partner with other congregations in this regard?

Credit Check

When my son was old enough to drive, he saved up his money and bought his first car. I was pleased with how responsible he had become. A few years later, some things started to go wrong with his vehicle, so he decided he wanted a new car. The problem was that he was only 19 and had no credit.

As a character reference, I could vouch for how responsible he was. But that doesn't cut it in the realm of credit. The only way my assurance would mean anything was if I cosigned the loan—and Proverbs 22:26-27 warns of the dangers of doing so. The only reason I decided to do so was because I knew my son. I had watched him demonstrate his responsibility over the years, and his actions showed me that he deserved this risk I was taking.

The request by the elders of the Jews can be seen as their "cosigning" the centurion's request for aid. Those elders knew the man's heart, as evidenced by his actions. For Jewish leaders to vouch for a commander in a Gentile occupying army was astounding! Their reason for so doing even more so.

Jesus said, "Ye shall know them by their fruits" (Matthew 7:16). What "fruits" did you produce this past week that would cause others to vouch enthusiastically for your character? —P. L. M.

II. Unmatched Faith

(Luke 7:6-10)

A. Insightful Centurion (vv. 6-8)

6a. Then Jesus went with them. And when he was now not far from the house, the centurion sent friends to him, saying unto him.

Capernaum was not a large city. Crossing from one end to the other would not have taken more than 15 minutes. Therefore, the time between when the elders spoke to Jesus and when the *friends* did so must have been very short.

Since the group was *not far from the house* of *the centurion*, the man may have seen Jesus and His entourage approaching before he dispatched delegation number two. These friends may have been either Gentile, Jewish, or both (compare Acts 10:24; 19:31). The message they brought was surprising! This act demonstrated, among other things, knowledge of and respect for Jewish law, customs, and sensibilities on the part of the centurion (compare John 18:28; Acts 10:28).

The parallel in Matthew 8:5 has the centurion himself speaking to Jesus personally. One way to resolve the tension between the accounts is to consider how that first-century culture would have viewed a messenger commissioned to speak on behalf of another person. In other words, when the centurion's friends talked to Jesus, it was as if Jesus was conversing with the centurion himself since that man had commissioned his friends to do so on his behalf. Matthew's Gospel, in a way, merely simplifies the account of the interactions.

6b-7. Lord, trouble not thyself: for I am not worthy that thou shouldest enter under my roof: Wherefore neither thought I myself

worthy to come unto thee: but say in a word, and my servant shall be healed.

As the centurion (through his friends) addressed Jesus as *Lord*, we should not automatically presume that the centurion acknowledged Jesus as the Lord God. The Greek word translated "Lord" occurs more than 700 times in the New Testament, and it is often used as simply a polite address of respect. In such cases, it is equivalent to our modern word *sir* (examples: Matthew 27:63; John 4:11).

The centurion's friends brought Jesus the unexpected message we see in the verses before us. Two things should be considered. First is the centurion's humility in admitting his unworthiness. Other admissions of unworthiness (same Greek word) occur in the parallel passages Matthew 3:11; Mark 1:7; and Luke 3:16. The tension created between the theme of unworthiness here and the theme of worthiness in Luke 7:4-5 is interesting! Second, some students propose that in addition to admitting personal unworthiness, the centurion was demonstrating sensitivity in avoiding a potentially awkward cross-cultural meeting under the *roof* of a Gentile (compare John 4:9; 18:28; Acts 10:28; 11:3).

What Do You Think?

How will you show humility as you come before God in prayer?

Digging Deeper

In what ways is humility crucial for your formation into Christlikeness? How does James 4:6-10 inform your response?

First Resort or Last Resort?

In 2001, the very first telerobotic surgery was performed. The so-called Lindbergh operation involved a surgeon in New York City performing the surgery on a patient in Strasbourg, France! The ensuing years saw further advances in this technology.

To heal without needing to be in the same room as the patient is certainly a feat worthy of accolades and awards. We wonder how much faith that first patient must have had to agree to such an experiment! One glitch and chaos could have ensued. Would any of us have such faith in this technology? Knowing human nature as we do, it's easy to envision almost everyone agreeing to undergo such an experiment if (1) there was no other option and (2) the medical condition was quite serious or terminal.

We see both conditions met in the situation of today's text. But that brings up a question: Do we bring our problems to Jesus in prayer from the beginning or only as a last resort when nothing else works? —P. L. M.

8. For I also am a man set under authority, having under me soldiers, and I say unto one, Go, and he goeth; and to another, Come, and he cometh; and to my servant, Do this, and he doeth it.

The centurion's plea was based on a hierarchical view of authority—a view that came from his military experience. See the discussion of the centurion's status in the commentary on Luke 7:2, above. Earlier in Capernaum, Jesus had commanded a demon to come out of a man (Luke 4:31-37). Those who had witnessed it acknowledged Jesus' authority and power as a result (4:36). The centurion was undoubtedly aware of this miracle and thereby recognized an analogy to his own authority. Moreover, the statement of the centurion admitted the limitations of his authority. The centurion had authority over his soldiers. However, Jesus has unlimited authority over the world. Regardless of how we perceive the centurion's words, they emphasize Jesus' authority over all things—even sickness.

What Do You Think?

How can you use the positions of leadership in which God has placed you to worship and serve Him?

Digging Deeper

How do you discern the limitations of your leadership and use those limitations as an opportunity to depend on God?

B. Astonished Jesus (v. 9)

9. When Jesus heard these things, he marvelled at him, and turned him about, and said unto the people that followed him, I say unto you, I have not found so great faith, no, not in Israel.

The four Gospels do not often speak of Jesus

himself being amazed at something or someone. Almost always, it's the other way around: people *marvelled* at Jesus or something He did. The two exceptions are the *faith* of the Gentile centurion (today's text plus parallel in Matthew 8:10) and the lack of faith of the people of Nazareth (Mark 6:6).

Furthermore, Jesus did not actively seek to minister to Gentiles, only to fellow Jews (compare Matthew 10:5-6 with its parallel in Mark 6:7 and Luke 9:1-2). Even so, Gentiles sought Him out in a few cases (in addition to today's text, see Matthew 15:28 and John 12:20-21). Jesus' initiative to the Samaritan (a person who was ethnically half Jewish) in John 4:1-42 is unique. As far as Luke is concerned, the centurion's faith is the greatest miracle in this passage.

What Do You Think?

How can you demonstrate "great faith" in your neighborhood? your city? your country?

Digging Deeper

What distractions do you need to remove in order to live with "great faith"?

C. Remote Healing (v. 10)

10. And they that were sent, returning to the house, found the servant whole that had been sick.

Jesus' healing miracles in the Gospels have been categorized in various ways. These include healings by touch (example: Matthew 8:15), command (example: Luke 5:24), and prayer (example: John 11:41-42). One interesting way of healing, not often considered, is miracle healing from a distance. There are three such: the ones involving (1) the Gentile centurion's servant in today's text and Matthew 8:5-13, (2) the Gentile woman's daughter in Matthew 15:21-28 (lesson 9), and (3) the nobleman and his son in John 4:46-54. In all three cases, faith was vindicated.

Conclusion

A. Centurion Faith

When we offer up intercessory prayer for the healing of a friend or family member, are we exercising the faith of the centurion? Without a doubt, any forthcoming healing will be a "remote healing" since Jesus is not here in the flesh, so that is not the issue.

The issue, instead, is one of believing in Jesus' authority. That's the essence of what we might call "Centurion Faith." Our intercessory prayers must have more than a "maybe" or "hope so" tone. When we fix our eyes on Jesus, we demonstrate "Centurion Faith" that God will answer our prayers. When we are distracted from Him and wring our hands in despair, nothing good happens (Matthew 14:25-31). Jesus taught, "Whatsoever ye shall ask in prayer, believing, ye shall receive" (21:22).

The centurion's background speaks loudly. He had cultivated friendships within his community for years. He had treated his neighbors with respect and honor, not pulling his rank as a Roman officer to get his way. In many ways, the significant gap between the Jews and Gentiles of Jesus' day was bridged on that day in Capernaum. The centurion had used his wealth and influence to protect the Jews and provide a gathering place for their study of Scripture. He played "the long game" in the most sincere and authentic manner possible. When his household was in need, his character and actions were remembered. Can the same be said of ours?

What Do You Think?

How will you have "Centurion Faith" in situations when it seems that God doesn't answer your prayers in a preferred or expected way?

Digging Deeper

What about in situations when God's presence seems altogether gone?

B. Prayer

Heavenly Father, our lives constantly need Your support and healing. Our churches and homes need Your presence. May we honor You in all ways and never doubt. May we have a simple faith like the centurion! We pray in the name of Jesus, Your Son. Amen.

C. Thought to Remember

Have "Centurion Faith"!

Involvement Learning

Enhance your lesson with KJV Bible Student *(from your curriculum supplier) and the reproducible activity page (at www.standardlesson.com or in the back of the* KJV Standard Lesson Commentary Deluxe Edition*).*

Into the Lesson

Ask learners to pair up and answer the following questions: 1–What was an honor that you received that was a total surprise? 2–What is an example of praise you received that you would not otherwise give yourself? Allow one minute for each learner to share.

Reconvene the class and ask for volunteers to share their answers. For whole-class discussion, ask, "How does it feel to be praised or honored when you don't feel worthy?"

Lead into Bible study by saying, "Today we'll learn about a man who came to Jesus, desperate for help. However, this man didn't feel he was worthy to receive that help. Perhaps some of you will be able to identify with his feelings."

Into the Word

Before class, ask a volunteer to prepare a five-minute report on Capernaum and its role in the ministry of Jesus. Encourage the volunteer to use the Lesson Context portion of the commentary, Bible encyclopedias, and other online resources.

Organize a dialogic reading of today's text. Choose four volunteers and assign them the following verses from Luke 7: Narrator (vv. 1-3, 4a, 6a, 9a), Elders (vv. 4b-5), Friends (vv. 6b-8), and Jesus (vv. 9b-10). Have volunteers read aloud through the lesson Scripture, each volunteer reading their assigned verses in the appropriate order. Encourage volunteers to "act out" their readings with emotion.

Distribute handouts (you prepare) to each learner with the following questions: 1–How did the centurion demonstrate faith? 2–How did the centurion show respect for Jesus? for the Jews? 3–Compare and contrast the elders' description of the centurion with his description of himself. 4–Why was Jesus impressed with the centurion's faith?

Invite learners to pay attention to answers to these questions as they listen to the Scripture reading. After the reading, have learners join the same pairs as in the previous activity to answer the questions. After several minutes, ask volunteers to share their answers with the whole class.

Option. Distribute copies of "The Centurion, the Servant, and the Savior" exercise from the activity page, which you can download. Have learners work in small groups to complete as indicated.

Into Life

Write the following question on the board: *What are ways that we can exhibit faith as analogous to that of the centurion?* In the same pairs as before, ask learners to brainstorm answers to this question. After five minutes, reconvene the class and ask volunteers to give their responses to this question. Write the responses on the board.

Then ask the class to divide into groups of four. Assign one response to each group and have each group create a plan so that class members can develop and exhibit that faith in the upcoming week. After five minutes, ask a volunteer from each group to share their group's plan with the class.

Option. Write the following question on the board: *What are untruths that we tell ourselves that prevent us from going to Jesus with our needs?* Conduct a brainstorming exercise to answer the question. Write responses on the board. Ask the following question for whole-class discussion: "How does today's lesson encourage us to ask Jesus for the help we need?"

Alternative. Distribute copies of the "Jumbled Words, Clear Messages" activity from the activity page. Have learners work with a partner to complete as indicated. If time allows, have pairs present their findings to the whole group. Conclude class with a time of prayer, thanking God for the truths stated in the unscrambled messages and asking God for the courage to share those truths with someone in the upcoming week.

April 21
Lesson 8 (KJV)

Faith of an Anointer

Devotional Reading: Romans 8:1-16
Background Scripture: Luke 7:36-50

Luke 7:36-39, 44-50

36 And one of the Pharisees desired him
that he would eat with him. And he went into
the Pharisee's house, and sat down to meat.
37 And, behold, a woman in the city, which
was a sinner, when she knew that Jesus sat at
meat in the Pharisee's house, brought an ala-
baster box of ointment,
38 And stood at his feet behind him weep-
ing, and began to wash his feet with tears, and
did wipe them with the hairs of her head, and
kissed his feet, and anointed them with the
ointment.
39 Now when the Pharisee which had bid-
den him saw it, he spake within himself, say-
ing, This man, if he were a prophet, would have
known who and what manner of woman this is
that toucheth him: for she is a sinner.

---

44 And he turned to the woman, and said
unto Simon, Seest thou this woman? I entered
into thine house, thou gavest me no water for
my feet: but she hath washed my feet with tears,
and wiped them with the hairs of her head.
45 Thou gavest me no kiss: but this woman
since the time I came in hath not ceased to kiss
my feet.
46 My head with oil thou didst not anoint:
but this woman hath anointed my feet with
ointment.
47 Wherefore I say unto thee, Her sins,
which are many, are forgiven; for she loved
much: but to whom little is forgiven, the same
loveth little.
48 And he said unto her, Thy sins are
forgiven.
49 And they that sat at meat with him began
to say within themselves, Who is this that for-
giveth sins also?
50 And he said to the woman, Thy faith
hath saved thee; go in peace.

Key Text

He said to the woman, Thy faith hath saved thee; go in peace. **—Luke 7:50**

Examining

Our Faith

Unit II: The Measure of Faith

Lessons 6–9

Lesson Aims

After participating in this lesson, each learner will be able to:

1. Identify what "saved" the woman.

2. Compare and contrast the mindsets of Jesus, the Pharisee, and the woman.

3. Evaluate his or her own mindset in light of those three.

Lesson Outline

Introduction
- A. A Person's Value
- B. Lesson Context

I. Three People (Luke 7:36-39)
- A. An Invited Guest (v. 36)
- B. An Uninvited Guest (vv. 37-38)
- C. An Ungracious Host (v. 39)

II. Different Actions (Luke 7:44-50)
- A. Criticism and Praise (vv. 44-46)
  Feet Worth Kissing
- B. Little and Much (vv. 47-48)
- C. Forgiveness and Peace (vv. 49-50)
  The Right Rock

Conclusion
- A. Who Needs Forgiveness?
- B. Prayer
- C. Thought to Remember

Introduction

A. A Person's Value

The "smiley face killer" (so-called because of notes he sent to the police) was a self-appointed vigilante. As depicted in the TV documentary series *Forensic Factor,* he seemed determined to put an end to prostitution in his town by murdering those who engaged in that immoral trade. By the time this otherwise ordinary citizen was caught, he had murdered 13 women.

The investigation into the murders was initially hampered because there wasn't much concern from the general public over the fate of missing prostitutes. In the first place, few people noticed that the women were missing. Second, most people seemed to view prostitutes as the dregs of society.

Today's text features a law-abiding citizen and a sinful woman who both met the merciful Savior. Jesus' interaction with them reveals an important link between forgiveness and love.

B. Lesson Context

Just prior to the events of today's lesson, Luke summarized two viewpoints toward Jesus that had emerged. Those viewpoints are revealed by reactions to John the Baptist. On the one hand, "All the people that heard [Jesus], and the publicans, justified God, being baptized with the baptism of John" (Luke 7:29). On the other hand, "the Pharisees and lawyers rejected the counsel of God against themselves, being not baptized of him" (7:30). Rejection of John the Baptist, the Christ's forerunner (1:15-17; 3:1-20; 7:33-35), meant rejecting the Christ as well (Matthew 17:12). This set the stage for a contrast between those who held these polar-opposite viewpoints.

As an oversimplification, we can see "the publicans" (tax collectors) as a demographic that represented the first view above. These Jews had chosen to work with the Romans to extract taxes from their fellow Jews, thereby earning great scorn as collaborators. Tax collectors could become wealthy by overcharging taxes (see Luke 19:2, 8).

The Pharisees, by contrast, can be seen as primary representatives of the second viewpoint above. Pharisees advocated strict and scrupulous observance of the Law of Moses. Over time, this resulted in human traditions being added to that law. See Jesus' critique of this fact in Matthew 23:1-36 and Mark 7:1-23.

The first-century Jewish historian Josephus estimated that there were only about 6,000 Pharisees throughout the Roman empire. Perhaps no more than a few hundred lived in the villages of Galilee. Yet they exerted an influence out of proportion to their numbers, as witnessed by their being mentioned about 100 times in the New Testament. (By contrast, Sadducees are mentioned only 14 times.)

Today's lesson takes us to an early point in Jesus' ministry when things had gotten serious enough for Pharisees to come from "every town of Galilee, and Judaea, and Jerusalem" to investigate Him (Luke 5:17). The nearest example up to the point of today's lesson is Jesus' having been in the village of Nain, about 25 miles southwest of Capernaum (7:11). Combining that fact with information in Luke 8:1, 22, and 26, we conclude that a village in Galilee was the location of today's lesson.

I. Three People

(Luke 7:36-39)

A. An Invited Guest (v. 36)

36. And one of the Pharisees desired him that he would eat with him. And he went into the Pharisee's house, and sat down to meat.

The first use of the word *him* refers to Jesus. This is one of three times in Luke that Jesus was invited to a meal at the home of a Pharisee (see Luke 11:37; 14:1). On whether the Pharisee's invitation included other guests, see commentary on 7:49, below.

The motive behind the invitations seemed to be that of scrutinizing Jesus more closely, noting any violations of the Law of Moses as interpreted by *the Pharisees.* In so doing, they were asking the wrong question of themselves. That question was: *Is Jesus on the side of truth as we know it?* But their question should have been: *Are we on the side of truth as Jesus is witnessing to it?*

B. An Uninvited Guest (vv. 37-38)

37a. And, behold, a woman in the city, which was a sinner, when she knew that Jesus sat at meat in the Pharisee's house.

Some students have identified this *woman* as Mary Magdalene, who is introduced in the following chapter (Luke 8:2). But this identification is speculative. Unless the woman's arrival at *the Pharisee's house* was a "set up" to trap Jesus (compare 20:20-26), it is safe to assume that she had not been invited. Therefore, the host did not welcome her presence at his dinner.

The scandal factor was multiplied by the fact that she *was a sinner.* Such a reputation probably suggests (but does not require) that the woman was a prostitute. Prostitution and harlots are mentioned about 100 times in the Old Testament and a dozen times in the New Testament. Sometimes this immorality is blended with the sin of adultery (example: Hosea 3:1-3). Prostitution is frequently used figuratively to refer to idol worship (example: Ezekiel 16:15-34). And although prostitution is sometimes presented in a matter-of-fact way (examples: Genesis 38; Joshua 2), the activity as such is never commended (Leviticus 19:29; 21:7, 9, 14; 1 Corinthians 6:15; etc.).

37b. Brought an alabaster box of ointment.

This action indicates preparation for the woman's encounter with Jesus. The woman who later anointed Jesus in Bethany also had *an alabaster box* (Matthew 26:7; Mark 14:3; see also John 12:1-3). These were appropriate containers for various oils. The woman's vessel held *ointment,* which is an aromatic perfume that could be rubbed into the hair or onto the skin. On that other occasion, Mark 14:3-5 establishes both the nature and value of the ointment. But no such specifics are noted in

How to Say It

alabaster	al-uh-*bas*-ter.
Capernaum	Kuh-*per*-nay-um.
Josephus	Jo-*see*-fus.
Magdalene	*Mag*-duh-leen or Mag-duh-*lee*-nee.
Nain	*Nay*-in.

the scene before us. Even so, this may be at a great expense on her part.

38a. And stood at his feet behind him weeping, and began to wash his feet with tears.

What happened must have surprised everyone. With no spoken word recorded, the woman went from a posture of standing to one of kneeling near Jesus—that's the only way for her to have been able to be in a position to wash *his feet*. It was customary to take off one's sandals during a meal, and people would sit around the low table on their knees with their feet behind them. The text says nothing about why she was *weeping*. We can only speculate that her tears come out of a repentant heart.

What Do You Think?

When have you been reduced to tears in Jesus' presence?

Digging Deeper

What blessing did you experience after being vulnerable at Jesus' feet?

38b. And did wipe them with the hairs of her head, and kissed his feet, and anointed them with the ointment.

There's more than meets the eye here as the woman used *the hairs of her head* as a washcloth. Women's hair in this era was typically bound up. Therefore this woman's letting her hair down was a departure from propriety. This act further suggests that she was lost in the moment with Jesus. She did not consider what anyone else might see or think.

C. An Ungracious Host (v. 39)

39. Now when the Pharisee which had bidden him saw it, he spake within himself, saying, This man, if he were a prophet, would have known who and what manner of woman this is that toucheth him: for she is a sinner.

Identities of local prostitutes were likely well known since the activities of such persons could not be secret for long in small villages. If the woman was indeed a prostitute, it explains why *the Pharisee* was scandalized that Jesus would not recognize her as *a sinner*. The Pharisee himself recognized her immediately.

The Pharisee's unspoken thoughts condemned both the woman and Jesus (contrast Luke 7:16). The Pharisee reasoned from a certain presupposition that he wouldn't allow to be overturned: if Jesus doesn't fit the Pharisee's idea of how a prophet should conduct himself, then Jesus can't be one. Jesus was thought to have carelessly allowed the woman's touch. The Jews' understanding of what made them unclean was often tied to touching (example: Numbers 9:6; 19:11). In general, touching anything considered unclean made the toucher unclean as well (see Isaiah 52:11; Haggai 2:13). Pharisees were obsessed with the avoidance of anything unclean or violations of the Law of Moses. This woman was the living embodiment of everything they warned against. The contrast between the woman, who expresses her love for Jesus, and the Pharisee, who views her with disdain, could hardly be sharper.

In the verses not included in today's lesson (Luke 7:40-43), Jesus told Simon a parable about a money lender pardoning debtors. While Jesus turns to the woman, He still speaks to Simon, but He is getting ready to make the parable a reality.

II. Different Actions

(Luke 7:44-50)

A. Criticism and Praise (vv. 44-46)

44. And he turned to the woman, and said unto Simon, Seest thou this woman? I entered into thine house, thou gavest me no water for my feet: but she hath washed my feet with tears, and wiped them with the hairs of her head.

An awkward situation ensued: Jesus *turned to the woman*, but His words were for the Pharisee. We also learn that the Pharisee's name was *Simon*, a common Jewish name. Simon (or "Simeon") was the second-born son of Jacob (Genesis 29:33), a patriarch of the tribes of Israel. Jesus had two disciples named Simon (Matthew 10:2, 4) as well as a brother (Mark 6:3), but this Pharisee was none of these.

Foot-washing was a centuries-old cultural practice (Genesis 18:4; 19:2; 43:24; etc.). It was an act of hospitality for guests in one's house. Footwear of the era did not keep dust and dirt out. Walking on unpaved roads resulted in feet getting filthy quickly, thus the expedience of the foot-washing courtesy—or at least providing water and a towel for the guest to do the foot-washing himself. Yet Simon had not even provided those to Jesus! Simon's actions were cold and calculated; both he and Jesus knew it. What a contrast to the woman, whose actions were those of spontaneous gratitude.

45. Thou gavest me no kiss: but this woman since the time I came in hath not ceased to kiss my feet.

As difficult as it may be for us to understand the ancient cultural practice of foot-washing, understanding the significance of a *kiss* is scarcely any easier! The missing *kiss* at issue here would have been an expression of greeting and welcome, customarily offered by a host to his guest (see Luke 15:20; compare Romans 16:16; contrast Luke 22:47-48). As with the absence of foot-washing water, the lack of a kiss indicates something less than full acceptance by the host.

The kissing of *feet* rather than the cheeks was not a part of hospitality expectations. But its presence here shows the woman's humility and her desire to serve Jesus.

Feet Worth Kissing

You will be hard-pressed to find a culture where kissing someone's feet in public is a normal, everyday expectation! It's a universal truth that feet stink, especially when people wear open sandals and walk on streets also used by animals. Most kissing aims for the face, cheek, or hand for a variety of reasons. And surely one of those reasons is that if we want to put our lips on something, clean is better.

To kiss feet eagerly indicates total devotion. The one whose feet are worthy of being kissed is special. It's uncomfortable to display affection in a way that breaks cultural norms unless the esteem of the object of one's love requires it. When was the last time your level of devotion to Jesus caused you to exceed your "embarrassment threshold" in an act of loving service to Him? —D. D.

46. My head with oil thou didst not anoint: but this woman hath anointed my feet with ointment.

To offer one's *head* to be anointed *with oil* also seems strange to us, something we would never expect when visiting a friend's home. But this, too, was a gesture of hospitality in first-century Palestine. The practice communicated favor (see Psalm 23:5; Ecclesiastes 9:8). Simon had withheld this level of courtesy as well.

The oil to which Jesus referred was olive oil, the multipurpose liquid used for cooking, fueling lamps, and medicinal purposes. By contrast, the woman anointed the *feet* of Jesus with perfumed *ointment* from her alabaster container. This might have been nard oil, which was highly prized and expensive in Palestine—much more so than household olive oil (compare Mark 14:3; John 12:3). The contrast of anointing the feet rather than the head demonstrated the great humility of the woman. Her actions were unsolicited.

> **What Do You Think?**
> When do you practice hospitality? Keep in mind that this is not limited to hosting dinners.
> **Digging Deeper**
> How does your hospitality honor Jesus?

B. Little and Much (vv. 47-48)

47. Wherefore I say unto thee, Her sins, which are many, are forgiven; for she loved much: but to whom little is forgiven, the same loveth little.

The Pharisee Simon had doubted Jesus' credentials as a prophet. But at this point, Jesus spoke with prophetic insight. The moral status of the woman as "a sinner" is uncontested—it is a given. But the scene depicted here illustrates the astonishing power and magnitude of God's forgiveness and its realization by the recipient. The woman's great love demonstrated that she knew she had much for which to be forgiven (see Luke 7:42-43, not in our printed text).

By contrast, Simon *loveth little* because his scrupulous attention to the Law of Moses had resulted in few sins to be forgiven of. Simon was proud of his tidy lifestyle as a Pharisee. He believed that he was vindicated by his success in keeping the Law of Moses strictly and by his descent from Abraham (John 8:39). The Pharisee understood neither why he needed to love (and be loved by) Jesus nor how the woman's *sins, which are many* could be forgiven, especially by Jesus (see Mark 2:7). In His encounters with sinners, Jesus walked the fine line between affirming the person while not condoning the sin (examples: John 4:17-18; 5:14; 8:10-11), and that's what we see Him do here.

What Do You Think?

What danger is there in not acknowledging one's own sins as serious or many?

Digging Deeper

How do you guard against both excessive pride in your own efforts and debilitating awareness of your sin?

48. And he said unto her, Thy sins are forgiven.

Jesus then spoke directly to the woman, but His words were for everyone in the room to hear. No such declaration of *thy sins are forgiven* is recorded for Simon the Pharisee.

C. Forgiveness and Peace (vv. 49-50)

49a. And they that sat at meat with him began to say within themselves.

The Pharisee's invitation in Luke 7:36 above does not mention the presence of friends or colleagues of the host or whether any of Jesus' disciples were invited. But others were indeed present at the dinner, as evidenced by the phrase *they that sat at meat with him.*

49b. Who is this that forgiveth sins also?

This is not the first time that Luke records controversy resulting from Jesus' forgiving *sins.* In the story of a paralyzed man of lesson 6, Jesus both healed the man and pronounced his sins to be forgiven (Luke 5:20; compare Matthew 9:2). The audience of scribes and Pharisees were outraged. But they spoke better than they knew with their rhetorical question, "Who can forgive sins, but God alone?" (Luke 5:21).

Similarly, Simon and his other guests in today's lesson are startled by Jesus' declaration. The pronouncement of forgiveness of sins in both texts forces a choice on the religious leaders: if Jesus indeed had the power to forgive sins, then He is God-in-the-flesh. But if Jesus did not have such power, then He was guilty of blasphemy.

50. And he said to the woman, Thy faith hath saved thee; go in peace.

The episode is closed with a final two-part word from Jesus to the woman. First, He clarifies the underlying reason for her forgiveness: her *faith,* which is the source of her love. By devoting herself to Jesus, she has yielded her heart to Him in repentance.

Second, Jesus' telling her to *go in peace* reminds us of His words to a sinful woman caught in adultery. After that woman's accusers left the scene, Jesus said to her, "Go, and sin no more" (John 8:11). Neither woman would have found peace if they had departed only to resume lives of sin.

What Do You Think?

What circumstances make it difficult to experience peace in your salvation?

Digging Deeper

If Jesus told you to "go in peace," how would that impact your daily activities?

The Right Rock

The most important test of Carl's life neared, but he wasn't nervous. He had no reason to be as long as he still had his lucky rock. Once upon a time, the smoothest oval-shaped stone he had ever laid his eyes on sat under a tree in his yard. Ever since then, from first grade to college, he never took a test without the lucky rock in his pocket. He earned straight A's.

So when Carl flunked his first test in over a decade, he was shocked. The rock had been in his pocket the whole exam! The failure shook his faith.

Faith has no power in itself. It's only as powerful as the object of one's faith. Faith in a rock to help you ace a test is silly and impotent. Rocks don't do that. Our faith in something does not magically activate what we believe it can do.

Faith in Christ Jesus is what matters. He is the ultimate Rock (Psalms 18:31, 46; 19:14; 28:1; 95:1;

etc.). He will never fail us. The faith of the sinful woman was not faith in her ability to convince Jesus to do something by means of her power of persuasion. Rather, her faith was focused on her Savior. Where is your faith focused? On your horoscope? On your retirement nest egg? On the government? Or on Jesus? —D. D.

Conclusion

A. Who Needs Forgiveness?

Many unbelievers today are involved in unholy, unbiblical activities. Some even make their living doing things that Christians know are immoral. It is easy for those within the church to take a dim view of these people, judging them to be incorrigible sinners. To be sure, a judging function does (or should) exist legitimately within the church (Matthew 7:16; 1 Corinthians 5:1–6:5; Titus 1:10-16; 3:10; etc.). But this judging function bears little, if any, resemblance to the one used by Simon the Pharisee. His viewpoint was that of complete rejection, thinking of himself more highly and being confident of his own righteousness (compare Luke 18:9-14).

But Simon was not completely sinless. As a student of the Law of Moses, he should have realized, as the Pharisee Paul did, that "all have sinned, and come short of the glory of God" (Romans 3:23; compare Acts 23:6). Another way to look at it is to imagine a survey being taken in Pharisee Simon's village. The survey question is, "Who needs to be forgiven, Simon or the immoral woman?" The villagers would predictably respond overwhelmingly to "the immoral woman." But this is really a trick question since it presents a false choice. It is not a matter of "either/or," but one of "both/and." They both needed to be forgiven of sin. They both needed a humble faith that would bring them to God with hearts full of love. They both needed to follow Jesus, love God, and serve others. The tragedy of this story is that only one of these people left the banquet forgiven. Simon's apparent pride in seeing himself superior to the woman blocked any realization of needing forgiveness.

Christians are to flee from sin and obey God. We show our love for God when we keep His commandments (1 John 5:2-3). But does this justify us when we reject and condemn those who struggle with sin? Are sinners welcome in our fellowship if they are seeking to love Jesus? Or must they clean up their sinful lives before they enter the doors of our church? Jesus taught that even the vilest of sinners can be forgiven if they turn to Him in faith and love. Are we willing to follow Him in His love for sinners and help them as they strive to follow Jesus, however imperfectly?

Visual for Lesson 8. *Allow learners to ponder this question and what their love for Christ suggests about the answer before praying to end class.*

What Do You Think?

What makes a good dinner guest?

Digging Deeper

Do Jesus' words and actions at this dinner change your answer? How, or why not?

B. Prayer

Heavenly Father, You have shown us Your willingness to forgive sinners. May we not keep that message to ourselves! And let us not be selective in pretending to know who will accept and who won't. Help us to love our neighbors as you love us by taking the good news of Your Son to them. In His name we pray. Amen.

C. Thought to Remember

To have forgiveness, we must first realize that we need it.

Involvement Learning

Enhance your lesson with KJV Bible Student *(from your curriculum supplier) and the reproducible activity page (at www.standardlesson.com or in the back of the* KJV Standard Lesson Commentary Deluxe Edition*).*

Into the Lesson

Write on the board *Rejection / Acceptance* as the headers of two columns. Divide learners into pairs or triads and ask them to brainstorm books, songs, TV shows/episodes, and/or movies that have themes fitting under one or both columns. Invite them to use smartphones to help them if needed. After five minutes, let groups share their conclusions while you write them on the board. Discuss with the whole class: 1–How common is rejection in our culture? 2–What have you learned by being accepted just as you are by someone in your life?

Lead to Bible study by saying, "Today's lesson will show us someone who was known for her sinfulness. Yet she risked further rejection to honor Jesus. As we look at the story, try to imagine what she, and those around her, were thinking as the incident unfolded."

Into the Word

Distribute a handout (you create) with the title "What Were They Thinking?" The chart should have four columns with the headers *Scripture / Pharisee / Woman / Jesus.* In the *Scripture* column, list four references from today's text: Luke 7:36-38; 7:39; 7:44-47; 7:48-50. Using the same groups as earlier in the lesson, ask learners to complete the chart together. Ask them to use their "sanctified imaginations" to consider what each person might have been thinking and feeling.

After six to eight minutes, ask learners to share their answers, jotting down any they hear from another group that are particularly compelling. Then have them circle the reactions on their charts that they find most surprising and put an exclamation point beside the sections they find most troubling. Then call the groups together once again to discuss as a whole class.

Alternative. Distribute copies of the "An Encounter with Jesus" exercise from the activity page, which you can download. Have groups work together to complete as indicated.

Into Life

Have learners refer back to the Bible-study chart they completed above. Ask them individually to put a star beside any emotions or thoughts recorded on their charts that they have ever had themselves. After a minute, ask volunteers to share.

Divide the learners into two groups. Assign a different discussion question to each group: 1–What leads Christians today to sometimes think like the Pharisee in this story? How can Christians react more like Jesus and less like the Pharisee? 2–What leads Christians today to react to Jesus with the passionate conviction this sinful woman displayed? What would prompt us to relate to Him more as she did? Give groups several minutes for this discussion.

Alternative. Distribute copies of the "Scripture Story, Contemporary Attitudes" exercise from the activity page. Have learners complete it individually in a minute or less before discussing conclusions with a partner.

After either activity, call the class together and urge as many as possible to share their reactions and conclusions after comparing the characters in today's story with their own life experiences.

Distribute slips of paper to each learner to write down one or more of the following prompts:

1. Lord, help us to have the compassion of Jesus for those who may not feel worthy to seek Him.
2. Lord, help us to overcome our preoccupation with ourselves that keeps us from boldly expressing our love for Jesus.
3. Lord, forgive us when we've looked down on others who need Jesus as much as we do.

Invite participants to use the prayer slips as part of their prayer time this week.

April 28
Lesson 9 (KJV)

Faith of a Canaanite

Devotional Reading: Psalm 61
Background Scripture: Matthew 15:21-28

Matthew 15:21-28

21 Then Jesus went thence, and departed into the coasts of Tyre and Sidon.

22 And, behold, a woman of Canaan came out of the same coasts, and cried unto him, saying, Have mercy on me, O Lord, thou Son of David; my daughter is grievously vexed with a devil.

23 But he answered her not a word. And his disciples came and besought him, saying, Send her away; for she crieth after us.

24 But he answered and said, I am not sent but unto the lost sheep of the house of Israel.

25 Then came she and worshipped him, saying, Lord, help me.

26 But he answered and said, It is not meet to take the children's bread, and to cast it to dogs.

27 And she said, Truth, Lord: yet the dogs eat of the crumbs which fall from their masters' table.

28 Then Jesus answered and said unto her, O woman, great is thy faith: be it unto thee even as thou wilt. And her daughter was made whole from that very hour.

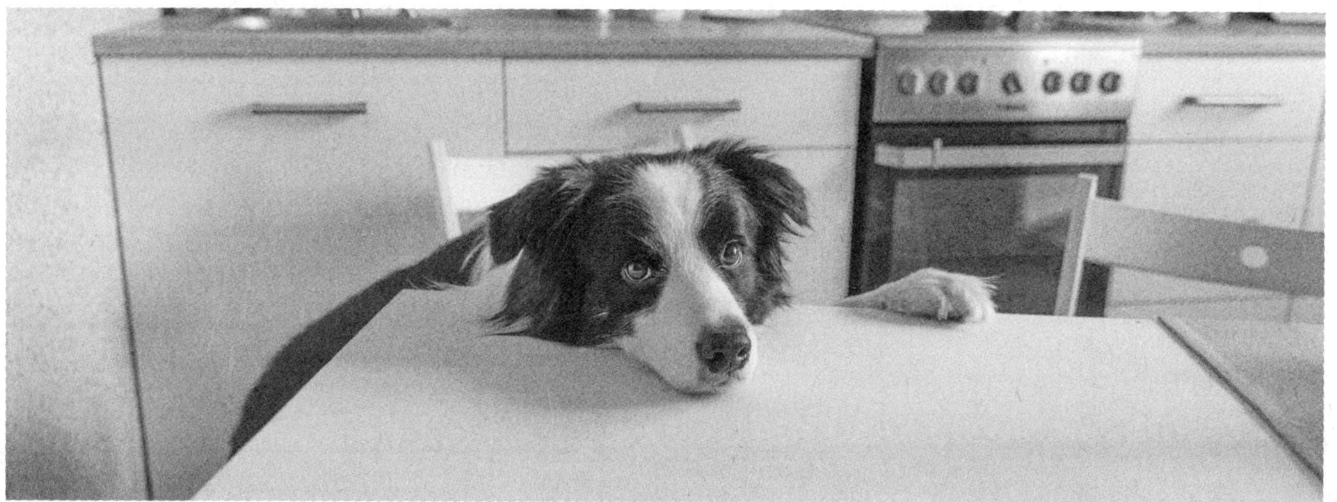

Key Text

Then Jesus answered and said unto her, O woman, great is thy faith: be it unto thee even as thou wilt. And her daughter was made whole from that very hour. **—Matthew 15:28**

Examining

Our Faith

Unit II: The Measure of Faith

Lessons 6–9

Lesson Aims

After participating in this lesson, each learner will be able to:

1. Summarize the interaction between Jesus and the Canaanite woman.

2. Explain Jesus' response in verse 24.

3. Brainstorm situations where a parent should and should not intervene on behalf of a child.

Lesson Outline

Introduction
- A. Blessing an "Outsider"
- B. Lesson Context

I. First Request (Matthew 15:21-24)
- A. Woman's Mission (vv. 21-22)
  - *A Mother's Care*
- B. Jesus' Mission (vv. 23-24)

II. Second Request (Matthew 15:25-28)
- A. Great Need (v. 25)
- B. Greater Priority (vv. 26-27)
- C. Great Faith (v. 28)
  - *No Surprises Here*

Conclusion
- A. Great Faith for God's People
- B. Prayer
- C. Thought to Remember

Introduction

A. Blessing an "Outsider"

The Rain Gutter Regatta was one of the highlights of my time in Cub Scouts. Competitors built tiny sailboats small enough to be placed in a rain gutter. These boats were human-powered by our blowing on the sails. Competitors risked blowing too hard or at the wrong angle lest they face disqualification.

One year, another boy showed up to the regatta with an unfinished boat that was barely "seaworthy." It hardly floated, and the boy was upset. My dad noticed the boy's frustration and offered to help him fix his boat into a more appropriate vessel. After a few minutes of work, my dad turned the barely "seaworthy" vessel into a regatta-winning craft. It even beat my boat in the process.

My dad blessed that boy with generosity. I had difficulty, however, accepting my dad's actions. I was upset because he had helped a boy I barely knew—a boy I considered an "outsider" to our family.

As you read today's lesson, consider which character in the story with whom you most identify. Do you align with the (outsider) woman or the (insider) disciples? Either option will affect how you view God's gracious and generous blessings.

B. Lesson Context

The Gospel of Matthew does not explicitly identify its author. The early church, however, attributed authorship to Matthew, a tax collector who became one of the apostles (Matthew 9:9; 10:3). Other Gospels mention this person by his given name: Levi (Mark 2:14; Luke 5:27-28), named after one of the sons of Jacob (see Genesis 29:34; 35:23).

As a tax collector, Matthew worked with the foreign occupiers of Palestine: the Romans. During the first century AD, tax collectors (also known as *publicans*) were despised by their fellow countrymen (example: Luke 18:11). They were seen as traitors to the Jewish people because they assisted the Romans in taking tax money. They were also held in low regard because they frequently enriched themselves at the expense of others (example: 19:2, 8).

The only other information we have about this

apostle is that he was the "son of Alphaeus" (Mark 2:14). The apostle James was also the "son of Alphaeus" (Matthew 10:3; Mark 3:18; Luke 6:15). These two may have been brothers, but none of the Gospels make that relationship apparent like they do with other sets of brothers (Matthew 4:21; 10:2; Mark 1:19).

Matthew's Gospel contains the most quotations from the Old Testament of the four Gospels. The Gospel of Matthew has about 65 Old Testament quotes; Mark has about 30; Luke has about 26, and John has about 16. As such, students frequently call Matthew the "most Jewish" of the four Gospels. It is thought that Matthew intended his Gospel to be received by a primarily Jewish audience.

Although this Gospel emphasized the Jewish context of Jesus's ministry (see Matthew 10:6; 15:24), its message reveals that the gospel of Jesus Christ was intended for both Jew and Gentile. Matthew is the only Gospel to record the visit of the Gentile wise men (2:1-12). It is also the only one to include Jesus' commission to His disciples that they "teach all nations" (28:16-20).

The events leading to today's Scripture reveal the intended expansion of the gospel message. As Jesus' ministry in Galilee drew to a close, it became evident that His people would reject Him and His mission (see Matthew 13:53-58). His disciples displayed little faith regarding His identity (see 14:22-32). They also failed to understand His teaching (15:12-20). Even the religious leaders were offended by Jesus' message (15:1-9). The people most expected to accept Jesus and His mission failed to understand. Mark 7:24-30 is a parallel account of Matthew 15:21-28.

I. First Request
(Matthew 15:21-24)

A. Woman's Mission (vv. 21-22)

21. Then Jesus went thence, and departed into the coasts of Tyre and Sidon.

This verse is not the first time Matthew's Gospel states that Jesus *went* from one area to another (compare Matthew 4:12; 12:15; 14:13). After He confronted the religious leaders (15:1-9), He *departed* from their midst.

Jesus frequently withdrew from crowds of people so that He could pray in solitude (examples: Matthew 14:23; Luke 5:16). He also removed himself from those who might misunderstand His ministry (example: John 6:15).

Tyre and Sidon were two prominent cities located on the coast of the Mediterranean Sea north of Galilee, in the region that is modern-day Lebanon. Following the exodus, much of the area was designated for the tribe of Asher (Joshua 19:24-31). But that tribe didn't drive out the inhabitants as directed (Judges 1:31-32). Tyre was about 125 miles north of Jerusalem, with Sidon being an additional 25 miles farther. The cities are mentioned together as "Tyre and Sidon" about 30 times in the Bible.

Because of their access to maritime trade, the cities attained great wealth—especially Tyre (also called "Tyrus"; see Zechariah 9:3). However, their prideful leaders had acted unjustly (see Ezekiel 26–28). As a result, the Old Testament prophets strongly condemned the cities (examples: Isaiah 23:1-18; Joel 3:4; Amos 1:9-10).

Jesus mentioned these cities in His indictment of the Jewish towns of Chorazin, Bethsaida, and Capernaum (Matthew 11:20-24; Luke 10:13-14). His contrast to the Gentile cities was to make a lesser-to-greater argument. If Gentile cities would have repented from sin and thereby avoided judgment, how much more should the Jewish towns do the same?

The Law of Moses taught the Israelites to avoid following the pagan practices of other people

How to Say It

Bethsaida	Beth-*say*-uh-duh.
Canaanite	*Kay*-nu-**nite**.
Capernaum	Kuh-*per*-nay-um.
centurion	sen-*ture*-ee-un.
Chorazin	Ko-*ray*-zin.
Deuteronomy	Due-ter-*ahn*-uh-me.
Mediterranean	*Med*-uh-tuh-**ray**-nee-un.
omniscient	ahm-*nish*-unt.
Phoenicians	Fuh-*nish*-unz.
Syrophenician	*Sigh*-roe-fih-**nish**-un.
Zarephath	*Zair*-uh-fath.

groups (Leviticus 18:3). By withdrawing into the *coasts* near those cities, Jesus ensured that no Jewish person would follow Him into a Gentile region.

Centuries before, this region was the location of two events involving the prophet Elijah (1 Kings 17:7-24). While in the town of Zarephath, that prophet demonstrated God's provision for a widow and resurrected the son of another woman. Perhaps the author Matthew had this story in mind as he wrote his account of the events that occurred to Jesus and His followers.

What Do You Think?

How do you decide whether or not to withdraw from a situation for your own spiritual, physical, or emotional health?

Digging Deeper

How might the example of Jesus help inform your decision?

22a. And, behold, a woman of Canaan came out of the same coasts, and cried unto him.

The crowds that followed Jesus included people from the region of Tyre and Sidon (see Mark 3:7-8). This *woman* undoubtedly had heard of Jesus and His work because of His popularity, as evidenced by those crowds.

Matthew describes her as being *of Canaan*, but Mark is more specific, noting that "the woman was a Greek, a Syrophenician" (Mark 7:26). The Canaanites were an ancient people who had settled in Palestine before the arrival of the Israelites (see Exodus 3:8). During the time of the ancient Israelites, the Canaanites were considered the enemies of Israel (example: Deuteronomy 7:1-6). Their descendants became the Phoenicians—people living in the regions of Tyre and Sidon. This woman was certainly not of Jewish heritage, and her ethnic background would have been seen in a negative light by most first-century Jewish people (compare Acts 10:28).

Mark's Gospel provides other details not given by Matthew. Mark states that Jesus "entered into an house" (Mark 7:24). This house was likely not the woman's (compare 7:30). That Gospel also reveals that Jesus had intended for His presence in that region to be a secret, but "he could not be hid" (7:24). The fact that Jesus desired secrecy reveals that He did not initially intend for His journey into Gentile territory to be a teaching mission.

22b. Saying, Have mercy on me, O Lord, thou Son of David; my daughter is grievously vexed with a devil.

The form of the designation *Son of David* appears 17 times in the Gospels. Matthew's Gospel contains 10 of those instances. In 1 of those 10, the reference is to Joseph (Matthew 1:20); in the other 9, people use that title about the Messiah (here and 1:1; 9:27; 12:23; 20:30-31; 21:9, 15; 22:42). Jesus never directly applied the designation to himself, but He did so indirectly (22:42; Mark 12:35; Luke 20:41).

The designation comes from the hope that a descendant of Israel's King David would someday rule with peace and justice (see 2 Samuel 7:12-16; Isaiah 9:6-7; Jeremiah 23:5-6; Ezekiel 34:23; compare Psalm 110). During the time between the Old and New Testaments, the Jewish people had strong expectations of this individual. They hoped the Son of David would come as a political leader to cleanse Jerusalem (see the nonbiblical Psalms of Solomon 17:22-28).

Because this designation reflected a uniquely Jewish expectation, it is shocking that a Gentile woman used it about Jesus. She would have been the most unexpected person to recognize Jesus as the long-awaited descendant of David. Before this event, some people had questioned whether Jesus was the Son of David (Matthew 12:23). This woman spoke in a way that reflected her genuine belief about Jesus' identity and mission.

The woman's cry for *mercy* resulted from seeing her daughter suffer demon possession. The New Testament writers understand devils and unclean (evil) spirits as the same thing (examples: Luke 8:2, 29). Neither Matthew nor Mark describes the daughter's symptoms. Others who experienced demonic possession also experienced physical disorders (examples: Matthew 9:32; 12:22). Therefore, we can assume that the daughter suffered similarly.

The way that Matthew's Gospel presents the woman's request is notable. She did not explicitly ask Jesus to heal her *daughter*, thus freeing the daughter from demonic possession (contrast Mark

7:26). Instead, the mother desired to experience *mercy* herself. She was likely her daughter's primary caretaker, and the weight of that work had become an unbearable burden.

What Do You Think?

What steps can we take to increase our faith in God before we see Him act?

Digging Deeper

How do cautionary admonishments, such as that of Luke 12:22-23, help inform your answer?

A Mother's Care

My mother was the most influential woman in my life. As a single parent, she was solely responsible for caring for my sibling and me. She worked hard to give us the best life possible. She began a new business, formed new relationships, and adopted new habits to care for us.

We know very little about the caring mother in today's lesson text. But caring for her daughter had taken its toll on the mother. By reaching out to Jesus, the mother displayed the extent that she was willing to go for the good of her daughter.

Who went to great lengths to care for you as a child? Maybe that person was your mother. Or perhaps that person was your father, an extended family member, or someone else altogether. Regardless of who that earthly caretaker was, remember God is the ultimate source of care: "As one whom his mother comforteth, so will I comfort you" (Isaiah 66:13). What prevents you from accepting God's care or being an agent of it to another? —O. P.

B. Jesus' Mission (vv. 23-24)

23a. But he answered her not a word.

Jesus' refusal to answer the woman might seem cruel, but His silence reflects some cultural differences of His day. At that time, it would be considered inappropriate for a Jewish rabbi to answer a woman—and a Gentile woman, no less (compare John 4:9)!

His silence could also be considered a test of the strength and quality of the woman's faith. Jewish teachers and rabbis sometimes tested their students, and Jcsus was no exception (examples: John 5:6; 6:6). The strategic silence created space for the woman to continue talking and explaining her desires.

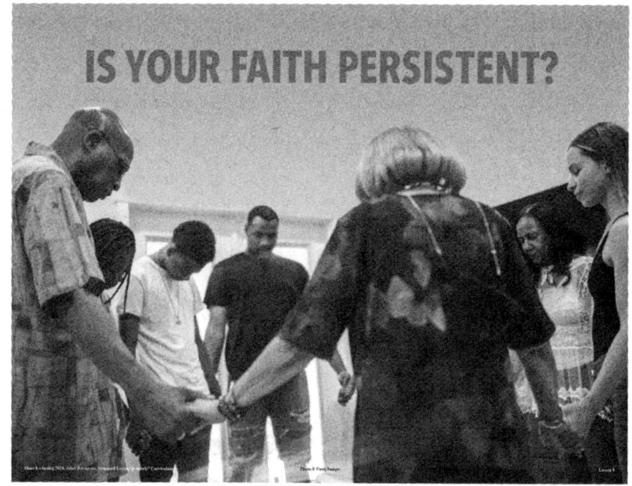

Visual for Lesson 9. *Have this visual on display as you pose the discussion question that is associated with Matthew 15:28a.*

23b. And his disciples came and besought him, saying, Send her away; for she crieth after us.

The woman had become a nuisance to Jesus' *disciples*. They did not address whether they thought Jesus should grant her request. Instead, the disciples wanted the woman out of their midst. Did they not think she was worthy of Jesus' aid because she was a Gentile woman? Or was it how *she crieth after* them that led to their dismissive attitude? Either way, the disciples tended to want to dismiss people they considered annoying or distracting (compare Matthew 19:13).

24. But he answered and said, I am not sent but unto the lost sheep of the house of Israel.

Jesus did not send the woman away as His disciples requested. The text is unclear regarding whom He *answered*. If His answer was directed at the disciples, He was reminding them about the mission for which His heavenly Father had *sent* Him (Matthew 10:5-6).

Jesus' primary mission before His resurrection focused on *the house of Israel*. They were like *lost sheep* without a shepherd (examples: Numbers 27:17; 1 Kings 22:17; Ezekiel 34:5-6; Zechariah 10:2; Matthew 9:36). As a result, Jesus came as a shepherd for the people. He provided spiritual care and guidance, like a shepherd caring for sheep (see Ezekiel 34:23; Luke 15:1-7; John 10:1-18, 27-30).

Central to Jesus' mission as a shepherd was His preaching on the need for repentance and the presence of God's kingdom (Matthew 4:17). This mission was first revealed to the people of Israel. God's blessing would be offered first to them. Then through them would blessing be available to all peoples (see Genesis 12:1-3; Isaiah 42:1-7; 49:6-7).

To be clear, Matthew's Gospel is not conveying an anti-Gentile sentiment. Old Testament prophets proclaimed that the Messiah's mission would include Gentiles (examples: Isaiah 19:16-25; Hosea 2:23; Zechariah 14:16). With a few exceptions (example: Matthew 8:5-13), Jesus' earthly ministry focused on the people of Israel. He acknowledged that His mission would reach Gentiles (see 24:14; 25:31-33; 28:19-20).

II. Second Request

(Matthew 15:25-28)

A. Great Need (v. 25)

25. Then came she and worshipped him, saying, Lord, help me.

The woman did not debate Jesus on the direction of His mission. Instead, she sought relief in a way that could only come from a desperate mother.

B. Greater Priority (vv. 26-27)

26. But he answered and said, It is not meet to take the children's bread, and to cast it to dogs.

Jesus responded with a metaphor to the woman's request for help. The statement highlights that the *bread* is given to the children of the household first and foremost. It is inappropriate for sustenance to be handed out *to dogs* when it would deprive the children. Most of Scripture's references to dogs carry a negative meaning (examples: 2 Samuel 9:8; Philippians 3:2). Unlike today's house pets, dogs in biblical times were scavengers (examples: Exodus 22:31; 1 Kings 14:11).

When we read this text today, we might feel that Jesus spoke harshly to the Gentile woman by comparing her people to dogs. But a study of the verses that follow may cause us to conclude otherwise.

In this statement, Jesus highlighted expectations regarding the order of the mission of God. Some Jewish people considered that the Messiah's mission came first and foremost for the people of Israel. Therefore it would have been inappropriate for Jesus to do anything concerning this Gentile woman.

27. And she said, Truth, Lord: yet the dogs eat of the crumbs which fall from their masters' table.

The Gentile woman accepted that Jesus was sent to Israel (Matthew 15:24, above). But she did not accept that He was *exclusively* sent to Israel, and she did not take Jesus' answer as a *no*. Instead, she built on His words, pointing out that *the dogs* did not have to take food from children in order to receive the blessing of *the crumbs*.

> **What Do You Think?**
> What metaphors or analogies might we use to help someone understand the depth of God's grace and mercy?
> **Digging Deeper**
> What are some dangers of using these comparisons?

C. Great Faith (v. 28)

28a. Then Jesus answered and said unto her, O woman, great is thy faith.

Rarely do we read in Matthew's Gospel of instances when *Jesus* publicly commended someone for their faith (see Matthew 9:22, 29). More often, Jesus challenged people for their lack of faith (examples: 6:30; 8:26; 14:31; 16:8). It is two Gentiles—this woman and a Roman centurion (8:10; Luke 7:9 [see lesson 7])—whom Jesus proclaims to have exceptional *faith.*

We should not interpret the designation of *woman* to be one of harshness. It could be used as a term of endearment (example: John 19:26).

> **What Do You Think?**
> How will you exhibit great and persistent faith in the upcoming week?
> **Digging Deeper**
> What steps will you take to address possible roadblocks that challenge your faith?

No Surprises Here

In 2021, I was hired as a university professor to help mentor and teach Latino and Hispanic students. These groups had increased in number at my university. Therefore, the administration felt it was appropriate to have a faculty member who could focus on their needs. I developed a plan that I thought would best reach these students. One of the first tasks was to create a course to educate all students regarding the cultures, religions, and histories of Latino and Hispanic peoples.

Student conversations soon went beyond the classroom. Even in my wildest dreams, I could have never planned for the students' positive response to the course. What I had designed to help *some* students soon turned into a way for *all* students to grow. I was caught unaware by the results and remain hopeful for the welfare and growth of my students!

Jesus, however, is never caught unaware. He is all-knowing (omniscient). He was not caught unaware when the Gentile woman approached Him and asked for mercy. He was not caught unaware when His disciples wanted to send her away. And He was not caught unaware when the Gentile woman demonstrated great faith. He is never unaware of our concerns—He knows them before we do! Do you have a great faith willing to bring your cares to Jesus? —O. P.

28b. Be it unto thee even as thou wilt. And her daughter was made whole from that very hour.

There is another parallel point between this story and Jesus' healing of the Roman centurion's servant in Matthew 8:5-13. In both instances, the healing occurred from a distance. The woman's *daughter was made whole*, and the centurion's servant was healed (Matthew 8:13) without Jesus being in the immediate proximity of the ailing person.

Those two occasions and Jesus' healing of the son of a certain nobleman in John 4:46-54 are the only times in the Gospels when a distance healing occurred. Further, all three instances may each describe the healing of a Gentile. As such, these accounts prefigure the apostles' ministry to the Gentiles described in Acts 13:14-52; 17:1-4, 12; etc.

Conclusion

A. Great Faith for God's People

The woman in today's text was the ultimate "outsider" to a first-century Jewish audience. She was aware of the biases against her. The deck would be stacked against her if she approached a Jewish teacher. Despite that awareness, she came to Jesus anyway. Her desperate situation and her suffering daughter necessitated a bold response.

The woman's behavior revealed a persistent and great faith. As a result, she received mercy from the Son of David. She was considered an "outsider" to some people, but she was an "insider" because of her life of faith.

This Scripture invites us to desire a life of great faith. What blessings do we fail to receive because we limit or misplace our faith? A life of great faith requires steadfast confidence that God will show mercy to everyone. How does your perspective need to change in this regard?

What Do You Think?

Considering this quarter's title, "Examining Our Faith," what's the most important thing you can do to complete a self-examination of your faith?

Digging Deeper

Who will you recruit as an accountability partner to help with that examination?

B. Prayer

Heavenly Father, we are grateful to be part of Your family. Reveal to us the things that prevent us from having great faith. Encourage us when we feel unable to show persistent faith. Give us eyes to see people we consider "outsiders" so we can invite them to experience Your great mercy. In Jesus' name, we pray. Amen.

C. Thought to Remember

Live by great faith!

Involvement Learning

Enhance your lesson with KJV Bible Student *(from your curriculum supplier) and the reproducible activity page (at www.standardlesson.com or in the back of the* KJV Standard Lesson Commentary Deluxe Edition*).*

Into the Lesson

Before class, set aside one index card for each learner. On one side of each card, write the name of a different group of people. (*Examples*: city-dwellers, farmers, oldest children, youngest children, business executives, small-business owners, empty nesters, dog owners, cat owner, public school teachers, church attendees, etc.)

Distribute one card to each learner. Begin the exercise by saying, "We frequently have certain assumptions regarding different groups of people. Write a commonly held assumption about the group on your card." Have learners spend one minute writing down their responses.

After time has passed, ask volunteers to provide their written responses. Then ask the following questions for whole-class discussion: 1–Are these assumptions accurate? Why or why not? 2–What are the dangers of holding these assumptions? 3–How can these assumptions lead to the exclusion of that group?

Lead to Bible study by saying, "Different groups of people have sometimes felt excluded. In today's lesson, we will read about the experience of a woman who was considered an outsider by some people."

Into the Word

Option. Distribute copies of the "Consider the Background" exercise from the activity page, which you can download. Have learners work in pairs to complete as indicated.

Distribute a handout (you create) with the following statements:

1. A woman from Capernaum approached Jesus.
2. The woman asked Jesus to heal her daughter.
3. Jesus did not answer the woman with a word.
4. Jesus' disciples eagerly welcomed the woman into their midst.
5. Jesus said He was sent only to "the lost sheep" of Israel.
6. Jesus responded with a metaphor about dogs eating bread from children.
7. Jesus considered the woman's faith to be "great."
8. Jesus went to the woman's house to heal her daughter.

(*Answers*: 1. False [v. 22a]; 2. False [v. 22b]; 3. True [v. 23a]; 4. False [v.23b]; 5. True [v. 24]; 6. True [v. 26]; 7. True [v. 28a]; 8. False [v. 28b])

Have learners read Matthew 15:21-28 and work in pairs to decide whether the statements are true or false. After no more than 10 minutes, ask pairs to give their answers.

Option. Distribute copies of the "Challenging Her Faith" exercise from the activity page. Have learners work in pairs to complete as indicated.

Into Life

Write the following sentences on the board:

1. *Everyone can receive God's mercy regardless of their background.*
2. *Parents sometimes risk everything for the good of their children.*
3. *God celebrates when people show great faith.*

Place learners in pairs and say, "Imagine you are writing a devotional on Matthew 15:21-28. On the board are three takeaways from this Scripture. With your partner, choose one and write points of application." After five minutes, reconvene the class.

For pairs who responded to the first prompt, ask: 1–What group has our congregation failed to reach with the gospel? 2–How can we remedy this?

For pairs who responded to the second prompt, ask: 1–How can a parent discern whether to let a child fend for themselves or to intervene for the child? 2–If you are a parent, has your opinion on this issue changed?

For pairs who responded to the third prompt, ask: 1–How do you live with great faith? 2–What obstacles to faith do you face, and how do you overcome them?

May 5
Lesson 10 (KJV)

Justified by Faith

Devotional Reading: John 3:1-8, 13-17
Background Scripture: Romans 3:21-30

Romans 3:21-30

21 But now the righteousness of God without the law is manifested, being witnessed by the law and the prophets;

22 Even the righteousness of God which is by faith of Jesus Christ unto all and upon all them that believe: for there is no difference:

23 For all have sinned, and come short of the glory of God;

24 Being justified freely by his grace through the redemption that is in Christ Jesus:

25 Whom God hath set forth to be a propitiation through faith in his blood, to declare his righteousness for the remission of sins that are past, through the forbearance of God;

26 To declare, I say, at this time his righteousness: that he might be just, and the justifier of him which believeth in Jesus.

27 Where is boasting then? It is excluded. By what law? of works? Nay: but by the law of faith.

28 Therefore we conclude that a man is justified by faith without the deeds of the law.

29 Is he the God of the Jews only? is he not also of the Gentiles? Yes, of the Gentiles also:

30 Seeing it is one God, which shall justify the circumcision by faith, and uncircumcision through faith.

Key Text

Even the righteousness of God which is by faith of Jesus Christ unto all and upon all them that believe: for there is no difference: For all have sinned, and come short of the glory of God; Being justified freely by his grace through the redemption that is in Christ Jesus. —**Romans 3:22-24**

Examining

Our Faith

Unit III: Standing in the Faith

Lessons 10–13

Lesson Aims

After participating in this lesson, each learner will be able to:

1. Identify what is "excluded" and why.
2. Explain the concept of *propitiation.*
3. Brainstorm ways to explain the concept of *propitiation* to an unbeliever.

Lesson Outline

Introduction

A. Always Going Downhill

B. Lesson Context

I. God's Righteousness (Romans 3:21-24)

A. Attested by Law and Prophets (v. 21)

B. Obtained in Christ (v. 22a)

C. Universally Required (vv. 22b-23)

Report Cards

D. Freely Given (v. 24)

II. Christ's Sacrifice (Romans 3:25-26)

A. For Righteousness (v. 25)

B. For Justification (v. 26)

III. Human Boasting (Romans 3:27-30)

A. "It Is Excluded" (vv. 27-28)

Bragging Rights

B. God of All (vv. 29-30)

Conclusion

A. Things We All Have in Common

B. Prayer

C. Thought to Remember

Introduction

A. Always Going Downhill

The Greek poet Homer (lived in the ninth or eighth century BC) recorded a myth about a king named Sisyphus. The human king figured out a way to cheat his death: by capturing the god of death, Thanatos, and thereby preventing anyone from being able to die. The consequences of this imprisonment were grisly, and the other gods could not allow the situation to persist.

Thanatos did not stay inactive forever. And when Sisyphus did die, he received an interesting punishment. He was to roll a heavy stone up a hill. But, just as he was about to reach the top of the hill, the stone would roll back down again. And this punishment would go on forever. This is the origin of characterizing an unachievable task as Sisyphean.

Surely we have all experienced a Sisyphean task, like having the carrot of a raise or promotion dangled just ahead, always out of reach, or family harmony always seeming just beyond the next therapy session or fight. Trying to earn salvation is another Sisyphean task we all know, whether we have struggled with it ourselves or only seen others in the midst of this impossible quest. There must be another way! And Paul teaches that other way in our lesson text today.

B. Lesson Context

Paul's letter to the Romans was written in about AD 58, most likely from Corinth during his third missionary journey. He had not planted the Roman church, and the letter's origins are something of a mystery. It could be that believers who were present at the first Pentecost brought it back from their Jerusalem pilgrimage to their home in Rome (Acts 2:10). The nature of the church in Rome was influenced by an edict, issued by Emperor Claudius in about AD 49, that had forced Jews living in the city to leave (18:2). The Roman historian Suetonius tells us that Claudius "banished from Rome all the Jews, who were continually making disturbances at the instigation of one Chrestus," the word *Chrestus* likely referring to *Christ.*

This experience probably fostered a certain division within the Roman church between Gentile and Jewish believers, with each group contending that it had a better claim of salvation in Christ than the other (compare Romans 11:13-24). The expulsion of Jews from Rome resulted in Gentile Christians being in the majority in the church there, if they had not been the majority already (1:5-6, 13). Their majority status seems to have continued even after the death of Claudius in AD 54 allowed Jews to return to the imperial city (compare Acts 18:2 with Romans 16:3-5). Much of Paul's letter was therefore directed specifically to the Gentile believers there (11:13).

Paul hoped to visit Rome soon, so his letter served as an introduction of himself and the gospel he would teach in Rome and abroad, God willing. Part of Paul's purpose in writing to the Roman Christians was to inform them of his desire to meet them (Romans 1:11-15) and to gain support for his planned travel to Spain (15:23-28). But the body of the letter is all gospel, making Romans perhaps the closest thing in the Bible to a systematic exploration of Christian doctrine. Our lesson today cuts straight to the heart of the matter: what is required for salvation.

I. God's Righteousness

(Romans 3:21-24)

A. Attested by Law and Prophets (v. 21)

21. But now the righteousness of God without the law is manifested, being witnessed by the law and the prophets.

But now builds on the thought that came before, that "by the deeds of the law there shall no flesh be justified in his sight: for by the law is the knowledge of sin" (Romans 3:20). For some, the law offers a surefire way to become righteous in God's eyes—by perfectly obeying it. But anyone with true understanding of God and the purpose of His laws knows that the law was never intended to make a person righteous and thus justify that person. If lawful action cannot justify a person, what can?

For the first time in this letter, Paul separates law from righteousness and affirms that his argument is not new; it aligns with *the law and the prophets*. This was a way to refer to all of the Old Testament (examples: Matthew 22:40; Luke 16:29; Acts 13:15). The law was intended to make people aware of their sin, and the prophets explicitly called out the people when they became blind to their sinfulness. Paul expanded on that idea in Galatians 3:19-29, which refers to the law as "our schoolmaster," teaching what God is like and keeping us safe until Jesus came to reveal *the righteousness of God* (see Romans 3:22a, below). Likewise, the writer of Hebrews said that the law was a shadow of the good things to come (Hebrews 10:1).

What Do You Think?

What texts in the law can explain that God's righteousness cannot be attained through obedience to it?

Digging Deeper

How do the words of the Old Testament prophets build on this idea?

B. Obtained in Christ (v. 22a)

22a. Even the righteousness of God which is by faith of Jesus Christ unto all and upon all them that believe.

The righteousness of God mentioned in verse 21 is here revealed to be the gift believers receive. There is some challenge in understanding the phrase *faith of Jesus Christ*. The Greek could imply that the faith is Jesus' own, as in His faithfulness to His promises. However, the context suggests that Paul is referring to one's faith in Jesus Christ. Faith is not just a collection of beliefs but is connected to the person of Jesus Christ.

Beginning in Romans 3:9, Paul makes clear that no person is righteous. The issue at hand is not Jesus' faithfulness, but how *all them that believe* can be called righteous (Romans 5:19). By faith in Jesus, we are eligible to and do, in fact, receive the gift of being called righteous (compare Genesis 15:6; Romans 4:3-8; Ephesians 3:12). The contrast is with the attempt to be made righteous through works, including keeping the law (compare Galatians 2:16). And we do well to remember that righteousness described here is being made right with God, despite our continued imperfect efforts.

C. Universally Required (vv. 22b-23)

22b-23. For there is no difference: for all have sinned, and come short of the glory of God.

Paul likely begins an aside here (see commentary on Romans 3:24, below). The phrase *for there is no difference* looks back to Paul's arguments about the fallenness of both Gentiles and Jews. Because both groups (which encompass all of humanity) are lost in sin and living counter to God's will, salvation for both must be attained in the same way (compare 3:9; Galatians 3:28).

The expression *all have sinned* is also found in Romans 5:12 (compare 1:18-21). In the Old Testament, *the glory of God* can be used in two primary ways: to refer to an experience of God (examples: Exodus 16:10; Ezekiel 1:28) or to give God the worship that is due Him and extolling others to do the same, implicitly or explicitly (examples: Joshua 7:19; 1 Chronicles 16:28-29). In these examples, there is a sense of God's revealing himself through His glory so that people might experience Him and honor Him. The glory of God can be defined as His presence with His people (compare John 1:14). God's glory is a true and holy representation of God's character, in contrast to any idol or other falsehood (see Romans 1:23-25). As His image-bearers, we were meant to reflect well on our Creator by living lives that reflect His holy character, His glory (Genesis 1:26; Leviticus 20:26; Isaiah 43:7; 1 Peter 1:13-25). Sin prevents us from accurately modeling God's glory.

Report Cards

Growing up, I never liked school. Starting in kindergarten, I would invent all kinds of excuses to stay home. For instance, I'd run home from my bus stop and tell my mother I needed a hug that inevitably lasted *just* long enough to miss my ride. My mom passed away recently, and I ran into some of my old report cards as we cleaned up her belongings. My struggles and failures were preserved and filed among mom's other essential papers. But something I found in the filing cabinet changed my initial embarrassment. Mom had kept her report cards from elementary school to high school. These papers revealed that my mother struggled in school as I did!

Failure can make us feel isolated. But if we were to compare our "report cards" of righteousness, we would see we are all in the same dismal position. How does knowing that we have all sinned and not attained God's glory change your attitude when you speak of Jesus to your friends and neighbors?

—J. M.

D. Freely Given (v. 24)

24. Being justified freely by his grace through the redemption that is in Christ Jesus.

Some have misunderstood this verse as teaching universal salvation. The argument usually ties *being justified* to "all [who] have sinned" in Romans 3:23. However, this reading cannot be preferred, as Jesus himself warned His listeners regarding eternal punishment (Matthew 7:13; 25:31-46; etc.). In keeping with other scriptural teachings—Paul's included—it is far more likely that much of Romans 3:22-23 (above) is a parenthetical thought. This links being justified not to verse 23 but to "all them that believe" in verse 22a (above; compare 1:17).

When one is justified, God considers that person righteous. There is a stark difference between works-based salvation and justification *by his grace.* In a works-based salvation, one strives as hard as one can and hopes at the very end that he or she has done enough to earn God's pardon. This suggests that salvation can be earned, like a wage, and can only be withheld if the work was not up to snuff. In contrast, justification by God's grace is given *freely . . . through the redemption that*

How to Say It

Claudius	*Claw*-dee-us.
propitiation	pro-*pih*-she-**ay**-shun.
Sisyphean	Si-suh-*fee*-uhn.
Suetonius	Soo-*toe*-nee-us.
Thanatos	*Tha*-nuh-toes.

is in Christ Jesus (Romans 4:4-5; 6:23; Galatians 3:13).

Redemption for Paul's audience would call up an image of a slave being purchased out of bondage into freedom (compare Hebrews 9:15). To the Jewish recipients of this letter, redemption also meant payment to free a prisoner sentenced to death (Exodus 21:29-30). The metaphor of being slaves, either to sin or to righteousness, occurs later in this very letter (Romans 6). Elsewhere, Paul compares redemption to adoption, the act through which we become God's sons and daughters (Galatians 4:4-5).

II. Christ's Sacrifice

(Romans 3:25-26)

A. For Righteousness (v. 25)

25. Whom God hath set forth to be a propitiation through faith in his blood, to declare his righteousness for the remission of sins that are past, through the forbearance of God.

Propitiation can be defined as the sacrifice that God requires to forgive His people. This was a major part of the process of atonement. In Israel, sacrifices were offered throughout the year and for various purposes. The mercyseat of the ark of the covenant was the center of the sacrificial system. But only the head priest could go into the holy of holies and only on the Day of Atonement, once every year, to sprinkle blood on the mercy seat. This sacrifice was a mercy from God so that He would forgive their sins (Leviticus 16:2, 13-15).

The sacrificial system was a temporary solution, made obsolete by Jesus' sacrificial death on the cross (Hebrews 9:11-14). When we respond *through faith*, Jesus' *blood* accomplishes the atonement we require for *the remission of sins* (John 1:29; Hebrews 10:19-22; Revelation 7:13-17; etc.).

Forbearance points to God's patience (2 Peter 3:9). Taking into account the cycle of sacrifices necessary before Jesus' death, God's forbearance was seen in His allowance for animal sacrifice to forgive sins, even though these only looked forward to Jesus' sacrifice (Hebrews 10:4). The past sacrifices were a shadow of the true sacrifice to come. God did not overlook sins, but He withheld judgment of those sins until Jesus' death—the sacrifice that took away sins once and for all (9:26; 10:10). This understanding of God's patience works well with the image Paul painted in Acts 17:30-31 of God's holding all people to account because there was no more excuse for ignorance regarding what He required.

What Do You Think?

How have you experienced God's patience?

Digging Deeper

How can we balance God's patience toward sinners with the urgency of accepting Jesus' sacrifice when witnessing to a nonbeliever?

B. For Justification (v. 26)

26. To declare, I say, at this time his righteousness: that he might be just, and the justifier of him which believeth in Jesus.

At this time refers to the time since Christ's sacrifice (comparable to "in this world" as a contrast to "that which is to come" in Ephesians 1:21). God's *righteousness* and justice go hand in hand (Job 37:23; Psalm 11:7; Isaiah 5:16; etc.). A remarkable tension is created, then, when God, in His perfect character, desires both justice and mercy for sinners. He could not accurately be called *just* if He simply turned a blind eye to wrongdoing. Through Jesus' sacrifice, a path forward is created. Those who *believeth in Jesus* experience God's mercy and are justified when they are covered in Christ's blood and made new.

III. Human Boasting

(Romans 3:27-30)

A. "It Is Excluded" (vv. 27-28)

27. Where is boasting then? It is excluded. By what law? of works? Nay: but by the law of faith.

This verse would have resonated with Jewish Christians who heard it. They took great pride in

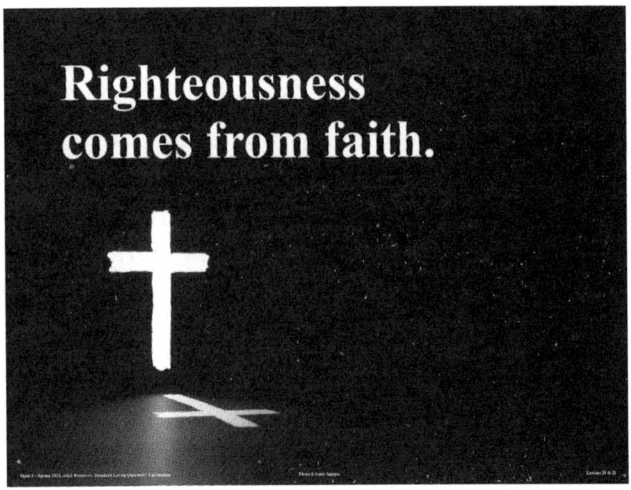
Righteousness
comes from faith.

Visual for Lessons 10 & 11. *Discuss why God's righteousness needs to be known before we can be called righteous through faith.*

God's having chosen them and revealed His desires through the Law of Moses. Some even boasted about their own success in following that law faithfully. If a person could earn his or her salvation, that person would have reason to boast because they measured up to the *law of works* (compare Romans 4:4-8). If anyone could boast about his adherence to the law, it was Paul (Galatians 1:14).

Since salvation is not accomplished by anything a sinful person can achieve, no person has the right to boast (Ephesians 2:8-9). For this reason, even Paul counted all things "dung, that I may win Christ, and be found in him, not having mine own righteousness, which is of the law, but that which is through the faith of Christ, the righteousness which is of God by faith" (Philippians 3:8-9). *The law of faith* supersedes the prior laws and accomplishes what a law of works could not: salvation in Christ.

Bragging Rights

When is it acceptable to boast? Hiring experts assert that the resume is an appropriate place to talk oneself up and make a big deal out of one's accomplishments. Indeed, what would a potential employer think if candidates did not bring up college degrees, prior work experience and accolades, and other pertinent information that qualified them for the job and made them the best candidates for the position? But, of course, too much zeal in touting one's accomplishments can backfire. For instance, in my hometown, the health director was forced to step down because of his resume: he allegedly oversold his college education.

Paul never weighed in on the merits of an effective resume. But on boasting in general, he reminds us that we have nothing to boast about when we stand before God. No matter what good works we could put on a resume documenting our lives, we fall short of what God requires. Bearing that in mind, how will you guard against illicit boasting? —J. M.

28. Therefore we conclude that a man is justified by faith without the deeds of the law.

This verse represents a summary of Paul's argument to this point. Keeping *the law* does not accomplish righteousness; trying to keep the law makes us aware of our shortcomings. Justification only comes *by faith*. The works that result are evidence of faith (Galatians 5:22-25); they are integral to a living faith (James 2:17), but they are not saving actions.

What Do You Think?

What evidence can you point to that you are being made new in Christ?

Digging Deeper

In what areas are you still trusting that the Spirit is recreating you in Jesus' image?

B. God of All (vv. 29-30)

29. Is he the God of the Jews only? is he not also of the Gentiles? Yes, of the Gentiles also.

Paul frequently uses rhetorical questions to further his argument (examples: Romans 6:1; 8:31). On the most basic level, *God* created everything (Genesis 1:1), and so He is the rightful God *of the Gentiles also*. Paul's Jewish audience would have agreed with this. But *the Jews* sometimes assumed that, because *God* had chosen them specially, He was opposed to all other people and chose the Jews *only*. Assuming that God's special care for Israel was an exclusionary concern for Israel ignores God's love for all people (Isaiah 42:5-7), expressed both in law (examples: Leviticus 19:10, 33-34; Numbers 15:15-16; Deuteronomy 10:18-19) and in His provision (examples: Genesis 16; 2 Kings 5; Jonah 3). Jesus made clear God's care for all in both His words and deeds (examples: Matthew 5:43-38; Mark 7:24-30; John 3:16-18).

What Do You Think?

Do you affirm in thought, word, and deed that God is the God of all?

Digging Deeper

If not, what repentance and repair might be called for?

30. Seeing it is one God, which shall justify the circumcision by faith, and uncircumcision through faith.

One God calls to mind the Shema: "The Lord our God is one Lord" (Deuteronomy 6:4). The command that follows is to "love the Lord thy God with all thine heart, and with all thy soul, and with all thy might" (6:5; compare Mark 12:29-30). The Shema was recited multiple times a day by observant Jews in pursuit of teaching the command and keeping it in their hearts (Deuteronomy 6:6-9). If there were many (real) gods, maybe there were different ways to justify the Jews and the Gentiles. But since there is only one God, He chose only one way to *justify* all people in the same way: *through faith.*

The circumcision refers to the Jews, as this was the physical sign of the covenant between God and Israel (Genesis 17) and often a badge of pride for Jews. *The uncircumcision* refers to any Gentiles. This made the practice a relatively clear-cut (pun intended) way to distinguish between the two groups. But there is only one way to the Father, no matter one's background: Jesus Christ himself (John 14:6).

Conclusion

A. Things We All Have in Common

All human brokenness and sorrow can be traced back to sin. That's something that everyone has in common. Rumors of wars create us-versus-them mentalities and the potential of violence through stoked hatred; war makes that violence a state-sanctioned reality and sows fear and destruction, reducing people to statistics of the dead and displaced. Even in times of relative peace, the seemingly conflicting hopes and fears for a nation's future can become polarizing calls to action, preventing the respect and cooperation necessary for cooperation and thriving within communities.

Even when we are not facing existential threats of war or violence, we are all broken by sin. It's sad that we are all united in this, but fortunately, the cure is also something we all have in common. Our own efforts cannot heal us. Like Sisyphus, we can make every effort to roll our stones to the top of a hill. Nevertheless, those sins we try to conquer through constant effort will always drag us back down, always requiring us to try again—unless we call on Jesus, who removes the stone and gives our efforts a whole new meaning.

We all need Jesus. He is the one person we can all have in common and in whom we can find unity outside of our sinfulness (John 17:20-23). He is the only one who can transform our efforts from futility in sin and death to Spirit-led works of hope and life.

What Do You Think?

What futile efforts toward earning salvation can you commit to abandoning?

Digging Deeper

How will unity with other believers in Christ help you in this endeavor?

B. Prayer

Gracious Lord, thank You for Your gift of salvation through faith in Jesus. Thank You that it is a gift offered to everyone regardless of race or status. Forgive us when we think we have to earn this gift. In Jesus' name through whom we have our salvation. Amen.

C. Thought to Remember

Stop struggling to earn the gift of salvation that Christ offers.

Involvement Learning

Enhance your lesson with KJV Bible Student *(from your curriculum supplier) and the reproducible activity page (at www.standardlesson.com or in the back of the* KJV Standard Lesson Commentary Deluxe Edition*).*

Into the Lesson

Write the word *Boast* on the board. Ask learners, "What are some things that come to mind when you see this word?" Learners may discuss achievements, possessions, abilities, or feelings of jealousy or pride. Ask learners to think of the most ridiculous thing they've ever seen someone boast about. Remind them that this is not a place for gossip, and so they should be careful with these examples. Have learners share the boasts, along with what made them ridiculous.

After the discussion, say, "Today, we're going to talk about something else that would be ridiculous to boast about."

Into the Word

As you read Romans 3:21-30 aloud, ask learners to think about what ridiculous boast Paul may be describing. Expected responses include boasting about all the good works we have done and efforts to earn salvation by following the law of works. Divide the class into groups of two or three. Ask the groups to discuss Paul's ridiculous boast as well as search for other passages that describe this same idea (examples: 1 Corinthians 1:30-31; Ephesians 2:8-9).

After calling time, have groups present their findings in a whole-class discussion. Continue talking about the topic with the following questions: 1–Why does Paul say boasting is to be excluded (Romans 3:27)? 2–Why does the law of works not support boasting (3:23)? 3–What does *propitiation* mean, and how does the word apply to Jesus (3:24-25)? 4–What can we do to be justified (3:22, 28)?

Option. Distribute index cards as well as copies of the "Coming Up Short" exercise from the activity page, which you can download. Give learners a minute to work individually, then as a group, complete as indicated.

Option. Distribute copies of the "God of All" exercise from the activity page. Give pairs of learners time to complete and discuss the activity as indicated.

Into Life

Write on the board *Misunderstandings / Metaphor / Action* as the headers of three columns. Conduct a whole-class brainstorming session on how to explain *propitiation* to an unbeliever. Remind learners that unbelievers may not be familiar with terms such as "satisfaction," "remission of sins," and "propitiation." *Option.* If you used the "Coming Up Short" activity earlier in the lesson, discuss why acknowledging one's sin might be helpful as we explain propitiation to an unbeliever.

If needed, continue further brainstorming by asking: 1–What common misunderstandings or misconceptions might unbelievers have about propitiation, and how can you sort those out? 2–What metaphors, comparisons, or verbal explanations can you use with words in a conversation? 3–What tangible, relational explanations might you use, accomplished over time through deed and action? Write responses in the appropriate column. Request that learners be specific. (For example, follow the non-specific response of "God's satisfaction" with the question "What is satisfied?")

Have learners practice explaining propitiation to each other in pairs, as if the other were unfamiliar with the concept. They may use either ideas from the board or their own thoughts. Ask pairs to pray for each other during the week as they talk to unbelievers.

Once they have finished practicing, bring the groups back together. Lead the whole group in a prayer, thanking God for His propitiation given through Jesus on our behalf. Pray for strength to live by faith rather than boasting in works. Pray that we let God's forgiveness make a difference in our lives and our communities.

May 12
Lesson 11 (KJV)

Counted as Righteous

Devotional Reading: Genesis 15:1-6
Background Scripture: Romans 4

Romans 4:13-25

13 For the promise, that he should be the
heir of the world, was not to Abraham, or to
his seed, through the law, but through the righteousness of faith.
14 For if they which are of the law be heirs,
faith is made void, and the promise made of
none effect:
15 Because the law worketh wrath: for
where no law is, there is no transgression.
16 Therefore it is of faith, that it might be by
grace; to the end the promise might be sure to
all the seed; not to that only which is of the law,
but to that also which is of the faith of Abraham; who is the father of us all,
17 (As it is written, I have made thee a
father of many nations,) before him whom
he believed, even God, who quickeneth the
dead, and calleth those things which be not as
though they were.
18 Who against hope believed in hope, that
he might become the father of many nations;
according to that which was spoken, So shall
thy seed be.
19 And being not weak in faith, he considered not his own body now dead, when he was
about an hundred years old, neither yet the
deadness of Sara's womb:
20 He staggered not at the promise of God
through unbelief; but was strong in faith, giving glory to God;
21 And being fully persuaded that, what he
had promised, he was able also to perform.
22 And therefore it was imputed to him for
righteousness.
23 Now it was not written for his sake alone,
that it was imputed to him;
24 But for us also, to whom it shall be
imputed, if we believe on him that raised up
Jesus our Lord from the dead;
25 Who was delivered for our offences, and
was raised again for our justification.

Key Text

He staggered not at the promise of God through unbelief; but was strong in faith, giving glory to God; And being fully persuaded that, what he had promised, he was able also to perform. —**Romans 4:20-21**

Examining
Our Faith

Unit III: Standing in the Faith

Lessons 10–13

Lesson Aims

After participating in this lesson, each learner will be able to:

1. Summarize Paul's view of Abraham.
2. Explain faith's role in being counted as righteous.
3. Brainstorm ways to celebrate with loving actions God's blessing of grace through faith.

Lesson Outline

Introduction

A. "The Primitive"

B. Lesson Context

I. True Heirs of Abraham (Romans 4:13)

A. Not by the Law (v. 13a)

B. The Righteousness of Faith (v. 13b)

II. Supporting Arguments (Romans 4:14-25)

A. Not the Promise (vv. 14-15)

B. Abraham's Trust (vv. 16-22)

Against All Hope

Fully Persuaded

C. Our Basis of Hope (vv. 23-25)

Conclusion

A. We Are Not Alone

B. Prayer

C. Thought to Remember

Introduction

A. "The Primitive"

German theologian Dietrich Bonhoeffer's resistance to Nazi rule cost him his life in 1945. While directing an illegal seminary, Bonhoeffer wrote to his brother-in-law about his practice of daily Bible reading. He found that practice drew him back to the basics, or what he called "the primitive." "In matters of faith," he said, "we are always consistently primitive." He meant that however elaborate our ideas or practices may be, we must always come back to our starting point: a fundamental attitude of trust in God's mercy. Our text today focuses on this primitive foundation.

B. Lesson Context

Romans 4 is part of Paul's overall argument supporting his statement in Romans 1:16-17:

> I am not ashamed of the gospel of Christ: for it is the power of God unto salvation to every one that believeth; to the Jew first, and also to the Greek. For therein is the righteousness of God revealed from faith to faith: as it is written, The just shall live by faith.

Romans 1–3 explores God's primary challenge in keeping the ancient promises, namely, the profound sinfulness of all human beings (3:23).

Chapter 4 begins the discussion of the remedy to universal sin. Far from facing a hopeless situation, humans have a model available to them of how to approach God. That model is the life of Abraham. When God promised that He would bless the world through Abraham, Abraham chose to respond in faith (Genesis 15:6; quoted in Romans 4:3, 9, 22; Galatians 3:6; James 2:23). Paul's readers, especially those of Jewish heritage, would have agreed that Abraham's legacy was important and valuable. The question in dispute is precisely what that legacy is. Paul argues that Abraham had a relationship with God because he placed his faith in God and trusted God's promises. Nothing else. In the New Testament, faith equals trust in God as the one who has promised to bless humanity. Jesus modeled that trust by submitting to His sacrificial death on a cross, being confident that God would work for good through Jesus' shame and suffering. That trust is the basis for any relationship with the same merciful God.

I. True Heirs of Abraham

(Romans 4:13)

A. Not by the Law (v. 13a)

13a. For the promise, that he should be the heir of the world, was not to Abraham, or to his seed, through the law.

Paul does not exclude the Jewish people from God's concern, nor does he minimize the importance of the Torah (the Law of Moses). But Paul builds on the insight that *the promise* predates *the law* (see lesson 10) since *Abraham* lived before Moses (about 2167–1992 BC and 1530–1410 BC, respectively) and the giving of the law (Exodus 19–20). Thus, it follows that the promise was the foundation of the law rather than the other way around (see Galatians 3:17).

The idea that Abraham would inherit *the world* comes in part from Genesis 12:1-3, which describes Abraham's offspring as a blessing to the world. This was sometimes interpreted as meaning that Abraham's family would literally govern all the world. But we see that Jesus' followers—Abraham's true *seed* (Galatians 3:7)—inherit the world (1 Corinthians 3:21-23; see Romans 4:17, below).

B. The Righteousness of Faith (v. 13b)

13b. But through the righteousness of faith.

Faith, which biblically might be defined as trust in God and His ability and intention to keep His promises, can characterize any person, not only those who were given the law. God is the God of all, both Jews and Gentiles (Romans 3:29). The relationship between God and humans rests on something deeper than the law, the thing that characterizes one group but not the other. That deeper reality is faith in Jesus. God chooses to credit us with righteousness when we come to Him through such faith. *Through the righteousness* that only comes from God's gift to us, we also stand to inherit the world as promised to Abraham.

What Do You Think?

How does your life reflect your trust in God?

Digging Deeper

What difference does it make that you cannot and do not need to try to earn righteousness?

II. Supporting Arguments

(Romans 4:14-25)

A. Not the Promise (vv. 14-15)

14. For if they which are of the law be heirs, faith is made void, and the promise made of none effect.

Salvation comes from God's *promise* since God saves "the ungodly" (Romans 4:5; 5:6). Nothing that we can do can save us. This radical confession has roots in the Old Testament, which also affirms that human achievement does not deliver in the final analysis. The analogy of earthly deliverance (examples: Psalms 44:3; 106:6-8; Hosea 11:7-11) is a precursor to the reality of eternal salvation (examples: Numbers 21:4-9; John 3:14-15).

Rather, the Law of Moses leads one to love God and fellow human beings (Leviticus 19:18; Deuteronomy 6:5; see Matthew 22:37-40). Paul does not mean that Jews or Gentile converts who keep *the law* cannot also trust God. But what was promised because of faith still required faith; law-keeping could not substitute for trusting God (Galatians 3:18).

Paul's language seems very strong here. He does not reject keeping the Torah for Jews, only the insistence that Gentiles must do so as well (Acts 15). One of the ironies of history has been that the

How to Say It

Abraham	*Ay*-bruh-ham.
Deuteronomy	Due-ter-*ahn*-uh-me.
Dietrich Bonhoeffer	*Dee*-truck *Bahn*-hahf-ur.
Isaac	*Eye*-zuk.
Moses	*Mo*-zes or *Mo*-zez.
Torah	*Tor*-uh.

situation reversed itself in the centuries after Paul so that Judaism and Christianity became separate religions, with Christians often persecuting Jews and using this and other texts to justify doing so. In Paul's setting, that situation had not arisen, and his statements must be understood in his different context without condoning any religious violence.

What Do You Think?

When have you experienced someone "voiding" a promise?

Digging Deeper

What gives you confidence that God has not voided the promise He made based on Abraham's faith?

15. Because the law worketh wrath: for where no law is, there is no transgression.

At the same time, *the law* has limitations. No one can violate a law that does not exist (Romans 5:13). The law could define sin's precise contours and clarify what effects it has, but it cannot save. It *worketh wrath*, that is, it provokes God's anger when humans break His law. Since God's wrath is justified and necessary to bring about justice, the law's function to notify us of boundaries serves a spiritually useful purpose.

Romans 1:18-32 catalogs the results of a life of sin, the terrible list of ways humans have of harming each other and themselves. These actions provoke God's righteous indignation, but also lead to God's mercy toward precisely all of us caught up in such evils (Romans 6:1-4). The Law of Moses emphasizes God's sense of justice and desire for humans to live together with justice and righteousness—the appropriate responses to a genuine love for God.

B. Abraham's Trust (vv. 16-22)

16. Therefore it is of faith, that it might be by grace; to the end the promise might be sure to all the seed; not to that only which is of the law, but to that also which is of the faith of Abraham, who is the father of us all.

It refers to the promise (see Romans 4:13, above). This verse makes two interrelated points. First, God's saving work extends to all who will receive it in *faith* by trusting God's promises and counting on God's mercy, justice, and protection. The Law of Moses was a gift from God for previously enslaved people so that they could experience a life of real freedom (Deuteronomy 30:11-20). Its many provisions tended toward building a community of mutual support and justice (examples: Exodus 22; Deuteronomy 15).

Second, the promise to bless the world (Genesis 12:1-3) extends to all who imitate *Abraham* in trusting God. Descent from the patriarch involves not ancestral DNA (Luke 3:8) but a similar faith-filled life. God's work was bigger than the law could accommodate, and God's *grace* extends to both Jews and Gentiles who trust Him.

17. (As it is written, I have made thee a father of many nations,) before him whom he believed, even God, who quickeneth the dead, and calleth those things which be not as though they were.

Verse 17 offers evidence for the previous verses' assertions by quoting Genesis 17:5. Part of a story of renewed promises to Abraham, this statement reveals the enormous consequences of the then-soon-to-be-fulfilled promise of a child, Isaac (see Genesis 21:1-7). The promise extends even to the raising of *the dead*. This happened metaphorically for Abraham and Sarah, who were long past child-bearing age (see also Hebrews 11:12), and literally for Jesus as "the firstfruits of them that slept" (1 Corinthians 15:20). The entire story of Israel and the church is one of unimagined possibilities coming to life thanks to God's saving work.

The final clause alludes to the story of God's creation of the world (Genesis 1:1–2:4), through which nonexistent things became realities. God's creative work did not cease long ago but continues until all things are made new (Revelation 21:5). Creation and redemption form two sides of the same coin because both come from God's love and proceed toward the well-being of the creature.

18. Who against hope believed in hope, that he might become the father of many nations, according to that which was spoken, So shall thy seed be.

Genesis repeats the promises to Abraham three times (Genesis 12; 15; 17). Paul moves backward from the third to the second occurrence, quoting Genesis 15:5 with *so shall thy seed be.* Paul interprets the quoted text in two ways simultaneously. First, the promise of offspring came to Abraham, and it was fulfilled. And second, the offspring would be like Abraham, full of hope for God's redemptive work.

Hope in the Bible is never simply wishful thinking. It is the expectation that something is to occur that is neither a given nor impossible. Two examples illustrate this: sunrise is a given, so we do not hope for it; flying under one's own power is impossible, so we do not hope for that, either. Nor is hope simply an emotional or intellectual state. For Paul, hope is an anticipation of an objective reality, the thing expected as much as the feeling of expectation. Hope can be laid up for us in God's presence (Colossians 1:5).

To hope *against hope* means that Abraham had no natural basis for believing he and Sarah could have a child. He and his wife had long passed the age of childbearing, and Sarah was postmenopausal (Genesis 17:17). The childbirth required a miracle, and the couple trusted God to provide that without knowing how it would occur.

What Do You Think?

How often do you speak of hope as a wish or a dream?

Digging Deeper

How could your witness of hope be strengthened if you only used the word to refer to hope based on God's promises?

Against All Hope

The nurse couldn't find a heartbeat. Doctors and attendants surrounded my wife's hospital bed, and one of them insisted that she could feel the baby moving. They rushed my wife away for an emergency C-section. These surgeries are not performed for babies who would be stillborn; faint heartbeats indicated that our daughter was practically gone.

Many doctors would have refused to operate, our doctor said. Our daughter would likely not survive. Even if she did, she would have profound brain injuries. "Wrongful life" suits chilled some doctors from acting as our doctor did. But she was a Christian, and she believed strongly in life. She thought, *Even if this child only lives for two days, it is still life.* Against all hope, she delivered our daughter.

Rebekah just turned eight years old.

Is your faith leading you to make a decision "against all hope"? —N. G.

19. And being not weak in faith, he considered not his own body now dead, when he was about an hundred years old, neither yet the deadness of Sarah's womb.

Paul ignores indications of Abraham's doubts in Genesis 15:2-3 and his ill-conceived attempt to "help" God by impregnating Hagar (Genesis 16). We might be encouraged that such major lapses in judgment and trust did not nullify Abraham's faith.

Instead, Paul's argument focuses on Abraham's ultimate acceptance of God's trustworthiness. For Abraham to focus on his or *Sarah's* limitations rather than the divine promises would have equaled weakness *in faith.* While Abraham recognized his and Sarah's physical states, he did not see that natural limit as the end of the possibilities available to God. Paul asks his readers to embrace this same mixture of realism and hope. As creatures of God, we know our limits but recognize that God's freedom and mercy need not always be channeled within those limits.

20. He staggered not at the promise of God through unbelief, but was strong in faith, giving glory to God.

This verse restates the ideas of the previous sentences but adds two dimensions. First, it clarifies what Abraham believed when he trusted God's *promise.* The grammar of the Greek text serves to emphasize the promise that Abraham trusted rather than his act of believing God. God's action precedes and forms the basis for Abraham's faith.

Second, this verse also proposes that Abraham's trust equaled glorifying *God.* Words of praise, no matter how beautiful, do not really bring honor to God unless the one who is praising lives in the hope that God's promises will be fulfilled.

21. And being fully persuaded, that what he had promised, he was able also to perform.

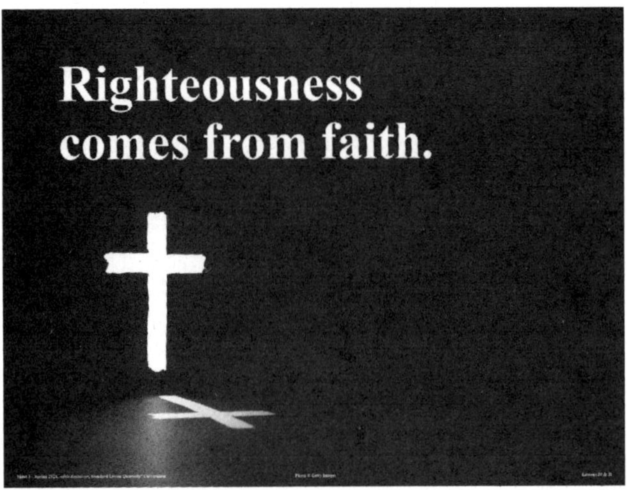
Righteousness
comes from faith.
Visual for Lessons 10 & 11. *Point to this visual as you discuss verse 22 and the discussion questions associated with it.*

Here concludes the analysis of Abraham's trust as confidence in God's ability and willingness to act benevolently for the benefit of human beings. The verse also describes an aspect of God's promises: they are not idle words.

> **What Do You Think?**
> Do you react differently to a broken promise if the promise-maker lacks the power rather than the will to fulfill it? Why or why not?
> **Digging Deeper**
> What other examples can you provide of both God's willingness and ability to fulfill His promises?

Fully Persuaded

Philip Bliss published the hymn "Almost Persuaded" in 1871. The first stanza has a lost soul telling the Spirit, "Go Thy way, / Some more convenient day / on Thee I'll call." The song emphasizes that the time to call on Jesus in faith is short. Bliss's own life was cut short when, on December 30, 1876, he and his wife were killed in a train crash. He was only 38.

Bliss's life and work indicate that he, like Abraham, lived fully persuaded that God could and would fulfill His promises. And like Abraham, Bliss's faith has inspired generations. Hymns he penned are still sung. His home in Rome, Pennsylvania, is now the Phillip P. Bliss Gospel Songwriters Museum, a testament to his ongoing influence.

The time is still short! Consider what your legacy will be. Will family, friends, colleagues, and others remember you as being fully persuaded to follow Jesus? —N. G.

22. And therefore it was imputed to him for righteousness.

Paul refers here to Genesis 15:6: "[Abram] believed in the Lord; and [God] counted it to him for righteousness." The word translated *imputed* also is translated elsewhere in this chapter as "counted" (Romans 4:3, 5) and "reckoned" (4:4, 9-10), which clarifies that God accepted Abraham's faith as righteous action. God *imputed to* Abraham *righteousness*, not because Abraham had done good deeds or avoided evil, but because he had staked his life and his family's future on God's promises starting in Genesis 12.

Paul uses Genesis 15:6 to paint a sharp contrast between a relationship built on command and obedience (under the Law of Moses) and one built on promises and trust. Many of his Jewish audience would probably have thought Paul overstated the case, since keeping the law ideally did show one's trust in, and love for, God. Yet Paul makes this distinction because he wishes to show that God keeps the ancient promises through the faithfulness of the Messiah, Jesus, and that the promises embrace both Jews and Gentiles.

> **What Do You Think?**
> What does it mean to have righteousness *imputed* based on faith?
> **Digging Deeper**
> What other verses can you point to that support your answer?

C. Our Basis of Hope (vv. 23-25)

23. Now it was not written for his sake alone, that it was imputed to him.

If God was to keep the promise to Abraham that he would become the ancestor of many nations, then the act of imputing righteousness to him based on faith must extend to others who do the same thing. Otherwise, God would be a respecter of persons, a player of favorites (contrast Acts 10:34; Romans 2:11-16; Galatians 2:6; Ephesians 6:9).

Whereas Abraham trusted God's promise of descendants who would bless the world, Paul's readers, ancient and modern, trust in the promise God sealed by raising Jesus from the dead. Simply believing that the resurrection of Jesus happened historically does not equate to having saving faith (compare James 2:19). To believe in the resurrection means to imitate Christ in His sufferings (2 Corinthians 13:4; Galatians 2:19-20; Philippians 3:10-11; 1 Thessalonians 1:6; 2:14). It means to trust in the final resurrection of the dead, of which Jesus' resurrection is the promissory note (1 Corinthians 15:20-28).

24. But for us also, to whom it shall be imputed, if we believe on him that raised up Jesus our Lord from the dead.

When does God reckon us as righteous? The verb tense of the underlying Greek could indicate a future time, such as the last judgment. But the Greek may also indicate something just about to happen or a certainty with uncertain timing. Perhaps Paul does not mean to be overly precise, as there are mysteries about the future that no one knows (Matthew 24:36). Or perhaps he signals the fact that justification occurs now *and* later as God continuously sustains a relationship with those who trust in His promises. This latter interpretation is in keeping with what can be referred to as the now/not yet of God's kingdom. We are *now* part of God's kingdom, but we are *not yet* experiencing its fullness (see Romans 8:22-25).

25. Who was delivered for our offences, and was raised again for our justification.

Paul's language echoes Isaiah 53:6, 12, which anticipated that the suffering servant would be handed over to His enemies to make "intercession for the transgressors" (compare similar language in 1 Corinthians 15:3). Isaiah's prophecy of the suffering servant was a key text for early Christians in understanding Jesus not as a tragic figure or a victim of state violence, but as the Messiah who died on behalf of others. His death was necessary to pay the price for sins, but it would have been incomplete without a resurrection (1 Corinthians 15:12-19). Jesus joined in the suffering brought about by sin in order to free from sin's power those who trust God's promises.

Conclusion

A. We Are Not Alone

God counts us as righteous when we, like Abraham, trust the promises of redemption and live accordingly. We are not righteous because of the good we do or the evil we avoid, but because God acknowledges us as loyal to Him, staking all our hopes on His promises. And His offer of salvation extends to all because sin has wrecked us all. We stand together in both our need and our hope.

This unity of humanity may show itself in different ways. We might wallow together in our sin, growing increasingly hostile to each other and sacrificing our common humanity on the altar of greed, envy, pride, and hatred. Or we might acknowledge our need, trust in God's mercy, and so join in a community built on such a faith. The choice belongs to us.

How do we build a community on such a basis? A church full of people who trust in God's promises live generous, open-hearted, kind lives. They, like Abraham, show hospitality to strangers as though they were angels (Hebrews 13:2). Such a church values the whole trajectory of a person's life of faith, emphasizing neither failures nor heroic successes but faithfulness in the face of adversity (James 1:2-3) and God's seeming slowness to act (2 Peter 3:9). This community of believers knows itself to be saved, not because of its own merits but because of God's mercy.

B. Prayer

God of Abraham and all who trust You, focus our minds not on our own limitations but on Your great love for Your creation. Thank You for Jesus' sacrifice, which we accept in faith as reconciling us to You. In His name we pray. Amen.

C. Thought to Remember

Justification by faith is not an abstract idea but a reality for life.

Involvement Learning

Enhance your lesson with KJV Bible Student *(from your curriculum supplier) and the reproducible activity page (at www.standardlesson.com or in the back of the* KJV Standard Lesson Commentary Deluxe Edition*).*

Into the Lesson

Before the learners enter, place a mini-size candy bar or similar treat under an opaque bowl on a table in the front of the room. Make sure no one looks underneath the bowl as they enter, and if anyone asks questions, simply respond, "Trust me."

When the class begins, tell the learners, "There is a candy bar under this bowl. You will receive not just this candy bar but enough for everyone, if you believe me. You can choose to look under the bowl at any point. If you look, and it turns out I was telling the truth, you will not receive any candy bars. If you don't look and I'm telling the truth, you will receive what I promised. Do you believe me? Why or why not?" Encourage learners to give reasons for their answers.

Pull out the bag of candy bars to show they do exist. Ask, "What about now? Do you believe that there is a candy bar under this bowl?" Again, encourage learners to respond fully. Have the learners share what makes them believe you or not. Then expand the discussion to what makes a promise trustworthy or untrustworthy. At the end of the activity, distribute candy bars to any learners who want them.

Transition by saying, "Today's study looks at how trustworthy God's promises are."

Alternative. Distribute copies of the "Promises" exercise from the activity page, which you can download. Have learners complete it individually in a minute or less before discussing responses in small groups. Not all prompts need answers if learners run out of time.

Into the Word

Introduce the words *imparted* (to give or convey) and *imputed* (to credit or ascribe to someone). Ask, "What was Abraham's righteousness based on?" Ask volunteers to read these texts out loud: Romans 4:13-25; Genesis 12:1-3; 13:14-17; 15–16; 21:1-21; and 22:1-19. Then divide the class into small groups. Distribute handouts (you create) with the preceding Scripture references and the following questions for in-group discussions: 1–What is Paul's view of Abraham and his faith? 2–What does the rest of Scripture show about Abraham's faith? 3–What doubts did Abraham have, and what did he do in the face of those doubts? 4–How did Abraham's actions ultimately show that he trusted God's promises? Give the groups time to answer the questions before bringing the groups back together for whole-class discussion.

Check back in on the question of the basis of Abraham's righteousness. The expected response should include God's character and promises and His imputing righteousness to Abraham, not based on Abraham's own merit or abilities.

Into Life

Distribute index cards and pens to all learners. Have each person write at the top of one side the name of someone who exhibited faith in the face of doubt or other challenges. This could be a biblical or other historical person or someone he or she knows personally. Ask learners to write down the action this person took in response to a specific hardship. Ask learners to record on the other side of the index card how God demonstrated His continued faithfulness and righteousness in that circumstance.

Alternative. Distribute copies of the "A 90-Year-Old Bucket List" exercise from the activity page. Have learners complete it individually in a minute or less before discussing the conclusion in small groups.

In pairs, have learners share situations in which they either are experiencing God's faithfulness. Have them brainstorm ways to celebrate God's grace with loving and faithful action. Close with a prayer that learners will have faith like Abraham to believe God's promises and trust in His faithfulness.

Reconciled to God

Devotional Reading: Acts 2:37-47
Background Scripture: Romans 5:1-11

Romans 5:1-11

1 Therefore being justified by faith, we have peace with God through our Lord Jesus Christ:

2 By whom also we have access by faith into this grace wherein we stand, and rejoice in hope of the glory of God.

3 And not only so, but we glory in tribulations also: knowing that tribulation worketh patience;

4 And patience, experience; and experience, hope:

5 And hope maketh not ashamed; because the love of God is shed abroad in our hearts by the Holy Ghost which is given unto us.

6 For when we were yet without strength, in due time Christ died for the ungodly.

7 For scarcely for a righteous man will one die: yet peradventure for a good man some would even dare to die.

8 But God commendeth his love toward us, in that, while we were yet sinners, Christ died for us.

9 Much more then, being now justified by his blood, we shall be saved from wrath through him.

10 For if, when we were enemies, we were reconciled to God by the death of his Son, much more, being reconciled, we shall be saved by his life.

11 And not only so, but we also joy in God through our Lord Jesus Christ, by whom we have now received the atonement.

Key Text

Therefore being justified by faith, we have peace with God through our Lord Jesus Christ. **—Romans 5:1**

Examining

Our Faith

Unit III: Standing in the Faith

Lessons 10–13

Lesson Aims

After participating in this lesson, each learner will be able to:

1. Identify what Christians have through faith.

2. Compare and contrast reconciliation with God to reconciliation between people.

3. Commit to sharing with an unbeliever a personal story of what life was like before and after being reconciled to God.

Lesson Outline

Introduction

A. Boasting Now and Then

B. Lesson Context

I. Effects of Justification (Romans 5:1-5)

A. Peace with God (v. 1)

B. Standing in Grace (v. 2)

C. The Realm of Boasting (vv. 3-5)

II. Effects of the Cross (Romans 5:6-11)

A. Reconciled to God (vv. 6-10)

The Right Time

Forgiveness

B. We Rejoice (v. 11)

Conclusion

A. Hope vs. Shame

B. Prayer

C. Thought to Remember

Introduction

A. Boasting Now and Then

Boasting in modern American culture is often seen as unattractive, even offensive. We tend to see it as a mark of insecurity, arrogance and superiority, and/or a disregard for the self-respect of others. We do make certain exceptions, such as when an underdog in a sporting event predicts a win for his or her team or celebrates an unexpected victory.

In ancient societies, however, boasting was part of the culture of warriors as they overcame their foes. Of course, the one boasting had to deliver on the words or risk looking foolish (1 Kings 20:11). But boasting itself did not seem problematic. People often thought of honor as a zero-sum game—"For me to increase my honor, I must diminish yours." Boasting allowed individuals to position themselves in society, as long as they could deliver.

Paul offers a radical alternative to the Greco-Roman understanding of self-promotion, based on his understanding of Jesus' death on the cross. He excluded it altogether because all are in the same position with respect to God (Romans 3:27; see lesson 10). Then Paul opened a new possibility for boasting, but not about our triumphs.

B. Lesson Context

Romans 5 depends entirely on Paul's previous discussion of the human response to the gospel found in Romans 4. Paul has argued, based on the experience of Abraham, that the true basis for a relationship with God is trust in His promises, that is, faith (see lesson 11). Chapter 5 extends the argument.

Our text today makes an important argument about why followers of Jesus both build their lives based on trust in God's promises yet still experience hardship. Those suffering might wonder whether the new era of God's mercy had dawned or not. In the past, prophets had revealed certain hardships to be God's judgment on sin (examples: Numbers 14:20-23; Jeremiah 21:4-14). Is a Christian's suffering also God's judgment?

Elsewhere, Paul boasted about his own suffering as evidence of God's work in his life (2 Corinthians 4:7-12; 11:23-30). Paul would go on to be executed in Rome in AD 67 or 68. In his estimation, this surely was another opportunity to imitate Christ (Philippians 1:21; 3:7-11). The transformation to be like Christ has several parts, including a new understanding of suffering, reconciliation, growing friendship with God, and ultimately rescue from the power of sin and death. Paul explores each dimension of these implications in today's text.

I. Effects of Justification

(Romans 5:1-5)

A. Peace with God (v. 1)

1. Therefore being justified by faith, we have peace with God through our Lord Jesus Christ.

Because God declares us accepted based on our *faith* in the Messiah, Jesus, this trust yields certain effects. Justification is not simply an accounting trick God makes. It begins a transformation of life.

We includes both Jews and Gentiles, with God showing no partiality to either. Because of God's work to keep the ancient promises to Abraham, everyone can have the kind of *peace* of which Paul speaks. The concept of peace had political implications for first-century subjects of Rome. By a mixture of force and political maneuvering, the Roman Empire had built the *Pax Romana* ("the Roman peace," lasting from 27 BC to AD 180). In contrast to peace enforced at the point of the sword, God offers genuine reconciliation of all people to himself through Jesus' faithful obedience (see Romans 5:19). Paul exhorts the Romans to have peace among themselves (14:19). Peace with God leads to (or should lead to) peace among followers of God when exhibiting the fruit of the Spirit (see Galatians 5:22-23).

What Do You Think?

How do you experience peace with God?

Digging Deeper

What practices might you adjust to have a deeper awareness of your reconciled status with God?

B. Standing in Grace (v. 2)

2a. By whom also we have access by faith into this grace wherein we stand.

Access to God's *grace* does not derive from an accident of birth or even from doing good deeds. It comes *by faith* in God's gracious offer of mercy. When *we stand*, we take confidence in God's promise, building our lives on it (compare Matthew 5:24-25). Because Jesus trusted God, those who follow him may do so as well. Regarding the access that results, see also Ephesians 2:18; 3:12.

2b. And rejoice in hope of the glory of God.

We come to the major assertion of our passage. The word *glory* draws on an old biblical theme with several dimensions. Some texts use the word to refer to God's overwhelming presence among human beings (examples: Exodus 40:34; 1 Kings 8:11; Ezekiel 1:28). The Psalms use the term to refer to God's splendor in Heaven, which is accessible in controlled ways to humans on earth (examples: Psalms 24:8-10; 29:9; 79:9). God's glory also appears when saving humans (example: Isaiah 40:5).

The final example is especially fitting here. The glory of God comes to light in the saving work of Jesus in his crucifixion and resurrection (Romans 6:4). God's glory is also evident in the life of the church (see 1 Corinthians 10:31; 2 Corinthians 4:6) and at the final judgment, when all things will become subject to God and open to His full presence (see Romans 8:18; 9:23). For this reason, we *rejoice* in expectant *hope* that God has forgiven us and given us new life now and in Heaven.

C. The Realm of Boasting (vv. 3-5)

3. And not only so, but we glory in tribulations also: knowing that tribulation worketh patience.

This second translation *glory* creates a wordplay that does not exist in the original Greek text since the words being translated aren't the same. The word translated "glory" here is translated "boast" in 2 Corinthians 10:8, 13; etc.; that is the sense here as well. With this word, Paul opens the possibility that Christians might celebrate, not only while experiencing pleasant things but also *in tribulations*. These words do not refer to mild annoyances or everyday problems but to devastating experiences. Tribulation can result from doing evil (Romans 2:9), though this is not the sense here. Instead, we think of tribulation that confronts the faithful who overcome it by the power of Christ's love (see 8:35; compare 2 Corinthians 1:4; 2:4; 4:17) and patience (Romans 12:12). Such hardship is an opportunity for God's grace to be revealed.

Many ancient people believed in the value of bearing suffering, not as an absolute good but as an important feature of the wise life. Paul is not arguing for a masochistic view of life, but instead that troubles and pain need not diminish our joy in Christ nor define our self-understanding. Suffering can nurture *patience* if we face the tribulation with the proper spiritual attitude. For Paul, growth occurred in the context of the mutual love between God and humankind (see Romans 5:5, below). It does so because the suffering itself is part of God's movement in the present age to bring about the new era that commenced at Calvary and comes to full blossom at the Last Judgment.

Boasting in tribulation makes sense not because of the suffering itself but because of the consequences of endurance. Yet such boasting would have seemed mad to Paul's ancient audience, just as it may to a modern one. Proper boasting should focus on God's achievements, which become most visible in human weakness (2 Corinthians 12:1-10).

What Do You Think?

What role does "glorying" in tribulations play in producing the characteristics that Paul lists?

Digging Deeper

What cautions should you heed when sharing this verse with someone currently going through tribulations?

4. And patience experience; and experience, hope.

The chain of words in verses 4-5 does not imply a straightforward progression from one virtue to another. Rather, the apparent progression reveals the close relationship among the qualities Paul lists. A willingness to endure hardship strengthens a person's *experience* and makes it possible to *hope* in a better future. In context, the translation *experience* is difficult. When we consider that the same Greek word is translated "proof" in reference to Timothy's character (Philippians 2:22; compare 2 Corinthians 2:9; 13:3), we can conclude here that experience is not the neutral event itself but the positive effect it can have on forming one's character. Experience should be understood in the positive sense of a high level of integrity that has developed through difficulties. Paul uses the same word several other times in his letters, always to praise people who have faced hardship with courage and love for God and their fellow human beings ("trial" in 2 Corinthians 8:2; etc.).

5. And hope maketh not ashamed; because the love of God is shed abroad in our hearts by the Holy Ghost which is given unto us.

Here Paul draws on an old biblical theme according to which God vindicated His people's *hope* through their restoration to a right relationship with Him (examples: Isaiah 49:5-7; Jeremiah 33:6-26; Ezekiel 20:33-44). Those who have hope in God's saving work, even if they experience social isolation or persecution, still have God's approval. Therefore, they cannot be shamed in any lasting way.

God's love is the source of honor. The Greek verb translated *shed abroad* often refers to the way *the Holy Ghost* comes to followers of Jesus (examples: Acts 2:17, 33; 10:45; Titus 3:6). Here, God's *love* is shed abroad, indicating the abundance that believers receive.

In the Old Testament, the heart indicates the seat of thinking and reason, not primarily of emotion (example: Genesis 17:17). God had promised to recreate Israel's heart so the nation could live in harmony with God and one another (Jeremiah 32:39; Ezekiel 11:19; 36:26). The prophets called the people to repentance while also making clear that Israel's heart surgery depended on God. Paul expands that vision even further by including the Gentiles. Paul clarifies that older tradition by speaking not of observing Torah with a new heart but of dwelling in God's love and loving Him in return (compare Matthew 22:37-40).

II. Effects of the Cross

(Romans 5:6-11)

A. Reconciled to God (vv. 6-10)

6. For when we were yet without strength, in due time Christ died for the ungodly.

Many scholars believe this verse quotes a saying that was circulating in the Roman church. The main argument for this position is that elsewhere Paul speaks of weakness as a positive attribute rather than as something to be overcome (2 Corinthians 12:5-10; 13:4). If this proposal is correct, it is in keeping with Paul's working to build bridges to his audience, especially when it included many strangers (example: Romans 1:8-15).

The evidence for Paul's claim that suffering borne faithfully produces spiritual growth comes from the life of *Christ* himself (compare Hebrews 5:8). Christ suffered patiently and voluntarily in part because He knew what would be accomplished through His death (see Philippians 2:6-11). His followers may imitate Him in that action (see 2:5).

Paul describes the prior status of all Jesus-followers as both weak and *ungodly*. This is a very strong term in a Greco-Roman context. It might refer to those who ignored the gods or even committed sacrilege against holy places. Christ did not die for the righteous but for the wicked (Hebrews 3–10; etc.). We were helpless to overcome death and evil until God's presence among humankind overcame those dangerous forces. God's mercy extends to those who need it most.

The Right Time

My young children were excited because their mother and I had purchased tickets to ride an Amtrak train for our midwestern vacation. We had never traveled by train before, so I made sure we arrived at the station much more than an hour prior to the arrival of the train so we would have no snafus. We sat in the empty building and waited eagerly for the train to arrive.

We did not know, and there was no one to tell us, that we should have been standing outside the building near the tracks in order to be seen and able to board. When the train arrived right on time, it sped straight past. The children cried, and I felt helpless. I was holding a train ticket that was no longer worth the paper it was printed on.

Unlike that train, Christ arrived on time *and* picked up those who were not even at the station to wait for Him. He died for the ungodly! And now is the right time to make sure you've boarded His train!

—J. M.

7. For scarcely for a righteous man will one die: yet peradventure for a good man some would even dare to die.

The distinction between *a righteous man* and *a good man* is a bit unclear. Probably the latter term refers to a benefactor, or more generically, someone who has done tremendous good for someone else. One might die for such a person as an act of appreciation, loyalty, or simple nobility of heart.

What Do You Think?

What is the biggest sacrifice you would consider making for someone you know and love?

Digging Deeper

What sacrifice would you make on behalf of someone you don't know? someone you consider an enemy?

8. But God commendeth his love toward us, in that, while we were yet sinners, Christ died for us.

The motives described in verse 7 do not apply to Jesus. Christ's death does not fit the normal pattern of brave, noble deaths for a good cause or as acts marking people as superior to others. Such deaths do occur in the ordinary world, and while they often deserve praise, Jesus' death is not comparable to theirs. It far exceeds them: *Christ died for* those who had done nothing for Him and never could. Paul's point is not found in the difference between a righteous person and a good one but instead between those for whom some person might die and those for whom Jesus died.

It is, therefore, highly inappropriate, or in fact, blasphemous, to compare Jesus' death to any other. Christ's death has no parallel because the reason for it has no parallel. The sustained human commitment to sin necessitated Christ's saving work. God shows love toward us by the radical nature of Jesus' death for strangers and enemies.

> **What Do You Think?**
> What circumstances make it challenging to show God's love to unbelievers?
>
> **Digging Deeper**
> Which verses lead you to pray regarding these difficulties?

9. Much more then, being now justified by his blood, we shall be saved from wrath through him.

Much more (also in Romans 5:10, below) introduces an argument from the most difficult task to one less difficult. God has overcome the power of sin and death. Since Jesus has already done the hard work of saving us from the power of sin and death, He can do the much easier work of saving us from God's *wrath* against unrighteousness (see 1:18). Wrath in this context refers to the last judgment (see 2:5-9), in which the true distinctions between good and evil become unmistakable to all. In that moment of truth-telling, the truth of God's mercy shown in Christ's death will win through. Those who trust God's promises to save through His Son will see their hope become a reality.

The substitutionary death of Jesus paid the price for our sins, a price we could never pay on our own (see Romans 3:25; 1 John 2:2; 4:10). Rather, by entering the world of sin and death that humans experience (Hebrews 2:17), God in Christ overcame those great evils and ended the estrangement that separated humanity from our creator. The end of that alienation from God came about because of His actions, not ours. We can be at peace with God. We are new creatures (2 Corinthians 5:17); we wear a new name, and we have a new destiny.

10. For if, when we were enemies, we were reconciled to God by the death of his Son, much more, being reconciled, we shall be saved by his life.

The final two verses of this section build on the idea of salvation in two ways. First, Paul asserts that Christ's death has made possible our reconciliation *to God*. While Paul did consider humans as active participants in the process (example: 2 Corinthians 5:20), here he emphasizes God's work rather than human responses. It is puzzling that Paul includes himself among God's (former) enemies since he had always obeyed God with a sincere heart even when he badly misunderstood God's desires (see Acts 22:3-4; Philippians 3:4-6). Yet this understanding reflects his conclusion that "all have sinned" (Romans 3:23) and that keeping the Law of Moses could not reconcile one to God without God's mercy.

Paul's new thought is that humanity can be saved by Christ's *life*. We participate in the life He has brought about through His actions at Calvary. Those who trust God can anticipate rescue from the forces of evil. They will experience Christ's life in their own lives (see also Galatians 2:19-20).

> **What Do You Think?**
> How do you participate in Jesus' ministry of reconciliation?
>
> **Digging Deeper**
> What role does your congregation play in calling your community to reconciliation in Christ?

Forgiveness

On October 22, 2006, 11-year-old Kathryn Miller rode with her Amish family in their horse-drawn buggy, returning home from a hymn sing. Mark Vandyke had been drinking. Just after 9:00 p.m., he smashed into the buggy with his truck. The impact killed Kathryn and injured her seven family members. Mark fled the scene, only stopping when he crashed into a car. Mark was arrested and charged for his crimes.

While in prison, Mark received an unexpected visitor: Kathryn's dad, Levi Miller. Even more shocking was Levi's mission: to offer Mark forgiveness. The day Mark was convicted, the judge referred to this forgiveness, offering it as a source of peace to Mark as he served his sentence.

Without our sin, the cross would not have been necessary. However, the Father chose to forgive us and not hold His Son's death against us. And God went beyond what Levi could offer: God *pardoned* us and took away our penalty! Do you experience the peace of God's forgiveness? If so, do you pass it along? See Colossians 3:13. —J. M.

B. We Rejoice (v. 11)

11. And not only so, but we also joy in God through our Lord Jesus Christ, by whom we have now received the atonement.

Salvation has tangible results in one's attitude toward daily life. The word translated *joy* is also translated "boast" in Romans 2:17, 23, and that is the sense here. Verse 3 raised the possibility of celebrating even the worst parts of life as opportunities to experience God's mercy. But here, the rejoicing focuses on the mercy itself. Those who trust God celebrate the fact that God's mercy extends to all, not just to themselves. They see themselves as part of the grand story of redemption from the power of evil and share that joy with others. Most importantly, their joy comes *through our Lord Jesus Christ*. That is, He is the author, inspirer, and basis of their words of celebration.

The Greek word translated *atonement* is the noun form of the verb translated "reconciled" in Romans 5:10 (above). Elsewhere, the *King James Version* translates this noun as a form of the word *reconciliation*, and that is the sense here (compare Romans 11:15 and 2 Corinthians 5:18-19). The last reference is relevant here: God's act of reconciliation involved not counting our sins against us. God does not pretend them away, but He refuses to let them define the relationship with us.

Conclusion

A. Hope vs. Shame

All human groups believe certain actions are respectable and others unrespectable, with many gradations in between the two poles of honor and shame. Because they followed a crucified Messiah, early Christians had to rethink their cultures' understanding of honor and shame from the ground up. This rethinking allowed them to endure the suffering that families and governments imposed on them for their faith. They concluded that human life was not a contest for a limited supply of honor and that the true fount of honor was God. The God who raised Jesus from the dead would raise them too. They endured suffering, not for its own sake, but because in suffering, they could imitate Jesus Christ. That radical hope allowed them to face public disgrace or private strife with generous hearts and confident minds.

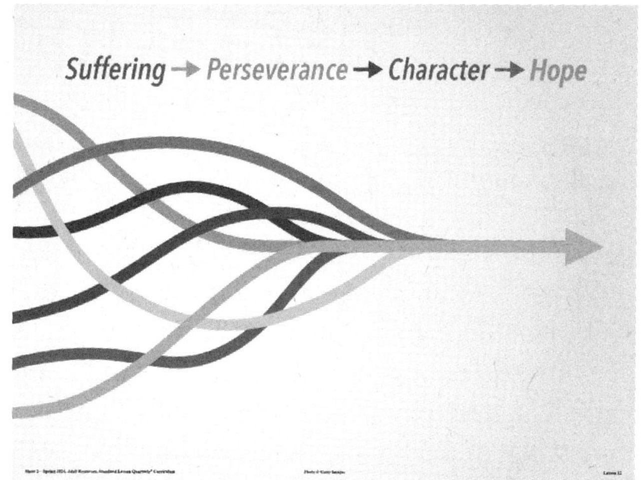

Visual for Lesson 12. *Discuss as a class how the threads of suffering, perseverance, and character can come together to produce hope.*

It still can today. The ability to endure suffering as Christ did shows that the new era is in the process of dawning and that God's promises to protect those who trust Him are reliable.

B. Prayer

God of our Lord Jesus Christ and of all who follow Him, we thank You for not allowing us to be shamed by our failures or even our sins. You have welcomed us into Your household as honored members, and for that, we are grateful. In Jesus' name we pray. Amen.

C. Thought to Remember

We have peace with God because Christ paid sin's price for us.

How to Say It

Messiah	Meh-*sigh*-uh.
Pax Romana *(Latin)*	*Pahks* Ro-*mah*-nah.

Involvement Learning

Enhance your lesson with KJV Bible Student *(from your curriculum supplier) and the reproducible activity page (at www.standardlesson.com or in the back of the* KJV Standard Lesson Commentary Deluxe Edition*).*

Into the Lesson

Write the words *peace* and *truce* on the board. As a class, define the concepts, paying attention to similarities and differences between them. Expect to hear that peace is a state of reconciliation, whereas a truce can be only a kind of cease-fire before hostilities resume. Ask for examples of peace and of truce. Then ask which word best describes reconciliation. What other words can be added to describe reconciliation?

Alternative. Distribute copies of the "Vocabulary Quiz" exercise from the activity page, which you can download. Have learners work in pairs to complete the exercise as indicated. When pairs have finished discussing, give the class an opportunity to share their responses.

After either of these activities, say, "Reconciliation between God and us required His action on our behalf. Today's lesson will explore what our reconciliation required and what it means for us."

Into the Word

Ask volunteers to read Romans 5:1-11. Divide the class into small groups and distribute to each group a handout (you create) with the following questions to help them compare reconciliation with God and reconciliation between people: 1–Who is responsible for initiating the reconciliation? (God; one of the people involved) 2–What occurs in the process of reconciliation, and how is reconciliation achieved? (Christ reconciles us to God through His sacrifice; one or both parties compromise.) 3–What is the goal of the reconciliation, or what does it lead to? (Peace and relationship.) 4–What happens if the reconciliation is not achieved? (We remain in sin, separated from God; our relationship with others is broken.) 5–What is the relationship like before reconciliation? (Lost, alone, dead in sin; broken, upset.)

Encourage learners to ask and answer other questions as well to compare and contrast the two types of reconciliation more fully. Remind participants that these questions are just prompts; they don't need to answer every question.

Bring the groups back together for whole-class discussion. Draw two large interlocking circles on the board, with one labeled "God" and the other labeled "People." Using learners' responses, fill in the diagram with the similarities and differences between reconciliation with God and reconciliation between people.

Into Life

Distribute index cards and pens to the learners. Challenge them to quickly outline what life was like before they were reconciled to God compared to after. It might help to think of a specific personal story from before reconciliation and then contrast it to a similar situation after and how it was different because of their reconciliation. Remind them to only write enough to remember the basic ideas. After a minute, have them practice sharing their story in pairs. Once both people have shared, switch to another set of pairs. If time allows, ask for one or two volunteers to share their stories with the entire class. Encourage the learners to share this story with an unbeliever sometime in the next week.

Option. Ask volunteers from the class to share their own stories of difficult life circumstances and how God used those to develop godly characteristics in their lives.

Alternative. Distribute copies of the "Not Only So!" exercise from the activity page to be worked on individually and completed at home. Inform learners that you will allow time for volunteers to share at the beginning of next week's class.

After either activity, pray for learners to experience the peace of reconciliation with God in the week to come.

May 26
Lesson 13 (KJV)

Who Has Believed?

Devotional Reading: Deuteronomy 30:11-20
Background Scripture: Romans 10:1-21

Romans 10:1-17

1 Brethren, my heart's desire and prayer to God for Israel is, that they might be saved.

2 For I bear them record that they have a zeal of God, but not according to knowledge.

3 For they being ignorant of God's righteousness, and going about to establish their own righteousness, have not submitted themselves unto the righteousness of God.

4 For Christ is the end of the law for righteousness to every one that believeth.

5 For Moses describeth the righteousness which is of the law, That the man which doeth those things shall live by them.

6 But the righteousness which is of faith speaketh on this wise, Say not in thine heart, Who shall ascend into heaven? (that is, to bring Christ down from above:)

7 Or, Who shall descend into the deep? (that is, to bring up Christ again from the dead.)

8 But what saith it? The word is nigh thee, even in thy mouth, and in thy heart: that is, the word of faith, which we preach;

9 That if thou shalt confess with thy mouth the Lord Jesus, and shalt believe in thine heart that God hath raised him from the dead, thou shalt be saved.

10 For with the heart man believeth unto righteousness; and with the mouth confession is made unto salvation.

11 For the scripture saith, Whosoever believeth on him shall not be ashamed.

12 For there is no difference between the Jew and the Greek: for the same Lord over all is rich unto all that call upon him.

13 For whosoever shall call upon the name of the Lord shall be saved.

14 How then shall they call on him in whom they have not believed? and how shall they believe in him of whom they have not heard? and how shall they hear without a preacher?

15 And how shall they preach, except they be sent? as it is written, How beautiful are the feet of them that preach the gospel of peace, and bring glad tidings of good things!

16 But they have not all obeyed the gospel. For Esaias saith, Lord, who hath believed our report?

17 So then faith cometh by hearing, and hearing by the word of God.

Key Text

That if thou shalt confess with thy mouth the Lord Jesus, and shalt believe in thine heart that God hath raised him from the dead, thou shalt be saved. —**Romans 10:9**

Examining

Our Faith

Unit III: Standing in the Faith

Lessons 10–13

Lesson Aims

After participating in this lesson, each learner will be able to:

1. Identify the seven Old Testament passages that Paul quotes.

2. Summarize how those seven quotations undergird Paul's argument.

3. State his or her personal responsibility in light of verses 14-15.

Lesson Outline

Introduction

A. Life Is a Gigantic Prayer

B. Lesson Context

I. Paul's Prayer (Romans 10:1-4)

A. Heart's Desire (v. 1)

B. Zeal Without Knowledge (vv. 2-3)

C. Christ and the Law (v. 4)

II. The Word of Salvation (Romans 10:5-13)

A. Righteousness by Faith (vv. 5-8)

B. Trust in God (vv. 9-10)

The Language of Faith

C. Faith Includes All (vv. 11-13)

III. Preaching Leads to Faith (Romans 10:14-17)

A. How Will They Hear? (vv. 14-15)

The Lawyer of Good News?

B. Who Has Believed? (vv. 16-17)

Conclusion

A. Who May Be Saved?

B. Prayer

C. Thought to Remember

Introduction

A. Life Is a Gigantic Prayer

Preaching that does not come out of love for the people being addressed ultimately does not benefit the listening crowd. The Catholic activist Dorothy Day once commented on preaching that, "If people will not listen, one can still love, one can still find Christ in them to love." We need not strain ourselves in order to provide examples of leaders whose message sounded good but whose practice turned out to be destructive. In these instances, whatever good was done because of the beautiful words is largely undone because of the harm of the speaker's actions. As with all Christian practice, preaching without love is worthless (see 1 Corinthians 13).

The same is true for prayer. We might think of preaching as a prayer shared with an audience. The speaker presents the good news in the hope and prayer that God will work in the hearts of those who hear. And, when we find ourselves unable to preach in words, our actions can still be a prayer that the people who interact with us will find themselves turning to God.

B. Lesson Context

Just how comprehensive *is* the good news of Jesus the Messiah? The entire book of Romans is concerned with this question. Romans 1–8 sets forth proof of the need and extent of God's mercy available to those who trust Him with their lives. God has announced salvation for all who trust (see Romans 1:16-17). The gospel of grace has come to light for all. The extension of God's offer of salvation to Gentiles does not exclude Jews. Chapters 9–11 advance the discussion in part by considering the fate of Israel. The depth of God's love extends to Israel as well as the Gentiles (11:33-36).

Romans 10 reflects on Paul's hope that the good news that Jesus is the Messiah and Lord will also come to his fellow Jews. God promised salvation to Israel, and God keeps promises at all times. Therefore, the promise of salvation must come to Israel. The hard division between Jews and Christians did not occur until several generations after Paul's lifetime. Paul himself never used the word "Christians" in his writings, though it had begun to circulate within the church. He likely did not anticipate the centuries of hostility between the two groups or the habit of those thinking themselves to be Christians of insulting and even persecuting Jews. The hard division that Paul experienced and wrote about was between Jews (whether Christ-followers or not) and Gentiles (whether God-fearers or not). The gospel of reconciliation and peace in Christ reaches all, allowing God both to keep the ancient promises to Israel and to add the Gentiles to the faithful community.

I. Paul's Prayer

(Romans 10:1-4)

A. Heart's Desire (v. 1)

1. Brethren, my heart's desire and prayer to God for Israel is, that they might be saved.

Praying for God's salvation *for Israel* was probably habitual for Paul. His concern for his people—including family and friends—was reason enough to pray for the nation. The Scriptures he long had studied modeled praying for deliverance for Israel from its various foes (examples: Psalms 79; 85:4-7; 130:7-8). And there was an expectation, found particularly in the prophets' writings, that the nation would be restored after suffering for their sins (Isaiah 40:1-2; 49:14-26; Jeremiah 30:10-11; Ezekiel 40–48; etc.). Paul's prayers expanded to include that his people would turn to Christ and find eternal salvation in Him.

> **What Do You Think?**
> What group of people do you belong to that you long to see come to be saved?
>
> **Digging Deeper**
> How does your status in that group allow you to witness to the good news in ways that might be difficult for someone from "outside"?

B. Zeal Without Knowledge (vv. 2-3)

2. For I bear them record that they have a zeal for God, but not according to knowledge.

This verse and the next summarize Paul's understanding of the state of his Jewish contemporaries. Paul did not suggest that his fellow Jews were all pursuing evil ends, because that was clearly not true. Jews who did not follow Jesus still desired to follow God. But, Paul asserts, they misunderstood the trajectory of God's work and how their own Scriptures pointed to Jesus as their Messiah (compare Luke 24:25-32). Paul does not dismiss *zeal* for God as insignificant; he knew from personal experience that misdirected zeal could be turned to God's purposes (Acts 22:3-21; Galatians 1:13-14; Philippians 3:6). Still, his people's zeal without *knowledge* of Christ prevented them from recognizing that God's long-anticipated provision for deliverance of His people (and indeed all nations) had finally been revealed (compare Acts 2:17-36).

> **What Do You Think?**
> When have you experienced zeal without knowledge?
>
> **Digging Deeper**
> Is there an occasion when zeal without knowledge only needs time and experience rather than intervention? Explain.

3. For they being ignorant of God's righteousness, and going about to establish their own righteousness, have not submitted themselves unto the righteousness of God.

Paul has argued that *God's righteousness* consists of extending salvation to all on the basis of trust in the work of Christ (Romans 4; see lesson 11). This verse echoes Romans 2:17-24, in which Paul criticized the attempt to make Jews out of Gentiles. Attempts to come to God on the basis of anything other than Christ, and especially on the basis of any human achievement, fail (compare Philippians 3:9). An approach to saving the Gentiles that tried to compel them to keep the Law of Moses (the Torah) neglected the deeper reality that the relationship to God always depends on faithful trust, not on the works themselves.

C. Christ and the Law (v. 4)

4. For Christ is the end of the law for righteousness to every one that believeth.

The word translated *end* can have the sense of

"the ultimate goal" in Greek, as it does here (compare Romans 6:22; 1 Timothy 1:5; 1 Peter 1:9). The coming of the *Christ* (the Hebrew Messiah) and His activity in revealing God's salvation to all human beings was always the goal *of the law*. And the Law of Moses itself pointed Israel to the work of God, as opposed to the law's existing for its own sake. Paul did not expect the abolition of Torah but the completion of God's promises (compare Matthew 5:17-20). Those who trust God's work through Jesus have fulfilled the Torah's overarching objectives.

II. The Word of Salvation

(Romans 10:5-13)

A. Righteousness by Faith (vv. 5-8)

5. For Moses describeth the righteousness which is of the law, That the man which doeth those things shall live by them.

Here and in Galatians 3:12, Paul quoted Leviticus 18:5: *The man which doeth those things shall live by them*. Paul did not oppose Jews keeping *the law*, and he accepted the idea that its instructions can guide a person to a wiser, more faithful life (see Romans 2:25; compare Psalm 119; James 1:22; 2:10-13). In this way, Jews who kept the Torah in faith did *live by them* and could experience the limited *righteousness* of striving to accomplish God's will.

6-7. But the righteousness which is of faith speaketh on this wise, Say not in thine heart, Who shall ascend into heaven? (that is, to bring Christ down from above.) Or, Who shall descend into the deep? (that is, to bring up Christ again from the dead.)

Paul next quotes Deuteronomy 30:12-13: *Say not in thine heart, Who shall ascend into heaven?... Who shall descend into the deep?* These verses are part of God's promise that He would extend mercy to Israel after the nation experienced the consequences of breaking covenant and turned to Him in repentance and faith (see commentary on Romans 10:8, below).

Paul adds to these quotations two comments, the first being *that is, to bring Christ down from above*. This is characteristic of a typical Jewish style of reading. In this style, the reader-scholar supplemented the original text by connecting it to a larger doctrinal point. Here, Paul's point is that Christ's descent into the human world (Philippians 2:7-8) was God's work, not that of striving human beings. Salvation, therefore, comes from God and not from humans. The second comment, *to bring up Christ again from the dead*, connects the ancient text to the core Christian story of Jesus' resurrection (Mark 16:6-7; etc.).

8. But what saith it? The word is nigh thee, even in thy mouth, and in thy heart, that is, the word of faith, which we preach.

The quotation continues, this time from Deuteronomy 30:13. In Deuteronomy *the word* (in context, the Law of Moses) is nearby, entering into the heart of those who love God with all their "heart, . . . soul, . . . and . . . might" (6:5). The Lord asserted His laws are neither hard to understand nor difficult to carry out (30:14), though people's experience showed that perfect adherence was not possible (example: Acts 15:10). This puts keeping the law into stark contrast with the heroics of mythic people like Gilgamesh, who needed to climb to Heaven or cross the ocean depths to please their supposed gods. Unlike mythical ancient heroes, ordinary people could not go to Heaven or survive in the waters, but they didn't need to in order to keep the Torah. It was accessible —as long as it was written on their hearts and not just in a book (consider 4:29; compare Jeremiah 31:33; Ezekiel 11:19).

The word of faith that comes to believers, both Jews and Gentiles, is the trustworthy message that Paul has been preaching. The end of the verse sets up the next several sentences.

What Do You Think?

How do you keep the Word in your mouth and in your heart?

Digging Deeper

How do you balance your efforts with the Spirit's work in this regard?

B. Trust in God (vv. 9-10)

9. That if thou shalt confess with thy mouth the Lord Jesus, and shalt believe in thine heart

that God hath raised him from the dead, thou shalt be saved.

Paul links the confession of faith from one's *mouth* with the belief in one's *heart* and thus to the commitments of the whole person (compare Deuteronomy 6:5; see commentary on Romans 10:8, above). To confess *Jesus* as *Lord* is a radical commitment. It was obviously so in the first century AD when the Roman emperors claimed to be sons of their gods, and many gods were worshipped as sovereign. The confession "Jesus is Lord" was almost certainly a part of early Christian worship; it was definitely a statement used to indicate one's ultimate allegiance (see 1 Corinthians 12:3; Philippians 2:11). Anyone who can sincerely make that confession with their mouth and heart will see a changed life over time.

To *believe* that God has raised Jesus *from the dead* also means to trust that God has overcome the power of death itself (see Revelation 1:18). Salvation involves both the present and the future. We can understand being *saved* as a shorthand for the entire relationship that the redeemed person enjoys with God. The effects begin in our Spirit-led lives now and will culminate in everlasting life in Heaven.

This verse is sometimes interpreted as a description of the entry point into the Christian life. Yet Paul's vision goes beyond beginnings. Confession of Christ's lordship occurs daily, both in the face of opposition or hardship and in more peaceful times. It also involves witnesses (1 Timothy 6:12), making it a public commitment (Acts 19:18). The message of the gospel connects deeply to real lives, and those who hear it must internalize it and proclaim it.

What Do You Think?

What biblical examples come to mind of people who called on the Lord and were saved?

Digging Deeper

Do these examples suggest anything about the process of being saved? Why or why not?

10. For with the heart man believeth unto righteousness; and with the mouth confession is made unto salvation.

The prior verse followed the sequence confess/believe in the order of Deuteronomy 30. But this verse follows a more intuitive order, with the commitments of *the heart* leading to the words of *the mouth*. (On the heart, see lesson 12 commentary on Romans 5:5.) When the heart and the mouth align in acknowledging the saving work of Christ, it becomes possible to experience both *righteousness* and *salvation*. Paul does not separate the realities of righteousness and salvation any more than he separates trust and confession (see 10:9, above). These all interconnect, each supporting the other.

The Language of Faith

I've taught all levels of Spanish as a second language. At higher levels, language acquisition assesses a person's ability to use their new vocabulary based on several elements. Among them are writing, reading, and imagining things with words.

It's always speaking that makes the difference in language learning. The ability to think in a second language is a form of high cognition because it's internalized. But speaking words that sound foreign takes boldness and courage. After all, the change of just one letter can be comical or downright embarrassing.

Paul encourages us to confess with our mouths, making a bold, courageous step in our faith. Have you learned the language of faith? What are you keeping to yourself instead of boldly proclaiming?

—O. P.

C. Faith Includes All (vv. 11-13)

11. For the scripture saith, Whosoever believeth on him shall not be ashamed.

Paul quotes Isaiah 28:16 (also in Romans 9:33), which is part of a promise that God would rebuild Zion after its destruction. The quotation may not quite match how our English Bibles state Isaiah 28:16 because Paul is quoting from the ancient

How to Say It

Gilgamesh	*Gil*-guh-mesh.
Septuagint	Sep-*too*-ih-jent.
Torah *(Hebrew)*	*Tor*-uh.

Greek version known as the Septuagint. Paul may have read that text metaphorically so that the promised "stone" laid in Zion became a reference to the Messiah (compare Acts 4:11), although Paul does not spell out this connection.

The Bible often conceives of shame as a social condition, visible to all, rather than an inner, more private emotion (examples: Psalms 35:26; 132:18; Isaiah 42:17). Paul understands trust in God as the opposite of public humiliation. At the final judgment, those who trust in Jesus for deliverance from sins *shall not be ashamed* because our hope of salvation will be fully realized.

12. For there is no difference between the Jew and the Greek: for the same Lord over all is rich unto all that call upon him.

This verse returns to the thesis statement of the book in Romans 1:16-17. The theme of God's richness also appears in 2 Corinthians 8:9, which describes the work of Christ in terms of the foregoing of wealth. The image in both texts is of a king who bestows goods on subjects whenever they need them. By calling Jesus *Lord over all*, the verse emphasizes His close relationship to the Father and the universal scope of His kingdom.

13. For whosoever shall call upon the name of the Lord shall be saved.

This verse quotes Joel 2:32 (see also Acts 2:16-21), which is part of a passage about one instance of God's rescuing Israel. Both Joel and Paul understand God as one who answers the sincere cries of people longing for help. Because Jesus is "Lord over all" (Romans 10:12), *whosoever* may *call upon* Him.

III. Preaching Leads to Faith

(Romans 10:14-17)

A. How Will They Hear? (vv. 14-15)

14-15a. How then shall they call on him in whom they have not believed? And how shall they believe in him of whom they have not heard? And how shall they hear without a preacher? And how shall they preach, except they be sent?

How do people know to *call on* God? The answer becomes a sustained explanation of the nature and purpose of Christian preaching. The act of proclaiming the gospel ultimately comes from the God who sends out proclaimers, not from their own concerns or abilities. Paul always understood his own mission as following God's leading (examples: Romans 1:1; Galatians 1:1; 1 Timothy 1:1). Here, we see a logical progression: a preacher must be sent so that an audience can hear the gospel and come to faith.

15b. As it is written, How beautiful are the feet of them that preach the gospel of peace, and bring glad tidings of good things!

The evidence Paul offers for God's calling messengers to preach is a quotation of Isaiah 52:7. That text, in turn, is part of a long discussion of the *glad tidings* to ancient Israel: God was ending the suffering of the Babylonian exile. The exiled people would soon return home and rebuild the ruined cities, especially Jerusalem (examples: Ezra 6:13-18; Nehemiah 6:15). The people would experience a good life in their own land, complete with the healing of physical and social ills (see Isaiah 61:1-4).

An important characteristic of Christian preaching is the proclamation of *peace* between God and humanity. When one experiences reconciliation with the Lord, it becomes possible to be reconciled to other people as well. Christian teaching and preaching should, therefore, be filled with joy and hope because of the *good things* God wants to accomplish in us and through us.

What Do You Think?

What books of the Bible most heavily informed your faith? Explain.

Digging Deeper

What books of the Bible have influenced you least? What value might you anticipate from giving one of those books another look?

The Lawyer of Good News?

A few years ago, my aunt received a vague voicemail from a lawyer. Her first reaction was worry; why was this person reaching out? She had some ideas, none of them good. For this reason, my aunt decided to call the lawyer back, with her family in the same room for moral support.

To their collective amazement, the call was about some money she was inheriting. Her sister, whom she had not seen in decades, had passed. Because her sister had no other family, my aunt received the entire inheritance. When the call was finished, my aunt resolved to express her appreciation to the lawyer who had shared this unexpected news.

Messengers who bring good news are welcomed and appreciated because of what they carry, regardless of who they are. And regardless of who *we* are, Paul challenges us to carry out the beautiful job of telling others the gospel. How will *you* proclaim the glad tidings this week? —O. P.

B. Who Has Believed? (vv. 16-17)

16. But they have not all obeyed the gospel. For Esaias saith, Lord, who that believed our report?

Paul quotes Isaiah 53:1, a text that is part of the prophetic reflection on the fact that people do not always listen to God's Word (compare Isaiah 6:9-11; compare John 12:37-41). In its immediate context, Isaiah 53:1 continues the account of the Suffering Servant, noting the disbelief of many.

In spite of that disbelief, Paul's job, and the job of all Christ-followers, is to keep celebrating the good news and to live lives that reflect our faith in Jesus (see 2 Corinthians 4). After all, we might plant the seed and water it, but God gives the increase (1 Corinthians 3:6). Our responsibility is not the outcome but our faithfulness to report *the gospel.*

17. So then faith cometh by hearing, and hearing by the word of God.

There is a contrast between verses 16 and 17. Both draw on an idea from the Old Testament prophets regarding how their audience would react. Verse 16 emphasizes the negative side of unbelief, while verse 17 understands the power of *the word* to be so great that it leads people to trust *God.* Paul was confident that both Jews and Gentiles would learn to trust God once they understood the nature of the gospel.

Conclusion

A. Who May be Saved?

The offer of salvation comes through the preaching of the Word as one of hope and expectation. God is *for* us and wishes to be *with* us. When we trust the reliability of that offer, we can enter into a life of joyful hope, which the Bible calls salvation. That life begins now and extends into eternity.

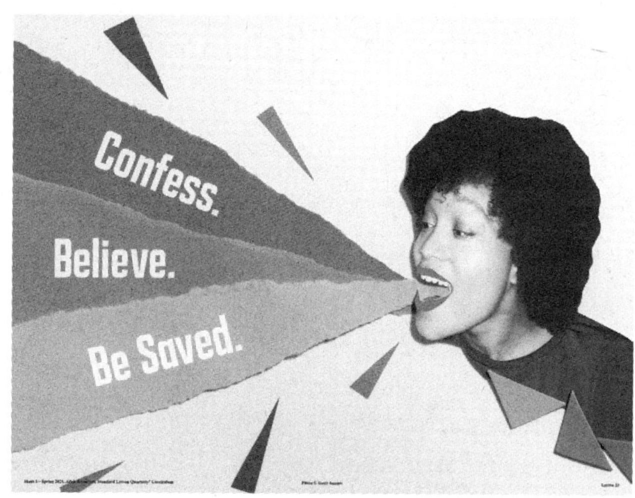

Visual for Lesson 13. *While discussing the questions with verse 9, talk about how the first two imperatives on this visual relate to the third.*

In Romans 10, Paul speaks of those who cry out to God, confess Jesus as Lord, and so receive salvation. Like the prophets of Israel, who called on their people to turn from evil toward good, Paul makes a direct connection between the words that humans speak and God's willingness to save. The words must be sincerely uttered, but the key actor in the drama of salvation is God. Preaching connects closely to prayer as we seek to conform our desires to God's desires. It must be full of hope, inviting listeners to trust a gracious God.

This readiness to hear comes from God's passionate love for the creation. In truth, God created the world originally out of love, and He sustains the creation out of the same love. In an environment of love, a needy humanity crying out for help receives a willing ear.

B. Prayer

O God who makes promises and keeps them over generations and long centuries, our prayer is for all people near and far to come to know Jesus. Send us! In Jesus' name we pray. Amen.

C. Thought to Remember

Confess and believe that Jesus is Lord!

Involvement Learning

Enhance your lesson with KJV Bible Student *(from your curriculum supplier) and the reproducible activity page (at www.standardlesson.com or in the back of the* KJV Standard Lesson Commentary Deluxe Edition*).*

Into the Lesson

Option. If you used the "Not Only So!" exercise from lesson 12, allow volunteers to share now.

Write on the board *Real-Life Heroes* and *Heroes in Mythology* as the heads of two columns. Have the class brainstorm people who belong in both categories. (In addition to characters known from ancient stories, *Heroes in Mythology* could include comic book, movie, or folk heroes, among others.) Once two sizable lists have been created, ask learners to consider which characteristics are likely shared between the groups (bravery, a sense of moral duty, honesty, and so on) and which characteristics more likely belong to one or the other.

Decide as a class whether the following statement is true: heroes in mythology conquer *impossible* odds with *supernatural* abilities, while real-life heroes conquer *great* odds through the extraordinary application of *natural* human abilities. Tweak as desired to highlight the differences between a mythic hero and a real-life hero. Lead into the lesson by saying, "God does not require us to be heroes to live according to His will. Our lesson focuses on the good news of the hero who accomplished what we could not do for ourselves."

Alternative. Distribute copies of the "Zeal Without Knowledge" exercise from the activity page, which you can download. Have learners work in pairs to complete as indicated. Say, "Paul wrote to the Romans about the importance of understanding what Jesus has done for us—and of sharing that knowledge."

Into the Word

Distribute printed copies of Romans 10:1-17 (you create), with a list of the following Old Testament passages. Leave out the references in parentheses–they are for the leader's reference only: Leviticus 18:5 *(v. 5)*; Deuteronomy 30:12 *(v. 6)*; Deuteronomy 30:13 *(v. 8)*; Isaiah 28:16 *(v. 11)*; Joel 2:32 *(v. 13)*; Isaiah 52:7 *(v. 15)*; and Isaiah 53:1 *(v. 16)*. In pairs or groups of three, have participants match up each Old Testament quotation to its use in today's Scripture passage.

Ask the following discussion questions: 1–What is Paul's overall argument? 2–How is Paul using each quotation to bolster his argument? 3–What steps does Paul describe in the progression of salvation? 4–What is the difference between the actions of the heart and the mouth? Bring the class back together to discuss. Consult the commentary for answers to these questions, as well as any that arise from learners. Tie this discussion back to the Into the Lesson exercise you chose by exploring together how that concept (either heroics or zeal without knowledge) relates to the gospel proclamation.

Into Life

Have the learners think through the progression Paul describes in verses 14-15 (hearing, believing, preaching), and ask, "Based on these verses, what is your personal responsibility?" Give learners a one-minute time limit to think individually, and then share their reflections with a partner. Ask: 1–Does Paul's progression seem complete? Why or why not? 2–What, if anything, would you add to this progression? Provide verses to support this assertion. 3–Where are you in this progression? 4–What, if any, next steps should you take? If there are no next steps, why not?

Alternative. Distribute copies of the "Who Has Believed?" exercise from the activity page. Have learners complete it individually in a minute or less before sharing their answers with a partner.

After either activity, lead the class in a closing prayer that learners will be attentive to the Spirit's leading this week as they find opportunities to grow in their belief in and preaching of the gospel in both word and deed.

Hope in the Lord

Special Features

Lessons

Unit 1: Experiencing Hope

Unit 2: Expressing Hope

Unit 3: Eternal Hope

Quarterly Quiz

Use these questions as a pretest or as a review. The answers are on page iv of This Quarter in the Word.

Lesson 1

1. Paul was filling up Christ's ______ in his flesh. *Colossians 1:24*

2. In Christ, all the treasures of wisdom and knowledge are hidden. T/F. *Colossians 2:3*

Lesson 2

1. The ______ kills, but the spirit gives life. *2 Corinthians 3:6*

2. Moses hid his face with what? (nothing, a veil, a mask) *2 Corinthians 3:13*

Lesson 3

1. The ______ ought to bear the infirmities of the ______. *Romans 15:1*

2. Paul quoted Jeremiah regarding the root of Jesse. T/F. *Romans 15:12*

Lesson 4

1. God promised to bless and multiply who? (Abraham, Jacob, Moses) *Hebrews 6:14*

2. God confirmed His promise with an ______. *Hebrews 6:17*

Lesson 5

1. Agrippa gave Paul permission to speak for himself. T/F. *Acts 26:1*

2. Who did Paul put into prison? (criminals, Gentiles, the saints) *Acts 26:10*

Lesson 6

1. "We are not consumed" because of the Lord's what? (mercies, judgment, inattention) *Lamentations 3:22*

2. Great is God's what? (faithfulness, wrath, indifference) *Lamentations 3:23*

Lesson 7

1. The psalmist began to learn from God at what stage of life? (his youth, during his marriage, on his deathbed) *Psalm 71:17*

2. The psalmist trusted that God would bring him home from a foreign prison. T/F. *Psalm 71:20*

Lesson 8

1. God's ______ made the psalmist. *Psalm 119:73*

2. God's law is the psalmist's delight. T/F. *Psalm 119:77*

Lesson 9

1. The psalmist cried out to God from where? (his home, a mountaintop, the depths) *Psalm 130:1*

2. "My soul waiteth for the Lord ______ than they that watch for the morning." *Psalm 130:6*

Lesson 10

1. The word the Thessalonian believers received was from men. T/F. *1 Thessalonians 2:13*

2. Paul called the Thessalonian believers his ______ and ______. *1 Thessalonians 2:20*

Lesson 11

1. We are now called God's what? (treasure, sons, soldiers) *1 John 3:2*

2. Jesus came to destroy the devil's work. T/F. *1 John 3:8*

Lesson 12

1. God promised the hope of what kind of life before the world began? (eternal, easy, fair) *Titus 1:2*

2. God's grace offers salvation to most people. T/F. *Titus 2:11*

Lesson 13

1. We are saved because of God's ______. *Titus 3:5*

2. Our works, good or bad, no longer matter when we have believed in God. T/F *Titus 3:8*

Quarter at a Glance

by Jon Miller

One dictionary defines *hope* as "to want something to happen or be true" or "to desire with the expectation of obtainment or fulfillment." In popular use, hope is often closely associated with a wish; there is not necessarily an expectation that this "hope" will come true. But Christian hope is based on nothing less than God's promises and the confidence we have based on His faithfulness to His promises. We do not *wish* God would honor His promises; we *hope* He will. This quarter of study traces the concept of hope through the generations.

Hope and the Church

The five lessons of Unit I, "Experiencing Hope," consider hope through the lens of those whose faith in Christ gave shape to the early church. In Colossians 1:27 (lesson 1), Paul tells the Colossians that the mysteries of God become known to them as their hope in Christ transforms their lives. In 2 Corinthians (lesson 2), hope in Christ leads to an even greater boldness than was possible for Moses because believers are able to see the glory of God "with open face" (3:18). Lesson 3 points to the hope that is inspired in those around us when they see the salvation that is being worked out in us by the Holy Spirit (Romans 15:1-13). In lesson 4, we find encouragement, as did the writer of Hebrews, in the spiritual lifeline we have to God through Christ (see Hebrews 6). The unit closes with a lesson from Acts 26:1-11 and a testimony of Christian hope from Paul's own lips as he defends himself before King Agrippa.

Praise and Hope

Unit II, "Expressing Hope," turns attention to the prayers of ancient Israel as a model for offering to God our praise and petitions. These Hebrew prayers are also expressions of Christian hope. The first lesson of the unit is from a song of lament in Lamentations 3. The author of Lamentations describes hope as fleeing from the people of Israel until the author remembers God's faithfulness. This memory leads the author to worship God and proclaim, "great is [God's] faithfulness" (Lamentations 3:23, lesson 6).

The remaining lessons of the unit are drawn from the Psalms. These ancient songs express hope in God's intervention (lesson 7), graceful giving of the law (lesson 8), and forgiveness (lesson 9). These hopes find their fulfillment in Christ.

Hope and the Future

The four lessons of Unit III, "Eternal Hope," consider facets of the promised future that God is preparing for those who call on the name of Jesus. What does hope look like as we wait for Jesus to come again in glory and finally set things right? Paul anticipates the nearness of Christ's return when he tells the Thessalonians how excited he is to brag about them (lesson 10), even as he worries about the problems that might rock their faith in his absence from them. Similarly, 1 John (lesson 11) anticipates Christ's return so that in seeing Christ, we might become like Him.

> *We do not* wish *God would honor His promises; we* hope *He will.*

The final two lessons of the quarter are from Titus, where we hear Paul's appeal to live out the present moment with a hope rooted in God's grace-filled future, made certain in Christ's death and resurrection. Our hope will be fulfilled at the second coming of the Lord Jesus Christ (see Titus 2:13, lesson 12). Thus, the foundation of hope is Jesus Christ. Through the death and resurrection of Christ and the promise of His coming, believers live in daily encouragement and strength. The knowledge of Christ's second coming prevents us from complacency in our present situation.

Get the Setting

by Jon Miller

When we read the New Testament letters, we are reading someone else's mail. Of the 27 books in our New Testament, 21 of them are messages between the author and a particular church or individual. In the Greco-Roman world, letters served a personal function and were considered a substitute for the writer's physical presence. The letters were commonly read aloud by the deliverer to the community (Colossians 4:16; 1 Thessalonians 5:27).

The challenge for the modern reader is the attempt to interpret the texts and understand them in the same way as the first-century audience. The letters best serve us after we know the historical and literary world in which these letters originated.

Historical Context

Persecution plagued the first-century church. Not long after the events of Pentecost (Acts 2:1-41), the apostles were arrested and threatened (5:17-41), and other church leaders were executed (example: 7:54-60). As a result, many early believers fled Jerusalem and scattered throughout the eastern Mediterranean region (example: 11:19).

Following his own transformation from persecutor to apostle (1 Corinthians 15:9), Paul clashed doctrinally with the Jews in the synagogues, which led to his persecution and imprisonment (Acts 13:45-52; 16:16-24; 24:27). While in prison, Paul wrote four of his letters, which are collected in our New Testament (Ephesians, Philippians, Colossians, and Philemon), and which are still prized as letters of encouragement and hope for believers facing persecution.

Literary Context

Greco-Roman letters generally followed a standard format. First, ancient letters contained a salutation in which the writer briefly introduced himself and identified the recipient of the letter (examples: 1 Corinthians 1:1-3; James 1:1). Next came a prayer of thanks or greeting (examples: Romans 1:7; Colossians 1:2). Then followed the body of the text that ended with a benediction (examples: Philippians 4:21-23; 1 Peter 5:14).

The book of Hebrews is unique compared to other New Testament letters. This book breaks the mold of the standard letter by excluding the routine introduction, including the name of the author. Therefore, some students believe the text aligns with the genre of a sermon rather than a letter. The writer of Hebrews knew that his or her recipients had a strong understanding of the Old Testament, which the writer cites more than 30 times. The original audience had endured great suffering and conflict, and the writing was intended to encourage them.

One of the ways the text of Hebrews encouraged the original audience was by using the Greco-Roman rhetorical skill of comparison (example: Hebrews 9:11-13). The author uses this literary device wisely and does not compare two opposite things. Instead, the author of Hebrews compares the good things of Judaism with the best of Christianity, Jesus. In the final chapter, Hebrews 13, the author concludes with an appeal. The recipients are reminded that they are connected to Christ in persecution and expectation of a future city (13:13-14). The connection to Christ in persecution is a literary way to remind the Christians of the words of Jesus (John 15:18-27).

Conclusion

Given the often-personal connections that the Christians of the first century had with those who wrote the letters that are now the New Testament, it is clear how these letters brought them hope and encouragement. Keeping in mind the *who* (both the writer and the audience) and *why* of a letter can help us better understand how the Spirit wants to encourage and teach us through reading the early believers' mail.

Mon, Aug. 12	**The Lord Is Just and Upright**	Deuteronomy 32:1-6
Tue, Aug. 13	**Bought with a Price**	1 Corinthians 6:9-20
Wed, Aug. 14	**A Godly Life Overcomes Evil**	Romans 12:9-21
Thu, Aug. 15	**Walking a Straight Path**	Proverbs 15:20-25
Fri, Aug. 16	**God Rescues the Righteous**	Psalm 37:27-40
Sat, Aug. 17	**Salvation Comes from the Lord**	Jonah 2:1-9
Sun, Aug. 18	**God Redeems and Purifies**	Titus 1:1-3; 2:11-15
Mon, Aug. 19	**Do Good Wherever You Can**	Proverbs 3:27-35
Tue, Aug. 20	**Defend the Poor and Needy**	Proverbs 31:1-9
Wed, Aug. 21	**Saved by God's Rich Mercy**	Ephesians 2:1-10
Thu, Aug. 22	**Faith Without Works Is Dead**	James 2:14-26
Fri, Aug. 23	**Walk in God's Way**	Isaiah 30:18-26
Sat, Aug. 24	**Shine Your Light Before Others**	Matthew 5:13-20
Sun, Aug. 25	**Saved by God's Mercy**	Titus 3:3-11

Answers to the Quarterly Quiz on page 338

Lesson 1—1. afflictions. 2. True. **Lesson 2**—1. letter. 2. a veil. **Lesson 3**—1. strong, weak. 2. False. **Lesson 4**—1. Abraham. 2. oath. **Lesson 5**—1. True. 2. the saints. **Lesson 6**—1. mercies. 2. faithfulness. **Lesson 7**—1. his youth. 2. False. **Lesson 8**—1. hands. 2. True. **Lesson 9**—1. the depths. 2. more. **Lesson 10**—1. False. 2. glory, joy. **Lesson 11**—1. sons. 2. True. **Lesson 12**—1. eternal. 2. False. **Lesson 13**—1. mercy. 2. False.

This Quarter in the Word

Mon, May 27	**God's Witnesses**	Isaiah 43:8-13
Tue, May 28	**Praise the Lord!**	Psalm 113
Wed, May 29	**God's Children Through Faith**	Galatians 3:19-29
Thu, May 30	**The Lord's Blessing Makes Rich**	Proverbs 10:19-25
Fri, May 31	**Your Treasure Is with Your Heart**	Matthew 6:19-24
Sat, June 1	**Seek First God's Kingdom**	Matthew 6:25-34
Sun, June 2	**Christ, the Most Precious Gift**	Colossians 1:24–2:3
Mon, June 3	**Boldly Proclaiming the Kingdom**	Acts 28:23-31
Tue, June 4	**The Awesome Presence of God**	Exodus 19:9-11, 16-25
Wed, June 5	**The Consuming Fire**	Hebrews 12:18-29
Thu, June 6	**The Church Prays for Boldness**	Acts 4:23-31
Fri, June 7	**Transfigured by the Power of God**	Exodus 34:28-35
Sat, June 8	**Be Strong and Courageous**	Deuteronomy 31:1-8
Sun, June 9	**Ministers of a New Covenant**	2 Corinthians 3:5-18
Mon, June 10	**Servant Leadership**	Luke 22:25-30
Tue, June 11	**You Shall Receive Power**	Acts 1:1-11
Wed, June 12	**Anointed by God**	Isaiah 61
Thu, June 13	**How Pleasant to Live in Unity**	Psalms 133–134
Fri, June 14	**Bear with One Another in Love**	Ephesians 4:1-7
Sat, June 15	**Embrace the Mind of Christ**	Philippians 2:1-13
Sun, June 16	**Prayer for Hope, Joy, and Peace**	Romans 15:1-13

Mon, June 17	**Hope in God Our Help**	Psalm 42
Tue, June 18	**Whoever Has the Son Has Life**	1 John 5:1-13
Wed, June 19	**Boldness in Christ**	1 John 5:14-21
Thu, June 20	**The Lord Is My Shepherd**	Psalm 23
Fri, June 21	**Trust in God Our Salvation**	Isaiah 12
Sat, June 22	**Maturing in Christ**	Hebrews 6:1-8
Sun, June 23	**Trust God's Promises**	Hebrews 6:9-20
Mon, June 24	**My Heart Shall Not Fear**	Psalm 27
Tue, June 25	**The Treasure of Knowing Christ**	Philippians 3:1-14
Wed, June 26	**Jesus Makes a Difference**	Galatians 1:13-24
Thu, June 27	**God Will Help the Fearful**	Isaiah 41:1-15
Fri, June 28	**The Wise Shall Shine Brightly**	Daniel 12
Sat, June 29	**Encounter with Christ**	Acts 9:1-9
Sun, June 30	**An Apostle's Defense**	Acts 26:1-11
Mon, July 1	**Our Father in Heaven**	Matthew 6:9-15
Tue, July 2	**Judah's Fate Sealed**	Jeremiah 52:1-15
Wed, July 3	**God's People Face Exile**	Jeremiah 52:16-30
Thu, July 4	**Boldly Approach the Throne of Grace**	Hebrews 4:12-16
Fri, July 5	**God Will Remember Sins No More**	Hebrews 8:6-13
Sat, July 6	**Joy Comes with the Morning**	Psalm 30
Sun, July 7	**Hope in God's Steadfast Love**	Lamentations 3:16-24
Mon, July 8	**The Fragrance of Knowing God**	2 Corinthians 2:12-17
Tue, July 9	**The Testimony of the Redeemed**	Psalm 107:1-9
Wed, July 10	**Sing of God's Deeds with Joy**	Psalm 107:10-22
Thu, July 11	**Hope Laid Up in Heaven**	Colossians 1:3-12
Fri, July 12	**Proclaim Christ's Boundless Riches**	Ephesians 3:1-13
Sat, July 13	**Refuge in the Lord**	Psalm 71:1-11
Sun, July 14	**Hope and Praise Continually**	Psalm 71:12-21

Mon, July 15	**Equipped for Every Good Work**	2 Timothy 3:10-17
Tue, July 16	**Resist Temptation**	Matthew 4:1-11
Wed, July 17	**Every Word of God Proves True**	Proverbs 30:1-9
Thu, July 18	**Let Christ's Word Abound in You**	Colossians 3:12-17
Fri, July 19	**Doers of the Word**	James 1:19-27
Sat, July 20	**Lord, Teach Me Your Statutes**	Psalm 119:57-72
Sun, July 21	**Hope in God's Word**	Psalm 119:73-80
Mon, July 22	**Await the Dawning Day**	2 Peter 1:16-21
Tue, July 23	**Hasten God's New Creation**	2 Peter 3:1-15a
Wed, July 24	**God Is My Fortress**	Psalm 59:1-9, 17
Thu, July 25	**Watch and Be Ready**	Matthew 25:1-13
Fri, July 26	**Watch and Work Faithfully**	Matthew 25:14-21, 24-30
Sat, July 27	**Wait for God's Salvation**	Lamentations 3:25-36
Sun, July 28	**Wait and Hope in the Lord**	Psalm 130
Mon, July 29	**Promise of Hope**	1 Thessalonians 4:13-18
Tue, July 30	**Encourage One Another**	Hebrews 10:19-25
Wed, July 31	**A Joyous Celebration**	2 Chronicles 30:21-27
Thu, Aug. 1	**Two Are Better Than One**	Ecclesiastes 4:7-12
Fri, Aug. 2	**Bear One Another's Burdens**	Galatians 6:1-10
Sat, Aug. 3	**My Help Comes from the Lord**	Psalm 121
Sun, Aug. 4	**Encouraged in Faith**	1 Thessalonians 2:13–3:5
Mon, Aug. 5	**The Love of Christ Compels Us**	2 Corinthians 5:16-21
Tue, Aug. 6	**Love the Lord Your God**	Deuteronomy 6:4-13
Wed, Aug. 7	**Fulfill the Royal Law of Love**	James 2:8-13
Thu, Aug. 8	**Love One Another**	John 13:31-35
Fri, Aug. 9	**Renewed in Love**	Zephaniah 3:14-20
Sat, Aug. 10	**An Everlasting Love**	Jeremiah 31:1-9
Sun, Aug. 11	**God's Beloved Children**	1 John 3:1-10

Chart Feature

How are you living?

Do (Virtue): Live self-controlled, righteous, godly lives	Do Not (Vice): Embrace ungodliness and worldly desires
Galatians 5:22-25	Galatians 5:19-21, 26
James 3:13, 17-18	2 Timothy 3:2-5
2 Peter 1:5-7	James 3:14-16
Titus 2:11-13	Titus 2:11-13
Titus 3:1-2	Titus 3:3, 9-11

Sheet 2—Summer 2024, *Adult Resources*, Standard Lesson Quarterly® Curriculum

Lesson 12

10,000 Hours?

Teacher Tips by Ronald L. Nickelson

When I look back on all the teachers I've had from high school through all the classroom situations that followed, I can name the truly excellent teachers instantly. Unfortunately, I can also name the truly unskilled ones almost as fast. There are fewer than five teachers in each category. All the rest fall in the middle area of *average* or *mediocre.*

Perception for Improvement

Your own experiences might naturally make you wonder how your students perceive you as a teacher. That perception could be valuable feedback for improvement—and don't we all have room for improvement? But were we to ask our students for such feedback, they may reply with more kindness than our teaching skills deserve! Such graciousness is appreciated, of course, but it doesn't do much to help us improve as teachers. We need something else.

Precepts for Improvement

Our motivation for constant improvement as teachers is the importance of our task. Think about it: *What's more important than leading others to eternal life in Jesus?* Nothing! This fact lies behind the great teaching-imperative texts of Proverbs 9:9; 22:6; Matthew 28:19-20; Romans 12:7; Colossians 3:16; 1 Timothy 1:3-7; 4:11-13; 6:2b-5; 2 Timothy 2:2, 24; Titus 1:10-11; 2:1-15; James 3:1; etc.

Precedents for Improvement

Improvement as a teacher of God's Word will come in the two areas of *content* (*what* is taught) and *form* (*how* content is taught). To be good at the form your teaching method takes but lousy in the area of content is to end up being condemned as a false teacher (see Romans 10:2; 1 Timothy 1:7; Titus 1:11; 2 Peter 2:1; etc.).

On the other hand, to be good at having the appropriate and correct knowledge of the Bible but mediocre (or worse) in your teaching technique is to have students say to one another (out of your earshot, of course), "He knows his stuff, but he just can't teach it!" (I can't count how many times I've heard that one; I've even said it myself!) Biblical examples of those who excelled at both form and content of Bible teaching include Ezra (Ezra 7:6, 10, 25; Nehemiah 8), Paul (Acts 17:22-33; 19:1-9), Apollos (18:24-28), and, of course, Jesus (Matthew 13:10-11, 34; Luke 2:46-47; 19:47-48; etc.).

Practice as Improvement?

So . . . how do we improve both the form and content of lessons as Bible teachers? In 2008, Malcolm Gladwell published a book titled *Outliers: The Story of Success* in which he introduced the concept of the "10,000-hour rule." This axiom proposes that expertise in any skill is attained after practicing that skill for 10,000 hours. So if we need to spend 10,000 hours studying the content of the Bible and another 10,000 hours practicing our teaching methods, that means . . . well . . . you can do the math!

Proposal for Improvement

One fallacy of the 10,000-hour rule is that it focuses only on the *quantity* of hours practiced. The *quality* of our Bible study and teaching practice is equally vital, if not more so. And said quality can be improved when you recruit a coach or mentor. It's been said that a good coach can get more out of you than you can get out of yourself.

I have been privileged twice to have good coaches to help improve my teaching skills. The first time was when I was enrolled in seminary. The second time was when I attended the Air Force's "Academic Instructor School." Both venues involved practice-teaching that was videotaped and critiqued. My teaching skills improved noticeably. Get a teaching-coach today!

Glorious Riches

Devotional Reading: Galatians 3:19-29
Background Scripture: Colossians 1:19–2:5

Colossians 1:24–2:3

24 Who now rejoice in my sufferings for you, and fill up that which is behind of the afflictions of Christ in my flesh for his body's sake, which is the church:

25 Whereof I am made a minister, according to the dispensation of God which is given to me for you, to fulfil the word of God;

26 Even the mystery which hath been hid from ages and from generations, but now is made manifest to his saints:

27 To whom God would make known what is the riches of the glory of this mystery among the Gentiles; which is Christ in you, the hope of glory:

28 Whom we preach, warning every man, and teaching every man in all wisdom; that we may present every man perfect in Christ Jesus:

29 Whereunto I also labour, striving according to his working, which worketh in me mightily.

1 For I would that ye knew what great conflict I have for you, and for them at Laodicea, and for as many as have not seen my face in the flesh;

2 That their hearts might be comforted, being knit together in love, and unto all riches of the full assurance of understanding, to the acknowledgement of the mystery of God, and of the Father, and of Christ;

3 In whom are hid all the treasures of wisdom and knowledge.

Key Text

That their hearts might be comforted, being knit together in love, and unto all riches of the full assurance of understanding, to the acknowledgement of the mystery of God, and of the Father, and of Christ; In whom are hid all the treasures of wisdom and knowledge. **—Colossians 2:2-3**

Hope in the Lord

Unit I: Experiencing Hope

Lessons 1–5

Lesson Aims

After participating in this lesson, each learner will be able to:

1. Identify the "mystery."
2. Explain why Paul discusses the "mystery."
3. State a way to pass along spiritual comfort that he or she once received during a time of distress.

Lesson Outline

Introduction
- A. Moving to a New House
- B. Lesson Context

I. Paul's Status (Colossians 1:24)
- A. In Suffering (v. 24a)
- B. For the Church (v. 24b)

II. Paul's Intent (Colossians 1:25-29)
- A. By Design of God (v. 25)
- B. For Maturity of Believers (v. 26)
  (Re)solving Mysteries
- C. In Hope of Glory (v. 27)
- D. With Goal-Directed Wisdom (v. 28)
  Adulting—It's for Everyone
- E. Through Divine Power (v. 29)

III. Paul's Labor (Colossians 2:1-3)
- A. Everywhere (v. 1)
- B. Everyone (v. 2)
- C. Everything (v. 3)

Conclusion
- A. Then and Now
- B. Prayer
- C. Thought to Remember

Introduction

A. Moving to a New House

It's not fun to move. Preparing boxes and furniture for movers is a lot of work! But moving old things or dragging old pictures out of the basement can bring pleasant memories back to life, providing comfort during these times of transition. According to professional movers, it's a good idea to use this opportunity to assess everything you own.

The people of the church at Colosse hadn't made a physical move, but a spiritual one. Those of Gentile background had moved from their polytheistic (meaning "many gods") outlook to acknowledge the one, true God. Those of Jewish background had been challenged to move on from the Law of Moses that had defined their existence. Both groups were moving into a new "house"—the same house! That house was and is known as the church.

Predictably, some folks brought old, obsolete "stuff" with them that didn't belong in the church. At best, it was just useless clutter; at worst, it could lead a person to make another move—a move out of the church. If anyone had good reason to leave the church, it was the apostle Paul (see Philippians 3:4-6). Today's lesson lets us glimpse his level of commitment.

B. Lesson Context

Colossians and Philemon are two of the four letters we call the Prison Epistles, the other two being Ephesians and Philippians. Paul wrote them from prison in Rome in the early AD 60s. There is no indication that Paul planted the church in Colosse (Colossians 2:1). Instead, a certain Epaphras probably did so after Paul had visited nearby towns (1:3-8; 4:12). According to most scholars, the church in Colosse was likely planted as a result of Paul's third missionary journey (Acts 18:23–21:16). Paul refers to the nearby towns of Hierapolis and Laodicea in Colossians 2:1; 4:13-16.

The congregations of Paul's day faced the dual threat of their members returning either to pagan deities or to superseded Jewish practices

(Romans 7:6; etc.). A more insidious heresy was *syncretism*—a blending of old beliefs and practices with new ones. Teachers of this system would say something like, "Having Christ is important, but to be saved, you also need . . . ." That sentence might be completed by one or more Jewish practices of the Law of Moses. Or it might be finished with speculative elements of Greek philosophy. Both seemed to have been problems at Colosse per Colossians 2:8-15. But before he confronted those problems, Paul first needed to ensure that his readers understood his own status, intent, and work.

I. Paul's Status

(Colossians 1:24)

A. In Suffering (v. 24a)

24a. Who now rejoice in my sufferings for you.

By use of the word *who*, Paul refers to himself, as the closing phrase of the previous verse indicates. From the outset, Paul's ministry was to be characterized by *sufferings* (Acts 9:16). That reality is a recurring theme in his letters (2 Corinthians 1:5-7; 6:3-10; 11:23-27; Ephesians 3:13; Philippians 3:10; 2 Timothy 1:12; 3:11; etc.). But Paul was not complaining about random aches and pains as we might do. Rather, his sufferings had a purpose: they were *for you*, as the next thought indicates.

B. For the Church (v. 24b)

24b. And fill up that which is behind of the afflictions of Christ in my flesh for his body's sake, which is the church.

As we read this half-verse, we may come away with more questions than answers! What does *fill up* mean in this context? How can Paul be so bold as to connect his own sufferings to *the afflictions of Christ*? How can Paul's sufferings be a benefit to the believers in Colosse (that is, *for his body's sake*)? Recognizing that the word *behind* refers to something lacking (as it does in the English translation of the same Greek word in 1 Corinthians 16:17; 2 Corinthians 11:9), what is the "lack" in the afflictions of Christ that Paul's sufferings fill up?

Dealing with the last question first, Paul is crystal clear elsewhere in this letter that there is nothing lacking about Christ's afflictions regarding what they were intended to accomplish (Colossians 2:9-15; compare Romans 6:9-10; Hebrews 7:27; 9:12, 28). One proposal is that the phrase *in my flesh* is the key to understanding here: that which is lacking completeness is not Christ's sufferings in and of themselves, but rather it is Christ's sufferings in Paul that are not yet complete. The church is the body of Christ, and Paul suffered for that body as he traveled around the Mediterranean world to preach the truth of the gospel. As more sufferings came his way, they filled up what the Lord had predicted in Acts 9:16.

What Do You Think?

What do Paul's words in 2 Corinthians 12:1-10 suggest about enduring suffering?

Digging Deeper

What factors affect how you counsel someone who is experiencing ongoing suffering? Keep Job 42:1-8 in mind.

II. Paul's Intent

(Colossians 1:25-29)

A. By Design of God (v. 25)

25a. Whereof I am made a minister.

This is now the second time Paul has identified himself as a *minister* in this letter (the first time is in Colossians 1:23). This self-identification is quite similar to his statements in Ephesians 3:2, 7-8. The English word translated "minister" comes from the Greek word *diakonos,* from which we also derive the word *deacon.* Paul is not using this word to refer to an office of the church (as he does in 1 Timothy 3:8, 12). Rather, he is depicting himself as a "servant," which is how the word is translated in Matthew 23:11; Mark 9:35; John 12:26; and elsewhere.

How to Say It

Colosse	Ko-*lahss*-ee.
Epaphras	*Ep*-uh-frass.
Laodicea	Lay-*odd*-uh-**see**-uh.
polytheistic	*pohl*-ih-thee-iz-tik.

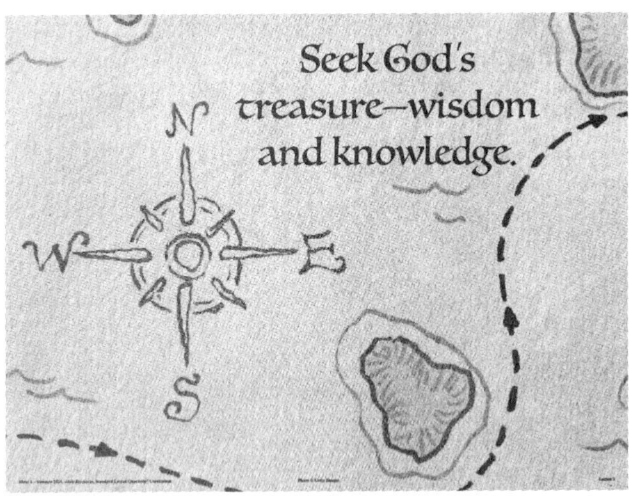

Visual for Lesson 1. *While discussing Colossians 2:3, ask how learners seek Jesus and His treasures of wisdom and knowledge.*

25b. According to the dispensation of God which is given to me.

The dispensation of God of which Paul speaks is recorded in Acts 9:15; 22:14-15; and 26:16-18. We could call those passages Paul's "mandate" or "marching orders."

What Do You Think?

In what ways was Paul's commission by God similar to and different from your own?

Digging Deeper

Compare and contrast your commission with the accounts found in Matthew 28:19-20; Acts 9:15; 22:14-15; and 26:16-18.

25c. For you, to fulfil the word of God.

The phrase *for you* establishes the believers at Colosse to be the beneficiaries of Paul's tasks; the phrase *to fulfil the word of God* establishes the benchmark by which to measure the accomplishment of those tasks. Both facts are stated in very general terms here. This serves as an introduction to specifics, which we will see below.

B. For Maturity of Believers (v. 26)

26. Even the mystery which hath been hid from ages and from generations, but now is made manifest to his saints.

Paul uses the word *mystery* numerous times in his letters in different ways. The passages that are closest to the usage of that word in the verse before us are Romans 16:25-26; 1 Corinthians 2:7; and Ephesians 3:3-9. In those, as here, the word refers to the content of Paul's preaching that is foundational: the good news of Jesus, once hidden but now revealed. In doing so, Paul was drawing on Jewish ideas about the mystery of God's plans, which culminate in Christ. It's possible that Paul's audience, especially the Gentiles, heard a contrast between God's mystery with the "mystery religions" of the Greco-Roman world.

The gospel message of Jesus Christ indeed was a mystery until it began to be disclosed by Jesus (compare 1 Timothy 3:16). But even though He brought, modeled, and explained the gospel message personally, people often did not comprehend (examples: Matthew 16:5-12; Mark 7:17-18; John 14:9), even right up to the day of His ascension (Acts 1:6).

Broadly speaking, the gospel message deals with two issues: (1) the *person* of Christ and (2) the *work* of Christ. The four Gospels (that is, Matthew, Mark, Luke, and John) focus almost wholly on the "person" issue; they are concerned primarily with evidence and belief that Jesus was (and is) the divine Son of God (John 20:30-31; etc.). The meaning and significance of Jesus' "work"—referring primarily to why His death, burial, resurrection, and ascension were (and are) essential—are largely unaddressed in the Gospels. A rare exception is Mark 10:45: "the Son of man came . . . to give his life a ransom for many." Even there, however, there's no explanation of who the ransom is to be paid to and how the ransom actually works.

The meaning and significance of Jesus' work received full treatment after His ascension as the apostles received further revelation and the rest of the New Testament was written (examples: Acts 10; Galatians 1:11-12). In that sense, the mystery *now is made manifest to his saints*—the word *saints* referring to all Christians.

(Re)solving Mysteries

When my husband and I started having children, we didn't agree on much. But there was one thing we both felt very strongly about: keeping the gender of our unborn children a mystery until the day of the birth.

The nine months of anticipation were exciting and well worth the wait! Even while friends and family expressed frustration and exasperation at being kept in the dark about our baby's gender, we did not relent. And when each of our babies was born, the revelation at the end was every bit as rewarding as we could have imagined.

God doesn't reveal His mysteries to us on our timetable but on His (Daniel 12:8-9; Acts 1:7; 1 Peter 1:10-12; etc.). But we want to know! And our unholy desire can lead to all kinds of problems. These range from professional embarrassment (remember the booklet *88 Reasons the Rapture Will Be in 1988*?) to divine condemnation (see 1 Corinthians 6:9).

Despite desires and attempts to unravel earthly or heavenly mysteries, the main question is this: *What are you doing with the mysteries God has* already *revealed?* —P. M.

C. In Hope of Glory (v. 27)

27. To whom God would make known what is the riches of the glory of this mystery among the Gentiles; which is Christ in you, the hope of glory.

In Greek, this verse is a continuation of the preceding verse rather than the beginning of a new sentence. The phrase *among the Gentiles* acknowledges the inclusiveness of the gospel message. Not all Gentiles accepted the message, of course, even though the truth of *this mystery* was available to them. Paul wants his readers to make no mistake regarding the content of the mystery: it's *Christ.* Not only Christ in and of himself, but Christ *in you.* Not only is Christ in us (2 Corinthians 13:5; Galatians 2:20; 4:19; Ephesians 3:17), but we are also in Him (John 17:21; Romans 8:1; 16:7; 1 Corinthians 1:30; etc.).

Thus what has been made known in terms of *the riches of the glory of* the mystery is explained in terms of the presence of Christ being *the hope of glory.* This is the future orientation that fulfills God's promise to Abraham (Genesis 15:5-6). Christ is the believer's hope for participation in the glory of Heaven.

We see the importance to Paul of the concept of "glory" when we read Romans 2:7, 10; 3:21; 8:17-18, 23, 30. The concepts of "hope" and "glory" are also connected in Romans 5:2 and Titus 2:13. Some students propose that the phrase "the riches of the glory" was standard in the worship settings of the first-century church, given similar expressions in Ephesians 1:18 and Philippians 4:19. In this context, the word *riches* refers to spiritual blessings (see Romans 2:4; 9:23; 11:33; Ephesians 1:7, 18; 2:7; 3:8, 16; Philippians 4:19).

D. With Goal-Directed Wisdom (v. 28)

28. Whom we preach, warning every man, and teaching every man in all wisdom; that we may present every man perfect in Christ Jesus.

The opening word of this verse tightly connects its content to "Christ" per His mention in the previous verse. Following that word *whom* comes a statement of two methods of conveying the message of the Christ: *preach[ing]* and *teaching.* Which of those two was more important to Paul? If word-count is any indication, it was *teaching*—a word he uses about twice as often as *preaching* or *proclaiming.*

The content of the message—whether preached or taught—has a singular goal of presenting everyone as *perfect in Christ Jesus.* But how is it possible to be perfect, even though Jesus commanded it in Matthew 5:48 (compare 19:21; Ephesians 5:27)? The word in the original language translated "perfect" occurs 20 times in the New Testament. Depending on the context, it can mean "perfect," "mature," or "something that has reached its goal." As we sift through the options, it's important to remember that "explaining" which is correct runs the danger of "explaining away" alternatives that we don't like. In the case at hand, it's best to leave the word *perfect* just like that. Indeed, it's not possible to attain perfection in this life (Romans 3:23). *But that doesn't mean we lower the standard!* We keep aiming for perfection, and we ask forgiveness when we fall short.

Aiming for the target of perfection is aided by the application of *wisdom.* Paul explains the connection between wisdom, perfection, and mystery in 1 Corinthians 2:6-7. As one becomes devoted to pursuing godly wisdom, he or she is able to distinguish between true wisdom (Colossians 2:2-3) and its counterfeits (2:23).

> **What Do You Think?**
> What is the difference between preaching and teaching? What are the overlaps between them?
> **Digging Deeper**
> What is preaching able to accomplish that teaching cannot, and vice versa? Consider Acts 4:2 as you answer.

Adulting—It's for Everyone

Out of all my children, it seems my youngest is having the most trouble growing up. At 20 years old, he still won't sit still long enough for me to teach him about basic life skills such as budgets, vehicle maintenance, credit cards, etc.

Because he refuses to be taught, he constantly makes bad choices and then comes to his father and me to bail him out. And we have the unfortunate job of telling him *no*. While that may seem harsh and unhelpful, his father and I both know what would happen if we caved: he would not grow out of this stage of unwise decisions.

We must not shy away from "speaking the truth in love" (Ephesians 4:15). All truth and no love makes us hard, legalistic people. All love and no truth results in tolerance of sinful behavior. What can you do today to bring those into balance?

—P. M.

E. Through Divine Power (v. 29)

29. Whereunto I also labour, striving according to his working, which worketh in me mightily.

The church has God's power or energy working within it. Paul's successful evangelist endeavors are evidence of that fact (Ephesians 3:7, 20; Philippians 4:13). This power is not exclusive to the apostle Paul; it was working through others as well (Galatians 2:8; Philippians 2:13). The purpose of the church is for her members to be not only reconciled (justified) but also to be complete in holiness (sanctified). God's working is directed toward both (compare 1 Corinthians 6:11).

III. Paul's Labor

(Colossians 2:1-3)

A. Everywhere (v. 1)

1. For I would that ye knew what great conflict I have for you, and for them at Laodicea, and for as many as have not seen my face in the flesh.

Paul desires that his readers know of his ministry of prayer on their behalf (see Colossians 1:9-12). The word translated *conflict* is a form of the same word translated "striving" in 1:29 (speaking of Paul's own labor) and "fervently" in 4:12 (speaking of Epaphras's laboring for them in prayer). Paul greets someone by name in Colossians 4:17, and he knows other Christians in Colosse (compare Philemon 1-2 with Colossians 4:10-17). Even so, the phrase *for as many as have not seen my face in the flesh* is widely accepted to mean that Paul had not been to Colosse (see Lesson Context).

Laodicea, approximately 10 miles from Colosse, is another city in the Lycus River valley. Although many within this letter's audience are strangers to Paul, they are still objects of Paul's concern that arises from the unity believers have in Christ (1 Corinthians 1:2; Ephesians 4:4; Colossians 4:16).

B. Everyone (v. 2)

2a. That their hearts might be comforted.

Scripture often uses the word *heart* to designate the person, especially one's center of moral and ethical deliberation, will, and attitudes (Genesis 6:5; Exodus 4:21; Matthew 9:4; 12:34; etc.). The verb translated *comforted* communicates more than offering solace; one is encouraged and strengthened in the kind of comfort Paul means (see also Ephesians 6:22; Colossians 4:8).

2b. Being knit together in love.

Knit together suggests a unity of purpose and thought. The same term appears in Ephesians 4:15-16 and Colossians 2:19 to speak of a unity derived from the church's attachment to its head, Christ. The love that unites believers has its source in their devotion to Christ, who empowers us to love one another (Ephesians 3:19; 4:1-4; 1 John 4:11). Only a love built on the knowledge of what Christ has done and a desire to serve others can unite the church (John 13:34-35).

2c. And unto all riches of the full assurance of understanding, to the acknowledgement of the mystery of God, and of the Father, and of Christ.

Paul desires his readers to have the confidence and power that comes from an ability to distinguish between true and false teaching (see Acts 9:22). The focus of this *understanding* is to be *the acknowledgement of the mystery of God*. Regarding Paul's use of the word *mystery,* see above on Colossians 1:26-27 (compare 4:3).

What Do You Think?

What is your goal when contending for other believers?

Digging Deeper

How well does your goal align with Paul's?

C. Everything (v. 3)

3. In whom are hid all the treasures of wisdom and knowledge.

This verse speaks against any false teachers who claim to have hidden truth to which only the spiritual elite have access. In contrast, Christ is the one *in whom are hid all the treasures of wisdom and knowledge* (Isaiah 11:2). Wisdom and knowledge are not the same, although they are related. Knowledge is the mental grasp of truth; wisdom is the ability to use knowledge appropriately. Believers can access the wisdom and knowledge revealed in Christ, but that remains hidden from those who reject Him (Matthew 13:13-15, quoting Isaiah 6:9-10).

What Do You Think?

What role does the Bible's wisdom literature play in your seeking wisdom?

Digging Deeper

How can Old Testament texts aid in growing in maturity in Christ?

Conclusion

A. Then and Now

God's care for the first-century church came primarily through human hands. The apostle Paul is, of course, the primary example of this. But what Paul set in motion needed the help of others to carry it out on a long-term basis, to finish what he had started (Titus 1:5; etc.). We see some of those potential helpers in the names listed in passages such as Colossians 4:16 and in the unnamed persons of 1:2. What Paul wrote to them was a call to alertness and action. They needed to remain alert to wrong views of Christ, wisdom, power, glory, mystery, etc. Only with such alertness could they be prepared to act to protect the church.

So how well did the church at Colosse do in this regard? We don't really know, but the church in nearby Laodicea received criticism decades later for being lukewarm in Revelation 3:14-22. Lukewarmness manifests itself in the form of complacency.

Do you see signs of complacency in your church? How do we know when complacency is setting in—what are its signs? To be able to answer such questions is an issue of alertness, which must precede action. And who do you expect to take the corrective or preventative action? Perhaps you?

B. Prayer

Heavenly Father, remind us constantly of Your presence and available power! May we never exchange Your Son and His wisdom for counterfeits. Let us become experts in Christ to be able to stay alert to those pretenders! We pray in the name of Your Son, Jesus. Amen.

C. Thought to Remember

Access the mystery of Christ!

Visuals FOR THESE LESSONS

The visual pictured in each lesson (example: page 348) is a small reproduction of a large, full-color poster included in the *Adult Resources* packet for the Summer Quarter. Order No. 9780784740637 from your supplier.

Involvement Learning

Enhance your lesson with KJV Bible Student *(from your curriculum supplier) and the reproducible activity page (at www.standardlesson.com or in the back of the* KJV Standard Lesson Commentary Deluxe Edition*).*

Into the Lesson

Read or display the following quote from Fred Rogers: "When I was a boy, and I would see scary things in the news, my mother would say to me, 'Look for the helpers. You will always find people who are helping.'" Have the class brainstorm the answers to this question: "Where are the helpers in our world today?"

Tell the class, "Mr. Rogers could move through a scary world when he heeded his mother's advice to look for helpers. Today's text shows us grand thoughts about hope from the apostle Paul."

Into the Word

Invite a volunteer to read today's text. Distribute handouts (you create) of the sentences below *without* the verse citations. Ask learners to mark them as True or False. Include space for additional written responses between sentences.

1–Paul knows he's supposed to suffer, and it has ruined his life. (1:24)

2–Paul is repeating here what most people had understood for many centuries. (1:26)

3–Believing in Christ makes little difference. (1:27)

4–Maturity comes in many ways; Jesus can help. (1:28)

5–What Christ did is easily and universally understood. (1:25-26)

6–Paul's suffering is very personal and private; he doesn't expect much result for the church. (2:1)

Share that each sentence is false. In pairs, challenge learners to write verse references that show the falsehood of each statement and write out true sentences based on the verse(s) referenced. After calling time, bring the class back together. Let pairs share their corrected sentences.

Alternative. Distribute copies of the "Paul's Hope" exercise from the activity page, which you can download. Allow learners to work individually for one minute before pairing up to complete the exercise.

In the same pairs from either alternative, ask learners to use Bible concordances to look up information about *mystery* in the New Testament. Have them answer how *mystery* is applied to Jesus, what other concepts are referred to as *mysteries,* and how these concepts of *mystery* are similar to or different from *mystery* as it might be used in pop culture. When pairs are finished, ask them to share what they found most eye-opening or helpful from their research.

Into Life

Write the following sentence on the board: *Hope came from suffering.* Ask class members to break into small groups to share experiences in their lives that illustrate the concept. Have them consider whether the statement could be true without Christ's work in that situation. What difference did their faith in Him make as they experienced pain?

After five minutes, discuss with the whole class: "How do we find hope in suffering without elevating suffering as good in itself?" As class members share ideas, write a few words on the board to summarize a principle or strategy for spiritual comfort. Ask the whole group, "What is one way we can pass along the type of spiritual comfort we received in our times of distress?" Group learners in pairs. Challenge pairs to come up with a plan to share hope with others during the week. Close with the pairs praying for each other.

Alternative. Distribute copies of the "My Hope" exercise from the activity page. Have learners complete it individually in a minute or less before discussing conclusions with a partner. *Option.* Have learners complete the page at home during the week.

Conclude with prayer that the class will experience joy as they grow in Christ this week.

Bold Ministers

Devotional Reading: Deuteronomy 31:1-8
Background Scripture: 2 Corinthians 3:5-18

2 Corinthians 3:5-18

5 Not that we are sufficient of ourselves to think any thing as of ourselves; but our sufficiency is of God;

6 Who also hath made us able ministers of the new testament; not of the letter, but of the spirit: for the letter killeth, but the spirit giveth life.

7 But if the ministration of death, written and engraven in stones, was glorious, so that the children of Israel could not stedfastly behold the face of Moses for the glory of his countenance; which glory was to be done away:

8 How shall not the ministration of the spirit be rather glorious?

9 For if the ministration of condemnation be glory, much more doth the ministration of righteousness exceed in glory.

10 For even that which was made glorious had no glory in this respect, by reason of the glory that excelleth.

11 For if that which is done away was glorious, much more that which remaineth is glorious.

12 Seeing then that we have such hope, we use great plainness of speech:

13 And not as Moses, which put a vail over his face, that the children of Israel could not stedfastly look to the end of that which is abolished:

14 But their minds were blinded: for until this day remaineth the same vail untaken away in the reading of the old testament; which vail is done away in Christ.

15 But even unto this day, when Moses is read, the vail is upon their heart.

16 Nevertheless when it shall turn to the Lord, the vail shall be taken away.

17 Now the Lord is that Spirit: and where the Spirit of the Lord is, there is liberty.

18 But we all, with open face beholding as in a glass the glory of the Lord, are changed into the same image from glory to glory, even as by the Spirit of the Lord.

Key Text

We all, with open face beholding as in a glass the glory of the Lord, are changed into the same image from glory to glory, even as by the Spirit of the Lord. —**2 Corinthians 3:18**

Hope in

the Lord

Unit I: Experiencing Hope

Lessons 1–5

Lesson Aims

After participating in this lesson, each learner will be able to:

1. Identify the nature of the hope to which Paul refers.

2. Explain the transformational change that is to occur as one matures in faith.

3. Make a plan to push toward that transformational change personally.

Lesson Outline

Introduction

A. A Pile of "Glory Stuff"?

B. Lesson Context

I. Paul's Expertise (2 Corinthians 3:5-6)

A. Source: God (v. 5)

B. Focus: New Covenant (v. 6)

No "False Choice" Here!

II. Paul's Interpretation (2 Corinthians 3:7-11)

A. First If-Then Argument (vv. 7-8)

Faded Glory?

B. Second If-Then Argument (vv. 9-10)

C. Third If-Then Argument (v. 11)

III. Paul's Application (2 Corinthians 3:12-18)

A. With Face Covering (vv. 12-15)

B. Without Face Covering (vv. 16-18)

Conclusion

A. The Few

B. Prayer

C. Thought to Remember

Introduction

A. A Pile of "Glory Stuff"?

An adult Christian was overheard commenting on a certain confusion he experienced when watching various televangelists as a child. He would occasionally hear a preacher say, "Give glory to God!" The child wondered about the meaning of this imperative. All he could think of was a pile of this "glory stuff" somewhere, and he was supposed to go there, get a double handful of it, and offer it to God. But didn't God have enough glory already? How was it possible to give Him more than what He already had? And what was this "glory stuff," anyway?

Such childhood thinking eventually was replaced with adult thinking, of course (compare 1 Corinthians 13:11). But a certain element of the question remained to be addressed: How does the concept of "glory" come into play as we live before God in a fallen world? The apostle Paul has the answer.

B. Lesson Context

By AD 57, the year that Paul wrote the letter we call 2 Corinthians, he had developed a multiyear relationship with the church he had planted in Corinth. He had established that congregation on his second missionary journey of AD 52–54 (Acts 18:1-11). Bible experts recognize this letter as the most difficult to understand among all 13 of Paul's epistles. This letter and others to the church in Corinth (see 1 Corinthians 5:9; 2 Corinthians 2:3-4; 7:8, 12) reveal that Paul had stayed in touch. Such was the nature of his church-planting ministry.

The letters of 1 and 2 Corinthians show a congregation troubled on several fronts. Challenges to Paul's apostolic authority aggravated those troubles, and his letters to that church feature responses to personal criticisms leveled at him (1 Corinthians 9:1-2; 2 Corinthians 10:10; 11:5; 12:11-12; etc.). Therefore, Paul used much ink in 2 Corinthians to defend the legitimacy of his apostolic calling. Indeed, the more than 500 words of 2 Corinthians 2:12–3:18 set the stage for longer defenses of his apostolic ministry later in the epistle. Today's lesson covers a majority of those 24 verses.

I. Paul's Expertise

(2 Corinthians 3:5-6)

A. Source: God (v. 5)

5. Not that we are sufficient of ourselves to think any thing as of ourselves; but our sufficiency is of God.

As Paul further explores the nature of his apostolic ministry, he uses a word that is translated *sufficient* and *sufficiency* several times in this letter (here and in 2 Corinthians 2:6, 16; compare also 1 Corinthians 15:9; Colossians 1:12; and 2 Timothy 2:2). In so doing, he makes clear that although he has confidence in the results of his ministry (2 Corinthians 1:15; 2:3; 3:4), it is God who must have the credit, not Paul and his fellow apostles. Any sufficiency is from *God*. This "credit where credit is due" acknowledgment is also reflected in 2 Corinthians 2:17 (compare 1 Corinthians 15:10).

What Do You Think?

If God makes us sufficient for the work He desires of us, what responsibilities are we left with as a result?

Digging Deeper

What verses support your answer?

B. Focus: New Covenant (v. 6)

6. Who also hath made us able ministers of the new testament; not of the letter, but of the spirit: for the letter killeth, but the spirit giveth life.

The English words *minister* and *ministers* occur four times (here and in Colossians 1:7; 4:7; and 1 Timothy 4:6) as a noun in describing the leadership function of those commonly designated today as "pastors." These ministers were tasked primarily with preaching the Word, while other leaders—commonly called "shepherds"—attended primarily to non-preaching tasks of caring for the church (example: James 5:14).

The term *new testament* refers to the new covenant (note how it is translated that way in Hebrews 8:6, 8; 10:16; 12:24). Several Old Testament passages refer to God's plan for such a covenant. Particularly clear on this point is Jeremiah 31:31-34. The covenant foreseen by Jeremiah was brought into being by Jesus himself (see Luke 22:20; Hebrews 8). A primary feature of the old covenant—the Law of Moses—was that it brought death by condemning people as lawbreakers (Romans 2:27; 7:5; 1 Corinthians 15:56). This was through no fault of the law; the benefit of following *the letter* of the law was learning God's ways, not earning salvation. The new covenant, by contrast, *giveth life*. Therefore, life under the new covenant is connected with *the spirit*, a concept introduced by Jesus (see John 6:63) and stressed by Paul (see Romans 2:29; 7:6).

No "False Choice" Here!

On March 23, 1775, legislator and orator Patrick Henry delivered one of the most famous speeches in American history. The American colonies were on the verge of revolution, and colonial legislators were trying to decide how to respond to a series of British policies deemed oppressive, intolerable, and coercive. While there is some doubt about the exact wording of his speech, most agree on its fiery ending: "I know not what course others may take, but as for me, give me liberty or give me death!"

While Henry was certainly talking about fighting the British in a revolution, his statement bears an ironic resemblance to today's lesson text. There are only two options when it comes to one's standing before God: death from the letter of the law or life in the Spirit of God through Jesus.

In the study of logic, we are careful to note what is called "the fallacy of the false choice." This is where a limited set of alternatives are offered from which to choose, when in fact, other, unstated choices are available. Neither Patrick Henry nor the apostle Paul was guilty of committing this fallacy. Henry had decided that there were only two ways his life could proceed; it was either death or liberty, nothing in between. Paul's view was the same, from a spiritual rather than an earthly perspective. Make no mistake: there is no alternative, no third or fourth choice available. How do you keep yourself from slipping into a "half and half" fiction in this regard?

—C. S.

II. Paul's Interpretation

(2 Corinthians 3:7-11)

A. First If-Then Argument (vv. 7-8)

7-8. But if the ministration of death, written and engraven in stones, was glorious, so that the children of Israel could not stedfastly behold the face of Moses for the glory of his countenance; which glory was to be done away. How shall not the ministration of the spirit be rather glorious?

Paul now begins a series of conditional if-then statements, a style of argument that also goes by the designation *a fortiori*, meaning "from [the] stronger." This type of logic is well documented in the ancient literature of Jews and Greeks. The argument is formed when the truth of a greater assertion is based on a lesser reality that is commonly agreed on. In other words, this kind of argument takes the form of "if such-and-such is true, then so-and-so must be true as well." Often the word *then* does not appear in this kind of argument, but its intent is understood to be present nonetheless. In the case at hand, the force of the word *then* occurs just before the word *how*.

Paul often walks a tightrope when he talks about the old law (the old covenant of the Law of Moses). He knows that the new covenant—*the ministration of the spirit*—is far superior to the old one—*the ministration of death* (see Romans 7:10). But that doesn't mean that the old covenant was defective or had failed in some way (9:6). Indeed, the old covenant of law was flawless in what it was intended to accomplish: establishing God's expectations in no uncertain terms (7:7; Galatians 3:24). This left Israel with no excuse regarding knowledge of sin. It's reasonable that in creating humans in His own image (Genesis 1:26), God would expect us to be holy because He is holy (Leviticus 11:44-45; quoted in 1 Peter 1:16). That expectation resulted in God's giving His requirements for holiness not just to *the children of Israel* but to Gentiles as well (Romans 1:18-20; 2:14-15).

But what constitutes a holy life? That's the question that the old law answered in terms of a code of behavior. That body of law was so important that it was *engraven in stones* (Exodus 32:16; 34:1-5, 28; contrast Romans 4:15; 5:13). Contrast that with our modern expression "it's not written in stone" when we want to stress that a document is just a first draft or that it is otherwise changeable. If anyone *could* keep the law perfectly, that person would have led a perfectly holy life. A person is not made holy by the corruptible things or the tradition of the elders. One is made holy by the precious blood of Christ (1 Peter 1:17-22).

Exodus 34:29-35 is the touchstone for Paul's illustration regarding *the face of Moses for the glory of his countenance*. The point of contrast is that the radiance of Moses' face, like the covenant he had received, was temporary. It faded with time. By contrast, the new covenant doesn't fade (1 Peter 1:3-4). God would not replace something "more" glorious with something "less" glorious!

What Do You Think?

What biblical examples come to mind when you consider the glory of the Spirit's ministry?

Digging Deeper

What examples can you give from your congregation?

Faded Glory?

A brand of denim jeans called "Faded Glory" hit the marketplace in 1972. Various articles of clothing under that brand name can still be purchased today. The success and longevity of this apparel line is curious at first glance since the name *Faded Glory* has a negative connotation. Things that are faded are in a state of deterioration; whatever glory was once present has become hard to discern.

Perhaps the attraction lies in being a contrarian —one who relishes doing something different than the majority of people would do. Today, we still see for sale new denim jeans of various brands that are sold "distressed," with intentional rips and holes.

I have no favorites when it comes to brands of denim jeans since I don't own any and never wear them. I have a contrarian mindset on many things, but not the Bible. I don't want to be the one in James 1:11 who fades away. Instead, I embrace the inheritance and crown that will never fade away (1 Peter 1:4; 5:4). This means I must reject any substitute. And to be able to do that, I must be able to recognize the danger (see Romans 1:25; 2 Thessalonians 2:1-12; etc.). Have you trained yourself to do so? —R. L. N.

Visual for Lesson 2. *As you close class time, ask learners how this statement can impact their witness this week.*

B. Second If-Then Argument (vv. 9-10)

9-10. For if the ministration of condemnation be glory, much more doth the ministration of righteousness exceed in glory. For even that which was made glorious had no glory in this respect, by reason of the glory that excelleth.

Paul moves to his second if-then conditional statement. Again, the word *then* isn't explicitly used, but its force is understood to be present nevertheless, just before the word *much*. The point about the *glory* of the old covenant in relation to the glory of the new covenant is essentially the same as in 2 Corinthians 3:7-8, just considered above. What's new here is the introduction of parallel descriptions: the "ministration of death" in 3:7 is the same as the *ministration of condemnation* here in describing the old covenant (Deuteronomy 27:26). And the "ministration of the spirit" in 2 Corinthians 3:8 is the same as the *ministration of righteousness* here in describing the new covenant in Christ. Therefore, the new covenant is superior because those who merit condemnation for sin receive instead imputed righteousness because of Christ (Romans 3:21-22; 2 Corinthians 5:21).

B. Third If-Then Argument (v. 11)

11. For if that which is done away was glorious, much more that which remaineth is glorious.

This is the third and final if-then argument that contrasts the old covenant (*that which is done away*) with the new covenant (*that which remaineth*). As mentioned above, the word *then* does not appear as such.

But its force is understood to occur just after the comma. The law could not make humanity perfect because of the weakness of the fallen nature (Psalm 19:7; Romans 8:3). It was meant to reveal that which is best, salvation by faith in Christ. In Him, sin was condemned in the flesh, and the righteous requirements of the law were accomplished (8:4; Hebrews 7:19; 10:1).

III. Paul's Application
(2 Corinthians 3:12-18)

A. With Face Covering (vv. 12-15)

12. Seeing then that we have such hope, we use great plainness of speech.

Hope is an important theme for Paul. Indeed, he uses the noun and verb forms of that word more than 60 times in his 13 letters! Certainty derives from hope. A person with a sincere hope of finishing a race has a significantly better chance of doing so than someone who enters the race convinced that he won't be able to finish. In Paul's case, his hope reveals itself in his boldness, expressed as *great plainness of speech* (compare Romans 5:4-5; 8:24-25). Imagine how ineffective Paul's message of the gospel would be if his voice conveyed the lukewarm overtones of "maybe," "perhaps," and "possibly"!

13. And not as Moses, which put a vail over his face, that the children of Israel could not stedfastly look to the end of that which is abolished.

Exodus 32–34 continues to be Paul's source of illustration to demonstrate the superiority of the new covenant over the old. Specifically, the reference here is to Exodus 34:33, 35. The illustration and its intended effect on Paul's first-century audience are essentially the same as in 2 Corinthians 3:7-8 above, but with the detail of *a vail* (veil) added. We know it was some face covering, but it is difficult to determine what it was made of, its shape, etc.

14-15. But their minds were blinded: for until this day remaineth the same vail untaken away in the reading of the old testament; which vail is done away in Christ. But even unto this day, when Moses is read, the vail is upon their heart.

The Scriptures often use figurative language to describe a lack of perception. Such language often involves the senses of seeing and hearing. Considering the word *blinded* in the verse at hand, we see the same word used in Romans 11:7 and 2 Corinthians 4:4. Hearts are said to be hardened in Mark 6:52; 8:17. Blindness and hardening are mentioned together in John 12:40. Hearts and ears are said to be "uncircumcised" in Acts 7:51. These are just a few examples—the list goes on and on.

All this speaks to spiritual insensitivity. A person with this self-inflicted disposition may refuse to hear physically; consider Acts 7:57, where people used their hands and loud voices to drown out and not hear Stephen's testimony. They refused to hear it both spiritually and physically. Regarding the two verses at hand, Paul's opponents were doing their best (or worst?) to retain the *vail* that had been *done away in Christ.* How foolish!

B. Without Face Covering (vv. 16-18)

16. Nevertheless when it shall turn to the Lord, the vail shall be taken away.

Paul says the same thing in Romans 11:23, using an agricultural comparison: "They also, if they abide not still in unbelief, shall be graffed in: for God is able to graff them in again." The way this happens is when hearts *turn to the Lord.* It's not enough merely to turn away from sin; that's only half the solution. The full solution is to turn to the Lord in repentance (Luke 1:17; Acts 9:35; 1 Thessalonians 1:9).

> **What Do You Think?**
> What "veils" prevent nonbelievers from coming to Christ today?
>
> **Digging Deeper**
> Do you have a role to play in taking the "veil" away? Why or why not?

17. Now the Lord is that Spirit: and where the Spirit of the Lord is, there is liberty.

The phrase *the Lord is that Spirit* reflects Isaiah 61:1, quoted by Jesus in Luke 4:18-19. Both passages stress the freedom or *liberty* that Christ has brought. In contrast to the Israelites, who most often had a human leader mediating between them and God (compare Hebrews 8), Paul's audience had access to God through the indwelling Spirit. Paul stresses that it is through the Spirit that they have freedom. Through the covenant of the Spirit, they were liberated from the veil. Unlike Moses, they did not have to place a veil over their face. The same face that Paul turned to the Lord was the same face that the people were able to see. Because now the glory never wears off.

When set alongside passages such as John 8:32; Romans 8:2; 2 Corinthians 13:9; and Galatians 5:1, 13, we get the full-orbed picture of the nature of this freedom.

> **What Do You Think?**
> What other verses help you define what it means to have freedom in the Spirit?
>
> **Digging Deeper**
> What popular definitions of freedom might hinder either experiencing or understanding freedom in the Spirit?

18. But we all, with open face beholding as in a glass the glory of the Lord, are changed

into the same image from glory to glory, even as by the Spirit of the Lord.

Paul now moves to contrast specifically those who erroneously choose to remain veiled with those who wisely choose not to (*we all, with open face*). Unlike the glory of the old covenant that was only given to Moses, the benefits of the new are available to everyone in Christ. In this sense, we can see at least a glimpse of *the glory of the Lord.* Our current view of Him is not crystal clear, given that we yet view Him as a reflection in a mirror (*as in a glass*; compare 1 Corinthians 13:12). We do not yet have the full view that we will eventually be blessed to have: "Beloved, now are we the sons of God, and it doth not yet appear what we shall be: but we know that, when he shall appear, we shall be like him; for we shall see him as he is" (1 John 3:2).

Even so, our reflected view is sufficient in this life for conforming us ever more closely to the *image* of the Son of God (Romans 8:29). Could there be any greater tragedy for choosing not to do so? See 2 Corinthians 4:4-6.

> **What Do You Think?**
> Have you experienced any "growth spurts" in your transformation into God's image?
>
> **Digging Deeper**
> What pitfalls might a believer experience if he or she found all growth in the Spirit to happen quickly or dramatically?

Conclusion

A. The Few

The larger context of Exodus 34—the source of Paul's illustrations regarding glory—is the sin of the Israelites in chapter 32. From Exodus 32:9 to 34:9, the Lord characterizes the people as "stiffnecked" four times. The face covering Moses needed is noted only after Moses returned from the mountain a second time, following the incident of the golden calf. Thus that great sin was answered with a sign of great holiness: the radiant glory of Moses' face, which needed to be covered.

But despite the greatness and holiness that that radiance symbolized, another episode of glory, the advent of Christ, was yet to be. Some 15 centuries later, Christ arrived in God's perfect timing. Few, if any, people expected Him in the way He came. And relatively few allowed Him to remove the veil from their hearts so they might see Him clearly.

And so it is yet today. Think of someone who believes that he or she will have no problem getting into Heaven because he or she is basically "a good person." Whether consciously or unconsciously, that attitude comes from a salvation-by-works mentality. Such thinking often presents itself when a person compares himself or herself to another who is relatively "more evil." But that's not how salvation works; that is not the criteria for entrance. Those stuck in this mode of belief have a veil they refuse to remove. They need to encounter the great veil-remover, Jesus Christ (Matthew 27:51; Mark 15:38; Luke 23:45).

How will you seek out someone who is lost in this way this week?

B. Prayer

Thank You, Heavenly Father, for the lesson's perspective on what is true and necessary. Deliver us from the worldly mindset that repeatedly tries to take our thoughts captive. May we be alert to spiritual blindfolds that we willingly put on so readily and easily. This week, provide us with opportunities to help remove the veil from someone's heart. We pray as Your servants in the name of Your Son, Jesus. Amen.

C. Thought to Remember

Be unveiled.
Be bold.

How to Say It

a fortiori *(Latin)*	eh four-she-*or*-eye or ah four-she-*or*-ee.
apostolic	ap-uh-*stahl*-ick.
Colossians	Kuh-*losh*-unz.
Corinth	*Kor*-inth.
Corinthians	Ko-*rin*-thee-unz (*th* as in *thin*).

Involvement Learning

Enhance your lesson with KJV Bible Student *(from your curriculum supplier) and the reproducible activity page (at www.standardlesson.com or in the back of the* KJV Standard Lesson Commentary Deluxe Edition*).*

Into the Lesson

Write the following sentences on the board:

After sunrise, streetlights are useless.

The enemy of the best is the second best.

Form learners into groups of four to discuss the two sentences. Ask class members to think of examples from history, current events, or everyday life to illustrate why the sentences are true. Make a transition by saying, "Today, we will look at a vital truth that echoes the truth of these two statements. It is a truth that changes lives for eternity."

Alternative. Distribute copies of the "Two Paraphrases" exercise from the activity page, which you can download. Allow no more than one minute for learners to complete as indicated. Use the second of the two paraphrases to lead into the lesson.

Into the Word

Have two class members alternate verses in reading aloud today's lesson text, 2 Corinthians 3:5-18. Then assign one of the following activities to each group formed earlier. As time allows, you can have groups complete more than one activity.

Activity 1—Covenants Compared

Distribute handouts (you create) with the terms *Old Covenant / New Covenant* as headers of two columns. Include the following instructions: "Compare and contrast Exodus 24:1-8; 34:29-30 with 2 Corinthians 3:5-18. Record similarities and differences under the appropriate heading."

Activity 2—Which Is Better?

Distribute handouts (you create) with the following instructions: "Create a devotional that emphasizes the benefits of living under the New Covenant. Use 2 Corinthians 3:5-18 to list points to be made before writing the devotion."

Activity 3—Regarding Veil and Curtains

Distribute handouts (you create) with these instructions: "Compare and contrast the veil of 2 Corinthians 3:5-18 with the curtain in Matthew 27:51; Mark 15:38; and Luke 23:45. What does each one signify that the other does not?"

Allow at least 10 minutes for groups to complete their tasks before reconvening for whole-class discussion. Give each group an opportunity to share its conclusions.

Ask a volunteer to read aloud 2 Corinthians 3:18. Talk through how the verse fits into the conclusions you just discussed.

Into Life

Whole-class brainstorming. Pose this question: "When people looked at Jesus, what did they see?" List responses on the board. After a few responses, categorize the replies in terms of what the people saw *physically* and what they perceived *spiritually.* Be sure to interject Isaiah 53:2 at an appropriate point in the discussion. Explore how these conclusions underline how unbelievers still see or perceive Jesus today. Ask for examples of modern "veils" that cover their hearts.

Next, pose the following questions (write them on the board) for potential application of 2 Corinthians 3:18. Allow for responses to each question before asking or revealing the question that follows it. (Larger classes can distribute handouts to small groups.)

1–How does the image of transformational change in 2 Corinthians 3:18 relate to that noted in Romans 12:2?

2–What are some ways to recognize the Spirit's desire to change us?

3–What can we do to open ourselves to that work of the Spirit?

Option. Distribute copies of the "I'm Changing!" activity from the activity page. Have learners complete it individually in a minute or less before sharing it with a partner.

Close with a time of silent prayer for transformational change.

June 16
Lesson 3 (KJV)

Empowered Servants

Devotional Reading: Philippians 2:1-13
Background Scripture: Romans 15:1-13

Romans 15:1-13

**1 We then that are strong ought to bear
the infirmities of the weak, and not to please
ourselves.
2 Let every one of us please his neighbour
for his good to edification.
3 For even Christ pleased not himself; but,
as it is written, The reproaches of them that
reproached thee fell on me.
4 For whatsoever things were written aforetime were written for our learning, that we
through patience and comfort of the scriptures
might have hope.
5 Now the God of patience and consolation
grant you to be likeminded one toward another
according to Christ Jesus:
6 That ye may with one mind and one
mouth glorify God, even the Father of our
Lord Jesus Christ.
7 Wherefore receive ye one another, as
Christ also received us to the glory of God.
8 Now I say that Jesus Christ was a minister of the circumcision for the truth of God, to
confirm the promises made unto the fathers:
9 And that the Gentiles might glorify God
for his mercy; as it is written, For this cause I
will confess to thee among the Gentiles, and
sing unto thy name.
10 And again he saith, Rejoice, ye Gentiles,
with his people.
11 And again, Praise the Lord, all ye Gentiles; and laud him, all ye people.
12 And again, Esaias saith, There shall be a
root of Jesse, and he that shall rise to reign over
the Gentiles; in him shall the Gentiles trust.
13 Now the God of hope fill you with all joy
and peace in believing, that ye may abound in
hope, through the power of the Holy Ghost.**

Key Text

Now the God of patience and consolation grant you to be likeminded one toward another according to Christ Jesus: That ye may with one mind and one mouth glorify God, even the Father of our Lord Jesus Christ.

—Romans 15:5-6

Hope in
the Lord

Unit I: Experiencing Hope
Lessons 1–5

Lesson Aims

After participating in this lesson, each learner will be able to:

1. Identify who set the ultimate example of acceptance.
2. Contrast the Christian concept of empowerment with secular concepts of that term.
3. Suggest a way to react to a common failing of new Christians ("the weak").

Lesson Outline

Introduction
- A. Diversity? Unity?
- B. Lesson Context: The Big Picture
- C. Lesson Context: The Letter Itself

I. What to Do, Part 1 (Romans 15:1-4)
- A. Bear Burdens (v. 1)
  - *Reciprocal Weakness—and Strength*
- B. Please Neighbors (v. 2)
- C. Follow Example (v. 3)
- D. Have Hope (v. 4)

II. What to Do, Part 2 (Romans 15:5-12)
- A. Be Unified in Mind (vv. 5-7)
  - *Unity in Volume*
- B. Embrace Diversity for God (vv. 8-12)

III. How God Can Help (Romans 5:13)
- A. Nature of the Kingdom (v. 13a)
- B. Power of the Spirit (v. 13b)

Conclusion
- A. Doctrinal? Practical?
- B. Prayer
- C. Thought to Remember

Introduction

A. Diversity? Unity?

Which is better for a country or community: to promote diversity or unity? Actually, that's a trick question because it presents those two options as being mutually exclusive, as if those were the only choices. Another choice would be to promote "diversity that embraces unity." A fourth choice might be "unity that honors diversity." You can probably think of other options as well.

The tension between the concepts of diversity and unity confronted the apostle Paul continually as he traveled throughout the Mediterranean world on his missionary journeys. The primary tension within the churches he planted was how those Christians of Jewish background were to relate to those of Gentile background. The text for today's lesson adds another tension to the mix.

B. Lesson Context: The Big Picture

The apostle Paul probably wrote his letter to the Romans while in the city of Corinth during his third missionary journey. That would have been about AD 58. Paul had not yet visited the church in Rome; others had planted it many years before.

The nature of the church in Rome was influenced by an edict issued by Emperor Claudius in about AD 49 that forced Jews living in the city to leave (Acts 18:2). This experience probably fostered a certain division within the Roman church between believers of Gentile and Jewish backgrounds. We can imagine each group contending that it had a better claim on salvation in Christ than the other (compare Romans 11:13-24).

The expulsion of Jews from Rome resulted in Christians of Gentile background being in the majority in the church there, if they had not been the majority already (Romans 1:5, 6, 13). Their majority status seems to have continued even after the death of Claudius in AD 54, which allowed Jews to return to the imperial city (compare Acts 18:2 with Romans 16:3-5a).

C. Lesson Context: The Letter Itself

Douglas J. Moo, scholar on the book of Romans, analyzes the structure of the book this way:

I. The Letter Opening (1:1-17)
II. The Heart of the Gospel (1:18–4:25)
III. The Assurance Provided by the Gospel (5:1–8:39)
IV. The Defense of the Gospel (9:1–11:36)
V. The Transforming Power of the Gospel (12:1–15:13)
VI. The Letter Closing (15:14–16:27)

This outline challenges us to consider how today's lesson from chapter 15 fits into the letter to the Romans. As we take up this challenge, we do well to resist the common practice of seeing everything in Romans through the lens of a favored doctrine or doctrinal category. More valuable is to recognize what Moo calls the "logical movement in the letter," as each topic introduced builds on, clarifies, and/or implements those previously discussed.

I. What to Do, Part 1
(Romans 15:1-4)
A. Bear Burdens (v. 1)

1. We then that are strong ought to bear the infirmities of the weak, and not to please ourselves.

The fact that chapter 15 occurs almost at the end of the letter doesn't mean it's an afterthought or a "P.S." In fact, it's quite the opposite. Paul thinks the attitude of the *strong* toward *the weak* in this verse is so important that it's a variation of what he has already said in Romans 14:1: "Him that is weak in the faith receive ye." And he will repeat this theme in 15:7, below.

Note the all-encompassing nature of this imperative: the two groups of strong and weak means that it applies to everyone. So far in this letter, there have been three issues dividing these two groups: what kinds of food can be eaten (Romans 14:2), the value of certain days (14:5), and the use of wine (14:21; see 14:17).

These don't seem to be random examples of how to get along with fellow Christians; rather, it's much more likely that these were actual problems in the church in Rome. What needed to be addressed was the basis for these points of tension.

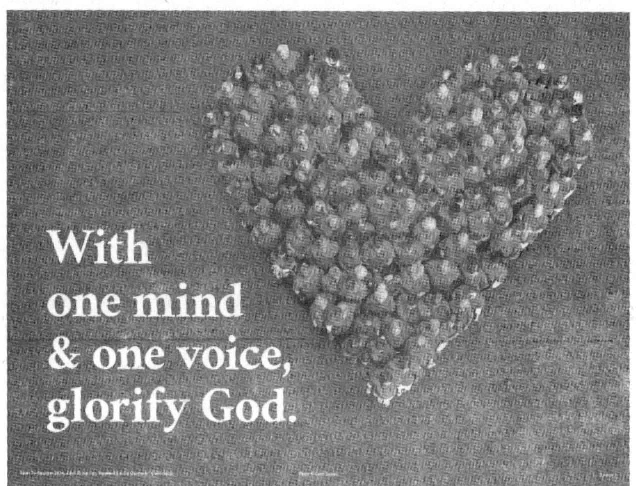

Visual for Lesson 3. *Display this visual as you discuss the questions associated with verse 6. Ask for Bible verses that support learners' answers.*

Who were the "strong" and the "weak"? And what made them that way? There is no shortage of opinions on these questions! But the most likely explanation is that the weak were Christians of Jewish background who maintained their devotion to the Law of Moses. The strong, therefore, would be primarily those Christians of Gentile background. We say "primarily" because Christians of Jewish background who realized they had been freed from that law could be numbered among the strong. Paul was one such, as the opening *we* of this verse establishes.

Note that Paul is not talking about merely tolerating those who are weak in the faith. Rather, the strong ought to *bear* the infirmities of those weaker in the faith. The nature of this verb is seen in Galatians 6:2, a passage about carrying one another's burdens (compare Isaiah 53:4; 1 Corinthians 10:24). Our stance toward others is active, not passive, pursuing unity in positive support, not just coexistence through benign neglect.

Reciprocal Weakness—and Strength

Opening jars with tight lids is a task that I do with a fair amount of regularity at home. There are times when my wife cannot open a jar, and she needs my help. But there is something that we all need to remember: those who are weaker than us may be stronger in other areas.

Today's passage wasn't talking about physical strength, but issues of conscience. Those who had more understanding knew that eating or abstaining from certain food wasn't what made a person faithful. Our challenge, whether stronger or weaker, is to build up each other so that all of us will please God in the Christian life. By helping one another, we accomplish the goal. —C. S.

B. Please Neighbors (v. 2)

2. Let every one of us please his neighbour for his good to edification.

The phrase *please his neighbour* here is the flip side of the imperative "not to please ourselves" in the previous verse. Elsewhere Paul condemns the idea of pleasing ourselves rather than God (Galatians 1:10; 1 Thessalonians 2:4). But the idea here is that of pleasing a fellow believer rather than ourselves. Living that way will build the faith of one's fellow Christians (Romans 14:15, 20).

Before moving on, we should note that the word *neighbour* in this context refers to fellow believers. It echoes the command of Leviticus 19:18 to love our neighbor as we love ourselves. If God's love compels love for all around us, how much more does it compel love for our sisters and brothers in Christ!

C. Follow Example (v. 3)

3. For even Christ pleased not himself; but, as it is written, The reproaches of them that reproached thee fell on me.

Paul moves directly from the exhortation of the previous two verses to the example of *Christ* (compare 1 Corinthians 10:33–11:1). The quote from Psalm 69:9b illustrates this further. The psalmist, recounting the way the righteous are often blamed for the sins of the wicked, anticipated the work of Christ, who took the guilt of sinful humanity on himself on the cross. Christ's sacrifice is the supreme expression of God's love that overcomes divisions and boundaries.

What Do You Think?

How should Christians respond to being insulted?

Digging Deeper

What biblical examples inform your answer?

D. Have Hope (v. 4)

4. For whatsoever things were written aforetime were written for our learning, that we through patience and comfort of the scriptures might have hope.

If anyone asks you what value there is in studying the Old Testament now that we're in the New Testament era, the answer is in this verse. But we should not view this verse in isolation in that regard since Paul writes it immediately after quoting from the Old Testament.

Another passage that affirms this value is 1 Corinthians 10:11. As we note the Old Testament's limitations for application to today (see Romans 6:14-15; 7:4), we do not throw the baby out with the bathwater by ignoring it altogether.

There is a process between *our learning* from *the scriptures* and the *hope* that ultimately results. That process involves (at least) the two intermediate effects of *patience and comfort.* The word *patience* is closely related to *endurance* and *perseverance* (examples: Romans 9:22; 2 Corinthians 1:6; 12:12; Ephesians 6:18). Through the Scripture, God works to give patience and endurance to Christians.

The word translated "comfort" in the verse at hand is the same word translated "consolation" in the next. Although the word *encouraged* does not appear in the *King James Version* of the New Testament, a form of that same Greek word in the old Greek version of the Old Testament (the Septuagint) is translated "encouraged" in Deuteronomy 3:28; that's the sense here as well.

II. What to Do, Part 2

(Romans 15:5-12)

A. Be Unified in Mind (vv. 5-7)

5. Now the God of patience and consolation grant you to be likeminded one toward another according to Christ Jesus.

If the church is to be unified in its diversity and diverse in its unity, it will only be so because of the good news of Jesus and the work of God the Father. God is characterized by *patience*, His capacity to bear with the failures and rebellions of humanity while continuing to offer them forgiveness. God is characterized by *consolation* or encouragement,

His constant provision of the tangible and intangible resources His people need as they navigate life's challenges. The supreme expression of God's patience and consolation is in Jesus, God's true king, who willingly gave His life for the unworthy.

This is the God who calls His people to pursue unity in their diversity. Paul recognizes that it is not within the flesh's capacity to unite with one another. Thus, this verse requests God to *grant* or give readers this ability (see John 15:5; Romans 7:18). Because of who God is and what He has done in Christ, His people can remain faithful to Him only if they have the same mind and heart, characterized by patience and encouragement for one another. That person may be different from me, but Christ died for that person, so I need to love that person just as God does. That likemindedness goes beyond merely being agreeable. As Paul says in Philippians 2:4, it will mean putting others' interests above our own.

The story of God has always been one of patience and comfort. That story came to its pinnacle in Jesus. Now we continue the story as the church that pursues a shared life filled with patience and consolation fitting our Lord.

6. That ye may with one mind and one mouth glorify God, even the Father of our Lord Jesus Christ.

The unified *mind* of God's people leads to the unified praise of *God*. Paul gives us an image of a church gathered with members from every imaginable background and identity but with every voice raised in praise to God (compare Acts 2:46-47). But that expression of praise is not simply in corporate worship. It is vividly expressed in the concern for others more than oneself that each Christian demonstrates, the exercise of the unified mind in all the Christian's relationships. To glorify God is to praise God for what He truly is and has truly done. The true God is the *Father of our Lord Jesus Christ*, who died and rose for unworthy humanity. That one is the ruler of all, the one to whom all God's people and ultimately all of humanity will bow. To bow to Him as Lord can only mean that we surrender our rights, customs, privileges, and desires to put others first. When we do, God is truly glorified, for in our actions the world sees what God has done.

What Do You Think?

To what degree do you consider Christian unity to be a reality versus an ideal?

Digging Deeper

What role does the Spirit play in unifying Christians? What responsibiilty does that leave us?

Unity in Volume

The one and only time I have been in a stadium was September 29, 2014. It was Arrowhead Stadium in Kansas City, Missouri, the home field of the Kansas City Chiefs professional football team. On the day I was there, the stadium's fans cheered so loudly that they hit 142.4 decibels. That is louder than a jet taking off from an aircraft carrier. There are plenty of times I am unable to hear one voice, but there is no way I could miss 50,000 united voices!

The unity of Christians' voices in praise of God should be grander still. If the cheers and shouts in a football stadium are impossible to miss, imagine what it would be like if all Christians united to glorify God with one mind and mouth. I wonder how many people would come to recognize Jesus as Lord if Christians were all more of one mind and mouth. —C. S.

7. Wherefore receive ye one another, as Christ also received us to the glory of God.

Paul ends this section with a pointed summary. What should I do with this person who prefers things I do not like, accepts things I reject, and rejects things I accept? The answer is to respond to that person as *Christ* responded to us. Christ did not forgive us because we started pleasing Him. No, He forgave us in our sins. In our gratitude, we sought to please Him, but first, He received us as we are. Of course, He continues to receive us, even

How to Say It

circumcision	sur-kuhm-*si*-zhn.
Esaias	E-*zay*-us.
Gentiles	*Jen*-tiles.

in our ongoing failure. That is the supreme model of how *God* calls us to respond to one another.

What Do You Think?

Which biblical teachings inform what it means to accept one another?

Digging Deeper

Which biblical teachings offer guidance about unacceptable behaviors or attitudes and how to react in such situations?

B. Embrace Diversity for God (vv. 8-12)

8. Now I say that Jesus Christ was a minister of the circumcision for the truth of God, to confirm thc promises made unto the fathers.

Paul now puts the work of *Christ* in the frame of the major division in the Roman church, between Jewish and Gentile Christians. He affirms that Christ's work fulfilled God's promises to Israel, and that Christ was a servant (*minister*) of those who received circumcision as a sign of God's covenant and promise. The God of Israel was never content to be just the God of one tribe. He always pointed forward to the peoples of the world joining with that tribe to be God's people. The story of the Old Testament is peppered with God's repeated promises to make himself known to the nations of the world through Israel. God fulfilled those promises in Jesus, the true Israelite (compare Genesis 22:18; Galatians 3:15-16).

9. And that the Gentiles might glorify God for his mercy; as it is written, For this cause I will confess to thee among the Gentiles, and sing unto thy name.

Paul now cites several passages from Israel's sacred Scriptures. This reminds readers that God always intended His *people* to be diverse and inclusive. Furthermore, this section connects to Paul's earlier comment (see verse 4). Paul's ministry was built around this divine intention. To believers in Jesus of different backgrounds, he repeatedly taught that Christ's church must express the promise of God to redeem all people as the church expresses love across lines of ethnicity, class, and custom.

Quoted here is David's song of praise in 2 Samuel 22:50, repeated in Psalm 18:49. Paul drew a lesson for the Roman church from the history of David, inviting defeated Gentile nations to praise God with Israel. This would have resonated with the original audience because of their reverence for both David and the Scripture.

10. And again he saith, Rejoice, ye Gentiles, with his people.

This quotation comes from Deuteronomy 32:43, as rendered in the Greek translation of the Hebrew Bible (see also Psalm 18:49). Again, the picture is of former pagans who have joined with God's people in worship of the true God. God has always sought diverse people to worship Him in unity. The picture is not of Gentiles becoming Israelites to join God's people but of Gentiles joining Israelites to praise God as His diverse people.

11. And again, Praise the Lord, all ye Gentiles; and laud him, all ye people.

The third quotation comes from Psalm 117:1. This very short psalm, merely two verses long, calls on people from all the world's ethnicities and tribes to join in God's praise. It is little wonder that so short a song of praise would focus on the promised diversity of God's people. The God who created the world and its diverse peoples ultimately seeks for all the diverse peoples of the world to worship Him together as one.

12. And again, Esaias saith, There shall be a root of Jesse, and he that shall rise to reign over the Gentiles; in him shall the Gentiles trust.

The final quotation comes from the great prophet *Esaias*, also known as Isaiah. In Isaiah 11:10, the root of Jesse refers prophetically to Jesus, the descendant of David, the son of Jesse. Jesus, as that root, is the one who fulfills God's promise of David's descendant who will rule over the nations without end (2 Samuel 7:12-16; Jeremiah 23:5; 33:15; Luke 1:32). His reign is not tyrannical or incompetent, like many of Israel's kings. People of all nations will trust Him as a good, wise, and powerful ruler, just as He demonstrates in making the nations His people despite their rebellion against Him. True submission to Jesus as king means that His people must pursue unity in their diversity just as He pursues it.

What Do You Think?

What other passages give you confidence in God's faithfulness and power to accomplish what He promises?

Digging Deeper

How can you align your own commitments with God's purposes?

III. How God Can Help

(Romans 15:13)

A. Nature of the Kingdom (v. 13a)

13a. Now the God of hope fill you with all joy and peace in believing.

God's *peace* is not merely the absence of hostility. Rather, it is positive, active goodwill toward others, living in active harmony and active service for one another. Likewise, God's *joy* is more than a pleasant state of mind. In joy, we respond to the experience of God's love as we receive it from God and as we receive it through one another. The peace and joy will be in each of them and shared among them as they express Christ's reign by living in harmony, deferring to one another in love (compare Romans 5:1; 14:17).

B. Power of the Spirit (v. 13b)

13b. That ye may abound in hope, through the power of the Holy Ghost.

The prayer continues, asking for abundant hope and a positive view of the future based on the believer's confidence in God's goodness and power. The hope of the future is grounded in the experience of the present. The *Holy Ghost* living in the Christian provides the proof of God's commitment to His people, assuring us that He will complete at Christ's return the salvation He began at our conversion (Romans 5:5; 8:11; Philippians 1:25). God's hope is not mere optimism. It is grounded in what God has done and is doing, expressing confidence in what God promises yet to do.

Hope binds God's people together in the present. By Christian hope, we affirm that we will spend eternity together in the fullness of Christ's kingdom. If we will be unified in eternity, pursuing unity in the present is our only faithful, hopeful alternative.

What Do You Think?

Where do you see the Spirit at work to shape your perspectives and actions?

Digging Deeper

In what specific ways can you cultivate an attitude that encourages you to follow the Spirit's guidance?

Conclusion

A. Doctrinal? Practical?

A teacher of an adult Bible study class announced that when their current study of the book of Mark was concluded, the class would study a certain doctrine. This announcement resulted immediately in an objection from a participant who said that every church she had been part of had had divisions over doctrine. Her objection was along the lines of "Give us something practical, not doctrinal!"

This statement, like the "Unity? Diversity?" question we posed at the very beginning of this lesson, is a false choice. Doctrine (what we believe) is the basis of practice (how we behave; compare 1 Timothy 1:3-10; 4:16; 2 Timothy 4:3-5; Titus 1:9; 2:1-14).

The doctrine of the church's global, multinational, multiethnic, inclusive, and diverse membership is grounded in the even more foundational doctrines of creation and redemption. God created all people of every nation, and Christ died and rose for all people of every nation. Those doctrinal foundations leave us with a practical question: Are we willing to surrender our privilege and defer to those unlike us to express our faith in and submit to the Creator God and the crucified Christ?

B. Prayer

Dear God, we celebrate Your love that made us one body of Christ composed of many tribes and nations. Empower us to live according to Your plan for Your kingdom. In Jesus' name we pray. Amen.

C. Thought to Remember

Christ creates one church united in Him.

Involvement Learning

Enhance your lesson with KJV Bible Student *(from your curriculum supplier) and the reproducible activity page (at www.standardlesson.com or in the back of the* KJV Standard Lesson Commentary Deluxe Edition*).*

Into the Lesson

Form learners into research pairs and distribute a newspaper or magazine to each pair. Challenge pairs to find pictures or headlines that show or imply a weak person. *Alternative:* Have pairs do their research using their smartphones.

After five minutes, call for discoveries in whole-class discussion. Pose one or more of the following questions to the class: 1–What was it about the person that indicated "weakness"? 2–How do stronger people react to those in your example? 3–How easy is it to respond positively to those who are weak?

Lead into Bible study by saying, "The apostle Paul has something to say about how Christians should respond to weakness in one another. Let's see what he had to say."

Into the Word

Have two volunteers read Romans 15:1-13, alternating with each verse. Then combine the pairs formed earlier into groups of four. Name the groups and distribute to them handouts (you create) with instructions as follows:

Commands and Reasons Group. Provide the group a handout (you create) with *What Paul Commands / Reason to Obey* as the headers of two columns. Instructions: "For each command you find in the text, write it in the first column; then write in the other column a reason why, also from the text. Include verse references." **Jesus Group.** Instructions: "List everything Romans 15:1-13 says about Jesus." **Church Group.** Instructions: "List everything Romans 15:1-13 has to say about the church."

After sufficient time, reconvene for whole-class discussion of findings and conclusions. Here are possible discussion questions: 1–In what ways is the picture of the church as presented here a contrast to the examples we discussed to begin class? 2–Why do you suppose Paul had to remind the Roman Christians to bear with the weak? 3–Why are Christians sometimes less tolerant of weakness than non-Christians?

Into Life

Write this prompt on the board and ask each learner to jot down a response: "One way I'm a stronger Christian today than I was several years ago is ________." Inform learners that you will collect the slips and that they should not put their names on them.

After collecting the slips, redistribute them so that no one receives his or her own slip back. Display or distribute the following two discussion questions to the groups of four formed earlier: 1–How well do you identify with the response on the slip you now hold? Why? 2–How can the weaknesses we've discussed be turned into strengths?

Allow time for groups to consider their responses before the whole-class sharing that follows. Use these two questions to conclude this discussion: 1–How can bearing with the weak lead them to be stronger? 2–In what ways can we "bear with" their weaknesses?

List the answers on the board as they are suggested.

Alternative. Distribute copies of the "I Once Was Weak, but Now I'm Strong" exercise from the activity page, which you can download. Have learners complete it individually in a minute or less as indicated before working with a partner to finalize.

After calling time under either alternative, challenge learners to choose one way to "bear with the weak" throughout the week. Begin next week's lesson by allowing learners time to share what happened.

As learners depart, distribute copies of the "Reasons to Serve, Foundations for Unity" crossword puzzle from the activity page. Close with prayer appropriate to today's topic.

June 23
Lesson 4 (KJV)

Full Assurance

Devotional Reading: Psalm 23
Background Scripture: Hebrews 6:9-20

Hebrews 6:9-20

9 But, beloved, we are persuaded better
things of you, and things that accompany salvation, though we thus speak.
10 For God is not unrighteous to forget
your work and labour of love, which ye have
shewed toward his name, in that ye have ministered to the saints, and do minister.
11 And we desire that every one of you do
shew the same diligence to the full assurance of
hope unto the end:
12 That ye be not slothful, but followers of
them who through faith and patience inherit
the promises.
13 For when God made promise to Abraham, because he could swear by no greater, he
sware by himself,
14 Saying, Surely blessing I will bless thee,
and multiplying I will multiply thee.
15 And so, after he had patiently endured,
he obtained the promise.
16 For men verily swear by the greater: and
an oath for confirmation is to them an end of
all strife.
17 Wherein God, willing more abundantly
to shew unto the heirs of promise the immutability of his counsel, confirmed it by an oath:
18 That by two immutable things, in which
it was impossible for God to lie, we might have
a strong consolation, who have fled for refuge
to lay hold upon the hope set before us:
19 Which hope we have as an anchor of
the soul, both sure and stedfast, and which
entereth into that within the veil;
20 Whither the forerunner is for us entered,
even Jesus, made an high priest for ever after
the order of Melchisedec.

Key Text

Which hope we have as an anchor of the soul, both sure and stedfast, and which entereth into that within the veil; Whither the forerunner is for us entered, even Jesus, made an high priest for ever after the order of Melchisedec. **—Hebrews 6:19-20**

Hope in

the Lord

Unit I: Experiencing Hope

Lessons 1–5

Lesson Aims

After participating in this lesson, each learner will be able to:

1. List elements of the "diligence" Christians are to practice.

2. Explain the meaning and significance of Jesus as "forerunner" and "high priest forever."

3. Write a prayer of thanks for God's keeping of His promises.

Lesson Outline

Introduction

A. Seal the Deal

B. Lesson Context

I. Promise Made (Hebrews 6:9-12)

A. Declaration (v. 9)

B. Source (v. 10a)

C. Basis (vv. 10b-12)

The Vital Element of Initiative

II. Promise Fulfilled (Hebrews 6:13-20)

A. By God's Greatness (vv. 13-15)

On Swearing to God

B. By God's Faithfulness (vv. 16-20)

Conclusion

A. The Deal Is Sealed

B. Prayer

C. Thought to Remember

Introduction

A. Seal the Deal

In the early years of expansion on the North American continent, there were few written codes for pioneers to follow. In those days, a handshake was considered a person's contract and signature. Rather than having lengthy documents with multiple signatures and notarized stamps, a person's word was his or her bond. Those who didn't keep their word risked social ostracism.

The Bible occasionally depicts the keeping of contracts or the honoring of promises in a similar way. In the Old Testament, people might seal a deal by making a vow to the Lord. A Bible dictionary defincs a vow as "a voluntary promise to God to perform some service or do something pleasing to him in return for some hoped-for benefits" (examples: Genesis 28:20-22; Judges 11:30). A vow could be made to abstain from certain things (example: Numbers 6:1-8). The law demanded that those who uttered a vow were bound by it (Numbers 30; compare Deuteronomy 23:21-23; Ecclesiastes 5:4-5). That's crystal clear regarding human obligations. But what about God's promises? The answer is found in today's lesson.

B. Lesson Context

The book of Hebrews is unique in the collection of New Testament letters in that the author's name is never divulged. But *anonymous* doesn't mean *completely unknown* since the original readers had a personal relationship with that person (Hebrews 13:22-24). Throughout the centuries, scholars have speculated that the writer could have been Barnabas, Silas, Apollos, Luke, Paul, or Priscilla. Even so, the book's anonymity does not make it any less God's truth; not stating the identity of the author was a common practice at that time, especially when the original audience had a connection with the author. Even though we don't know the author's name, the original audience did!

The absence of a title to this letter in the earliest existing Greek manuscripts makes it challenging to identify the original recipients. Some scholars think that the author lived in Rome. This assertion is based on the writings of Clement of Rome (lived about AD 35–99), who cited numerous passages from Hebrews (see the many quotes from Hebrews 1 in the nonbiblical 1 Clement 36). In addition, there is a reference to Italy in Hebrews 13:24.

The lack of information regarding the recipients has resulted in no shortage of proposals! The passage of time alluded to in Hebrews 5:12 is thought to indicate that a second generation of believers is in view. The word *remember* in Hebrews 13:7 is taken to support this proposal, as this verse challenges the original audience to recall instructions from the leaders of the first generation of believers. This theory is viable as long as the word *remember* is intended to mean "recall information from memory." But the Greek word translated *remember* can also mean "keep thinking about," as it seems to intend in Hebrews 11:15. There, the same underlying Greek word is translated "mindful." In any case, the many references to the priesthood and numerous Old Testament personalities (Hebrews 11) point to an audience of Jewish background.

There are various ways to outline the book. One way is in terms of five passages of warning. These five are Hebrews 2:1-4; 3:7–4:13; 5:11–6:12; 10:19-39; and 12:14-29. Each warning section includes a call to salvation and a vivid description of the consequences if God's way is rejected.

Today's text includes part of the third warning. This passage consists of four sections split between negative and positive appeals. Hebrews 5:11-14 is negative, balanced by the positive 6:1-3. Hebrews 6:4-8 returns to a negative warning and is offset by the encouragement found in today's lesson.

I. Promise Made

(Hebrews 6:9-12)

A. Declaration (v. 9)

9. But, beloved, we are persuaded better things of you, and things that accompany salvation, though we thus speak.

The opening *but* indicates that what follows contrasts in some way with what has just been said. In the verse immediately before the one at hand, the writer of Hebrews wrapped up his or her negative cautions (see Lesson Context) to switch to a discussion of *better things*. The writer does not define or give specifics about these better things, saying only that they are things to anticipate.

In making the transition, the writer does not deny the applicability of the warning just given in Hebrews 6:4-8. We know this because of similar warnings given later (see Hebrews 10:26-28). Noteworthy is the fact that the writer is self-inclusive in using the plural *we*. This is sometimes called an "editorial we," as it is used when writers speak with the authority of their position.

One detail speaks to the connection between the writer and the original intended audience: the word *beloved*. The use of this word in similar contexts indicates a close connection and personal acquaintance (example: Romans 16:8-9, 12).

B. Source (v. 10a)

10a. For God is not unrighteous to forget.

Having declared the promise of better things, the writer transitions to speaking of the one who makes the promise: *God*. In using the description *not unrighteous*, the writer employs a form of rhetoric known as *litotes*. This device occurs when a writer or speaker creates an understatement by expressing an affirmative by means of a negative to the contrary. In other words, we might affirm that something is "good" by declaring it "not bad." Therefore, the fact communicated here is that God is righteous. The premise of God's righteousness is connected with His unwillingness *to forget*. What it is that God won't forget is stated next.

C. Basis (vv. 10b-12)

10b. Your work and labour of love, which ye have shewed toward his name, in that ye have ministered to the saints, and do minister.

How to Say It

Apollos	Uh-*pahl*-us.
Barnabas	*Bar*-nuh-bus.
Ecclesiastes	Ik-*leez*-ee-**as**-teez.
Ishmael	*Ish*-may-el.
litotes	*lie*-tuh-**teez**.
Melchisedec	Mel-*kiz*-eh-dek.
omnipotent	ahm-*nih*-poh-tent.
Silas	*Sigh*-luss.

The recipients of this letter had *ministered* in ways that visibly witnessed to their salvation. We know that good works result *from* salvation; they don't result *in* salvation. Salvation is by grace through faith and not by works (Ephesians 2:8-9). Jesus had said that the world would know His followers by their *love* for one another (John 13:35). The love we demonstrate is (or should be) a result of the grace and forgiveness received in Christ.

The phrase *shewed toward his name* harmonizes with the imperative that ministry is to be done as though doing it to Christ himself (see Matthew 25:40). Some students believe this is a preface for the work of prison ministry described in Hebrews 10:32-34. The author uses past and present tense verbs (*have ministered . . . and do minister*) to acknowledge the work of believers. From this, we can conclude that the recipients of this letter were consistent in living out their faith.

What Do You Think?

How will you show care and love to other believers in the upcoming week?

Digging Deeper

How will you show care and love to believers whom you may consider annoying or disagreeable?

11. And we desire that every one of you do shew the same diligence to the full assurance of hope unto the end.

The writer's concern for consistent and continuous pastoral care continues. This was not only for the benefit of the one receiving the care but also evidence of the recipients' *full assurance of hope.* So that they do not get discouraged in their work, the author directs their attention to the finish line (compare Hebrews 3:14; 12:1).

Scholars disagree about whether *the end* refers to the end of the lives of the original readers of Hebrews or the end of the age (compare and contrast Matthew 10:22; 13:39-40; 24:13; John 13:1). Either way, the imperative of uninterrupted faithfulness is paramount. The apostle Paul saw life as a race to be finished for the hope of reward (Acts 20:24; 1 Corinthians 9:24-27; 2 Timothy 4:7-8).

12. That ye be not slothful, but followers of them who through faith and patience inherit the promises.

The opposite of being diligent is being *slothful.* The underlying Greek word occurs in only two places in the New Testament: here and in Hebrews 5:11. There, the translation is the word *dull,* found in a context that warns against failing to hear. We know that a failure to listen will sometimes result in a failure to act accordingly. The author hopes the readers will both hear and minister according to the truth (compare James 1:22).

The author of Hebrews realizes that the readers may need more than a pep talk in this regard. Thus, the readers are encouraged to follow the example of those who have been faithful in ministry (compare 1 Corinthians 4:6; 11:1; Ephesians 5:1; 1 Thessalonians 1:6; 2:14).

What Do You Think?

What precautions do you take to be not only a *hearer* of God's Word but a *doer* of its commands as well?

Digging Deeper

Who will be an accountability partner so that you might "be not weary in well doing" (2 Thessalonians 3:13)?

The Vital Element of Initiative

Jim and Zach had been friends since middle school. They decided to attend the same Bible college, planning to become youth ministers. At college, they met Mike, a student who was a year older. Mike offered to mentor the two in a discipleship group. The three became inseparable.

Things changed, however, after they left college. Mike got married and spent less time with Jim and Zach. Jim and Mike both found ministry positions, while Zach struggled with his calling. He eventually took a non-ministry job to support himself.

The spiritual lives of all three began to suffer under changing realities. Mike began to feel his ministry was more of a job than a calling. Jim became increasingly disillusioned with his faith. Zach started to describe himself as agnostic regarding God and faith.

A cursory glance at their lives would not detect

laziness or lack of diligence. They had started with deep devotion, completed their education, and found ways to serve God. Yet, over time, their commitment to God wavered. They needed to be called back to be "followers of them who through faith and patience inherit the promises" (Hebrews 6:12). For that to have happened, who should have taken the initiative? How can you avoid the regret of not doing so regarding a struggling believer you know right now? —A. W.

II. Promise Fulfilled

(Hebrews 6:13-20)

A. By God's Greatness (vv. 13-15)

13. For when God made a promise to Abraham, because he could swear by no greater, he sware by himself.

The patriarch *Abraham* is mentioned by name 10 times in the book of Hebrews. Clearly, he is a pivotal figure to this writer. Even so, the emphasis here is on God, who *made* a certain *promise* to that man.

The promise in view is found in Genesis 22:15-18. Before we delve into the nature of that promise, we note that making a vow or swearing an oath is virtually the same thing. Psalm 132:2 depicts the two actions in parallel lines (compare Numbers 30:2, 10). It was permissible in the Old Testament era to swear by the name of Israel's God because He was the only true God (Deuteronomy 6:13; Isaiah 65:16). Thus, when God himself makes a promise or swears an oath, He must *swear . . . by himself* because no one *greater* in the universe exists by which to swear (45:23). The original readers would have been encouraged by this reminder that God's promises are assured since His unsurpassed greatness confirms them.

The fact that vows are not necessarily sinful in and of themselves in the New Testament era is established in Acts 18:18, which records Paul's taking of a vow. But the taking of vows and swearing of oaths were widely misused in the first century, as human tradition displaced God's Word. The result was self-serving oaths and vows; Jesus condemned such a practice in no uncertain words (Matthew 5:33-37; 15:4-6; 23:16-22; Mark 7:6-13).

On Swearing to God

There is one thing about the television show *Cops* that never seems to change: when suspects realize that their explanations and denials aren't being accepted at face value, they will escalate their claims by saying, "I swear to God." In one show, the arresting officer who heard this oath responded, "Well, you're lying to God!" In another episode, an experienced police officer noted that when suspects double down by saying, "I swear to God," that's the point when he's *certain* they are lying!

A review of particular Scripture passages would be invaluable to some, were they to understand those passages as God's warning to them. On oath-taking in general, Matthew 5:33-37 is a good start. On the forgivability of lying while swearing an oath, Mark 14:71 and John 21:15-19 provide insight. Concerning various sins, including lying, 1 Corinthians 6:9-10 and Revelation 21:8; 22:15 are brutally cautionary. But before we take these warnings to others, do we heed them ourselves? —R. L. N.

14-15. Saying, Surely blessing I will bless thee, and multiplying I will multiply thee. And so, after he had patiently endured, he obtained the promise.

The quotation from Genesis 22:15-18 continues. *The promise* from God was that through Abraham's vast number of descendants, all the nations of the world would be blessed (Genesis 18:18; 22:17-18). While Abraham (Abram) was at Haran, God had promised him many descendants (12:1-4; stressed anew in 15:5). God began fulfilling that promise 25 years later when the 100-year-old Abraham had a son named Isaac (21:5). The staggering result some 620 years later is seen in Numbers 1:1-46.

Abraham's main task during those 25 years was to wait *patiently*, as such would demonstrate his trust in God. That man's patience wore thin after 11 years of waiting when he tried to help push God's plan along through the conception and birth of Ishmael (Genesis 16). But, in God's timing, the promise was indeed fulfilled as Abraham learned patience over the course of an additional 14 years until the birth of Isaac.

As with other cases in the Bible, God's intent

was eventually distorted by self-serving human tradition and pride. By the first century AD, a widely held belief was that physical descent from Abraham was the ticket to being right with God (see Matthew 3:9; Luke 3:8; etc.). But the more important issue was (and is) to be a spiritual descendant of Abraham (see Romans 4:9-17; 9:6-8; Galatians 3:7-9).

What Do You Think?

How will you demonstrate patience in following God's plan, even if you don't fully understand it?

Digging Deeper

What steps will you take to strengthen your patience as the world grows increasingly impatient and hurried?

B. By God's Faithfulness (vv. 16-20)

16. For men verily swear by the greater: and an oath for confirmation is to them an end of all strife.

This verse reflects Exodus 22:10-11. A person swearing *an oath* in that context was inviting God to witness the truth of the testimony. Ideally, this served to put *an end to all strife* of the case at hand (compare Genesis 21:23). The compelling idea here is that people take oaths in light of something or someone who is *the greater.* And there is nothing or no one greater than God.

17. Wherein God, willing more abundantly to shew unto the heirs of promise the immutability of his counsel, confirmed it by an oath.

In taking the oath, *God* communicated on the level of humanity's understanding at the time. He did so in order that there would be no doubt regarding His intention and commitment to implement His plan. This resolve is reflected in the phrase *immutability of his counsel.* The word *immutable* means "unchanging." The underlying Greek word occurs in the New Testament only in this verse and the next.

18. That by two immutable things, in which it was impossible for God to lie, we might have a strong consolation, who have fled for refuge to lay hold upon the hope set before us.

A trick question sometimes asked of Christians is, "Do you believe that God can do anything?" The trap is that if the response is *no*, then the Christian has admitted to following a deity who is less than omnipotent (meaning "all-powerful"). But if the answer is *yes,* then the Christian can be asked a follow-up question such as, "So, you believe that God can make two plus two equal seven?"

The correct response to the first question is to state that God cannot do anything that would violate His own nature. God is the one who created all the rules that order the universe. This fact reveals Him to be a God of order, not disorder. Regarding the second question, to violate a rule that requires two plus two always to equal four would be for God to violate His own orderly nature. This is not a sign of weakness—in fact, quite the opposite! In the verse at hand, we see an affirmation of all this in the fact that it is *impossible for God to lie* (compare Numbers 23:19; 1 Samuel 15:29; Titus 1:2; see lesson 12). That is one of the *two immutable things* in view in the verse at hand.

The second of those two things is that God sealed the promise with an oath, as already discussed. We should not lose sight of the fact that an important goal of the writer is to prevent the readers from falling away from Christ (Hebrews 6:4-6). The stress on the absolute reliability of God's promises serves to achieve this goal. How foolish to abandon this *hope*!

What Do You Think?

How does knowledge of God's omnipotence strengthen your faith?

Digging Deeper

What other attributes of God have encouraged and strengthened your faith?

19-20. Which hope we have as an anchor of the soul, both sure and stedfast, and which entereth into that within the veil; Whither the forerunner is for us entered, even Jesus, made an high priest for ever after the order of Melchisedec.

The focus on *hope* continues as the author weaves metaphors together to illustrate the message. Anchors bring to mind thoughts of stability (compare and contrast Acts 27:13-17). This verse is the only instance in the New Testament where *an anchor* is used to illustrate Christian hope.

The second metaphor involves the temple *veil*. The veils in the temple in Jerusalem served to divide areas. As the writer later notes, behind "the second veil" was "the tabernacle which is called the Holiest of all" (Hebrews 9:3; compare Exodus 26:33). Rules for going behind that veil to enter the Holiest place were highly restrictive (see Leviticus 16; Hebrews 9:7). The Gospels record that the temple's veil was torn from the top to the bottom when *Jesus* died on the cross (Matthew 27:51; Mark 15:38; Luke 23:45). Thus Jesus was in some sense *the forerunner . . . for us* in that regard. The writer of Hebrews explains this further in Hebrews 10:19-25.

The primary reference in the Old Testament to the mysterious *Melchisedec* is Genesis 14:18, with another one found in Psalm 110:4. The writer closes this section of the book of Hebrews by reflecting on the imagery of this psalm, as he did earlier in Hebrews 5:6, 10. Reference to this ancient person invites further explanation—an explanation that follows immediately in Hebrews 7:1-17.

What Do You Think?

How would you explain Christian hope to an unbeliever by using the metaphor of an anchor?

Digging Deeper

What other metaphors can you use to communicate Christian hope?

Conclusion

A. The Deal Is Sealed

The state of Alaska covers some 586,000 square miles of land, which is more than 375 million acres. In 1867, the United States purchased Alaska from Russia for $7.2 million in one of the largest land deals in history. Adjusted for inflation, the purchasing power of that sum of money was about $122.2 million in 2018. That was the year that Amazon purchased the home security company Ring for an undisclosed amount that many experts estimate to be approximately $1 billion.

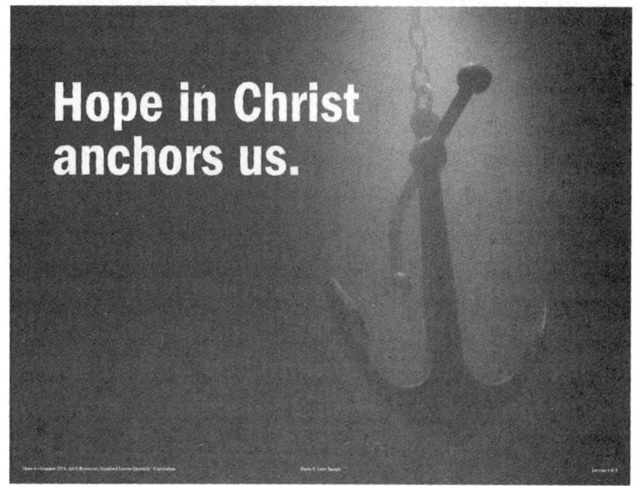

Visual for Lesson 4 & 5. *Have this visual on display as you discuss the commentary and discussion questions associated with Hebrews 6:19-20.*

Therefore, Amazon's purchase was about 90 times what was paid for Alaska! There are many differences between these two transactions. But they had one thing in common: money needed to change hands to seal the deal.

When God promised Abraham that his offspring would bless all nations, that was the beginning of the Abrahamic covenant. It was a promise that reached beyond Abraham's immediate descendants to encompass the entire world. The fulfillment of the promise lay in the work of Jesus on the cross. Once humanity's debt of sin was paid, no further payment was required.

That means that we are invited to be heirs to the promise, not to be the purchaser of the promise. The question is whether or not we can live out this life-changing truth. To live this truth means that we rest in the work of Christ and cease trying to redeem that which we have already inherited through faith. Do you?

B. Prayer

Father, we thank You for the certainty of Your promises—promises based on Your Son's work on the cross. May this ever be a reminder to us that You will do the things You promised, even as we anticipate the return of Jesus. We pray in His name. Amen.

C. Thought to Remember

Be assured that our future is ensured.

Involvement Learning

Enhance your lesson with KJV Bible Student *(from your curriculum supplier) and the reproducible activity page (at www.standardlesson.com or in the back of the* KJV Standard Lesson Commentary Deluxe Edition*).*

Into the Lesson

Have the phrase *Elements of a contract* written on the board as learners arrive. Invite learners to name examples of contracts that they have signed. Then ask volunteers to name common elements of those contracts; write responses on the board.

After about five minutes of discussion, ask: "What are legitimate reasons to breach a contract?" If no one mentions it, say that the contract itself may have "escape clauses" built in. Another legitimate reason to breach a contract is if one or more of its provisions are unconscionable.

Alternative. Distribute copies of the "Let's Make a Deal" exercise from the activity page, which you can download. Ask pairs to complete the exercise as indicated.

Lead into the lesson by saying, "People make deals, but God makes promises!" Note that some of His contractual promises include escape clauses (example: Jeremiah 39:18), and some do not (example: Ezekiel 17:18). And God's covenantal promises are never unconscionable. God will not break His covenant with humanity, nor will He impose impossible conditions to meet.

Make a transition by saying, "Let's see how the writer of Hebrews draws on these ideas."

Into the Word

In advance, reproduce the 12 verses of the lesson text, along with their verse numbers, on 12 slips of paper, one verse per slip. Have learners draw slips blindly from a container, with slips distributed evenly in proportion to class size. Have learners read their drawn verse(s) aloud in numeric order.

Then divide the class into three teams: **God Researchers, Audience of Hebrews Researchers**, and **Abraham Researchers**. Have each team list the many characteristics of the individual(s) assigned to them by looking in and beyond the lesson text. Provide aids for the research as the nature of your class and your advance study dictate. Allow several minutes for teams to work.

Reread Hebrews 6:9-20 aloud, stopping at the end of each verse. Allow time for the individual groups to share any attributes found in that verse. Lead a discussion as to why the author of Hebrews chose to describe specific characteristics of God by stating what God is not.

Discuss why the author of Hebrews described the various attributes of God, the letter's original readers, and Abraham. *Option.* For further discussion, ask, "What advantage do the characteristics of individuals bring to the story, and how does this help readers today in terms of diligence to be exercised?" *(Expect responses to mention their faithfulness as enduring models to emulate.)*

Dig deeper by asking how the mention of the Melchisdec priesthood, an anchor, and the temple relate to these attributes. Be prepared to explain these yourself. Make a transition to the Into Life section by discussing the significance of Jesus as a "forerunner" and a "high priest for ever" (Hebrews 6:20).

Into Life

Distribute index cards that have *THANKS* written vertically (you prepare). Challenge learners to take no more than one minute to write a thank you note to God using the word on the card as an acrostic. Have learners complete it individually in a minute or less.

Option. Time allowing, have learners write on the back of their index cards some life situations that have caused them to doubt the promises of God *(examples: sickness, job loss)*. Then have them write a promise or declaration from the lesson text that encourages them about that situation. Invite learners to take the cards home and consult them throughout the week when discouragement and doubt arise.

June 30
Lesson 5 (KJV)

Fearless Witness

Devotional Reading: Philippians 3:1-14
Background Scripture: Acts 26:1-11

Acts 26:1-11

1 Then Agrippa said unto Paul, Thou art permitted to speak for thyself. Then Paul stretched forth the hand, and answered for himself:

2 I think myself happy, king Agrippa, because I shall answer for myself this day before thee touching all the things whereof I am accused of the Jews:

3 Especially because I know thee to be expert in all customs and questions which are among the Jews: wherefore I beseech thee to hear me patiently.

4 My manner of life from my youth, which was at the first among mine own nation at Jerusalem, know all the Jews;

5 Which knew me from the beginning, if they would testify, that after the most straitest sect of our religion I lived a Pharisee.

6 And now I stand and am judged for the hope of the promise made of God unto our fathers:

7 Unto which promise our twelve tribes, instantly serving God day and night, hope to come. For which hope's sake, king Agrippa, I am accused of the Jews.

8 Why should it be thought a thing incredible with you, that God should raise the dead?

9 I verily thought with myself, that I ought to do many things contrary to the name of Jesus of Nazareth.

10 Which thing I also did in Jerusalem: and many of the saints did I shut up in prison, having received authority from the chief priests; and when they were put to death, I gave my voice against them.

11 And I punished them oft in every synagogue, and compelled them to blaspheme; and being exceedingly mad against them, I persecuted them even unto strange cities.

Key Text

Now I stand and am judged for the hope of the promise made of God unto our fathers: —**Acts 26:6**

Hope in the Lord

Unit I: Experiencing Hope

Lessons 1–5

Lesson Aims

After participating in this lesson, each learner will be able to:

1. Summarize Paul's actions (as Saul) before his conversion.

2. Explain why Paul characterized the Pharisees as a "sect."

3. Identify the most important "takeaway" from the lesson to practice personally.

Lesson Outline

Introduction

A. The Rules of Debate

B. Lesson Context

I. Paul Begins His Defense (Acts 26:1-8)

A. What Agrippa Knew (vv. 1-3)

B. What the Jews Knew (vv. 4-5)

C. What the Accusation Was (vv. 6-8)

II. Paul Summarizes His Error (Acts 26:9-11)

A. Opposed the Name (v. 9)

B. Persecuted Christians (vv. 10-11)

Tact—The Lost Art?

On Being an Extremist

Conclusion

A. Greatest Shame, Greatest Strength

B. Prayer

C. Thought to Remember

Introduction

A. The Rules of Debate

The rules of debate team were simple: one team defended a stated proposition while the other team opposed it. The rules prevented either side from changing an argument or modifying a position. A team could bring more evidence to support a position, but an unsupported argument was not to deter the debaters. By pointing out the other side's weaknesses, a team could put points on the board and hope to sway the judge's decision in its favor. It was unthinkable for a team to admit that its perspective had changed because the other team had a stronger argument! Ultimately, debate team was not about which side was "right"; rather, it was about debating skills as they contributed to winning or losing.

We often see the same focus in today's debates, which frequently come in the form of point-counterpoint sound bites on the evening news. If such "debates" ever change the mind of someone prominent, that person is dismissed as having "flip-flopped." Yet it should not be disqualifying to admit when we have changed our minds based on changed awareness of facts. If anything, the person who has shifted away from a certain viewpoint is demonstrating an openness to new information. The apostle Paul was such a person.

B. Lesson Context

The book of Acts relates one of the most significant mindset changes made by an individual throughout history. That change involved a man named Saul, who was a deadly enemy of Christianity at first (Acts 7:60b–8:3). But after an encounter with the risen Lord, Saul became Christianity's chief proponent. The specifics of how the change came about are recorded in Acts 9:1-19; 22:3-21; and 26:12-18. Today's lesson is the preface to the third of these accounts.

Saul was converted to Christianity in about AD 34. He subsequently traveled around the Mediterranean world on three missionary journeys, as recounted in Acts 12:25–14:28; 15:36–18:22; and 18:23–21:9. Perhaps desiring to leave his old identity in the past, Saul became known as Paul early in these journeys (13:9). Shortly after the third journey ended in Caesarea Maritima, Paul traveled down to Jerusalem. There he was sighted by enemies who incited a riot to silence him (21:17-29). Paul's subsequent arrest undoubtedly saved his life (21:30-36). The year was probably AD 58.

After another riot or near-riot, Paul used his Roman citizenship to avoid being flogged (Acts 22:22-29). An inquest and a murder plot ensued (22:30–23:22), so Paul was transferred under heavy guard to Caesarea Maritima—about 75 miles road distance from Jerusalem—for trial under Governor Felix (23:23–24:26). That trial was inconclusive, and Paul was held in prison for two years until Governor Festus replaced Felix (24:27).

That change in leadership resulted in another trial (Acts 25:1-9), Paul's appeal to Caesar (25:10-12), high-level consultation (25:13-22), and appearance before King Agrippa II (25:23-27). That's the immediate backdrop to today's lesson; the year was about AD 60.

I. Paul Begins His Defense
(Acts 26:1-8)

A. What Agrippa Knew (vv. 1-3)

1. Then Agrippa said unto Paul, Thou art permitted to speak for thyself. Then Paul stretched forth the hand, and answered for himself.

Agrippa is short for Herod Agrippa II, the last of the line of Herodian kings. They ruled Judea as the clients of Rome. Paul had reason to fear this king: his father, Herod Agrippa I, had arrested and killed the apostle James (Acts 12:2).

But Paul was no novice at interacting with authorities. By this time, his 26 years as Christianity's chief proponent had made him a seasoned debater (examples: Acts 9:29; 13:45; 17:1-5, 16-34; 18:4-6; 19:8-10). Thus, he was practiced in the habits of defending his actions, counteracting personal attacks, and dividing his opposition (23:6-10).

Paul's case was difficult for civic authorities to grapple with, somewhat like the case of Jesus was 30 years earlier. The authorities were primarily interested in maintaining law and order. But how was order to be maintained when it involved bodily harm due to issues of personal religious belief and practice? Should the authorities insert themselves into such disputes, or should they leave it up to the Jews and their own religious authorities to sort things out (compare John 18:31; Acts 18:14-17; 25:18-21)?

Paul was well aware of this point of tension, and he used his Roman citizenship as leverage in his defense on at least two occasions (Acts 16:37-38; 22:23–23:30). We also see a personal characteristic of Paul at this point as he gestures with his *hand* in some way to open his defense (compare 13:16; 21:4).

> **What Do You Think?**
> Do Christians need to wait for an authority to give permission to talk about our faith? Why or why not?
>
> **Digging Deeper**
> What attitude(s) might make others curious to hear what you have to say, whether or not you have "permission" to speak?

2. I think myself happy, king Agrippa, because I shall answer for myself this day before thee touching all the things whereof I am accused of the Jews.

Exhibiting deference to a judge is wise, and Paul indicates that he is *happy* to do so. (We note that the word translated "happy" is more often translated "blessed.") His defense will comprehensively address *all the things the Jews* have *accused* him of. Those charges to this point in the narrative are that Paul has (1) been causing divisions among the Jews and (2) desecrated the temple (Acts 24:5-6). More accusations will be mentioned below.

3. Especially because I know thee to be expert in all customs and questions which are among the Jews: wherefore I beseech thee to hear me patiently.

Paul acknowledges Agrippa's familiarity with Jewish matters, as Paul does again in Acts 26:26. Herod's family was outwardly Jewish. They made a point of following aspects of the Law of Moses.

But it was equally obvious they were more interested in being loyal to Rome.

Even so, Paul showed him respect and asked politely to be heard. Paul probably knew that Agrippa's marriage to that man's own sister was not lawful. That sister, Bernice, is mentioned in Acts 25:13, 23; 26:30; therefore, she was present to hear Paul. Years earlier, Herod Antipas had had John the Baptist beheaded, at the instigation of his wife Herodias, because of John's declaration of the immoral nature of their marriage (Matthew 14:1-12). Paul does not travel down this same road!

What Do You Think?

What can be learned from Paul's defense of himself about the importance of being able to give a clear explanation of one's faith?

Digging Deeper

What opportunities do you have to practice communicating your faith with respect and humility?

B. What the Jews Knew (vv. 4-5)

4-5. My manner of life from my youth, which was at the first among mine own nation at Jerusalem, know all the Jews; which knew me from the beginning, if they would testify, that after the most straitest sect of our religion I lived a Pharisee.

Paul's *manner of life* in being brought up as a Jewish boy was beyond reproach. A detailed account of that upbringing is found in Philippians 3:5-6. By mentioning his upbringing in Jerusalem, Paul noted his previous status as an "insider." He had been zealous for his faith (Galatians 1:14). Although born in Tarsus in Cilicia, Paul was "brought up in [Jerusalem] at the feet of Gamaliel, and taught according to the perfect manner of the law of the fathers" (Acts 22:3). Furthermore, Paul described himself as a Pharisee, the son of a Pharisee (23:6).

The word translated *sect* is something of a chameleon, able to "change color" depending on the context. The word in the original language appears nine times in the New Testament, and it may take on a positive, neutral, or negative overtone in its various possible meanings of "faction," "sect," "school," or "heresy." Along these lines, the first-century Jewish historian Josephus mentions five branches of Judaism of his day: Pharisees (right-wing formalists), Sadducees (left-wing aristocrats), Essenes (ultra-right-wing purists), Zealots (militants), and Herodians (supporters of the Herods).

What Do You Think?

What are some examples of hopes and dreams your ancestors passed on to you?

Digging Deeper

How can you pass along your hope and faith to future generations?

C. What the Accusation Was (vv. 6-8)

6-7. And now I stand and am judged for the hope of the promise made of God unto our fathers: Unto which promise our twelve tribes, instantly serving God day and night, hope to come. For which hope's sake, king Agrippa, I am accused of the Jews.

What Paul is referring to in his three uses of the word *hope* in these two verses is found in Acts 23:6-8; 24:15: *The hope of the promise* is the resurrection of the dead. The *fathers* are the patriarchs: Abraham, Isaac, and Jacob. According to Hebrews 11:10, 13, their faith in things far off was an example of faith. Resurrection was viewed as a reward that Jews were seeking, which is why they gave such devoted service to God *day and night* (Hebrews 11:35). Since what Paul is being *accused* of by *the Jews* is part of Jewish belief, there is no wrongdoing—at least from the viewpoint of the Pharisees' doctrine (Acts 23:8). What drew the ire of the Pharisees is Paul's claim that the resurrection of Jesus is the basis of the future resurrection of people (1 Corinthians 15).

8. Why should it be thought a thing incredible with you, that God should raise the dead?

This rhetorical question binds together even tighter the "hope" of the previous two verses with belief in resurrection. Again, the basis of Paul's claim is the fact that the resurrection of Jesus anticipates and guarantees our own (compare Acts 25:19). In this light, Paul could mean, "Since you, King Agrippa, accept that God will *raise the dead,* why is it so strange that God started with Jesus?" Or perhaps Paul is still referring to a belief in the general resurrection. In any case, Paul is seeking common ground with his audience, which is an important strategy when trying to persuade.

What Do You Think?

How does your hope in the resurrection help you face the future with optimism and peace?

Digging Deeper

How could you respond to someone who finds it difficult to believe in the resurrection of the dead?

II. Paul Summarizes His Error

(Acts 26:9-11)

A. Opposed the Name (v. 9)

9. I verily thought with myself, that I ought to do many things contrary to the name of Jesus of Nazareth.

The designation *Jesus of Nazareth* occurs more than a dozen times in the New Testament. Indeed, Jesus identified himself this way to Paul (as Saul) on the road to Damascus (Acts 22:8). People who lived in ancient times did not have last names, so they had to be identified in other ways, particularly if a person's name was common. The name *Jesus* was fairly common, being an adaptation of the Old Testament name Joshua, meaning "save"—thus the need to use other methods to distinguish one person from another who had the same name (compare Matthew 27:56; John 14:22). The designator used for Jesus was a fulfillment of prophecy (Matthew 2:23).

Designators can be used to cast something or someone in a positive or negative light. In the case of Jesus, the designator "of Nazareth" was probably used by opponents in a negative, dismissive sense, given the poor reputation of that town (compare John 1:46; 19:19; Acts 6:14). We might also propose that believers embraced the designator as a term of honor and devotion (3:6; 4:10). There's also the use of this designator by a third category of people: those who think they're on Jesus' side, but are not (Luke 21:8).

We may also see a negative use of the name of the town of Nazareth applied to Christians in general in Acts 24:5. There, Paul's opponents label him as "a ringleader of the sect of the Nazarenes." Believers, however, seemed to have preferred to be known as "Christians" (Acts 11:26) or "this way" (9:2; 19:9, 23; 24:22).

B. Persecuted Christians (vv. 10-11)

10. Which thing I also did in Jerusalem: and many of the saints did I shut up in prison, having received authority from the chief priests; and when they were put to death, I gave my voice against them.

There is a subtle connection between this verse and the one just before it that we should not miss. In the previous verse, Paul spoke of having done "many things contrary to the name of Jesus of Nazareth"; that is what he is referring to when he admits the actions we see in the verse before us. To persecute or neglect Jesus' followers is to persecute or neglect Jesus personally (compare Matthew 25:45; Acts 22:7-8; 26:14-15).

Prior to his experience on the road to Damascus (Acts 9:1-9), Paul (as Saul) was eager to defend the Jewish faith against the supposed threat of Christians (7:60b–8:3). The arrest and crucifixion of Jesus had been an attempt to protect vested interests (see especially John 11:48). Additionally, a pagan attempt to maintain a *status quo* is seen Acts 19:23-41. Human nature seems rather predictable when vested interests are threatened!

Paul's persecution of Christians was so notorious that his infamous reputation had spread at least as far as Damascus (Acts 9:13-14; compare 11:19), a road distance of some 225 miles from Jerusalem. Earlier, Paul had publicly admitted his culpability in the stoning death of Stephen (22:19-20; compare 7:54-60).

The phrase *I gave my voice against them* would seem to imply that Paul (as Saul) possessed voting authority concerning punishments meted out, even though he was "young" (Acts 7:58). On the other hand, this phrase could be a rhetorical device to indicate Paul's sense of responsibility in intending to highlight his role. In either case, the phrase *received authority from the chief priests* lines up with Acts 9:1-2 in leaving no doubt that Paul had been authorized to stamp out this new belief system.

Tact—The Lost Art?

A dictionary definition of the word *tact* is "the ability to do or say things without offending or upsetting other people." This ability seems to be something of a lost art today. This seems particularly true of posts on social media.

Influencing or correcting others is tricky, particularly regarding those who have more power and authority than we do. We want to speak the facts truthfully but do so in a way that gains us a hearing. The axiom "It's not what you say, but how you say it" applies, although the word *just* should be added before the word *what.*

Paul's interaction with King Agrippa illustrates this. Paul waited for permission to speak rather than interrupting. He acknowledged the king's authority and knowledge of Jewish customs. Paul spoke with humility, admitting his own mistakes.

How might you apply this example in your life?

—A. W.

11. And I punished them oft in every synagogue, and compelled them to blaspheme; and being exceedingly mad against them, I persecuted them even unto strange cities.

To his horror, Paul had been harming people who were in the right. He was so threatening that many could not believe his change of heart at first (Acts 9:26). Paul carried the weight of this sin for the rest of his days (1 Corinthians 15:9).

How to Say It

Caesarea Maritima	Sess-uh-*ree*-uh Mar-uh-*tee*-muh.
Gamaliel	Guh-*may*-lih-ul or Guh-*may*-lee-al.
Herodians	Heh-*roe*-dee-unz.

This admission reveals the extent of the Jewish leaders' plan to root out Christians; to be *punished* in synagogues was a continuing fulfillment of what Jesus predicted in Matthew 10:17. For Christians to attend *synagogue* shows they still considered themselves Jewish, even while accepting Jesus as Messiah.

The author does not clarify the meaning of *blaspheme* as used here. But examining the Greek word's approximately 35 uses in the New Testament, we get the idea that it is equivalent to our modern word *slander.* Such speech results in the slandered person being reviled or defamed. Forcing a Christian to deny Christ was undoubtedly one of the goals of the persecution campaign of Paul (as Saul). We note in passing that the phrase *strange cities* refers to foreign cities; compare how the words *strangers* and *foreigners* are used almost as parallel terms in Ephesians 2:19.

We may think that Paul had an odd way of defending himself before King Agrippa! What good did it do to admit to the bloody and oppressive details of his former way of life? But this method of beginning his defense at trial served an important purpose—a purpose Paul had two years to perfect (Acts 24:27). That purpose seems to have been to convince Herod Agrippa that a man who would admit doing such horrible things wouldn't be lying about anything else.

As Agrippa listened to Paul, one cannot help but imagine that the testimony brought up memories of the persecution of Christians conducted by his father, King Herod Agrippa I, about 16 years prior (Acts 12:1-4). The son knew all too well the blood on his father's hands. And now here was someone by the name of Paul admitting to doing much the same thing!

This fact introduced complications. If it had been OK for his father to do such things, was it not permissible for Paul to have done so as well, as long as he didn't violate Roman law (compare John 18:31)? But more importantly, what could have accounted for such a massive change of heart—a change so profound that Paul's men who were once colleagues were now his deadly enemies? Paul hinted at the answer in Acts 26:8 (see comments on which above). He explains the reason in the text that follows the passage of today's lesson: Paul's intent is to vindicate himself and evangelize (Acts 26:28-29).

On Being an Extremist

A radio commentator was heard to remark that politics in the democracy of his country was fought "between the 40-yard lines." By this, he was using imagery from American football to illustrate the point that extremists usually don't win elections and don't have much influence. The area between the 40-yard lines is midfield. It is the area of "the moderates." To engage in the political struggle in this area is to make modest, incremental changes, not drastic ones. The majority of voters usually fear extremists and won't elect them.

Indeed, history witnesses to the failure of many extremists (examples: Acts 5:36-37). Some extremists succeed for a while as they do a great deal of harm; that was Saul before he became Paul. But some extremists do a massive amount of good; that was the renamed and recommissioned Paul.

The currents of history sometimes work against change (Amos 5:13). But sometimes they demand it (1 Chronicles 12:23, 32). When such times come, every Christian must be ready to do his or her part, whether big (as in Esther 4:14) or small (consider Jason in Acts 17:7). How are you preparing for your part? And how will you know that the timing is right in that regard? —R. L. N.

Conclusion

A. Greatest Shame, Greatest Strength

All believers who have turned to God were once God's enemies (Romans 5:10). This means having opposed what God was doing. God desires to make peace, find reconciliation, and move forward in life's newness. Unlike participating on the debate team mentioned earlier, we should seek reconciliation rather than victory. And we don't have to look very hard to find it—it's right there in the Bible. See Romans 5:11; 2 Corinthians 5:18-20; Ephesians 2:14-22; and Colossians 1:19-23. Paul, the onetime deadly enemy of the church, wrote all those texts on reconciliation.

Though Paul was ashamed of his past behavior,

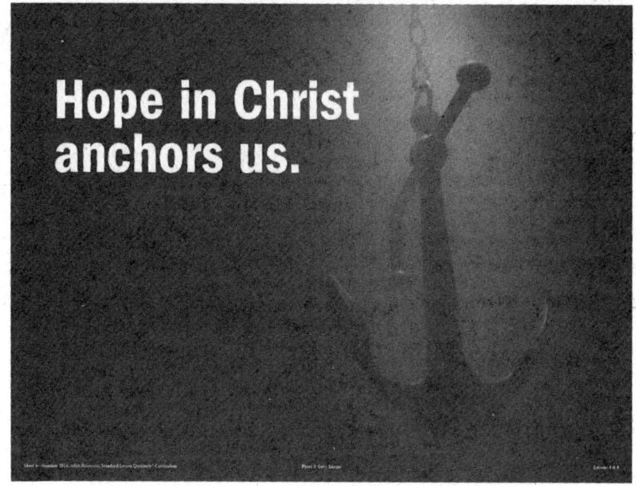

Visual for Lessons 4 & 5. *Ask learners to consider how faith in Christ anchored Paul during his trial and how that same faith anchors us.*

this did not hinder his ministry. One result was a certain set of sad ironies in that ministry. He who had had blindness inflicted upon him (Acts 9:8-9) found it necessary to inflict it on another in turn (13:11). He who beat others (22:19) was in turn beaten (16:22). He who imprisoned others (8:3) was himself imprisoned—more than once (16:23; etc.). He who approved the death of others (8:1) was eventually executed for that same faith.

Through it all, he followed the call of God to bring the gospel to the ends of the earth. In what ways can you follow in Paul's footsteps?

What Do You Think?

When have you acted out of deep conviction only to repent of your deeds later?

Digging Deeper

What did you learn from the experience that helps you avoid a repeat offense?

B. Prayer

Father in Heaven, we were once Your enemies, but You sent Jesus to die for our sins. Make us skillful in communicating Your reconciliation to others. Make us eager to make disciples rather than to win arguments. We pray this in Jesus' name. Amen.

C. Thought to Remember

If God is for us, no one can stand against us!

Involvement Learning

Enhance your lesson with KJV Bible Student *(from your curriculum supplier) and the reproducible activity page (at www.standardlesson.com or in the back of the* KJV Standard Lesson Commentary Deluxe Edition*).*

Into the Lesson

Read the following statements to the group. Ask learners to stand (or raise hands) for each one that is true of them.

1–I have been wrongly accused of a crime.
2–I'm a different person than I was 20 years ago.
3–Specific difficulties have prepared me for life now.
4–One big event changed my life.

Lead a short discussion of what causes a person to consider a certain event as a defining moment. (Caution: learners may have lots of stories to tell; don't let this drag out.)

Lead to the Bible study by saying, "When forced to defend himself, the apostle Paul referred to a singular event that changed the direction of his life. Let's see how and why."

Into the Word

Have two learners alternate in reading aloud the verses of today's text. Then form learners into three small groups of two or three to describe the life and reign of either Festus, Felix, or Agrippa, one official to be studied per group. (Larger classes can form more groups and give duplicate assignments.) Provide Bible-study resources in hard copy and/or links to online tools as necessary.

After several minutes, have a spokesperson from each group present discoveries for whole-class discussion. To enhance clarity, research in advance a time line on each official's time in office. Draw a blank time line on the board, and fill it in from your research as groups present their discoveries.

Next, distribute to the same groups a handout (you prepare) titled *Paul's Life, Paul's Defense.* Have the following questions on the handout:

1–How is Paul's use of the word *sect* in Acts 26:5 similar to and/or different from the way that word is commonly used today?
2–What three words would you pick to describe Paul's life while he was still called Saul, considering also Acts 7:58–8:3; 22:2-5?
3–Why did Paul begin his defense as he did?

Depending on the time available, you can either assign all questions to all groups or assign just one question to each group. Compare and contrast conclusions in the ensuing whole-class discussion.

Option. If you wish to consider the entirety of Paul's defense in Acts 26, distribute copies of the "A Defense and a Testimony" exercise from the activity page, which you can download, to be completed in the same small groups. During or after presentations of conclusions in whole-class discussion, write the following questions on the board:

1–How can a defense be a testimony?
2–Why was Paul's testimony more important to him than his defense?

Jot responses on the board as they are voiced.

Into Life

Give each of your groups one of the following statements. Challenge them to use today's text to help them construct a response to the statement assigned.

1–*Dealing with the past.* "I know you say the church is for those who need to be forgiven, not those who already have their act together. But you don't know all the sordid details about my past."
2–*Trying to testify.* "I try to tell my friends about Jesus, but I feel if they knew some of my secrets, they'd never believe in Him. My failures are keeping me from sharing the gospel."
3–*Intimidated by authority.* "My boss is a good enough man, but he's not a Christian. I feel I can't talk to him about faith in Jesus. It's like he holds my future in his hands, and I can't risk losing my job."

Alternative. Distribute copies of the "My Key Takeaway" exercise from the activity page. Have learners complete it individually in a minute or less. Assure learners in advance that you will not put anyone on the spot to share with the entire class, nor will you collect the completed exercise.

After the minute is up, allow the opportunity for volunteers to share their takeaways.

July 7
Lesson 6 (KJV)

Ceaseless Love

Devotional Reading: Psalm 30
Background Scripture: Lamentations 3:16-24; Psalm 30; Jeremiah 52:1-30

Lamentations 3:16-24

16 He hath also broken my teeth with gravel stones, he hath covered me with ashes.

17 And thou hast removed my soul far off from peace: I forgat prosperity.

18 And I said, My strength and my hope is perished from the LORD:

19 Remembering mine affliction and my misery, the wormwood and the gall.

20 My soul hath them still in remembrance, and is humbled in me.

21 This I recall to my mind, therefore have I hope.

22 It is of the LORD's mercies that we are not consumed, because his compassions fail not.

23 They are new every morning: great is thy faithfulness.

24 The LORD is my portion, saith my soul; therefore will I hope in him.

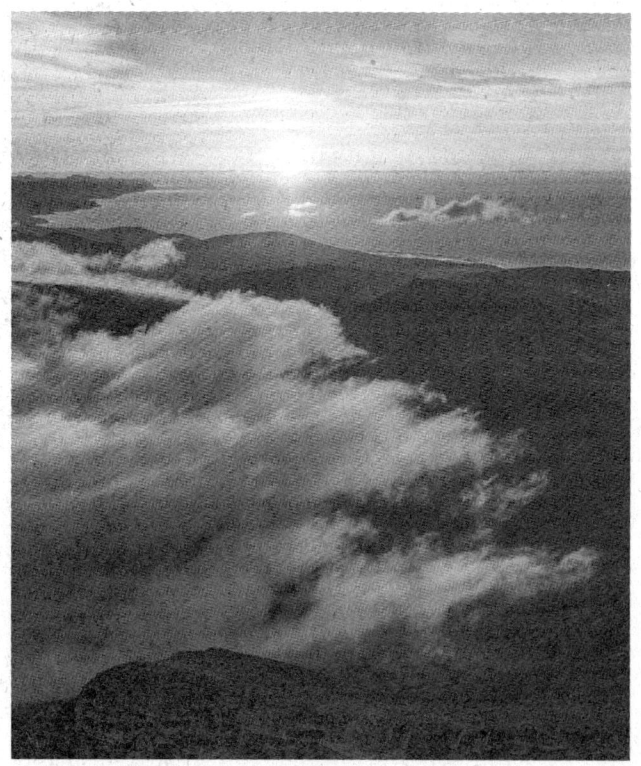

Key Text

This I recall to my mind, therefore have I hope. It is of the LORD's mercies that we are not consumed, because his compassions fail not. **—Lamentations 3:21-22**

Hope in
the Lord

Unit II: Expressing Hope

Lessons 6–9

Lesson Aims

After participating in this lesson, each learner will be able to:

1. Identify by color coding elements of hope (green) as interspersed with elements of despair (yellow).

2. Contrast those oppositional elements in terms of how God sees things.

3. Write a prayer of thanks for God's faithfulness in having led him or her through a time of despair.

Lesson Outline

Introduction

A. The Truth About Trauma

B. Lesson Context

I. Remembering Judgment (Lamentations 3:16-20)

A. Memories of Humiliation (v. 16)

Broken Teeth

B. Memories of Despair (vv. 17-18)

C. Memories of Bitterness (vv. 19-20)

II. Remembering Mercy (Lamentations 3:21-24)

A. Memories of Ceaseless Love (vv. 21-23)

Great Is Thy Faithfulness

B. Memories of Sufficiency (v. 24)

Conclusion

A. Remembering the Whole Truth

B. Prayer

C. Thought to Remember

Introduction

A. The Truth About Trauma

Physician Bessel van der Kolk, a world leader in the study of trauma's impact on the brain, made the following penetrating observation:

> Breakdown of the thalamus explains why trauma is primarily remembered not as a story, a narrative with a beginning, middle, and end, but as isolated sensory imprints: images, sounds, and physical sensations that are accompanied by intense emotions, usually terror and helplessness.

Poetry is the perfect medium for sensory impressions that cannot yet be remembered as a coherent plotline or story. Poems require no plot; rather, they are an artistic means of processing intense emotions. They can mirror the experience of remembering trauma too. These memories so overwhelm our brains with intense sensations and emotions that we cannot quite narrate them. We can only remember them in patches and fragments as images, sounds, and sensations. It is extremely difficult to remember the whole truth about trauma.

The poetry of Lamentations wrestles with the people's trauma and what the whole truth—about the people and about God—really is.

B. Lesson Context

The book of Lamentations commemorates the devastating destruction of Jerusalem that occurred when Nebuchadnezzar, king of Babylon, invaded Judah in 586 BC. A long siege left many dead from starvation, and a significant number of the remaining population was brutalized and taken captive to Babylon. The city itself was leveled after Nebuchadnezzar's forces successfully breached the city. Especially hurtful to the inhabitants of Jerusalem was the utter destruction of the temple, the centerpiece of their city and the symbol of their special relationship with God (Jeremiah 7:4-14; 52:12-23).

The five poems of Lamentations are one person's attempt to sort through his confusion and questions as well as to find a reason for hope. Though traditionally, this person has been identified with the prophet Jeremiah, the book of Lamentations is anonymous. We cannot know with certainty who expressed the community's grief with such vivid images and powerful poetry. What is clear, however, is that the poet was a master of metaphors with an unusual awareness of his people's pain. The poet's experience is representative of the people as a whole. In fact, throughout Lamentations 3, the speaker presents himself as an authoritative figure with an official role as the people's representative with a responsibility to lead them in expressing and processing their pain. This leads eventually to his leading them in a liturgy of repentance, appealing to divine mercy, and seeking restoration to divine favor (Lamentations 3:40-42).

The first four of these five laments are acrostic poems: they use the Hebrew alphabet as their organizational scheme by having the first word of each stanza begin with the successive letter of the alphabet. The third lament, the one in which our text is located, intensifies the acrostic so that the first word of each line of each stanza features the successive letter of the Hebrew alphabet. This technique aided the community's collective memory of the trauma. It was also a means of trying to order the chaotic emotions and make sense of the horrific experience in terms of the people's covenant with God.

While the people of Judah certainly had to express their grief and wrestle with the difficult theological questions raised by their intense suffering, they also had to remember God's character and His long track record of faithfulness and love if they were to avoid succumbing to despair. This latter task dominates the poet's concerns in Lamentations 3:16-24. These verses are a climax for the collection of poems that make up the book of Lamentations.

I. Remembering Judgment

(Lamentations 3:16-20)

A. Memories of Humiliation (v. 16)

16a. He hath also broken my teeth with gravel stones.

Our text begins amid an extended reflection on how God has behaved like one of Judah's vicious enemies, seemingly seeking the people's annihilation (Lamentations 3:3-15, not in our printed text). The imagery is of extreme humiliation. Breaking

God's compassions are
new every morning.

Visual for Lesson 6. *Ask learners to consider what in their faith journeys gives them the confidence to say this no matter what the days bring.*

teeth with *gravel* conveys the experience of being thrown to the ground with such force that the rock-covered ground knocked the victim's *teeth* out.

The poet's physical posture of lying injured on the ground points to the more profound and lasting reality of being brought low spiritually. Ironically, David twice requested that God break the teeth of his wicked enemies (Psalms 3:7; 58:6). Though this fate may have once been reserved for David's and Judah's enemies, it now enters Judah's own experience as David's descendants and the nation they governed became enemies of God through their persistent rebellion.

Broken Teeth

When I was in junior high, my youth group hosted a lock-in. Someone had the *bright* idea of playing hide-and-seek in the basement—in the pitch dark. I was "it," and as I was blindly searching, a girl ran straight into me. The top of her head collided with my teeth. She got eight stitches, and I got frequent dentist appointments. Eating was painful, temporarily robbing meals of joy. Today my front two teeth are made of porcelain and gold.

My experience gives me some physical insight into the pain described here, if not the utter humiliation. The people's misery was not just broken or missing teeth, but also the loss of joy and nearly of hope as well. God had once granted them many good things to eat (Exodus 3:8), but now their teeth—and spirits—were broken. As you continue with this lesson, consider the juxtaposition of *this* pain with the faithful declarations to come (see Lamentations 3:21-24, below). —C. S.

16b. He hath covered me with ashes.

The humiliating experience is exacerbated by the poet's sense that God has personally forced him down into the dust. *Covered me with ashes* does not convey the full violence of this image. The Hebrew indicates the act of forcing someone down and keeping him down, perhaps by pressing one's foot down on his back. A contemporary way of putting it might be, "He made me eat dirt."

The poet attributes this action directly to God, though no doubt it was the Babylonian invaders who treated the poet and his fellow Judeans harshly. In one sense, this is due to our human tendency to project onto God the cruelty we experience at the hands of human beings. While this is an understandable reaction insofar as God was using the Babylonians as agents of His judgment (Jeremiah 25:8-11), it also indicates how traumatic experiences and suffering tend to cloud and confuse our perception of God. We, like the poet, believe that God is in control and might erroneously attribute the evil actions of others to God's own hand (compare Job 1:12, 22; 2:6, 10; 42:1-6).

B. Memories of Despair (vv. 17-18)

17. And thou hast removed my soul far off from peace: I forgat prosperity.

Here the poet reflects on the significant losses he and his community sustained in the wake of their tragedy. Chief among them was any sense of well-being or hope for future prosperity. The poet uses the familiar Hebrew word *shalom* (translated *peace*), known to most English speakers as the common greeting in Israel to this very day. The word conveys a broad sense of holistic well-being, of both material security and deep spiritual contentment. Not only had all sense of this security and contentment fled the poet's experience, but he could not even remember what *prosperity* was.

While this could be an example of poetic hyperbole or exaggeration for effect, it also underscores a well-documented effect of trauma. The tragedy of Jerusalem's destruction significantly altered how the poet and his community viewed their past. Their present pain threatened to eclipse all memory of past prosperity and permanently cast a dark shadow over the entire story of their emergence as a people and of their relationship with God.

18. And I said, My strength and my hope is perished from the LORD.

It is not clear to whom the poet *said* this. Did he speak to himself, share with fellow sufferers, or address it to God in prayer (see Lamentations 3:23b, below)? Whatever the case, it captured the utter despair that inevitably followed the poet's loss of any sense of well-being, contentment, or even the ability to recall pleasant memories from Judah's past.

In strikingly absolute terms, the poet dismisses any possibility of a future return to *strength* or reason for *hope.* Whereas the previous verse emphasized the impact the poet's trauma had on his recollection of the past, the present verse emphasizes the effect his trauma had on his vision for the future. In the immediate aftermath of Jerusalem's destruction and all the pain and suffering that came with it, the poet saw no way forward, no path by which he could imagine God advancing His plans for His people.

C. Memories of Bitterness (vv. 19-20)

19. Remembering mine affliction and my misery, the wormwood and the gall.

The poet captures a nauseating sense that all of life has turned sour and lost all of its taste and delight with the use of two vivid words: *wormwood* and *gall.* These two extremely bitter-tasting plants were often used in medicinal elixirs and teas, as referenced in the Mishna (an important Hebrew extrabiblical text); the plants were notoriously hard to swallow without gagging or vomiting.

But in Scripture, these plants are rarely associated with healing and are viewed negatively as having no redeeming value. They are considered toxic (compare Deuteronomy 29:18; Proverbs 5:4; Lamentations 3:15; Revelation 8:11). The one possible exception is the occasion when gall was offered to Jesus on the cross, presumably as an anesthetic (Matthew 27:34), though His rejection of it does not speak highly of the substance.

> **What Do You Think?**
> What situation have you experienced that gives you empathy for the writer's despair?
> **Digging Deeper**
> How can empathy be a ministry aid?

20. My soul hath them still in remembrance, and is humbled in me.

The poet reflects on the overall effect this all-consuming memory from Lamentations 3:3-19 had on the poet. (See lesson 9 regarding the *soul* in Hebrew thought.) The vivid memories served only to darken the poet's outlook further and depress him. Indeed, they were hardly memories at all, but more like flashbacks, as though the poet relived the experience each time he recalled it.

> **What Do You Think?**
> How do the feelings of despair described in this passage relate to your own experiences?
> **Digging Deeper**
> What can you learn from the author's example about how to express pain and frustration to God?

II. Remembering Mercy

(Lamentations 3:21-24)

A. Memories of Ceaseless Love (vv. 21-23)

21. This I recall to my mind, therefore have I hope.

As if recognizing the danger of continuing down the dark path of bitterness, the poet suddenly turns his thoughts in a very different direction. He draws from the rich tradition of prayer and praise that he undoubtedly knows from his own education beginning in his boyhood. His recollection interrupts the downward spiral of despair with memories that are deeply ingrained through years of study and more profoundly formative than the traumatic memories of recent suffering (see commentary on Lamentations 3:22a, below). The poet can call to *mind* convictions powerful enough to challenge and hold in check the despondency threatening to dominate his thoughts and determine his outlook. His *hope* is revived as he begins to view his situation from the perspective of revelation and tradition rather than personal experience.

> **What Do You Think?**
> What are some biblical examples of God's love you can recall to bolster your hope?
> **Digging Deeper**
> What are some personal examples?

22a. It is of the LORD's mercies that we are not consumed.

The poet confessed the truth of divine mercy with language reminiscent of the book of Psalms, Israel's hymnal and prayerbook. The phrase *the Lord's mercies* recalls, among others, Psalms 89:2 and 107:43 (where *mercies* is translated as "lovingkindnesses") and refers to God's long track record of forgiveness and grace that had preserved Israel by withholding the full penalty of the people's sin (compare Ezra 9:13; Psalm 103:10). This sentiment seemed to inspire the poet to turn his attention to this traditional recitation of the long list of God's merciful actions and faithful interventions on his people's behalf and to remind his fellow sufferers of this. With this in mind, the poet can see that his survival and the survival of his fellow sufferers is no accident of history but is instead evidence of God's enduring love.

The poet caught himself in a common theological error—the error of pitting God's love against God's wrath as if the two were mutually exclusive. However, divine wrath is a function of divine love. God's anger over Judah's persistent sin was his love taking disciplinary form. His purpose was not to destroy Judah, nor was it to forsake her and give up on his covenant. Rather, the judgment was a kind of radical surgery performed to save the patient.

22b. Because his compassions fail not.

The poet uses the plural form *compassions* to hint at numerous, discrete divine actions motivated by God's amazing tenderness for Judah. The word the poet uses for divine compassion is related to the Hebrew word for "womb" and has strong connotations of warmth, intimacy, and maternal tenderness. This is a striking and unexpected choice of words on the heels of such vivid descriptions of the carnage and destruction that the poet and his community recently endured, seemingly at God's hand (see Lamentations 3:16, above)!

23a. They are new every morning.

The significance of the poet's use of the plural "compassions" (verse 22b) again takes center stage here with the assertion that God's compassions *are new every morning* (compare Psalm 92:2). In other words, a new expression of divine compassion greeted the poet daily. The poet's previous experiences of the manifold nature of divine mercy assured him that he and his community would somehow experience yet another new depth of divine mercy. God's mercy would be equal to the task of healing the deep wounds of Jerusalem's destruction.

23b. Great is thy faithfulness.

This is the only one of the poet's statements expressed directly to God as a prayer. In the rest of the text, the poet either addressed himself in an attempt to keep his own faith afloat (example: verse 21, above), or he addressed his community in an attempt to rally them to persevere in faith with him (example: verse 22a, above). This is an interesting shift in the poet's rhetoric, considering that elsewhere he seemed to view prayer as an impossibility (see Lamentations 3:8, 44). Nonetheless, between those two statements asserting God's unwillingness to hear, the poet prays quite confidently, if briefly. While this may strike readers as odd and perhaps even contradictory, it makes sense considering the circumstances under which the poet wrote these words. In this time of crisis, his faith waxed and waned, ebbed and flowed as it does for us in our moments of intense trial.

The fact that the poet prayed these words rather than addressing them to himself or others raises the possibility that he was looking for reassurance from God that His *faithfulness* really is *great*. Perhaps the statement was half assertion and half question: "Great is thy faithfulness! Right?" Either way, the poet was determined to hold on to this hope.

How to Say It

Mishna *(Hebrew)*	*Mish*-nuh.
Nebuchadnezzar	*Neb*-yuh-kud-**nez**-er.
shalom *(Hebrew)*	shah-*lome*.

Great Is Thy Faithfulness

One of my oldest friends is a Haitian national. His favorite hymn, "Great Is Thy Faithfulness," is based on Lamentations 3:23. But looking at Haiti, one might question God's faithfulness. It is the poorest country in the Western Hemisphere and has suffered through severe earthquakes and hurricanes in recent years. Voodoo practice keeps many shackled to false gods and dangerous religious practices. The government has yet to find an effective way to govern, especially regarding armed gangs.

But if you could spend some time with my friend, you might begin to understand why he loves this hymn. He would tell you of the great victories and unexpected blessings and provisions that cross into the realm of the miraculous. There is much to lament, but in the middle of it all, my friend sees that God has not abandoned Haiti. He is faithful to the work He is doing there. Whatever your lament today, remember—great is *His* faithfulness. —C. S.

B. Memories of Sufficiency (v. 24)

24a. The Lord is my portion, saith my soul.

The poet drew once again from Israel's prayerbook as he desperately sought resources to support his faith through this trial, this time from Psalm 16:5. The word *portion* refers to the land plots distributed to the various tribes of Israel according to Moses' instructions (Joshua 18–19). This is significant considering that the original land distribution had been disrupted by the exiles of first Israel and then Judah due to their sin (2 Kings 17:7-23; 25:1-21). With the land under the control of the foreign power by which God judged His people (Habakkuk 1:6), these original land grants were effectively rendered meaningless. Aware that Judah had now forfeited the physical manifestation of God's fidelity to His promise due to sin, the poet made perhaps one of the boldest and most beautiful assertions of faith in all of Lamentations.

As great a loss as the seizure of the land by foreigners was, it was survivable if the poet and his people could only maintain their relationship with God. The assertion was a surprising generalization of a principle originally modeled only by Levites. Of all the tribes of Israel, they alone received no portion of land as did the other tribes. God's explanation for this was that He was Levi's portion. The special privilege this tribe had of maintaining the sanctuary made it a model for all of Israel of dependence on God's all-sufficiency. The Levites lived lives of deprivation and dependence, relying on Israel's sacrifices and tithes for their livelihood (Numbers 18:20-24).

24b. Therefore will I hope in him.

The poet concluded these reflections with a simple statement of his determination to fix all of his hopes on God. Given all that he remembered of God's past faithfulness, both from his personal experience and from the collective memory of previous generations carefully preserved in Scripture, liturgy, and tradition, the poet can find reasons to *hope*. His was a hope that all the evil in the world could not ultimately sink. After the tears had been shed and the grief, anger, bitterness, and doubt expressed, hope remained.

What Do You Think?

What does it mean to wait on the Lord? Provide biblical examples.

Digging Deeper

How might your faith grow as a result of waiting on God? What personal or biblical examples can you provide?

Conclusion

A. Remembering the Whole Truth

Lamentations 3:16-24 can be thought of as an exercise in remembering the whole truth. The text does not shy away from the ugly reality of the community's suffering. Honest and vivid expression is given to the pain, disillusionment, and bitterness experienced by the poet and his people.

This, however, is not the whole truth. Experience is important and sheds valuable light on reality, but it is not the only or final word. The poet balanced his experience with revelation Scriptures, prayers, and traditions he had learned since his youth. Though the tension created by their juxtaposition at times seems greater than our hearts can bear, the internal dialogue between our lived experience and the Spirit's testimony in Scripture is essential to our arriving at the whole truth and to the survival of our hope.

When enduring great trials and suffering, we cannot isolate ourselves in an echo chamber of despair. Never is it more crucial to participate in the worshipping community than when we are wrestling with intense doubts regarding God's goodness and love. Many people of faith have survived harrowing experiences only to rebound from them with greater assurance of God's love. We must not ignore their testimony. All of these form a great cloud of witnesses testifying that faith in God's ceaseless love need not wither and die in the face of the world's horrors. The secret to their resilient faith was that they trained their memories to recall not only the pain of their experience but also the many pieces of evidence of God's enduring love, both in their own lives and in the lives of believers who preceded them.

What Do You Think?

How can remembering God's faithfulness change how you respond in heartbreaking circumstances?

Digging Deeper

What would it take for you to surrender the illusion of control over the future?

B. Prayer

Our Father, we thank You for the testimonies of the cloud of witnesses who remind us of Your enduring love even in our darkest moments. May Your Spirit awaken in us memories of Your faithfulness and love to balance the memories of our heartbreak and pain. In Jesus' name we pray. Amen.

C. Thought to Remember

Have hope in God's compassions and faithfulness.

Involvement Learning

Enhance your lesson with KJV Bible Student *(from your curriculum supplier) and the reproducible activity page (at www.standardlesson.com or in the back of the* KJV Standard Lesson Commentary Deluxe Edition*).*

Into the Lesson

Ask learners to brainstorm events that they now recognize as creating a "before" time and an "after" time. As a class, choose one event to discuss further. Write *Before* and *After* as headers on your board. Then brainstorm words and phrases to describe what before was like and what after was like. Then discuss to what degree life felt like it normalized sometime in the after, and if so, what repercussions they still sense from the chosen event.

Transition to the Bible study by saying, "The writer of Lamentations had experienced a horrific split between before and after. Our study today contains poetry written as he grappled with what these events meant for his faith in God."

Into the Word

Prepare a short presentation on the historical background of Lamentations, especially concerning Babylon's siege, the destruction of Jerusalem and the temple, and the exile that followed; use the Lesson Context. Then read Lamentations 3:16-24 out loud.

Alternative. Distribute copies of the "Hope and Despair" exercise from the activity page, which you can download. Have learners complete as indicated.

Focus the class on Lamentations 3:16-24 to answer the following questions; encourage them to provide Bible verses to support their answers when possible: 1–What evidence can you give that the writer was *correct* in saying that God did these things to him? (Expected answers might include God's judgment on sins or His use of the Babylonians as instruments of judgment.) 2–What counterevidence can you provide that the writer was *incorrect* in saying that God did these things? (Expected answers might include God's characteristics as the writer knew them [see vv. 21-24] or God's acknowledgment that Babylon deserved judgment for their cruelty.)

Lead into the next activity by rereading Lamentations 3:21-24 and asking the following question: 3–How did the writer turn his despairing thoughts in a hopeful direction?

Divide the class into groups as follows: the **Ezra Group**; the **Nehemiah Group**; and the **Minor Prophets Group** (including Joel, Obadiah, Haggai, Zechariah, and Malachi). Then ask the groups to choose one or two key events or attitudes from their assigned text(s) that address the hope found in Lamentations 3:21-24. For instance, they might note how the Lord demonstrated His mercies or faithfulness or how the people demonstrated that they would wait for the Lord. After calling time, allow groups to share their key insights. Then consider together how the writer of Lamentations might have felt if he had known what the future held for Judah.

Divide each previous group in half. One half of each group will be the **Luke Group**, while the other half will be the **Acts Group**. The two groups will repeat the above activity, focusing on key events recorded in Luke or Acts as assigned. Once again, gather as a whole class to share the groups' key insights and to consider how the writer might have felt about all that happened from Jesus' birth through the early church.

Into Life

Distribute note cards to learners and invite each person to take one minute to write down a time when God led him or her through despair. Have learners write down a prayer of thanks for God's faithfulness in that time.

Alternative. Distribute copies of the "This I Recall" exercise from the activity page. Give learners a minute or less to complete as indicated before discussing with a partner.

Close class with a prayer, thanking God that we can lament to Him and still be confident in His love and promises.

Continual Proclamation

Devotional Reading: Ephesians 3:1-13
Background Scripture: Psalm 71:12-21

Psalm 71:12-21

12 O God, be not far from me: O my God, make haste for my help.

13 Let them be confounded and consumed that are adversaries to my soul; let them be covered with reproach and dishonour that seek my hurt.

14 But I will hope continually, and will yet praise thee more and more.

15 My mouth shall shew forth thy righteousness and thy salvation all the day; for I know not the numbers thereof.

16 I will go in the strength of the Lord GOD: I will make mention of thy righteousness, even of thine only.

17 O God, thou hast taught me from my youth: and hitherto have I declared thy wondrous works.

18 Now also when I am old and grayheaded, O God, forsake me not; until I have shewed thy strength unto this generation, And thy power to every one that is to come.

19 Thy righteousness also, O God, is very high, who hast done great things: O God, who is like unto thee!

20 Thou, which hast shewed me great and sore troubles, shalt quicken me again, And shalt bring me up again from the depths of the earth.

21 Thou shalt increase my greatness, and comfort me on every side.

Key Text

I will hope continually, And will yet praise thee more and more. —**Psalm 71:14**

Hope in
the Lord

Unit II: Expressing Hope

Lessons 6–9

Lesson Aims

After participating in this lesson, each learner will be able to:

1. Summarize what the biblical writer does to maintain hope.

2. Contrast the biblical basis for hope with secular ones.

3. Role-play a debate regarding conclusions from Lesson Aim 2.

Lesson Outline

Introduction
- A. Experiencing Hope
- B. Lesson Context

I. God of Help (Psalm 71:12-16)
- A. Request for Presence (vv. 12-13)
- B. Worshipper's Commitment (vv. 14-16)

II. Lifelong Learning (Psalm 71:17-21)
- A. From Youth to Old Age (vv. 17-18)
  Not Forsaken
- B. Of God's Incomparability (vv. 19-21)
  Inspiration to Worship

Conclusion
- A. God the Teacher
- B. Prayer
- C. Thought to Remember

Introduction

A. Experiencing Hope

The German theologian Jürgen Moltmann once remarked, "Hell is hopelessness." He was 16 when he was drafted into the German Air Force during World War II. Upon his surrender, Moltmann spent time as a prisoner of war, during which he learned of the atrocities his country perpetrated in concentration camps. Into this hell of hopelessness—his country in shambles and guilty of unspeakable crimes, the unfathomable suffering inflicted on millions of families, the guilt and shame of having had any part to play in evil—stepped a chaplain. This man was the first to share the gospel with Moltmann. That Moltmann went on to write a book entitled *Theology of Hope* speaks to the fundamental change he experienced when Jesus found him.

Some of us also have experienced times when hope seemed out of reach. To believe oneself to have no possibility for redemption, forgiveness, or mercy is the worst state of life. Fortunately, Psalm 71 (and the rest of the Bible) affirms that a hopeless life is not inevitable for any human being. This psalm lays out the perspective of someone who has not yet reached a perfect world but believes in its possibility—because of God's continued efforts.

B. Lesson Context

Psalm 71 is part of a long string of prayers (going back at least to Psalm 50) that express the hope that God will help those who trust in Him. This section of Psalms addresses the suffering of either individuals or Israel as a people in lament after lament. These psalms call God's attention to the human need for a continuing relationship of rescue. And the psalms remind the people of Israel of their constant need for self-examination, repentance, and hopeful action. Psalm 71 is the last in this series of laments; Psalm 72 brings Book II of the Psalms (Psalms 42–72) to a hopeful conclusion.

Because this psalm is not attributed to a specific person, we can refer to him (or her) as "the psalmist." Psalm 71 is a psalm of individual lament, in which a single person addresses God while seeking help during a time of danger or catastrophe (compare Psalms 3, 22, 43, etc.). Even though the psalm does not explicitly name an audience, the psalmist likely had in view a public performance of the psalm (perhaps set to music) along with other texts like it. The audience would be the assembly of Israel gathered in the temple, especially during the great feasts noted in Exodus 23:14-19.

While this poem is a lament, we can also speak of it as a prayer. Psalm 71 interweaves requests for help with statements about the problems faced and expressions of trust in God. The psalmist expresses trust in God's righteousness (v. 2) and reliability throughout life (vv. 5-6). Verses 10-11 (not in our printed text) describe the insults of the psalmist's critics and enemies. They slandered not only the psalmist but also God, whom they accused of abandoning the faithful (compare Psalm 22:7-8). The psalmist's real experiences are revealed in general terms, without naming names, so we are invited to consider our own experiences as we consider the psalmist's troubles and how he responded in faith.

I. God of Help

(Psalm 71:12-16)

A. Request for Presence (vv. 12-13)

12. O God, be not far from me: O my God, make haste for my help.

On the heels of these insults, verse 12 responds to the enemies not by returning their insults but by asking for God's presence (compare Psalm 22:19). The psalmist asserted the enemies' accusations were baseless and false, and that God would prove their error and vindicate their victim.

The verse's two requests are closely related. First, God's nearness allows Him to save the psalmist. Making *haste* emphasizes God's nearness and His desire to respond to the prayerful request for *help*. Requests like these also occur in other psalms of lament or petition (Psalms 38:22; 40:13; 70:1, 5; etc.).

This standard appeal for God's merciful presence depends on two prior ideas. First, God has shown himself to be a helper as defined by His being the one who provides needed aid unobtainable from anyone else (examples: Deuteronomy 33:7, 26, 29; Psalms 115:9-11; 121:1-2). Second, humans often experience the need for God's aid as urgent, not as a pleasant future desire but as a present need. God's relative speed in responding to such pleas is less about a timeline than about attentiveness and care. The psalmist assumed that God wants to help in ways that bring hope—not from afar and not with needless delay.

What Do You Think?

How do you react when you do not sense God nearby?

Digging Deeper

In such times, what habits and relationships help you to wait on the Lord?

13. Let them be confounded and consumed that are adversaries to my soul; let them be covered with reproach and dishonour that seek my hurt.

Verses 10-11 (not in our printed text) identify the psalmist's *adversaries* as the source of mistreatment. Whether the psalmist had any power in the relationship with these enemies, the psalm itself suggests a lack of power. As such, God is the one who shifts the power from the evildoers to the psalmist who has been mistreated (compare Romans 12:19-21). This change of fortune is entirely in God's hands.

The verse at hand turns back to those people (or the attitudes they represent) and asks God to change *them* in two ways: by altering their minds (confounding them) so that they can no longer sustain their attacks and by exposing their sins to public scrutiny (*reproach and dishonour*). This second request would lead to everyone else recognizing the injustice and cruelty of the enemies' words and deeds. The language of shame does not refer only to individuals' internal feelings but to their status in society. Part of the pursuit of justice in the Old Testament involved ensuring that society does not reward evil behavior (example: Isaiah 32:5-8).

How to Say It

Jürgen Moltmann	*Yahr*-gehn *Molt*-mawn.
psalmist	*sawlm*-ist.

The prayers of the faithful do not personalize attacks on evil people, but they do ask for God's help in real-life interpersonal struggles. This verse asks God to somehow turn the enemies' wishes for the psalmist back on them. It does not ask for their physical harm but seeks their exposure as evildoers.

What Do You Think?

Should Christians pray for their enemies' demise? Why or why not? Give New Testament verses to support your answer.

Digging Deeper

How can growing in God's wisdom help you reconcile different biblical approaches to conflict?

B. Worshipper's Commitment (vv. 14-16)

14a. But I will hope continually.

But marks a shift from the request for God's vindication to what the psalmist promises to God. Verses 14-16 work together as a vow of *praise*, in direct contrast to the enemies' insults. The faithful person commits to a life of celebrating God's gracious deeds. That commitment implies a willingness to look for evidence of grace and reasons for *hope* in all aspects of life. This expresses the poet's desire for steady confidence in God's promises. The statement is also a commitment to God and a bid for favor. The faithful person's desire is always to live in hopefulness, even when events and feelings challenge that attitude.

14b. And will yet praise thee more and more.

This second clause of verse 14 is difficult to translate. A more literal translation (and more difficult reading) would be, "I will continue your praise in all." But all of what? "All situations" or "before all people" would be reasonable completions of the translation. Regardless, the psalmist commits to learning the art of praising God with *more and more* skill.

Humans do not praise God for His sake, since God neither requires flattery (Psalm 50:12-15) nor needs to be informed about our lives (139:1-6). We *praise* God as an act of truth-telling and orientation to reality. This praise happens primarily in a community of like-minded people who encourage each other to see the joyful world God seeks to create for humanity. The commitment is to a lifetime of praise, whether in the midst of trouble or peace (compare Acts 16:22-25).

15a. My mouth shall shew forth thy righteousness and thy salvation all the day.

Verse 15 builds on the ideas of verse 14 by clarifying the content of praise. God's *righteousness* and actions to save all become the subject of these praises. The psalmist could enumerate evidence of God's justice and compassion in specific terms. But we can imagine that the psalmist needed a manageable psalm at the end of the day and so did not go into every detail of God's saving work. Therefore, it becomes necessary to speak *all the day* long (compare 1 Thessalonians 5:16-17).

15b. For I know not the numbers thereof.

The Hebrew word used here for *numbers* occurs only here in the Old Testament, though related words from the same Hebrew root are common. The main idea is clear: God's deeds are so numerous that humans should spend time enumerating them while also realizing our inability to finish the list (compare Job 5:9; Psalm 40:5).

16. I will go into the strength of the Lord God: I will make mention of thy righteousness, even of thine only.

Go here means to go to the temple for worship, as it also does in verse 3. The psalmist joins the community of the faithful at prayer in the place where Israel could gather for prayer (compare Psalms 5:7; 42:2; 66:13; 95:6). The one praying does not enter timidly, fearful of God's rejection or indifference, but confidently drawing on God's *strength* (compare Hebrews 4:16).

While in the presence of God in the worshipping community, the psalmist will carry out the commitment made in the previous two verses to mention God's fundamental commitment to fair and loyal treatment for all. Since God's *righteousness* will be the subject of each individual's prayer, the whole community of faith will praise God's pursuit of justice (a concept closely linked with righteousness; compare Psalms 7:11; 9:4; etc.) and join in it themselves.

Even of thine only qualifies the statement in a meaningful way. Prayer is not an occasion for human boasting. Admittedly it often becomes that when we thank God for carrying out the plans we had already agreed upon. Proper prayer, however, focuses on the unexpected signs of God's mercy and questions our tendency to baptize our actions as though they were God's.

What Do You Think?

Why should people praise God?

Digging Deeper

How much do "the right reasons" matter when praising God? Explain your answer.

II. Lifelong Learning

(Psalm 71:17-21)

A. From Youth to Old Age (vv. 17-18)

17a. O God, thou hast taught me from my youth.

A shift begins with a new address to *God*, paralleling the one that began in the previous section in verse 12 (above). Furthermore, this verse begins a new section in the psalm, shifting the imagery from prayer to learning. Verses 17-19 explore the extent and content of the process of spiritual education that the psalmist experiences.

Once again, the prayer turns to God, this time as the teacher. The learning process begins early (see Ecclesiastes 12:1-11) and operates through the many dimensions of life. Some learning may occur in school, but that environment is only part of the whole. Learning occurs everywhere, just as long as the person pays attention to life's experiences and receives proper guidance from wise teachers. Thus, the elderly psalmist reflects on a life of learning from the days of his youth.

17b. And hitherto have I declared thy wondrous works.

Here the psalmist states the core curriculum in God's school: the *wondrous works* of creation and salvation. The (one) Hebrew word translated *wondrous works* can refer to the liberating plagues in Egypt (Exodus 3:20; Micah 7:15; etc.), relief in an invasion (Jeremiah 21:2; etc.), or repeated acts of deliverance (Psalms 9:1-6; 75; etc.). The marvels also include the sustenance of the creation itself (Job 5:9-10; 37:6-13; etc.).

The psalmist did not advocate mouthing empty phrases but instead expressed a deep respect for the many ways in which God works in the world. The wonders in question are diverse and deep, and we must think carefully about what each of them implies about humanity's place in God's creation. That process of thinking is precisely what the psalmist celebrates. God has gradually taught the lessons of life to an attentive pupil, but those lessons never end.

18. Now also when I am old and grayheaded, O God, forsake me not; until I have shewed thy strength unto this generation, and thy power to every one that is to come.

The psalmist's education began in youth and continues in *old* age. The psalmist seeking wisdom asks God never to *forsake* the role of teacher, not because the writer believes God might do so, but because it is valuable to express the human desire for God's presence during all phases of life.

The psalmist aims to learn and become wise in part so that he can teach the next *generation* as well. The psalmist takes responsibility for the learning he has acquired, seeing it as a sacred trust rather than just a chance for self-promotion or even self-satisfaction.

How will the psalmist show God's *strength*? Surely the very words that the psalmist utters perform that task. So, the last part of this verse refers to itself, or rather to the poem as a whole. By speaking as it does, this psalm carries out the task of teaching about God's work by celebrating its depth, breadth, and impact on each individual who learns of it.

Not Forsaken

One of my earliest memories is singing songs in Sunday school. And one of my favorite songs was "Jesus Loves the Little Children." This song planted the seed that grew into a life-changing conviction: that our God *does* love all the world. This knowledge became one of my first inspirations to pursue full-time mission work and later become a missions professor.

Today, my hair is turning gray. My life lacks the

color and adventure it had when I was younger. Sometimes I look back over the colorful years and wonder whether any of those efforts made a difference. But when I speak to my Russian neighbors, send messages of encouragement to our friends in Ukraine, or just say hello to a stranger speaking in a tongue I don't understand, I feel grateful. If God has not changed the whole world through me, at least He has changed me. —A. W.

B. Of God's Incomparability (vv. 19-21)

19. Thy righteousness also, O God, is very high, who hast done great things: O God, who is like unto thee!

Some people could be said to have done *great things*, but by questionable means. God's *righteousness* permeates all His actions; every incredible act of creation or recreation, of love or mercy or justice, is done perfectly by the Lord. Unlike human beings, *God* does not waste time on trivialities but works for the good in all things. God's righteousness becomes tangible in ways that humans can identify and understand. For this reason, the poem speaks of God's incomparability (compare Exodus 15:11; 1 Kings 8:23; Micah 7:18). No one else in Heaven or on earth can bring about the good outcomes righteous people experience every day.

What Do You Think?

What characteristics of God most remind you that He is unlike any other being?

Digging Deeper

Why is it important to balance our knowledge of God with the understanding that He is ultimately incomprehensible to His creatures?

20. Thou, which hast shewed me great and sore troubles, shalt quicken me again, and shalt bring me up again from the depths of the earth.

This verse amplifies the role of God as the teacher. God has allowed the faithful person to experience *troubles*, since much learning can occur under difficult circumstances (see 1 Peter 1:7). But God can also bring a person back to life, in this case figuratively (Deuteronomy 32:39; 1 Thessalonians 4:15-18). The psalmist acknowledges such an experience. A person's trials may seem to resemble death itself, but God can revive even the dead (compare 1 Kings 17:17-22). For a similar idea, see the song Jonah sang while in the belly of the great fish (Jonah 2:3-10).

The depths of the earth can refer to a space that God has created (Genesis 1:2) or overcome through creation (Psalms 33:7; 77:16; Isaiah 51:10). It can also be a metaphor for extreme suffering and death (Jonah 2:6; see lesson 9) as well as for the magnitude of God's mercy (Psalm 36:6). Suffering cannot have the last word because God has the power to *quicken* a person *again* and *bring* that person out of whatever depth he or she experiences.

Inspiration to Worship

Humans have long looked to the creation and been inspired to worship (examples: Psalms 8:3-9; 33:6-9; Romans 1:20). We serve a God who has created galaxies of stupendous size and distance. But we can be equally inspired by our own bodies. Ninety-nine percent of the human body comprises just six common elements: oxygen, hydrogen, nitrogen, carbon, calcium, and phosphorus. And over a lifetime, many of our cells will be replaced over and over again—yet we still remain ourselves.

On our path through life, we can be encouraged that we have a God who reaches to the furthest expanses of the universe yet is mindful of us, small as we are and insignificant as we feel. When life is difficult, bombards us with problems, and even hits us with terrible calamities that we may feel we can never survive, God is here to help us through it. In fact, when we face the ultimate calamity, the destruction of our bodies in the grave, even then, God can revive us again from the very depths of the earth.

God is indeed a great God. So, worship!

—A. W.

21a. Thou shalt increase my greatness.

The psalmist expects God to increase the praying person's *greatness* rather than allow him or her to suffer social isolation and disgrace. This is not the request of a boastful or already successful person for even more power. Rather, this is the hope of an oppressed, downtrodden person to receive the honor due to all human beings who trust in God. This hope is rooted in God's character. The prayer asks God to reverse the painful situation that the psalmist experienced because of the slanders of the enemies (see Psalm 71:9-11, not in our printed text).

21b. And comfort me on every side.

The psalmist will find peace of mind at last. This request provides a fitting ending for the reading. Verse 21 is the beginning of the psalm's final turn (see Psalm 71:22-24). As in most other psalms of individual lament, Psalm 71 concludes by praising God. The terrible present, with its rivalries among human beings and its moral struggles, gives way at the end to a world of healthy, ordered social relationships and deep spiritual engagement. Fittingly, this prayer and others like it conclude by either praising God or promising to praise God (71:22-24, not in our printed text; compare 22:19-31).

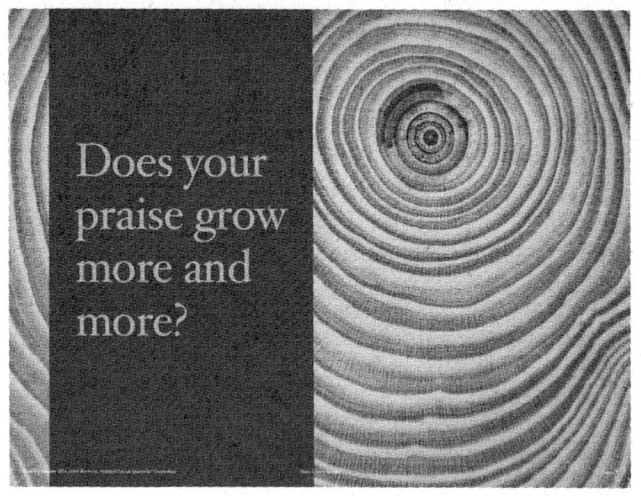

Visual for Lesson 7. *Ask the class to consider how a tree's growth can be an analogy for our growth in wisdom and praise.*

Conclusion

A. God the Teacher

This psalm, like others, portrays God as the head teacher in the school of life. The attentive student enters enthusiastically into the lessons even when they are difficult, even when they involve real suffering. When other people seem bent on our destruction, when everything we attempt fails, or when our most cherished plans crumble into the dust, even then, there is hope. Hope is possible because this life does not fully belong to human beings, and whatever evil we may dream of, carry out, or merely tolerate will not prevail in the end. God reigns in life. He works steadily for the good, building a world in which love prevails over hate.

Hardships can teach us hope because we trust the teacher to provide valuable learning that will transform our lives and lead to a better situation (Romans 8:28). As the good teacher, God cares deeply about the welfare of His students and leads us at a pace at which we can successfully proceed toward the ultimate goal, a life of goodness and peace before Him (compare 5:3-5).

A more righteous world begins by improving our use of language as people of faith. We refuse to join in the fearful, hateful barrage of words that does so much damage. Instead, we fill the air with praise for God's justice and mercy, as this psalm does. Better words lead to better actions and better relationships. Hope spreads from life to life to create a new world. The social alienation and pain caused by human greed, pride, and envy will give way to social harmony wrought by mutual love and full of praiseworthy actions. May God grant us this comfort and bring His kingdom to earth as it is in Heaven (Matthew 5:10).

What Do You Think?

Where do you see the seeds of the gospel of Jesus Christ in this psalm?

Digging Deeper

What worship will you offer to God this week as a result of this study?

B. Prayer

O God, our teacher, help us to learn to read the signs of Your grace everywhere, to add up the evidence of Your mercy, and to subtract the fears that overwhelm us so easily. Write on our hearts the words of joyful expectation You have opened to us. We pray in Jesus' name. Amen.

C. Thought to Remember

Cry out to God and be comforted.

Involvement Learning

Enhance your lesson with KJV Bible Student *(from your curriculum supplier) and the reproducible activity page (at www.standardlesson.com or in the back of the* KJV Standard Lesson Commentary Deluxe Edition*).*

Into the Lesson

Ask partners to share with each other the Bible stories they remember most vividly from their childhood and why they made such an impression. Encourage students who were not raised in the church to discuss a Bible story that was instrumental in their coming to faith. *Option.* Bring several children's Bibles for participants to flip through as they discuss. Allow several volunteers to share their responses. Lead a discussion to answer the following questions: 1–How has that story helped form your faith in adulthood? 2–How do favorite stories or verses today help when you are feeling stressed, guilty, or shameful?

Alternative. Distribute copies of the "Biggest Sources of Stress" exercise from the activity page, which you can download. Have learners complete it individually in a minute or less before discussing conclusions in pairs.

Transition into the next part of the lesson by saying, "Today's Scripture text shows how one poet maintained hope in the face of adversity. Let's see what that looks like."

Into the Word

As a class, read aloud Psalm 71:12-21, inviting each learner to read one verse (allow learners to pass if they feel uncomfortable reading aloud). *Option.* Read the entirety of Psalm 71 together, then reread the verses for today's study. As the psalm is being read, have learners make note of the reasons the psalmist might be feeling stressed out or afraid, plus any other themes they hear. These could include the desire for God to come close, for the psalmist to be vindicated, and for the psalmist to praise God. In small groups, have learners discuss their observations.

Distribute handouts (you create) with the following headers: *Reasons for Fear* and *Reasons for Praise.* Encourage the groups to watch for any overlap in the two categories as they work together to fill in the answers below the headers. For example, verse 20 describes that the psalmist has seen troubles (a reason for fear) but that he also expects God will restore his life (a reason for praise). Allow about ten minutes for this exercise.

Ask the groups to create two new headers on the back of their handouts: *Faithful Reasons for Hope* and *Secular Reasons for Hope.* Have the groups identify reasons found in Psalm 71 for the *Faithful* list. Encourage them to consider other biblical examples as well, providing references. They should also offer contrasting reasons that fit under the *Secular* list. Tell learners these answers will be used in the next activity.

Into Life

Divide the small groups into halves. One half of the class will work together to debate why faithful reasons for hope are superior to secular reasons; the other half will take the opposing side, why secular reasons are better. Encourage the teams to quickly brainstorm an opening statement, prepare to argue their case, and then offer a closing statement.

When the class has finished debating, ask what (if any) compelling reasons were given in favor of secular hope. Then discuss how these hopes might point to faithful hope, and how faithful hope might seem more difficult but, in the end, is the only real hope.

Alternative. Distribute copies of the "Continual Proclamation" exercise for individuals to complete. *Option.* Offer this as a take-home activity, and remind students that they will have time to share in the next class if they desire.

After either activity, close class by reading Psalm 71:12-21 once more as a prayer to God. Allow time for one minute of silence for learners to add their private supplications before dismissing the class.

Delightful Precepts

Devotional Reading: Proverbs 30:1-9
Background Scripture: Psalm 119-73-80

Psalm 119:73-80

73 Thy hands have made me and fashioned me: give me understanding, that I may learn thy commandments.

74 They that fear thee will be glad when they see me; because I have hoped in thy word.

75 I know, O Lord, that thy judgments are right, and that thou in faithfulness hast afflicted me.

76 Let, I pray thee, thy merciful kindness be for my comfort, according to thy word unto thy servant.

77 Let thy tender mercies come unto me, that I may live: for thy law is my delight.

78 Let the proud be ashamed; for they dealt perversely with me without a cause: but I will meditate in thy precepts.

79 Let those that fear thee turn unto me, and those that have known thy testimonies.

80 Let my heart be sound in thy statutes; that I be not ashamed.

Key Text

Thy hands have made me and fashioned me: give me understanding, that I may learn thy commandments.

—Psalm 119:73

Hope in
the Lord

Unit II: Expressing Hope
Lessons 6–9

Lesson Aims

After participating in this lesson, each learner will be able to:

1. Identify the reason(s) for the psalmist's comfort.
2. Explain why following the law is more than rule-keeping.
3. Select one of the eight verses of the text as most personally meaningful and explain why it is so.

Lesson Outline

Introduction
- A. The Power of Knowledge
- B. Lesson Context

I. Request for Wisdom (Psalm 119:73-76)
- A. God and His Pupils (vv. 73-74)
  - *Child of the Father*
- B. Trust in God (vv. 75-76)

II. Hope for the Future (Psalm 119:77-80)
- A. The Righteous and the Wicked (vv. 77-78)
- B. Trust in God (vv. 79-80)
  - *Vindication*

Conclusion
- A. Learning to Trust, Trusting to Learn
- B. Prayer
- C. Thought to Remember

Introduction

A. The Power of Knowledge

"Knowledge is power." The statement can mean many different things. Awareness of how we are being misled gives us freedom from outside control. Possessing the right skills allows a person to lead or even dominate others. Or withholding information from others can allow us to control them. The vagueness of this proverb reminds us that knowledge can take many forms and serve many purposes.

A better statement might be, "Knowledge can support goodness." Instead of thinking of knowledge as the path to power, might we think of knowledge as a way of learning to do good and build a better world? Some forms of knowledge and methods of acquiring it have great potential for good.

Knowledge comes to us, of course, through some process of education, whether in formal schools or elsewhere. Healthy patterns of education draw together good teachers and eager students working around a series of questions and concerns that will produce knowledge and transform the lives of those involved in the learning process. In wisdom texts like Psalm 119 or Proverbs or Job, the disciplined pursuit of knowledge involves all sorts of concerns. A wise person might study many things, ranging from what we would today call the sciences, to languages, to arts and crafts. But most of all, the wise person described in these texts cultivates the art of living.

B. Lesson Context

Psalm 119 takes up the art of living in an almost obsessive way, as it repeatedly turns to the same ideas and figures of speech. It emphasizes the Law of Moses (the Torah) as a guidebook to a life of dignity and moral integrity. It invites faithful people to delight in such a life, not merely endure it.

Psalm 119 is by far the longest poem in the Bible. Its length is due in part to the psalmist's decision to write an acrostic psalm, in which lines would begin with successive letters of the Hebrew alphabet. This technique was a form used to display a comprehensive approach to the subject of the poem. The same convention appears in various forms in other Old

Testament texts, such as Psalms 37, 111, 112, and Lamentations 1–4, among others. Psalm 119 takes the form to its extreme by including eight consecutive lines beginning with the same Hebrew letter. In English, this would mean eight poetic lines that start with the letter *A*, then eight more with *B*, and so on. Twenty-two Hebrew letters multiplied by eight lines equals the 176 verses found in Psalm 119.

While the alphabetically-structured sections are relatively self-contained, several themes and keywords repeatedly appear throughout the psalm. These include various words for the Law of Moses ("commandments" [Psalm 119:73]; "judgments" [v. 75]; "precepts" [v. 78]; "statutes" [v. 80]; etc.) and the response of the faithful person to the law ("delight" [v. 77]; "comfort" [v. 76]; etc.). In its expression of such ideas, verses 73-80 all begin with the Hebrew letter *yodh*. This section focuses on the psalmist's hope and prayer for a future that will be better than the past.

Like Psalm 71, this section of Psalm 119 portrays God as the teacher and the human praying as the student in the school of life. The student learns the commandments, the Law of Moses, not merely as a set of arbitrary rules, but as a window into the meaning of life. By providing a clear structure to everyday life, the law invites a person to inner peace and openness to the work of the creator God. These commandments rest on God's prior commitment to justice (often paired with or assumed to accompany righteousness). God's deep desire for a fair and fertile world for human beings underlies everything in the revelation at Sinai (Exodus 20; etc.), and it can underlie everything in human life. So this psalm affirms.

I. Request for Wisdom
(Psalm 119:73-76)

A. God and His Pupils (vv. 73-74)

73a. Thy hands have made me and fashioned me.

One of the challenges that Scripture writers encountered was communicating God's works in earthly terminology. Here the psalmist uses a common practice of ascribing human traits to God, anthropomorphism, even though the reader would know that God is a spirit and does not have a human physique (compare Exodus 7:5; Numbers 6:25; Psalm 34:15; etc.).

What Do You Think?

Why is it helpful to attribute human characteristics to God?

Digging Deeper

What dangers can overidentifying God with human attributes pose?

The yodh section opens by confessing belief in God as the Creator. God did not create only *me* (the psalmist), but the psalmist is representative of any person who acknowledges God's work in the world, which begins by giving life to every creature therein. The two verbs of creation mean essentially the same thing, though the Hebrew word translated *fashioned* emphasizes the ongoing nature of God's work. It could be paraphrased, "You have put the finishing touches on me." God's creative work did not end long ago at creation (Genesis 1) but continues in each individual life through creation and re-creation (examples: Psalm 139:13-16; Jeremiah 18:1-6; Ezekiel 11:19; John 3:3-8).

73b. Give me understanding, that I may learn thy commandments.

Since the psalmist acknowledges God as the source of life, it makes sense to ask Him for the gift of *understanding* that life (compare James 1:5). Unlike all other creatures known to us, human beings are self-aware and capable of curiosity and existential questioning. We desire to understand. The psalmist knows, of course, that we can learn from many sources, but the plea here is for God to take up the role of a teacher (compare Psalms 25:4-5; 86:11). As Creator, God knows all things and cares deeply for all creatures. Therefore, God is in the best position to teach a person how to live.

This is why the psalmist asks for God's help to grow in knowledge, especially about His *commandments* and their requirements (see Psalm 119:80, below). Like Psalms 1 and 19, this text assumes that God's laws are not simply orders that compliant people obey without question or feeling. Quite to the contrary, the commandments invite the believer into a world of wholeness and wonder. Understanding their meaning and interconnectedness requires a lifetime of attentiveness. That attentiveness, in turn, requires God's help if comprehension is to result.

> **What Do You Think?**
> What emotions does your study of God's commandments inspire in you?
>
> **Digging Deeper**
> Imagine how the psalmist feels about studying God's commandments. Do your emotions mirror these? If not, why not?

Child of the Father

Based on an Italian children's book, Disney's *Pinocchio* tells the story of a puppeteer named Geppetto who created a marionette of a little boy. Geppetto wished the toy he named Pinocchio was a living, breathing, loving son. When Pinocchio magically came to life, Geppetto experienced great joy. Great pain came when the boy used his freedom to leave his father and follow a dangerous path. Eventually, the two were reunited, and Pinocchio did become Geppetto's living, breathing, loving son.

The psalmist knows that he is a creature, made by a loving Father whose commands give him understanding. And like Pinocchio, we have a choice: to look to our Father for wisdom to live lives that glorify Him, or to look to our own desires and face lives of boundless danger. Which path will you choose? —A. W.

74. They that fear thee will be glad when they see me: because I have hoped in thy word.

Psalm 119 often mentions the wicked who resist God (119:53, 61, 95, etc.), but here our text introduces a different group: those who *fear* God (see 119:79, below; also 119:63). These people share the speaker's confidence in God's promises (example: 33:18-22), and they rejoice in finding a like-minded person in the psalmist.

But when do they *see* such a person? Most likely, this is a reference to an audience hearing the psalmist read or sing his praise at the temple. In such a situation, they would *be glad* because they recognized the truth of the psalmist's words. This was only possible because the psalmist *hoped in* God's *word*, not human sources of knowledge or wisdom (compare 1 Corinthians 3:19).

From another point of view, this verse underscores the nature of the faithful community. This community exists because it has found hope in God's promises, learning from divine revelation the vastness of God's care for the creation and each human in it. The members of that community have come to see the world not as totally evil but as potentially good. They find their lives meaningful. That is why they rejoice in finding a like-minded person (compare Luke 15:7; Philippians 2:2). This emphasis on acceptance by other faithful people contrasts with the theme in psalms of lament of persecution by evil persons (see lesson 7).

> **What Do You Think?**
> Whose walk with Jesus is so exemplary that you feel happy when you see or think of that person?
>
> **Digging Deeper**
> Are you likely to be that sort of person for someone else? If not, what prevents your example from bringing another joy?

B. Trust in God (vv. 75-76)

75a. I know, O Lord, that thy judgments are right.

Alongside words of hope come words of evaluation and reformation (Psalm 119:75b, below). The Hebrew word translated *judgments* can also mean "custom" (1 Samuel 2:13) or "manner" (Joshua 6:15). This verse seems to play with these nuances and on judgments as God's ordinances for His people. *Right* should be understood as "righteous" (Psalm 119:106, 138, 160, 164) or "just" (Deuteronomy 16:20); the image of the righteous life as following a straight and narrow path is fitting here (Matthew 7:13-14). Following God's instructions creates the conditions required for human thriving. God's prescribed patterns of life create in those following them a commitment to just dealings with all others (example: Deuteronomy 16:19-

20), without which no one can please God (Micah 6:6-8; example: James 2:14-17).

75b. And that thou in faithfulness hast afflicted me.

The second clause repeats the basic idea of the first but takes it in a new direction. The psalmist perceives God's judgments as naturally flowing from God's *faithfulness*. Another way of saying this would be that if God did not judge sin, He would be unfaithful to His character and word (compare Psalm 33:4; Revelation 19:11). God has rightly *afflicted* (with the sense of being humbled, as in Exodus 10:3) the person praying.

Humility before God is always the appropriate posture for His creatures, and the humble person accepts the resulting suffering as an opportunity for education (compare James 4:10). Like all good teachers, God does not shy away from allowing the pupil to struggle in order to learn important lessons (Romans 8:24-28). And the good student recognizes adversity as a chance to learn. The psalmist had personally experienced the judgment of the Lord when he lost his way. This verse reflects that experience (compare Psalm 119:67).

The book of Psalms considers suffering from various angles. Suffering may be punishment for sin, or it may come undeserved from evil persons. In the first case, the one praying seeks forgiveness (example: Psalm 51:10-17), and in the second, deliverance (example: 55:1-3).

76. Let, I pray thee, thy merciful kindness be for my comfort, according to thy word unto thy servant.

In a third case (see Psalm 119:75b, above), the person praying may thank God for the lesson contained in affliction while also seeking some relief (example: 2 Corinthians 12:7-10).

The *kindness* of God is not a random act but is better understood as the expression of His covenant loyalty. It comes from a deep relationship based on God's promises and the human acceptance of those promises. Just as Abraham and Sarah had a child in their old age after they trusted God to do the impossible (Genesis 21:1-7), the psalmist stands in a relationship of deep trust in the Creator, whose promises come true in time.

The last clause assumes that God has promised to console and that God's *word* can be counted on. Based on the psalmist's knowledge of God's promises, he asks that God in mercy will work to *comfort* the psalmist amid suffering. The heavenly teacher provides proper support when the lesson is the hardest to learn. Therefore, the person of faith can count on God's statements of favor and promises to deliver, just as Moses did when arguing for God to forgive Israel after the episode of the golden calf (Exodus 33:12-16).

II. Hope for the Future

(Psalm 119:77-80)

A. The Righteous and the Wicked (vv. 77-78)

77a. Let thy tender mercies come unto me, that I may live.

The idea that God shows mercy is common in the Psalms and texts about Israelite worship more generally (Exodus 34:6; Nehemiah 9:31; Psalms 111:4; 112:4; etc.). Without such mercy, no one could not survive, let alone thrive.

77b. For thy law is my delight.

The second part of this verse explains the basis for the prayer and the confidence that God will answer it. The psalmist takes pleasure in the *law* (compare Psalm 1:2). The Hebrew word translated *delight* is relatively rare in the Old Testament. Isaiah 5:7 uses it (there translated "pleasant") to refer to Judah. Proverbs 8:30 speaks of Wisdom herself as God's source of delight, similar to a favorite child, and then 8:31 speaks of the pleasure God and Wisdom take in the human race. Most occurrences, however, appear in Psalm 119 itself (vv. 24, 77, 92, 143, 174). In each of those cases, the human being finds pleasure in God's commandments because they can preserve life, protect from various enemies, and provide stability in an unstable world.

The instructions in wise and righteous living that the Torah—given to Moses by God for Israel's benefit (Deuteronomy 4:1-2)—provides foster joy in the person dedicated to following those laws. The person who pursues life in and with God will experience joy, even amidst trials (1 Thessalonians 5:16-18). Far from being a burden to be endured, the law orients a faithful person to a deeply meaningful pattern of life (example: Psalm 1:1-3). By taking seriously the role of the student (see also 119:73b, above), the psalmist enters into a deep relationship with God. This relationship is filled with delight at learning God's ways.

> **What Do You Think?**
> What about God's Word delights you?
>
> **Digging Deeper**
> What do you need from God to experience more joy when studying His Word?

78. Let the proud be ashamed; for they dealt perversely with me without a cause: but I will meditate in thy precepts.

In contrast, some people become so consumed by their pride that they attack those like the psalmist who try to live virtuously. To deal *perversely without a cause* can be understood as slandering or lying (like "falsifying" in Amos 8:5). In doing so, *the proud* brought the righteous person harm. By meditating on God's *precepts*, the psalmist can avoid becoming a perpetrator of the abuse he suffered at others' hands.

God's instructions provide a different mindset and pattern of life for the faithful person. We can imagine how, if all people were striving to keep God's laws, we would be more protected against evil. But even without others committing to a righteous path, those who choose it can learn to reject unjust words and actions and find a centered, joy-filled, meaningful life even during a time of trouble.

B. Trust in God (vv. 79-80)

79. Let those that fear thee turn unto me, and those that have known thy testimonies.

This verse picks up the theme of verse 74, bringing the yodh section of the psalm full circle (see also Psalm 119:80, below). Focus turns from the individual back to the group. It invites anyone listening to join the psalmist in a way of life—to enroll in God's school, as it were. The congregation hearing this psalm, the ones who *fear* God, should *turn* to the psalmist and join in the song (compare Jeremiah 15:19). These fellow worshippers have the correct stance toward God and the correct knowledge. They are fellow students of their Creator, aware of the long legacy of promises and fulfillments in Israel's history, steeped in its stories and ethical and spiritual commitments.

80. Let my heart be sound in thy statutes; that I be not ashamed.

The yodh section ends as it began, by asking for help in learning with not just the right intellectual skills but the right attitudes and dispositions of the *heart* (see Psalm 119:73, above). The Hebrew word translated *sound* can imply perfection (example: Genesis 6:9), being without blemish or spot (examples: Exodus 12:5; Numbers 19:2), and/or sincerity (example: Joshua 24:14). The attitude matters as much as the method of thinking or the results of learning God's *statutes*.

All of these elements must go together for the educational experience to succeed fully—*that I be not ashamed*. The psalmist is fully committed to learning and carrying out the details of the law. In doing so, he would not suffer social stigma or be humiliated. Rather, the person who does this joins a great company of like-minded persons across the ages.

> **What Do You Think?**
> How has following the Lord guarded you against public shame?
>
> **Digging Deeper**
> Has following Him also prevented your feeling ashamed of your own actions? Why or why not?

Vindication

Kenneth Bae, a Korean-American missionary, was arrested in North Korea in 2012 under false charges of trying to overthrow Kim Jung Un's government. In reality, Kenneth's only "crime" was spreading the gospel in North Korea. Sentenced to 15 years of hard labor, Kenneth was forced to do 8 hours of farm labor 6 days a week under grueling conditions. He lost weight and suffered other medical complications. In 2014, Kenneth was released and returned home to the United States, where he continued his ministry.

Being falsely accused and arrested based on unjust laws in a foreign country is a frightening experience. But even in his imprisonment, Kenneth, like the psalmist, knew that God's laws are just and righteous, motivated by love and compassion. He continued to lean on the Lord. In the end, Kenneth did not suffer shame but was vindicated. We can experience the same if we trust what we have learned from the Lord. —A. W.

Conclusion

A. Learning to Trust, Trusting to Learn

The psalmist did not simply obey rules. He enjoyed a relationship with God. That relationship was full of dignity and moral depth. The Law was not just a set of rules but a guide to a meaningful life. God's Law contains the secrets of spiritual growth for the people of Israel and, to a certain extent, for Christians as well. We affirm this when we learn from the writers of Scripture who grew and learned because of their reverence for God's Law. A life of obedience should not be burdensome but joyful.

Still, Psalm 119 acknowledges the presence of hostile forces, in this case, fellow human beings who sought the righteous person's harm in some unspecified way. The pursuit of wise living does not guarantee that one will enjoy universal respect. In fact, when we seek God and follow His ways, we should expect to be very unpopular, at least sometimes. Yet the faithful person perseveres without fear or anger, confident in the ultimate triumph of God's mercy and goodness.

Beyond the psalmist, these verses assumed the existence of a faithful community of like-minded people. They trusted each other and worked toward building a better world that expects goodness from its Creator. They did so in part by fostering a life of celebration. While they did not ignore or pretend away the negative dimensions of life, they saw something more behind them. Their hopeful, trusting attitude inspires us to live similarly.

Such an education requires faithful persons to free themselves from fear, prejudice, anger, greed, lust, and other vices. One of the principal causes of social discord in modern societies is the loss of trust in others and their honorable intentions. Certainly, some people cannot be trusted. But an

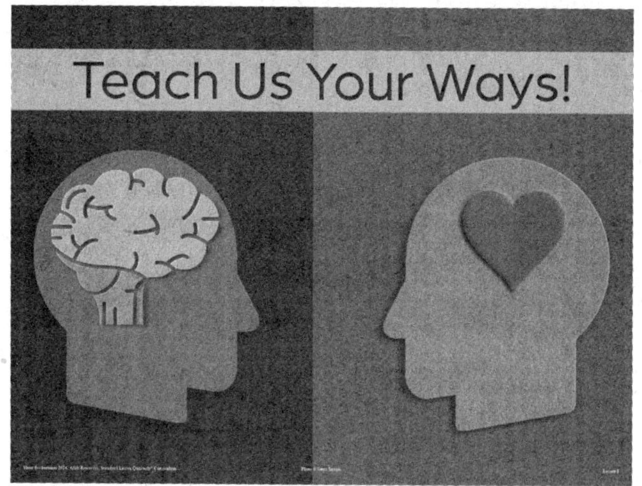

Visual for Lesson 8. *Discuss why it is important for head knowledge of God to become heart knowledge and how that transfer can happen.*

attitude of mistrust can spread like cancer and divide even those whose actions are honorable and whose intentions are good. In resistance to such a tendency, Psalm 119 and others like it open the door to the possibility of mutual trust. This stance of informed, reasonable trust begins with trust in God as the Creator and educator, who draws anyone willing into a meaningful life. That stance allows us to learn from others, to check our pride, and to weed out our prejudices and fears. In short, true education for life requires trust. Only then can the delight in God become a reality in our lives.

B. Prayer

Father God, our Creator, You have fashioned us and continue to shape us into the image of Christ. Help us to understand to whatever degree we can Your gracious movements in Your creation, Your care for all things, Your love for us, and Your desire that we grow in wisdom. In Jesus' name we pray. Amen.

C. Thought to Remember

Learn what the Lord desires!

How to Say It

Moses	*Mo*-zes or *Mo*-zez.
Torah *(Hebrew)*	*Tor*-uh.
yodh *(Hebrew)*	yode.

Involvement Learning

Enhance your lesson with KJV Bible Student *(from your curriculum supplier) and the reproducible activity page (at www.standardlesson.com or in the back of the* KJV Standard Lesson Commentary Deluxe Edition*).*

Into the Lesson

Option. If you sent the class home with last week's second exercise, allow a few minutes to discuss their impressions.

Divide the class into two groups. Have one group brainstorm rules or laws they are usually content to keep *(example: not committing murder).* Ask the other group to brainstorm rules or laws they do not enjoy obeying *(example: paying taxes).* After a few minutes, ask learners to break into smaller groups comprised of people from both of the original halves. These small groups should share the rules they thought of. Then the groups should summarize what delightful laws have in common and what the others have in common.

Alternative 1. Write on the board, *Good laws encourage human flourishing.* As a class, discuss to what degree students agree or disagree with this statement, as well as any caveats or amendments they might make to improve the statement.

Alternative 2. Distribute copies of the "Why Do People Break Traffic Laws?" exercise from the activity sheet, which you can download. After completing the activity, bring the class together to discuss the prompts at the bottom of the exercise.

After any of these activities, lead into Bible study by saying, "Obedience to laws rarely elicits great joy. But the psalmist experienced delight from his quest to learn God's ways and obey them. Our study today encourages us to do the same."

Into the Word

Using the commentary, give a background summary of Psalm 119, its structure, and how today's Scripture fits into the psalm. *Option.* Ask a volunteer to prepare this ahead of time. Then read Psalm 119:73-80 in the form of a responsive reading: the teacher (or a volunteer) should read the odd-numbered verses aloud, while the rest of the class will read in unison the even-numbered verses.

Ask learners to list the qualities and actions of God in today's passage that gave the psalmist confidence and hope. Write these on the board. Have learners try to group the qualities. They might notice the following: God is the Creator; He gives understanding of His commands; His laws are righteous; He is characterized by faithfulness, unfailing love, and compassion. Ask, "Which of these qualities or actions is most meaningful to you?" Invite volunteers to elaborate with examples from their lives.

Divide the class into pairs. Based on today's verses, have the pairs discuss what characteristics they think the psalmist exhibited. They should consider when those characteristics mimic God, are a reaction to God's characteristics, or fall into some other category. After several minutes, bring the class back together to discuss what they found.

Into Life

Distribute a note card and pen to each learner. Allow quiet time for learners to reread Psalm 119:73-80 silently. Invite them to write down one of the verses that is the most personally meaningful. Challenge them to write a word or two that helps them identify why that verse is meaningful and briefly write why that is so. Encourage learners to refer to their cards throughout the week for hope and encouragement in following God.

Alternative. Distribute copies of the "Delightful Precept" exercise from the activity page. Have learners complete it individually in a minute or less before discussing conclusions in pairs.

Ask two members of the class to close the lesson in prayer. The first prayer should focus on thanking and praising God for His qualities and actions described in today's Scripture and how they give us hope. The second prayer should implore God for help in handling situations where we are persecuted, shamed, or unjustly accused by people. Ask God for wisdom to handle those situations in a way that would honor Him.

July 28
Lesson 9 (KJV)

Expectant Watchfulness

Devotional Reading: Matthew 25:1-13
Background Scripture: Psalm 130

Psalm 130

**1 Out of the depths have I cried unto thee,
O LORD.**
**2 Lord, hear my voice: Let thine ears be
attentive to the voice of my supplications.**
**3 If thou, LORD, shouldest mark iniquities,
O Lord, who shall stand?**
**4 But there is forgiveness with thee, That
thou mayest be feared.**
**5 I wait for the LORD, my soul doth wait,
And in his word do I hope.**
**6 My soul waiteth for the Lord More than
they that watch for the morning: I say, more
than they that watch for the morning.**
**7 Let Israel hope in the LORD: For with the
LORD there is mercy, And with him is plenteous redemption.**
**8 And he shall redeem Israel From all his
iniquities.**

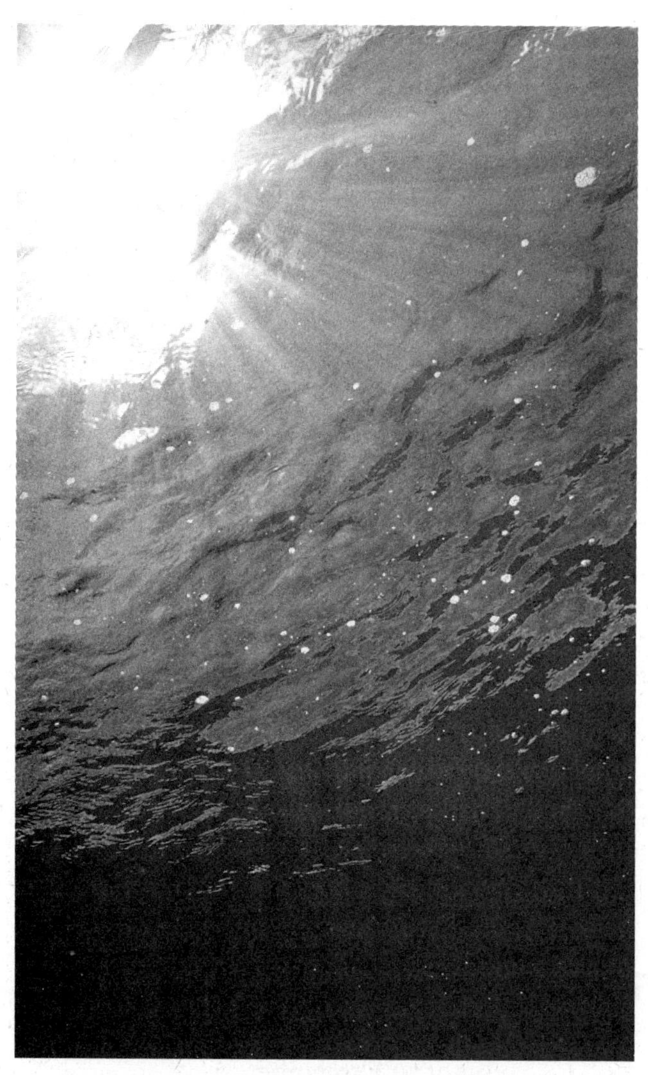

Key Text

Let Israel hope in the LORD: For with the LORD there is mercy, and with him is plenteous redemption.

—Psalm 130:7

Hope in
the Lord

Unit II: Expressing Hope

Lessons 6–9

Lesson Aims

After participating in this lesson, each learner will be able to:

1. Identify elements of cause and effect in the text.

2. Define the genre of lament using Psalm 130 as an example.

3. Personalize, in writing, one of the verses without changing the psalmist's original intent.

Lesson Outline

Introduction

A. Out of the Depths

B. Lesson Context

I. Address to the Lord (Psalm 130:1-6)

A. God Listens (vv. 1-2)

B. God Forgives (vv. 3-4)

Records of Wrongdoing

C. Waiting for God (vv. 5-6)

II. Address to Israel (Psalm 130:7-8)

A. Hope in God (v. 7)

B. Receive Redemption (v. 8)

The Bridge to Nowhere

Conclusion

A. The Power of Waiting

B. Prayer

C. Thought to Remember

Introduction

A. Out of the Depths

For such a short prayer, Psalm 130 covers a lot of ground. It begins by acknowledging the terrifying possibilities of human life and ends with hope for a different future. Yet, in reading it, we should not skip too quickly to the end.

In this psalm, the focus does not lie on outside, terrible forces but precisely on human sin. The terror that the psalmist faces comes from the human tendency to allow vices to overcome us. That tendency threatens to take over everything we do and are, thwarting our best plans and spoiling our best intentions. What can be done about this problem of sin?

As Dietrich Bonhoeffer noted in *The Cost of Discipleship*, "Together, they [the disciples, the church] bring their guilt before God and pray together for grace. May God forgive not only me my sins, but us our sins." That sense that both our sin and the possibility of forgiveness unite us is central to this psalm and to the Bible as a whole.

B. Lesson Context

Psalm 130 is part of a larger cluster, usually called the Psalms of Ascents or, less often, the Pilgrimage Psalter (Psalms 120–134). The psalms in the group may have originated at different times and places (as would be true of a modern hymnal) but functioned together as songs for the pilgrims entering the Jerusalem temple in the period following the Babylonian exile.

The group of psalms falls into three subgroups (Psalms 120–124, 125–129, and 130–134). Perhaps the pilgrims sang them at different stops on the road from the Mount of Olives, through the Kidron Valley, and into the precinct around the temple itself. Psalm 130, in particular, may have served as part of a night vigil as the pilgrims awaited the dawn, which in turn would symbolize the dawning of God's light in their lives (see 130:6, below). Those hypotheses are reasonable but hard to prove. Yet they would explain the varying moods of these psalms and their progressive closeness to the temple itself.

More certain is that the psalms together address

a wide range of concerns and moods. Together, they allow the worshipping community to express anxiety and hope, fear and trust, sorrow and joy. That is, they help worshippers bring their entire lives to God, share their lives with each other, and eagerly await God's transforming work.

Psalm 130 moves the pilgrims from an attitude of despair (v. 1, below) to one of supreme confidence in God's saving work (vv. 7-8, below). When the one singing focuses on his or her personal suffering, fear and sorrow can overtake faith. But when the focus shifts toward God's inclination to save and the consequent hope that the entire people may enjoy, the mood may change to hope. So it is here.

The poem, though very short, moves in several steps, from a statement of need addressed to God, to an acknowledgment of God's mercy and confession of hope, to an address to all of Israel. Psalm 130 begins with a cry to God, as most laments do. Here the attitude is one of deep need and expectation of help. It differs from some psalms of lament by being briefer and jumping to praise without much preparation. In these songs born of distress, the singer either promises to praise God or does so. The promise or the praise is born out of gratitude for God's generous response to the petition for help.

Psalm 130 seems like a very condensed lament that shades into something different altogether. Perhaps that difference from other psalms reflects this one's placement in a larger group. It does not have to do all the work a "normal" lament does because it does not stand alone. Psalm 129 describes long-standing attacks on faithful Israelites and expects God's deliverance, while Psalm 130 expresses contrition before God. Collectively, these psalms together position the one praying as someone in the correct spiritual position before God.

How to Say It

Babylonian	Bab-ih-*low*-nee-un.
Dietrich Bonhoeffer	*Dee*-trik *Bawn*-haw-fer.
Ketchikan	*Keh*-chuh-kan.
Kidron	*Kid*-ron.
Psalter	*Sawl*-ter.
Sheol *(Hebrew)*	*She*-ol.

I. Address to the Lord

(Psalm 130:1-6)

A. God Listens (vv. 1-2)

1. Out of the depths have I cried unto thee, O LORD.

The phrase *out of the depths* might be a shorter form of the phrase "the depths of the waters" (Ezekiel 27:34; compare Psalm 69:2, 14). Isaiah 51:10 speaks of "the depths of the sea." While the Hebrew word here translated *depths* only occurs in these instances in the Bible, images of the watery deep were frequently used as an image of danger or chaos, especially the horror of drowning (examples: Exodus 15:5; Psalm 69:2).

Additionally, the concept of depth is linked to Sheol, the place of the dead. Depths and Sheol should not be conflated, but neither should the possible link between them be neglected. Like Jonah crying from the belly of the great fish (Jonah 2:2-5), the psalmist here speaks metaphorically of having descended to the realm of death, to Sheol. Though not an equivalent of the place we would call hell, Sheol was under the earth and generally considered far from God's presence (Numbers 16:30-33; Psalm 6:5; contrast 139:8); no one worshipped God there (88:10-12). These characteristics of Sheol give insight into what death entailed to ancient Israelites' way of thinking. The cry from the gates of the realm of death, Sheol itself, points to the many sorts of problems humans may face, including our mortality and proneness to sickness, as well as the hostile attitudes of wicked people or the irresistible power of some historical or natural events. The depths may take many forms.

From there, the psalmist now addresses God in hopes of being heard and saved (compare Psalm 49:15). A call asking God to listen comes early on in many of David's laments (examples: 4:1; 55:1-2; 61:1; 86:1; 141:1). The psalm before us is not attributed to David, nor is the request to hear repeated word for word. But each instance shares the idea that God will be inclined to listen, that the human being ought to seek God's attention,

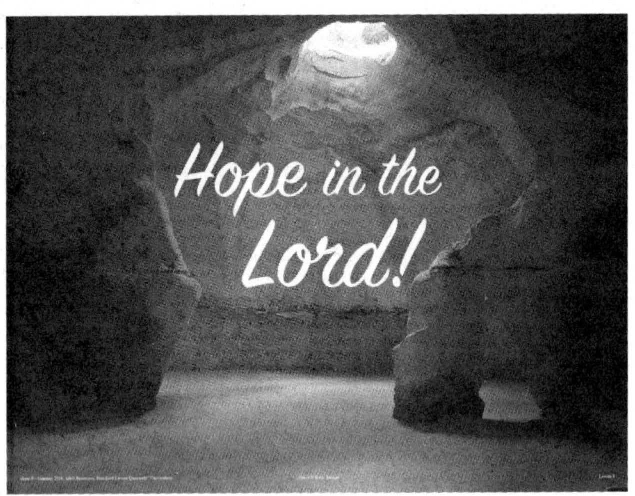

Visual for Lesson 9. *At the end of class, allow one minute of silence for learners to cry to God, no matter what depth they are experiencing.*

and that each supplicant may do so freely and in the company of others (see 130:7-8, below).

The psalmist is not in danger of drowning (or how could he write?) and may not literally be about to die (see commentary on Psalm 130:3). But many different forms of suffering can feel like a death—from physical ailments to relational estrangements and beyond. In all circumstances—even as far from God as Israelites could imagine, at the bottom of a body of water—we can still call on the *Lord.*

2. Lord, hear my voice: let thine ears be attentive to the voice of my supplications.

The opening address to the *Lord* continues with a petition to listen. These two clauses express essentially the same thing, repeating both the sense of the verb *hear* and the direct object *my voice.* This poetic device of synonymous parallelism reinforces the importance the psalmist places on receiving God's full attention.

The second clause asks for tangible but unspecified expressions of God's favor. His care begins with listening attentively to the content of the *supplications* and acting to alleviate those specific concerns. As is common in psalms, we do not know the specific occasion for writing—a feature of the poems that invites us to consider our supplications.

Similar language appears several times in psalms of lament (examples: Psalms 86:6; 140:6; 143:1). Psalm 28:6, for example, offers a counterpart to the request for God to hear by celebrating that God already had heard (compare 31:22; 116:1; etc.). All these psalms expect that God desires to listen to sincere requests for help and will respond with speed and compassion. We do well to remember, however, that God's timing is not our own (2 Peter 3:9), and a perceived lack of an answer from God does not mean He has not heard or has no intention of acting (examples: Habakkuk 1:2-5; John 11:21-22).

What Do You Think?

What situation might you describe as "the depths" from which you call to God?

Digging Deeper

What gives you confidence that God is attentive to your cries?

B. God Forgives (vv. 3-4)

3. If thou, Lord, shouldest mark iniquities, O Lord, who shall stand?

The psalmist affirms God's mercy in the form of a question, as if to remind Him of His choice to exhibit mercy. God could obsess over human sin to keep meticulous tabs on every stray thought, word, and deed. A similar use of the verb *mark* appears in 1 Samuel 1:12, which says that Eli "marked" Hannah's mouth when she prayed for a son. In the context of 1 Samuel, the verb suggests close observation, as it does here. If God decided to *mark iniquities,* no person could be counted as righteous (Psalm 14:2-3; Ecclesiastes 7:20; Romans 3:10-12).

Furthermore, a God who rigorously punished all evil immediately would leave no space for human survival (compare Genesis 6:5-7; 7:21-22). But a God who ignored evildoing altogether would cause great harm to humanity; we might consider the fear of God's abandoning His people as exemplified in Lamentations. The God of Israel, however, engages with human beings to reform their lives (example: Ezekiel 11:19-20).

The psalmist's question is not merely a theoretical discussion of divine mercy. Mentioning sin also likely touches on the psalmist's reason for writing:

to repent of sinful behavior and seek God's forgiveness. The psalmist assumes that God delights in forgiveness and the repair of human life that it makes possible (compare Ezekiel 33:11; Acts 2:17-39). By appealing to God's mercy, the person praying also commits to reform (see Romans 2:4).

> **What Do You Think?**
> On a scale of 1 to 10, how aware are you of your own sinfulness?
>
> **Digging Deeper**
> What benefit is there in being more aware of your own sin? less aware?

4. But there is forgiveness with thee, that thou mayest be feared.

But ties this verse closely to verse 3, implying a sequence of closely related events. The experience or even observation of God's forgiveness and its consequences for human life create a sense of awe in the impressionable human. Here the psalmist's knowledge of God's inclination toward mercy becomes clear.

But the sequence of thoughts may seem odd at first. How does the reality of *forgiveness* create an awe-filled sense of fear? Contrary to the possible view that God's hatred of sin or ferocity toward evil will so terrify people that they will live better lives, this verse suggests that God's mercy toward sinners inspires them to honor Him more. Instead of being mired in sins and paralyzed to choose or do better, forgiveness creates a new path (example: Isaiah 42:16). Divine gentleness with the people inspires awe in part because it seems so different from human inclinations toward one another. In contrast to the pitiless ways in which we often respond to mistreatment or wrongdoing, God exercises mercy.

Records of Wrongdoing

I took the carpenter at his word and paid him $5,000. He had the plans for the custom cabinets my wife and I hired him to build for our new home; the down payment would cover materials so he could begin work. When months later we still had neither updates nor cabinets, I drove three hours to his shop—only to discover the carpenter had gone out of business and left town.

Like a detective, I gathered evidence and built my case to get our money back. For years, I saved all my records of the man's crimes, getting angry every time I saw the growing pile on my desk. It wasn't until I threw the paperwork in the garbage that I could forgive him for wronging us.

God could pile up the evidence of our guilt too. But He chooses instead to throw out the evidence against us and forgive us (Hebrews 9:11-15). Are there any wrongdoings that you continue to keep records of? What prevents you from throwing out these records, as God did for you? —J. M.

C. Waiting for God (vv. 5-6)

5a. I wait for the LORD, my soul doth wait.

The Hebrew word translated *soul* has a more robust meaning than we might consider in English. Ancient Israelites did not believe in a soul that merely inhabited a body (like Greek thinking). Instead of a divide between body and soul, the Israelites thought of the human being as an integrated whole, a body-and-soul unity. The soul was the animating force, the piece of the body that made a person alive. This integration of body and soul remains central to Christianity, which rests on the hope of our bodily resurrection (1 Corinthians 15:50-57) rather than the immortality of a disembodied spirit or soul.

In saying *my soul doth wait,* then, the psalmist claims to anticipate God's saving work with every fiber of his being. The psalmist's faith involves an orientation to a future in which the problems of the moment find a solution (see commentary Psalm 130:5b-6, below).

5b. And in his word do I hope.

To *hope* here is a synonym for waiting on God (see Psalm 130:5a, above). We never hope in vain when we place our hope in His promises. God's *word* refers here, not to the law as it might, but to His promise of salvation given first to Abram (Genesis 12:2-3), which becomes the focus of the faithful person's life. Having confidence in that promise shapes behavior for a lifetime as well.

6. My soul waiteth for the Lord more than they that watch for the morning: I say, more than they that watch for the morning.

This verse repeats *more than they that watch for*

the morning for rhythmical purposes; we might recognize this convention in our hymns. The repetition also expresses the intensity of waiting for God's saving act. The waiting involves a person's entire being (see Psalm 130:5a, above, regarding the Hebrew concept of the *soul*).

What this particular phrase means, however, is less than obvious. The emphasis could be on waiting at a specific time—during the night. Or it could be emphasizing *they*—the sentinels who are watching. In either case, an analogy is drawn. Just as nighttime sentries eagerly await the dawn and the relative safety of daytime, so does the one praying wait for a new day in which God will act. Once again, the psalmist's faith requires hope in God's future action.

What Do You Think?

What metaphor would you use to describe what it feels like to wait on the Lord?

Digging Deeper

How is waiting on God different from other kinds of waiting?

II. Address to Israel

(Psalm 130:7-8)

A. Hope in God (v. 7)

7a. Let Israel hope in the LORD: for with the LORD there is mercy.

In the last two verses, the psalm shifts focus from an individual psalmist to the whole community. This sort of shift frequently occurs in psalms of lament (see Lesson Context, above). But this one lacks any transition, as the psalm turns from the address to God to the address to the people. The hope, especially in God's *mercy*, that the psalmist expressed for his personal circumstances is prescribed for the gathered community.

7b. And with him is plenteous redemption.

The Hebrew behind this phrase is difficult to understand and translate. One reason for this is the scarcity of biblical uses of the precise Hebrew word translated *redemption* (Psalm 111:9; translated "sever" in Exodus 8:22 and "redeem" in Isaiah 50:2). However, the related verb is more common, which gives us confidence that redemption is the appropriate translation here.

While we don't often think of it this way, redemption is a legal metaphor. In ancient Israel, the term often applied to the purchase of slaves to free them. The language is prevalent in texts describing God's liberation of the Israelites from Egyptian bondage (examples: Deuteronomy 7:8; 9:26; 15:15; 2 Samuel 7:23; Micah 6:4). Here, however, the liberation does not involve political oppression (or at least not just that), but the oppression of human sin in all its forms. The psalm anticipates God acting to free Israel from sin's power. This redemption is the ultimate fulfillment of God's ancient covenant with the ancestors (see commentary on Psalm 130:5b, above; compare Luke 1:46-55).

B. Receive Redemption (v.8)

8. And he shall redeem Israel from all his iniquities.

As laments often do, the psalm ends with an expression of deep trust in God (example: Psalm 22). This ending repositions the whole poem because it moves readers from focusing on the individual to God's care for the whole people. In God's great mercy lies hope for *Israel* and everyone within it. This psalm probably lies behind the promise of the angel to Joseph in Matthew 1:21: "Thou shalt call his name Jesus: for he shall save his people from their sins." For Matthew, Jesus became the sign and instrument of God's redemption of Israel and to the larger world.

There is a tight connection between the individual's experience and the community's proclamation. The people of Israel were the community whom God rescued from evil in all its manifestations, of which we are the spiritual descendants. The people announced and celebrated the good news that such deliverance had occurred (example: Exodus 15), and they sought more of it. And of course, that understanding also applies to the church, the community grafted into Israel (Romans 9–11). We also experience, both as individuals and as a community, the power of God's forgiveness, which we imitate in our dealings with others.

What Do You Think?

Imagine you were the psalmist anticipating God's redemption. What would you think of Jesus?

Digging Deeper

How has studying the Psalms deepened your appreciation for Christ?

The Bridge to Nowhere

Like many Alaska towns, Ketchikan is not connected to the rest of the state by roads, but instead by air. The phrase "off-the-road system" describes towns like this. The unique thing about Ketchikan is that its airport is situated on a small island. A ferry shuttles travelers between the airport and the town.

Between 2006 and 2015, Alaska policymakers discussed the construction of a bridge to replace the ferry. Twenty-eight million dollars were spent constructing a road to the bridge. But in 2015, it was determined that the financially responsible decision was to cancel the bridge project and upgrade the city's ferries. This project became known as the "Bridge to Nowhere," though what actually exists is a *road* to nowhere.

The work of God in our lives is not a road to nowhere or an abandoned bridge project. God does not enthusiastically begin to transform us only to neglect His work later. We experience full redemption and restoration because of His work in our lives. Is there a bridge-to-nowhere project in your life that you need God to finish? Or would it be wiser to repent of your misguided work and start over?

—J. M.

Conclusion

A. The Power of Waiting

Psalm 130 speaks to faith that involves waiting for God's grace to make itself known. During such a time, the person may doubt God's ability or willingness to save, question the integrity of other human beings, and even lose self-respect. Waiting for salvation challenges every fiber of a person's being.

Yet, that challenge itself strengthens faith in the long run. As this psalm makes clear, trust in God does not come without some doubts. Will God listen? Biblical faith is not a Pollyanna attitude about life. It is realistic and honest about hardship. Yet it does not remain there. The spiritual challenges we face—the depths—become opportunities for grace. Therefore, learning the discipline of waiting is part of learning to live with God and all others who are also awaiting God's help. This psalm, in short, exposes an important truth about human beings: our profound need and desire for God's presence.

As part of a community of pilgrims seeking God's presence, the faithful person can speak to God even in the most desperate moments of life. The communal worship of the Israelite community acknowledges that fact. God does not skimp on acts that will benefit human beings but rather frequently engages in them. Worship in the community still reminds us of God's mighty acts. May we, in our darkest moments and in the grasp of the sins that don't want to let us go, cry out to our God and heed the call to hope in His saving works.

What Do You Think?

What key idea will you take away from these three lessons in the Psalms?

Digging Deeper

How will you continue to seek knowledge and wisdom from the Lord?

B. Prayer

O, God who hears the cries of broken people and sees our tear-stained faces, who sutures broken hearts and shattered relationships, hear every cry from the depths of us as well. Do not forget us in our day of distress, and help us not forget to be thankful when You have rescued us with one of the many methods at Your disposal. In Jesus' name we pray. Amen.

C. Thought to Remember

Faith celebrates our hope in God's forgiveness and calls others to do the same.

Involvement Learning

Enhance your lesson with KJV Bible Student *(from your curriculum supplier) and the reproducible activity page (at www.standardlesson.com or in the back of the* KJV Standard Lesson Commentary Deluxe Edition*).*

Into the Lesson

Ask for volunteers to share about a time when they had to wait for something as a child or young adult. Were they waiting for something they needed or just wanted? What made it easier or harder to wait? Did they display patience as they waited? Then ask the same questions but from a more recent example. Follow up by asking whether waiting has become easier with age. Why or why not? *Option.* Have learners pair up to answer the prompts.

After hearing from several people, talk together about what made waiting hard in those situations. Then discuss what factors make waiting easier or harder. Answers might include who they are waiting on (someone trustworthy or not, for example), whether they need or only want what they're waiting for, and how guaranteed it is that they will eventually receive what they desire.

Transition to the next portion of the lesson with the statement, "We're going to read Psalm 130 now, in which the psalmist waits hopefully for God's answer to His prayer for forgiveness."

Into the Word

Distribute to the class handouts (you create) of Psalm 130, along with pens. As you read the psalm aloud to the class, ask them to mark phrases that stand out by underlining them and any that seem unclear or confusing with a question mark. After hearing from volunteers about what they marked, start by addressing any questions with information found in the commentary. Then discuss together why the underlined phrases stood out in particular.

Finally, ask how the psalmist's experience of waiting on God is like or unlike the personal stories that were shared in the previous exercise. What phrases suggest that the psalmist found waiting difficult? Do any suggest he found it easy?

Alternative 1. Have learners work in pairs to identify several themes found in Psalm 130. These should include the psalmist's need for God to hear and act on his behalf, the psalmist's awareness of his own sin, and the psalmist's hope for his own redemption as well as that of Israel. Then ask the pairs to compare and contrast Psalm 130 to Psalms 71:12-21 (lesson 7) and 119:73-80 (lesson 8). They should focus on themes found in these three psalms. After calling time, have the class come back together to discuss what they found. What do the common themes suggest about waiting for God then and now?

Alternative 2. Distribute copies of the "God's Response" exercise from the activity sheet, which you can download. Ask pairs to complete as indicated.

After any of these activities, bring the class together to consider the following questions: 1–Does God make us wait a long time before He answers our petitions? 2–How can Psalm 130 help one continue to hope when our sins seem insurmountable? 3–What should we do as we wait on the Lord's answer to the longings of our hearts?

Into Life

Have students reread Psalm 130 from the handout you distributed (above). Ask them to circle the verse that speaks to them the most and write a brief note in the margin explaining their choice. Then have them paraphrase that verse to personalize it without changing the psalmist's original intent. Allow volunteers to share their answers.

Option. Distribute copies of the "Expectant Watchfulness" exercise. Have learners work individually for one minute as indicated. Encourage learners to refer to the exercise throughout the week as they wait on the Lord.

Finally, lead the class in a closing prayer, including elements of praise, requests for help, confession, and thanks.

August 4
Lesson 10 (KJV)

The Word of God

Devotional Reading: Psalm 121
Background Scripture: 1 Thessalonians 2:13–3:5

1 Thessalonians 2:13–3:5

**13 For this cause also thank we God with-
out ceasing, because, when ye received the
word of God which ye heard of us, ye received
it not as the word of men, but as it is in truth,
the word of God, which effectually worketh
also in you that believe.**
**14 For ye, brethren, became followers of the
churches of God which in Judaea are in Christ
Jesus: for ye also have suffered like things of
your own countrymen, even as they have of the
Jews:**
**15 Who both killed the Lord Jesus, and
their own prophets, and have persecuted us;
and they please not God, and are contrary to
all men:**
**16 Forbidding us to speak to the Gentiles
that they might be saved, to fill up their sins
alway: for the wrath is come upon them to the
uttermost.**
**17 But we, brethren, being taken from
you for a short time in presence, not in heart,
endeavoured the more abundantly to see your
face with great desire.**
**18 Wherefore we would have come unto
you, even I Paul, once and again; but Satan
hindered us.**
**19 For what is our hope, or joy, or crown of
rejoicing? Are not even ye in the presence of our
Lord Jesus Christ at his coming?**
20 For ye are our glory and joy.

**1 Wherefore when we could no longer for-
bear, we thought it good to be left at Athens
alone;**
**2 And sent Timotheus, our brother, and
minister of God, and our fellowlabourer in the
gospel of Christ, to establish you, and to comfort you concerning your faith:**
**3 That no man should be moved by these
afflictions: for yourselves know that we are
appointed thereunto.**
**4 For verily, when we were with you, we told
you before that we should suffer tribulation;
even as it came to pass, and ye know.**
**5 For this cause, when I could no longer for-
bear, I sent to know your faith, lest by some
means the tempter have tempted you, and our
labour be in vain.**

Key Text

For this cause also thank we God without ceasing, because, when ye received the word of God which ye heard of us, ye received it not as the word of men, but as it is in truth, the word of God, which effectually worketh also in you that believe. —**1 Thessalonians 2:13**

Hope in

the Lord

Unit III: Eternal Hope

Lessons 10–13

Lesson Aims

After participating in this lesson, each learner will be able to:

1. Summarize Paul's concerns regarding the believers in Thessalonica.

2. Compare and contrast the Jews and Gentiles as Paul describes them in the lesson text.

3. Commit to offering Christian encouragement to a fellow believer in the week ahead.

Lesson Outline

Introduction

A. The Power of Encouragement

B. Lesson Context

I. Thanksgiving (1 Thessalonians 2:13-16)

A. Accepting God's Word (v. 13)

Reacting to the Word

B. Imitating God's Churches (v. 14)

C. Seeing God's Justice (vv. 15-16)

II. Encouragement (1 Thessalonians 2:17–3:5)

A. Paul's Desire to Return (v. 17)

B. Desire Thwarted (v. 18)

C. Paul's Joy in Them (vv. 19-20)

D. Paul Sends Timothy (vv. 1-5)

Love Letter

Conclusion

A. Encouraging One Another

B. Prayer

C. Thought to Remember

Introduction

A. The Power of Encouragement

When I was a sophomore in high school, I qualified for the state championship in swimming. Two days before the swim meet, my father became ill and ended up in the hospital. We quickly realized that he would not be able to come to the meet, and I was distraught. My father had never missed a meet since I started swimming at 8 years old. Now he would miss the biggest competition of my career.

On the morning of the meet, my mother came with a letter my father had written for me. The letter was filled with encouragement. He shared words of faith in me and my abilities. I was so touched by his letter that I swam my fastest times. I even placed in the finals. Even though my father was absent, he still encouraged me through my mother and his letter.

B. Lesson Context

Because it was written around AD 51, the epistle we call 1 Thessalonians was probably the first of the New Testament's 27 books to be written. Although the four Gospels detail earlier events, most research agrees that those four were not written until the AD 60s and later.

Thessalonica was (and is) a Macedonian port city where Paul founded a church during his second missionary journey. His visit was quite controversial (Acts 17:1-9). The commotion Paul stirred was so intense that he had to escape by night (17:10). That was not the first time he had had to do so (9:23-25), nor would it be the last (23:31).

The city was on an important trade route and prospered as a result. Those of Greek, Roman, and Jewish heritage constituted its population. Paul and Silas had entered the synagogue in Thessalonica and argued from the Scriptures that Jesus was the Messiah. They ultimately persuaded some Jews and many Gentiles (Acts 17:1-4). Other Jews in the city became envious of Paul and Silas' success. They persuaded the governing authorities to persecute the residents who believed in Christ. While the church in Thessalonica grew, it continued to face challenges in the form of persecution (1 Thessalonians 2:14; 3:3-4). Paul wrote this letter to comfort and encourage the Thessalonian believers in their trials.

I. Thanksgiving

(1 Thessalonians 2:13-16)

A. Accepting God's Word (v. 13)

13. For this cause also thank we God without ceasing, because, when ye received the word of God which ye heard of us, ye received it not as the word of men, but as it is in truth, the word of God, which effectually worketh also in you that believe.

The phrase *this cause* introduces the reason for Paul's thankfulness: the Thessalonians' receptiveness to *the word of God* as being just that. Today we rightly identify the Bible as the Word of God, which acknowledges its divine origin and character. The same was true in the first century AD (Mark 7:13; 1 Corinthians 2:13; 14:37). But when Paul began his missionary journeys, none of the 27 books of the New Testament had yet been written (see Lesson Context). Therefore the Word of God they heard was Paul's oral testimony to them. In Galatians 1:11-12, he explains why his preaching was to be taken as divinely authoritative: "the gospel which was preached of me is not after man . . . . but by the revelation of Jesus Christ." Vital to their salvation and sanctification was their response of "belief of the truth" (2 Thessalonians 2:13). Paul's original readers recognized the supernatural origin of Paul's message and responded fittingly. For a "sharper" description of how the Word of God *effectually worketh*, see Hebrews 4:12.

> **What Do You Think?**
> Considering that the Bible is the Word of God, how do you approach your study of the Bible?
>
> **Digging Deeper**
> When you encounter difficult or challenging passages in the Bible, how do you respond? Who can you turn to for help with those passages?

Reacting to the Word

As a child, I enjoyed Sunday night services at my small-town church. People wore their regular street clothes, not the dresses and suits they wore on Sunday mornings. It felt like a gathering of good friends having fun together. Not only that, but if special speakers visited, they usually took center stage on Sunday evenings.

My favorite of these services happened when missionaries visited. They told stories of people in far-off places, people who spoke different languages and had different traditions. They brought trays of slides for the overhead projector to illustrate their presentations. Sometimes they wore traditional clothes from the country where they ministered.

Even though the missionaries were admired, the real focus was on the people who heard and accepted the Word of God. Their eternities were changed because they believed the gospel message the missionaries brought to them. The new Christians realized that what they heard did not originate with men but was from God. They applied it to their culture, honoring God in the process.

It's all too easy to become "ho-hum" about the Bible. Those who live in Western democracies have unlimited access to it in its numerous translations, sizes, and bindings. You probably have several Bibles around your house right now and one or more Bible apps installed on your smartphone. What lesson(s) can we learn from the first-century Thessalonians about not taking the Word of God lightly?

—L. M. W.

B. Imitating God's Churches (v. 14)

14. For ye, brethren, became followers of the churches of God which in Judaea are in Christ Jesus: for ye also have suffered like things of your own countrymen, even as they have of the Jews.

The conjunction *for* links this verse closely with the preceding one. It also alerts the reader that what follows is the evidence that the Word of God is working daily in their lives. To be active *followers* of someone else's example is sometimes a good thing (1 Corinthians 4:16; 11:1) and sometimes a bad thing (Hebrews 4:11). Paul has already acknowledged the readers' wise choice in this

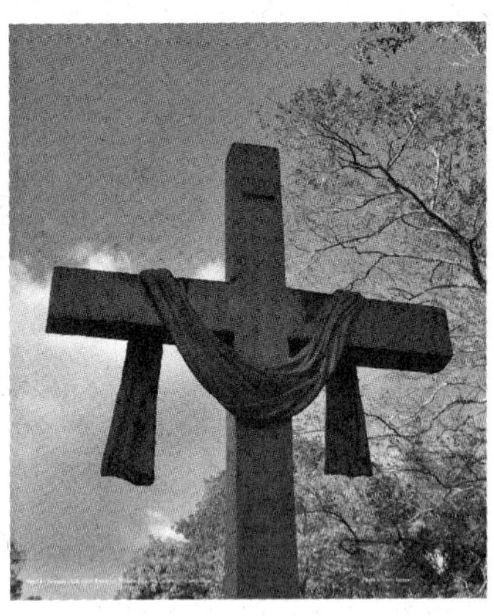

Visual for Lesson 10. *After discussing verse 13, allow learners one minute to silently consider this question and any action they might take.*

regard (1 Thessalonians 1:6). We might call that "active imitation."

But active imitation doesn't seem to be the sense of the verse before us. Paul here seems to have in view more of a "passive imitation" in that the Thessalonian believers are undergoing the same kind of persecution as are *the churches of God which in Judaea are in Christ Jesus.* The Thessalonians had not chosen to be persecuted; rather, persecution has been inflicted on them. Paul doesn't minimize this fact (see 2 Thessalonians 1:4). Instead, this seems to be his way of providing assurance, comfort, and encouragement by telling his readers that they are not alone.

The parallel between *your own countrymen* and *the Jews* is interesting for comparing and contrasting the sources and nature of the persecutions. We may wonder to which group or groups the word *countrymen* refers exactly, since Romans, Greeks, and Jews all inhabited the area in significant numbers (see Lesson Context). The answer lies in Acts 17:5; the instigators of the persecution in Thessalonica are "the Jews which believed not." The mindset of those who inflicted the *like things* is the subject of the following verse.

C. Seeing God's Justice (vv. 15-16)

15. Who both killed the Lord Jesus, and their own prophets, and have persecuted us; and they please not God, and are contrary to all men.

A small group of Jewish leaders had ensured the judicial murder of *the Lord Jesus* (compare John 11:45-53; 18:28-31; Acts 2:23; 13:28; etc.). This was entirely consistent with how the *prophets* in the Old Testament had been rejected and condemned (Luke 11:47-48; Acts 7:52; example: Jeremiah 26:20-23).

In such context, Paul noted the Jewish leaders' culpability in continuing this pattern of opposition not only to *God* but to *all men* who opposed their agenda—an agenda seen in our next verse.

16a. Forbidding us to speak to the Gentiles that they might be saved, to fill up their sins always.

The general hostility of Jews toward *the Gentiles* of the time is well known. Such hostility reaches back into the approximately 400 years between the Old and New Testaments. The literature of that time tells of the periodic desecration of the temple and Jerusalem by Gentiles. Those transgressions eventually resulted in the Maccabean revolt of about 167–160 BC. The animosity between Jews and Gentiles is detectable in various places in the New Testament (examples: Luke 21:24; Acts 10:28).

The Thessalonians had personally witnessed persecution against Paul and Silas (Acts 17:5-9). Paul's criticism of his persecutors here echoes Jesus' pushback on the scribes and Pharisees in His final week (Matthew 23:13).

16b. For the wrath is come upon them to the uttermost.

The divine *wrath* that *is come upon* the Jewish leaders may include a future punishment, but the main idea is that of the present at the time Paul writes. The word translated *uttermost* can take at least eight meanings, depending on how it is used in a given context. A reasonable conclusion here is that *uttermost* is to be understood in the sense of "completely."

Luke 18:5 is another case that shares this same likelihood: "Yet because this widow troubleth me, I will avenge her, lest by her continual coming she weary me." The phrasing at issue is the translated word *continual.* The sense of "continuing to pester me until I'm completely worn out" is a very reasonable interpretation.

II. Encouragement

(1 Thessalonians 2:17–3:5)

A. Paul's Desire to Return (v. 17)

17. But we, brethren, being taken from you for a short time in presence, not in heart, endeavoured the more abundantly to see your face with great desire.

After spending at least 15 days in Thessalonica (Acts 17:2), mob violence had resulted in Paul's hasty exit from the city under cover of darkness (17:5-10). The phrasing *being taken from you* indicates a departure that was less than voluntary. This fact undoubtedly was a key factor in Paul's intense desire to return.

But Paul quickly reassured his readers that "out of sight, out of mind" was not his method of operation. The phrase of being absent *in presence, not in heart* indicates quite the opposite (similar are 1 Corinthians 5:3 and Colossians 2:5). In other cities, Paul spent months teaching and preaching the truths of the gospel (Acts 18:11; 19:8); he undoubtedly realized that his having been in Thessalonica for less than a month was inadequate. His hasty, secretive departure had necessarily left work undone, as witnessed by 1 Thessalonians 3:10.

B. Desire Thwarted (v. 18)

18. Wherefore we would have come unto you, even I Paul, once and again; but Satan hindered us.

Paul's inability to make a return visit was not due to a lack of desire on his part. *Satan* was to blame, although the text does not tell us what specific method he used. Some propose that it was an illness (as also possible in 2 Corinthians 12:7). Others theorize that the city leaders of Thessalonica may have forbidden his return, given the disturbance his work in the city caused (Acts 17:5-9).

Both options are merely guesses. Neither should distract us from the main point: Satan, the enemy and accuser of God's people (Revelation 12:10b), was responsible for Paul's extended absence. He may have been responsible for other travel hindrances, but some cases involved Paul's juggling his ministry priorities (Romans 1:13; 15:22).

What Do You Think?

How do you handle situations when your plans or desires are thwarted or delayed? Consider James 4:13-17 as you think about your answer.

Digging Deeper

How does James 4:13-17 inform your answer?

C. Paul's Joy in Them (vv. 19-20)

19-20. For what is our hope, or joy, or crown of rejoicing? Are not even ye in the presence of our Lord Jesus Christ at his coming? For ye are our glory and joy.

Old Testament prophets sometimes received no assurance that their ministries would result in changed hearts and changed behavior. In fact, the prophet Jeremiah was told that his prophetic ministry would *not* succeed (Jeremiah 7:27-28; 18:11-12)! No wonder Jeremiah is called "the weeping prophet." To be assigned a task predicted to fail would strain anyone's emotions to the maximum.

Paul's ministry was not like that of Jeremiah's, however. Paul did have opposition, but he also had a successful harvest of souls that was evidence of a God-given ministry (compare 1 Corinthians 9:1). And Paul does not take this for granted. Rather, he communicates its results loud and clear with the rhetorical question: *For what is our hope, or joy, or crown of rejoicing?* The answer comes by the declaration, *For ye are our glory and joy.* As affirming as this harvest is, Paul knows that it's not all due to his efforts (see 3:6-9). An apt summary of all this is found in 1 Thessalonians 2:4a.

The mention of *our Lord Jesus Christ at his coming*

How to Say It

Berea	Buh-*ree*-uh.
Gentiles	*Jen*-tiles.
Maccabean	Mack-uh-*be*-un.
Macedonian	Mass-eh-*doe*-nee-un.
Silas	*Sigh*-luss.
Thessalonica	*Thess*-uh-lo-**nye**-kuh (*th* as in *thin*).

sets another event-context for the text before us. It refers to Jesus' future advent when He returns to earth. It's the same day referred to in Philippians 1:6, 10; 2:16. Paul thinks so highly of his Thessalonian readers that he can count them as already on the right side when that event comes to pass.

What Do You Think?

How do you find hope and joy in the midst of difficult circumstances?

Digging Deeper

How can you be a source of hope and joy for others, especially for those who are struggling or in need?

D. Paul Sends Timothy (vv. 1-5)

1-2. Wherefore when we could no longer forbear, we thought it good to be left at Athens alone; and sent Timotheus, our brother, and minister of God, and our fellowlabourer in the gospel of Christ, to establish you, and to comfort you concerning your faith.

Having escaped from Thessalonica by night, Paul and Silas then traveled 45 miles to the west to preach the gospel in Berea (Acts 17:10-12). They would have made that trek in three days if they had maintained an average walking pace of two miles per hour, eight hours per day (17:10).

But Paul was soon forced out of that town as well, making his way south to *Athens* under escort (Acts 17:13-16). As he dismissed his escort, their task having been completed, he sent instructions back to Berea with them for "Silas and Timotheus . . . to come to him with all speed" (17:15).

There is some debate regarding whether that reunion took place in Athens or happened later in Corinth (compare Acts 18:5). The latter seems more likely, as there is no hint of Timothy's coming to Athens. Research indicates that Paul wrote his letters to the Thessalonians while in Corinth, perhaps in AD 51 (see Lesson Context).

The phrase *we could no longer forbear* indicates that Paul was on pins and needles, wondering how the new Christians in Thessalonica were doing. He knew their need for him and did his best to plan for a return visit. But his best wasn't good enough, and he seemed nearly to have reached a breaking point. Ultimately, Paul made what undoubtedly seemed to him a "second best" decision: if the apostle couldn't go back to Thessalonica personally, he would send Timothy instead. Thus Timothy could carry Paul's correspondence to the Thessalonians.

After Timothy's conversion in Acts 16:1-3, Paul often trusted him with special tasks. This involved travel that was unaccompanied by Paul himself (Acts 19:22; 1 Corinthians 4:17).

What Do You Think?

What situations of frustration or weariness have you recently experienced in your own life?

Digging Deeper

How can you broaden and deepen a network of true friends who will encourage you in difficult times?

Love Letter

I opened the large envelope and pulled out the old photos my mom had given me. Among the family pictures was a letter written in 1948, even before my mother was born. My grandfather had gone to the city for a hospital stay, and while he was there, he wrote to my grandmother back home with the children. My grandparents were young at the time, in their twenties, and they had only been married a few years. His love for her was evident. He called her "honey" and his "little lump of sugar," and he told her how much he missed her cooking. He penned greetings to the children and admonished them to be good for their mom while he was away. He assured them he would return soon.

I smiled as I read the words exchanged between the two people who started our family as I know it. I read it to my children, and we laughed at how he asked her to send a few toothpicks in her next letter since "they don't seem to have any here."

Just as I cherished the letter and shared it with my children, the Thessalonians must have cherished the letters from Paul, their spiritual father in the faith (1 Thessalonians 2:11-12; compare 1 Timothy 1:2).

If challenged to pick five words to describe your

attitude toward the Bible, would the word *cherish* be a candidate for one of those five? —L. M. W.

3. That no man should be moved by these afflictions: for yourselves know that we are appointed thereunto.

In speaking of *afflictions* as they intersect the Christian life, a more modern way to say what Paul says here might be, "The limits of tyrants are prescribed by the endurance of those whom they oppress" (Frederick Douglass, 1818–1895). The Bible itself has much more to say about oppression. Consider Jesus' words in John 15:18: "If the world hate you, ye know that it hated me before it hated you." Paul used to be one of the haters (Acts 8:3), and he's been on the receiving end of hatred as well (16:22-23). So he knows what he's talking about when he says, "All that will live godly in Christ Jesus shall suffer persecution" (2 Timothy 3:12).

4. For verily, when we were with you, we told you before that we should suffer tribulation; even as it came to pass, and ye know.

Having been forewarned, the Thessalonians should not have been surprised when the predictions of *tribulation* came true (*even as it came to pass*). This theme of "don't be surprised" is echoed by the other apostles as well (compare 1 Peter 4:12; 1 John 3:13). In fact, Paul later argues that suffering with Christ is linked to eventual glory with Him (Romans 8:17). Suffering was (and is) unavoidable; it is a key part of the way that God makes us into Jesus' image. Hardship can result in distinguishing between those of deep and shallow faith (Matthew 13:5-6, 20-21). It's an issue of counting the cost of becoming a disciple (Luke 14:26-27).

5. For this cause, when I could no longer forbear, I sent to know your faith, lest by some means the tempter have tempted you, and our labour be in vain.

At the same time, Paul was concerned about the state of the Thessalonians' faith. He had been with them such a short time! Now having received the left foot of fellowship from Thessalonica, he feared the worst. Since Satan had been hindering Paul from visiting them (1 Thessalonians 2:18), what harm might he be doing in Thessalonica?

When Paul wrote that he feared *the tempter had tempted* them, he probably was not referring to the common temptations to sin. Paul knew that such temptations were part of earthly life (1 Corinthians 10:13). What concerned Paul was the temptation to reject Christ to escape suffering. If that happened, Paul's ministry in Thessalonica might turn out to be *in vain* (compare Philippians 2:16). The antidote for the tempter's poison was encouragement, so Paul sent his trusted "son in the faith" (1 Timothy 1:2) to bring that encouragement to the Thessalonians.

What Do You Think?

How can you resist temptations that would draw you away from Christ?

Digging Deeper

Why is it important to encourage and support other believers who are also facing temptations?

Conclusion

A. Encouraging One Another

Suffering is part of the Christian life. But sometimes, we fall into the habit of dealing with suffering alone. We think we need to just grit our teeth and bear it. While God does call us to endure suffering, He does not ask us to suffer alone. Paul talks more about suffering for Christ than anyone else in the New Testament. Yet his solution was not telling people to buck up but encouraging them. Because the church is Christ's body, we share in each other's sufferings (1 Corinthians 12:26). By encouraging one another, we can help bear the burdens of our brothers and sisters in Christ (Galatians 6:2). We will also keep sufferings from becoming temptations, leading one another away from following Christ.

B. Prayer

Father, help us to seek and comfort the discouraged in our midst. Let their burdens be ours as well. In Jesus' name we pray. Amen.

C. Thought to Remember

Encouragement is a defense against despair.

Involvement Learning

Enhance your lesson with KJV Bible Student *(from your curriculum supplier) and the reproducible activity page (at www.standardlesson.com or in the back of the* KJV Standard Lesson Commentary Deluxe Edition*).*

Into the Lesson

Give learners envelopes and have them write their names on them. Collect and shuffle the envelopes, then redistribute them randomly, making sure no one receives his or her own envelope. Distribute note cards and ask learners to write a short note of encouragement to the person named on the envelope, then seal the note card in the envelope. Collect the envelopes to deliver at the end of class. *Option.* Have learners write their mailing addresses on the envelopes; mail the cards in the week ahead.

Pose this question for whole-class discussion: "What's your reaction to being asked to write a note like this?"

Transition to Bible study by saying, "Sometimes it's challenging to know how to encourage others from a distance. But it is important for those needing encouragement to know that they haven't been forgotten."

Into the Word

Ask two volunteers to read aloud 1 Thessalonians 2:13–3:5, alternating between verses. Focus on 2:13 as you distribute handouts (you create) with these two phrases as column headers:

Word of God | *Word of Men*

Form learners into three groups—**Noun Group**, **Verb Group**, and **Adjectives Group**. Give these instructions: "According to your group's name, put in one column some words or phrases that describe the effect of that column's header; then put its opposite in the other column." Should your learners need examples to get started, here are possibilities: **Noun Group**: Christian | pagan; **Verb Group**: pleases God | displeases God; **Adjective Group**: reliable | unreliable.

After allowing a few minutes to make lists, invite a volunteer from each group to write their responses in the columns on the board. Then pose this question for whole-group discussion: "What levels of resistance have you seen for accepting the Word of God as being just that?"

Alternative. Distribute copies of "The Word at Work" exercise from the activity page, which you can download. Divide learners into study pairs to complete as indicated.

Focusing on 1 Thessalonians 2:17-20, pose these questions for whole-class discussion: 1–What frustrations did Paul express to the Thessalonians? 2–When have you experienced a time when you were unable to be with someone who cared about you? 3–How can knowing Paul's story help you deal with future frustrations? Allow time to discuss each question before voicing the one that follows.

Focus on 1 Thessalonians 3:1-5. Brainstorm ways that Paul's letter encouraged the Thessalonians. Have each participant write on a slip of paper a favorite encouraging verse of Scripture, leaving the selection anonymous. Put all slips of paper in a container. Draw one out, read the text aloud, and ask for a show of hands from those who find that passage especially encouraging. Repeat with other slips of paper as time allows.

Into Life

Challenge learners to suggest ways to offer encouragement to fellow believers. Write their ideas on the board. Ask learners to think of a fellow Christian whom they haven't seen in a while. Challenge them to encourage at least one of those people in the week ahead. Invite learners to use one of the brainstormed ideas written on the board or another one that occurs to them. Have learners write their idea on a slip of paper as a reminder.

Alternative. Distribute copies of the "Ideas for Encouragement" exercise from the activity page. Have learners complete it within one minute before discussing conclusions with a partner.

The Love of God

Devotional Reading: 2 Corinthians 5:16-21
Background Scripture: 1 John 3:1-10

1 John 3:1-10

1 Behold, what manner of love the Father hath bestowed upon us, that we should be called the sons of God: therefore the world knoweth us not, because it knew him not.

2 Beloved, now are we the sons of God, and it doth not yet appear what we shall be: but we know that, when he shall appear, we shall be like him; for we shall see him as he is.

3 And every man that hath this hope in him purifieth himself, even as he is pure.

4 Whosoever committeth sin transgresseth also the law: for sin is the transgression of the law.

5 And ye know that he was manifested to take away our sins; and in him is no sin.

6 Whosoever abideth in him sinneth not: whosoever sinneth hath not seen him, neither known him.

7 Little children, let no man deceive you: he that doeth righteousness is righteous, even as he is righteous.

8 He that committeth sin is of the devil; for the devil sinneth from the beginning. For this purpose the Son of God was manifested, that he might destroy the works of the devil.

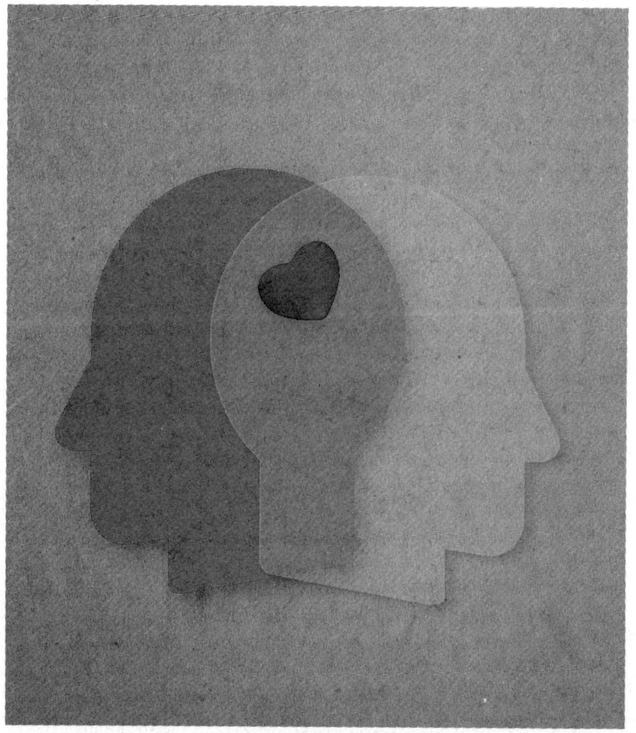

9 Whosoever is born of God doth not commit sin; for his seed remaineth in him: and he cannot sin, because he is born of God.

10 In this the children of God are manifest, and the children of the devil: whosoever doeth not righteousness is not of God, neither he that loveth not his brother.

Key Text

Behold, what manner of love the Father hath bestowed upon us, that we should be called the sons of God: therefore the world knoweth us not, because it knew him not. —**1 John 3:1**

Hope in

the Lord

Unit III: Eternal Hope

Lessons 10–13

Lesson Aims

After participating in this lesson, each learner will be able to:

1. State the reason the Son of God came.
2. Explain the significance of Christ's purity.
3. Recruit an accountability partner for mutual resistance to sin.

Lesson Outline

Introduction

A. Using Rubrics

In education, a *rubric* is a guide for specifying criteria for academic assignments. A well-written rubric can be a lifesaver for both students and teachers. For the student, these tools provide expectations, goals, and guidance. For the teacher, rubrics help ensure fair and consistent grading. However, a poorly written or overly complicated rubric can create uncertainty and difficulty for teachers and students.

As a college professor, I frequently create rubrics for my students. In one such rubric, I accidentally used unclear directions for the assignment. As students worked on the project, they filled my email inbox with complaints and requests for help. Addressing their concerns and clarifying the rubric required a whole weekend of unplanned work. The next time I taught the class, I double-checked to be sure that the revised rubric did not contain unclear directions.

Today's Scripture reveals a rubric for living as beloved children of God. Unlike the rubric I created, this one is clear and straightforward. As you read the Scripture, consider this question: Will you pass or fail the final assignment?

B. Lesson Context

Five books of the New Testament have traditionally been attributed to the apostle John, who was one of the original 12 disciples (Matthew 10:2). Three of the five—the ones we designate 1 John, 2 John, and 3 John—are letters from the apostle to various believers in the first century AD.

Church history strongly associates John with the church in Ephesus, located in modern-day Turkey. Tradition says he died in this city in the AD 90s. The three letters were probably written in the region of Ephesus. The letters date from the AD 80s or 90s. John would have been an older man by this time (compare the self-designation "the elder" in 2 John 1; 3 John 1). The dignity of his age peeks through in 1 John as he addresses his readers as "little children" nine times (examples: 1 John 2:1; 3:7).

We are unsure of the issues that faced the letter's original audience. Apparently, they had been confronted with threats to their faith. Some of these threats included the temptation from an early form of the attractive heresy we call Gnosticism. Among other things, gnostics taught that it did not matter whether a person had morality or love—as long as he or she had "secret knowledge." To combat this false teaching, John emphasized the connection between right belief, right actions, and right love. The child of God must believe the truth, obey the commands, and love the brethren. False teachers were so bold that John referred to them as having a "spirit of antichrist" (1 John 4:3; compare 2:18, 22). John wanted their influence eliminated lest they split the church further (see 2:19).

The church also faced more general threats, including the denial that Jesus is Christ (1 John 2:22), a return to idol worship (5:21), and a general lack of love for one another (4:7).

I. The Love of God

(1 John 3:1-3)

A. Our Identity (v. 1)

1a. Behold, what manner of love the Father hath bestowed upon us, that we should be called the sons of God.

John had established that God is righteous and that "every one that doeth righteousness is born of him" (1 John 2:29). John draws the attention of his audience to the *love* of God *the Father*. This love was *bestowed* on humanity through the Father's sending of His only Son, Jesus, to earth for our sins (Romans 3:25; 1 John 2:2; 4:10). There was nothing that humanity could do to deserve God's love. No amount of human love for God could influence *what manner of love* God has for humanity (4:9-10).

When people demonstrate faith in Jesus, they become *sons* and daughters *of God* (John 1:12-13; Galatians 3:26). This adoption occurs through the transforming power of the Holy Spirit so that we might share in God's glory (Romans 8:14-17). Therefore, adoption into God's family comes not through physical birth but spiritual birth (John 3:5-8).

1b. Therefore the world knoweth us not, because it knew him not.

The underlying Greek word translated *world* appears 23 times in 1 John. If we were to count all the uses of this word in the writings of John, it would total over 100 uses. In John's writings, the term can refer to all humanity in general (examples: John 3:16; 1 John 2:2), the location where humanity lives (example: John 17:11), or to the sinful individuals and structures that oppose God and His people (examples: 1 John 2:16-17; 3:13; 5:4-5).

It is the final option to which this verse refers. In contrast to the children of God, *the world* has failed to know God and His abundant love revealed through Christ Jesus. Therefore, the world is also unable to know the children of God. As a result, believers can anticipate facing hatred from the world (John 15:18-25).

Known or Unknown?

Employees typically change their behavior in the presence of a supervisor. Workers sit up straighter, adopt a more pleasant attitude, or try to appear busier to impress the boss. What happens, though, when the supervisor makes a surprise appearance?

One holiday season, I was in my office when the door opened, and a person in an elf costume entered. The "elf" greeted us and handed us each a sugar packet. My coworkers and I laughed, but several minutes passed until I recognized the person in the costume: my boss's boss. When I realized the identity of the person in the elvish ears and outfit, I exhaled, relieved that I hadn't embarrassed myself!

Unlike my boss's boss, God has not hidden or disguised himself. He has revealed himself

How to Say It

Colossians	Kuh-*losh*-unz.
Corinthians	Ko-*rin*-thee-unz (*th* as in *thin*).
Ephesus	*Ef*-uh-sus.
Galatians	Guh-*lay*-shunz.
Gnosticism	Nahss-tih-*sizz*-um.
gnostics	*nahss*-ticks.
Philippians	Fih-*lip*-ee-unz.
rubric	*rew*-brik.

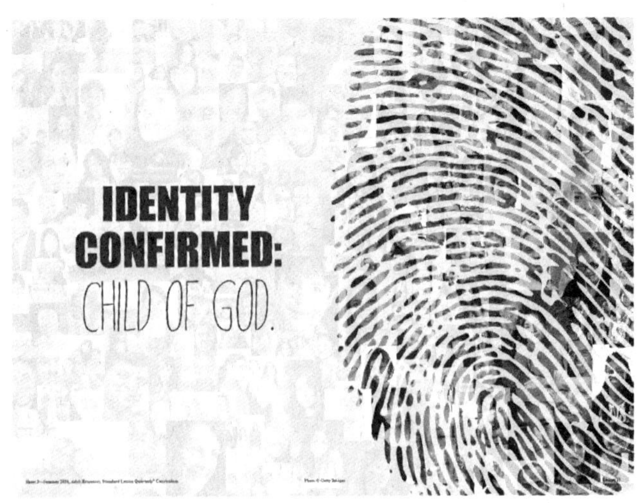

Visual for Lesson 11. *At the close of class, point to this visual and give time for learners to silently pray for guidance on how to live as a child of God.*

through general revelation to His creation (see Romans 1:19-20) and through specific revelation through the incarnation of Jesus (see John 1:18). Although the world has received God's self-disclosure, it has failed to know Him.

However, the world sees us: God's people. Do your actions and speech point others to God (compare Matthew 5:16)? Eventually, all people will see and know Christ (Revelation 1:7). What are you doing to point others to God as we wait for that moment? —L. M. W.

B. God's Purity (vv. 2-3)

2a. Beloved, now are we the sons of God.

John uses the greeting *beloved* five times in this epistle (here and in 1 John 3:21; 4:1, 7, 11). The greeting reveals the relationship that John had with his audience. Although he was an older man when writing this epistle, he felt a close connection with them. He counted himself with them (*we*) as being children *of God*.

2b. And it doth not yet appear what we shall be: but we know that, when he shall appear, we shall be like him; for we shall see him as he is.

As God's children, we do not fully know God's plan for our lives. But we know we will someday be changed (1 Corinthians 15:51-54). What we eventually *shall be* has not yet been disclosed fully. Even so, we know this: when Jesus *shall appear* at His second coming, *we shall see him as he is* because we will see Him face-to-face.

At that time, *we shall be like him*. Christ will transform our bodies into something glorious (Philippians 3:20-21). In and through this transformation, we will share in Christ's glory (Romans 8:17; Colossians 3:4).

What Do You Think?

How will you live differently in the upcoming week in light of this verse's promise regarding our future glory?

Digging Deeper

How does the hope that you will someday be "like" Christ affect your life today?

3a. And every man that hath this hope in him purifieth himself.

The verse before us contains the only usage of the underlying Greek noun *hope* in any of the writings of John. In contrast, the apostle Paul uses the term about three dozen times throughout his epistles. *This hope* comes from what has been promised to believers regarding the future return of Christ. Hope, however, is not simply a positive outlook or feeling. Instead, our hope comes from the trustworthiness of God's character. We have hope because of what God has promised to do *in* Christ (see Titus 2:13-14, lesson 12).

This verse contains only the second usage of the Greek word translated *purifieth* in the writings of John. Thus, we have two rare (for John) words back-to-back, drawing our attention. *Purifieth* refers either to (1) ceremonial purification per the Law of Moses (John 11:55; Acts 24:18), (2) taking a vow when the word is used with a particular grammatical construction (21:23-24, 26), or (3) moral purification (James 4:8; 1 Peter 1:22). Its usage in the verse before us reflects the third option.

3b. Even as he is pure.

The antecedent of the word *he* isn't the "man" of 1 John 3:3a, just considered. Instead, "he" refers to Christ. It is He who *is pure*, meaning He is sinless (see commentary on 1 John 3:5, below). Christ's blood shed on the cross is the means through which our purification from sin occurs (1:7). This does not mean believers are "off the hook" from living upright and righteous lives. Instead, believers should purify themselves and avoid the stain of sin (see 2 Corinthians 7:1; 1 Timothy 5:22). Such purification occurs when believers put an end to all sinful behaviors (Colossians 3:5). As we do so, we develop lives of righteousness (James 1:19-20).

John's directives in this verse mirror Jesus' teachings: "Be ye therefore perfect, even as your Father which is in heaven is perfect" (Matthew 5:48). Human perfection is impossible on earth. However, we should make every effort to live pure and upright lives as children of our perfect heavenly Father.

What Do You Think?

How will you be more attentive to the Holy Spirit's leading as you pursue a life of purity?

Digging Deeper

How will you get rid of distractions that prevent you from noticing the guidance of the Holy Spirit?

II. The Mission of God

(1 John 3:4-6)

A. Our Situation (v. 4)

4. Whosoever committeth sin transgresseth also the law: for sin is the transgression of the law.

Having established the life of purity required for God's children, John presents the danger that believers face: that of sin. The human inclination toward sin is unavoidable for all people—believers included. Scripture describes *sin* in various ways. Sin is foolishness (Proverbs 24:9), the opposite of faith (Romans 14:23), falling short of God's glory (3:23), a willful failure to do good (James 4:17), or any "unrighteousness" (1 John 5:17). Ultimately, sin turns people into enemies of God.

Perhaps you remember from high-school English classes that when you see the verb *is*, you can almost think of it as an equal sign (=) that equates the two sides of the sentence. That is indeed true here: *sin = the transgression of the law*. This verse is the clearest definition of sin in the New Testament. Perhaps you've heard *sin* vaguely defined as "to miss the mark" or some such. But right before us now is the biblical definition of sin.

B. God's Solution (vv. 5-6)

5. And ye know that he was manifested to take away our sins; and in him is no sin.

The Greek word translated *know* appears 15 times in 1 John. Its use reveals the apostle's emphasis on knowing the person and work of Jesus Christ. But simply having knowledge of Jesus is not enough (compare James 2:19). Instead, believers should seek understanding of Christ and conform their lives to that knowledge (see 1 John 5:18-20).

Only one person could take away humanity's sins: Jesus Christ (John 1:29). Only Jesus has the power to deal with sin because He was the sinless Son of God (2 Corinthians 5:21; compare Isaiah 53:9-10). He and He alone could *take away our sins* through His sacrifice on the cross (see Hebrews 9:28; 1 Peter 2:22-24).

6a. Whosoever abideth in him sinneth not.

John begins a contrast of two types of people. The first is the person who *abideth in* Christ. Jesus taught that believers should remain in Him because He is the source of spiritual life (John 15:4-7). Believers do so by receiving His teachings (1 John 2:24) and obeying them (John 14:23; 15:10; 1 John 3:24). Doing so does not mean that believers will be perfect and without any sin (compare 1:8, 10). Rather, when we follow the perfect, sinless Savior, we can pursue lives of holiness and righteousness.

6b. Whosoever sinneth hath not seen him, neither known him.

The second type is the person who has neither *seen* Christ nor *known him*. Some people in John's original audience had apparently claimed that they could know God but continue to live sinful lives. This false belief led to a strong correction from the apostle: it was not possible to both love God and love sin (1 John 1:6; 2:4).

III. The Children of God

(1 John 3:7-10)

A. Our Warning (vv. 7-8)

7. Little children, let no man deceive you: he

that doeth righteousness is righteous, even as he is righteous.

The phrase *little children* is a favorite greeting of the apostle John. His nine uses of the expression in 1 John reveal the care that he felt for the original recipients of the letter (examples: 1 John 2:1, 12, 28; 3:18; 5:21). They were all children of God, but John had a unique relationship with his audience—one like a spiritual father and his children.

Some people in the community had attempted to *deceive* the believers and lead them astray from the truth (see Lesson Context; see also 1 John 2:26). Although we do not know the content of their teaching, we can do a "mirror reading" of 1 John to determine aspects of their false doctrine. Based on this verse, we can assume that these teachers had wrongly taught that a person could be *righteous* without behaving righteously.

However, this verse does not mean that John taught a form of works-righteousness. Humans cannot attain righteousness through their behavior (Romans 3:10). Only Christ Jesus is completely *righteous* (2 Corinthians 5:21). People can become righteous before God through faith in Christ (see Romans 3:21-26; 5:17). As a result of their being declared righteous by God, believers should live upright lives in obedience to Him (1 John 2:3-5).

8a. He that committeth sin is of the devil; for the devil sinneth from the beginning.

In contrast to the righteous person is the person who *committeth sin* and disobeys God's law. People who willfully oppose God and His truth are following the devil's lies (see John 8:44; Acts 13:10). This spirit of disobedience results in a person's spiritual death (see Ephesians 2:1-2).

The devil is another name for Satan (see Revelation 12:9). Since the introduction of sin at *the beginning*, the devil has opposed God and the people of God. The devil's opposition comes through temptation (examples: Genesis 3:1; Luke 4:1-13; John 13:2). Therefore, believers should not "give place to the devil" (Ephesians 4:27). Instead, we should make every effort to resist the work of the devil (see Ephesians 6:10-17; James 4:7; 1 Peter 5:8-9).

What Do You Think?

How does each part of the armor of God (Ephesians 6:10-17) help believers resist the work of the devil?

Digging Deeper

In what ways is a community of believers necessary to help each member resist the work of the devil?

8b. For this purpose the Son of God was manifested, that he might destroy the works of the devil.

Jesus Christ, *the Son of God*, came to earth as a sacrifice for human sin (1 John 3:5, above). By doing so, He triumphed over the devil (Colossians 2:13-15; Hebrews 2:14-15). Although Christ has already won the victory (Galatians 1:4), the devil has power in the world for a time (1 John 5:19). That power, however, is limited. Someday, Christ will return to *destroy* the devil and the *works of the devil* (see Romans 16:20; Revelation 20:1-10).

B. God's Seed (vv. 9-10)

9. Whosoever is born of God doth not commit sin; for his seed remaineth in him: and he cannot sin, because he is born of God.

The underlying Greek word translated *born* appears 10 times in 1 John. All instances of that word in this letter refer to a person's spiritual birth into being a child *of God*. People who have experienced this spiritual birth do what is right (1 John 2:29), know God and love others (4:7), believe that Jesus is the Christ (5:1), overcome the world (5:4), and will not continue to sin (5:18).

God's children will continue to wage war against sin and its effects (see 1 Peter 2:11). Although we have been released from sin and freed from its condemnation (Romans 6:1-14; 8:1), our sinful nature will continue until Christ returns to deliver us (7:14-25). When John says that believers *doth not commit sin*, he does not mean that we will live perfect lives. Instead, John's words are meant to encourage us to seek godly and upright lives.

Believers can avoid a life of sin because they have the *seed* of God in them. This seed is "planted" when believers receive the gospel (see 1 John 2:24) and the Holy Spirit (see 3:24). Only through the power of God's Spirit that *remaineth in* us can we fight sin (Romans 8:5-16; Galatians 5:16-17; etc.).

> **What Do You Think?**
> How would you explain the concept of being "born of God" to an unbeliever?
> **Digging Deeper**
> In what ways are Ezekiel 11:19-20; John 1:12-13; 3:1-15; Romans 6:1-14; 2 Corinthians 5:17; and Titus 3:4-7 relevant to your explanation?

What Makes You Different?

Every day, the brother and sister drove to school together. The siblings had always gotten along with each other, with other students, and with their teachers. Every morning, they walked past the same security guard at school. He had seen many high schoolers in his years of service, so he knew well the temperaments and habits of teenagers.

One morning, the guard approached the siblings and said, "You two are different from other students. What makes you different?"

The sister froze, unsure how to respond. How would she be able to explain the truth? Would she dare tell him that they were children of God?

"I try to keep a positive attitude," said the brother, smiling at the man.

As they walked down the hall, the sister said, "Just a 'positive attitude,' huh?"

Do others see your behavior and wonder what makes you different? God's children do more than keep positive attitudes; they lead lives of righteousness. Do you? —L. M. W.

10. In this the children of God are manifest, and the children of the devil: whosoever doeth not righteousness is not of God, neither he that loveth not his brother.

This verse presents a rubric to distinguish *the children of God* from *the children of the devil.* That status is revealed by a person's actions: children of God act with *righteousness* (1 John 2:29; compare 3:7, above). Further, a person's status is also measured by how he or she loves other members of the family of God. As the love of God fills believers, there will be a natural outpouring of love among believers (3:11-24; 4:7-21). The person who habitually fails to act with righteousness or demonstrate love is not a child *of God.* The rubric is clear, and it is pass-or-fail in this regard.

> **What Do You Think?**
> How do you ensure that you are living according to this rubric?
> **Digging Deeper**
> Who will you ask to be an accountability partner for you in this regard?

Conclusion

A. Spiritual Rubrics

Rubrics help learners understand expectations and how to achieve an assignment's intended goals. Today's Scripture gives us a rubric for whether or not we live as though we have been filled by God's love. If His love has changed our lives, then we will seek lives of holiness and demonstrate love for others.

God's love has transformed us, but we are still affected by the presence of sin. Until the ultimate defeat of Satan, we will fail to behave or love as we ought. In the meantime, God has given us tools to help us grow spiritually. He has given us His Spirit to transform us into Christ's likeness. God has also provided us with a spiritual "family": other children of God. These spiritual "siblings" can encourage us to live according to the rubric of life that God has given us.

B. Prayer

Loving God, You have shown us tremendous mercy and brought us into Your family. We repent of the times when we have failed to love You and our neighbors. Show us how we might better notice the Spirit's leading so that we will not remain in sin. In Jesus' name, we pray. Amen.

C. Thought to Remember

The rubric is clear: God's children love Him and seek lives of righteousness.

Involvement Learning

Enhance your lesson with KJV Bible Student *(from your curriculum supplier) and the reproducible activity page (at www.standardlesson.com or in the back of the* KJV Standard Lesson Commentary Deluxe Edition*).*

Into the Lesson

Write this sentence on the board and ask volunteers to complete it:

A frequently appearing trait in my family is . . .

Encourage volunteers to consider physical or personality traits that appear in their family. Write responses on the board.

Lead into Bible study by saying, "When we exhibit inherited family traits, others can recognize which family we belong to and whose children we are. As we study today's Scripture, consider the 'family traits' that the children of God possess."

Into the Word

Announce a Bible-marking activity. Provide copies of 1 John 3:1-10 for those who do not want to write in their Bible. Provide handouts (you create) with these instructions:

- Draw a circle around any word or phrase related to children or offspring.
- Underline any word or phrase that refers to the work of God.
- Double underline any word or phrase that refers to the work of believers.
- Triple underline any word or phrase that refers to the devil.
- Draw a thin line through any word or phrase that refers to sin or sinful behavior.
- Draw a square around any word or phrase that describes the appropriate behavior for the children of God.
- Draw a question mark next to any word or phrase you find challenging to understand.

Read the Scripture aloud slowly (or ask volunteers to do so) at least twice and as many as four times. As the Scripture is read, class members should mark their copies in the ways noted.

After the final reading, divide class members into groups of three. Have triads answer the following questions: 1–What does it mean to be a child of God? 2–What is the connection between spiritual maturity and purity? 3–How does this Scripture describe the work of God? the work of the devil? the behavior of the children of God? 4–What steps would you take to understand this Scripture better or address difficult-to-understand words or phrases?

Write on the board the following headers: *Doing Right / Loving Others.* Lead into the exercise by saying, "First John 3:10 states that one way to recognize a child of God is by looking at a person's actions and how he or she loves." Ask each triad to brainstorm ways that a believer can act righteously ("Doing Right") and show love toward other believers ("Loving Others"). After five minutes, have a representative from each triad give their responses as you write them under the appropriate header.

Alternative. Distribute copies of the "The Children of God" exercise from the activity page, which you can download. Have learners work in pairs to complete as indicated.

Into Life

Begin this portion of the lesson by asking, "Based on today's study, why should believers consider having an accountability partner?"

Ask learners to partner with another class member for mutual resistance to sin. Remind the class that being an accountability partner requires trust and discretion. Distribute index cards and pens to learners and have them write down specific ways their accountability partner can encourage resistance to sin. Have partners trade cards and make a plan to follow up at least once during the upcoming week and again at the beginning of the next class.

Conclude class by having pairs pray that each other will not continue to live in sin but live as children of God.

Alternative. Distribute the "Resist Sin" exercise from the activity page. Challenge learners to complete the exercise throughout the upcoming week. Invite volunteers to report at the beginning of class next week.

The Rules of Life

Devotional Reading: Psalm 37:27-40
Background Scripture: Titus 1:1-3; 2:11-15

Titus 1:1-3

1 Paul, a servant of God, and an apostle of Jesus Christ, according to the faith of God's elect, and the acknowledging of the truth which is after godliness;

2 In hope of eternal life, which God, that cannot lie, promised before the world began;

3 But hath in due times manifested his word through preaching, which is committed unto me according to the commandment of God our Saviour.

Titus 2:11-15

11 For the grace of God that bringeth salvation hath appeared to all men,

12 Teaching us that, denying ungodliness and worldly lusts, we should live soberly, righteously, and godly, in this present world;

13 Looking for that blessed hope, and the glorious appearing of the great God and our Saviour Jesus Christ;

14 Who gave himself for us, that he might redeem us from all iniquity, and purify unto himself a peculiar people, zealous of good works.

15 These things speak, and exhort, and rebuke with all authority. Let no man despise thee.

Key Text

The grace of God that bringeth salvation hath appeared to all men, Teaching us that, denying ungodliness and worldly lusts, we should live soberly, righteously, and godly, in this present world; Looking for that blessed hope, and the glorious appearing of the great God and our Saviour Jesus Christ. **—Titus 2:11-13**

Hope in
the Lord

Unit III: Eternal Hope

Lessons 10–13

Lesson Aims

After participating in this lesson, each learner will be able to:

1. Recall the "blessed hope."
2. Contrast godly and ungodly lives of Paul's day.
3. Make a plan to eliminate one ungodly element in his or her life.

Lesson Outline

Introduction
- A. Struggle for Godliness
- B. Lesson Context

I. The Messenger (Titus 1:1-3)
- A. Servant and Apostle (v. 1)
- B. Commanded by God (vv. 2-3)

II. The Message (Titus 2:11-15)
- A. Grace Appeared (vv. 11-12)
  - *Ever Learning*
- B. Hope Promised (vv. 13-14)
  - *Waiting for Hope*
- C. Leader Encouraged (v. 15)

Conclusion
- A. The Gift of Grace
- B. Prayer
- C. Thought to Remember

Introduction

A. Struggle for Godliness

A glance through the news would make it seem like the church is consistently plagued by ungodly behavior from both without and within. Recent scandals of greed, abuse, and misuse of power remind us that the church is not immune from ungodly behavior.

But the people of God have always struggled against ungodliness. The church has sought ways to live godly lives, even in an ungodly culture. This issue is as much an issue in the twenty-first century as it was in the first century.

B. Lesson Context

Paul's letter to Titus comes from a part of the New Testament called the Pastoral Epistles. Whereas Paul wrote other letters to specific groups of believers in particular locations (examples: Galatians 1:1, 1 Thessalonians 1:1), the Pastoral Epistles were written to particular individuals: Timothy (1 Timothy 1:2; 2 Timothy 1:2) and Titus. The latter was a church leader Paul designated "mine own son after the common faith" (Titus 1:4).

The letter to Titus involved events that occurred after the conclusion of the book of Acts, but we have no exact knowledge of the sequence. By the time Paul wrote to Titus, the apostle had been released from his imprisonment in Rome and had found an occasion to visit the island of Crete. While visiting, Paul evangelized and started some churches. It is likely, however, that the gospel had already reached Crete many years earlier through unnamed believers (see Acts 2:11).

Crete was famous in antiquity as a source of culture and religion. The Cretan people, however, were not highly esteemed in the Roman world. In Titus 1:12, Paul quotes a native Cretan "prophet" who describes his own people as "liars, evil beasts, [with] slow bellies." While Paul does not name this source, one possibility is the sixth-century BC writer Epimenides. This statement has been called the Cretan Paradox because if all Cretans are liars, and Epimenides was a Cretan, then was he lying when he made the statement?

Paul was accompanied on Crete by one of his

most trusted associates, a Gentile believer named Titus (Galatians 2:3). The book of Acts does not mention Titus by name. Still, he figures prominently in the letters of Paul. In 2 Corinthians, Titus is named (in Greek) nine times (example: 2 Corinthians 8:23). Paul wrote his letter to Titus in about AD 65 after departing from the island. Paul had left Titus behind to correct a chaotic situation in the Cretan churches. Most importantly, Titus needed to place an eldership in each congregation (Titus 1:5).

The church in Crete was troubled by people who professed to know God but lived demonstrably different lives (see Titus 1:16). Such people had deceived others, disrupted the community (1:10-11), and brought needless controversy to the church (3:9-10).

Today's lesson reveals Paul's solution to this challenging situation. What the church in Crete needed was "sound doctrine" (Titus 1:9; 2:1) and training in godliness (see 1:1; 2:12). This is the nitty-gritty of helping believers mature into godly men and women. Paul wanted Titus to grow the church by grounding them in the truth of the gospel and encouraging lives of holiness.

I. The Messenger

(Titus 1:1-3)

A. Servant and Apostle (v. 1)

1a. Paul, a servant of God, and apostle of Jesus Christ.

An ancient letter typically began by naming its author and its intended recipients. Paul's other New Testament epistles reflect this tendency (examples: 1 Corinthians 1:1-2; 1 Timothy 1:1-2). In the first verses of this particular letter, *Paul* identified himself as its author and named his intended audience: Titus (Titus 1:4, not in our printed text).

In Romans 1:1 and Philippians 1:1, Paul identifies himself as a servant of Jesus Christ. But nowhere else in the New Testament does he identify himself as *a servant of God* (compare James 1:1). His self-description reflects his humility—a required attitude for a leader of Christ's church (see Matthew 20:26-28). Humility did not preclude him from leading the church. Instead, it was a prerequisite to being an *apostle of Jesus Christ.* Paul—a former Pharisee and persecutor of Christians—had been chosen to be Christ's messenger (see Acts 9:15). Through the letter's introduction, Paul demonstrated humility, affirmed his allegiance to God, and reminded Titus of his apostolic mission.

1b. According to the faith of God's elect, and the acknowledging of the truth which is after godliness.

Paul's purpose in writing was to strengthen *God's elect* people. This designation is rooted in God's gracious and generous choice of a people to be His own (see Romans 8:29-33; Ephesians 1:4-14; 1 Peter 2:9-10). Paul's mission as an apostle was to strengthen the elect's *faith* so that they may better understand their salvation (see 2 Timothy 2:10).

Paul also wrote to mature their knowledge of *the truth* of their salvation through Christ Jesus. Doing so was part of his task as an apostle (compare 1 Timothy 2:3-7). When people understand and accept the truth of salvation, they will repent and live new lives rightly ordered by God's truth (see 2 Timothy 2:25).

Together, faith and knowledge produce *godliness*: behavior that follows God's standards revealed by Christ Jesus (see 1 Timothy 4:7-8; 6:3-4). Ten of the fifteen uses in the New Testament of the underlying Greek word translated *godliness* are found in the Pastoral Epistles. Its usage reveals that Paul considered it crucial for leaders of the church to develop godliness.

Some Cretans were known for their ungodly behavior (see Titus 1:10-13). Therefore, it was appropriate for Paul to address such behavior from the start of his letter. Paul expected that Titus would take on the mission of leading the church in Crete to maturity through the gospel message.

B. Commanded by God (vv. 2-3)

2. In hope of eternal life, which God, that cannot lie, promised before the world began.

The word *hope* often implies wishful thinking, like, "I hope it doesn't rain tomorrow." That is not how Paul uses the word in this verse. For Paul, *hope* is an assurance because the subject of this hope was Jesus Christ. Jesus is life, and He has life in himself (John 11:25; 1 John 5:20). God has promised that people can experience *eternal life* when they enter into a saving relationship with Him (John 17:3).

This promise is sure because it comes from the all-perfect, all-powerful God. He is trustworthy and faithful and *cannot lie* (see 1 Samuel 15:29; Hebrews 6:18). Further, it is rooted in God's eternal nature. He gives life and desires to be in a relationship with His creation. Even when sin and death entered the world, God had prepared a way of salvation through Christ Jesus *before the world began* (see 2 Timothy 1:9).

3. But hath in due times manifested his word through preaching, which is committed unto me according to the commandment of God our Saviour.

Though God's promise existed since before creation, only *in due times* did He reveal Christ as the fulfillment of that promise (see Galatians 4:4-5). God's timing in this regard was perfect; Christ came to earth at just the right time and in just the right context (see Romans 5:6; 1 Timothy 2:6). Thus, Paul emphasizes that God is at work in human history to accomplish His plan and purpose.

The underlying Greek word translated *preaching* conveys the idea of both the act of proclaiming the good news and the content of that proclamation. Part of Paul's task as an apostle was to commit himself *according to the commandment of God our Saviour* to proclaim that salvation had come in and through Christ Jesus. *Through* Paul's *preaching*, he served as a herald, announcing the good news of salvation (compare Romans 16:25; 1 Corinthians 2:4; 2 Timothy 4:17).

In this verse, Paul unpacks the basis for his ministry as an apostle. He could claim apostleship because he had experienced a particular calling to proclaim holiness and grace. Elsewhere, the apostle further unpacks this authority in his letter to his protégé, Timothy (2 Timothy 1:9-11).

How to Say It

Cretans	*Cree*-tunz.
Crete	Creet.
Epimenides	Ep-ih-*men*-ih-deez.
Pharisee	*Fair*-ih-see.
Septuagint	Sep-*too*-ih-jent.
Titus	*Ty*-tus.

What Do You Think?

In what ways has the preaching of the gospel in your local church deepened your love for God?

Digging Deeper

How will you increase your exposure to God's Word and its teaching in your daily life?

II. The Message

(Titus 2:11-15)

The first half of Paul's letter addressed several needs that faced the church at Crete: godly leadership in the church (Titus 1:5-9), a rebuke of ungodly behavior (1:10-16), and sound doctrine that leads to godly behavior (2:1-10).

A. Grace Appeared (vv. 11-12)

11. For the grace of God that bringeth salvation hath appeared to all men.

Having described how believers should live, Paul then explains the reason *for* that way of living: *the grace of God*. Such grace is a gift given to us by God for our justification and *salvation* (see 2 Timothy 1:9; Titus 3:7). Grace is necessary for salvation because, without it, we are incapable of attaining salvation by our own merit. Grace is not deserved or earned. Instead, it is based exclusively on the love of God (see Ephesians 2:4-10).

The underlying Greek word for *appeared* shows up only four times in the New Testament, two of which are in the letter to Titus (here and in Titus 3:4; see lesson 13). The word carries the connotation of light appearing and shining in darkness (compare its usage in Luke 1:79 and Acts 27:20). The grace of God, revealed in Christ Jesus, has *appeared* to bring salvation to a sin-darkened world (see John 1:9; Colossians 1:13). The gift of grace is available to all people (see 1 Timothy 2:3-4), but not everyone will accept it. For those who do receive this gift, their lives will bear the fruit of godliness (see Ephesians 5:8-20).

What Do You Think?

How will you share the message of God's grace and salvation with someone this upcoming week?

Digging Deeper

How will you tailor your communication of that message to have maximum appeal and persuasiveness?

12a. Teaching us that, denying ungodliness and worldly lusts.

God's grace has a formative effect on His people. Not only has this grace appeared for our salvation, but it has become our instructor, *teaching us* the habits of righteousness and godly living.

The Cretans were not the only ungodly people. Outside of Christ, *everyone* stands condemned for their sins (Romans 3:23). When we accept the gift of grace, God gives us His Spirit to teach us. The Spirit bears the fruits of righteousness through us (see John 14:26; 15:5; Galatians 5:22-24).

God's grace forms us to want to renounce personal and systemic sin. *Ungodliness* is a generic word for any evil behavior blatantly against God's righteous nature (see Romans 1:18-23). *Worldly lusts* refer to the selfish passions of the flesh (compare Galatians 5:16). Because God calls believers to a life of righteousness, we should deny any such behavior that opposes God or is inconsistent with His character.

12b. We should live soberly, righteously, and godly, in this present world.

God's grace instructs believers to replace ungodly behavior with righteous behavior. Living *soberly* suggests prudence regarding our passions and desires. Paul lists it as a standard for the believers in Crete (Titus 1:8; 2:2, 5-6), and it should be our standard as well. To live *righteously* and *godly* summarizes the required attitudes and behaviors that conform to God's standard. It is the opposite of "ungodliness" (2:12a, above). Righteousness is God's standard, and He desires the same from His people (see 2 Timothy 2:22; compare Ephesians 6:14).

Paul frequently includes "virtue lists" in his writings (examples: Galatians 5:22-23; Ephesians 4:32; Philippians 4:8). This verse is the only such list that mentions all three of these attributes together. These three are not simply things to attain in future eternal life. Instead, we should seek to develop them *in this present world*—a world that actively opposes God and God's people (see Ephesians 6:10-12).

What Do You Think?

In what ways are you attentive to the voice of the Holy Spirit to lead you into godliness?

Digging Deeper

Who will you ask to be a role model for you in this regard?

Ever Learning

What do a cook, a pruner, a construction worker, a customer service representative, and a student have in common? This question seems like the start of a bad joke, but it's not. It's a list of some jobs I held after high school.

These diverse jobs had a common denominator. They each required some level of specialized training. For example, the restaurant required detailed training for its kitchen staff, and the construction company mandated that I know building codes. Because of these experiences, I've learned that life is a continuous process of learning and growing.

The Christian life is also one of learning and growing. God's grace teaches us to avoid ungodliness and to pursue righteous living. Are you willing to learn more about what God requires for the Christian life, or have you decided that you've learned all you can? What would your closest friends say about you? —J. M.

B. Hope Promised (vv. 13-14)

13. Looking for that blessed hope, and the glorious appearing of the great God and our Saviour Jesus Christ.

Many unbelievers dread what the future may bring (see 1 Thessalonians 4:13). Believers, however, have a *blessed hope* of Christ's return and eternal life in the presence of God (see 2:19; Titus 1:2, above; 2 Timothy 1:10). Even though we may experience trials and suffering on earth, we can take hope that God will be faithful to His promises and bring redemption and renewal to us and our world (see Romans 8:18-21; Philippians 3:20-21). This hope will be fulfilled at the *glorious appearing* of Christ to earth (see Matthew 16:27). At His return, we will experience glorious renewal and resurrection life.

God revealed His grace through the incarnation of Jesus (see 2 Corinthians 8:9; 1 Timothy 3:16; Hebrews 2:9). This very same grace will again be on display at the return of our *great God and our Saviour Jesus Christ.* As a result, we are to have lives of holiness and godliness in eager anticipation (see Colossians 3:4-5; 1 John 2:28).

What Do You Think?

How would you respond to someone who says that the return of Jesus Christ is inconsequential for a believer?

Digging Deeper

How do Matthew 24:14; 25:31-46; 1 Corinthians 1:4-9; 1 Thessalonians 1:3; 4:15-18; and Hebrews 10:24-25 inform your response?

Waiting for Hope

"We can walk or ride a bike wherever we need to go" was my proposal to my wife when we first arrived in rural Alaska. At that time, there were only five miles of paved highway in our area, and a gallon of gas cost over seven dollars, so owning a car seemed unreasonable to me. Fortunately, my wife accepted my proposition. Walking and cycling became our primary forms of transportation.

After several years, however, we learned that five miles is a long distance to bike or walk during subzero temperatures. We settled on buying a used vehicle and hired a shipping company to deliver it to our remote location via a barge. As the barge slowly made its way to rural Alaska, we kept a close eye on its location with the help of the Internet. Over several months, the barge made numerous stops before arriving with our vehicle. The time we spent waiting for the arrival of the barge felt longer than the years spent without a car.

Jesus will return to earth, but we don't know its timing. Therefore, we wait for that "blessed hope" (Titus 2:13) and live in an "in-between" period between Christ's first and second coming. But this "in-between" time is not a time for us to wait aimlessly. Instead, during this time, we worship God and develop lives of godliness. How will you grow in godliness as you wait for Christ? —J. M.

14. Who gave himself for us, that he might redeem us from all iniquity, and purify unto himself a peculiar people, zealous of good works.

Believers eagerly await Christ's glorious return, and our hope is based on what He accomplished for us in His first coming to earth. God's grace was displayed when Jesus *gave himself for us* on the cross. In Jesus' giving of himself, He voluntarily did something that no one else could: rescue us from the grasp of sin and death and give us life (see Galatians 1:4; 2:20).

The purpose of Christ's self-giving was two-fold. First, He came to *redeem us.* He did this by being the ransom that sin requires (Mark 10:45). The underlying Greek word for *redeem* is also used in the Septuagint to describe how God ransomed His people from their bondage (examples: Exodus 6:6; 15:13; 2 Samuel 7:23; Psalm 130:8). Christ's death on the cross paid the ransom for our sin and freed us from the bondage of our *iniquity* and ungodliness (Romans 6:22; 1 Timothy 2:6).

Second, the shedding of Christ's blood cleanses us from the impurity of our sins (see Hebrews 9:12-14; 1 John 1:7, 9). Our purification from sin leads to our sanctification into holiness and godly behavior (see 2 Corinthians 7:1).

The result of our redemption and purification is that we become identified as the people of God. In the antique English of the *King James Version,* the word translated *peculiar* doesn't mean "odd" or "eccentric." Instead, it conveys a deep sense of ownership. (See also 1 Peter 2:9, although a different Greek word is used there.) Christ's work has created an "elect" people (Titus 1:1, above)—redeemed and purified—as God's own.

As God's redeemed people, we wait for Christ's return and the resurrection of the body. In this season of waiting, we should become *zealous* to do *good works* that result from God's grace (see Ephesians 2:8-10). These good works flow from our love (see Romans 12:9-21; 1 Corinthians 13) that results from a life filled with God's Spirit (see Galatians 5:13-26; Colossians 3:12-15).

What Do You Think?

How will you live differently in light of the knowledge of your redemption and purification?

Digging Deeper

How will you make time to do the good works that result from this status?

C. Leader Encouraged (v. 15)

15. These things speak, and exhort, and rebuke with all authority. Let no man despise thee.

Paul concludes this section of his letter by imploring Titus to action to encourage people to lead holy lives. First and foremost, Titus needed to address the problems at Crete. God had set Paul apart to preach the gospel of Jesus Christ (Acts 9:15; 26:15-18; Galatians 1:11-16). From this position of authority, Paul encouraged Titus to strengthen the faith of the believers.

Titus would *exhort* other believers to do good works indicative of their life in Christ. Exhortation was an aspect of Paul's mission (see Colossians 1:28), and so would be the mission of Titus.

This verse is the third time in this letter that Paul uses the underlying Greek word translated here as *rebuke* (see also Titus 1:9, 13). Ungodly behavior had abounded in Crete (see 1:12). Therefore, Titus would have to call it out and offer a correction for godliness (compare Galatians 6:1; Ephesians 5:11).

Titus could exhort and rebuke because of the *authority* that Paul had given him. There was a specific "chain of command" in this letter. Titus received authority from Paul, who had received his power as "a servant of God, and an apostle of Jesus Christ" (Titus 1:1, above). As Titus boldly and confidently proclaimed the gospel, he followed in the footsteps of Paul.

The command *let no man despise you* is very similar to Paul's command to Timothy in 1 Timothy 4:12. Although there is no mention of Titus's age, he was likely younger than Paul. Titus could have confidence that his words to the believers in Crete were authoritative and valuable for their growth in godliness.

How are you living?

Do (Virtue): Live self-controlled, righteous, godly lives	Do Not (Vice): Embrace ungodliness and worldly desires
Galatians 5:22-25	Galatians 5:19-21, 26
James 3:13, 17-18	2 Timothy 3:2-5
2 Peter 1:5-7	James 3:14-16
Titus 2:11-13	Titus 2:11-13
Titus 3:1-2	Titus 3:3, 9-11

Visual for Lesson 12. *Show this visual as you ask volunteers to read the Scripture texts to discover how believers should and should not live.*

Conclusion

A. The Gift of Grace

When we feel burdened by our failures and struggles, we can take hope because of the good news that the grace of God has arrived. It has come in Christ Jesus. Christ's giving of himself has redeemed and purified us. Therefore, we have hope of eternal life—a hope anchored in God's saving gift. God's grace is a gift to humanity.

God's gift teaches us to live godly lives and to seek Christlike behavior. We live in this manner as we wait for the blessed hope of the coming of Christ Jesus.

B. Prayer

God, our Savior, we thank You for the gift of grace that has appeared in Your Son, Jesus Christ. Thank You for Your gift of salvation and the hope that we have because of it. By the power of Your Spirit, help us to live godly and pure lives. In the name of Your Son, Jesus. Amen.

C. Thought to Remember

We have a "blessed hope"!

Involvement Learning

Enhance your lesson with KJV Bible Student *(from your curriculum supplier) and the reproducible activity page (at www.standardlesson.com or in the back of the* KJV Standard Lesson Commentary Deluxe Edition*).*

Into the Lesson

Write the following headers on the board: *Daily / Weekly / Quarterly / Yearly.* Ask learners to give examples of how they must wait during the time frame of each of the columns. (Possible examples: daily waiting at a traffic light, waiting for a weekly report, waiting at a doctor's office for a quarterly appointment, waiting for a yearly birthday party.) For whole-class discussion, ask learners how they feel as they wait during each of these periods of time.

Option. Distribute copies of the "Waiting Game" exercise from the activity page, which you can download. Have learners work in pairs to complete as indicated.

Lead into Bible study by saying, "Our lives are filled with seasons of waiting. Part of the Christian life is one of waiting—eagerly anticipating the glorious return of our Savior, Jesus Christ. In today's study, consider how we can be good stewards of the time in which we wait."

Into the Word

Ask a volunteer to read Titus 1:1-3 aloud. Divide learners into six groups: **Proverbs 8:12-26 Group, John 17:3-24 Group, 1 Corinthians 2:6-7 Group, Ephesians 1:4-6 Group, 2 Timothy 1:9-10 Group**, and **1 Peter 1:18-20 Group**. Have each group read their assigned text and answer the following questions: 1–What does your group's given text reveal about God's eternal nature? 2–How should the promise and hope of these eternal things impact how we live today? 3–What hope do you find in the passage from Titus and the assigned verses?

Divide the class into two groups: **Our Work Group** and **God's Work Group**. Have each group read Titus 2:11-15 and answer the following questions.

Our Work Group: 1–What should believers do while waiting for the "blessed hope" (Titus 2:13) of Christ's return? 2–What is the connection between our salvation and our good works? 3–How can we avoid ungodliness and worldly lusts? 4–How can we live soberly, righteously, and godly?

God's Work Group: 1–What things in this passage describe what God has done or what He is doing for us? 2–What is the connection between the grace of God and the presence of God's Spirit? 3–How is God's work in Christ Jesus one of redemption and purification? 4–What is the significance that God's work culminates in His creation of a people for himself?

After five minutes, ask a volunteer from each group to share their answers before the whole class. After each group has shared, ask the following question for whole-class discussion: "How does the work that God has done and is doing impact our work of becoming godly people?"

Option. Distribute copies of the "Personal Timeline" activity from the activity page. Have learners complete it individually in a minute or less before discussing conclusions with a partner.

Into Life

Distribute an index card to each learner. Ask them to reread Titus 2:12 and write down ways to live soberly, righteously, and godly in light of the grace of God. Then, have each learner write a step-by-step plan for how he or she will eliminate one area of ungodliness and pursue one area of godliness instead.

Place learners into pairs and have each of them pray that their partner will be attentive to the leading of the Holy Spirit as they pursue lives of godliness.

Note: Some learners may be apprehensive about sharing their plans with a partner. Encourage pairs not to spend time on the content of the plans but, instead, to focus on prayer for awareness of the Holy Spirit's work.

August 25
Lesson 13 (KJV)

The Washing of Regeneration

Devotional Reading: Ephesians 2:1-10
Background Scripture: Titus 3:3-11

Titus 3:3-11

3 For we ourselves also were sometimes foolish, disobedient, deceived, serving divers lusts and pleasures, living in malice and envy, hateful, and hating one another.

4 But after that the kindness and love of God our Saviour toward man appeared,

5 Not by works of righteousness which we have done, but according to his mercy he saved us, by the washing of regeneration, and renewing of the Holy Ghost;

6 Which he shed on us abundantly through Jesus Christ our Saviour;

7 That being justified by his grace, we should be made heirs according to the hope of eternal life.

8 This is a faithful saying, and these things I will that thou affirm constantly, that they which have believed in God might be careful to maintain good works. These things are good and profitable unto men.

9 But avoid foolish questions, and genealogies, and contentions, and strivings about the law; for they are unprofitable and vain.

10 A man that is an heretick after the first and second admonition reject;

11 Knowing that he that is such is subverted, and sinneth, being condemned of himself.

Key Text

But after that the kindness and love of God our Saviour toward man appeared, Not by works of righteousness which we have done, but according to his mercy he saved us, by the washing of regeneration, and renewing of the Holy Ghost; **—Titus 3:4-5**

Hope in
the Lord

Unit III: Eternal Hope

Lessons 10–13

Lesson Aims

After participating in this lesson, each learner will be able to:

1. List the means by which God saves.
2. Explain how to distinguish between profitable and unprofitable conversations from Paul's perspective.
3. Make a commitment to participate in conversations that only are profitable.

Lesson Outline

Introduction

A. Ever-Present Distractions

It seems that at almost every turn, we face new distractions. The latest television show, a spat on social media, or the day's most scandalous entertainment news story all become distractions. These fleeting things take our attention away from those things that are truly important, like our most valued relationships and the work that God has called us to do. A 1985 book by critic Neil Postman asks whether we are *Amusing Ourselves to Death*. Could we also be *distracting* ourselves to negative ends?

The same question could also apply to how we approach our faith in God. Rather than focus on the core of our faith, we might become too distracted by nonessential issues. As a result, social media fights among Christians ensue, churches divide, and believers become discouraged.

How can believers avoid distractions and focus on the thing that matters: the gospel that brings salvation? This question is not new; it has faced believers since the beginning of the church.

B. Lesson Context

The context surrounding the island of Crete and Paul's travels there has been covered in the Lesson Context of the previous lesson—lesson 12.

Paul had written this letter to address certain disturbances that faced the believers on that island. There had been a lack of godliness that had led to meaningless controversies and distractions (Titus 1:10-15). Paul instructed Titus to appoint godly leadership (1:5) to encourage others with gospel truth and refute the teachings of the opposition (1:9-16).

Old or young, male or female, husband or wife, free or enslaved, Paul instructed his readers to demonstrate self-control and pursue lives of godliness (see Titus 2:1-15). Paul also directed Titus to encourage the people to obey authority, be eager for good works, and live with gentleness and meekness (3:1-2). The worst thing that could occur would be for controversies to arise and distract the believers in Crete from focusing on the gospel.

I. Gospel Reminder

(Titus 3:3-8)

A. Our Situation (v. 3)

3a. For we ourselves also were sometimes foolish, disobedient, deceived, serving divers lusts and pleasures.

In order to highlight the power of the gospel, Paul first had to acknowledge the human situation. Every person has sinned (Romans 3:23), and no one is entirely righteous (3:10). By stating *we ourselves*, Paul included himself as among those who had sinned (compare 7:22-25).

Paul described the condition of human sin by using a "vice list." Such lists appear often in the writings of Paul (examples: Romans 1:29-31; 1 Corinthians 6:9-10; Galatians 5:19-21, 26; 2 Timothy 3:2-5). By one count, the New Testament contains 23 of these lists. Paul does not use these lists to imply that every person has committed every sin listed. Instead, the lists paint word pictures, reminding us of the many ways that sin has affected the world and our hearts.

This particular vice list begins by mentioning the *foolish* person who stubbornly refuses to accept God's truth (compare Galatians 3:1-3). Such a person becomes *disobedient* by rebelling against the standards of God (example: Titus 1:16) and others (example: Romans 1:30).

Sin can lead people to deceive themselves regarding right and wrong (see Isaiah 5:20). Therefore, Paul frequently warns against being *deceived* (examples: 1 Corinthians 15:33; Galatians 6:7). Such self-deception causes people to become captive to the *divers lusts and pleasures* of a sinful world (compare Titus 2:12, lesson 12).

3b. Living in malice and envy, hateful, and hating one another.

Sin affects not only a person's mindset and actions but also his or her relationships with others. *Malice and envy* are feelings of wickedness directed at another person. These two feelings tend to go hand-in-hand; the underlying Greek words occur together also in Romans 1:29 and 1 Peter 2:1. These feelings result from sinful desires and can lead to anger or other sins. Rather than be filled with love for others (see 1 Corinthians 13:4), the envious person becomes filled with hate that leads to further sin (James 3:14-16).

This verse is the only occurrence in the New Testament of the underlying Greek word translated as *hateful*. The same word is used twice in a letter from the early church leader Clement of Rome (lived AD 35–99). In one letter, Clement describes how unrighteousness is considered "hateful to God" (see the nonbiblical 1 Clement 35:5-6) and causes people to be considered "abominable" (45:7). God hates wickedness (Proverbs 6:16-19). Instead, God desires that people repent from sin and follow His Son.

Earlier in this letter, Paul remarked on the wickedness of the Cretans (Titus 1:12). In the verse before us, the apostle made it clear to Titus that without God's grace, all people—including Titus and Paul—were no better than the Cretans. They were *all* sinners.

> **What Do You Think?**
> What steps do you take to ensure that you do not harbor feelings of envy and malice toward others?
>
> **Digging Deeper**
> In what ways do the teachings of the "Love Chapter" (1 Corinthians 13) serve as an antidote to envy and malice?

B. God's Response (vv. 4-7)

4. But after that the kindness and love of God our Saviour toward man appeared.

The phrase *but after that* points to a change of status for humanity. The previous verse's description of human sin does not have to be the final status for humanity. Instead, God has provided a way to free us from sin and evil. This divine initiative for salvation arises from God's character, particularly His *kindness and love*. This truth is the core of our faith.

God has revealed His kindness through His gracious benevolence to help sinful humanity. Throughout history, God's kindness has been on display (examples: Ruth 2:20; Jeremiah 9:24). The ultimate example of His kindness has come through God's sending of His Son, Christ Jesus, to pay sin's price through the sacrifice of himself on the cross (Romans 3:21-26; Ephesians 2:7). This display of kindness would lead humanity to repentance (Romans 2:4).

The underlying Greek word translated *love* in this verse is unique. It is not one of the more frequently used Greek words for *love* found in the New Testament. A form of this particular Greek word is used in Acts 27:3 regarding the behavior of Julius. The term is also used in 28:2 regarding the "kindness" of the people of Malta toward Paul. We can experience salvation and a new life because of God's love and kindness for us.

This verse is the second and final occurrence in this letter of the underlying Greek translated *appeared*. The word is first used regarding the appearance of "the grace of God that bringeth salvation" (Titus 2:11; see lesson 12). Humanity no longer had to live in the darkness of sin. Instead, the grace, kindness, and love *of God our Saviour* have been displayed through Jesus Christ for our salvation (see 2 Timothy 1:9-10).

What Do You Think?

How would you explain God's love and kindness to someone who does not think of God as such?

Digging Deeper

What Scripture texts come to mind that would help inform your explanation?

The Love of a Parent

The teenager hoped her mom would not notice the long scratch on the family car. The damage had occurred as the girl had backed the car out of the garage that morning. She was sure her mom would be angry when she eventually saw the damage. The teenager feared losing her mother's respect—and maybe even love.

Eventually, the daughter came clean. She didn't maintain eye contact with her mother as she recounted the story of that morning. As the girl spoke, she felt her mother's hand gently raise her chin, forcing the daughter to look her mother in the eye.

Noticing the daughter's anxiety, the mother hugged her and said, "I'm just glad you're OK. I love you because of who I am, not because of what you do. I'm your mom; moms love their kids."

God does not base His love for us on anything we do—or do not do. Instead, His love comes from His nature as a loving heavenly Father who desires a relationship with us. Because of His love, God has shown His kindness to us for our salvation! How will you praise God for His kindness and love? —L. M. W.

5a. Not by works of righteousness which we have done, but according to his mercy he saved us.

The good things we do—*works of righteousness*—do not earn us salvation. Our righteous acts are like "filthy rags" (Isaiah 64:6) that do not benefit us for salvation (57:12).

Despite human sin, God delights in showing *mercy* (Micah 7:18; example: Daniel 9:9). This is because God is "rich in mercy" for our salvation (Ephesians 2:4-5). Our merciful God has provided a way for salvation that does not require our righteousness (Romans 9:15-16). Instead, He has initiated our salvation through His gift of grace (11:6; Ephesians 2:8-9; 2 Timothy 1:9). By His mercy and grace, we are justified by faith, and we are *saved*.

5b. By the washing of regeneration, and renewing of the Holy Ghost.

Students of the text have long discussed what Paul meant by the phrase *the washing of regeneration*. One possibility is that Paul was referring to the practice of baptism. Through baptism, we are "buried with [Christ]" (Colossians 2:12), and those who have been baptized "put on Christ" (Galatians 3:27). The other possibility is that Paul is generally referring to the spiritual cleansing from sin that results from our salvation. When we accept God's gift of grace, His Spirit fills us and transforms us (2 Corinthians 3:18). This transformation comes as the Spirit empowers us to remove the sinful self and receive new life (Ephesians 4:22-24; Colossians 3:10-11).

This new life is one where we are dead to the ways of sin (Romans 6:11). Our old selves were held captive to foolishness and disobedience. But because of God's gift of grace, salvation is available to us. When we accept that gift, *the Holy Ghost* transforms us into new people devoted to following God and obeying His commands.

Washing and Renewal

While spending a summer in a foreign country, a storm caused flooding in the city where I had been living. The flood destroyed the city's water purification system. Tap water became contaminated, unsafe for consumption. The city government had to distribute tanks of clean water to the residents for cooking, drinking, and washing.

After an entire summer with limited access to potable water, I left for home feeling dirty and exhausted. In a hotel room on the journey back home, I took my first real bath in months. To say that I felt washed and renewed would be an understatement—I never felt as clean as I did after that bath!

The apostle Paul wrote of "the washing of regeneration" (Titus 3:5b). As God's children, we have been washed and made clean. Does your behavior reflect your status in this regard? Why or why not? —L. M. W.

6. Which he shed on us abundantly through Jesus Christ our Saviour.

This verse reminds readers of the events of Pentecost when God poured out His Spirit (Acts 2:1-41). The underlying Greek word translated *shed* is also used in Acts 2 to describe how God promised to "pour out" His Spirit (2:17-18; compare Joel 2:28). By using the phrase *on us*, Paul includes both himself and Titus as among those who had experienced the presence of God's Spirit.

The pouring out of God's Spirit on His people is not like the trickle of water from a drying creek. Instead, God has *abundantly* poured His Spirit out as a rich resource of His grace and love (Romans 5:5). The Spirit's presence brings renewal and sanctification to the lives of believers. All people who have accepted God's grace are invited to receive and "drink" of God's Spirit (1 Corinthians 12:13).

Paul's explanation of our salvation in verses 5-6 reveals the work of the Triune God. All three persons of the Trinity are either mentioned or implied

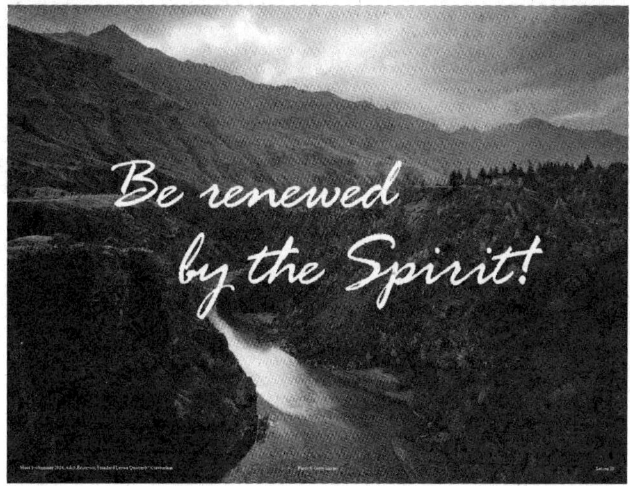

Visual for Lesson 13. *Point to this visual as you ask learners to consider if their behavior reflects their status as people renewed by God's Spirit.*

in these verses. The personal pronoun *he* refers to God the Father who has sent the Holy Spirit (John 14:16-17). The Holy Spirit proceeds from both God the Father and His only Son, *Jesus Christ our Saviour* (14:26; 15:26; 16:7). In this verse, Paul has affirmed the role of all three persons of the Triune God—Father, Son, and Holy Spirit—for our justification and sanctification.

7. That being justified by his grace, we should be made heirs according to the hope of eternal life.

Only through God's *grace* and our faith Christ's sacrifice are we *justified* (Romans 3:24; 5:9; 10:9-10; 11:6; Galatians 3:11; etc.). Although we are guilty of sin, we are counted righteous when we accept God's gift of grace (2:16). Our justification results in a new status and our hope for the future. Because of this justification, we become the children of God. As such, we are *made heirs* of God and become benefactors of God's promises regarding glory (Romans 8:17; Galatians 4:7).

As heirs, we have a unique hope as we await our future (Romans 8:23-25). To have *hope* does not mean wishful thinking. For Paul, *hope* is a certainty; it is a confidence that the promises made by God to His heirs will come true (15:4; see also commentary on Titus 1:2 and 2:13 in lesson 12). In this case, the hoped-for promise is that God's children will someday experience glorious *eternal life* with Him (2 Timothy 2:10; 1 Peter 1:3-4; 2 Peter 1:10-11; etc.).

What Do You Think?

How has your identity and purpose as a believer changed as you think of yourself as an "heir" in God's family?

Digging Deeper

How does your identity as an heir of eternal riches change your relationship with your material possessions?

C. Profitable Actions (v. 8)

8a. This is a faithful saying, and these things I will that thou affirm constantly.

The phrase *this is a faithful saying* or its equivalent is found in five places in the Pastoral Epistles (here and in 1 Timothy 1:15; 3:1; 4:9; 2 Timothy 2:11). As a mentor to both Timothy and Titus, Paul ought to remind them of the trustworthy doctrine that they could then proclaim in their churches.

These things include what Paul had taught up to this point in the letter. This teaching included the human condition, the kindness and love of God, salvation through grace, purification by the Spirit, and hope of eternal life (Titus 3:3-7). These points of doctrine are the core of the gospel message. Titus could trust Paul's teaching and, therefore, proclaim it to the Cretans. As Titus taught these things, the believers in Crete would hear and obey, thus becoming obedient children of God.

8b. That they which have believed in God might be careful to maintain good works. These things are good and profitable unto men.

When the gospel is proclaimed, heard, and *believed*, it will create a people devoted to obeying *God*. Having faith and doing good go hand-in-hand (James 2:14-21, 26). Believers doing good works that result from their salvation is a prominent theme in this letter (see also Titus 2:14; 3:1, 14).

The *good works* of a believer come as a result of the presence of God in that person's life (Philippians 2:12-13). Good works are the result of salvation, not the source of it. God has blessed us so that we might do good works (2 Corinthians 9:8; Ephesians 2:10). The good works that Paul has in mind *are good and profitable* for all people. By this, he means that good works are a way to obey God and are a benefit for others (examples: 1 Timothy 5:10; 6:18). When we are filled with the Holy Spirit and allow the Spirit to shape our habits and mindsets, we become eager to do good works. In the process, we please and obey God (Hebrews 13:16).

What Do You Think?

How do you pay attention to the leading of God's Spirit to guide your habits and mindset?

Digging Deeper

In what ways will you encourage other believers to do the same?

III. Gospel Behavior

(Titus 3:9-11)

A. Avoid Foolishness (v. 9)

9. But avoid foolish questions, and genealogies, and contentions, and strivings about the law; for they are unprofitable and vain.

Having established what defines "profitable" behavior in light of salvation (Titus 3:8, above), Paul describes those *unprofitable* behaviors for believers pursuing godliness. This list of behavior is related to the "unruly and vain talkers and deceivers, . . . who subvert whole houses, teaching things which they ought not" (1:10-11). In this verse, Paul addressed false teachers that had infiltrated the Cretan church. Their *foolish questions* and *contentions* had divided the church. Rather than being a community known for love and good works, the Cretan church risked conflict over *vain* debates by following these teachers.

The mention of *genealogies* and *strivings about the law* provides clues regarding the identity of the false teachers. Their teachings had been influenced by certain Jewish ideas from the people "of the circumcision" (Titus 1:10; see 1:14). Some of the teachings concerned aspects of the Law of Moses and human ancestry. Such things had no value for human salvation in light of the work of Christ Jesus.

In Paul's letters to Timothy, the apostle warns the young man regarding the dangers of empty talk (1 Timothy 1:6; 2 Timothy 2:16, 23) and meaningless stories and genealogies (1 Timothy 1:3-4). While we do not know specifics regarding the situations that faced Timothy and Titus, both men confronted false teachers in their communities. Part of Paul's ministry was to guide these younger leaders to lead their particular churches in the ways of godliness. This guidance meant they would have to call out dangerous teachings and divisive behaviors.

What Do You Think?

How do you discern what things are profitable for your spiritual maturity and what things are "unprofitable and vain"?

Digging Deeper

Who is a younger person to whom you can give profitable spiritual encouragement?

B. Admonish Divisiveness (vv. 10-11)

10-11. A man that is an heretick after the first and second admonition reject; knowing that he that is such is subverted, and sinneth, being condemned of himself.

We typically use the word *heretic* to refer to someone who espouses false teaching. However, that meaning is not in view in this verse's mention of *a man that is an heretick*. Instead, the underlying Greek word in this verse refers to someone who causes division. Rather than build up the body of Christ that is the church, this type of person creates discord and disruption. Therefore, believers should avoid such a person (see Romans 16:17; 2 Thessalonians 3:6).

In response to such a divisive person, Paul describes an early form of church discipline. Paul's directives reveal a certain level of patience. Divisive people could receive two warnings. After the *second* warning, the church should outright reject the person. By allowing two warnings, Titus would give the troublesome party ample opportunity to repent and change. Paul's warning in these verses recalls Jesus' teaching regarding dealing with sin in the church (Matthew 18:15-17). This event was not Paul's first experience handing out warnings and discipline. The church in Corinth had received such warnings from Paul (2 Corinthians 13:2).

By following Paul's directives in this regard, Titus would no longer give attention to those who brought distraction and division to the church. The false teachers' stubbornness and refusal to accept correction had *condemned* them. Their behaviors *subverted* the order Titus had been commissioned to create for the church at Crete. As a result, a strong response on the part of Titus was required.

Conclusion

A. Gospel Focus

When churches emphasize the gospel, the spiritual health of its members improves. Instead of being focused on distractions that lead to division, believers can become devoted to doing good works that result from godliness.

As if to remind believers of all eras, the apostle Paul retells the gospel message that begins with the kindness and love of God that results in our salvation and culminates with being made new through God's Spirit. This is the gospel message, and it is profitable for all believers.

In response to Paul's directives to Titus, we should reflect on his teachings and the practices of our churches. Ask yourself if your church focuses on the gospel and living out its teachings. Then, ask yourself the same question. Do you focus on the gospel and living out its teachings? Have distractions threatened your spiritual livelihood?

B. Prayer

Kind and loving God, we thank You for Your mercy and grace by which You have saved us. Help us be more attentive to the Spirit's leading into renewal and rebirth so that we might do good works in Your name. In Jesus' name, we pray. Amen.

C. Thought to Remember

The only thing truly profitable is the gospel!

How to Say It

Corinth	*Kor*-inth.
Ephesians	Ee-*fee*-zhunz.
Malta	*Mawl*-tuh.
Pentecost	*Pent*-ih-kost.

Involvement Learning

Enhance your lesson with KJV Bible Student *(from your curriculum supplier) and the reproducible activity page (at www.standardlesson.com or in the back of the* KJV Standard Lesson Commentary Deluxe Edition*).*

Into the Lesson

Begin by asking learners to share stories about the most significant messes they have ever encountered. Ask how they cleaned up the mess, including the tools, assistance, and steps for cleaning.

Alternative. Distribute the "What a Mess" exercise from the activity page, which you can download. Have learners work in their groups to complete the activity as indicated before discussing conclusions with the whole class.

Lead into Bible study by saying, "A large mess can sometimes seem daunting to clean. But as we read today's passage, let us consider how God has cleansed our lives."

Into the Word

Explain the background for today's lesson using the material for the Lesson Context section from lessons 12 and 13. If possible, recruit a class member ahead of time to present a three-minute summary of this material to set the stage for today's Bible study.

Announce a Bible-marking activity. Provide copies of Titus 3:3-11 for those who do not want to write in their own Bibles. Provide four different colored pencils to each learner and distribute handouts (you create) with these instructions:

- Underline with one color the words or phrases that describe sinful humanity.
- Underline with a second color the words or phrases that describe the work of God.
- Underline with a third color the words or phrases that describe the process of salvation.
- Underline with a fourth color the words or phrases that describe saved and redeemed humanity.

Read the Scripture aloud (or ask a volunteer to do so) slowly two to four times. As the Scripture is read, class members are to mark their copies of the Scripture text in the ways noted.

After all the responses to the underlining activity have been given, ask the following questions for whole-class discussion: 1–In light of the lesson context, what is notable about the ways that Paul describes sinful humanity? 2–How would you summarize the work of God described in this passage? 3–How would you summarize for an unbeliever the process of salvation as described in this passage? 4–What actions are "good and profitable" for your class to undertake in the upcoming week?

Alternative. Distribute copies of the "Profitable Responses" exercise from the activity page. Have learners complete the activity individually in a minute or less before discussing conclusions with a partner.

Into Life

Write two headers on the board: *Profitable Conversations / Unprofitable Conversations.* Ask volunteers to provide attributes for each type of conversation and write their responses on the board. After volunteers have shared, have another volunteer use the listed characteristics to write definitions for "profitable conversations" and "unprofitable conversations." Have the volunteer ask for feedback from the whole class regarding the definitions.

Divide the class into small groups. Using the definitions, ask groups to brainstorm ways to discern whether or not a conversation is profitable. After five minutes, have a volunteer from each group share their ideas before the whole class.

Place learners into pairs and have them commit to participate in conversations that only are profitable. Suggest that partners share about situations and relationships in which responding profitably could be a challenge. Conclude class by having learners pray that their partner will pursue those things that are profitable for his or her spiritual growth and maturity.

Alternative. Have small groups expand the "Profitable Responses" exercise and discuss how to practice responding to similar real-life scenarios in ways that are more in line with Scripture.